Frommer's®
Paris 2013

by Anna E. Brooke, Lily Heise, Sophie Nellis & Kate van den Boogert

WILEY

John Wiley & Sons, Inc.

Published by:
John Wiley & Sons, Inc.
111 River St.
Hoboken, NJ 07030-5774

ISBN 978-1-118-28764-4 (paper); ISBN 978-1-118-33370-9 (ebk); ISBN 978-1-118-33143-9 (ebk); ISBN 978-1-118-33198-9 (ebk)

Editor: Jennifer Polland
Production Editor: Michael Brumitt
Cartographer: Andrew Murphy
Photo Editor: Alden Gewirtz
Cover Photo Editor: Richard Fox
Graphics and Prepress by Wiley Indianapolis Composition Services

Front cover photo: Louvre Museum, Paris ©Shaun Egan Getty Images
Back cover photo: *Left:* Willi's Wine Bar, Rue des petits Champs, Paris ©Nicholas Mac Innes. *Middle:* Stained glass in the cathedral of Sainte-Chapelle, in Paris ©Elisabeth Blanchet. *Right:* Eiffel Tower ©Markel Redondo.

CONTENTS

LIST OF MAPS

ABOUT THE AUTHORS

After growing up in a Francophile household and studying French at university, **Anna E. Brooke** came to Paris in 2000 and hasn't looked back since. She's the author of seven Frommer's guidebooks, and a regular writer for the *Sunday Times Travel Magazine, Time Out*, and the *Financial Times*. When she's not travel writing, she's singing and song writing for Monkey Anna, her funky electro-pop group: www.reverbnation.com/monkeyanna.

Sophie Nellis has been living in Paris since 2007. After she completed her undergraduate degree in English Literature and History at Trinity College in Dublin, her love affair with Paris led her to a Masters in Paris Studies: History and Culture at the University of Paris in London (ULIP). She currently lives in Belleville and has her own blog about life in the capital today, elephantinparis.wordpress.com. She divides her time between writing, teaching, translating, and leading walking tours of Paris.

Lily Heise has been living in Paris for over 10 years, having refused to go back to Canada after studying art first in Italy and then in France. She has extensive experience in the travel and culture sectors and, in addition to contributing to *Frommer's Paris* and *Frommer's France,* she reports on Paris cultural news for local and international online and print publications. She lives in Montmartre and spends her free time exploring off-beat Paris and traveling around Europe.

Kate van den Boogert is the founding editor of the popular Paris blog gogoparis.com, an insider's guide to fashion, food, arts, gigs, and gossip in the French capital. Find the guides GogoParis and GogoLondon on the AppStore. Kate moved to Paris from Melbourne in 2000.

HOW TO CONTACT US

In researching this book, we discovered many wonderful places—hotels, restaurants, shops, and more. We're sure you'll find others. Please tell us about them, so we can share the information with your fellow travelers in upcoming editions. If you were disappointed with a recommendation, we'd love to know that, too. Please write to:

Frommer's Paris 2013
John Wiley & Sons, Inc. • 111 River St. • Hoboken, NJ 07030-5774
frommersfeedback@wiley.com

ADVISORY & DISCLAIMER

Travel information can change quickly and unexpectedly, and we strongly advise you to confirm important details locally before traveling, including information on visas, health and safety, traffic and transport, accommodations, shopping, and eating out. We also encourage you to stay alert while traveling and to remain aware of your surroundings. Avoid civil disturbances, and keep a close eye on cameras, purses, wallets, and other valuables.

While we have endeavored to ensure that the information contained within this guide is accurate and up-to-date at the time of publication, we make no representations or warranties with respect to the accuracy or completeness of the contents of this work and specifically disclaim all warranties, including without limitation warranties of fitness for a particular purpose. We accept no responsibility or liability for any inaccuracy or errors or omissions, or for any inconvenience, loss, damage, costs, or expenses of any nature whatsoever incurred or suffered by anyone as a result of any advice or information contained in this guide.

The inclusion of a company, organization, or website in this guide as a service provider and/or potential source of further information does not mean that we endorse them or the information they provide. Be aware that information provided through some websites may be unreliable and can change without notice. Neither the publisher nor author shall be liable for any damages arising herefrom.

FROMMER'S STAR RATINGS, ICONS & ABBREVIATIONS

Every hotel, restaurant, and attraction listing in this guide has been ranked for quality, value, service, amenities, and special features using a **star-rating system.** In country, state, and regional guides, we also rate towns and regions to help you narrow down your choices and budget your time accordingly. Hotels and restaurants are rated on a scale of zero (recommended) to three stars (exceptional). Attractions, shopping, nightlife, towns, and regions are rated according to the following scale: zero stars (recommended), one star (highly recommended), two stars (very highly recommended), and three stars (must-see).

In addition to the star-rating system, we also use **seven feature icons** that point you to the great deals, in-the-know advice, and unique experiences that separate travelers from tourists. Throughout the book, look for:

special finds—those places only insiders know about

fun facts—details that make travelers more informed and their trips more fun

kids—best bets for kids and advice for the whole family

special moments—those experiences that memories are made of

overrated—places or experiences not worth your time or money

insider tips—great ways to save time and money

great values—where to get the best deals

The following abbreviations are used for credit cards:

AE	American Express	**DISC**	Discover	**V**	Visa
DC	Diners Club	**MC**	MasterCard		

TRAVEL RESOURCES AT FROMMERS.COM

Frommer's travel resources don't end with this guide. Frommer's website, **www. frommers.com**, has travel information on more than 4,000 destinations. We update features regularly, giving you access to the most current trip-planning information and the best airfare, lodging, and car-rental bargains. You can also listen to podcasts, connect with other Frommers.com members through our active-reader forums, share your travel photos, read blogs from guidebook editors and fellow travelers, and much more.

THE BEST OF PARIS

Paris is unique in that it is a major global city—home to more than 10 million people in the greater region—yet it manages to synthesize the rhythms of village life with those of a cosmopolitan metropolis. Although the city is a center of European commerce, many shops are closed on Sundays, allowing for lazy brunches or shopping excursions at a local market. Paris is the capital of fashion, art, and people-watching. It's a culinary center where the waiters might be rude, but the food is *délicieux*. Your love affair begins once you look beyond the Eiffel Tower, explore the back streets, and make Paris your own.

Things to Do Comfy shoes are essential for this city of a thousand walks, landscaped gardens, and cavernous galleries. Reserve your ticket for speedy access to the **Louvre,** which sidles up to the sculpture-dotted **Jardin des Tuileries.** Across the Seine on the **Left Bank,** take your pick from Impressionist hangout **Musée d'Orsay, Notre-Dame's** Gothic grandeur, and **Musée Rodin's** *Kiss* sculpture. Okay, you really *can't* leave without seeing Paris light up from the **Eiffel Tower,** open till midnight.

Restaurants & Dining Good food is a birthright and its appreciation a rite of passage in Paris, where a meal—sometimes even coffee—can last hours. For a memorable splurge, book one of the city's opulent three-star palace restaurants, like **Le Bristol** or **L'Astrance,** or book ahead for a table at one of the trendy *bistronomiques* that combine gastronomy with bistro pricing—**Frenchie, Le Chateaubriand, Septime,** and **Spring** are all hot right now.

Shopping Parisians luxuriate in shopping, bidding shopkeepers *bonjour* and pausing to *lèche-vitrines* ("lick the windows," or window shop). Saunter the boutiquey **Marais** for home-grown fashion, or voguish **rue Saint-Honoré,** home to concept store **Colette,** for more high-end labels. Where else can you find such palatial department stores as chic **Bon Marché,** Art Nouveau **Printemps,** or monumental **Galeries Lafayette?** Antiques, bric-a-brac, vintage Chanel—it's all at the charming **Porte de Vanves weekend flea market;** arrive early for bargains and stay for brunch.

Nightlife & Entertainment Ballet and opera at the glittering **Opéra Garnier,** Molière classics at the **Comédie Française,** and cancan at the (in)famous **Moulin Rouge**—Paris nightlife reaches from sublime to borderline sleazy. A young, trendy crowd parties in the areas south of **Pigalle (SoPi),** gay **Marais,** and the effortlessly hip bars in **Oberkampf,** where DJs play at industrial-chic **Nouveau Casino.** Dress to the nines to slip past picky doormen in clubs around **Champs-Élysées** like celebrity-magnet **Le Baron,** and rock the Seine dancing to techno on moored party boat **Batofar.**

PREVIOUS PAGE: **A couple strolls along the picturesque quays of the Seine river.**

THE most unforgettable
PARIS EXPERIENCES

- **Whiling Away an Afternoon in a Parisian Cafe:** The cafes are where passionate meetings of writers, artists, philosophers, thinkers, and revolutionaries once took place—and perhaps still do. Parisians stop by their favorite cafes to meet lovers and friends, to make new ones, or to sit in solitude with a newspaper or book.

- **Taking Afternoon Tea à la Française:** Drinking tea in London has its charm, but the Parisian *salon de thé* is unique. Skip the cucumber-and-watercress sandwiches and delve into a luscious dessert such as macaroons and the Mont Blanc, a creamy purée of sweetened chestnuts and meringue. One of the loveliest Parisian tea salons is **Ladurée,** 16 rue Royale, 8e (☏ **01-42-60-21-79;** p. 260). Its version of the Mont Blanc includes blackcurrant and chocolate.

- **Strolling Along the Seine:** Such painters as Sisley, Turner, and Monet have fallen under the Seine's spell. On its banks, lovers still walk hand in hand, anglers cast their lines, and *bouquinistes* (secondhand-book dealers) peddle their mix of postcards, 100-year-old pornography, and tattered histories of Indochina.

- **Spending a Day at the Races:** Paris boasts eight tracks for horse racing. The most famous and the classiest is **Hippodrome de Longchamp,** in the Bois de Boulogne, the site of the Prix de l'Arc de Triomphe and Grand Prix (p. 102). These and other top races are major social events, so you'll have to dress up.

Diners at Les Deux Magots cafe.

- **Calling on the Dead:** You don't have to be a ghoul to be thrilled by a visit to Europe's most famous cemetery, **Père-Lachaise** (p. 115). You can pay your respects to the resting places of Oscar Wilde, Yves Montand and Simone Signoret, Edith Piaf, Isadora Duncan, Frédéric Chopin, Marcel Proust, Jim Morrison, and others. Laid out in 1803 on a hill in Ménilmontant, the cemetery offers surprises with its bizarre monuments, unexpected views, and ornate sculpture.

- **Window-Shopping in the Faubourg St-Honoré:** In the 1700s, the wealthiest Parisians resided in the Faubourg St-Honoré; today, the quarter is home to stores catering to the rich, particularly on rue du Faubourg St-Honoré and avenue Montaigne. Even if you don't buy anything, it's great to window-shop big names such as Hermès, Dior, Chanel, Gaultier, Vuitton,

Givenchy, and Yves Saint Laurent. If you want to browse in the stores, be sure to dress the part. See chapter 7.

o **Exploring Ile de la Cité's Flower Market:** A fine finish to any day (Mon–Sat) spent meandering along the Seine is a stroll through the **Marché aux Fleurs,** place Louis-Lépine (p. 243). You can buy rare flowers, the gems of the French Riviera—bouquets that have inspired artists throughout the centuries. On Sundays, the area is transformed into the **Marché aux Oiseaux,** where you can admire rare birds from around the world.

o **Going Gourmet at Fauchon:** An exotic world of food, **Fauchon** (p. 262) offers more than 20,000 products from around the globe. Everything you never knew you were missing is in aisle after aisle of coffees, spices, pastries, fruits, vegetables, and much more. Take your pick: Scottish smoked salmon, preserved cocks' combs, Romanian rose-petal jelly, blue-red Indian pomegranates, golden Tunisian dates, dark morels from France's rich soil, century-old eggs from China, and a creole punch from Martinique, reputed to be the best anywhere.

o **Attending a Ballet or an Opera:** Take your pick between the rococo splendor of the majestic **Opéra Garnier** (p. 110) or the more modern **Opéra Bastille** (p. 272), France's largest opera house. Established in 1989, the Opéra Bastille presents opera and symphony performances in its four concert halls (its main hall seats 2,700). The Opéra Garnier is the home of the Paris Opera Ballet, one of the best companies in the world, and it hosts opera, classical concerts, and ballet performances inside its stunning gold and red velvet auditorium. Dress for the occasion, with pomp and circumstance.

o **Sipping Wine at a Wine Bar:** You'll still find Paris first-timers arriving with a copy of Hemingway's *A Moveable Feast* and taking the author's endorsement to heart by heading for Harry's Bar at "Sank roo doe Noo." But today's chic crowds head to a new generation of wine bars like **Le Verre Volé** (p. 208), **Vivant** (p. 209), **Le Garde Robe** (p. 184), and **Coinstôt Vino** (p. 181).

Enjoying *vin* at a Paris wine bar.

A meat vendor at the market on rue Montorgueil.

Here, the sophisticated selection of often natural wines will take your taste-buds on a "terroir" tour throughout France.

o **Checking Out the Marchés:** A daily Parisian ritual is ambling through one of the open-air markets to buy fresh food—perhaps a properly creamy Camembert or a ripe plum—to be eaten before sundown. Our favorite market is the Marché d'Aligre. During mornings at this grubby little cluster of food stalls, we've spotted some of France's finest chefs stocking up for the day.

THE most unforgettable
FOOD & DRINK EXPERIENCES

o **Eating illicit cheese:** Many varieties of French *fromage* (cheese) are actually illegal in the United States because they're made with raw, unpasteurized milk—this adds depth of flavor to the cheese. While in France, sample the oozy Brie de Meaux (or Brie de Melun, if it's available), the pungent washed rind cheese Epoisses, or a very young and tangy snow-white chèvre. Our favorite cheese shop is **Androuet** (37 rue de Verneuil; ✆ **01-42-61-97-55**; www.androuet.com) in the 7th arrondissement, though there are other locations around the city.

o **Pairing that cheese with a warm baguette:** Just across the street from the Androuet cheese shop in the 7e is the **Eric Kayser** bakery (p. 222). Run by an acclaimed Alsatian who has patented several bread-making techniques, this bakery sells at least four different types of baguette, all chewy and delicious.

Fresh baguettes.

Picnicking in the Champ de Mars.

Sampling local wines.

o **Filling a box of chocolates:** It's impossible to walk into a chocolatarie and not be tempted to take home a box. Choose the size of the box, and then begin the fun task of pointing out whatever *pralinés* and *ganaches* you'd like to try. Our favorite *chocolatiers* are **Jacques Genin** (133 rue du Turenne, 3e; ℂ 01-45-77-29-01) and **Patrick Roger** (108 boulevard Saint-Germain, 6e; ℂ 01-43-29-38-42; www.patrickroger.com).

o **Going au naturel:** Natural wines, which are made from organic grapes and use few preservatives or stabilizing agents, are all the rage in Paris right now. The best place to learn about these (by drinking, of course) is **Vivant** (p. 209), a restaurant in the 10th arrondissement that's run by a leader in the *vins naturels* movement named Pierre Jancou.

The makings of a Parisian meal: cheese, charcuterie, cornichons, bread, and wine.

- **Surrendering control:** Tasting menus that offer no choices are becoming increasingly popular in Paris's restaurants. If you're ready to put yourself in the hands of a talented chef, try **Le Chateaubriand** (p. 203), **Cobéa** (p. 223), or **Spring** (p. 180).

- **Having a picnic:** When the weather is nice, the banks of the Seine River and the Canal St-Martin and the city's many parks become lined with Parisians enjoying a picnic in the open air. Bring a baguette, some cheese, and a bottle of wine (don't forget the bottle opener!), and join the locals for some of the cheapest fun to be had in Paris.

THE best MUSEUMS

- **Palais de Tokyo:** The Palais de Tokyo is a contemporary "art mall" that displays radical emerging art—even its hours (noon–midnight) are radical. After its 2012 renovation and expansion, the museum has become even more monumental, with double the exhibition space. You're bound to see thought-provoking exhibitions that you'd be unlikely to see elsewhere. See p. 108.

- **Musée du Louvre:** The Louvre's exterior is a triumph of French architecture, and its interior shelters an embarrassment of art, one of the greatest treasure troves known to Western civilization. Of the Louvre's more than 300,000 paintings, only a small percentage can be displayed at one time. The museum maintains its staid dignity and timelessness even though thousands of visitors traipse daily through its corridors, looking for the *Mona Lisa* or the *Venus de Milo.* I. M. Pei's controversial Great Pyramid nearly offsets the grandeur of the cour Carrée, but it has a real functional purpose. See p. 81.

- **Musée d'Orsay:** The spidery glass-and-iron canopies of a former railway station frame one of Europe's greatest museums of art. Devoted mainly to paintings of the 19th century, d'Orsay contains some of the most celebrated masterpieces of the French Impressionists, along with sculptures and decorative objects whose designs forever changed the way European artists interpreted line, movement, and color. This is also where *Whistler's Mother* sits in her rocker. See p. 136.

Musée du Louvre.

Centre Pompidou.

o **Centre Pompidou:** "The most avant-garde building in the world," or so it is known, is a citadel of modern art, with exhibitions drawn from more than 40,000 works. Everything seemingly is here—from Calder's 1928 *Josephine Baker* (one of his earliest versions of the mobile) to a re-creation of Brancusi's Jazz Age studio. See p. 90.

o **Musée des Arts Décoratifs:** In the northwest wing of the Louvre's Pavillon de Marsan, this imposing museum is home to a treasury of furnishings, fabrics, wallpaper, objets d'art, and items displaying living styles from the Middle Ages to the present. Notable are the 1920s Art Deco boudoir, bath, and bedroom done for couturier Jeanne Lanvin by the designer Rateau, plus a collection of the works donated by Jean Dubuffet. See p. 80.

o **Fondation Cartier:** This is a special place. The fine jeweler Cartier commissioned Pritzker Architecture Prize–winning architect Jean Nouvel to design a headquarters for its art foundation, and the result is an airy glass-and-steel structure. The foundation is known for presenting art from stars better known for their success in other fields, like Patti Smith or David Lynch. There is also a wild-looking garden surrounding the building, which is a pleasure to walk though. See p. 141.

The Lady and the Unicorn tapestries.

- **Musée Marmottan Monet:** On the edge of the Bois de Boulogne, this museum is home to 130 paintings, watercolors, pastels, and drawings of Claude Monet, the "father of Impressionism." A gift of Monet's son Michel, the bequest is one of the greatest art acquisitions in France. Exhibited here is the painting *Impression: Sunrise,* which named the artistic movement. See p. 106.

- **Musée Rodin:** Auguste Rodin, the man credited with freeing French sculpture from classicism, once lived at and had his studio in this charming 18th-century mansion across from Napoleon's tomb. Today the house and its garden are filled with his works, including *The Thinker* crouched on his pedestal, the *Burghers of Calais,* and the writhing *Gates of Hell.* See p. 138.

THE best FAMILY EXPERIENCES

- **Best for Keeping the Kids Quiet:** **Les Catacombes,** a creepy underground ossuary, will have the kids transfixed. Wander through almost 2km (1¼ miles) of labyrinthine corridors lined with 6 million bones, transferred here from Parisian cemeteries over 200 years ago. In the past, it served as a quarry, where stone was extracted for building, and during World War II, the French Resistance used the tunnel system to outsmart the German soldiers. See p. 141.

- **Best for History:** Originally a royal garden dedicated to medicinal plants, the **Jardin des Plantes,** set within a park that includes the **Natural History Museum,** offers a mesmerizing overview of the history of both sea and land creatures and gives an insight into the impact of man on nature by spotlighting different extinct and endangered animals. The Gallery of Paleontology presents a fascinating collection of fossils and specimens, including dinosaurs, mammoths, and even the skeleton of Louis XV's pet rhinoceros! Plus there's a charming zoo, featuring over 900 animals, everything from wallabies to pink flamingos to orangutans. See p. 125.

Les Catacombes.

- **Best for Wearing the Kids Out:** Europe's most visited theme park, **Disneyland Paris,** offers total sensory overload for the whole family in its five lands: Main Street, U.S.A.; Adventureland; Frontierland; Fantasyland; and Discoveryland. Fairy tales come alive in Sleeping Beauty's Castle, and adventurers will love Indiana Jones and the Temple of Peril. See p. 362.

Sleeping Beauty's Castle.

- **Best for a Picnic: Parc des Buttes Chaumont,** a large 19th-century park built by Napoleon III, is full of exciting features that the kids will love, like cliffs, a suspension bridge leading to a romantic stone belvedere, a lake with ducks and swans, and a massive grotto with a thundering waterfall. There are pony rides, a merry-go-round, an adventure playground, and a puppet theater too. See p. 120.

- **Best Gross Out:** Rémy the rat from the animated 2007 film *Ratatouille* made his way up from the Paris sewers to take the reins of the restaurant made famous by his gastronomic hero, Auguste Gusteau. Take the kids on this smelly tour through **Les Egouts,** the city's sewers, and give them a new perspective on the city and its history. See p. 135.

- **Best Climb: Basilique du Sacré-Coeur,** an impressive neo-Byzantine basilica, crowns the Montmartre hill, the highest point in the city. Give your calf muscles a workout getting to the top: Take the Metro to Anvers and walk up the hill to the gardens surrounding the church; from there, the funicular can take you up to the church, where around 500 steps await to take you to the very top of the edifice, and its panoramic views of the city below. See p. 111.

- **Best Place to Run and Play: Parc de la Villette,** Paris's largest park, includes 10 astounding gardens that guarantee the whole family a memorable day. Here you'll find the Garden of Childhood Fears, with its mysterious musical forest; the Garden of Acrobatics, with games involving balance and movement; the Dragon Garden; the Garden of Mirrors; and more. The park includes vast open spaces ideal for picnics and games. See p. 120.

- **Best High-Tech Experience:** Located within a beautifully restored and updated 19th-century Parisian theater in the heart of the city, the **Gaîté Lyrique** is a forward-thinking cultural institution devoted to exploring mixed-media and digital art forms. Kids will have a great time interacting with the rotating exhibits that range from music and multimedia performances to design and fashion to new media—there's even an interactive room dedicated to video games. See p. 92.

- **Best for Thrill-Seekers:** For the summer months of July and August, the **Jardin des Tuileries** hosts a **funfair** (www.feteforaine-jardindestuileries.com), a special amusement park that boasts all the classic amusements such as a

shooting gallery, trampolines, and a century-old wooden carousel. The enormous Ferris wheel provides superb views over Paris. See p. 78.

o **Best for a Hike: La Promenade Plantée,** a former railway line abandoned since 1969, has been transformed into a 4.5km (2.8-mile) pedestrian walkway that runs through the 12th arrondissement. It begins near Bastille at the avenue Dausmenil and ends at the Bois de Vincennes. Have fun cutting through the city on this elevated green path, planted with all sorts of plants and trees. See p. 114.

Walking through La Promenade Plantée.

THE best FREE & DIRT CHEAP PARIS

o **Meeting the Natives:** Meeting Parisians is one of the adventures of traveling to Paris—and it's free. Visitors often find Parisians brusque to the point of rudeness, but this hardened crust often protects a soft center. Compliment a surly bistro owner on her cuisine, and—9 times out of 10—she'll melt before your eyes. Admire a Parisian's dog and you'll find a loquaciously knowledgeable companion. Try to meet a Parisian halfway with some kind of personalized contact. Only then do you learn their best qualities: their famed charm, their savoir-faire—and, yes, believe it or not, the delightful courtesy that marks their social life.

o **Attending a Free Concert:** Summer brings a Paris joy: free festivals and concerts in parks and churches all over the city. The Paris Jazz Festival takes place in the Parc Floral in June and July; there's outdoor cinema at La Villette throughout August. Some of the best concerts are held at the **American Church in Paris,** 65 quai d'Orsay, 7e (*℃* 01-40-62-05-00; p. 273), which sponsors free concerts from September to June on Sunday at 5pm. You can also attend free concerts on Saturdays at 5:45pm at **Eglise St-Merri,** 76 rue de la Verrerie (*℃* 01-42-71-93-93; p. 273). These performances are staged based on the availability of the performers, from September to July on Saturday at 9pm and again on Sunday at 4pm.

o **Hanging Out at Place des Vosges:** Deep in the Marais, place des Vosges is more an enchanted island than a city square. Laid out in 1605 by order of Henri IV, this lovely oasis is the oldest square in Paris. In the middle is a tiny park where you can sit and sun, listen to the splashing waters of the fountains, or watch the kids at play. On three sides is an encircling arcaded walk, supported by arches and paved with ancient, worn flagstones. Sit sipping an espresso and people-watch as the day passes you by. See p. 96.

Strolling through the arcade at place des Vosges.

A contemporary art exhibit.

o **Viewing Contemporary Art:** Space is too tight to document the dozens of art galleries that abound in Paris, but the true devotee will find that not all great art in Paris is displayed in a museum. Our favorite galleries in the Marais include big guns **Emmanuel Perrotin,** 76 rue du Turenne, 3e (© **01-42-16-79-79;** www.galerieperrotin.com), and **Yvon Lambert,** 108 rue Vieille du Temple, 3e (© **01-42-71-09-330;** www.yvon-lambert.com). They display changing exhibits from both Parisian and international avant-garde artists. Many galleries dealing in modern art are in St-Germain-des-Prés, many along the rue de Seine.

o **Strolling the World's Grandest Promenade:** Pointing from place de la Concorde like a broad, straight arrow to the Arc de Triomphe at the far end, the **Champs-Élysées** (the main street of Paris) presents its grandest spectacle at night. Paris guidebook writers grow tired of repeating "the most in the world," but, of course, the Champs-Élysées is the world's most famous promenade. For the first third of the stroll from place de la Concorde, the avenue is lined by chestnut trees. Then it changes into a double row of palatial hotels and shops, office buildings, and endless sidewalk cafes.

o **Cooling Off in the Jardin des Tuileries:** Parisians head to the Tuileries Gardens to cool off on a hot summer day. The park stretches on the Right Bank of the Seine from the place de la Concorde to the doorstep of the Louvre. This exquisitely formal garden was laid out as a royal pleasure ground in 1564, but was thrown open to the public by the French Revolution. Filled with statues (some by Rodin), fountains, and mathematically trimmed hedges, its nicest feature is a series of round ponds on which kids sail armadas of model boats.

o **Seeing Paris from a Bus:** Most tours of Paris are expensive, but for only 1.70€ you can ride one of the city's public buses traversing some of the most scenic streets. Our favorite is no. 29, which begins at historic Gare St-Lazare, subject of Monet's painting *La Gare St-Lazare* at Musée d'Orsay and featured in Zola's novel *La Bête Humaine.* Aboard no. 29, you pass the famous Opéra Garnier and proceed into the Marais district, passing by the place des Vosges. You end up at the Bastille district, home of the new opera. It's a cheap way to see the city without a tour guide's commentary.

Relaxing in the Jardin des Tuileries.

THE best HISTORIC EXPERIENCES

- Invoking Ancient Rome at the Musée National du Moyen Age/Thermes de Cluny (Musée de Cluny): This museum associates two historic edifices: the medieval Hôtel of the Abbots of Cluny and the ruins of the city's Gallo-Roman baths. These ancient thermal baths date from when the city—then known as Lutetia—was under Roman rule, between the 1st and 3rd centuries. *Thermae*, or municipal baths, were at the center of daily life in Roman society, providing a social forum for citizens. These ruins, along with the nearby outdoor amphitheater, are the only significant traces of the city's Roman period. See p. 125.

- Discovering the Oldest Church in Paris at St-Germain-des-Prés: This is the oldest church in Paris, predating the Gothic Notre-Dame cathedral nearby by at least 600 years. The site was originally a Benedictine abbey founded in 542 by the Merovingian King Childebert to house a relic of the cross brought back from Spain. The Vikings pillaged the building in the 7th century, but the tower and nave were rebuilt 2 centuries later, and are now the only remaining vestiges of Romanesque architecture left in Paris. See p. 131.

- Remembering Marie Antoinette at the Conciergerie: The seat of royal power for 400 years, from the 10th to the 14th centuries, this is the oldest royal palace in the capital. After Charles V abandoned the palace for a new residence in the current Marais, it was converted into a prison, and during the French Revolution, Marie Antoinette was held there before being guillotined. It's a great example of the architecture of the Middle Ages; don't miss the Gens d'Armes room, the Guard room, and the kitchens. On the northeastern corner you can still see the city's first public clock, installed in 1370. See p. 91.

- Exploring the Musée du Louvre: The history of the Louvre and the history of Paris are practically one. This emblematic building has dominated

THE BEST OF PARIS

The Best Historic Experiences

1

13

The Conciergerie.

the center of the city since the 12th century, changing over the years from a medieval fortress (you can still see these foundations in the basement today) to the gargantuan palace it became under the Sun King, Louis XIV, in the 17th century. Today, the Louvre is one of the world's most important museums. See p. 81.

o **Commemorating Medieval Times at La Sainte-Chapelle:** This medieval monument on the Ile de la Cité was built to house Christ's Crown of Thorns, which King Louis IX (Saint Louis) bought from the emperor of Constantinople in the 13th century. Considered a veritable masterpiece of Gothic architecture, it features 600 sq. m (6,460 sq. ft.) of magnificent stained-glass windows. The architecture is so delicate that when you are inside the church, you feel as if you are in a palace entirely constructed of colored glass. See p. 96.

o **Reliving the French Revolution at Place de la Bastille:** The Bastille prison once stood here, and its storming on July 14, 1789, signaled the start of the French Revolution. In 1794, the revolutionary authorities beheaded 75 enemies of the state with its guillotine. Today the Bastille Square remains a powerfully symbolic site for Parisians and many marches and demonstrations start or finish here. See p. 114.

o **Honoring Napoleon at the Arc de Triomphe:** Napoleon commissioned this triumphal arch in 1806 in homage to his military victories. It is decorated with reliefs and sculptures representing scenes from his epic battles, and is the centerpiece of the place Charles de Gaulle-Etoile. Twelve majestic avenues commence at the base of the monument, most of which bear the names of famous battles fought by Napoleon (for example, Friedland and Wagram). The view from the top is incredible. See p. 100.

o **Drinking with the literary greats at Café de Flore:** The Café de Flore has been at the center of the city's intellectual life since it opened its doors in

The stained-glass windows of Sainte-Chapelle.

1887. The writer Charles Maurras wrote his book *Au signe de Flore* there. The cafe has been associated with poets Guillaume Apollinaire, Louis Aragon, and Jacques Prévert; philosopher Jean-Paul Sartre; and expat American writers Arthur Koestler, Ernest Hemingway, and Truman Capote. Today you can still order a glass of *vin* and toast to all the drinks, arguments, and ideas that have passed through this exceptional place. See p. 229.

THE best LOCAL EXPERIENCES

o **Picnicking on the Canal St-Martin:** On a nice day, pack a picnic lunch and head to the banks of the charming Canal St-Martin, where you'll find bohemian Parisians relaxing under the shady plane trees and dining with friends. You can even order pizza from Pink Flamingo (p. 209) and have it delivered to your picnic spot. See p. 116.

o **Feasting on Oysters and Chablis:** During oyster season (Sept–Apr), take the time for a briny lunch of *fines de claire* oysters washed down with a glass—or two—of chablis, a white wine from Burgundy. Many bistros and brasseries serve oysters during this period—you'll know by the heaping mounds of oysters set up on tables in front of these establishments.

o **Easting Asian in Chinatown:** While most visitors don't associate Paris with Asian food, the city has an important Asian community originating primarily from China, Laos, Vietnam, and Cambodia. There are two Chinatowns in the city; the smallest at Metro Belleville and the largest in the 13th arrondissement near Metro Porte d'Ivry. Here you can eat well (and cheaply) while seeing a different side of the city. See p. 213.

o **Riding a Bike:** The city's small size and predominantly flat terrain make it ideal for cycling. The city government actively encourages bike riding: you'll see bike paths around the city, and there's even an efficient municipal bike

Shopping at a local food market.

rental system, the **Vélib'** (www.velib.paris.fr). It's an invigorating way to see the city.

o **Bathing in a Hammam:** Bathhouses are common in Paris; this custom was imported by Paris's important communities from Maghreb, where hammams are prevalent. The best known and perhaps most beautiful hammam is the one inside the **La Grande Mosquée de Paris.** Strip down (it's women or men only) and relax in the succession of increasingly hot steam rooms, before plunging into a cold pool. Finish off the experience with a cleansing mint tea. See p. 122.

o **Perusing the Local Food Markets:** Possibly everything there is to say about the charm of the city's local food markets has already been said—it's a delight for all the senses. Get inspired by the variety of fresh French produce, from its cheeses to charcuteries to fruits, vegetables, seafood, meats, and world-class bread. See p. 243.

o **Hitting the Sales:** Twice a year Paris shops sacrifice their current collections, with up to 75% reductions, to make way for new stock. Summer sales start in the last week of June, and winter sales start in early January. Parisians stock up on everything from clothes to home goods to electronics at these city-wide sales. See p. 268.

o **Taking an Aperitif:** The *apéro* (predinner drink) is a common ritual in Paris, where Parisians meet in their favorite local bars and bistros for a chat and a drink, usually around 7pm. The aperitif is meant to open the appetite, and classic examples include white wine, champagne, pastis, or vermouth. See p. 275.

Bicycling along the Canal St-Martin.

THE best NEIGHBORHOODS FOR GETTING LOST

o **Montmartre:** Montmartre has a village-like atmosphere that you won't find elsewhere in Paris. The best way to appreciate its charm is to avoid the tourist traps and make your way slowly up *la butte* (the hill) along the winding, cobblestone streets. Admire Montmartre's two surviving windmills on **rue Lepic** and the tiny vineyard on **rue des Saules.** All over Montmartre are plaques, statues, and street names that pay homage to the great writers, artists, and musicians who have lived here, including van Gogh and Picasso. Many of these former residents are now buried in the **Montmartre cemetery,** perfect for a peaceful stroll.

o **The 5th arrondissement:** Stretching from the Seine to the Panthéon, most people come to the 5th to visit the historic Latin Quarter. But you'll see another, quieter side to the 5th if you head to the **place Monge** area. There are lots of narrow little back streets here worth exploring. Admire the picturesque **place de la Contrascarpe,** which leads into the lively market street **rue Mouffetard,** a popular student hangout. Have tea in the **Great Mosque of Paris** and stroll through the lovely **Jardin des Plantes.** History buffs should visit the old Roman amphitheater, **Arènes de Lutèce.**

A staircase in Montmartre.

o **Le Marais:** The Marais is one of the most fashionable districts in Paris, known for its boutiques, lively bars, elegant private mansions, "gay Paree," and strong Jewish community—you'll find all of this in the streets around **rue des Francs-Bourgeois, rue des Archives,** and **rue des Rosiers.** But these days it's the quieter, edgier upper Marais (in the 3rd arrondissement) that everybody is talking about, and it's a great place for an idle stroll. The streets around **rue de Bretagne** are full of trendy boutiques and contemporary art galleries and the **Marché des Enfants Rouge** is a great place to stop for food.

o **13th arrondissement:** If you're eager to get off the beaten track and see a different side of Paris, head to the **Olympiades** area. Immigrants from China, Vietnam, Cambodia, and Laos have transformed the area between **rue de Tolbiac, avenue de Choisy,** and **boulevard Massena** into a

A street in the Quartier Latin.

vibrant and exotic Chinatown. Explore the peaceful, cobblestoned streets around the picturesque **rue de la Butte aux Cailles** area, where you'll find a number of charming bars and cafes.

o **Belleville:** Belleville is a great starting point for exploring northeast Paris. Its working-class history and diverse immigrant populations have transformed it into one of the city's most vibrant neighborhoods. Cheap rents have attracted many artists and you're sure to come across artists' studios and colorful street art (head to **rue Denoyez** for some good examples). **Parc de Belleville** offers wonderful views of Paris and if you're a fan of green spaces, the lovely **Buttes Chaumont** is only a short-walk away. Around **rue de Menilmontant** you'll find cool bars and vintage shops. Further east is the renowned **Père-Lachaise** cemetery.

PARIS IN DEPTH

by Sophie Nellis

2

Paris is a city that is steeped in history, and its past is omnipresent throughout the city. Over the centuries, the city has been shaped by many great men, a few great women, and its rowdy and rebellious inhabitants: the Parisians. From Philippe Auguste, the first king to build a wall around the city, to François Mitterrand, the former French president responsible for I. M. Pei's glass pyramid in the Louvre, Paris's rulers have ensured their places in history by imprinting their tastes and their political visions on the city. But the Parisians have always been skeptical of authority. Whether they are building barricades, hurling cobblestones, or marching through the streets, Parisians have always made it clear that the city belongs to them. They remain very proud of Paris, and, thanks to the city's great art, fashion, and food, Parisians are some of the most cultured people on the planet.

However, over the past few decades, many Parisians have been complaining that the city has lost its soul, that it's turning into *Paris Ville-Musée* (Paris the Museum). Less edgy than Berlin and less hip than London, Paris seemed to be stagnating. But the city is fighting back, and is slowly reinventing itself as a 21st-century capital. From the young designers setting up shop in the 3rd arrondissement to the pioneering chefs who are experimenting with neo-bistros, and from new sustainability initiatives—such as the Vélib' bike-rental program—to a growing immigrant population, the city is rapidly changing and Parisian traditions are being injected with a new sense of dynamism. The future of Paris is far from certain, but one thing's for sure: Paris is a city on the move.

PARIS TODAY

Paris today is a dynamic, vibrant city, and much of that can be attributed to Bertrand Delanoë, the Socialist mayor who has been in office since 2001. The first openly gay mayor of a European capital, he was reelected in 2008 and is generally well liked and respected by Parisians. Although he did fail to win Paris's bid for the 2012 Olympic Games, he has done a lot to improve the city. He has implemented free Wi-Fi in many public places, and created programs such as Paris Plage (a fake beach set up alongside the Seine in the summer) and La Nuit Blanche (an all-night arts festival in October). He has also undertaken several environmentally-friendly initiatives; it was Delanoë who was responsible for both the highly popular **Vélib'** bike-rental program and the increase in the amount of bike lanes around the city. Encouraged by the success of the Vélibs, he recently launched another green initiative, the **Autolib',** which hopes to encourage Parisians to rent rather than own a car. With only 2 more years left in office, the

Street musicians.

mayor is now turning his attention to the Seine. From summer 2012, the section of the quays between Pont d'Alma and the Musée d'Orsay will be entirely closed to traffic and transformed into a pedestrian zone reserved for sports and cultural activities. A new boat network called **Voguéo** is also being developed, which will be incorporated into the city's public transport network and will offer commuters an alternative to the Métro and the RER; it is due to be completed in 2013.

Green is not just a popular color with the mayor. Paris has been undergoing a *bio* (organic) revolution for a few years, and being green, organic, and ethical is very much in fashion these days. You can find the health food store **Naturalia** (www.naturalia.fr) in nearly every neighborhood, and all major supermarkets now offer their own ranges of both organic and environmentally-friendly products. Restaurants that offer organic dishes are becoming increasingly popular, and organic wine is also in high demand. New, informal green spaces have started to appear around the city in the form of *jardins partagés* (community gardens), where people can grow vegetables, plant flowers, or simply enjoy the greenery. There's even a new music festival called We Love Green.

Tackling the housing crisis is another one of the key points on Delanoë's agenda for the next couple of years. Housing prices in Paris have been increasing for years and demand greatly outweighs supply. The new social housing initiatives that the mayor is experimenting with incorporate many of his ideas about sustainable development, but they might drastically change Paris's beloved skyline. Challenging a 1977 by-law that limits the height of buildings within Paris to 37m (121 ft.), he is convinced that tower blocks offer the best solution to the housing crisis. Several sites, including Porte de la Chapelle in the 18e and the Masséna-Bruneseau district of the 13e, have been chosen as potential locations for 50m (164 ft.) and 200m (656 ft.) towers.

Unsurprisingly, Delanoë is a keen advocate of the **Tour Triangle,** a 180m-tall (590 ft.) glass office building to be built at the Porte de Versailles in the 15e; the designers are Herzog & de Meuron, the same firm who did London's

Tate Modern. Planned for 2017, the tower is currently at the consultation stage. However, the project has already come under attack; some critics claim that the tower will ruin the city's skyline, while others argue that money should be spent on building housing not office blocks.

As rising house prices have made it virtually impossible for anyone other than the super wealthy to live in central Paris, you'll find a lot more life in the outer arrondissements. In recent years, there's been a shift toward the northern and northeastern arrondissements, which were traditionally home to the city's *quartiers populaires* (working-class districts). These neighborhoods tend to be edgy and dynamic, as prices are lower, rents are cheaper, and the nightlife is better. Here, you'll find a mix of students, artists, immigrants, middle-class families, and **bobos** (short for *bourgeois-bohèmes*, which means bourgeois bohemian). Who are the *bobos*? Usually liberal, the *bobos* are a creative and chic group, most of whom have a middle-class education and strong ambitions for success. Over the past decade, the *bobos* have been transforming the face of Paris, moving into the *quartiers populaires* and bringing with them chic boutiques, trendy bars, and organic restaurants. As more and more parts of Paris become gentrified, the *bobos* are now key players in the life and soul of the city.

What defines the Paris of today, and key to the city's evolution as a 21st-century capital, is Paris's interaction with the **banlieues** (suburbs). There are more than 10 million people living in the Parisian suburbs and only around 2.2 million in Paris. Some of the suburbs—such as Issy-les-Moulineaux, Levallois-Perret, and Montreuil—are nice, residential areas and many middle-class families prefer living outside Paris because property is cheaper and more spacious. But not every suburb is a leafy, suburban paradise. Northern suburbs such as St-Denis and Aubervilliers-La Courneuve are infamous for their sprawling housing estates (known as *cités*), poor transport connections, high unemployment, and high crime rate. Understandably, many young people living in these suburbs, particularly the children of immigrants, feel isolated and excluded from French society. These social tensions exploded in October 2005, when two teenage boys were electrocuted while hiding from police in an electricity substation in Clichy-sous-Bois. Their deaths sparked huge riots in the vast, run-down housing estates; the violence spread all over France, from Marseilles to Strasbourg, and lasted for several weeks. Since the 2005 riots, the *banlieues* have received a great deal of media attention but nobody is sure how to deal with what appears to be a profound sense of alienation. For young people living in

Bicycling is a popular means of transportation in Paris.

Bobos (short for bourgeois-bohèmes) are usually young, creative, and fashionable.

these troubled suburbs today, little has changed. It remains very difficult to get a job in Paris if your address places you in one of the *cités,* and in some of the racially diverse estates in Clichy-sous-Bois, unemployment for those under 25 is as high as 40%.

For people living in the suburbs, getting to Paris is often stressful, time-consuming, expensive and, occasionally, dangerous. A monthly transport pass for Paris (which is comprised of zones 1 and 2) now costs 63€. If you live in zone 5 it costs 116€. About 1 million people take the RER Line A everyday, making it the third-busiest route in the world; there are 800,000 on its B counterpart. Passengers are increasing by about 5% (about 25,000 people each year), so to maintain the same quality of service would require 25 new trains. But as the lines are already saturated none have been added. Strikes and breakdowns are frequent occurrences.

Many believe that the solution lies in better integrating Paris into the surrounding suburbs—or better integrating the surrounding suburbs into Paris, depending on how you look at it, and President Nicolas Sarkozy seemed to agree. In April 2009, he launched an ambitious urban renewal project, **Le Grand Paris,** which aims to improve transportation and housing in the Paris metropolitan region, while making Paris a greener, more sustainable 21st-century city. Internationally-renowned architects, like Jean Nouvel, Roland Castro, and Richard Rogers, lead teams that are responsible for generating new ideas and analyzing Paris's urban development. Ideas so far include a monorail-style Métro running above the *périphérique* (the ring road that surrounds Paris, known as the *périph*), green housing estates, and transforming Paris into a port city by linking it to Le Havre with a high-speed train. Le Grand Paris is an ambitious long-term project that will be implemented over the next decade, but the principal transport initiatives are being launched in 2012. The backbone of the transport network is going to be Métro Line 14; the plan is to extend it north and south, to both Charles de Gaulle airport and Orly airport. There is also talk of having a single tariff for all journeys in zones 1 to 5.

It is hoped that Le Grand Paris will not only breathe new life into the *banlieues* but also challenge existing notions of centrality and revitalize Paris's historic center. Given that just a few years ago, Parisians were afraid that their city was turning into a somewhat sanitized *Paris Ville-Musée* (Paris the Museum), this can only be seen as a good thing. The center of the city is currently dotted with building sites. The ugly shopping center **Forum Les Halles,** located on the site of the former food markets known as Les Halles, is currently undergoing a renovation which will cover the complex with a giant canopy; the project is slated to be completed in 2014. Nearby, on the rue de Rivoli, work is due to start on **La Samaritaine,** the legendary French department store opened by the Cognacq-Jay family in 1870. The site is now owned by the LVMH group (Louis Vuitton Moët Hennessy), which has decided to transform La Samaritaine into a luxury hotel, with some obligatory social housing and a municipal kindergarten thrown in for good measure.

Culturally, Paris still has a lot to offer. From opera houses to fashion houses and art galleries to theaters, culture remains an integral part of *la vie Parisienne.* Although the art scene is not as edgy or avant-garde as in London or New York, Paris remains an important city on the exhibition circuit, hosting several major exhibitions every year, as well as the **FIAC** (Foire International d'Art Contemporain; www.fiac.com) art fair in October. Several of Paris's most famous museums have been undergoing a makeover, or, as the French would say, a *relooking.* In October 2011 the **Musée d'Orsay** unveiled its new look after a 2-year renovation that cost 20€ million. The highlight is a new Impressionist gallery, which hopes to show the Impressionist masterpieces in a completely new light. Not to be outdone by its Left Bank rival, the **Louvre** is planning to open a new wing dedicated to Islamic Art in the summer of 2012. Although the budget is currently 10€ million short, the widely anticipated plans for this wing are progressing. However, these museum renovations often seem to involve inflated budgets and long delays—like the **Musée Picasso.** Although work on the Picasso museum began in 2009, the museum is not due to re-open until the spring of 2013.

Although a visit to Paris would be incomplete without visiting its major museums, it's also worth going a little further afield to check out newer cultural spaces. The **104** (www.104.fr; ☎ 01-53-35-50-00), a cultural center located in the former Municipal Funeral Service warehouses in the 19e, is home to a number of artists in residence and exhibition spaces; and the contemporary art gallery **Mac/Val** (www.macval.fr; ☎ 01-43-91-64-20) in the Parisian suburb of Vitry-sur-Seine has a great permanent collection and hosts interesting temporary exhibitions.

Paris remains a food lover's dream destination and Parisians are as passionate about food and eating out as ever. The big trend in Parisian dining at the moment is the **neo-bistrot.** Known for an innovative approach to cooking and a relaxed atmosphere, the neo-bistrot serves high-quality French food at reasonable prices (usually under 50€ per person). Rejecting the formalities of Michelin-starred restaurants, the neo-bistrots try to be more casual. One French chef, Alain Senderens, even went so far as to reject his Michelin stars. Popular neo-bistrots include **Frenchie** in the 2e (p. 181), **Claude Colliot** in the 4e, **Le Comptoir du Relais** in the 6e (p. 216), and **Jadis** in the 15e (p. 224).

THE new PARISIANS

Paris is often described as a melting pot, and the city is home to large numbers of immigrant communities. While some Parisians welcome immigrants and are keen to acknowledge the contributions that immigrants have made to French society, others have balked at the perceived drain on their resources and fear that immigrants are not prepared to integrate into French society.

Immigration first became a major political debate in the 1990s and since then it has become strongly associated with questions of national identity. Some would even go so far as to say that 21st-century France is suffering from an identity crisis. As a secular, republican state, France has always favored assimilation over multiculturalism. This is partly a result of the French concept of identity, which is based on the 1789 Declaration of the Rights of Man. If all citizens are equal, ethnicity and religion must remain outside of the political sphere, and all citizens are thus divested of their origins. Consequently, it is illegal to collect ethnic-based data in France and there are no statistics about the children of immigrants. In theory, if you are born in France, you're French.

In practice, however, it's very different and many second- and third-generation immigrants don't feel French. In November 2009, Sarkozy launched a debate about national identity. At the center of the debate was the question "What does it mean to be French?" The debate received a lot of media attention and public meetings were held across the country. However, many commentators felt that the debate ignored the colonial legacy, and that the real but unspoken question was "Can one be black, Arab, Asian, and still be French?" The debate is particularly pertinent in Paris because the majority of Paris's immigrant populations live on the other side of the *périphérique* in the *banlieues*. This means that there is a physical, as well as psychological, divide between Parisians and the Paris region's immigrant population. What is sure is that if Le Grand Paris or other urban renewal projects are to succeed, they must include these new Parisians.

Key to this identity debate is the position of Islam in France, which is home to the largest Muslim population in Europe—Muslims account for roughly 8% of the French population. In January 2010 the government began a campaign to ban the burqa (the veil that covers all of a woman's face). Sarkozy claimed that it was not welcome in France, a secular country that values gender equality. Once again, the campaign provoked an intense media debate and in April 2011 the burqa ban became legal. Any woman seen wearing a burqa in public risks being fined 150€, while husbands who force their wives to wear it face a fine of 15,000€ or even a prison sentence. Only about 2,000 women wear the burqa in France.

Another interesting and perhaps surprising food trend is the rising popularity of Anglo-Saxon food. **The Rose Bakery** in the 3e and 9e, **Bob's Juice Bar** in the 3e and 10e, and **Le Bal Café** in the 18e are all doing a pretty good job of introducing Parisians to the joys of British and American cuisine. There's even a gourmet food truck selling American-style hamburgers that is making the rounds in Paris; set up by a Californian chef, look out for **Le Camion qui Fume**

(p. 189). As people look for a more unique eating experience, underground restaurants and private supper clubs are becoming increasingly popular in cities all over the world, and Paris is no exception. Ranging from top-secret soirées that are notoriously difficult to find out about to well-known gatherings such as Paris's **Hidden Kitchen,** underground restaurants offer foodies an intimate dining experience with like-minded people.

This Anglo-Saxon influence is not limited to food. Younger Parisians are a fairly international bunch, most of whom can speak English and are interested in traveling and working abroad. They are also interested in English music and culture. Thanks to a 1994 law passed to protect French pop, at least 40% of the music played on the Paris radio stations has to be French. But despite this, more and more musicians are singing in English, such as Charlotte Gainsbourg, alternative rock band Phoenix, and electro-pop band Pony Pony Run Run. And following his 2010 Grammy Award, French DJ David Guetta is currently one of the most sought after music producers in the world. However, this year Parisians are turning their attention to classical music. Designed by Jean Nouvel, **La Philharmonie de Paris** (www.philharmoniedeparis.com) is due to open in 2013 in the 19th arrondissement, overlooking Parc de la Villette. The aluminum structure will be home to a 2,400-seat auditorium, which the city hopes will transform Paris into a world capital of music for the 21st century.

Going to the cinema remains a popular pastime for Parisians, and there is at least one cinema in each of the 20 arrondissements. Compared to other capitals, you can still find a lot of independent, art house cinemas in Paris, and a diverse range of films are always on offer in the city. Filmmakers are as fascinated by Paris as ever—Woody Allen's most recent film *Midnight in Paris,* with a cameo appearance by France's first lady Carla Bruni-Sarkozy, was a charming, romantic comedy full of nostalgia for the city's literary and artistic glory days. Recent box office successes include the silent film *The Artist,* which won the 2012 Oscar for the Best Picture, Best Actor, and Best Director categories, and *Intouchables,* a comedy which tackled hard-hitting themes such as the *banlieues,* race, and disability.

Dominique Strauss-Kahn's presidential hopes were dashed when he was arrested in New York for the attempted rape of a hotel maid in May 2011. Although the charges were later dropped, DSK was forced to resign as head of the IMF. At press time, he was under investigation for his alleged involvement in a prostitution ring centered on the Hotel Carlton in Lille, and it seemed unlikely he would make a political comeback. In December 2011, former president Jacques Chirac was given a 2-year suspended sentence for embezzling funds while he was Mayor of Paris from 1977 to 1995.

In the **2012 French Presidential Election,** the Parti Socialiste (Socialist Party) candidate **François Hollande** defeated the incumbent president Nicolas Sarkozy. At a time of severe economic crisis, unemployment, austerity, and national identity were all key issues during the campaign. Nicknamed "Mr. Normal," Hollande has promised to challenge the German-led austerity measures against the Eurozone crisis, create 60,000 new teaching jobs across France, reduce the deficit by taxing the wealthy, and pull French troops out of Afghanistan by the end of the year. With France's high public debt, record levels of unemployment, and poor growth, new President Hollande certainly has his work cut out for him. As Sarkozy put it in his presidency concession speech, "a new era of France has started."

THE MAKING OF PARIS
The Origins of Paris

Early humans were roaming the plains of Paris and hunting deer, boar, and bears as early as 700,000 years ago. In the 1990s, several dugout canoes dating from around 4500 B.C. were found in Bercy, and they revealed the importance of the river in the lives of these early societies. You can see some of these boats in the **Musée Carnavalet** (p. 93) in the Marais.

By 250 B.C., a tribe of Celts known as the **Parisii** had settled on the present-day Ile de la Cité. The Parisii were first and foremost river people and the Seine was a place of trade and exchange. Both the strategic location of the Parisii's fortified town and the relative wealth of the community soon attracted the attention of the Romans.

Roman Paris & Early Christianity (52 B.C.–A.D. 400)

By the time the Romans, led by Julius Caesar, conquered the Parisii in 54 B.C., much of southern Gaul had already fallen into Roman hands. The Roman occupation of Gaul was immortalized in the enormously popular *Asterix* comic books, written by René Goscinny and illustrated by Albert Uderzo. First published in 1959, the series follows a group of Gauls—led by Asterix and his friend Obelix—as they resist the Roman occupier.

Under the Romans, this thriving community became known as **Lutetia** (*Lutèce* in French). Most of the 8,000 inhabitants lived on the Left Bank, around today's rue St-Jacques and boulevard St-Michel. You can still see traces of Lutetia today: the site of the 15,000-seat amphitheater on rue Monge, the **Arènes de Lutèce** (p. 121), has been preserved, and the remains of the Roman baths are in the **Thermes de Cluny** (p. 125).

Christianity first came to Paris in the form of Saint Denis. In around A.D. 250 Denis was sent from Athens to Lutetia to convert the Gallo-Roman Parisians, who were notorious for their pagan ways. Denis founded the Parisian church and became the first Bishop of Paris. Beheaded near the Gallo-Roman temple of Mercury in Montmartre, legend has it that Denis picked up his head and carried it to the present-day suburb of St-Denis where he died. Denis's headless antics led to him becoming one of Paris's patron saints.

Roman ruins at the Thermes de Cluny.

Saint Geneviève, a pious virgin who is said to have defended Paris from Attila the Hun, is another important figure in Paris's history. From A.D. 275 onward, Lutetia was raided by wave after wave of barbarian invaders from across the Rhine river. Although the Romans managed to hold onto the town for two more centuries, Roman rule in Gaul began to disintegrate as a result of these Germanic invasions. In A.D. 451, Attila the Hun was threatening the city and its inhabitants were preparing to flee. Thanks to the intervention of young Geneviève, who prayed for Paris and encouraged the people to stay and defend the city, Attila backed off and Paris was spared. She was less fortunate in 486 when she had to surrender the city to Clovis, King of the Francs, after he had blockaded Paris for 10 years. There is a shrine dedicated to Ste-Geneviève in the church of **St-Etienne-du-Mont** (p. 127) in the 5e, and a statue of her on the Pont de la Tournelle, which was made by Paul Landowski in 1928. Ever wary of invaders, you'll notice that Ste-Geneviève is facing the east.

From Clovis to the Capetians (5th c.–10th c.)

Clovis, the first king of the Franks (a west Germanic tribe) ruled France in the 5th century. He chose Paris as the capital of his kingdom and founded the **Merovingian dynasty,** which ruled from 486 to 752. Clovis's wife, Clotilde, persuaded him to convert to Christianity and a spate of church building began the Christianization of the city. In 511 Clovis's son, **Childebert,** commissioned the cathedral of St-Etienne, the forerunner of Notre Dame. Its remains can be seen in the archaeological crypt under the place du Parvis Notre Dame. Childebert also brought the relics of Saint Vincent to Paris and placed them in a chapel on the Left Bank. He decided to build a basilica to house the relics, which eventually became known as **St-Germain-des-Prés.** Over the following centuries it became the Left Bank's most powerful abbey.

The Merovingians were succeeded by the militaristic **Carolingian dynasty,** which ruled from 752 to 987. The most famous of the Carolingians was **Charlemagne,** who conquered half of Europe but chose Aix-la-Chapelle (in present-day Germany), rather than Paris, as his capital. Exposed and badly defended, Paris was vulnerable to invasion and was repeatedly sacked and pillaged by the Normans in the 9th century. Many of the churches that had been built in the 6th century were destroyed. In the absence of the Carolingian kings Paris was ruled by the counts, and in 987 they elected a new king, **Hugues Capet.** This was the beginning of a new dynasty and a new era of great prosperity for Paris. Under the **Capetian dynasty,** which ruled France from 987 to 1328, Paris was once again the royal capital and the kings lived in a palace on the Ile de la Cité (on the site of the present-day Palais de Justice).

Five Paris Historical Reads

Andrew Hussey, *Paris: The Secret History* (Bloomsbury, 2006)
Colin Jones, *Paris: The Biography of a City* (Viking, 2004)
Graham Robb, *Parisians: An Adventure History of Paris* (Norton & Co., 2010)
Rod Kedward, *La Vie en Bleu, France and the French Since 1900* (Penguin, 2006)
Alistair Horne, *Seven Ages of Paris* (Knopf, 2002)

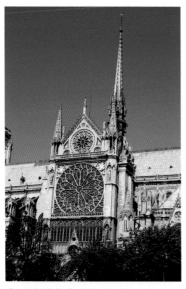

The **Cathédrale de Notre-Dame** is a prime example of Gothic architecture.

The Middle Ages (11th c.–15th c.)

During the Middle Ages, Paris flourished and became a center of politics, commerce, trade, religion, education, and culture. The "Queen of Cities" was divided into three parts: the Ile de la Cité remained the administrative heart of Paris and it was here that you could find the symbols of state power such as the royal palace and the cathedral; the Left Bank, thanks to the creation of the University of Paris, was a place of education and learning; and the Right Bank saw a boom in commercial activity and became the center of trade and commerce. These associations have continued throughout the history of Paris and, to a certain degree, remain true today.

The 12th and 13th centuries were a time of intense building activity, and it was in this period that **Gothic architecture** was born. Engineering developments had freed church architecture from the thick, heavy walls of Romanesque structures and allowed ceilings to soar, walls to thin, and windows to proliferate. Graceful buttresses and spires soared above town centers. Inside, the gothic interiors invited churchgoers to gaze upward at the high ceilings filled with light, and it was believed that building taller churches would bring people closer to God. The Gothic phase is believed to have begun with Abbot Suger's rebuilding of the **Abbey of St-Denis,** which was consecrated in 1144. However, it was the **Cathédrale de Notre-Dame** (p. 86) that made the style so influential. Work began on Notre-Dame in 1163, and it took 2 centuries to build; the Gothic style was preserved until the 17th century when, in the name of restoration, the church suffered a number of mutilations. Higher than any other building in the city, Notre-Dame dramatically altered the skyline of medieval Paris and could be seen from miles around. The success of **Victor Hugo's epic novel *Notre-Dame de Paris,*** published in 1831, led to a revival of interest in Gothic architecture and, more importantly, to the restoration of Notre-Dame. This was carried out by renowned 19th-century architect Eugène Viollet-le-Duc.

During the Middle Ages, the monarch who did the most to consolidate Paris's reputation as a great city was **Philippe Auguste,** who ruled France from 1180 to 1223. He built the **Louvre** (p. 81), a 33m-high (108-ft.) tower that was used to defend the city from attack and survey the surrounding area (the word Louvre is thought to have come from the old French word *louver,* which meant stronghold). He was also responsible for the first covered market at **Les Halles** (p. 243), which strengthened the reputation of the Right Bank as a center of commerce and trade. His greatest achievement, however, was the military fortifications he constructed around the city from 1190 to 1213. Running from the

A divided **CITY**

The dichotomies of Paris/*banlieue* (suburbs), center/periphery, inside/outside are particularly pertinent to Paris because of the physical boundary that separates the 20 arrondissements of the city from the rest of the Paris region. There has been a marker distinguishing *intra muros* (inside the wall) from *extra muros* (outside the wall) since fortifications were built around Paris in A.D. 300. The **Philippe–Auguste Wall,** built between 1190 and 1213, was predominantly a defensive measure but it also served to define and distinguish the city as a royal capital. Although the position and use of the fortifications changed throughout the centuries, the social geography of the city became increasingly determined by the existence of a barrier between Paris and the world outside. After the First World War, the **Thiers fortifications,** as the barrier was then known, were considered obsolete and were slowly dismantled over several decades. This was a golden opportunity to better integrate Paris into the surrounding *banlieues,* but what happened only served to reinforce the divide between the city and its suburbs. The space created by the removal of the ramparts was eventually used to build the **boulevard périphérique.** Although many modern cities are surrounded by a ring road, the history of Paris and its fortifications renders the *périph* a powerful symbol of the divide between the center and the suburbs of Paris—the inside and the outside. It could be read as a symbol of the social exclusion and alienation experienced by those living in the *banlieues,* far away from the luxury and glamour of Paris.

Louvre to the lower Marais on the Right Bank and encompassing the site of the present-day Panthéon and the area around Odéon on the Left Bank, the **Philippe–Auguste Wall** had the effect of consolidating and defining the space of the city. There are several places in Paris where you can see remains of this 12th-century wall, including rue Clovis in the 5th arrondissement and rue des Jardins St-Paul in the Marais.

By the time Philippe Auguste died in 1223, Paris was the undisputed cultural capital of Europe. This was largely due to its intellectual activity and the reputation of the University of Paris. In the 12th century, students from across Europe flocked to the city to study medicine, law, theology, and liberal arts. In 1253, Robert de Sorbon, a royal chaplain, established a new theology college that became known as the **Sorbonne.** It quickly became one of Paris's most prestigious colleges and a byword for the University of Paris. By 1300 there were 3,000 students living on the Left Bank, most of whom spoke Latin. This is how the Latin Quarter got its name.

The Hundred Years' War (1337–1453)

In 1328, Charles IV died without an heir, bringing the Capetian dynasty to a close—this marked the end of the medieval golden age and the beginning of a troubled period in the history of Paris. **Philippe de Valois,** Charles IV's cousin, became king, establishing the Valois dynasty. However, his claim was contested by Edward III of England and this instigated the **Hundred Years' War** between

Pierre Abélard

One of Paris's most famous medieval scholars was Pierre Abélard. After arriving in the city in 1108, Abélard quickly became one of most popular teachers and philosophers in Paris. He was employed by Canon Fulbert of Notre Dame to tutor his niece, Héloïse, in theology and philosophy. Abélard and Héloïse fell in love and eloped to Brittany where they got married and had a son.

However, Abélard was not ready to swap academia for domestic life and on his way back to Paris he sent Héloïse to a convent. Believing Abélard had abandoned his niece, Fulbert and a group of his cronies went to Abélard's house during the night and castrated him. Despite his scholarly brilliance, Abélard's reputation never quite recovered.

France and England. Although the Valois kings ultimately won the war, it brought financial ruin to the city of Paris. To make matters worse, the **Black Death** (bubonic plague) arrived in Paris in 1348, killing several hundred Parisians a day. Throughout the next century Paris was full of tension, violence, plots, and intrigue.

When Charles V came to the throne in 1364 he was determined to crush the unruly forces at work within the city. He decided to both strengthen and expand the Philippe–Auguste Wall and on the Right Bank the wall was extended to encompass a new fortress, the **Bastille** (p. 114). Charles V was also the first king to make the Louvre the home of the monarchy. He moved there in the late 1360s and transformed it into a luxurious and official residence.

The Renaissance & the Wars of Religion (16th c.)

Military escapades in Italy in the early 16th century brought the Renaissance style to France. Italian **Renaissance architecture** was characterized by its use of symmetry, decorative facades, columns and pilasters, and domes. In France, the continuing prevalence of the Gothic style, combined with the need for steep roofs and tall chimneys, created a Renaissance style with a particular French emphasis; this later evolved into a style known as French Classicism. The Renaissance style was instigated by **François I,** whose greatest achievement in Paris was the transformation of the **Louvre** (p. 81) into a Renaissance-style palace. It was intended to be a very public affirmation of the glory of the monarchy. In 1546, the medieval palace and fortress that were the existing Louvre were destroyed and the first stones of the present-day Louvre were laid by the architect Pierre Lescot in the Cour Carrée. For the next 3 centuries, François I's Renaissance palace served as the model for all subsequent extensions and additions to the Louvre.

The Reformation, the religious movement that was begun by Martin Luther in Germany in 1517 and led to the creation of Protestantism, had caused bitter conflict between Catholics and Protestants (known as Huguenots) in France. By the 1560s, this conflict had turned into civil war and the **Wars of Religion** lasted from 1562 to 1598. The bloodiest atrocity of these conflicts was the **St. Bartholomew's Day Massacre,** which took place in Paris on August 24, 1572. The scheming powerhouse at the heart of the French court, Catherine

The Louvre is a Renaissance-style palace.

de Medici, had arranged for her daughter Marguerite de Valois to marry Henri de Navarre, a Protestant aristocrat from the Bourbon family. While the official reason for the marriage was to join the two opposing religious forces in a union that would support the monarchy, Catherine had hidden motives. There were a large number of Huguenots in Paris for the wedding, and on the morning of August 24, the tolling of the bell in St-Germain l'Auxerrois acted as a signal for the Catholics to start massacring Huguenots. Between 1,500 and 2,000 Huguenots were killed, but Henri de Navarre was spared, thanks to his wife. Marguerite de Valois's turbulent life and the massacre were the inspiration for **Alexandre Dumas's 1845 novel, *La Reine Margot*,** which in turn inspired the 1994 film adaptation of the same name.

Henri IV (1589–1610)

After a dark and turbulent century Paris entered a dynamic period of growth in the late 16th century, under the guidance of Henri IV and, later, his son and successor Louis XIII. **Henri IV** became king in 1589 but it was 5 years before he entered Paris. Determined to win the Parisians over, the Huguenot king converted to Catholicism, announcing *"Paris vaut bien une messe"* ("Paris deserves a Mass"). In 1599 he signed the Edict of Nantes, which ended the Wars of Religion and led to long-lasting religious toleration and diversity in France.

Henri IV, who was known as *Le Vert Galant* (which roughly translates as "the old charmer") due to his fondness for the ladies, was very committed to Paris and was determined to restore the city to its earlier eminence. Like François I

📎 Five Paris Paintings

Eugène Delacroix, *La Liberté guidant le peuple* (1830)
Édouard Manet, *Olympia* (1863)
Claude Monet, *Le Pont de l'Europe–Gare St-Lazare* (1877)
Pablo Picasso, *Les Demoiselles d'Avignon* (1907)
Pierre-Auguste Renoir, *Bal du moulin de la Galette* (1876)

before him, Henri IV wanted the Louvre to be a testament to his power so he decided to link the Louvre with the Palais de Tuileries by building what is now known as the **Grande Galerie.** The Palais de Tuileries had been built by Catherine de Medici in 1559 and stood in between the current Jardin des Tuileries and the Arc de Triomphe du Carrousel (the palace burned down in 1871 and the space is now a garden, the Jardin du Carrousel). By the time Henri IV arrived in Paris, the Palais de Tuileries had become the home of the reigning monarch while the Louvre was the symbol of state power.

Henri IV was also responsible for the building of the **place des Vosges** (then known as the place Royale; p. 96), which transformed the Marais from a marshy wasteland into one of Paris's most fashionable areas. A number of the Marais's finest *hôtel particuliers* (private mansions) were built during this period.

Arguably, Henri IV's most important contribution to Paris was the **Pont Neuf** (p. 89). It was the first stone bridge to cross the Seine, and the first bridge that did not have houses or shops on it. Its unprecedented length and width (232m x 22m/761 ft. x 72 ft.) made it the longest bridge in Paris. At the time, its name (which means New Bridge) was deserved but today, as the other bridges across the Seine have all been replaced, it stands as the oldest bridge in Paris. Once completed, it became a hub of activity and in his *Tableau de Paris* in 1788, Louis-Sébastien Mercier declared the Pont Neuf to be "to the city what the heart is to the body: the center of movement and of circulation."

The Pont Neuf.

Henri IV was assassinated by a Catholic fanatic called François Ravaillac while his carriage was stuck in traffic on the rue de la Ferronnerie (near Les Halles). However, the city continued to expand and the population continued to increase after his death.

The Sun King & Versailles (1638–1789)

Louis XIV, known as *le Roi Soleil* (the Sun King), became king in 1638 at the age of 4. He ruled until his death in 1715 at the age of 76, making him the longest ruling monarch in the history of Europe. His reign marked the peak of absolute monarchy in France, and he is famous for asserting "I am the State." Early in his reign, he was attracted to the idea that the glorification of the capital city would both add to the prestige of his own dynasty and create a dominant royal presence. He built the two triumphal arches at Porte St-Denis and Porte St-Martin, and was

Grand Versailles is a testament to Louis XIV (The Sun King).

responsible for the Baroque-style **Hôtel des Invalides** (p. 132), a complex of buildings designed to house injured and elderly soldiers from the king's army. In addition, the hospital of Salpêtrière in the 13e was built to shelter fallen women.

However, Louis XIV soon abandoned Paris for **Versailles.** He spent colossal sums of money transforming the former hunting lodge of his father, Louis XIII, into a palace. Built in the excessive Baroque style, Versailles is the embodiment of grandeur and indulgence. The French court officially moved there in 1683, and from then on Paris was eclipsed by the courtly goings-on in Versailles. After the death of Louis XIV the infant **Louis XV** lived in Paris for several years, but he soon scuttled back to Versailles. Consequently, his successor, **Louis XVI,** had no intention of living in Paris. Over the years various additions were made to the palace, including the Hall of Mirrors, the Petit Trianon (which was built in the 1760s for Louis XV's mistress, Mme de Pompadour), and La Petite Ferme, where Louis XVI's wife, Marie Antoinette, played at being a milkmaid. **Sofia Coppola's 2006 film, _Marie Antoinette,_** despite its anachronisms and rock soundtrack, superbly captures the decadence and frivolity of Versailles and the last years of the _Ancien Régime._

Five French Novels

Muriel Barbery, _The Elegance of the Hedgehog_ (Europa Editions, 2008)
Michel Houellebecq, _Platform_ (Knopf, 2003)
Victor Hugo, _The Hunchback of Notre-Dame_ (1831)
Georges Perec, _Life: A User's Manual_ (1978)
Émile Zola, _The Belly of Paris_ (1873)

The Enlightenment (18th c.)

Despite the absence of the monarchy, the 18th century was one of the most prestigious and dynamic periods in Paris's history. Paris became the unofficial capital of the **Enlightenment,** the age of rational humanism. Philosophers and intellectuals, such as **Rousseau** and **Voltaire,** gathered in coffeehouses and bars to criticize the king and discuss alternative forms of government. The population soared from half a million in 1715 to more than 650,000 in 1789. Literacy rates were increasing and the number of books published increased threefold. This was also the heyday of the Palais Royal (p. 84), the Parisian residence of Philippe II, the duc d'Orléans. In the early 1780s, he transformed the Palais Royale into a semi-public space that became the meeting place of intellectuals, prostitutes, and sexual adventurers.

However, the increasing wealth of the city only served to highlight the vast gap between rich and poor. The ruling elite feared the *sans-culottes* ("without breeches"), members of the lower working classes who lived and worked in the warren-like alleys around rue du Faubourg St-Antoine (off place de la Bastille). Rumors of the excess and decadence of Versailles led people to perceive the court as increasingly corrupt and immoral. Louis XVI further aroused the hostility of the Parisian working classes by building a customs barrier around the city, known as the Farmers General Wall, from 1784 to 1787. Anyone bringing products into the city from outside Paris had to pay a tax. When a riot started on July 14, 1789, the mob attacked the **Bastille** and various outposts of the Farmers General Wall, thus starting the French Revolution.

The French Revolution (1789–1799)

The storming of the Bastille, on July 14, 1789, was the beginning of the French Revolution. The events that took place in Paris during the revolution would

The storming of the Bastille.

The Arc de Triomphe.

change France forever. The city was "reclaimed" by the people, who were more interested in destroying the symbols of the *Ancien Régime* than building anything new. This was exemplified by the destruction of a number of churches and abbeys, the desecration of the royal tombs at the Saint-Denis basilica, and the symbolic decapitation of the statues of the kings on the facade of Notre-Dame (the revolutionaries mistook them for the kings of France but actually they represent the kings of Judah). Church bells were melted down to make cannonballs, churches were renamed or given a new function—Notre-Dame became the Temple of Reason and the Eglise St-Germain was used to store gunpowder—and many streets across the city were given more revolutionary names. Place Louis XV became place de la Révolution—it was only given its current name, **place de la Concorde,** after the revolution (see p. 70).

In 1792 the revolution took a much more radical turn. The extremist **Jacobins,** led by Maximilien Robespierre, Georges Jacques Danton, and Jean-Paul Marat, instigated the period of the revolution known as **The Reign of Terror.** On January 21, 1793, Louis XVI was guillotined in the place de la Révolution. Marie Antoinette was kept prisoner in the Conciergerie, where the Revolutionary Tribunal presided over the revolution and decided who should be sent to the guillotine. Located next to Sainte-Chapelle on the Ile de la Cité, you can visit Marie Antoinette's cell in the **Conciergerie** (p. 91). She was executed in October 1793. By mid-1794, around 2,500 people had been beheaded in Paris.

Napoleon (1804–1814)

Taking advantage of the post-revolutionary chaos, **Napoleon Bonaparte** crowned himself emperor of the French in 1804. He famously declared that "Paris is short of monuments" and so "It must be given them." His desire to remake Paris into a city fit for an emperor led to an ambitious public building program. From 1802 onward, canals—including **Canal St-Martin**—were built to ensure that the city had a clean water supply. In 1806, Napoleon decided to build the **Arc de Triomphe** (p. 100), which was intended to celebrate his victory at Austerlitz but was only completed 2 decades after his downfall, and a neo-classical "Temple to the Glory of the Great Army," which was never fully completed and later became **La Madeleine** (p. 104).

Although the emperor failed to reshape Paris in the way that he had hoped, his military prowess—and the fact that he preserved the changes brought about by the revolution—mean that even today the French still consider him to be a great national hero. His reign provides the backdrop for Victor Hugo's classic tale of social oppression and human courage, *Les Misérables.*

The *Flâneur*

Idle strolling in London, Rome, or Madrid is simply idle strolling. Idle strolling in Paris is *flânerie*. The *flâneur* is an idle, aimless, and usually male stroller who wanders through the urban environment looking for distraction and pleasure. It was during the 19th century that the figure of the *flâneur* and the activity of *flânerie* became a key part of the Parisian experience. The archetypal Parisian *flâneur* was the poet Baudelaire, but modern writers are still inspired by this idea. Edmund White's book *The Flâneur* (Bloomsbury, 2001) uses the ideas of the *flâneur* and *flânerie* to delve into Paris's history and culture.

Food-wise, the 18th century was very important. It was during this period that the restaurant, as we know it today, first appeared. Thanks to the revolution, in the 1790s, chefs from aristocratic houses found themselves jobless and were forced to look for work. A number of them opened restaurants. Many restaurant conventions that we take for granted—such as flexible mealtimes, printed menus, and individualized meals—date from this period.

Napoleon III & Haussmann (1848–1870)

For several decades France gave the monarchy a second chance, but after the last French king, Louis-Philippe, abdicated in 1848, power fell into the hands of Louis Bonaparte, Napoleon's nephew. In December 1848, he was elected

A Haussmann-style boulevard.

president, and by 1852 he had moved into the **Palais des Tuileries** (p. 78) and declared himself **Emperor Napoleon III.** In 1853, he appointed **Georges-Eugène Haussmann** as prefect of Paris, placing under his control a city that, monuments aside, had changed little since the Middle Ages. Inadequate housing meant there was huge overcrowding in the poorer parts of the city. There was no efficient sanitation system; the Seine was still being used as a sewer, and only one in five houses had access to running water. There were no straight roads through Paris and congestion increasingly disrupted the social and economic life of the city. Haussmann had a very prestigious position; he had no superior other than the emperor and the two men met every day. Napoleon III wanted to create a city that was modern, aesthetically beautiful, and a magnificent monument to his power. Ultimately though, as it was Haussmann who oversaw this transformation, it is his name that has come to be associated with the Paris that emerged from it.

Haussmann improved circulation in the city by widening the streets and building the boulevards—a prime example of his work is the boulevard that was named after him, the boulevard Haussmann in the 9e. He was responsible for the standardization of the Parisian facade: all the buildings in a block were linked by symmetrical wrought-iron balconies, creating a long, horizontal perspective—examples of this architecture can be seen on boulevard St-Michel. He oversaw the renovation of the markets at **Les Halles** (p. 243) and the design of the eight iron- and glass-pavilions that were at the center of the project. He built 560km (348 miles) of sewers and vastly increased the amount of green space available to the public. Architecturally, Haussmann was inspired by French Classic architecture, but what distinguished him from others who had tried to reshape Paris in the past was the unprecedented scale of his transformation of the city.

However, not everybody was impressed by Haussmann, who described himself as a "demolition artist." He destroyed about 27,000 houses—including the house where he had grown up—and most of Medieval Paris was wiped off the map. The destruction of inner-city slums and the subsequent rise in property prices forced the working classes to move from the city center to the northeastern districts of the city. The poet Charles Baudelaire lamented the loss of *le vieux Paris* (old Paris) in his poem *Le Cygne* (The Swan), when he wrote "The old Paris is gone (the form a city takes more quickly shifts, alas than does the mortal heart)."

During the 19th century, Paris saw an extraordinary flourishing of art and literature, including the emergence of new forms of art. **Impressionism** was born during this time (you can see works by Impressionist artists such as Édouard Manet and Claude Monet at the **Musée d'Orsay;** p. 136), as was **Literary Naturalism,** with writers like Émile Zola, one of the first pioneers of the French realist novel, paving the way. Both Zola and the Impressionists frequently took Haussmann's transformation of Paris as their subjects, and their work reveals much about Parisian modernity.

The Paris Commune (1871)

Perhaps what is most incredible about Napoleon III's and Haussmann's transformation of the city is how much was achieved in such a short period of time. The **Franco Prussian War** (1870–1871), in which Paris was occupied, led to the fall of Napoleon III. After 17 years as prefect, Haussmann was out on his ear. What followed remains one of the bloodiest periods of Paris's history. The new, moderate republican government signed a peace treaty with the Germans, which angered many Parisians. When the new president, Adolphe Thiers, ordered his soldiers to enter the city and take away its cannons, the working classes rose up in protest and the government was forced to flee to Versailles. The Parisians elected their own governing body, the **Commune,** and from March to May 1871, the working classes occupied the city. When the government troops were finally able to enter the city, they showed no mercy; 200,000 people were killed in a single week, which became known as *la semaine sanglante* (the bloody week). The fighting finished in **Père Lachaise** (p. 115), where 147 Communards were lined up and shot against the Mur des Fédérés.

Despite its short life, the Commune succeeded in leaving its mark on the city. Napoleon's column in place Vedôme was pulled down, the **Hôtel de Ville** (p. 92) was burned to the ground, destroying all the state registers and archives, and the **Palais des Tuileries** (p. 78) was looted and the interior was set on fire. While the Hôtel de Ville was quickly rebuilt, the new government decided to knock down the ruins of the Palais des Tuileries because it was a symbol of the monarchy and they feared a royalist coup d'état.

La Belle Époque (1880–1914)

Memories of the Commune were soon swept away as Paris entered the period that later came to be referred to as *la belle époque* (the beautiful age). Lasting from roughly 1880 to World War I, this was the era of the *Expositions Universelles*

An Art Nouveau–style Métro sign.

The Eiffel Tower undergoing construction.

(the World Fairs), during which Paris was visited by millions of people from across the globe. The highlight of the 1889 *Exposition Universelle* was the **Eiffel Tower** (p. 139). At a height of 320m (1,066 ft.), it was the tallest structure in the world when it was completed in 1899, and it remains the tallest structure in Paris. Many people hated the tower when it was first unveiled, as it was considered too industrial-looking to be beautiful. The tower was supposed to be dismantled in 1909 but its value as a radio tower saved it from destruction. The Eiffel Tower remained, forever changing the Paris skyline. The stars of the 1900 *Exposition Universelle* were the **Grand Palais** (p. 109) and the **Petit Palais** (p. 109), which were built just off the Champs-Élysées. The huge iron- and glass-structure of the Grand Palais was typical of the architecture of the Industrial Age, and testified to the importance of these materials in 19th-century architecture.

In July 1900, the first **Métro** line was opened—Line 1—running from Vincennes to Porte Maillot. The station entrances were designed by Art Nouveau architect Hector Guimard. **Art Nouveau,** with its asymmetrical, curvaceous designs based on organic forms, was a reaction against the Industrial Age. Only a few of Guimard's original Métro entrances survive, at Porte Dauphine and Abbesses.

Although Paris had been overtaken by London in terms of size, the city remained Europe's cultural capital during *la belle époque*. This was the heyday of the **Impressionists,** most notably **Claude Monet, Auguste Renoir, Edgar Degas, Camille Pissarro,** and **Paul Cézanne.** They were given the name Impressionists, intended as an insult, by critics who thought their paintings were impressions rather than finished scenes. Interested in the effects of light, the

Gertrude Stein.

Impressionists often painted outside, capturing subjects both in the countryside and Haussmann's Paris. You can see many impressionist works at the **Musée d'Orsay** (p. 136).

With its cheap rents, booze, and cabarets, **Montmartre** (p. 153) had become the home of the literary and artistic avant-garde. All the big artists of the day—including **Picasso** and **van Gogh**—lived, drank, and painted in Montmartre. From 1904 to 1912, Picasso lived at the **Bateau-Lavoir** (p. 154), a former piano factory, and it was here that he painted *Les Demoiselles d'Avignon,* the painting that marked the beginning of Cubism. This was the era of absinthe (also known as "the green fairy") and the **Moulin Rouge** (p. 275). **Toulouse-Lautrec's** paintings of cabarets, circus freaks, and prostitutes perfectly capture the wild, heady spirit of the time.

In December 1895, the Lumière brothers showed the first moving images of Paris to the customers of the Grand Café on boulevard des Capucines. This was the birth of a new art form, and the beginning of the Parisian passion for **cinema.**

WWI & the Années Folles (1914–1938)

When the Germans broke through Belgium and entered France in September 1914, they very nearly made it to Paris. They were met by the French army at the **Battle of the Marne,** just 15km (9 miles) east of the capital. The Parisian taxi fleet came to the nation's rescue by taking 4,000 soldiers to the front. Paris was safe and by the end of that year, the fighting had turned into the trench warfare that came to characterize World War I. Although the city itself suffered very little from 1914 to 1918, victory came at a high cost: of the eight million French soldiers who fought in WWI, 1.3 million were killed, and another 1 million were crippled. In June 1919, the **Treaty of Versailles** was signed in the Hall of Mirrors in the **Palace of Versailles** (p. 346), officially bringing an end to the war.

In the interwar years, Paris became the avant-garde capital of the world. All the great writers, artists, and thinkers of the day gathered in Paris during the *années folles* (mad years), and the city was a whirlwind of decadence and creativity. Montparnasse had become the cultural epicenter of Paris, and the artistic community gathered here in bars and restaurants, including **Rotunde,** the **Dôme,** the **Select,** and the **Coupole**—all of which are still in business.

As Prohibition reached its peak in the U.S., American writers—including **Ernest Hemingway, F. Scott Fitzgerald, Henry Miller, Ezra Pound,** and **Gertrude Stein**—came to Paris in search of freedom, bohemia, and alcohol. It was here that Ernest Hemingway began his career as a writer, and his 1936

Five New Wave Films

François Truffaut, *Les Quatre Cents Coups* (1959)
Alain Resnais, *Hiroshima Mon Amour* (1959)
Jean-Luc Godard, *À bout de souffle* (1960)
Agnès Varda, *Cléo de 5 à 7* (1962)
François Truffaut, *Jules et Jim* (1962)

memoir, *A Moveable Feast,* is arguably the best Anglophone novel about 1920s Paris. Hemingway and Gertrude Stein (played by Kathy Bates) were key characters in Woody Allen's 2011 film *Midnight in Paris,* which perfectly captures the romance and spontaneity of the *années folles.* When they weren't at the bars of Montparnasse, these writers gathered in the English-language bookshop **Shakespeare & Co.** (p. 249), run by a young American woman called **Sylvia Beach.** In July 1920, Sylvia met the Irish writer **James Joyce,** and in March 1921, she offered to publish his modernist masterpiece, *Ulysses.*

WWII & Occupation (1939–44)

When World War II broke out, France believed that it would be protected by its concrete fortifications, known as the Maginot Line. However, in May 1940, the German army simply bypassed the fortifications and entered France by going through Belgium. Fear and panic led to a mass exodus from Paris toward the south of France, but by the autumn most Parisians had returned home. The chaos of this period is brilliantly portrayed in the first part of **Irène Némirovsky's novel *Suite Française;*** this book was never finished as Némirovsky died at the age of 39 in Auschwitz. A more romantic, but less historically accurate, portrayal of this time is the classic film *Casablanca.*

By June 1940, Paris was in German hands. Although Parisians had to get used to rationing, and the presence of both German soldiers and German street signs, Paris suffered little physical damage during the Occupation. As France was being liberated in 1944, Hitler famously gave the order for the retreating German army to blow Paris up, but the commander in charge, Von Cholitz, could not bring himself to destroy such a beautiful city.

The Occupation was a dark period in the history of both France and Paris, and it was many years before the French recognized the role they had played in the Holocaust. Anti-Semitism had been prevalent in France long before the Occupation, and the Germans found that many sections of society, as well as Marshall Pétain's Vichy Government, were more than happy to get involved in the deportation of the Jews. This culminated in July 1942, when the Parisian police rounded up 12,000 of the city's Jewish population. They were interned in the Vel' d'Hiv sports stadium before being deported to Auschwitz. Around 75,000 Jews were deported from France during the Occupation. Most of them passed through a temporary internment camp in Drancy, just outside Paris. The town of Drancy still exists and you can see it from the window of the RER B on your way out to Aéroport Roissy-Charles-de-Gaulle. Tatiana de Rosnay's novel *Sarah's Key,* which was released as a film starring Kristin Scott-Thomas in 2010, tells the story of a young girl's experiences during these events, describes France under Occupation, and highlights the degree to which the French were complicit in, and even enthusiastic about, the Vel' d'Hiv round-up.

Les Trentes Glorieuses (1945–75)

After the end of WWII, France embarked on a period of ambitious industrial modernization. The postwar economic boom that followed came to be known as *les trentes glorieuses* (the 30 glorious years). Wages were higher and increased spending on consumer goods radically changed the culture of everyday life, with

more and more French households being equipped with television sets, washing machines, and cars. Women became more independent, and younger people gained more freedom.

Many of the lifestyle changes brought about by *les trentes glorieuses* were explored in the films of the **French New Wave,** known as *la nouvelle vague,* which were a celebration of youth, Paris, and above all, cinema. New Wave film directors such as Jean-Luc Godard, François Truffaut, Claude Chabrol, and Agnès Varda used lighter, hand-held cameras to film in the streets rather than in studios; they challenged conventional editing practices and encouraged improvisation. It was through New Wave films, such as *À bout de souffle* (**Breathless**) and *Les Quatre Cents Coups* (**The 400 Blows**), that the world came to know the sights and sounds of 1960s Paris.

A scene from *À bout de souffle (Breathless)*.

The Algerian War (1954–62)

Although daily life was improving at home, France's empire was falling apart abroad. After the French army was defeated in the 1954 **French Indochina War,** they entered the **Algerian War,** a long and bloody war of decolonization in which Algeria fought France for its independence. The Algerian War lasted until 1962 and, like the Occupation, this was one of the more shameful periods of French history. Torture was used as an interrogation technique by the French army during the Algerian War, a fact that subsequent governments have never admitted.

By 1954 there were 350,000 Algerians living in France, most of whom were in Paris. Although the postwar economic boom depended on an immigrant labor force, the Algerian War made life very difficult for the Algerian community in Paris. Tensions between the leaders of the community and the police escalated, culminating in a protest by 20,000 Algerians in Paris on October 17, 1961. Under the orders of Maurice Papon, the police opened fire on the crowds and savagely assaulted protesters. Over 11,000 Algerian men were arrested and the bodies of a number of Algerians were thrown into the Seine. It is thought that around 200 people died in the massacre, which is commemorated on a plaque on the Pont St-Michel.

Many immigrants who came to Paris during *les trentes glorieuses* found themselves living in *bidonvilles* (shantytowns) on the peripheries of the city. Slowly, those living in the *bidonvilles* were relocated to huge housing estates, known as *grandes ensembles,* in the *banlieues.* However, these poorly built housing estates soon became sites of spatial isolation and economic exclusion, and

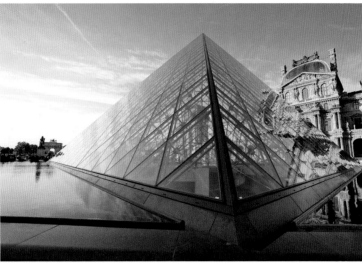

I. M. Pei's glass pyramid in the Louvre.

many people believe that the current problems in the *banlieues* date from this period.

May 1968

In May 1968, at a university campus in Nanterre, a suburb of Paris, students began to protest against the campus's overcrowded and dilapidated buildings, occupying some of the buildings for several days. When the ringleaders of the sit-in were brought before a disciplinary hearing held at the **Sorbonne** in Paris,

DATELINE

250 B.C. Parisii tribe lives on the Ile de la Cité and trades along the Seine.

52 B.C. Julius Caesar conquers the city during the Gallic Wars, renaming it Lutétia.

A.D. 250 St-Denis beheaded in Montmartre.

486 Clovis, king of the Franks, chooses Paris as his capital.

987 Hugh Capet becomes first king of the Capetian dynasty.

1253 Robert de Sorbon establishes the Sorbonne, a theology college.

1360s Charles V moves into the Louvre, making it a royal palace.

1546 First stones of present-day Louvre laid under François I.

1559 Construction begins on Catherine de Medici's Palais des Tuileries; building facades in Paris move from half-timbered to more durable chiseled stonework.

1572 The Wars of Religion reach their climax with the St. Bartholomew's Day massacre of Protestants.

1599 Henri IV endorses the Edict of Nantes, establishing religious toleration.

a riot broke out on the boulevard St-Michel and stones were thrown at police. As the protest gathered momentum, more and more students filled the streets, and TV crews arrived. They were soon joined by trade unions and secondary school students. The streets were full of graffiti and slogans challenging society such as "Métro, boulot, dodo" ("subway, work, sleep") and "Sous les pavés, la plage" ("Under the paving stones, the beach"). Despite the presence of the international media, the police frequently met protestors with violence.

By mid-May, nine million people were on strike, and the protest was threatening Charles de Gaulle's right-wing government. However, somewhat surprisingly, the revolts did not, as many people had feared, topple the government. In June 1968, de Gaulle called an election, and his party won by an overwhelming majority. Although May '68 challenged capitalist society and revived the 19th-century tradition of Parisian militancy, ultimately it confirmed France's middle-class commitment to capitalist values. Today, May '68 is remembered more for the iconic images and slogans it gave rise to than its political significance, although one of the leaders of the revolt, Daniel Cohn-Bendit, is now a member of the Green Party in the European Parliament. The student riots are only the backdrop to **Bernardo Bertolucci's 2003 film *The Dreamers,*** which tells the story of a young American student who gets caught up in a complicated conflict, but the film is an interesting portrayal of the violence and the idealism of May '68.

Modernizing Paris: From Pompidou to Mitterand (1969–85)

De Gaulle was succeeded by two more right-wing presidents: Georges Pompidou and Valéry Giscard d'Estaing. Pompidou strove to modernize Paris but many Parisians were far from keen on the results: the **Tour Montparnasse** (1972) has been voted the second-ugliest building in the world, the **Pompidou Centre** (1977) was described as a "wart" on the face of Paris, and the design of the **Forum Les Halles** (1979) was so heavily criticized that it is now being completely

1615	Construction begins on the Palais du Luxembourg for Henri IV's widow, Marie de Medici.	**1814**	Aided by a coalition of France's enemies, especially England, the Bourbon monarchy under Louis XVIII is temporarily restored.
1624	The Palais Royal is built in honor of Cardinal Richelieu.	**1848**	A violent working-class revolution deposes Louis-Philippe, who's replaced by autocratic Napoleon III.
1683	Louis XIV, the "Sun King," moves his court to the newly built Versailles.	**1853**	Napoleon III asks Baron Haussmann to modernize Paris.
1789	The French Revolution begins.	**1860s**	The Impressionist style of painting emerges.
1793	Louis XVI and his Austrian-born queen, Marie Antoinette, are publicly guillotined.	**1870**	The Franco-Prussian War ends in the defeat of France.
1804	Napoleon Bonaparte crowns himself emperor of France and embellishes Paris further with neoclassical splendor.		

continues

renovated. Despite having to inaugurate many of the buildings Pompidou had commissioned, Valéry Giscard d'Estaing did not share his predecessor's vision for Paris, and he opposed the erection of any more tower blocks in the city. He set the height for buildings in Paris at 25m (82 ft.) and buildings in the suburbs at 37m (121 ft.). Paris's skyline was safe.

Politically, it was a huge event when the head of the Parti Socialiste (PS), **François Mitterrand,** won the presidential election in 1981; he remained president until 1995. Like the great kings and emperors before him, Mitterrand understood how important it was for a great leader to leave his mark on the city. With his heart set on posterity, he launched a number of controversial initiatives known as the *Grands Projets* (big projects), including **I. M. Pei's glass pyramid in the Louvre** (p. 81), **La Grande Arche de La Défense** (p. 144), the **Opéra Bastille** (p. 272), and the **Bibliothèque Nationale de France (BNF)** in the 13e (p. 121). The use of glass in many of the *Grands Projets* was intended to be a manifestation of a new era of political transparency. Like Pompidou's modern buildings, many of the *Grands Projets* were hated when they were first unveiled. One critic accused Mitterrand of "treating the Louvre as if it were Disneyland." However, today these initiatives have been absorbed into the city's landscape, and Parisians have learned to appreciate, one could even go so far as to say love, the *Grands Projets.*

1871	Insurrectionary government known as The Paris Commune takes over Paris from March to May.	1954–62	War begins in Algeria and is eventually lost; refugees flood into Paris, and the nation becomes divided over its North African policies.
1878–1937	Several international expositions add monuments to the Paris skyline, including the Tour Eiffel.	1958	France's Fourth Republic collapses; General de Gaulle is called out of retirement to head the Fifth Republic.
1914–18	World War I rips Europe apart.		
1940	German troops invade Paris; the French government, under Marshal Pétain, evacuates to Vichy, while the French Resistance under Gen. Charles de Gaulle maintains symbolic headquarters in London.	1968	Paris's students start rioting in the Latin Quarter.
		1981	François Mitterrand is elected France's first Socialist president since the 1940s; he's reelected in 1988.
1944	U.S. troops liberate Paris; Charles de Gaulle returns in triumph.	1989	Paris celebrates the bicentennial of the French Revolution.

Contemporary Paris (1995–Present)

The 1990s were a difficult decade for Parisians. **Jacques Chirac** became president in 1995 but his presidency was almost immediately undermined by a series of strikes and protests that lasted for months on end. (These strikes were mainly in the public sector and were a response to Chirac's Prime Minister Alain Juppé's planned welfare cutbacks.) There was also a profound sense of fear in Paris, due to a wave of terrorist attacks carried out by the Armed Islamic Group (GIA) in 1995. The worst attack occurred in July '95 when the St-Michel Métro station was bombed, resulting in the death of 7 people and the injury of another 84 people.

The mood in Paris was more upbeat in 1998 when France's multi-ethnic football (soccer) team, led by Zinedine Zidane (the son of Algerian immigrants), won the World Cup. People were keen to celebrate France's ethnic diversity and many took the team's success as a sign that ethnic minorities had finally taken their rightful place in French society. However, this sense of pride was relatively short-lived.

After winning a second term in 2002, Chirac became even more popular in 2003, after he opposed the U.S.-led invasion of Iraq. However, his failed attempt to reform the public sector in the spring and his mismanagement of the deadly heat wave in August—which killed 14,000 elderly people—aroused a great deal of criticism.

Taking Mitterand's cue, Chirac commissioned the **Musée du quai Branly** (p. 137), which is dedicated to indigenous art from Africa, Asia, Oceania, and the Americas. The building was designed by renowned contemporary French architect Jean Nouvel and has a "living wall" on part of its exterior.

In October 2005, following the deaths of two teenagers in the suburb of Clichy-sous-Bois, riots broke out in the huge, run-down housing estates in the *banlieues*. Rioters—many of whom were the children of North African immigrants—torched cars, smashed buildings, and threw stones at the police. The violence spread all over France, from Marseilles to Strasbourg, and lasted for

1992 Euro Disney opens on the outskirts of Paris.

1994 Mitterrand and Queen Elizabeth II ride under the English Channel in the new Channel Tunnel.

1995 Jacques Chirac is elected president and Mitterrand dies the following year. Paris is crippled by a general strike and terrorists bomb the subway.

2002 France replaces its national currency, the franc, and switches to the euro, the new European currency.

2003 Attacks on French Jews mark the rise of anti-Semitism, the worst since World War II.

2005 Riots break out in the suburbs and spread across France.

2006 Massive demonstrations against a new labor law are held in Paris and other cities. Jacques Chirac revokes the law.

2007 Pro-American Nicolas Sarkozy becomes president of France, sparking riots.

2008 France bans smoking in public places.

2010 Economic woes and a battered euro plague France.

2012 François Hollande wins the French presidential election.

several weeks. Chirac was forced to declare a State of Emergency. **Nicolas Sarkozy,** then minister of the interior, intensified the anger of the rioters when he called them *"racaille"* (a very insulting expression, meaning "scum").

After 12 years of President Chirac, the French people were ready for a change. Promising to modernize and reform the country's employment law to make France more competitive, Sarkozy was elected president of France in 2007, but he has remained a very divisive figure. He has continued to take a hard line on immigration and national identity issues; this includes banning the burqa (the veil that covers all of a woman's face), which came into force in April 2011; and the controversial crackdown on Roma (gypsies), which has seen more than 10,000 people expelled from France. His attempt to reform the pension system by raising the age of retirement from 60 to 62 caused a wave of strikes and protests across France in the autumn of 2010 (despite widespread opposition to the legislation, the French parliament approved the reforms in October 2010). His presidency was undermined by several high profile political scandals, most notably the Bettencourt Affair, which involved illegal payments made by Liliane Bettencourt (the head of L'Oréal) to members of Sarkozy's party in the run-up to the 2007 presidential election.

Outside of politics, Parisians tend to look at Sarkozy's personal life with ridicule. His marriage to Italian-French pop singer Carla Bruni-Sarkozy and his vacations with the rich and famous have earned him the title of the "bling bling president," and stories of his aides putting boxes behind podiums to make him seem taller during his speeches have been met with derision. Despite a hard-fought campaign in the 2012 French Presidential Election, Sarkozy's flashy lifestyle and unpopular policies proved too much for the French electorate. The so-called "president of the rich" did not win a second mandate, making him the 11th European leader to be kicked out since the economic crisis and the shortest serving president since the Fifth Republic was created in 1958.

WHEN TO GO

With an average of 27 million visitors per year, Paris is the most visited city in the world. Although the city is bustling year-round, the summer (July–Aug) is the worst time to visit, because there are a lot of tourists and most Parisians flee the city. Paris is probably most pleasant to visit in the spring (Apr–June) or fall (Sept–Nov), but it is also lovely during December, when the city is all lit up with Christmas lights. Annual fashion shows and trade fairs bring a lot of people to the city in September and October, so it may be difficult to find a hotel room during this period. Hotels in Paris rarely advertise off-season rates, but rooms are often a little less expensive during the cold, rainy period from November to February. Airfares are cheaper during these months, and more promotions are available; airfares rise in the spring and fall, peaking in the summer, when tickets cost the most.

Weather

Although you'll often hear French people complaining about the weather in Paris, Parisian weather is usually quite stable, and the surrounding region boasts one of the lowest annual rates of precipitation in the country (640mm/25in.). In terms of weather, the best times to visit Paris are the spring (Apr–June) or the fall (Sept–Oct). Recently, Paris has seen extreme temperatures in both summer (when temperatures are around 90°F/30°C) and winter (when temperatures are around 30°F/below 0°C)—perhaps a result of global warming. The high temperatures in summer, combined with air pollution, can make it unbearable to visit Paris then—especially in the un-air-conditioned Métro.

For a reliable weather forecast, go to **Météo France** (www.meteofrance.com) or **Weather.com**, or tune into local radio stations.

Paris's Average Daytime Temperatures & Rainfall

	JAN	FEB	MAR	APR	MAY	JUNE	JULY	AUG	SEPT	OCT	NOV	DEC
Temp. °F	39	40	45	50	57	62	67	67	61	53	44	41
Temp. °C	4	4	7	10	14	17	19	19	16	12	7	5
Rainfall (in.)	2.2	1.8	1.4	1.7	2.3	2.1	2.3	2.5	2.1	1.9	2.0	1.9
Rainfall (mm)	56	46	36	42	57	54	59	64	55	50	51	50

Public Holidays

Holidays in France are known as *jours fériés.* Shops and banks are closed, as well as many (but not all) restaurants and museums. If a *jour férié* falls on a Thursday, for example, many French people *faire le pont* (literally "make the bridge") and take the Friday off work. For a list of major holidays, see "Fast Facts," p. 389.

Paris Calendar of Events

For an exhaustive list of events beyond those listed here, check http://events.frommers.com, where you'll find a searchable, up-to-the-minute roster of what's happening in cities all over the world.

JANUARY

January Sales. Over 1,000 shops, from boutiques to *grands magasins*, participate in the January sales, offering discounts as high as 70%. Sales begin around January 11 and last until mid-February.

International Circus Festival of Tomorrow. The annual International Circus Festival of Tomorrow at Paris's Pelouse de Reuilly (Métro: Liberté) offers the chance to catch the world's finest circuses under one roof. Young artists from such diverse schools as the Beijing Circus, the Moscow Circus, and France's own *Ecole Fratellini* compete at the festival in a bid to discover the stars of the future. To book, call ℰ **01-40-55-50-56;** www.cirquededemain.com. Four days at the end of January.

FEBRUARY

International Agricultural Show. Every February, the *terroir* (France's country-side) comes to Paris for the International Agricultural Show at the Porte de Versailles. It's a real institution (even the French president makes an official call) with exhibits featuring the top models of the animal world, meaty gastronomic delicacies from 22 French regions, and leisure, hunting, and fishing displays. Order tickets in advance online at www.salon-agriculture.com or call ℰ **01-49-20-45-12.** Mid-February.

Six Nations Rugby. France faces its European rivals (England, Scotland, Wales, Ireland, and Italy) in the Six Nations rugby union internationals at the humongous *Stade de France*. The championship is the oldest rugby tournament in the world, having existed in one form or another for 120 years. Since the advent of the Six Nations, France has been the most successful country, so come along and see whether they can be beaten on home territory. Check www.stadedefrance.com or www.rbs6nations.com for information. February and March.

MARCH

Paris Carnival. The annual *Carnaval de Paris* goes by many names, including the *Pantruche Carnaval*, the *Saint-Fargeau*, and the *Promenade du Boeuf Gras* (Fat Cow Parade). Led by the Fat Cow herself (yes, an actual cow), it revives an age-old tradition begun in 1274. Cheerful Parisians, trumpeters, and other musicians parade through the capital's streets to the Hôtel de Ville (Town Hall). Carnival buildup usually begins at 1:30pm at place Gambetta, and leaves at 3pm, arriving at the town hall at 7pm. For information, see www.carnavaldeparis.org. First Sunday of March.

Banlieues Blues. This annual music festival, in Paris's northern suburb of St-Denis, brings top-notch jazz and blues names to the traditionally culture-hungry suburbs. It's a fine way to discover lesser-known theaters as your feet swing to the sound of top-notch international musicians. Visit www.banlieuesbleues.org. Mid-March to mid-April.

Festival Chorus. Paris's Festival Chorus brings rock, pop, and French chanson to dozens of venues across the western Hauts-de-Seine suburb with some 120 artists taking part in more than 80 different concerts. The main stage is the Magic Mirror, an old-fashioned, circus-style big-top set on the esplanade between La Defense's modern towers. Buy tickets in advance by calling ✆ **01-47-74-64-64;** www.chorus92.fr. Two weeks from mid- to late-March.

APRIL

Paris Marathon. The Paris Marathon offers runners the chance to take in some of the city's most famous landmarks (cheered on by thousands of spectators), including the Champs-Élysées, the Tuileries garden, and place de la Bastille. If you'd like to get your kids involved, there is a 1.5km (1 mile) breakfast run for kids 5 to 10 years old, *La Course du P'tit Déj,* held the day before the marathon. Register for both online at www.parismarathon.com. One Sunday in April.

Salon des Réalités Nouvelles. The Parc Floral brings abstract art to the fore at its annual Salon des Réalités Nouvelles. More than 400 French and international avant-garde artists reveal the latest trends in the abstract world through their striking creations, which range from paintings and photos to weird and wonderful sculptures and installations. For information, visit www.realitesnouvelles. org. Mid-April.

Foire du Trône. Europe's largest temporary carnival, the Foire du Trône at the Pelouse de Reuilly attracts around five million visitors every year. Though it has roots stretching from the 12th century, since the 1950s the event has grown to epic proportions—every year, visitors down enough beer to fill an Olympic swimming pool. With its flashing lights, pumping music, freak shows, and greasy aromas, the Foire du Trône is a world away from the cultural clichés of the French capital, and sometimes that is the best thing about it. Visit www.foiredutrone.com. Early April to the end of May.

MAY

Nuit des Musées. During the Nuit des Musées (Museum Night), the city's museums stay open until 1am, offering you a chance to see the Louvre, and hundreds more, for free. For information, visit http://nuitdesmusees.culture.fr. One Saturday mid-May.

St-Germain-des-Prés Jazz Festival. The *Rive Gauche,* Paris's traditional jazz quarter, swings as local and international musicians perform at this jazz festival. Playing everything from boogie-woogie to blues, free concerts are held in St-Germain square with ticketed concerts taking place in local libraries, cafes, concert halls, and bars. Visit www.festivaljazzsaintgermainparis.com. Two weeks in May.

The French Open. For 2 weeks the world's best tennis players battle it out on Roland Garros's clay courts. The event is one of France's biggest sports competitions, so book in advance for a decent seat. The main matches are the most expensive, so if you want to save money, watch the unseeded players on the smaller courts—you could be watching the tennis stars of the future. Visit www.rolandgarros.com. Mid-May to early June.

Paris Wine Fair. Paris's Palais Brongniart (the city's beautiful neoclassical, former stock-exchange building) is the setting for the annual *Salon de la Revue du Vin de France* (French Wine Fair). Professionals and enthusiasts gather over 2 days to sample the country's best wines and some 200 winemakers attend—it's the perfect opportunity for you to learn how to tell your Bordeaux from your Bourgogne and build up your own dream cellar. Visit www.larvf.com. Mid-May.

JUNE

Jardin Shakespeare. Every year the Jardin Shakespeare in Paris's Bois de Boulogne hosts an open-air theater festival. Plays by the bard are performed in French and English, as well as works by other playwrights and the occasional concert or opera. You won't find a more charming spot for a summer night's entertainment. For information call ☎ **01-40-19-95-33;** www.jardin shakespeare.fr. June to September.

Paris Jazz Festival. This annual summer event presents a program of free jazz concerts in the beautiful surroundings of the Parc Floral. Gigs take place every Saturday and Sunday throughout June and July. The concerts begin at 3pm and are free to all those who have paid the standard park entry fee. Arrive early to ensure that you get 1 of the 1,500 seats available, or pack a picnic and bask by the park's miniature lake. Visit www.parisjazzfestival.fr. June to July.

Fête de la Musique. In Paris for the Fête de la Musique? Everywhere you go you'll hear music, from opera and jazz to techno and rock. The Fête unites big names at major venues with accordionists on street corners and choirs in church halls. All concerts are free and every year the Fête de la Musique website publishes a list of participating venues. For information, visit www.fetedelamusique.culture.fr. June 21.

Solidays. Solidarité SIDA is France's main charity promoting the cause of those with HIV. Its annual festival, Solidays, held at Paris's Hippodrome de Longchamp, has fast become one of the city's hippest cultural events attracting more than 100,000 visitors for a weekend of music and arts. The real stars of the show are the musicians—big names from the international pop and rock scene. Visit www.solidays.org for information. Late June.

Gay Pride. The flamboyant Paris Gay Pride parade traditionally goes from République to Beaubourg via the Marais, but final confirmation of the route is not usually given until the last minute. Paris has a large gay and lesbian population, with consequently one of the most liberal attitudes in France. Over the last few years the march has grown into a huge carnival, and the big day itself is the culmination of a series of events, including debates and masked balls. Visit www.accueil.gaypride.fr. Late June.

JULY

Paris Dance Festival. *Les Etés de la Danse* provides a series of breathtaking ballet performances at the Belle Époque Théâtre du Châtelet. A different world-renowned company is invited to perform every year. Expect everything from traditional ballet to contemporary modern dance. For information call ☎ **01-42-68-22-14** or visit www.lesetesdeladanse.com.

Bastille Day. France's national holiday commemorates the 1789 storming of the Bastille at the start of the French Revolution. Crowds line the Champs-Élysées for a military parade led by the president, during which jets fly in formation as top military brass bands march from the Arc de Triomphe to the place de la Concorde. Later Parisians party until dawn as fireworks explode over the Trocadéro. July 14.

Paris Plage. Every summer, 3.2km (2 miles) of the Seine (near the Pont Neuf) are turned into Paris Plage, a beach complete with golden sand and tanning beds. There are free sports, such as volleyball, and entertainment, from comedy to hip-hop. A second stretch of beach, along the Canal de l'Ourcq, also draws crowds with yet more concerts, outdoor games, canoeing, and sand. For information, visit www.paris.fr/parisplages. July to August.

Open-air Cinema at La Villette. Each summer, film fans converge on Paris's Parc de la Villette for its 4-week Open-Air Cinema. Pack a picnic, and watch movies with the locals—some are dubbed or subtitled and some are "VO" (original language). Visit www.villette. com. Mid-July to mid-August.

AUGUST

Classique au Vert. World-class classical musicians gather to serenade around 1,500 tourists and Parisians in the leafy Parc Floral (Métro: Château de Vincennes) during this event. Pack a picnic and savor it on the lawn as the sound fills the air—or, if you want a spot under the bandstand, get there around an hour before the concert. For information, visit www.classiqueauvert.fr. Weekends in August and September.

Arènes de Montmartre Festival. The Italian tradition of *commedia dell'arte* and traveling theater comes to Montmartre's Arènes (one of only two remaining Roman amphitheater ruins in Paris) for a 3-week festival. The Mystère Bouffe Theatre Company takes the lead with its colorful theatrical inventions. Plays are also performed in other spots around the Marais and the 10th and 20th arrondissements. For information, visit www.mysterebouffe.com.

Rock en Seine. This music festival, held in the Saint Cloud park just outside Paris (Métro: Boulogne–Pont de Saint-Cloud), offers a consistently excellent line-up of internationally renowned pop and rock stars, and its chilled-out atmosphere makes it a definite highlight of the city's musical calendar. Kids are welcome too, with a special "minirock" stage set aside for 6- to 10-year-olds. If you buy a festival pass, you can camp at the festival campsite (just bring your own tent). Visit www.rockenseine.com/en for information. Late August.

SEPTEMBER

Techno Parade. The annual Techno Parade turns up the volume and quickens the pace on Paris's streets. Around 20 floats carrying 150 musicians, DJs, and performers turn out to dance their way along the 4.8km (3-mile) route. This huge event forms part of the *Rendez-vous électroniques* (Electronic Festival) and attracts 400,000 hardcore partygoers. You can free your inner party animal afterwards too, in numerous bars and clubs across the capital. Visit www.techno parade.fr. Mid-September.

Journées du Patrimoine (Heritage Days). France's Heritage Days give visitors the chance to peek behind the doors of 14,000 buildings that are usually closed to the public. All over the country visitors can glimpse inside politicians' homes, private crypts and cellars, and the backstage of theaters; many museums open their doors for free as well. Paris has so many wonderful buildings to discover that there are tremendous crowds, so expect to line up and be patient—the wait will be worth it. For a full program of what to see, check www.journeesdu patrimoine.culture.fr. Late September.

Paris-Versailles Walk. Walkers and runners have been taking part in the annual Paris-Versailles Walk, *Grande Classique,* for more than 30 years. It starts on the quay in front of the Eiffel Tower and ends 16km (10 miles) away at the Château de Versailles. Changing rooms and refreshments are available all along the route. Anyone over the age of 16 is invited to enter, but French regulations dictate that you need to send in a medical certificate to prove you're up to the challenge. You'll also need to enroll online beforehand at www.parisversailles.com. Late September.

Paris Autumn Festival. Encompassing opera, film, dance, and performing arts, Paris's Autumn Festival incorporates more high-powered contemporary arts events than some other cities see in a whole year. Dip into this festival at any point and you'll discover the best productions Paris has to offer. Languages range from Japanese and Russian to French, German, and English (subtitled where necessary in French), so choose your productions wisely. Visit www.festival-automne.com. September to December.

OCTOBER

Nuit Blanche. See Paris as you've never seen it before, when museums, monuments, cinemas, parks, and swimming pools stay open from dusk to dawn (for 1 night only) as thousands of revelers celebrate Nuit Blanche. The Métro stays open later, and night buses serve all the main arteries until dawn. Visit www.paris.fr. Early October.

Prix de l'Arc de Triomphe. Paris's Hippodrome de Longchamp stages the Prix de l'Arc de Triomphe, the jewel in the crown of French horse racing, attended by around 48,000 onlookers. Part of the prestigious World Series Racing Championship, the Arc is popular with Brits, who cross the channel to watch the action. In addition to the excitement of the race, expect a wonderful display of horses, hats, and enough champagne to sink a ship. For information, visit www.prix arcdetriomphe.com. Early October.

Montmartre Grape Harvest Fest. The 5-day Montmartre Grape Harvest Festival *(Fête des Vendanges de Montmartre)* celebrates the new Cuvée Montmartre vintage wine (produced on Montmartre's very slopes). Each year, thousands of revelers come to see short film screenings, listen to concerts, and drink *vin*. Stalls selling regional produce set up

shop on the *Butte* (Montmartre's hill) and a colorful parade in honor of Bacchus fills the cobbled streets. Visit www.fetedesvendangesdemontmartre.com. Early October.

Salon du Chocolat. The Salon du Chocolat, at Paris's Porte de Versailles, is heaven for thousands of chocolate lovers who come to devour the international ambrosia and learn how it's made. You can also discover the latest in industry trends from a series of chocolate tastings, demonstrations, and symposiums while watching chefs making *douceurs* and chocolatiers create their fineries. This is a popular event so buy your ticket online before you go at www.salon-du-chocolat.com. Late October.

NOVEMBER

Orchestres en Fête. This annual classical music festival is celebrated nationwide, but as the capital city, Paris is the *real* center for classical music. Expect classics and lesser-known contemporary pieces played by 50-piece national orchestras as well as more intimate concerts by small Baroque ensembles in venues across the city. For information visit www.orchestresenfete.com. Mid- to late November.

Les Nuits Capitales. This event celebrates Paris's nightlife scene, recognizing all music genres, like jazz, electronica, hip-hop, rock, and pop. It's a fine opportunity to dance the night away in hip venues across the city and to discover new artists. *Tip:* All participating venues offer reduced prices to those registered on the Nuits Capitales' website (www.nuitscapitales.com). Call ✆ **01-43-58-38-50.** Late November.

DECEMBER

High Heel Race. As far as wackiness goes, Paris's High Heel Race is a winner. Each year preselected teams of women run as fast as they can in high heels (without breaking their necks), at a different Parisian Monument. It's the final leg of an international competition sponsored by the Sarenza shoe website. The winner gets thousands of British pounds to spend on Sarenza's shoes. Yes, it's marketing, but it's all good fun, and there is live music. For information, visit www.highheelrace.co.uk. Early December.

Ice-Skating. Get your skates on and get down to Paris's ice rinks, which pop up across Paris over the winter months. You'll find a mix of tourists and locals cutting up the ice, and best of all: it's free (skate rentals cost around 5€). Visit www.paris.fr for information. December to early March.

RESPONSIBLE TOURISM

In an age when environmental, ethical, and social concerns are becoming more important, Paris has embraced sustainability and has become a green city. It was recently ranked one of the top 10 cities committed to ecological issues by the European Green City Index.

The city of Paris has an excellent public transportation system, which is cheap and user-friendly, and most Parisians get around the city by public transport. With 16 lines and 300 stations, the Paris **Métro** is an efficient system that covers most of the city. Several Métro lines are currently being extended, as is the **Tramway** network, which is quiet, electric, and nonpolluting. There are also the **RER** (*Réseau Express Régional*), the **Suburban Rail,** and a widespread network of **buses.** Alternatively, since the city is relatively small, many people choose to get around simply by walking.

Bertrand Delanoë, Paris's mayor since 2001, has launched a series of initiatives aimed at making the city more environmentally friendly by reducing pollution and cutting down on traffic. In 2007, Delanoë introduced the **Vélib'** scheme (www.velib.paris.fr), a public bicycle rental program; with thousands of bicycles and bike rental stations spread throughout the city, it is a fast and inexpensive way to get around the city, and you will see both Parisians and visitors taking advantage of this program. Delanoë also expanded bike lanes throughout the city, and today you'll see more cyclists and cycle lanes in Paris than ever before. Following on the heels of the Vélib' program's success, Delanoë recently introduced the **Autolib'** scheme (www.autolib.fr), which offers the public a short-term, self-service car rental service. The 100% electric Bluecars mean no noise or air pollution, and if it leads to a reduction in the number of privately-owned cars, hopefully the scheme will reduce the number of traffic jams.

Paris is home to 400 green spaces, all of which are enhanced and maintained by the city council. The city is home to some beautiful parks, including the **Jardin du Luxembourg** in the 6e (p. 128) and the **Parc des Buttes Chaumont** in the 19e (p. 120), and these spaces offer a refuge from the urban environment. Over the last 15 years, the city government has spent a lot of money on transforming vacant land into parks (like Jardin Serge Gainsbourg at Porte des Lilas) and there are several parks currently undergoing renovation and expansion (like Parc Martin Luther King at Clichy Batignolles).

Many hotels in Paris have undertaken measures to preserve the environment, and those that have are awarded with a green label; in Paris, look for hotels with the title of **La Clef Verte** (Green Key; www.laclefverte.org) or the European Eco-Label. Both labels reward hotels that take a more environmental approach to water, energy, and waste, and raise the awareness of their guests. In Paris, the **Best Western Premier Regent's Garden** (p. 308) boasts a European Eco-Label and the **Radisson Blu Le Dokhan's Hotel** (p. 310) claims the title of *La*

Clef Verte, among others. Although there are currently only a few hotels that boast such labels, sustainable tourism is becoming increasingly important in the hotel industry. Even if you don't stay at a green hotel, you can still do your bit: turn down the air-conditioning when you leave the room, request that your sheets aren't changed every day, and use your towels more than once. Laundry makes up around 40% of an average hotel's energy use.

Responsible tourism means leaving a city in the same condition as you found it. You can do this by not dropping litter and respecting the recently created color-coded garbage bin system: Yellow bins are for recyclable materials, including paper, plastic, and aluminum cans, while gray bins are for garbage. Support the local economy and culture of the city by shopping in smaller, neighborhood shops, and eating in local, family-run restaurants rather than big chain stores and restaurants. Vegetarianism is still not particularly widespread in France, but organic food (*bio*) is becoming increasingly popular—look out for the *bio* tag in shops and restaurants. For more information about Paris's sustainability, go to http://en.parisinfo.com/sustainable-tourism.

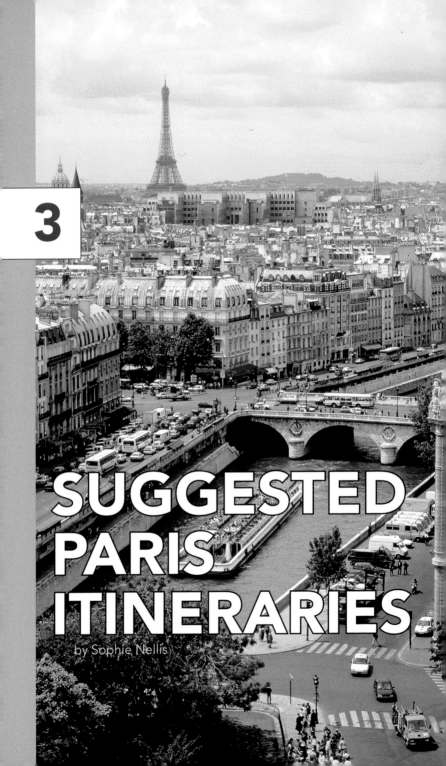

3

SUGGESTED PARIS ITINERARIES

by Sophie Nellis

From the Louvre to the Eiffel Tower, Paris is home to some of the world's most famous museums and monuments. All of these sights are well worth visiting, but the city is so much more than a mere collection of buildings. Visiting Paris is as much about soaking up the atmosphere and getting to know the city as it is about sightseeing. With all the layers of history, it's easy to forget that Paris is a 21st-century capital, but some of the more recent additions to the city, such as the Vélib' biking scheme, have injected Paris with a new sense of dynamism.

Each of Paris's 20 arrondissements possesses a unique style and character. Our guide to the different neighborhoods of Paris will give you an insight into the city and help you decide where you want to stay and what you want to see. Once you arrive in Paris, try to explore as many neighborhoods as you can in order to appreciate the diversity of the city. Our suggested itineraries will help you organize your time and discover new sides to the city. If you only have a few days, you'll probably spend most of your time in the center of Paris, seeing the major sites. In a week, you'll be able to wander off the beaten track and explore some of Paris's neighborhoods in a bit more depth. And if you're lucky enough to be able to stay for several weeks, you'll soon be an expert on *la vie parisienne.*

CITY LAYOUT

Compared to many capitals, Paris is surprisingly compact. The river Seine divides the city into the *Rive Droite* (**Right Bank**) to the north and the *Rive Gauche* (**Left Bank**) to the south. The larger Right Bank is where you find the city's business sector, stately monuments, and high-fashion industry. The smaller Left Bank has the publishing houses, universities, and a reputation as bohemian because students, philosophers, and creative types have been congregating here for centuries.

Paris is divided into 20 numbered municipal districts called **arrondissements.** The layout of these districts follows a distinct pattern. The first (abbreviated 1er for *premier*) arrondissement is the dead center of Paris, comprising an area around Notre-Dame and the Louvre. From there, the rest of the districts spiral outward, clockwise, in ascending order, like a snail shell. The lower the arrondissement number, the more central the location. If you want to be within walking distance of all the major sites and monuments, be sure to stay in one of the first eight arrondissements. There are only six arrondissements—the 5e, 6e, 7e, 13e, 14e, and 15e—on the Left Bank. The Right Bank is much larger, and it is comprised of the remaining 14 arrondissements.

Most city maps are divided by arrondissement, and addresses include the arrondissement number (in Roman or Arabic numerals and followed by "ème" or "e", for example, 10ème). Arrondissement numbers are key to locating an address in Paris, and this book lists addresses the way they appear in Paris, with the arrondissement number following the specific street address (for instance, 29 rue de Rivoli, 4e, is in the 4th arrondissement). Paris also has its own version of a zip code. The mailing address for a hotel is written as, for example, "Paris 75014." The last two digits, 14, indicate that the address is in the 14th arrondissement—in this case, Montparnasse. Arrondissements are indicated on the blue enamel street signs, above the street name.

Finding an address can be a complicated process in Paris, but once you know the arrondissement in which an address is located, finding that spot is much easier. Numbers on buildings running parallel to the Seine usually follow the course of the river east to west. On north-south streets, numbering begins at the river. To enter a building, you'll usually need a code for the outside door. Once inside, you'll need a letter indicating which staircase to take, the floor number, and the position of the apartment (right, left, last door, and so on). *Bis* and *ter* after a building number are the equivalent of "b" or "c" and indicate a separate address.

A good way to orient yourself is the Métro. As you're rarely more than a 10-minute walk away from a Métro station, it's easy to work out which part of Paris you're in by finding your nearest station.

There is a pull-out map showing Paris's neighborhoods at the back of this book. For a more detailed map of Paris, we recommend *Paris Pratique par arrondissement,* available at newsstands and bookshops for around 7€. This guide provides you with a Métro map and maps of each arrondissement, with all streets listed and keyed. Free maps of the Paris Métro, bus, and RER networks are available at all Métro stations.

NEIGHBORHOODS IN BRIEF
The Right Bank

LES HALLES, LOUVRE & PALAIS ROYAL (1ER & 2E)   Home to some of Paris's most important historical sites, the area around the **Louvre** and **Palais-Royal** is one of the most visited (but least residential) parts of the city. Whether you're strolling through the **Jardin des Tuileries** or admiring the classic beauty of the **place Vendôme,** this is one of the most elegant neighborhoods in the city. It's also one of the most luxurious, with designer boutiques filling the arcades of the Palais-Royal and *haute couture* lining the sidewalks of the **rue St-Honoré. Rue de Rivoli,** the main artery running through the 1st arrondissement, is one of the busiest streets in Paris, full of shops, cafes, and restaurants. For a little peace and quiet, head south for a walk along the banks of the Seine or take refuge in the gardens of the Palais-Royal.

North of the Palais-Royal is the **Bourse** (stock exchange). You'll find fewer tourists, but it still remains close to the center of the action. Like most financial districts, this area is lively during the week but much quieter at weekends. To the east is **Sentier,** the traditional center of the wholesale clothing trade, and the picturesque, cobbled market street, **rue Montorgueil.** Over the past few decades, the area around **Etienne Marcel** has gained a reputation as a trendy fashion district. For a more classic shopping environment, explore the various *passages* (covered arcades) that the 2nd arrondissement is famous for, the loveliest of which is Galerie Vivienne.

Les Halles was the name of Paris's great food market, which was located here from the Middle Ages to the 1960s, when the market was moved to Rungis, outside Paris. The 19th-century iron and glass pavilions were torn down and replaced by an ugly Seventies-style shopping complex,

ABOVE: **The view of the Louvre from the Jardin des Tuileries.** RIGHT: **An old doorway on the Ile de la Cité.**

Forum des Halles. Seen as one of central Paris's biggest eyesores, both the Forum and the surrounding gardens are currently being redeveloped. However, it'll be years before all the work is finished and at the moment most of this area is a building site. The huge underground shopping center and Métro/RER station means that Les Halles is always hectic and heaving with people. It's not the safest area and it's worth avoiding at night. The same is true of the seedy rue St-Denis, just east of Les Halles, as this is one of Paris's red light districts.

LE MARAIS, ILE ST-LOUIS & ILE DE LA CITÉ (3E & 4E) There's no better place to begin your exploration of Paris than at the Seine and the two islands in its center as it was here that Paris's history began all those thousands of years ago. There are magnificent views of the river from the Ile de la Cité and the Ile St-

Louis, but apart from that the two islands could not be more different from each other. Although the **Ile de la Cité** does have some quieter spots, such as the Square du Vert-Galant, as it is where you'll find the majestic Gothic cathedral **Notre-Dame** and the beautiful **Sainte-Chapelle,** it is visited by thousands of tourists every day. The **Ile St-Louis,** with its aristocratic town houses, is much calmer and more picturesque. Far removed from the hustle and bustle of Paris, the *quais* of the Ile St-Louis are perfect for a romantic stroll.

Having avoided Haussmann's 19th-century transformation of Paris, **Le Marais** has a more intimate atmosphere than other parts of Paris. It's home to the beautiful **place des Vosges** and is full of *hôtels particuliers* (private mansions that were built by the aristocracy). Stretching across the 3rd and 4th arrondissements, the southern part of Le Marais is a lively area, full of elegant boutiques and

The Marais is home to the city's Jewish community.

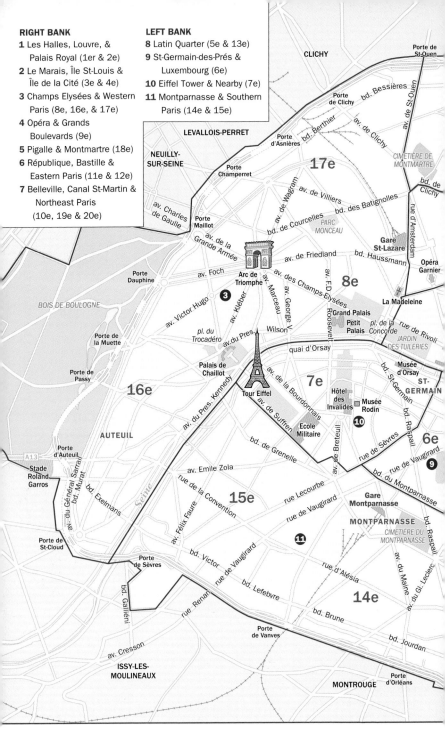

RIGHT BANK

1 Les Halles, Louvre, & Palais Royal (1er & 2e)

2 Le Marais, Île St-Louis & Île de la Cité (3e & 4e)

3 Champs Elysées & Western Paris (8e, 16e, & 17e)

4 Opéra & Grands Boulevards (9e)

5 Pigalle & Montmartre (18e)

6 République, Bastille & Eastern Paris (11e & 12e)

7 Belleville, Canal St-Martin & Northeast Paris (10e, 19e & 20e)

LEFT BANK

8 Latin Quarter (5e & 13e)

9 St-Germain-des-Prés & Luxembourg (6e)

10 Eiffel Tower & Nearby (7e)

11 Montparnasse & Southern Paris (14e & 15e)

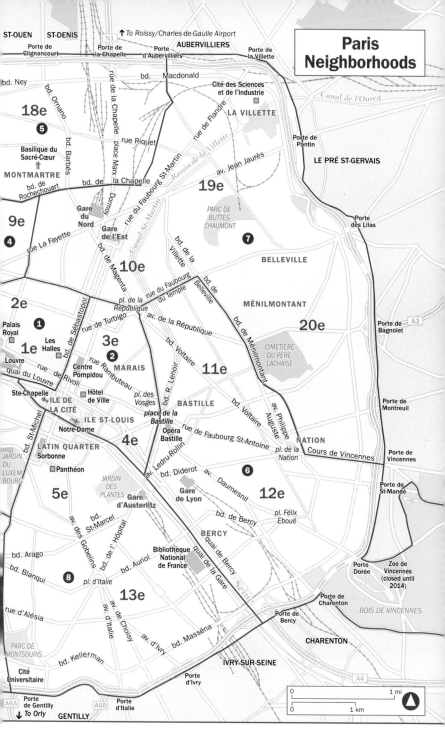

Paris Neighborhoods

small, contemporary art galleries. It's a great area for wining and dining, and very popular on Sundays as, unlike many other parts of Paris, most of the shops here are open. The area around **rue des Rosiers** has long been home to the city's Jewish community, while the **rues St-Croix-de-la-Bretonnerie, des Archives,** and **Vieille-du-Temple** are the center of Paris's gay and lesbian life.

The upper part of the Le Marais, north of the rue des Francs Bourgeois is more up and coming but considerably quieter than the 4th. The heart of the 3rd is the **rue de Bretagne.** There's a great antiques market along this street on Sunday mornings and it's here you'll find the **Marché des Enfants Rouge,** a food market full of delicious goodies. Nearby, the beautiful iron market hall designed by Gustave Eiffel, the Carreau du Temple, is undergoing restoration. The plan is for it to become a cultural center. The streets around this hall, such as **rue de Picardie,** are home to some cool bars and you'll also find a lot of small contemporary art galleries in this neighborhood.

CHAMPS-ÉLYSÉES & WESTERN PARIS (8E, 16E & 17E)   One of the most famous avenues in the world, the tree-lined avenue **des Champs-Élysées** is the embodiment of Parisian grandeur. While strolling along the Champs-Élysées may be something of a disappointment thanks to the fast-food restaurants, overpriced cafes, and chain stores, leading off to the south are **avenue George V** and **avenue Montaigne,** home to *haute couture* boutiques and several of Paris's most luxurious hotels. The Champs-Élysées continues to be a rallying point for parades and festivities, and there's a popular Christmas market here in winter.

You'll find similar levels of wealth and grandeur in the 16th arrondissement, which is full of embassies, diplomats, and exclusive residences. Fans of Art Nouveau will enjoy walking around the 16th as it was here that Hector Guimard built nearly all of his buildings, the most famous of which is Castel Béranger. There are several interesting museums, including the **Musée Guimet, Paris's Musée d'Art Moderne,** and the hip **Palais du Tokyo,** but this remains one of Paris's most bourgeois districts and can feel quite soulless and far from the action.

Heading north from the Champs-Élysées, you'll come to the picturesque **Parc Monceau** and the area known as **Batignolles.** This sophisticated neighborhood became fashionable during the 19th century and is full of elegant Haussmannian-style buildings. Today, it's a wealthy, predominantly residential area but there are some wonderful museums housed in *hôtels particuliers:* the **Musée Cernuschi,** the **Musée Nissim de Camondo,** and the **Musée Jacquemart-André.** The area around **place de Clichy** is more lively but a lot less elegant. On the nearby **rue des Dames** there are a number of hip bars and good restaurants.

OPÉRA & GRANDS BOULEVARDS (9E)   Sandwiched between the 2nd and 18th arrondissements, the 9th is a good base for exploring Paris's Right Bank. The area around the glitzy **Opéra Garnier** is one of the busiest, most commercial areas of Paris. It's a great place for shopping, and it's where you'll find the landmark 19th-century department stores **Galeries Lafayette** and **Printemps.** Heading east from Opéra you come to the area known as **Grands Boulevards.** This is the collective name for the streets that run from Madeline to République and they follow the lines of the ramparts built by Charles

V in the 14th century. This was one of the most fashionable neighborhoods of Paris in the 18th and 19th centuries as it was the epicenter of cafe and theater life. It was also, in the days before department stores, a popular shopping district thanks to the numerous covered *passages* (arcades). **Passage Jouffroy,** next to the waxworks museum the **Musée Grevin,** is well worth a visit. But although there is still lively nightlife here—bars, cinemas, and theaters—the grandeur of Grands Boulevards has faded and the area can seem rather shabby and inauthentic.

North of rue de Châteaudun, the 9th arrondissement becomes much quieter and more residential. **Rue Cadet** is a pretty market street and several of the streets leading up to Pigalle, such as **rue des Martyrs** and **rue de Rochechouart** are full of interesting boutiques, delicious food shops, and cozy cafes. The area around St-Georges is a quarter known as La Nouvelle Athènes (the New Athens). It got this name when a wave of Romantic artists and writers came to live here in the 19th century. Admire the mansions on the rue de la Tour des Dames, and head to the **Musée de la Vie Romantique** and the **Musée Gustave Moreau** for more insight into the cultural history of this neighborhood.

PIGALLE & MONTMARTRE (18E)   Located on a hill in the north of Paris, Montmartre's winding, narrow streets are a far cry from the wide avenues and boulevards of central Paris. Despite its distance from the center, **Montmartre**—or *la butte* (the hill), as it is affectionately referred to by locals—is one of the city's most popular neighborhoods for visitors and residents alike. At the end of the 19th century, Montmartre was full of avant-garde writers and artists, including Picasso, van Gogh, and Toulouse-Lautrec, who were attracted by the cheap rents and cheap booze. Despite the busloads of tourists who climb the hill to visit **Sacré Coeur,** this area has retained its bohemian atmosphere and if you avoid the tourist traps—such as place du Tertre—you'll find plenty of charm and romance. There's a great selection of bars and restaurants around **rue des Abbesses** and **rue Lepic,** and one of the advantages of being a little farther away from the center is that the prices are lower.

Place Pigalle was named after a French sculptor, Jean-Baptiste Pigalle, who is buried in a tiny cemetery at the top of *la butte.* Unfortunately for him, it's not usually art that springs to mind when you hear the name "Pigalle." This neighborhood has long been one of Paris's red light districts and between place Pigalle and place Blanche, you'll discover the seedier side of this neighborhood with flashing neon signs advertising sex shops and adult-only cinemas. There are lots of good music venues in **Pigalle,** such as Le Trianon and La Cigale, and although there are fewer dance halls and absinthe dens these days, the neighborhood is still a popular area for drinking and clubbing.

To the east of the 18th, around rue de la Goutte d'Or and Barbès-Rochechouart, there is a large North African community. There's a lively

Street performers in Montmartre.

atmosphere here but it's quite hectic, particularly on Saturdays when there is a popular fruit and vegetable market. If you do get off the Métro here, be wary of pickpockets. Located on the northernmost edge of the 18th is the city's most famous flea market, the **Marché aux Puces de Clignancourt.**

RÉPUBLIQUE, BASTILLE & EASTERN PARIS (11E & 12E)   The districts of eastern Paris—the 11th and 12th arrondissements—were traditionally home to Paris's working classes but over the last several decades they have become predominantly middle-class, residential neighborhoods. In spite of this, both place de la Bastille and **place de la République,** with its statue of the great symbol of the Revolution, *Marianne,* remain symbolic places for the French Left and are often the scenes of large public demonstrations.

To the east of République, is the leafy **boulevard Richard Lenoir,** which covers the southern section of Canal Saint-Martin as it makes its way to the Seine. The gardens along this boulevard, originally designed by Second Empire architect Gabrial Davioud and updated by David Mangin in 1993, make this a pleasant way to walk from République to Bastille. The area between Goncourt, Menilmontant, Parmentier, and Oberkampf is young and hip, and boasts some of the best nightlife in the city.

Place de la Bastille is dominated by the modern **Opéra Bastille,** which was met with mixed reactions when it opened in 1989. Nearby, in the streets around **rue de Lappe** and **rue de Roquette,** you'll find numerous bars and clubs, but compared to other areas in Paris the nightlife in Bastille can seem overpriced and inauthentic. To the east of the place is the **rue du Faubourg St-Antoine,** which has been the center of the furniture-makers district for centuries. It's now a pleasant shopping street, but if you go up some of the side streets you can still find some artisans at work. Head down the rue d'Aligre and you'll find the delightful food market the **Marché d'Aligre.** One of the most peaceful parts of the 12th arrondissement is the **Promenade Plantée,** a leafy walkway built along an old railway viaduct. It starts just south of the opera house and continues to Jardin de Reuilly before going on to the **Bois de Vincennes** just outside Paris. The 12th is also home to **Bercy Village.** Up until the 1980s, wine was unloaded from boats and stored in warehouses here, but the warehouses were recently renovated and are now home to shops, bars, and a multiplex cinema.

BELLEVILLE, CANAL ST-MARTIN & NORTHEAST PARIS (10E, 19E & 20E)   The 10th arrondissement is one of Paris's most multiethnic neighborhoods, and the streets around **rue du Faubourg Saint-Denis** are home to large numbers of Indians, Pakistanis, Bangladeshis, West Indians, Africans, and Turks. It's a vibrant, thriving area and the **passage Brady** is one of the best places in Paris to eat Indian and Pakistani food. However, the streets around Strasbourg St-Denis, Gare du Nord, and Gare de l'Est are not the safest parts of the city and should be avoided late at night.

The main attraction of the 10th is the increasingly popular **Canal Saint-Martin.** With its picturesque footbridges and cobbled, tree-lined *quais,* this is the ideal place for a summer picnic or Sunday stroll. There's a very *bobo* (short for *bourgeois bohemian*) atmosphere around here, thanks to the stylish boutiques and trendy bars and cafes.

Heading east from the Canal, you'll come to the traditionally working-class district of **Belleville,** which is home to large numbers of immigrants. North African Muslims and Jews, many of Tunisian origin, live alongside

Chinese and Vietnamese immigrants, and Belleville is Paris's second Chinatown. Cheap rents attracted a number of artists to this area and you'll come across a lot of artists' studios and street art. Sadly, Paris property prices mean that this area, like many others before it, is slowly being gentrified. There's a lively atmosphere in the streets of Belleville, and it's a great place to come for cheap bars and restaurants.

The 19th is not the most attractive of Paris's arrondissements, but there are some places that are worth visiting. At the top of the Canal St-Martin is the **Bassin de la Villette,** where two MK2 cinemas (MK2 is one of Paris's biggest movie theater chains) face each other across the canal. There's a pleasant atmosphere here during the summer, when people gather outside the local bars, picnicking or playing *pétanque*. If you continue along the Canal de l'Ourcq you'll reach the **Parc de la Villette,** which hosts an outdoor cinema festival in the summer and a jazz festival in September. A little farther south is one of Paris's loveliest green spaces, the **Parc des Buttes Chaumont.** If you continue south, the 19th becomes the 20th, a sprawling, predominantly residential district, some parts of which are not easily accessible on the Métro. The main attraction in the 20th is definitely the **Père-Lachaise Cemetery,** where the likes of Jim Morrison, Edith Piaf, and Chopin are buried. However, it's not just the dead who are drawing people to the 20th these days. There are several good bars and music venues both north of the cemetery, around **Menilmontant,** and south, around **place St-Blaise.**

The Left Bank

LATIN QUARTER (5E & 13E)   From a historical perspective, the Latin Quarter is not to be missed. From the Roman settlement of Lutetia to the heady days of May 1968, layers of Parisian history are visible in the 5th arrondissement. Home to the **Sorbonne**—the administrative center of the University of Paris—the Latin Quarter has been associated with education and learning since the Middle Ages. A number of academic institutions are still based in the 5th and parts of the neighborhood, particularly around rue Mouffetard and place de la Contrescarpe, are filled with students. There are lots of arthouse cinemas here that give the neighborhood an offbeat, indie vibe, and a trip to the charming English-language bookshop, **Shakespeare & Co.** (see p. 249), on rue de la Bûcherie, is a must for literature lovers.

Many visitors are disappointed by how tacky and commercial parts of the 5th have become. The area around place St-Michel and rue de la Huchette, although very central, is one of most touristy parts of the city. To do the Latin Quarter justice, it's best not to spend much time in these streets. Instead, admire Ile de la Cité from the terrace of the **Institut du Monde Arabe,** visit the hammam in the **Mosquée de Paris,** or take a leisurely stroll through the **Jardin des Plantes.** As you head further south you can see the quieter, more residential side of the 5th.

You'll see quite a different side of Paris in the 13th arrondissement. It's one of the few districts in the city where there are modern, high-rise tower blocks. It's also home to Paris's principal **Chinatown:** the area around place d'Italie, Tolbiac, and Olympiades is a great place to come for authentic Chinese and Vietnamese food. Just south of place d'Italie is the pretty, village-like neighborhood of **Butte-aux-Cailles.** The main streets of this area are the cobbled rue de la Butte aux Cailles and rue des Cinq

Diamants, and walking around you'll come across quaint old houses and charming bars and restaurants.

ST-GERMAIN-DES-PRÉS & LUXEMBOURG (6E)

Today one of the city's most exclusive neighborhoods, St-Germain oozes *Rive Gauche* glamour. For most of the 20th century, the area around the Eglise-St-Germain-des-Prés was the intellectual heartland of Paris, and everywhere you turn, you'll encounter historic and literary associations. Here you'll find three of Paris's most famous cafes, all within a few meters of one another. Known as **The Golden Triangle,** the **Brasserie Lipp, Les Deux Magots,** and **Café de Flore** were frequented by the likes of

One of the many famous cafes in St-Germain-des-Prés.

Hemingway and Picasso in the 1920s, and Jean-Paul Sartre and Simone de Beauvoir in the 1950s. However, the neighborhood has lost a lot of its intellectual appeal in the last few decades and nowadays, you'll find more *haute couture* (Christian Dior, Louis Vuitton, and more) than highbrow culture.

Despite being one of the smaller arrondissements (in terms of both surface area and population) you can find a little of everything in St-Germain. It's home to two of the city's most famous churches, **Eglise-St-Germain-des-Prés** and **St-Sulpice,** as well as the **Institut de France** and former mint, the **Hôtel des Monnaies.** There's art, thanks to the **Ecole des Beaux Arts** on rue Bonaparte, and you'll find an abundance of art dealers and small, private galleries on the nearby streets. If you want to go shopping you can choose from the designer names mentioned above, the smart, upmarket boutiques around St-Sulpice, or the more reasonably priced high street stores on rue de Rennes. Despite being a little on the pricey side, this neighborhood boasts some great bars and restaurants and there's a lively atmosphere in the evenings in the narrow streets around St-Germain and **Odéon.** Not forgetting one of Paris's largest and loveliest green spaces, the charming **Jardin du Luxembourg**—a 24-hectare (59-acre) park, the design of which is based in the Boboli Gardens in Florence—is full of 19th-century park furniture and allegorical statues. Popular with everyone, from toddlers to joggers to lovers, this park is well-worth strolling around.

EIFFEL TOWER & NEARBY (7E)

The 7th arrondissement is a calm, elegant, but rather formal neighborhood. The main attraction is, of course, the **Eiffel Tower.** Despite the fact that many people hated it when it was showcased at the 1889 Great Exhibition, the Eiffel Tower has become the symbol of Paris itself. The panoramic views from the top and the sheer magnificence of the structure attract thousands of visitors everyday. But where there are tourists there are pickpockets and you should be very vigilant when strolling around beneath the tower. Similarly, the Champ de Mars attracts some dodgy characters and it's not the safest place to hang out after dark.

The 7th arrondissement is also home to the world famous and recently renovated **Musée d'Orsay,** where you'll find many of the Impressionist masterpieces, as well as the **Musée Rodin.** In the center of the 7th, you'll also find the **Hôtel des Invalides,** where Napoleon's body was interred, the

Assemblée Nationale (National Assembly), and a number of key government ministries. Although there are a lot of civil servants running—or being chauffeured—around during the week, this makes it one of the quieter neighborhoods at the weekends. There's a bit more of life on either side of Invalides. **Rue St-Dominique** and **rue de Grenelle** are popular shopping streets and **rue Cler** is a busy, well-heeled market-street full of gourmet food shops and classy cafes. On the other side of the 7th, you'll find the chic **rue du Bac,** which winds its way down to the lively shopping district around Sèvres Babylone. It is impossible to come here without paying a visit to the beautiful 19th-century department store, **Le Bon Marché,** on the rue des Sèvres.

MONTPARNASSE & SOUTHERN PARIS (14E & 15E) After WWI, the artistic center of Paris shifted from Montmartre to Montparnasse, and this lively, cosmopolitan neighborhood witnessed the birth of Modernism. Picasso, Matisse, Modigliani, and Chagall, along with expats Ernest Hemingway, Henry Miller, and Gertrude Stein, were all well-known figures in Montparnasse. Today, it's difficult to imagine this area as a literary and artistic heartland. Montparnasse is a busy, commercial neighborhood dominated by the rather ugly **Montparnasse Tower,** which was built in the 1970s. It's still reasonably close to central Paris and is very well connected in terms of public transport but it has lost much of its former soul. Along boulevard Montparnasse you can find, however, several famous Art Deco brasseries—La Coupole, Le Select, and Le Dôme—which were patronized by the all the movers and shakers of the interwar period, including Hemingway, Picasso, and Trotsky.

Aside from shopping, the 14th arrondissement is home to some interesting art institutions, such as the **Fondation Cartier pour l'Art Contemporain,** which organizes interesting contemporary art exhibitions, and the **Fondation Henri Cartier-Bresson,** a must-see for photography lovers. You'll find some peace and quiet in the **Cimetière du Montparnasse,** the resting place of a number of artists, writers, and intellectuals, including Serge Gainsbourg, Samuel Beckett, and both Jean-Paul Sartre and Simone de Beauvoir. As you head south, the 14th becomes increasingly residential and there's very little to see or do down here. The same is true for the 15th arrondissement, which does not have any significant buildings or landmarks. There are a couple of nice parks including Parc André-Citroën and Parc Georges-Brassens, which hosts a book market on Saturdays and Sundays. You'll find a busy shopping district around **Métro La Motte Picquet Grenelle** and **rue du Commerce.**

SUGGESTED ITINERARIES
ICONIC PARIS

If you have limited time in Paris and want to sample the best the city has to offer, then this is the itinerary for you, taking you on a whistle-stop tour past 17 of the city's main attractions. If you don't linger too long in any one place, you could just about get through them all in a day—although why not take your time and spread things over 2 (or even 3) days? *Start: Métro to Cité on the Ile de la Cité. Exit the station, turn right and cross place Louis Lépine. You'll come to boulevard du Palais, where you'll see Sainte-Chapelle.*

1 Sainte-Chapelle

This sublime Gothic chapel built in 1242 is renowned for its breathtaking stained-glass windows. There are often long lines so it's good to get here as early as you can. See p. 96.

The spectacular stained-glass windows of Sainte-Chapelle.

2 Cathédrale de Notre-Dame

One of the supreme masterpieces of Gothic art, the majestic Notre-Dame, built between 1163 and 1250, is the main reason to visit the Ile de la Cité. See p. 86.

3 Ile St-Louis

Full of 17th-century aristocratic town houses, this small island is one of the calmest and most picturesque places in Paris. Stroll along rue Saint Louis en l'Ile, making sure to stop in at Maison Berthillon (nos. 29–31), Paris's most famous sorbet and ice-cream parlor. See p. 86.

4 The Quays of the Seine

Walking along the quays, you'll encounter the most splendid panoramic views that Paris has to offer. The city has 37 bridges, many of them landmarks in their own right. Admire the Pont Neuf, the oldest and most evocative of Paris's bridges.

5 Musée du Louvre

"I never knew what a palace was until I had a glimpse of the Louvre," wrote Nathaniel Hawthorne. The world's greatest art museum—and a former royal residence—the Louvre is the 1st arrondissement's main attraction. The museum's most famous works are the *Mona Lisa, Venus de Milo,* and *Winged Victory.* See p. 81.

Winged Victory.

A quiet street in Ile St-Louis.

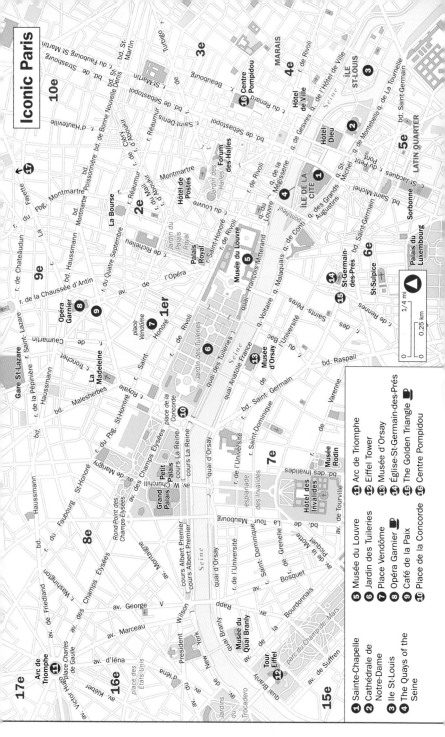

Iconic Paris

1 Sainte-Chapelle
2 Cathédrale de Notre-Dame
3 Île St-Louis
4 The Quays of the Seine
5 Musée du Louvre
6 Jardin des Tuileries
7 Place Vendôme
8 Opéra Garnier 🛍
9 Café de la Paix
10 Place de la Concorde
11 Arc de Triomphe
12 Eiffel Tower
13 Musée d'Orsay
14 Église-St-Germain-des-Prés
15 The Golden Triangle 🛍
16 Centre Pompidou

6 Jardin des Tuileries

It's worth strolling through this elegant French garden just to admire the sculptures and ornamental ponds. At the far end you'll find two galleries: the Jeu de Paume and the Orangerie. See p. 78.

7 Place Vendôme

Home of the Ritz hotel and top-of-the-range jewelers, including Cartier and Bvlgari, this square is the embodiment of Parisian luxury. At the center is a column celebrating Napoleon's Battle of Austerlitz in 1806.

8 Opéra Garnier

Be dazzled by the grand and ornate facade of the Opéra Garnier (p. 110), a testament to the excesses of the Second Empire.

9 Café de la Paix 🍵

On the left of the Opéra Garnier you'll see the glitzy **Café de la Paix** (corner of place de l'Opéra and boulevard des Capucines; www.cafedelapaix.fr; 🕐 **01-40-07-36-36**), also designed by Charles Garnier in the 19th century. Why not stop for lunch or a luxurious coffee in this beautiful Paris institution? The menu is different (and cheaper) if you sit on either the indoor or outdoor terrace rather than inside the restaurant.

10 Place de la Concorde

At the center of place de la Concorde is the 3,300-year-old Obelisk of Luxor. From here, you will have a spectacular view up the Champs-Élysées toward the Arc de Triomphe.

11 Arc de Triomphe

Begun by Napoleon in 1806, this triumphal arch is modeled on ancient Roman arches, and is dedicated to the French army. Beneath it is the tomb of the unknown soldier. See p. 100.

12 Eiffel Tower

Towering above Paris's skyline, Gustave Eiffel's cast-iron tower built for the 1889 Great Exhibition is one of the city's greatest symbols. See p. 139.

Arc de Triomphe.

Place de la Concorde.

13 Musée d'Orsay

A former railway station, the Musée d'Orsay houses an internationally renowned collection of 19th-century art, including key works by the masters of French Impressionism. See p. 136.

The interior of the Musée d'Orsay.

14 Église-St-Germain-des-Prés

This church is all that remains of the former Abbey of St-Germain. The clock tower dates from 1000 A.D., making it the oldest church in Paris. See p. 131.

15 The Golden Triangle ☕

Stop for an aperitif or a bite to eat at one of three elegant cafes known as The Golden Triangle: **Brasserie Lipp, Les Deux Magots,** and **Café de la Flore** (all of which are located on the boulevard St-Germain, just a stone's throw away from the church). Admire the beautiful Art Deco interiors and if you're lucky enough to get a table on the terrace, indulge in a bit of people-watching.

Les Deux Magots cafe.

16 Centre Pompidou

Described by some early critics as a "wart" on the face of Paris, the Centre Pompidou (built in 1977) still arouses mixed reactions. Architecture aside, it contains the impressive Musée National d'Art Moderne and often puts on prestigious temporary exhibitions. See p. 90.

The Centre Pompidou.

17 Sacré-Coeur

Standing in front of this kitsch 19th-century basilica gives you a magnificent view over Paris, day or night (p. 111). After visiting Sacré-Coeur, explore the winding, narrow streets of Montmartre. As you head back down the hill, finish your tour with a drink in one of the bars along rue des Abbesses.

HEMINGWAY & 1920S PARIS

"If you're lucky enough to have lived in Paris as a young man, then wherever you go for the rest of your life, it stays with you, for Paris is a moveable feast." So opens *A Moveable Feast*, Ernest Hemingway's memoir of the years he spent in Paris as a young and often penniless writer in the 1920s. He was one of many soon-to-be-great Anglophone writers drawn to Paris during this era, a number of

ABOVE: **Shakespeare & Co. bookshop;**
RIGHT: **Jardin du Luxembourg.**

whom were featured in Woody Allen's 2011 film *Midnight in Paris*. This tour will introduce you to some of the key players and places of this glorious decade. ***Start:*** *Place de la Contrescarpe.*

1 Place de la Contrescarpe

A Moveable Feast opens with a description of the grubby Café des Amateurs, which was located in this picturesque square. The cafe is no longer there, but there are plenty of student dives nearby on the rue Mouffetard.

2 Rue Cardinal Lemoine

Hemingway and his wife Hadley had the first Parisian apartment at no. 74. A little farther up, at no. 71, is where Irish writer **James Joyce** finished his modernist masterpiece *Ulysses* in the early 1920s.

3 Shakespeare & Co.

Opened in 1919 by a young American called **Sylvia Beach,** this wonderful English-language bookshop soon became a meeting place for all the Anglophone writers who were in Paris in the 1920s, including Joyce, Hemingway, and **Ezra Pound.** In 1922, Sylvia decided to publish Joyce's *Ulysses*. See p. 249.

4 Brasserie Lipp

The 1920s saw the literary and artistic center of Paris shift from Montmartre in the north of Paris to the cafes and brasseries of St-Germain and Montparnasse in the south. **Brasserie Lipp** (151 bd. St-Germain; www.ila-chateau.com/lipp; ✆ **01-45-48-53-91**) was one of Hemingway's favorite watering holes, and he occasionally came here to write. See p. 71.

5 Jardin du Luxembourg

Hemingway used to walk through the gardens on his way to visit renowned patron of the arts **Gertrude Stein** (who lived at 27 rue de Fleurus). When he was particularly strapped for cash, he used to hunt pigeons here with his son. See p. 128.

6 La Closerie des Lilas

Another of Hemingway's favorite cafes, **La Closerie des Lilas** (171 Blvd. Montparnasse; www.closeriedeslilas.fr; ✆ **01-40-51-34-50**) is where he and the novelist **F. Scott Fitzgerald** planned a crazy trip to Lyon to recover Fitzgerald's car. Today it's quite an upmarket restaurant.

La Closerie des Lilas.

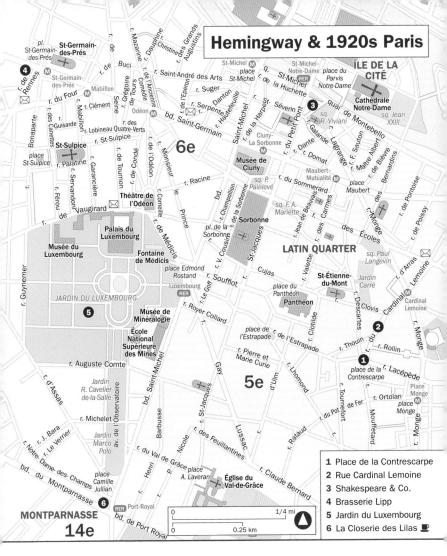

Hemingway & 1920s Paris

ÎLE DE LA CITÉ

6e

LATIN QUARTER

5e

JARDIN DU LUXEMBOURG

MONTPARNASSE
14e

1 Place de la Contrescarpe
2 Rue Cardinal Lemoine
3 Shakespeare & Co.
4 Brasserie Lipp
5 Jardin du Luxembourg
6 La Closerie des Lilas

PARISIAN ARCHITECTURE THROUGH THE AGES

Thanks to Baron Haussmann's modernization of the city in the 19th century, Paris is, in architectural terms, more homogenous than most capitals. The uniformity of Haussmannian architecture is undoubtedly key to Paris's charm and beauty, but you don't have to look far to find traces of other styles and periods. **Start:** *Ile de la Cité.*

1 Cathédrale de Notre-Dame

Built between 1163 and 1250, but added to over the centuries, Notre-Dame is the archetypal Gothic cathedral. The key features of **Gothic** architecture were flying buttresses, rose windows, and if you venture inside, vaulted ceilings. See p. 86.

73

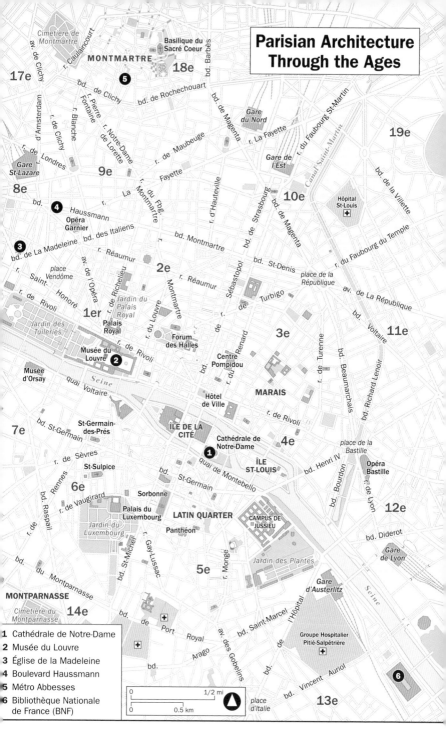

Parisian Architecture Through the Ages

Cimetière de Montmartre
av. de Clichy
r. Caulaincourt
Basilique du Sacré Coeur
bd. Barbès

17e

MONTMARTRE
18e

5

r. de Clichy
bd. de Clichy
r. Pierre Fontaine
r. Blanche
r. Notre-Dame de Lorette
bd. de Rochechouart
bd. de Magenta

Gare du Nord

19e

r. d'Amsterdam
r. de Clichy
r. de Londres

Gare St-Lazare

8e

r. de Maubeuge
r. La Fayette
r. du Faubourg St-Martin

Gare de l'Est

Canal Saint-Martin

bd. de la Villette

9e

La Fayette
r. du Fbg. Montmartre
r. d'Hauteville

Hôpital St-Louis ✚

4 Haussmann
Opéra Garnier
bd. Haussmann
r. de Strasbourg
bd. de Magenta

10e

3 bd. de La Madeleine
bd. des Italiens
r. Réaumur
bd. Montmartre
bd. St-Denis
r. du Faubourg du Temple

place de la République

av. de La République

place Vendôme
r. Saint-Honoré
av. de l'Opéra
r. de Richelieu
r. Réaumur
Montmartre
r. de
Sébastopol
place de la République
bd. Voltaire

2e

Turbigo

11e

1er
Jardin des Tuileries
Jardin du Palais Royal
Palais Royal
r. du Louvre
Forum des Halles
r. Renard
de
Turbigo
r. de Turenne
bd. Beaumarchais
bd. Richard Lenoir
bd. Voltaire

Musée du Louvre **2**
r. de Rivoli
Centre Pompidou

3e

Musée d'Orsay
Seine
quai Voltaire
Hôtel de Ville
MARAIS
r. de Rivoli

7e
bd. St-Germain
St-Germain-des-Prés
ÎLE DE LA CITÉ
Cathédrale de Notre-Dame
1
4e
place de la Bastille

Opéra Bastille

r. de Sèvres
St-Sulpice
r. de Rennes
6e
Sorbonne
bd. St-Germain
quai de Montebello
ÎLE ST-LOUIS
bd. Henri IV
bd. Bourdon
r. de Lyon

r. de Vaugirard
Palais du Luxembourg
LATIN QUARTER
CAMPUS DE JUSSIEU

12e

Jardin du Luxembourg
Panthéon
Sorbonne
St-Germain

bd. Raspail
r. de
bd. du Montparnasse
bd. St-Michel
Gay-Lussac
5e
r. Monge
Jardin des Plantes
bd. Diderot
Gare de Lyon

MONTPARNASSE
Cimetière du Montparnasse
14e
bd. de Port Royal
av. des Gobelins
bd. Saint-Marcel
Gare d'Austerlitz
Seine

✚
Arago
bd. de l'Hôpital
Groupe Hospitalier Pitié-Salpêtrière ✚

6

bd. Vincent Auriol
place d'Italie
13e

1	Cathédrale de Notre-Dame
2	Musée du Louvre
3	Église de la Madeleine
4	Boulevard Haussmann
5	Métro Abbesses
6	Bibliothèque Nationale de France (BNF)

0 ___ 1/2 mi
0 ___ 0.5 km

2 Musée du Louvre

The left-hand side of the façade opposite you is the oldest part of the Louvre. Built in the 1530s, it's a good example of **Renaissance** architecture. Admire the decorative bas-reliefs, the pilasters (shallow columns projecting from the wall), and the symmetry of the facade. See p. 81.

3 Église de la Madeleine

Inspired by ancient Rome, Napoleon I ordered the construction of this **neoclassicist** temple. He intended it to be a "Temple to the Glory of the Great Army," but as it was incomplete when he fell from grace, it became a church and was consecrated in 1842.

The Gothic Cathédrale de Notre-Dame.

4 Boulevard Haussmann

Named after the Baron who transformed Paris in the 19th century, this wide tree-lined boulevard demonstrates the key characteristics of **Haussmannian** architecture; look for wrought-iron balconies and the alignment of the windows and balconies to create a sense of perspective.

5 Métro Abbesses

This is one of the only two original Métro entrances that are left in Paris (the other is at Porte Dauphine). Designed by Hector Guimard in 1900, the Paris Métro entrances were a classic example of the **Art Nouveau** style.

6 Bibliothèque Nationale de France (BNF)

Designed by **contemporary** architect Dominique Perrault, this huge library opened in 1996. The reading rooms are underground, while the books are housed in four glass towers—the shape of each tower is supposed to symbolize an open book.

Boulevard Haussmann.

The towers of the Bibliothèque Nationale de France resemble open books.

EXPLORING PARIS

by Kate van den Boogert

4

The city of Paris has a long history: There has been civilization here for more than 2 millennia, ever since Julius Caesar's troops invaded the city in 52 B.C., snatching power from the Gaulish tribe, the *Parisii*. Two thousand years of art, architecture, war, religion, and politics—not to mention power, passion, and intrigue—have left their mark on the city. Paris counts hundreds of museums and monuments. There are irresistible stars such as the Louvre, *bien sûr*, but there are also many surprising, secret spots. It's a city that can transport you back centuries, where you can lose yourself in the labyrinth of royal power and opulence, or get captivated by the violence of the French Revolution. Or the city can bring you up to date, with the most avant-garde art, design, and architecture that the world has to offer today. But the special thing about Paris is that just walking the streets feels like visiting the world's most magical museum.

The year 2013 should see the much-missed Musée Picasso, Musée de l'Homme, Louxor cinema, and Musée Galliera reopen to the public after years of renovations. Paris's transport and shopping hub Les Halles is in the middle of a massive overhaul, expected to finish in 2016.

Area by area, the following pages will highlight the best that Paris can offer, from iconic sights known the world over to quirky museums and hidden gardens, from 1,000-year-old castles to galleries celebrating the most challenging contemporary art, and from the must-sees to the only-if-you've-seen-everything-else-sees. Here, then, is the best of Paris's attractions.

PARIS'S TOP 14 SIGHTS & ATTRACTIONS

- Arc de Triomphe (p. 100)
- Basilique du Sacré-Coeur (p. 111)
- Cathédrale de Notre-Dame (p. 86)
- Centre Pompidou (p. 90)
- Cimetière du Père-Lachaise (p. 115)
- Gaîté Lyrique (p. 92)
- Jardin du Luxembourg (p. 128)
- Musée d'Orsay (p. 136)
- Musée du Louvre (p. 81)
- Musée du Quai Branly (p. 137)
- Palais de Tokyo (p. 108)
- Parc de la Villette (p. 120)
- Sainte Chapelle (p. 96)
- Tour Eiffel (p. 139)

PREVIOUS PAGE: **A fountain in place de la Concorde.**

THE RIGHT BANK
Les Halles, Louvre & Palais Royal (1er & 2e)

Crowned by the Louvre, this central area that flanks the Seine packs in a high density of important museums, centered around the magnificent former royal palace and its expansive Jardin des Tuileries. Though the Louvre is on top of most visitors' to-do lists, don't forget that there are also some wonderful smaller museums close by, and great shopping too.

Jardin des Tuileries ★★ ☺ GARDEN   The spectacular statue-studded Jardin des Tuileries, bordering place de la Concorde, is as much a part of Paris as the Seine. Le Nôtre, Louis XIV's gardener and planner of the Versailles grounds, designed the gardens. Some of the gardens' most distinctive statues are the 18 enormous bronzes by Maillol, installed within the Jardin du Carrousel, a subdivision of the Jardin des Tuileries, between 1964 and 1965, under the direction of Culture Minister André Malraux.

About 400 years before that, Catherine de Medici ordered a palace built here, the **Palais des Tuileries;** other occupants have included Louis XVI (after he left Versailles) and Napoleon. Twice attacked by Parisians, it was burned to the ground in 1871 and never rebuilt. The gardens, however, remain. In orderly French manner, the trees are arranged according to designs, and even the paths are arrow-straight. Bubbling fountains break the sense of order and formality.

Each summer, over the months of July and August, the parks hosts a traditional **funfair** (www.feteforaine-jardindestuileries.com) alongside the rue de Rivoli—be sure to take a Ferris wheel ride for excellent views.

Near place de la Concorde, 1er. ✆ **01-40-20-90-43.** Free admission. Daily Apr–May 7am–9pm; June–Aug 7am–11pm; Sept 7am–9pm; Oct–Mar 7:30am–7:30pm. Métro: Tuileries or Concorde.

Jeu de Paume ★★ MUSEUM   After knowing many roles, this museum, in the northeast corner of the Tuileries gardens, has become a national center for photography and video, exploring "the world of images, their uses, and the issues they raise" from the 19th to the 21st centuries. It is one of the finest museums of its type in the world, and presents ever-changing exhibitions, many of them daringly avant-garde.

Originally, in this part of the gardens, Napoleon III built a ball court on which *jeu de paume,* an antecedent of tennis, was played—hence the museum's name. The most infamous period in the gallery's history came during the Nazi occupation, when it served as an "evaluation center" for works of modern art. Paintings from all over France were shipped to the Jeu de Paume; art condemned by the Nazis as "degenerate" was burned.

1 place de la Concorde, 8e. www.jeudepaume. org. ✆ **01-47-03-12-50.** Admission 8.50€ adults, 5.50€ students and children. Tues noon–9pm; Wed–Fri noon–7pm; Sat–Sun 10am–7pm. Métro: Concorde.

A video exhibit at Jeu de Paume.

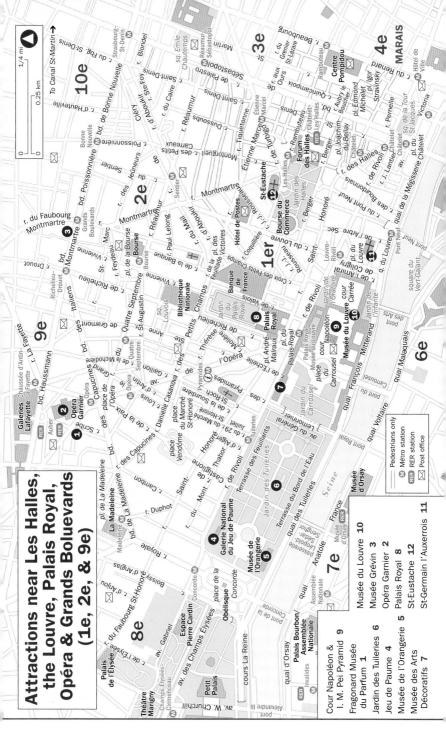

Attractions near Les Halles, the Louvre, Palais Royal, Opéra & Grands Boluevards (1e, 2e, & 9e)

Cour Napoléon & I. M. Pei Pyramid **9**
Fragonard Musée du Parfum **1**
Jardin des Tuileries **6**
Jeu de Paume **4**
Musée de l'Orangerie **5**
Musée des Arts Décoratifs **7**
Musée du Louvre **10**
Musée Grévin **3**
Opéra Garnier **2**
Palais Royal **8**
St-Eustache **12**
St-Germain l'Auxerrois **11**

Pedestrians only
Ⓜ Metro station
Ⓡ RER station
⊠ Post office

79

The New Les Halles

For 8 centuries, **Les Halles** was the city's primary wholesale fruit, meat, and vegetable market. In the 19th century, Zola famously called it "the belly of Paris." The smock-clad vendors, beef carcasses, and baskets of vegetables all belong to the past, for the original market was torn down in the early '70s and relocated to a massive steel-and-glass edifice at Rungis, a suburb near Orly. Today, Les Halles includes the city's chief transportation hub and a major shopping complex, the **Forum des Halles** (1–7 rue Pierre-Lescot, 1er). This large mall, much of it underground, contains shops, restaurants, and movie theaters. In 2010, the city embarked on a massive 810€-million renovation program that will overhaul the underground shopping and transportation zones as well as the garden above. Renovations are slated to be completed in 2016, but the complex should remain open and operational during the renovations. For more information, visit www.parisleshalles.fr.

Musée de l'Orangerie ★★ MUSEUM   In the Tuileries stands another gem among museums. It has an outstanding collection of art and one celebrated work on display: Claude Monet's exquisite *Nymphéas* (1915–27). The two galleries were purpose built by the French state to house eight massive murals by Monet, in which water lilies float amorphously on the canvas. The paintings are displayed as the artist intended them to be: lit by sunlight in large oval galleries that evoke the shape of the garden ponds at his former Giverny estate.

Creating his effects with hundreds and hundreds of minute strokes of his brush (one irate 19th-c. critic called them "tongue lickings"), Monet achieved unity and harmony, as he did in his Rouen Cathedral series and his haystacks. Artists with lesser talent might have stirred up "soup." But Monet, of course, was a genius. See his lilies and evoke for yourself the mood and melancholy as he experienced them so many years ago. Monet continued to paint his water landscapes right up until his death in 1926, although he was greatly hampered by failing eyesight.

The renovated building also houses the art collections of two men, John Walter and Paul Guillaume, who are not connected to each other, except that they were both married at different times to the same woman. Their collection includes more than 24 Renoirs, including *Young Girl at a Piano*. Cézanne is represented by 14 works, notably *The Red Rock*, and Matisse by 11 paintings. The highlight of Rousseau's nine works displayed here is *The Wedding*, and the dozen paintings by Picasso reach the pinnacle of their brilliance in *The Female Bathers*. Other outstanding paintings are by Utrillo (10 works in all), Soutine (22), and Derain (28).

It is possible to buy a joint ticket to both the Musée d'Orsay (p. 136) and the Musée de l'Orangerie, which is valid for 4 days and costs 14€.

Jardin des Tuileries, 1er. www.musee-orangerie.fr. ✆ **01-44-77-80-07.** Admission 7.50€ adults, 5€ students 25 and younger. Free 1st Sun of every month. Wed–Mon 9am–6pm. Métro: Concorde.

Musée des Arts Décoratifs ★★ MUSEUM   In the northwest wing of the Louvre's Pavillon de Marsan, this imposing museum is home to a treasury of furnishings, fabrics, wallpaper, objets d'art, and items displaying living styles from the Middle Ages to the present. Notable are the 1920s Art Deco boudoir, bath, and bedroom done for couturier Jeanne Lanvin by the designer Rateau, plus a collection of the works donated by Jean Dubuffet. Decorative art from the Middle Ages to the Renaissance is on the second floor; collections from the 17th, 18th, and

Musée du Louvre.

19th centuries occupy the third and fourth floors. The fifth floor has specialized centers, such as wallpaper and drawings, and exhibits detailing fashion, textiles, toys, crafts, and glass trends. The space also includes a lovely ground-floor shop, **107 Rivoli** (p. 246), selling all sorts of craft pieces, and a restaurant, Le Saut du Loup, which boasts an outdoor eating area in the Tuileries Gardens.

Palais du Louvre, 107 rue de Rivoli, 1er. www.lesartsdecoratifs.fr. ⓒ **01-44-55-57-50.** Admission 9.50€ adults, 8€ ages 18–25, free for children 17 and younger. Tues–Wed, Fri 11am–6pm; Thurs 11am–6pm; Sat–Sun 10am–6pm. Métro: Palais-Royal or Tuileries.

Musée du Louvre ★★★ MUSEUM   The Louvre is the world's largest palace and museum, and it houses one of the greatest art collections ever. To enter, pass through I. M. Pei's controversial 21m (69-ft.) **glass pyramid ★**—a startling though effective contrast of the ultramodern against the palace's classical lines. Commissioned by the late president François Mitterrand and completed in 1989, it allows sunlight to shine on an underground reception area with a complex of shops and restaurants.

People on one of those "Paris-in-a-day" tours try to break track records to get a glimpse of the Louvre's two most famous ladies: the beguiling *Mona Lisa* and the armless *Venus de Milo ★★★*. The herd then dashes on a 5-minute stampede in pursuit of *Winged Victory ★★★*, the headless statue discovered at Samothrace and dating from about 200 B.C. In defiance of the assembly line theory of art, we head instead for David's *Coronation of Napoleon,* showing Napoleon poised with the crown aloft as Joséphine kneels before him, just across from his *Portrait of Madame Récamier ★*, depicting Napoleon's opponent at age 23; she reclines on her sofa agelessly in the style of classical antiquity.

Viewing the *Mona Lisa*.

Then a big question looms: Which of the rest of the 30,000 works on display would you like to see?

Between the Seine and rue de Rivoli, the Palais du Louvre suffers from an embarrassment of riches, stretching for almost 1km (½ mile). In the days of Charles V, it was a fortress, but François I, a patron of Leonardo da Vinci, had it torn down and rebuilt as a royal residence. Less than a month after Marie Antoinette's head and body parted company, the

Winged Victory

Revolutionary Committee decided the king's collection of paintings and sculpture should be opened to the public. At the lowest point in its history, in the 18th century, the Louvre was home for anybody who wanted to set up housekeeping. Laundry hung in the windows, corners were pigpens, and families built fires to cook their meals in winter. Napoleon ended all that, chasing out the squatters and restoring the palace. In fact, he chose the Louvre as the site of his wedding to Marie-Louise.

So where did all these paintings come from? The kings of France, notably François I and Louis XIV, acquired many of them, and others were willed to or purchased by the state. Many contributed by Napoleon were taken from reluctant donors: The church was one especially heavy and unwilling giver. Much of Napoleon's plunder had to be returned, though France hasn't yet seen its way clear to giving back all the booty.

The collections are divided into seven departments: Egyptian Antiquities; Oriental Antiquities; Greek, Etruscan, and Roman Antiquities; Sculpture; Painting; Decorative Arts; and Graphic Arts. If you don't have to do Paris in a day, you might want to visit several times, concentrating on different collections or schools of painting. Those with little time should take a guided tour.

Acquired by François I to hang above his bathtub, Leonardo's *La Gioconda (Mona Lisa)* ★★★ has been the source of legend for centuries. Note the guard and bulletproof glass: The world's most famous painting was stolen in 1911 then found in Florence in 1913. At first, both the poet Guillaume Apollinaire and Picasso were

Venus de Milo.

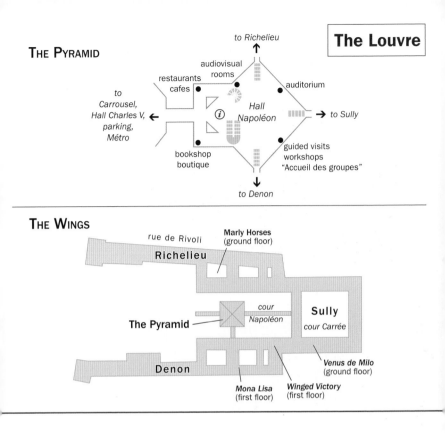

The Louvre

The Pyramid

to Richelieu ↑

audiovisual rooms

restaurants cafes

to Carrousel, Hall Charles V, parking, Métro ←

auditorium

(i) Hall Napoléon

→ to Sully

bookshop boutique

guided visits workshops "Accueil des groupes"

↓ to Denon

The Wings

rue de Rivoli

Marly Horses (ground floor)

Richelieu

cour Napoléon

Sully cour Carrée

The Pyramid

Denon

Venus de Milo (ground floor)

Mona Lisa (first floor)

Winged Victory (first floor)

---

suspected, but it was discovered in the possession of a former Louvre employee, who'd apparently carried it out under his overcoat. Two centuries after its arrival at the Louvre, the *Mona Lisa* in 2003 was assigned a new gallery of her own. Less well known (but to us even more enchanting) are Leonardo's **Virgin and Child with St. Anne ★** and the **Virgin of the Rocks.**

After paying your respects to the "smiling one," allow time to see some French works stretching from the Richelieu wing through the entire **Sully wing** and even overflowing into the **Denon wing.** It's all here: Watteau's **Gilles** with the mysterious boy in a clown suit staring at you; Fragonard's and Boucher's rococo renderings of the aristocracy; and the greatest masterpieces of David, including his stellar 1785 **The Oath of the Horatii** and the vast and vivid **Coronation of Napoleon.** Only Florence's Uffizi rivals the Denon wing for its Italian Renaissance collection—everything from Raphael's **Portrait of Balthazar Castiglione** to Titian's **Man with a Glove.** Veronese's gigantic **Wedding Feast at Cana ★**, a romp of

Leaping over the Louvre Line

If you don't want to wait in line for tickets to the Louvre, you can order tickets in advance by visiting **http://louvre.fnacspectacles.com** or calling ℂ **08-92-68-46-94;** tickets can be mailed to you, or you can pick them up at any Paris branch of the FNAC electronics chain. You can also order advance tickets and take a virtual tour at **www.louvre.fr.** Note that the Louvre is open until 10pm on Wednesday and Friday—usually a quiet time to visit.

83

Contemporary Art & the Louvre

With all those centuries-old masterpieces grabbing the spotlight, the museum's contemporary works can get overlooked—but they're worth seeking out. In 2010, the museum unveiled a painted ceiling in the Salle des Bronzes by American artist Cy Twombly, the third contemporary artist who was commissioned to install a permanent work at the Louvre.

(He was preceded by contemporary artists Anselm Kiefer and François Morellet.) Twombly's painting appears on the ceiling of one of the Louvre's largest galleries, and it covers more than 350 sq. m (3,770 sq. ft.). The ceiling depicts an immense blue sky that is dotted with spheres and white insets inscribed with the names of famous Greek sculptors.

Venetian high society in the 1500s, occupies an entire wall (that's Paolo himself playing the cello).

Of the Greek and Roman antiquities, the most notable collections, aside from the *Venus de Milo* and *Winged Victory,* are fragments of a **Parthenon frieze** (in the Denon wing). In Renaissance sculpture, you'll see Michelangelo's *Esclaves (Slaves),* originally intended for the tomb of Julius II but sold into other bondage. The Denon wing houses masterpieces such as Ingres's *The Turkish Bath,* the **Botticelli frescoes** from the Villa Lemmi, Raphael's *La Belle Jardinière,* and Titian's *Open Air Concert.* The Sully wing is also filled with old masters, such as Boucher's *Diana Resting After Her Bath* and Fragonard's *Bathers.*

The **Richelieu wing ★★★** houses northern European and French paintings, along with decorative arts, sculpture, Oriental antiquities (including a rich collection of both Islamic and Far Eastern Art), and the Napoleon III salons. One of its galleries displays 21 works that Rubens painted in a space of only 2 years for Marie de Medici's Palais de Luxembourg. The masterpieces here include Dürer's *Self-Portrait,* van Dyck's *Portrait of Charles I of England,* and Holbein the Younger's *Portrait of Erasmus of Rotterdam.*

When you tire of strolling the galleries, you may like a pick-me-up at the Richelieu Wing's **Café Richelieu** (*(C)* **01-47-03-99-68**) or, under the arcades and overlooking I. M. Pei's pyramid, at **Café Marly,** 93 rue de Rivoli, 1er (*(C)* **01-49-26-06-60**). Boasting Napoleon III opulence, the Marly is a perfect oasis. Try a cafe crème, a club sandwich, a pastry, or something from the bistro menu.

34–36 quai du Louvre, 1er. Main entrance in the glass pyramid, cour Napoléon. www.louvre.fr. *(C)* **01-40-20-53-17,** 01-40-20-50-50 for operator, or 08-92-68-46-94 for advance credit card sales. Admission 10€, children 17 and younger free, free to all 1st Sun of every month. Sat–Mon and Thurs 9am–6pm; Wed and Fri 9am–10pm. 1½-hr. English-language tours (Mon and Wed–Sun) 9€, 6€ children 12 and younger with museum ticket. Métro: Palais-Royal–Musée du Louvre.

Palais Royal ★★ HISTORIC SITE/GARDEN The Palais Royal was originally known as the Palais Cardinal, for it was the residence of Cardinal Richelieu, Louis XIII's prime minister. Richelieu had it built, and after his death it was inherited by the king, who died soon after. Louis XIV spent part of his childhood here with his mother, Anne of Austria, but later resided at the Louvre and Versailles. The palace was later owned by the duc de Chartres et Orléans (see Parc Monceau on p. 108), who encouraged the opening of cafes, gambling dens, and other public entertainment. Today the building is occupied by the French Culture Ministry.

The lovely **Jardin du Palais Royal** is at the center of the arcaded former palace, and features a fountain and gardens. Don't miss the main courtyard, close

The courtyard of the Palais Royal.

The black-marble tomb of Jean-Baptiste Colbert.

to the rue St-Honoré, with the controversial 1986 Buren sculpture—280 prison-striped columns, oddly placed. The arcades of the Palais Royal have become a high fashion destination over the last few years, with high-end boutiques such as Marc Jacobs and Stella McCartney.

Rue St-Honoré, 1er. No phone. Free admission. Gardens daily 7:30am–dusk. Métro: Palais Royal–Musée du Louvre.

St-Eustache ★★ CHURCH   This Gothic and Renaissance church completed in 1637 is rivaled only by Notre-Dame. Mme de Pompadour and Richelieu were baptized here, and Molière's funeral was held here in 1673. The church has been known for organ recitals ever since Liszt played in 1866. Inside rests the **black-marble tomb** of Jean-Baptiste Colbert, the minister of state under Louis XIV; atop the tomb is his marble effigy flanked by statues of *Abundance* by Coysevox and *Fidelity* by Tuby. Notable paintings are Rembrandt's ***The Pilgrimage to Emmaus,*** two versions of ***Disciples d'Emmaüs*** by Rubens, and a triptych by modern American painter Keith Haring—his last work before he died in 1990 of AIDS. The church has a side entrance on rue Rambuteau.

2 impasse St-Eustache, 1er. www.st-eustache.org. ✆ **01-42-36-31-05.** Free admission. Daily 9am–7pm; Sun 9am–7pm; Sun organ recitals 5:30pm. Métro: Les Halles.

St-Germain l'Auxerrois ★★ CHURCH   Once it was the church for the Palais du Louvre, drawing an assortment of royalty, courtesans, men of art and law, and local artisans. Sharing place du Louvre with Perrault's colonnade, the church contains only the foundation stones of its original 11th-century belfry. The chapel that had stood here was greatly enlarged in the 14th century by the addition of side aisles and became a beautiful church, with 77 sq. m (829 sq. ft.) of stained glass, including some rose windows from the Renaissance. The intricately carved **church-wardens' pews** are outstanding, based on 17th-century Le Brun designs. Behind them is a **15th-century triptych** and **Flemish retable,** so poorly lit you can hardly appreciate it. The organ was ordered by Louis XVI for Sainte-Chapelle. Many famous men were entombed here, including the sculptor Coysevox and the architect Le Vau. Around the chancel is an intricate **18th-century grille.**

The saddest moment in the church's history was on August 24, 1572, the evening of the St. Bartholomew Massacre. The tower bells rang, signaling the supporters of Catherine de Medici, Marguerite de Guise, Charles IX, and the future Henri III to launch a slaughter of thousands of Huguenots, who'd been invited to celebrate the marriage of Henri de Navarre to Marguerite de Valois.

2 place du Louvre, 1er. ℂ **01-42-60-13-96.** Free admission. Daily 8am–7pm. Métro: Louvre-Rivoli.

Le Marais, Ile St-Louis & Ile de la Cité (3e & 4e)

This historic neighborhood, home to royalty and aristocracy in the 17th and 18th centuries, preserves exceptional architecture—some of it dating back to the Renaissance. Its narrow, winding streets are from another age. While it features some blockbuster attractions, including the **Hôtel de Ville** and the **Centre Pompidou,** the Marais is notable for its density of charming smaller museums, where you hopefully won't be fighting through crowds. The two islands in the Seine—Ile St-Louis and Ile de la Cité—set the stage for some impressive medieval monuments, the **Cathédrale de Notre-Dame,** the **Conciergerie,** and the glorious **Sainte-Chapelle**. *Note:* the Musée Picasso, which has been closed for renovations over the past few years, should reopen in May 2013.

Cathédrale de Notre-Dame ★★ CATHEDRAL   Notre-Dame is the heart of Paris and even of the country itself: Distances from the city to all parts of France are calculated from a spot at the far end of place du Parvis, in front of the cathedral, where a circular bronze plaque marks **Kilomètre Zéro.**

The cathedral's setting on the banks of the Seine has always been memorable. Founded in the 12th century by Maurice de Sully, bishop of Paris, Notre-Dame has grown over the years, changing as Paris has changed; often falling victim to whims of taste. Its flying buttresses (the external side supports, giving the massive interior a sense of weightlessness) were rebuilt in 1330. Though many disagree, we feel Notre-Dame is more interesting outside than in, and you'll want to walk all around it to fully appreciate this "vast symphony of stone." Better yet, cross over the Pont au Double to the Left Bank and view it from the quai.

The histories of Paris and Notre-Dame are inseparable. Many prayed here before going off to fight in the Crusades. The revolutionaries who destroyed the Galerie des Rois and converted the building into a secular temple didn't spare "Our Lady of Paris." Later, Napoleon crowned himself emperor here, yanking the crown out of Pius VII's hands and placing it on his own head before crowning his Joséphine empress (see David's *Coronation of Napoléon* in the Louvre). But carelessness, vandalism, embellishments, and wars of religion had

Kilomètre Zéro.

Cathédrale de Notre-Dame.

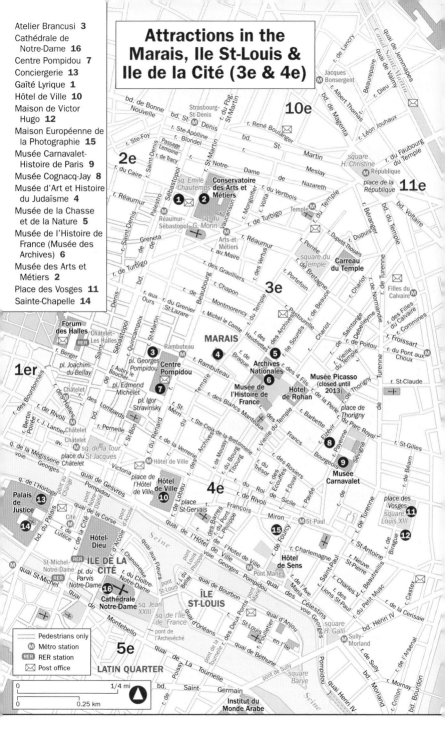

Attractions in the Marais, Ile St-Louis & Ile de la Cité (3e & 4e)

87

Notre-Dame de Paris

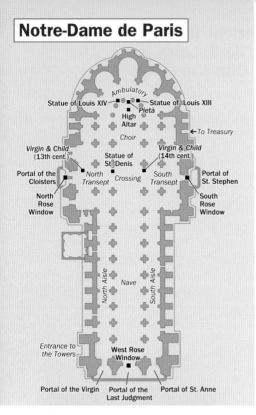

- Statue of Louis XIV
- Ambulatory
- Statue of Louis XIII
- Pietà
- High Altar
- Choir
- ← To Treasury
- Virgin & Child (13th cent.)
- Statue of St. Denis
- Virgin & Child (14th cent.)
- Portal of the Cloisters
- North Transept
- Crossing
- South Transept
- Portal of St. Stephen
- North Rose Window
- South Rose Window
- North Aisle
- Nave
- South Aisle
- Entrance to the Towers
- West Rose Window
- Portal of the Virgin
- Portal of the Last Judgment
- Portal of St. Anne

Rose window at the Cathédrale de Notre-Dame.

already demolished much of the previously existing structure.

The cathedral was once scheduled for demolition, but because of the popularity of Victor Hugo's *Hunchback of Notre-Dame* and the revival of interest in the Gothic period, a movement mushroomed to restore the cathedral to its original glory. The task was completed under Viollet-le-Duc, an architectural genius. The houses of old Paris used to crowd in on Notre-Dame, but during his redesign of the city, Baron Haussmann ordered them torn down to show the cathedral to its best advantage from the parvis. This is the best vantage for seeing the three sculpted 13th-century portals (the Virgin, the Last Judgment, and St. Anne).

On the left, the **Portal of the Virgin** depicts the signs of the zodiac and the coronation of the Virgin, an association found in dozens of medieval churches. The restored central **Portal of the Last Judgment** depicts three levels: the first shows Vices and Virtues; the second, Christ and his Apostles; and above that, Christ in triumph after the Resurrection. The portal is a close illustration of the Gospel according to Matthew. Over it is the remarkable **west rose window ★★**, 9.5m (31 ft.) wide, forming a showcase for a statue of the Virgin and Child. On the far right is the **Portal of St. Anne,** depicting scenes such as the Virgin enthroned with Child; it's Notre-Dame's best-preserved and most perfect piece of sculpture. Equally interesting (though often missed) is the **Portal of the Cloisters** (around on the left), with its dour-faced 13th-century Virgin, a survivor among the figures that originally adorned the facade. (Alas, the Child she's holding has been decapitated.) Finally, on the Seine side of Notre-Dame, the **Portal of St. Stephen** traces that saint's martyrdom.

Pont Neuf

Don't miss the ironically named **Pont Neuf (New Bridge)** at the tip of the Ile de la Cité, opposite from Notre-Dame. The span isn't new—it's Paris's oldest bridge, begun in 1578 and finished in 1604. In its day, it had two unique features: It was paved, and it wasn't flanked with houses and shops. Actually, with 12 arches, it's not one bridge but two (they don't quite line up)—one from the Right Bank to the island and the other from the Left Bank to the island. At the **Musée Carnavalet** (p. 93), a painting called *The Spectacle of Buffoons* shows what the bridge was like between 1665 and 1669. Duels were fought on it, the nobility's great coaches crossed it, peddlers sold

their wares, and entertainers such as Tabarin went there to seek a few coins from the gawkers. As public facilities were lacking, the bridge also served as a *de facto* outhouse.

If possible, see Notre-Dame at sunset. Inside of the three giant medallions warming the austere cathedral, the **north rose window ★★** in the transept, from the mid–13th century, is best. The main body of the church is typically Gothic, with slender, graceful columns. In the **choir,** a stone-carved screen from the early–14th century depicts such biblical scenes as the Last Supper. Near the altar stands the 14th-century *Virgin and Child ★*, highly venerated among Paris's faithful. In the **treasury** are displayed vestments and gold objects, including crowns. Exhibited is a cross presented to Haile Selassie, former emperor of Ethiopia, and a reliquary given by Napoleon. Notre-Dame is especially proud of its relics of the True Cross and the Crown of Thorns.

To visit the **gargoyles ★★** immortalized by Hugo, you have to scale steps leading to the twin **towers,** rising to a height of 68m (223 ft.). When there, you can inspect devils, hobgoblins, and birds of prey. Look carefully, and you may see hunchback Quasimodo with Esmeralda.

Approached through a garden behind Notre-Dame is the **Mémorial des Martyrs Français de la Déportation de 1945 (Deportation Memorial),** out on the tip of Ile de la Cité. Here, birds chirp and the Seine flows gently by, but the memories are far from pleasant. The memorial commemorates the French citizens who were deported to concentration camps during World War II. Carved into stone are these blood-red words (in French): "Forgive, but don't forget." The memorial is open Monday to Friday 8:30am to 9:45pm, and Saturday to Sunday 9am to 9:45pm. Admission is free.

6 place du Parvis Notre-Dame, 4e. www.notredamedeparis.fr. 🕐 **01-53-10-07-02.** Admission free to cathedral. Towers 8.50€ adults, 5€ seniors and ages 13–25, free for children 12 and younger. Treasury 3€ adults, 2.20€ seniors, 1.60€ ages 13–25, free for children 12 and younger. Cathedral year-round daily 8am–6:45pm (Sat–Sun 7:15pm). Towers and crypt daily 10am–6pm (until 11pm Sat–Sun June–Aug). Museum Wed and Sat–Sun 2–5pm. Treasury Mon–Fri 9:30am–6pm; Sat 9:30am–6:30pm; Sun 1:30–6:30pm. Métro: Cité or St-Michel. RER: St-Michel.

Centre Pompidou ★★★ ☺ MUSEUM When it first opened in the 1970s, the Centre Pompidou was hailed as "the most avant-garde building in the world," and today it still continues to pack in the art-loving crowds—about six million people visit it each year.

Conceived by former French president Georges Pompidou and designed by architects Renzo Piano and Richard Rogers, this building originally opened in 1977, and it underwent a major renovation in 2000, which expanded and improved the space. The building's exterior is very bold: brightly painted pipes and ducts crisscross its transparent facade (green for water, red for heat, blue for air, and yellow for electricity), and an outdoor escalator flanks the building, freeing up interior space for exhibitions.

Inside, the big attraction is the impressive **Musée National d'Art Moderne (National Museum of Modern Art) ★★**, which is home to some 40,000 works from the 20th and 21st centuries—though only about 850 works can be displayed at one time. If you want to view some real charmers, seek out Calder's 1926 *Josephine Baker,* one of his earlier versions of the mobile, an art form he invented. You'll also find two examples of Duchamps's series of Dada-style sculptures he invented in 1936: *Boîte en Valise* (1941) and *Boîte en Valise* (1968). And every time we visit, we have to see Dalí's *Hallucination partielle: Six images de Lénine sur un piano* (1931), with Lenin dancing on a piano. A new gallery, the Espace 315, is dedicated to exhibitions by a younger generation of international artists. A dedicated area for children, **La Galerie des Enfants** on the mezzanine, hosts great interactive artist-conceived projects for kids.

Other attractions inside the Centre Pompidou include: the **Bibliothéque Publique d'Information (Public Information Library),** a vast public library with a huge collection of French and foreign books, periodicals, films, music records, slides, and more; the **Institut de Recherche et de Coordination Acoustique-Musique (Institute for Research and Coordination of Acoustics/Music),** which brings together musicians and composers; and the **Atelier Brancusi ★,** a minimuseum that re-creates the Jazz Age studio of Romanian sculptor Brancusi. There are also performance halls that often host concerts and events, shops, restaurants, and a movie theater. The Centre Pompidou holds regularly changing public exhibitions and events, so check their website for information.

Centre Pompidou.

Brightly painted pipes on the facade of the Centre Pompidou.

LEFT: **The Stravinsky fountain**; RIGHT: **The Conciergerie.**

Outside, there is a large open **forecourt,** which is a free "entertainment center" often featuring mimes, fire-eaters, circus performers, and sometimes musicians. Here you can admire a monumental sculpture by Alexander Calder. Dating from 1974 and made in France, the piece *Horizontal* is one of Calder's last *stabiles-mobiles.* And don't miss the nearby **Stravinsky fountain,** containing mobile sculptures by Tinguely and Niki de Saint Phalle.

Place Georges-Pompidou, 4e. www.centrepompidou.fr. ℓ **01-44-78-12-33.** Admission 11€–13€ adults, students 9€–10€ students, free for children 17 and younger; admission varies depending on exhibits. Wed–Mon 11am–10pm. Métro: Rambuteau, Hôtel de Ville, or Châtelet–Les Halles.

Conciergerie ★★ HISTORIC SITE   London has its Bloody Tower, and Paris has its Conciergerie. Even though the Conciergerie had a long regal history before the French Revolution, it was forever stained by the Reign of Terror and lives as an infamous symbol of the time when carts pulled up constantly to haul off fresh supplies of victims of Dr. Guillotin's wonderful little invention.

Much of the Conciergerie was built in the 14th century as an extension of the Capetian royal Palais de la Cité. You approach through its landmark twin towers, the **Tour d'Argent** (where the crown jewels were stored at one time) and **Tour de César,** but the **Salle des Gardes (Guard Room)** is the actual entrance. Even more interesting is the dark and foreboding Gothic **Salle des Gens d'Armes (Room of People at Arms),** utterly changed from the days when the king used it as a banquet hall. However, architecture plays a secondary role to the list of prisoners who spent their last days here. Few in its history endured tortures as severe as those imposed on Ravaillac, who assassinated Henri IV in 1610. In the Tour de César, he received pincers in the flesh and had hot lead and boiling oil poured on him like bath water before being executed. During the revolution, the Conciergerie became a symbol of terror to the nobility and enemies of the State. A short walk away, the Revolutionary Tribunal dispensed a skewed, hurried justice—if it's any consolation, the jurists didn't believe in torturing their victims, only in decapitating them.

After being seized by a crowd of peasants who stormed Versailles, Louis XVI and Marie Antoinette were brought here to await their trials. In failing health and shocked beyond grief, *l'Autrichienne* ("the Austrian," as she was called with malice) had only a small screen (sometimes not even that) to protect her modesty from the gaze of guards stationed in her cell. By accounts of the day, she was shy and stupid, though the evidence is that on her death, she displayed the nobility of a true queen. (What's more, the famous "Let them eat cake," which she supposedly uttered when told the peasants had no bread, is probably apocryphal—besides, at the time, cake

4

EXPLORING PARIS

The Right Bank

flour was less expensive than bread flour, so even if she said this, it wasn't meant coldheartedly.) It was shortly before noon on the morning of October 16, 1793, when the executioners arrived, grabbing her and cutting her hair, as was the custom for victims marked for the guillotine.

Later, the Conciergerie housed other prisoners, including Mme Elisabeth; Mme du Barry, mistress of Louis XV; Mme Roland ("O Liberty! Liberty! What crimes are committed in thy name!"); and Charlotte Corday, who killed Marat while he was taking a sulfur bath. In time, the revolution consumed its own leaders, such as Danton and Robespierre. Finally, one of Paris's most hated men, public prosecutor Fouquier-Tinville, faced the guillotine to which he'd sent so many others. Among the few interned here who lived to tell the tale was American Thomas Paine, who reminisced about his chats in English with Danton.

1 quai de l'Horloge, 4e. www.monum.fr. ℂ **01-53-40-60-80.** Admission 8.50€ adults, 5.50€ ages 18–25, free for children 17 and younger. Mar–Oct daily 9:30–6pm; Nov–Feb daily 9am–5pm. Métro: Cité, Châtelet, or St-Michel. RER: St-Michel.

Gaîté Lyrique ★ ☺ CULTURAL INSTITUTION This modern cultural institution, which is devoted to exploring mixed-media and digital art forms, opened in March 2011 to much fanfare. This museum hosts rotating exhibits that range from music and multimedia performances to design, fashion, and architecture to new media—there's even an interactive room dedicated to video games. This forward-thinking institution is located within a beautifully restored and updated 19th-century Parisian theater in the heart of the city.

3 bis rue Papin, 3e. www.gaite-lyrique.net. ℂ **01-53-01-51-51.** Tues–Sun 2–8pm. Métro: Réaumur Sébastopol. Opening hours and admission prices vary according to the exhibitions and events.

Hôtel de Ville ★ HISTORIC SITE On a large square with fountains and early-1900s lampposts, the 19th-century Hôtel de Ville isn't a hotel, but Paris's grandiose City Hall. The medieval structure it replaced had witnessed countless municipally ordered executions. Henri IV's assassin, Ravaillac, was quartered alive on the square in 1610, his body tied to four horses that bolted in opposite directions. On May 24, 1871, the Communards doused the City Hall with gas, creating a blaze that lasted for 8 days. The Third Republic ordered the structure rebuilt, with many changes, even creating a Hall of Mirrors evocative of that at Versailles. For security reasons, the major splendor of this building is closed to the public. There are changing art, architecture, design, and photography exhibitions (usually free admission), which can be accessed through the back entrance on rue Lobau. In winter, you'll find a skating rink on the piazza in front of the building.

29 rue de Rivoli, 4e. No phone for information. Free admission. Métro: Hôtel-de-Ville.

Hôtel de Ville.

Maison de Victor Hugo.

A salon in the Musée Carnavalet-Histoire de Paris.

Maison de Victor Hugo ★ MUSEUM   Today, theatergoers who've seen *Les Misérables,* and even those who haven't read anything by Paris's 19th-century novelist, come to place des Vosges to see where Hugo lived and wrote. Some thought him a genius, but Cocteau called him a madman, and an American composer discovered that in his old age, he was carving furniture with his teeth! From 1832 to 1848, the novelist/poet lived on the second floor of the Hôtel de Rohan Guémené. The museum owns some of Hugo's furniture, as well as pieces that once belonged to Juliette Drouet, the mistress with whom he lived in exile on Guernsey, one of the Channel Islands.

Worth the visit are Hugo's drawings, more than 450, illustrating scenes from his own works. Mementos of the great writer abound, including samples of his handwriting, his inkwell, and first editions of his works. A painting of Hugo's 1885 funeral procession at the Arc de Triomphe is on display, as many portraits and souvenirs of his family. Of the furnishings, a chinoiserie salon stands out. The collection even contains Daumier caricatures and a bust of Hugo by David d'Angers, which, compared with Rodin's, looks saccharine.

6 place des Vosges, 4e. www.musee-hugo.paris.fr. ⓒ **01-42-72-10-16.** Free admission to the permanent collections. Tues–Sun 10am–6pm. Métro: St-Paul, Bastille, or Chemin-Vert.

Maison Européene de la Photographie ★★ ▮ MUSEUM   This major center for contemporary photography opened in the mid-1990s, and it features regularly changing photography exhibitions. The museum also has a permanent collection of about 15,000 works features works by well-known photographers such as Robert Frank and Raymond Depardon. You access the museum via a new wing built on the rue de Fourcy, but the majority of the museum is located within an 18th-century mansion, the Hôtel Hénault de Cantobre.

5–7 rue de Fourcy, 4e. www.mep-fr.org. ⓒ **01-44-78-75-00.** Wed–Sun 11am–8pm. 7€ adults, 4€ students and seniors, free for children 7 and under. Free entry Wed 5–8pm. Métro: St-Paul.

Musée Carnavalet-Histoire de Paris ★★ ☺ MUSEUM   If you enjoy history, but history tomes bore you, spend some time here for insight into Paris's past, which comes alive in such details as the chessmen Louis XVI used to distract himself while waiting to go to the guillotine. The comprehensive and lifelike exhibits are great for kids. The building, a Renaissance palace, was built in 1544 and later acquired by Mme de Carnavalet. François Mansart transformed it between 1655 and 1661.

The palace is best known for one of history's most famous letter writers, Mme de Sévigné, who moved here in 1677. Fanatically devoted to her daughter (she moved in with her because she couldn't bear to be apart), she poured out nearly every detail of her life in her letters, virtually ignoring her son. A native of the Marais district, she died at her daughter's château in 1696. In 1866, the city of Paris acquired the mansion and turned it into a museum. Several salons cover the Revolution, with a bust of Marat, a portrait of Danton, and a model of the Bastille (one painting shows its demolition). Another salon tells the story of the captivity of the royal family at the Conciergerie, displaying the bed in which Mme Elisabeth (the sister of Louis XVI) slept and the Dauphin's exercise book.

Exhibits continue at the **Hôtel le Peletier de St-Fargeau,** across the courtyard. On display is furniture from the Louis XIV period to the early 20th century, including a replica of Marcel Proust's cork-lined bedroom with his actual furniture, including his brass bed. This section also exhibits artifacts from the museum's archaeological collection, including some Neolithic pirogues, shallow oak boats used for fishing and transport from about 4400 to 2200 B.C.

23 rue de Sévigné, 3e. www.carnavalet.paris.fr. (℃) **01-44-59-58-58.** Free admission. Special exhibits from 5€ adults, 4.20€ students and children. Tues–Sun 10am–6pm. Métro: St-Paul or Chemin Vert.

Musée Cognacq-Jay ★ MUSEUM   The founders of the defunct La Samaritaine department store, Ernest Cognacq and his wife, Louise Jay, were fabled for their exquisite taste. To see what they accumulated from around the world, head for this museum in the 16th-century Hôtel Denon, with its Louis XV and Louis XVI paneled rooms. Some of the 18th century's most valuable decorative works are exhibited, ranging from ceramics and porcelain to delicate cabinets and paintings by Canaletto, Fragonard, Greuze, Chardin, Boucher, Watteau, and Tiepolo.

In the Hôtel Donon, 8 rue Elzévir, 3e. www.cognacq-jay.paris.fr. (℃) **01-40-27-07-21.** Free admission to permanent collection; variable charges for temporary shows. Tues–Sun 10am–6pm. Métro: St-Paul.

Musée d'Art et Histoire du Judaisme ★★ MUSEUM   Security is tight, but it's worth the effort. In the Hôtel de St-Aignan, dating from the 1600s, this museum of Jewish history has been handsomely and impressively installed. The development of Jewish culture is traced not only in Paris, but also in France itself, as well as in Europe. Many of the exhibitions are devoted to religious subjects, including menorahs, Torah ornaments, and ark curtains, in both the Ashkenazi and Sephardic traditions. For us, the most interesting documents relate to the notorious Dreyfus case. Also on parade is a collection of illuminated manuscripts, Renaissance Torah arks, and

An exhibit at the Musée d'Art et Histoire du Judaisme.

paintings from the 18th and 19th centuries, along with Jewish gravestones from the Middle Ages. The best display is of the artwork by leading Jewish painters and artists ranging from Soutine to Zadkine, from Chagall to Modigliani.

Hôtel de St-Aignan, 71 rue du Temple, 3e. www.mahj.org. ℂ **01-53-01-86-53.** Admission 6.80€ adults, 4.50€ ages 18–26, free for children 17 and younger. Mon–Fri 11am–6pm; Sun 10am–6pm. Métro: Rambuteau.

Musée de la Chasse et de la Nature ★★ 🏛☺ MUSEUM   This surprising little "hunting and nature" museum explores the relationship between humans and nature via the art of hunting, which remains quite popular in France. Established by French industrialist and avid hunter Francois Sommer and his wife, Jacqueline, in 1964, the museum features a collection of art in different mediums that celebrates the natural world. There is also a large collection of stuffed animals—you'll see everything from pigeons to polar bears. The museum is housed in a beautiful 18th-century mansion.

2 rue des Archives, Hôtel de Mongelas, 3e. www.chassenature.org. ℂ **01-53-01-92-40.** Admission 6€ adults, 4.50€ students, children 17 and under free. Tues–Sun 11am–6pm. Métro: Rambuteau.

Musée de l'Histoire de France (Musée des Archives Nationales) ★
MUSEUM   The official home of the archives that reflect the convoluted history of France, this small but noteworthy palace was first built in 1371 as the **Hôtel de Clisson** and later acquired by the ducs de Guise, who figured prominently in France's bloody wars of religion. In 1705, most of it was demolished by the prince and princesse de Soubise, through their architect, the much-underrated Delamair, and rebuilt with a baroque facade. The princesse de Soubise was once the mistress of Louis XIV, and apparently, the Sun King was very generous, giving her the funds to remodel and redesign the palace into one of the most beautiful buildings in the Marais. *Tip:* Before entering through the building's main entrance, the gracefully colonnaded Cour d'Honneur (Court of Honor), walk around the corner to 58 rue des Archives, where you'll see the few remaining vestiges—a turreted medieval gateway—of the original Hôtel de Clisson.

In the early 1800s, the site was designated by Napoleon as the repository for his archives, and it has served that function ever since. The archives contain documents that predate Charlemagne. But depending on the policies of the curator, only some of them are on display at any given moment, and usually as part of an ongoing series of temporary exhibitions that sometimes spill out into the **Hôtel de Rohan,** just around the corner on the rue Vieille du Temple.

Within these exhibitions, you're likely to see the facsimiles of the penmanship of Marie Antoinette in a farewell letter she composed just before her execution; Louis XVI's last will and testament; and documents from Danton,

The turreted medieval gateway at the Musée de l'Histoire de France (Musée des Archives Nationales).

Robespierre, Napoleon I, and Joan of Arc. The archives have the only known sketch of the Maid of Orléans that was completed during her lifetime. Even the jailers' keys from the long-since-demolished Bastille are here. Despite the undeniable appeal of the documents it shelters, one of the most intriguing aspects of this museum involves the layout and decor of rooms that have changed very little since the 18th century. One of the finest is the **Salon de la Princesse** (aka the Salon Ovale), an oval room with sweeping expanses of gilt and crystal and a series of artfully executed ceiling frescoes by Van Loo, Boucher, and Natoire.

In the Hôtel de Soubise, 60 rue des Francs-Bourgeois, 3e. 🕻 **01-40-27-60-96.** Admission 4€ adults, 2€ ages 18–25, free for children 17 and younger; temporary exhibitions 6€ adults, 4€ ages 18–25 Mon and Wed–Fri 10am–12:30pm and 2–5:30pm; Sat–Sun 2–5:30pm. Métro: Hôtel-de-Ville or Rambuteau.

Musée des Arts et Métiers ☺ MUSEUM   Paris's Arts and Industry museum was founded in 1794 within the church Saint-Martin-des-Champs. It features exhibits on the history of technological development. Highlights of its collection include an original version of Foucault's pendulum from 1851, which still swings eternally and that earned the museum a mention in Umbert Eco's novel *Foucault's Pendulum.* The museum includes an additional building adjacent to the abbey.

60 rue Réaumur, 3e. www.arts-et-metiers.net. 🕻 **01-53-01-82-00.** Admission 6.50€ adults, 4.50€ students, children under 18 free. Temporary exhibitions 5.50€ adults, 3.50€ students. Tues–Sun 10am–6pm (until 9:30pm Thurs). Métro: Arts et Métiers or Réaumur Sébastopol.

Place des Vosges ★★ ☺ SQUARE   The exquisite place des Vosges was built by Henri IV and inaugurated in 1612 to celebrate the wedding of Louis XIII to Anne of Austria. It is Paris's oldest planned square and is in the heart of the Marais, actually marking the division between the 3rd and 4th arrondissements. Lined with large buildings of red brick and blue-tiled roofs, the square was previously named "place Royale" under the reign of Henri IV, then "place des Fédérés," "place de la Fabrication-des-Armes," and "place de l'Indivisibilité" during the French Revolution. It was only in 1800 that it was given the name it has today, in honor of the French department the Vosges. Adorned with Linden trees, water fountains, and an equestrian statue of Louis XIII, it makes a charming spot for a picnic *en famille.* There's free Wi-Fi here too.

Place des Vosges.

4e. Métro: St-Paul.

Sainte-Chapelle ★★★ CHURCH   Countless writers have called this tiny chapel a jewel box, yet that hardly suffices. Go when the sun is shining, and you'll need no one else's words to describe the remarkable effects of natural light on Sainte-Chapelle. You approach the church through the cour de la Sainte-Chapelle of the Palais de Justice.

Begun in 1246, the bi-level chapel was built to house relics of the True Cross, including the Crown of Thorns acquired by St. Louis (the Crusader King, Louis IX) from the emperor of Constantinople. (In those days, cathedrals throughout Europe were busy acquiring relics for their treasuries, regardless of their authenticity. It was a seller's, perhaps a sucker's, market.) Louis IX is said to have paid heavily for his relics, raising the money through unscrupulous means. He died of the plague on a crusade and was canonized in 1297.

You enter through the *chapelle basse* (**lower chapel**), used by the palace servants; it's supported by flying buttresses and ornamented with fleur-de-lis designs. The king and his courtiers used the *chapelle haute* (**upper chapel**), one of the greatest achievements of Gothic art; you reach it by ascending a narrow spiral staircase. On a bright day, the 15 stained-glass windows seem to glow with Chartres blue and wine-colored reds. The walls consist almost entirely of the glass, 612 sq. m (6,588 sq. ft.) of it, which had to be removed for safekeeping during the revolution and again during both world wars. In the windows' Old and New Testament designs are embodied the hopes and dreams (and the pretensions) of the kings who ordered their construction. The 1,134 scenes depict the Christian story from the Garden of Eden through the Apocalypse; you read them from bottom to top and from left to right. The great rose window depicts the Apocalypse.

Sainte-Chapelle stages **concerts** from March to November, daily at 7 and 8:30pm; tickets cost 19€ to 25€. Call ℂ **01-44-07-12-38** from 11am to 6pm daily for details.

Palais de Justice, 4 bd. du Palais, 4e. www.monum.fr. ℂ **01-53-40-60-80.** 8.50€ adults, 5.50€ ages 18–25, free 17 and younger. Mar–Oct daily 9:30am–6pm; Nov–Feb daily 9am–5pm. Métro: Cité, St-Michel, or Châtelet–Les Halles. RER: St-Michel.

Champs-Élysées & Western Paris (8e, 16e & 17e)

Money and power dominate this neighborhood and its emblematic avenue, the Champs-Élysées. There is also a wealth of exceptional museums here from the **Musée d'art Moderne,** a testament to Paris's Modernist glory days, to the **Palais de Tokyo,** a pioneering contemporary art space. In this area, you'll also find the **Maison Baccarat,** the **Musée Nissim de Camondo,** and the **Musée Jacquemart-André.**

American Cathedral of the Holy Trinity CATHEDRAL   This cathedral is one of Europe's finest examples of Gothic Revival architecture and a center for the presentation of music and art. It was consecrated in 1886, and George Edmund Street, best known for the London Law Courts, created it. Aside from the architecture, you'll find remarkable pre-Raphaelite stained-glass windows illustrating the *Te Deum,* an early-15th-century triptych by an anonymous painter (probably a monk) known as the Roussillon Master; a needlepoint collection including kneelers depicting the 50 state flowers; and the 50 state flags in the nave. A **Memorial Cloister** commemorates Americans who died in Europe in World War I and all the victims of World War II. Documentation in several languages explains the highlights. The cathedral is also a center of worship, with a schedule of Sunday and weekday services in English. Les Arts George V, a cultural organization, presents reasonably priced choral concerts, lectures, and art shows.

23 av. George V, 8e. www.americancathedral.org. ℂ **01-53-23-84-00.** Free admission. Mon–Fri 9am–5pm. Métro: Alma-Marceau or George V.

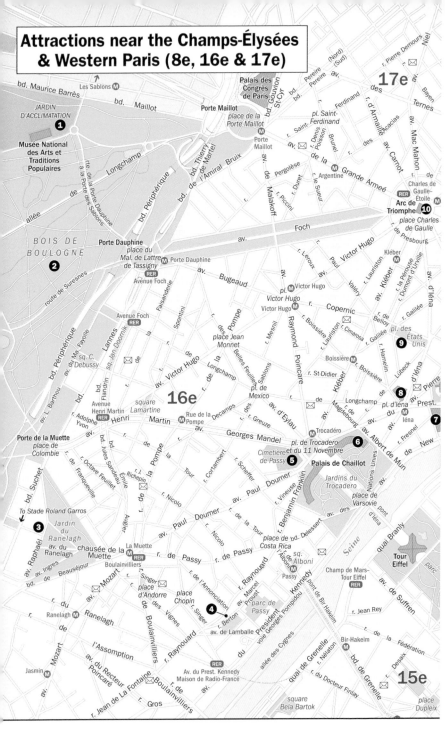

Attractions near the Champs-Élysées & Western Paris (8e, 16e & 17e)

American Cathedral of the Holy Trinity **12**	Musée d'Art Moderne de la Ville de Paris **11**
Arc de Triomphe **10**	Musée Jacquemart-André **15**
Bois de Boulogne **2**	Musée Marmottan Monet **3**
Cimetière de Passy **5**	Musée National des Arts Asiatiques Guimet **8**
Grand Palais **19**	
Jardin d'Acclimatation **1**	Musée Nissim de Camondo **14**
La Cité de l'Architecture et du Patrimoine **6**	Palais de Tokyo **7**
La Madeleine **17**	Parc Monceau **13**
Maison Baccarat **9**	Petit Palais **18**
Maison de Balzac **4**	Pinacothèque de Paris **16**

Arc de Triomphe ★★ MONUMENT   At the western end of the Champs-Élysées, the Arc de Triomphe suggests an ancient Roman arch, only it's larger. Actually, it's the biggest triumphal arch in the world, about 49m (161 ft.) high and 44m (144 ft.) wide. To reach it, *don't try to cross the square,* Paris's busiest traffic hub. With a dozen streets radiating from the "Star," the roundabout has been called by one writer "vehicular roulette with more balls than numbers"; death is certain! Take the underground passage, and live a little longer.

Commissioned by Napoleon in 1806 to commemorate the victories of his Grand Armée, the arch wasn't ready for the entrance of his empress, Marie-Louise, in 1810 (he divorced Joséphine because she couldn't provide him an heir). It wasn't completed until 1836, under the reign of Louis-Philippe. Four years later, Napoleon's remains, brought from St. Helena, passed under the arch on their journey to his tomb at the Hôtel des Invalides. Since then, it has become the focal point for state funerals. It's also the site of the tomb of the Unknown Soldier, in whose honor an eternal flame burns.

The greatest state funeral was Victor Hugo's in 1885; his coffin was placed under the arch, and much of Paris came to pay tribute. Another notable funeral was in 1929 for Ferdinand Foch, commander of the Allied forces in World War I. The arch has been the centerpiece of some of France's proudest moments and some of its most humiliating defeats, notably in 1871 and 1940. The memory of German

Arc de Triomphe.

The view from the Arc de Triomphe.

troops marching under the arch is still painful to the French. Who can forget the 1940 newsreel of the Frenchman standing on the Champs-Élysées weeping as the Nazi storm troopers goose-stepped through Paris? The arch's happiest moment occurred in 1944, when the liberation-of-Paris parade passed beneath it. That same year, Eisenhower paid a visit to the tomb of the Unknown Soldier, a new tradition among leaders of state and important figures. After Charles de Gaulle's death, the French government (despite protests from anti-Gaullists) voted to change the name of this site from place de l'Etoile to place Charles de Gaulle. Today it's often known as place Charles de Gaulle–Etoile.

Of the sculptures on the monument, the best known is Rude's *Marseillaise,* or *The Departure of the Volunteers.* J. P. Cortot's *Triumph of Napoléon in 1810* and Etex's *Resistance of 1814* and *Peace of 1815* also adorn the facade. The monument is engraved with the names of hundreds of generals (those underlined died in battle) who commanded French troops in Napoleonic victories.

You can take an elevator or climb the stairway to the top, where there's an exhibition hall with lithographs and photos depicting the arch throughout its history, as well as an observation deck with an exceptional view.

Place Charles de Gaulle–Etoile, 8e. www.monum.fr. (✆) **01-55-37-73-77.** Admission 9.50€ adults, 6€ for those 18–24. Apr–Sept daily 10am–11pm; Oct–Mar daily 10am–10:30pm. Métro: Charles-de-Gaulle–Etoile. Bus: 22, 30, 31, 52, 73, or 92.

Bois de Boulogne ★★ ☺ PARK One of the most spectacular parks in Europe is the **Bois de Boulogne,** often called the "main lung" of Paris. Horse-drawn carriages traverse it, but you can also drive through. You can discover its hidden pathways, however, only by walking. You could spend days in the Bois de Boulogne and still not see everything.

Porte Dauphine is the main entrance, though you can take the Métro to Porte Maillot as well. West of Paris, the park was once a forest kept for royal hunts. It was in vogue in the late 19th century: Along avenue Foch, carriages with elegantly attired and coiffured Parisian damsels would rumble along with their foppish escorts. Nowadays, it's more likely to attract run-of-the-mill picnickers. (Be careful at night, when hookers and muggers proliferate.)

When Napoleon III gave the grounds to the city in 1852, they were developed by Baron Haussmann. Separating Lac Inférieur from Lac Supérieur is the **Carrefour des Cascades ★** (you can stroll under its waterfall). The Lower Lake contains two islands connected by a foot-bridge. From the east bank, you can take a boat to these idyllically situated grounds, perhaps stopping off at the cafe/restaurant on one of them.

Restaurants in the *bois* are numerous, elegant, and expensive. The **Pré Catelan ★** contains a deluxe restaurant of the same name (✆ **01-44-14-41-00;** www.precatelanparis.com), occupying a gem of a Napoleon III–style château, and also a Shakespearean

The Bois de Boulogne.

theater in a garden planted with trees mentioned in the bard's plays. Nearby is **La Grande Cascade** (📞 **01-45-27-33-51**), once a hunting lodge for Napoleon III.

Jardin d'Acclimatation (📞 **01-40-67-90-82**; www.jardin dacclimatation.fr), at the northern edge of the park, is for children, with a zoo, an amusement park, and a narrow-gauge railway (see listing below for more information).

Two racetracks, the **Hippo-drome de Longchamp ★★★** and the **Hippodrome d'Auteuil,** are in the park. The Grand Prix is run in June at Longchamp (the site of a medieval abbey). Fashionable

Parc de Bagatelle.

Parisians always turn out for this, the women in their finest haute couture. To the north of Longchamp is the **Grand Cascade,** an artificial waterfall.

In the western section of the *bois*, the 24-hectare (59-acre) **Parc de Baga-telle ★** (📞 **01-43-28-47-63**) owes its existence to a bet between the comte d'Artois (later Charles X) and Marie Antoinette, his sister-in-law. The comte wagered he could erect a small palace in less than 3 months, so he hired nearly 1,000 craftsmen (cabinetmakers, painters, Scottish landscape architect Thomas Blaikie, and others) and irritated the locals by requisitioning all shipments of stone and plaster arriving through Paris's west gates. He won his bet. If you're here in late April, it's worth visiting the Bagatelle just for the tulips. In late May, one of the finest rose collections in Europe is in full bloom.

16e. Métro: Porte d'Auteuil, Les Sablons, Porte Maillot, or Porte Dauphine.

Cimetière de Passy CEMETERY This cemetery runs along Paris's old northern walls, south and southwest of Trocadéro. It's a small graveyard sheltered by chestnut trees, but it contains many gravesites of the famous—a concierge at the gate can guide you. Painters **Edouard Manet** and **Romaine Brooks** and composer **Claude Debussy** are tenants. Many great literary figures since 1850 were interred here, including **Tristan Bernard, Jean Giraudoux,** and **Fran-çois de Croisset.** Also present are composer **Gabriel Fauré;** aviator **Henry Farman;** actor **Fernandel;** and high priestess of the city's most famous literary salon, **Natalie Barney,** along with **Renée Vivien,** one of her many lovers.

2 rue du Comandant-Schloesing, 16e. 📞 **01-53-70-40-80.** Free admission. Mar–Nov Mon–Fri 8am–6pm, Sat 8:30am–6pm, Sun 9am–6pm; Nov–Feb Mon–Fri 8am–5:30pm, Sat 8:30am–5:30pm, Sun 9am–5:30pm. Métro: Trocadéro.

Grand Palais ★★ HISTORIC SITE Built for the 1900 Universal Exhibition, this giant exhibition hall spans a total area of 72,000 sq. m (775,000 sq. ft.), with the biggest glass roof in Europe—an elegant lighting solution, since the building was constructed prior to electricity. After years of renovations, the Grand Palais reopened in 2007, and today it hosts a changing array of sporting and cultural events, including FIAC (Paris's annual contemporary art fair), "Monumenta" (an annual event which commissions and displays an original monumental work by a contemporary artist in the Grand Palais' nave), the Hermès horse jumping competition, and fashion shows; check their website for events. The Grand Palais faces the Petit Palais (p. 109).

1 av. Géneral Eisenhower, 8e. www.grandpalais.fr. ⓒ **01-44-13-17-17.** Opening hours and admission prices vary according to the exhibitions and events. Métro: Champs-Élysées Clémenceau.

Jardin d'Acclimatation ★ ☺ AMUSEMENT PARK/GARDEN This
20-hectare (49-acre) children's park in the northern part of the Bois de Boulogne is the kind of place that amuses tykes and adults but not teenagers. The visit starts with a ride on a narrow-gauge train from Porte Maillot to the Jardin entrance, through a stretch of wooded park. The train operates at 10-minute intervals daily from 10:30am until the park closes; round-trip fare costs 2.70€. En route you'll find a **house of mirrors,** an **archery range,** a **miniature-golf**

Children's rides in the Jardin d'Acclimatation.

course, zoo animals, a **puppet theater** (performances Wed, Sat–Sun, and holidays), a **playground,** a **hurdle-racing course, junior-scale rides, shooting galleries,** and **waffle stalls.** You can trot the kids off on a **pony** (Sat–Sun only) or join them in a **boat** on a mill-stirred lagoon. **La Prévention Routière** is a miniature roadway operated by the Paris police: Youngsters drive through in small cars equipped to start and stop, and are required by two genuine gendarmes to obey street signs and light changes. Inside the gate is an easy-to-follow map.

In the Bois de Boulogne, 16e. www.jardindacclimatation.fr. ⓒ **01-40-67-90-82.** Admission 2.90€, free for children 3 and younger. Apr–Sept daily 10am–7pm; Oct–Mar daily 10am–6pm. Métro: Sablons.

La Cité de l'Architecture et du Patrimoine ★ MUSEUM After a
decade-long makeover, the City of Architecture and Heritage was opened by President Nicolas Sarkozy in 2007. With its trio of galleries and vast space, the museum is the largest architectural museum in the world. It lies in the east wing of the Palais de Chaillot on a hill overlooking a curve of the Seine, with panoramic views of Paris in all directions. The Eiffel Tower looms just across the river.

Exhibits are devoted to 12 centuries of French architecture, the most stunning of which is the reproduction of the **stained-glass window ★★** in the Gothic cathedral at Chartres. Other exhibits include a walk-in replica of Le Corbusier's mid-20th-century Cité Radieuse in Marseille.

In all there are 350 plaster cast reproductions of some of the greatest achievements in French architecture, going back to the Middle Ages. One gallery reproduces France's remarkable paintings and frescoes from the 12th to 16th centuries. A third gallery is devoted to modern architecture right up to a turn-of-the-millennium cultural center in New Caledonia in the South Pacific. Children can build their own architectural masterpieces with Legos and other materials.

1 place du Trocadéro, 16e. www.citechaillot.fr. ⓒ **01-58-51-52-00.** Admission to permanent collection 8€ adults, 5€ students, free ages 18 and younger; temporary exhibitions 8€ adults, 5€ students. Wed and Fri–Mon 11am–7pm; Thurs 11am–9pm. Métro: Trocadéro.

La Madeleine ★★ CHURCH   La Madeleine is one of Paris's minor landmarks, dominating rue Royale, which culminates in place de la Concorde. Though construction began in 1806, it wasn't consecrated until 1842. Resembling a Roman temple, the building was intended as a monument to the glory of the Grande Armée (Napoleon's idea, of course). Later, several alternative uses were considered: the National Assembly, the Bourse, and the National Library. Climb the 28 steps to the facade, and look back: You'll be able to see rue Royale, place de la Concorde and its obelisk, and (across the Seine) the dome of the Hôtel des Invalides. Don't miss Rude's *Le Baptême du Christ,* to the left as you enter.

Rude's *Le Baptême du Christ.*

Place de la Madeleine, 8e. www.eglise-la madeleine.com. ✆ **01-42-65-52-17.** Free admission. Mon–Sat 9:30am–7pm; Sun services at 9:30, 11am, and 7pm. Métro: Madeleine.

Maison Baccarat ★★ MUSEUM   The fine French crystal maker Baccarat opened this magnificent Philippe Starck–designed flagship store and museum in 2003, in the former mansion of avant-garde art patron Marie-Laure de Noailles, who worked with artists like Salvador Dalí and Piet Mondrian. Starck integrated the building's avant-garde history with the more traditional style of Baccarat to design this whimsical building.

Baccarat first opened a glass factory, authorized by Louis XV, in 1764; in 1816, it began to manufacture crystal. The company quickly gained a reputation for its fine crystal works, and by the end of the 19th century, it was being commissioned to create pieces for various monarchies. One of those pieces—an elaborate 775kg (1,705-lb.) chandelier created for Czar Nicolas II—lights up an antechamber to this museum. Another sensational crystal chandelier adorns the entrance to the building—but this one is submerged in an aquarium. The design of the building is playful and contemporary, yet it still feels opulent and classic.

Maison Baccarat comprises a boutique on the ground floor selling the brand's tableware and jewelry, and an upstairs museum and restaurant, Cristal Room.

11 place des États-Unis, 16e. www.baccarat.com. ✆ **01-40-22-11-00.** Museum admission 5€ adults, 3.50€ seniors, free for ages 17 and under. Museum open Mon, Wed–Sat 10am–6.30pm. Métro: Iéna or Boissière.

Maison de Balzac MUSEUM   In the residential district of Passy, near the Bois de Boulogne, sits this modest house with a courtyard and garden. Honoré de Balzac fled to this house in 1840, after his possessions and furnishings were seized, and lived there for 7 years (to see him, you had to know a password). If a creditor knocked on the rue Raynouard door, Balzac was able to escape through the rue Berton exit. The museum's most notable memento is Balzac's "screech-owl" (his nickname for his tea kettle), which he kept hot throughout the night as he wrote *La Comédie Humaine.* Also enshrined are Balzac's writing desk and chair, and a library of special interest to scholars. The little house is filled with caricatures of Balzac. A biographer once wrote: "With his bulky baboon silhouette, his blue suit with gold buttons, his famous cane like a golden crowbar, and his abundant, disheveled hair, Balzac was a sight for caricature."

47 rue Raynouard, 16e. www.balzac.paris.fr. ℂ **01-55-74-41-80.** Admission free for permanent collection. Temporary exhibition admission 4€ adults, 3€ seniors and students, 2€ ages 14–26, free for children 13 and younger. Tues–Sun 10am–6pm. Métro: Passy or La Muette.

Musée d'Art Moderne de la Ville de Paris ★★ MUSEUM Paris's Modern Art Museum borders the Seine and is in fact housed in the Eastern Wing of the monumental Palais de Tokyo (p. 108), a building designed for the 1937 World Fair. The museum opened in 1961, and it is home to works of modern art, including Henri Matisse's *The Dance,* Pierre Bonnard's *Nude in the Bath* and *The Garden,* and Fernand Léger's *Discs.* There are also works by Chagall, Rothko, Braque, Dufy, Picasso, Utrillo, and Modigliani. Seek out Pierre Tal Coat's **Portrait of Gertrude Stein,** and keep Picasso's version of this difficult subject in mind. The museum also presents excellent ever-changing exhibits on individual artists from all over the world or on contemporary international trends.

11 av. du Président-Wilson, 16e. www.mam.paris.fr. ℂ **01-53-67-40-00.** Free admission to general collections, temporary exhibition admission 5€–11€. Tues–Sun 10am–6pm. Métro: Iéna or Alma-Marceau.

Musée Jacquemart-André ★★ MUSEUM This is the finest museum of its type in Paris, the treasure-trove of a couple devoted to 18th-century French paintings and furnishings, 17th-century Dutch and Flemish paintings, and Italian Renaissance works. Edouard André, the last scion of a family that made a fortune in banking and industry in the 19th century, spent most of his life as an army officer stationed abroad; he eventually returned to marry a well-known portraitist of government figures and the aristocracy, Nélie Jacquemart, and they went on to compile a collection of rare decorative art and paintings in this 1850s town house.

A sumptuous room in the Musée Jacquemart-André.

105

In 1912, Mme Jacquemart willed the house and its contents to the Institut de France, which paid for an extensive renovation and enlargement. The salons drip with gilt and are the ultimate in *fin-de-siècle* style. Works by Bellini, Carpaccio, Uccello, Van Dyck, Rembrandt *(The Pilgrim of Emmaus)*, Tiepolo, Rubens, Watteau, Boucher, Fragonard, and Mantegna are complemented by Houdon busts, Savonnerie carpets, Gobelin tapestries, Della Robbia terra cottas, and an awesome collection of antiques.

Take a break with a cup of tea in Mme Jacquemart's high-ceilinged dining room, where you'll find the outstanding 18th-century Tiepolo frescoes of spectators on balconies viewing Henri III's 1574 arrival in Venice. Salads, tarts, *tourtes* (pastries filled with meat or fruit), and Viennese pastries are served during museum hours to a steady stream of tourist and school groups.

158 bd. Haussmann, 8e. www.musee-jacquemart-andre.com. (℃ **01-45-62-11-59.** Admission 11€ adults, 9.50€ children 7–17, free for children 6 and younger. Daily 10am–6pm. Métro: Miromesnil or St-Philippe-du-Roule.

Musée Marmottan Monet ★★

MUSEUM   In the past, an art historian or two would sometimes venture here to the edge of the Bois de Boulogne to see what Paul Marmottan had donated to the Académie des Beaux-Arts. Hardly anyone else did until 1966, when Claude Monet's son Michel died in a car crash, leaving a then $10-million bequest of his father's art to the little museum. The Académie suddenly found itself with 130-plus paintings, watercolors, pastels, and drawings. Monet lovers could now trace the evolution of the great man's work in a single museum. The collec-

An exhibit at the Musée Marmottan Monet.

tion includes more than 30 paintings of Monet's house at Giverny and many of water lilies, his everlasting fancy, plus **Willow** (1918), **House of Parliament** (1905), and a **Renoir portrait** of a 32-year-old Monet. The museum had always owned Monet's *Impression: Sunrise* (1872), from which the Impressionist movement got its name. Paul Marmottan's original collection includes fig-leafed nudes, First Empire antiques, assorted objets d'art, Renaissance tapestries, bucolic paintings, and crystal chandeliers. You can also see countless miniatures donated by Daniel Waldenstein. The works of other Impressionists are also included, among them Degas, Manet, Pissarro, Renoir, Auguste Rodin, and Alfred Sisley.

2 rue Louis-Boilly, 16e. www.marmottan.com. (℃ **01-44-96-50-33.** Admission 10€ adults, 5€ ages 8–24, free for children 7 and younger. Wed–Sun 11am–6pm; Tues 11am–9pm. Métro: La Muette. RER: Bouilainvilliers, line C.

Musée National des Arts Asiatiques-Guimet ★★ MUSEUM   This is

one of the most beautiful Asian museums in the world, and it houses one of the world's finest collections of Asian art. Some 3,000 pieces of the museum's 45,000 works are on display. The Guimet, opened in Lyon but transferred to Paris in 1889, received the Musée Indochinois du Trocadéro's collections in 1931 and

An exhibit at the Musée National des Arts Asiatiques-Guimet.

the Louvre's Asian collections after World War II. The most interesting exhibits are Buddhas, serpentine monster heads, funereal figurines, and antiquities from the temple of Angkor Wat. Some galleries are devoted to Tibetan art, including fascinating scenes of the Grand Lamas entwined with serpents and demons.

6 place d'Iéna, 16e. www.guimet.fr. ℂ 01-56-52-53-00. Admission to permanent exhibition 7.50€ adults, 5.50€ students, free for ages 17 and younger; admission to temporary exhibitions 8€ adults, 6€ students, free for ages 7 and under. Wed–Mon 10am–6pm. Métro: Iéna.

Musée Nissim de Camondo ★ 🎁 MUSEUM   Visit this museum for fascinating insight into the decorative arts of the 18th century. Originally the home of Moïse de Camondo, a wealthy Parisian banker during the Belle Époque, this museum displays Camondo's excellent collection of 18th-century French furniture and decorative arts. (On his death, Camondo donated the home and its contents to the state in memory of his only son Nissim, who died in the First World War.) This museum offers an interesting glimpse into what a late 19th–century aristocratic home would have looked like; you'll see the home's enormous kitchen, hung with copper utensils, as well as spectacular furniture, clocks,

A room in the Musée Nissim de Camondo.

An exhibit at the Palais de Tokyo.

Parc Monceau.

chandeliers, vases, and tableware. The museum is home to a silver dinner service commissioned by Catherine II of Russia from the silversmith Roettiers in 1770.

63 rue de Monceau, 8e. www.lesartsdecoratifs.fr. ✆ **01-53-89-06-40.** Admission 7.50€ adults, 5.50€ ages 18–25, free for children 17 and younger. Wed–Sun 10am–5:30pm. Closed Jan 1, May 1, Bastille Day (July 14), and Dec 25. Métro: Villiers.

Palais de Tokyo ★★★ ☺ MUSEUM   This art center, which opened in 2002, is one of the most original and avant-garde in Europe. Dedicated to "emerging" art and artists, the Palais de Tokyo emphasizes edgy, contemporary art and ideas. Its monumental raw concrete architecture immediately sets it apart from a classic museum, and its opening hours (noon to midnight) are radical too. The installations and vast open spaces invariably appeal to kids. The exhibits change frequently, so check to see what's showing—perhaps a video or sculpture exhibition, fashion events, or performance art. The space also includes a bookshop, a cafeteria, and a first-rate restaurant and bar called Tokyo Eat. In 2012 the Palais de Tokyo underwent a major expansion—its surface area expanded from 8,000 square meters (86,111 sq. ft.) to 22,000 square meters (236,806 sq. ft.)—and it is now one of the largest sites devoted to contemporary creativity in Europe.

13 av. du Président-Wilson, 16e. www.palaisdetokyo.com. ✆ **01-47-23-54-01.** Admission 6€ adults, 4.50€ students, free for ages 18 and younger. Tues–Sun noon–midnight. Métro: Iéna.

Parc Monceau ★ PARK   Much of Parc Monceau is ringed with 18th- and 19th-century mansions, some evoking Proust's *Remembrance of Things Past*. Carmontelle designed it in 1778 as a private hideaway for the duc d'Orléans (who came to be known as Philippe-Egalité), at the time the richest man in France. The duke was noted for his debauchery and pursuit of pleasure, so no ordinary park would do. It was opened to the public in the days of Napoleon III's Second Empire.

Monceau was laid out with an Egyptian-style obelisk, a medieval dungeon, a thatched farmhouse, a Chinese pagoda, a Roman temple, an enchanted grotto, various chinoiseries, and a waterfall. These fairy-tale touches have largely disappeared except for a pyramid and an oval naumachia fringed by a colonnade. Now the park is filled with solid statuary and monuments, including one honoring Chopin. In spring, the red tulips and magnolias are breathtaking.

35 bd. de Courcelles, 8e. Free admission. 8am–sundown. Métro: Monceau or Villiers.

Petit Palais HISTORIC SITE   Like its neighbor the Grand Palais, the Petit Palais was built for the 1900 Universal Exhibition, and it became a fine arts museum in 1902. Designed by architect Charles Girault, the Petit Palais indeed feels like a "little palace." Its eclectic collections include paintings, sculpture, and objets d'art from ancient times through WWI. You'll see paintings by such French masters as Ingres, Delacroix, Manet, Monet, Courbet, and Sisley. The space also hosts temporary exhibits dedicated to everything from contemporary photography to fashion.

Avenue Winston Churchill, 8e. www.petitpalais.paris.fr. ℂ **01-53-43-40-00.** Free admission to the permanent collections; charges vary for temporary exhibitions. Tues–Sun 10am–6pm. Métro: Champs-Élysées Clémenceau.

Pinacothèque de Paris MUSEUM   This privately funded gallery manages to rival some of the city's major institutions with its blockbuster shows—think Picasso, Pollock, or Munch—that get people lining up down the street. (The quietest days to visit are Mon and Wed, or at lunch time the rest of the week.) The impressive space covers 2,000 sq. m. (21,528 sq. ft.) over three levels, and is located between the two Fauchon delicatessens on the place de la Madeleine.

28 place de la Madeleine, 8e. www.pinacotheque.com. ℂ **01-42-68-02-01.** Daily 10:30am–6pm (until 8pm Wed). Admission 10€ adults, 8€ students. Métro: Madeleine.

Opéra & Grands Boulevards (9e)

The impressive **Opéra Garnier** dominates its dynamic neighborhood, which delivers perhaps more opportunities for outstanding retail experiences than for cultural ones.

Fragonard Musée du Parfum MUSEUM   This perfume museum is in a 19th-century theater on one of Paris's busiest thoroughfares. As you enter the lobby through a courtyard, the scented air will remind you of why you're there—to appreciate perfume enough to buy a bottle in the ground-floor shop. But first, a short visit upstairs introduces you to the rudiments of perfume history. The copper containers with spouts and tubes were used in the distillation of perfume oils, and the exquisite collection of perfume bottles from the 17th to the 20th century is impressive.

9 rue Scribe, 9e. www.fragonard.com. ℂ **01-4742-04-56.** Free admission. Mon–Sat 9am–6pm; Sun 9am–5pm. Métro: Opéra.

An exhibit in the Fragonard Musée du Parfum.

Musée Grévin ☺ MUSEUM   This wax museum presents French history in a series of tableaux. Depicted are the 1429 consecration of Charles VII in the Cathédrale de Reims (armored Joan of Arc, carrying her standard, stands behind the king); Marguerite de Valois, first wife of Henri IV, meeting on a secret stairway with La Molle, who was soon to be decapitated; Catherine de Medici with Florentine alchemist David Ruggieri; Louis XV and Mozart at the home of the marquise de Pompadour; and Napoleon on a rock at St. Helena, reviewing his victories and

An exhibit in the Musée Grévin.   Opéra Garnier.

defeats. Visitors will also find displays of contemporary sports and political figures, as well as 50 of the world's best-loved film stars.

Two shows are staged frequently throughout the day. The first, called the **"Palais des Mirages,"** starts off as a sort of Temple of Brahma and, through magically distorting mirrors, changes first into an enchanted forest and then into a fête at the Alhambra in Granada. A magician is the star of the second show, **"Le Cabinet Fantastique"**; he entertains children of all ages.

10 bd. Montmartre, 9e. www.grevin.com. ℂ **01-47-70-85-05.** Admission 22€ adults, 19€ students, 15€ children 6–14. Mon–Fri 10am–6:30pm; Sat–Sun 10am–7pm. Ticket office closes at 5:30pm. Métro: Grands Boulevards.

Opéra Garnier ★★ OPERA HOUSE   This neobaroque masterpiece was built in 1875, under Napoleon III, by architect Charles Garnier, and was known as the Palais Garnier. The stunning grand foyer, restored in 2004, is lined with mirrors and adorned with crystal chandeliers; it resembles the famous Galerie des Glaces at Versailles. It has a magnificent painted ceiling by Paul Baudry portraying themes from the history of music. The gilded auditorium has 1,900 seats and is lit by an immense crystal chandelier that hangs below a once-controversial ceiling painted by Marc Chagall in the 1960s. Today, the venue is home to the fine Paris Opera Ballet. The site also famously hosts beehives on its roof, and the exclusive honey from those hives can be purchased from the Opéra's souvenir store.

8 rue Scribe, 9e. www.operadeparis.fr. ℂ **01-40-01-17-89.** Admission 9€ adults, 6€ students, children under 10 enter for free. Daily 10am–5pm. Métro: Opéra.

Pigalle & Montmartre (18e)

Perched on the city's highest point, the **Sacré-Coeur** basilica may be the area's only significant monument, but Montmartre's cobblestone streets and unique, villagelike architecture are an attraction in themselves. The harmless red-light district of neighboring Pigalle can't be reduced to a single attraction either, but it is an exciting area to explore.

Basilique du Sacré-Coeur ★★ ☺ CHURCH   Sacré-Coeur is one of Paris's most characteristic landmarks and has been the subject of much controversy.

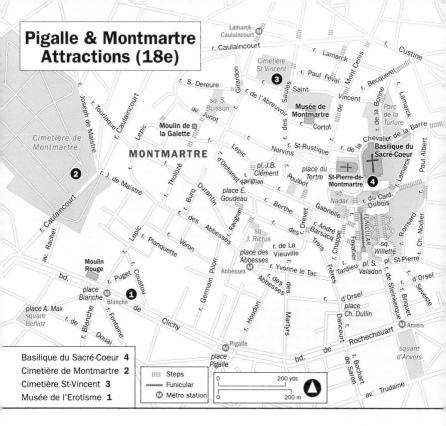

Pigalle & Montmartre Attractions (18e)

Basilique du Sacré-Coeur **4**
Cimetière de Montmartre **2**
Cimetière St-Vincent **3**
Musée de l'Erotisme **1**

||||| Steps
••••••• Funicular
Ⓜ Métro station

0   200 yds
0   200 m

One Parisian called it "a lunatic's confectionery dream." An offended Zola declared it "the basilica of the ridiculous." Sacré-Coeur has had warm supporters as well, including poet Max Jacob and artist Maurice Utrillo. Utrillo never tired of drawing and painting it, and he and Jacob came here regularly to pray. Atop the *butte* (hill) in Montmartre, its multiple gleaming white domes and campanile (bell tower) loom over Paris like a 12th-century Byzantine church. But it's not that old. After France's 1870 defeat by the Prussians, the basilica was planned as a votive offering to cure France's misfortunes. Rich and poor alike contributed money to build it. Construction began in 1876, and though the church wasn't consecrated until 1919, perpetual prayers of adoration have been made here day and night since 1885. The interior is brilliantly decorated with mosaics: Look for the striking Christ on the ceiling and the mural of his Passion at the back of the altar. The stained-glass windows were shattered during the struggle for Paris in 1944 but have been well replaced. The crypt contains what some of the devout believe is Christ's sacred heart—hence, the name of the church. Kids will delight in taking a turn on the merry-go-round, then taking the funicular up the hill to the church.

    Insider's tip: Although the view from the Arc de Triomphe is the greatest panorama of Paris, we also want to endorse the view from the gallery around the inner dome of Sacré-Coeur. On a clear day, your eyes take in a sweep of Paris

FROM TOP: **Basilique du Sacré-Coeur; the dome of Basilique du Sacré-Coeur.**

extending for 48km (30 miles) into the Ile de France. You can also walk around the inner dome, an attraction even better than the interior of Sacré-Coeur itself.

Place St-Pierre, 18e. www.sacre-coeur-montmartre.com. ℰ **01-53-41-89-00.** Free admission to basilica, joint ticket to dome and crypt 8€/5€. Basilica daily 6am–11pm; dome and crypt daily 9am–6pm. Métro: Abbesses; take elevator to surface and follow signs to funicular.

Cimetière de Montmartre ★ CEMETERY   This cemetery, established in 1795, lies west of Montmartre and north of boulevard de Clichy. Russian dancer **Vaslav Nijinsky,** novelist **Alexandre Dumas *fils,*** Impressionist **Edgar Degas,** and composers **Hector Berlioz** and **Jacques Offenbach** are interred here, along with **Stendhal** and lesser literary lights such as **Edmond** and **Jules de Goncourt** and **Heinrich Heine.** A more recent tombstone honors **François Truffaut,** film director of the *nouvelle vague* (new wave). We like to pay our respects at the tomb of **Alphonsine Plessis,** heroine of *La Dame aux Camélias,* and **Mme Récamier,** who taught the world how to lounge. **Émile Zola** was buried here, but his corpse was exhumed and promoted to the Panthéon in 1908. In 1871, the cemetery was used for mass burials of victims of the Siege and the Commune.

20 av. Rachel (west of the Butte Montmartre and north of bd. de Clichy), 18e. ℰ **01-53-42-36-30.** Mon–Fri 8am–6pm; Sat 8:30am–6pm; Sun 9am–6pm. Métro: La Fourche.

Cimetière St-Vincent CEMETERY   Because of the artists and writers who have their resting places in the modest burial ground of St-Vincent, with a view of Sacré-Coeur on the hill, it's sometimes called "the most intellectual cemetery in Paris"—but that epithet seems more apt for other graveyards. Artists **Maurice Utrillo** and **Théopile-Alexandre Steinien** were buried here, as were musician **Arthur Honegger** and writer **Marcel Aymé.** More recently, burials have included the remains of French actor **Gabriello,** film director **Marcel Carné,** and painter **Eugène Boudin.**

6 rue Lucien-Gaulard, 18e. ℂ **01-46-06-29-78.** Mar 6–Nov 5 Mon–Fri 8am–6pm, Sat 8:30am–6pm, Sun 9am–6pm; Nov 6–Mar 5 Mon–Fri 8am–5:15pm, Sat 8:30am–5:15pm, Sun 9am–5:15pm. Métro: Lamarck-Caulaincourt.

Musée de l'Erotisme MUSEUM   A tribute to the primal appeal of human sexuality, this art gallery/museum is in a 19th-century town house that had been a raunchy cabaret. It presents a tasteful but risqué collection of art and artifacts, with six floors boasting an array of exhibits such as erotic sculptures and drawings. The oldest object is a palm-size Roman *tintinabulum* (bell), a phallus-shaped animal with the likeness of a nude woman riding astride it. Modern objects include resin, wood, and plaster sculptures by French artist Alain Rose and works by American, Dutch, German, and French artists. Also look for everyday items with erotic themes from South America (terra-cotta pipes shaped like phalluses) and the United States (a 1920s belt buckle that resembles a praying nun when it's fastened and a nude woman when it's open).

72 bd. de Clichy, 18e. www.musee-erotisme.com. ℂ **01-42-58-28-73.** Admission 10€ adults, children 17 and younger not permitted. Daily 10am–2am. Métro: Blanche.

République, Bastille & Eastern Paris (11e & 12e)

The two public squares, place de la République and place de la Bastille, provide a historical and geographical heart to these two largely residential neighborhoods.

An exhibit from the Musée de l'Erotisme.

Jogging on La Promenade Plantée.

La Maison Rouge ★ MUSEUM
Created by art collector Antoine de Galbert, the "Red House" offers a quality program of rotating exhibitions focusing on contemporary art. Solo shows alternate with thematic shows, and many of the exhibitions, conceived by independent curators, are sourced from major international private collections. The charming space also includes a cafe that is managed by the hip Rose Bakery.

10 bd. de la Bastille, 12e. www.lamaison rouge.org. ✆ **01-40-01-08-81.** Admission 7€ adults, 5€ ages 3 to 18 and senior citizens. Wed–Sun 11am–7pm (until 9pm Thurs). Métro: Quai de la Rapée.

La Promenade Plantée ★ ☺
WALKING TRAIL Look up, above the Viaduc des Arts running along the avenue Daumesnil, and you'll glimpse this 18th-century railway line. Unused since 1969, this old railway line has been converted into a 4.5km (2.8-mile) pedestrian path that runs from Bastille to the Bois de Vincennes. This pleasant path is overrun with various fruit and nut trees, including lime and hazel, climbing plants, rosebushes, and other flowering plants.

Leaves from the beginning of Avenue Daumesnil, 12e.

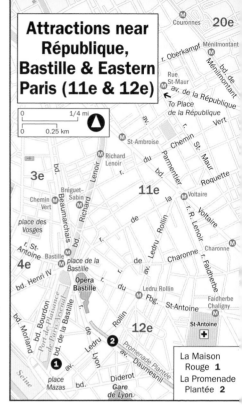

Place de la Bastille

This square is symbolic of the French Revolution, which began here with the storming of the Bastille prison on July 14, 1789. (This date continues to mark Bastille Day, a French national holiday.) Almost nothing remains of the prison, except for a few foundations—you can see one from the platform of line 5 at Bastille Métro station. The statue in the middle of the square, the July Column, was inaugurated in 1840 in commemoration of the Trois Glorieuses, or 3 days of insurrections in 1830 that brought down the French monarchy for a second time. The square's rich political symbolism makes it a preferred location for various public meetings and demonstrations, hosting everything from the Gay Pride Parade to Socialist Party events. Former president François Mitterrand even celebrated his 1981 election victory here. Note that the city's second national opera house, l'Opéra Bastille, is located on the southeastern rim of the square; it's regularly criticized for its architecture and reportedly average acoustics.

The colossal bronze monument in the middle of the place de la République was inaugurated on July 14, 1883, in celebration of the French Republic. The figure of Marianne, a symbol of the French state, sits on a carved stone column that is decorated with allegories of *liberté*, *égalité*, and *fraternité*. Marianne holds an olive branch as a symbol of peace in her right hand, and in her left, a tablet inscribed with the Rights of Man *(les Droits de l'Homme)*. Because of its powerful symbolism, the monument is the preferred departure point for many left-wing demonstrations.

Belleville, Canal St-Martin & Northeast Paris (10e, 19e & 20e)

Perhaps the greatest attraction in this area is the picturesque **Canal St-Martin** itself. Beyond that is **La Villette,** which encompasses Paris's biggest park, Parc de la Villette. It is also an exceptional 21st-century cultural compound including museums, concert halls, circus tents, and exhibition spaces that host a great year-round program. The lure of this former industrial zone is its outdoor attractions: In addition to La Villette, the renowned **Père-Lachaise cemetery** and the wonderful **Buttes Chaumont park** are also located in this area. Note that the area around the Belleville Métro station is also home to one of the city's bustling Chinatowns.

Cimetière du Père-Lachaise ★★★ ☺ CEMETERY When it comes to name-dropping, this cemetery knows no peer; it has been called the "grandest address in Paris." Everybody from Sarah Bernhardt to Oscar Wilde to Richard Wright is resting here, along with Honoré de Balzac, Jacques-Louis David, Eugène Delacroix, Maria Callas, Max Ernst, and Georges Bizet. Colette was taken here in 1954; her black granite slab always sports flowers, and legend has it that cats replenish the roses. In time, the "little sparrow," Edith Piaf, followed. The lover of George Sand, poet Alfred de Musset, was buried under a weeping

FROM LEFT: **Jim Morrison's tomb; Cimetière du Père-Lachaise.**

The Canal St-Martin

The Canal St-Martin is a picturesque waterway that connects the river Seine, near Bastille, to the Canal de l'Ourcq, near the Villette in the 19th arrondissement. When Parisians talk about *le canal*, they are usually referring to the popular stretch of the quais Jemmapes and Valmy, which begins just above République and runs up by the Gare de l'Est. The canal was inaugurated in 1825 with the aim of bringing fresh drinking water to the heart of the city. During the 19th and early 20th centuries, this water highway attracted much commerce and industry to the surrounding areas. Painter Alfred Sisley was inspired by this canal—you can admire his painting "Vue du canal Saint-Martin à Paris" (1870) at the Musée d'Orsay (p. 136). After almost being destroyed in the 1970s to make way for more roads, the canal was classified as a historic monument in 1993, and today, visitors can explore the canal at their leisure. If you'd like to take a scenic boat tour of the canal, contact **Paris Canal** (www.pariscanal.com; ☎ **01-42-40-96-97**) or **Canauxrama** (www.canauxrama.com; ☎ **01-42-39-15-00**).

willow. Napoleon's marshals, Ney and Masséna, lie here, as do Frédéric Chopin and Molière. Marcel Proust's black tombstone rarely lacks a tiny bunch of violets (he wanted to be buried beside his friend/lover, composer Maurice Ravel, but their families wouldn't allow it).

Some tombs are sentimental favorites: Love-torn graffiti radiates 1km (½ mile) from the grave of Doors singer **Jim Morrison** and could appeal to jaded teens. The great dancer **Isadora Duncan** came to rest in the Columbarium, where bodies have been cremated and "filed" away. If you search hard enough, you can find the tombs of that star-crossed pair **Abélard** and **Héloïse,** the ill-fated lovers of the 12th century—at Père-Lachaise, they've found peace at last. Other famous lovers also rest here: A stone is marked **"Alice B. Toklas"** on one side and **"Gertrude Stein"** on the other; and eventually, France's First Couple of film were reunited when **Yves Montand** joined his wife, **Simone Signoret.**

Covering more than 44 hectares (109 acres), Père-Lachaise was acquired by the city in 1804. Nineteenth-century sculpture abounds, as each family tried to outdo the others in ostentation. Monuments also honor Frenchmen who died in the Resistance or in Nazi concentration camps. Some French Socialists still pay tribute at the **Mur des Fédérés,** the anonymous gravesite of the Communards who were executed in the cemetery on May 28, 1871. When these last-ditch fighters of the Commune, the world's first anarchist republic, made their final desperate stand against the troops of the French government, they were overwhelmed, lined up against the wall, and shot in groups. A few survived and lived hidden in the cemetery for years, venturing into Paris at night to forage for food.

A free map of Père-Lachaise is available at the newsstand across from the main entrance (additional map on p. 118).

16 rue de Repos, 20e. www.pere-lachaise.com. ℂ **01-55-25-82-10.** Mon–Fri 8am–6pm; Sat–Sun 8:30am–6pm (closes at 5pm Nov to early Mar). Métro: Père-Lachaise or Philippe Auguste.

Cité des Sciences et de l'Industrie

★★ ☺ MUSEUM   A city of science and industry has risen here from unlikely ashes. When a slaughterhouse was built on the site in the 1960s, it was touted as the most modern of its kind. It was abandoned in 1974, and the location on the city's northern edge presented the government with a problem. What could be built in such an unlikely place? In 1986, the converted premises opened as the world's most expensive ($642-million) science complex, designed to "modernize mentalities" in the service of modernizing society. It is located within the Parc de La Villette compound (see below).

The place is so vast, with so many exhibits, that a single visit gives only an idea of the scope of the Cité. Busts of Plato, Hippocrates, and a double-faced Janus gaze silently at a tube-filled riot of high-tech girders, glass, and lights. The sheer dimensions pose a challenge to the curators of its constantly changing exhibits. Some exhibits are couched in Gallic humor—imagine using the comic-strip adventures of a jungle explorer to explain seismographic activity. **Explora,** a permanent exhibit, occupies the three upper levels

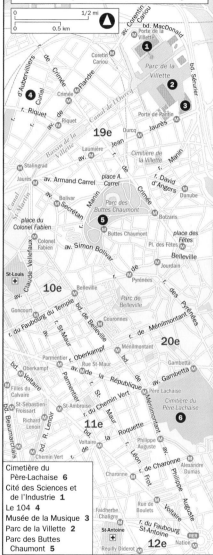

Attractions in Belleville, Canal St-Martin & Northeast Paris (10e, 19e & 20e)

Cimetière du Père-Lachaise **6**
Cité des Sciences et de l'Industrie **1**
Le 104 **4**
Musée de la Musique **3**
Parc de la Villette **2**
Parc des Buttes Chaumont **5**

Cimetière du Père-Lachaise

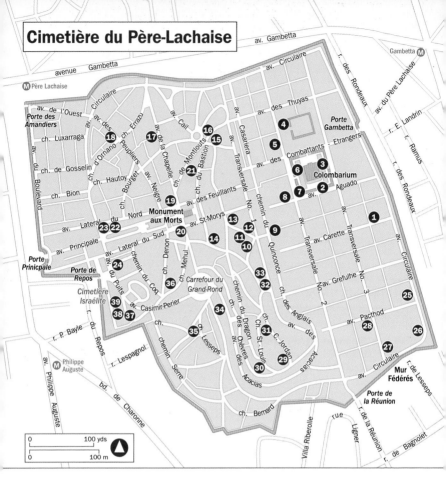

Cité des Sciences et de l'Industrie.

of the building and examines four themes: the universe, life, matter, and communication. The Cité also has a **multimedia library,** a **planetarium,** and an **"inventorium"** for kids. The silver-skinned geodesic dome called **La Géode**—a 34m-high (112-ft.) sphere with a 370-seat theater—is the city's IMAX theater, regularly screening 3-D films on a giant 400 sq. m (4,305 sq. ft.) screen.

In the Parc de La Villette, 30 av. Corentine-Cariou, La Villette, 19e. www.cite-sciences.fr. ℂ **01-40-05-70-00.** Varied ticket options 11€–21€ adults, 8€–16€ ages 7–24, free 6 and younger. Tues–Sat 10am–6pm; Sun 10am–7pm. Métro: Porte de La Villette.

Le 104 ★ ☺ CULTURAL INSTITUTION   Built in 1873, this colossal site on the outskirts of Paris was once the city's Municipal Funeral Service. In 2008, it became a contemporary arts center called Le 104. The place displays art to the public, while also supporting artists in the development of their work. Therefore over a quarter of the space is dedicated to creation and production, with workshops, performance spaces, and production offices. Le 104 oversees artists during the whole creative process, from research to production to exhibition. The site also houses a quality bookshop, a second-hand shop run by local charity Emmaüs, a chic restaurant called Les Grandes Tables, and a cool cafe called Le Café Caché. There's an organic market on Sundays from 11am.

104 rue d'Aubervilliers & 5 rue Curial, 19e. www.104.fr. ℂ **01-53-35-51-00.** Free entry to the site, varied ticket options for the exhibitions and performances. Tue–Fri noon–7pm; Sat–Sun 11am–7pm. Métro: Riquet.

Musée de la Musique MUSEUM   In the stone-and-glass Cité de la Musique, this museum serves as a tribute and testament to music. You can view 4,500 instruments from the 16th century to the present, as well as paintings, engravings, and sculptures that relate to musical history. It's all here: cornets disguised as snakes, mandolins, lutes, zithers, music boxes, even an early electric guitar. Models of the world's great concert halls and interactive display areas give you a chance to hear and better understand musical art and technology. The museum is located within the Parc de la Villette (see below).

In the Cité de la Musique, 221 av. Jean-Jaurès, 19e. www.cite-musique.fr. ℂ **01-44-84-44-84.** Admission 8€ adults, 5€ students 18–25 and children 17 and younger, free for children 5 and younger. Tues–Sat noon–6pm; Sun 10am–7pm. Métro: Porte de Pantin.

FROM LEFT: **An exhibit from the Musée de la Musique; Parc de la Villette.**

Parc de la Villette ★★★ ☺ PARK This modern 21st-century park, designed by architect Bernard Tschumi, cleverly combines nature and architecture. Twice the size of the Jardin des Tuileries, it is Paris's largest park. The Canal de l'Ourcq runs through the park, feeding into various waterfalls, fountains, and ponds. Two walkways crisscross the park: the first runs from the Porte de Pantin to the Porte de la Villette, and the second is elevated and runs along the southern bank of the canal. The park is famous for its 26 red "follies," a contemporary version of the 18th-century gazebo, which are both ornamental and functional. In the center of the park are large grassy areas known as the circle and the triangle, where people can relax; during the summer, the triangle hosts a popular outdoor cinema program.

211 avenue Jean Jaurès, 19e. www.villette.com. ℅ **01-40-03-75-75.** Daily 6am–1am. Métro: Porte de Pantin or Porte de la Villette.

Parc des Buttes Chaumont ★★ ☺ PARK Napoleon III transformed a quarry into this magical park, full of almost ridiculous (if they weren't so charming) artificial features, such as lakes, waterfalls, and grottos—there's even an imitation of Etretat's coastline. Inaugurated during the 1867 World Fair, the Buttes Chaumont has century–old trees and is home to ducks, swans, geese, and fish. Parisians come here throughout the year to jog, walk their dogs, read books, picnic, or simply to hide out from the city. The park is home to two restaurants: **Rosa Bonheur** serves tapas-style snacks to a younger crowd, while **Le Pavillon du Lac** is a more serious dining affair with

Parc des Buttes Chaumont.

table service but equally lovely views. There are pony rides for the kids on weekends and Wednesdays, plus a puppet theater, a carousel, and two playgrounds.

Rue Manin, 19e. Open 7am–11pm May 1–Sept 30; 7am–9pm Sept 30–Apr 30. Métro: Botzaris or Buttes Chaumont.

THE LEFT BANK

Latin Quarter (5e & 13e)

This leafy neighborhood is defined by the medieval university at its heart: the Sorbonne. In fact, it gets its name from the Latin the students spoke in their classes there up until 1793. The Roman occupation, from 52 B.C. until A.D. 486, remains visible too; the rue Saint-Jacques and boulevard Saint-Michel mark the former Roman cardo, and you can explore Roman ruins at the Cluny Museum. French architect Dominique Perrault is behind the massive new national library out in the 13th arrondissement, signaling the resurrection of this former industrial heartland.

Arènes de Lutèce RUINS   Discovered and partially destroyed in 1869, this amphitheater is Paris's most important Roman ruin after the baths in the Musée de Cluny (p. 125). Today, the site is home to a small arena—not as grand as the original—and gardens. You may feel as if you've discovered a private spot in the heart of the city, but don't be fooled. Your solitude is sure to be interrupted, if not by groups of students playing soccer, then by parents pushing strollers down the paths. This is an ideal spot for a picnic; bring a bottle of wine and baguettes to enjoy in this vestige of the ancient city of Lutetia.

At rues Monge and Navarre, 5e. ✆ **01-40-71-76-60.** Free admission. Mon–Fri 8am–9pm; Sat–Sun 9am–9pm. Métro: Jussieu.

Bibliothèque Nationale de France, Site Tolbiac/François Mitterrand
LIBRARY   The French National Library opened in 1996 with a futuristic design by Dominique Perrault: the library is built into four 24-story towers evoking the

The towers of the Bibliothèque Nationale de France, Site Tolbiac.

121

look of open books. This is the last of the *grands projets* of the late François Mitterrand. It boasts the same grandiose scale as the Cité de la Musique and houses the nation's literary and historic archives; it's regarded as a repository of the French soul, replacing outmoded facilities on rue des Archives. The library incorporates space for 1,600 readers at a time, many of whom enjoy views over two levels of a garden-style courtyard that seems far removed from Paris's urban congestion.

Sweet mint tea and baklava at the Restaurant de la Mosquée de Paris.

This is one of Europe's most user-friendly academic facilities, emphasizing computerized documentation and microfiche—a role model that will set academic and literary priorities well into the future. The public has access to as many as 180,000 books, plus thousands of periodicals, with an additional 10 million historic (including medieval) documents available to qualified experts. Though the appeal of this place extends mainly to serious scholars, a handful of special exhibits might interest you, as well as concerts and lectures. Concert tickets rarely exceed 15€; a schedule is available at the library.

Quai François-Mauriac, 13e. www.bnf.fr. ✆ **01-53-79-59-59.** Admission 3.50€. Children 15 and under not admitted. Mon 2–8pm; Tues–Sat 10am–7pm; Sun 1–7pm. Closed Sept 8–21. Métro: Bibliothèque François-Mitterrand.

La Grande Mosquée de Paris ★ MOSQUE   This beautiful pink marble mosque was built in 1922 to honor the North African countries that had given aid to France during World War I. Today, North Africans living in Paris gather on Friday, the Muslim holy day, and during Ramadan to pray to Allah. Short tours are given of the building, its central courtyard, and its Moorish garden; guides present a brief history of the Islamic faith. However, you may want to just wander around on your own and then join the students from nearby universities for couscous and sweet mint tea at the Muslim **Restaurant de la Mosquée de Paris** (✆ **01-43-31-18-14**), adjoining the grounds, open daily from noon to 3pm and 7 to 10:30pm. The mosque also features a charming if slightly decrepit traditional hammam or Turkish baths (18€ entry). The Byzantine decor features mosaic, marble, and a porphyry stone fountain; open to men or women only on alternate days (men Tues & Sun).

2 bis place du Puits-de-l'Ermite, 5e. www.mosquee-de-paris.net. ✆ **01-45-35-97-33.** Admission 3€, free for children 7 and younger. Sat–Thurs 9am–noon and 2–6pm. Métro: Place Monge.

Manufacture Nationale des Gobelins ★ MUSEUM   Did you know a single tapestry can take 4 years to complete, employing as many as three to five full-time weavers? The founder of this dynasty, Jean Gobelin, came from a family of dyers and clothmakers; in the 15th century, he discovered a scarlet dye that made him famous. By 1601, Henri IV imported 200 weavers from Flanders to make tapestries full time. Until this endeavor, the Gobelin family hadn't made any tapestries. Colbert, Louis XIV's minister, bought the works, and under royal patronage the craftsmen set about executing designs by Le Brun. After the revolution, the industry was reactivated by Napoleon. Today, Les Gobelins is a viable

Attractions in the Latin Quarter & Southern Paris (5e & 13e)

Hôtel-Dieu

St-Michel

place St-Michel

r. St-André des Arts

r. Suger

St-Michel-Notre-Dame

Cathédrale Notre-Dame

ÎLE DE LA CITÉ

sq. Jean XXIII

sq. de l'Île de France

Seine

Pont Marie

voie Georges Pompidou

quai des Célestins

r. de Rivoli

r. de Fourcy

r. de Charlemagne

St-Paul

r. St-Antoine

r. St-Paul

4e

ÎLE ST-LOUIS

r. du Petit Musc

bd. St-Germain

Odéon

r. Serpente

r. du Petit Pont

quai de Montebello

square R. Viviani

r. Dante

r. du Sommerard

Maubert-Mutualité

place Maubert

r. des Bernardins

r. de Pontoise

r. de Poissy

quai de La Tournelle

bd. St-Germain

r. des Fossés St-Bernard

Cardinal Lemoine

r. des Deux Ponts

quai de Béthune en l'île

pont de Sully

square Barye

bd. Henri IV

Sully-Morland

bd. Morland

quai Henri IV

Seine

6e

Cluny-La Sorbonne

Monsieur le Prince

r. Racine

bd. St-Michel

Sorbonne

sq. F.A. Mariette

place Edmond Rostand

r. de Médicis

pl. de la Sorbonne

Luxembourg

r. St-Jacques

Cujas

r. Soufflot

place du Panthéon

Panthéon

r. Clotilde

r. de l'Estrapade

r. Descartes

r. Thouin

LATIN QUARTER

sq. Paul Langevin

des Écoles

Jardin Carré

du

Cardinal Lemoine

place Jussieu

Jussieu

CAMPUS DE JUSSIEU (Université Pierre-et-Marie-Curie, Université Paris Diderot, Institut de Physique du Globe de Paris)

Musée de la Sculpture en Plein Air

quai St-Bernard

Cuvier

Ménagerie

5e

r. Pierre et Marie Curie

r. d'Ulm

r. Lhomond

Lussac

r. Gay-Lussac

place de la Contrescarpe

r. Rollin

r. Lacépède

r. Linné

JARDIN DES PLANTES

Gare d'Austerlitz

r. des Feuillantines

place A. Laveran

Église du Val-de-Grâce

VAL-DE-GRÂCE

r. St-Jacques

r. Tournefort

Mouffetard

r. Lhomond

place Monge

Place Monge

Grande Mosquée de Paris

Geoffroy

Saint Hilaire

r. Buffon

r. Poliveau

r. Censier

Censier-Daubenton

r. du Fer à Moulin

bd. Saint-Marcel

St-Marcel

r. de l'Hôpital

GROUPE HOSPITALIER PITIÉ-SALPÊTRIÈRE

14e

HÔPITAL COCHIN

bd. de Port Royal

r. Berthollet

Claude Bernard

r. Broca

bd. de la Santé

r. de la Glacière

bd. Arago

av. des Gobelins

Les Gobelins

r. Le Brun

av. Jeanne d'Arc

bd. de la Santé

Campo Formio

r. du Banquier

r. Watteau

de Campo Formio

R. Pinnel

r. Jenner

r. Jeanne d'Arc

Esquirol

Nicole

bd.

Arago

13e

place d'Italie

Place d'Italie

bd. Vincent Auriol

National

0   1/4 mi

0   0.25 km

A weaver working in the Manufacture Nationale des Gobelins.

business entity, weaving tapestries for museums and historical restorations around the world. Throughout most of the week, the factories are closed to casual visitors, who are never allowed to wander at will. But if you'd like insight into this medieval craft, you can participate, 3 days a week (Tues, Wed, Thu), in one of two guided tours, each lasting 90 minutes and each conducted in French. The factory also includes the **Galerie des Gobelins,** which displays exhibits that are generally sourced from the extraordinary furniture and arts collections of the Mobilier National.

42 av. des Gobelins, 13e. www.mobiliernational.culture.gouv.fr. © **01-40-13-46-46.** Admission to the Galerie des Gobelins 10€, 7.50€ students. Tues–Sun 10am–6pm. Métro: Gobelins.

Musée de l'Institut du Monde Arabe ★ MUSEUM   Many factors have contributed to France's preoccupation with the Arab world, but three of the most important include trade links that developed during the Crusades, a large Arab population living today in France, and the memories of France's lost colonies in North Africa. For insights into the way France has handled its relations with the Arab world, consider making a trek to this bastion of Arab intellect and aesthetics. Designed in 1987 by architect Jean Nouvel and funded by 22 different, mostly Arab, countries, it includes expositions on calligraphy, decorative arts, architecture, and photography produced by the Arab/Islamic world, as well as insights into its religion, philosophy, and politics. In 2011 Chanel donated to the museum an avant-garde "mobile art container" designed by the Iraqi-British architect

The facade of the Musée de l'Institut du Monde Arabe.

Zaha Hadid; this avant-garde pod sits on the site's piazza, providing another exhibition space. And in 2012 the museum spaces housing the permanent collection underwent a major renovation. There's a bookshop on site, a replica of a medina selling high-quality gifts, art objects, and archival resources. Views from the windows of the roof-top Moroccan cafe encompass Notre-Dame, l'Ile de la Cité, and Sacré-Coeur. Guided tours start at 3pm Tuesday to Friday or at 4:30pm on Saturday and Sunday.

1 rue des Fossés St-Bernard, 5e. www.imarabe.org. (*) **01-40-51-38-38.** Admission to permanent exhibitions 7€, 5€ students, free for children 11 and under. Tues–Sun 10am–6pm. Métro: Jussieu, Cardinal Lemoine, Sully-Morland.

Musée National d'Histoire Naturelle (Museum of Natural History) ★ ☺

MUSEUM   This museum in the Jardin des Plantes, founded in 1635 as a research center by Guy de la Brosse, physician to Louis XIII, has a range of science and nature exhibits. At the entrance of the **Grande Gallery of Evolution,** two 26m (85-ft.) skeletons of whales greet you. Kids will love the display containing the skeletons of dinosaurs and mastodons, dedicated to endangered and vanished species. Galleries specialize in paleontology, anatomy, mineralogy, and botany. Within the museum's grounds are **tropical hothouses** containing thousands of species of unusual plant life and a **menagerie** with small animals in simulated natural habitats.

36 rue Geoffrey, 5e. www.mnhn.fr. (*) **01-40-79-54-79.** Admission 9€ adults; 7€ students, seniors 60 and older, and children 4–13. Wed–Mon 10am–6pm. Métro: Jussieu or Gare d'Austerlitz.

Musée National du Moyen Age/Thermes de Cluny (Musée de Cluny) ★★

MUSEUM   Along with the Hôtel de Sens in the Marais, the Hôtel de Cluny is all that remains of domestic medieval architecture in Paris. Enter through the cobblestoned **Cour d'Honneur (Court of Honor),** where you can admire the flamboyant Gothic building with its vines, turreted walls, gargoyles, and dormers with seashell motifs. First, the Cluny was the mansion of a rich 15th-century abbot, built on top of/next to the ruins of a Roman bath. By 1515, it was the residence of Mary Tudor, widow of Louis XII and daughter of Henry VII and

The Lady and the Unicorn tapestries.

Elizabeth of York. Seized during the Revolution, the Cluny was rented in 1833 to Alexandre du Sommerard, who adorned it with medieval artworks. After his death in 1842, the government bought the building and the collection.

This collection of medieval arts and crafts is superb. Most people come to see *The Lady and the Unicorn* tapestries ★★★, the most acclaimed tapestries of their kind. All the romance of the age of chivalry—a beautiful princess and her handmaiden, beasts of prey, and house pets—lives on in these remarkable yet mysterious tapestries discovered only a century ago in Limousin's Château de Boussac. Five seem to deal with the senses (one, for example, depicts a unicorn looking into a mirror held by a dour-faced maiden). The sixth shows a woman under an elaborate tent with jewels, her pet dog resting on an embroidered cushion beside her, with the lovable unicorn and his friendly companion, a lion, holding back the flaps. The background forms a rich carpet of spring flowers, fruit-laden trees, birds, rabbits, donkeys, dogs, goats, lambs, and monkeys.

The other exhibits range widely: Flemish retables; a 14th-century Sienese John the Baptist and other sculptures; statues from Sainte-Chapelle (1243–48); 12th- and 13th-century crosses, chalices, manuscripts, carvings, vestments, leatherwork, jewelry, and coins; a 13th-century Adam; and recently discovered heads and fragments of statues from Notre-Dame de Paris. In the fan-vaulted medieval chapel hang tapestries depicting scenes from the life of St. Stephen.

Downstairs are the ruins of the **Roman baths,** from around A.D. 200. The best-preserved section is seen in room X, the frigidarium (where one bathed in cold water). Once it measured 21×11m (69×36 ft.), rising to a height of 15m (49 ft.), with stone walls nearly 1.5m (5 ft.) thick. The ribbed vaulting here rests on consoles evoking ships' prows. Credit for this unusual motif goes to the builders of the baths, Paris's boatmen. During Tiberius's reign, a column to Jupiter was found beneath Notre-Dame's chancel and is now on view in the court; called the "Column of the Boatmen," it's believed to be the oldest sculpture created in Paris.

6 place Paul Painlevé, 5e. www.musee-moyenage.fr. ℂ **01-53-73-78-00.** Admission 7.50€ adults, 5.50€ youths 18–25. Add 2€ for access to the temporary exhibitions. Wed–Mon 9:15am–5:45pm. Métro: Miromesnil or St-Philippe-du-Roule.

Panthéon ★★ CHURCH   Some of the most famous men in French history (Victor Hugo, for one) are buried here on the crest of the mount of St. Geneviève. In 1744, Louis XV vowed that if he recovered from a mysterious illness, he'd build a church to replace the Abbaye de St. Geneviève. He recovered but took his time fulfilling his promise. It wasn't until 1764 that Mme de Pompadour's brother hired Soufflot to design a church in the form of a Greek cross with a dome reminiscent of St. Paul's in London. When Soufflot died, his pupil Rondelet carried out the work, completing the structure 9 years after his master's death.

After the revolution, the church was converted to a "Temple of Fame" and became a pantheon for the great men of France. Mirabeau was buried here, though his remains were later removed. Likewise, Marat was only a temporary tenant. Voltaire's body was exhumed and placed here—and allowed to remain. In the 19th century, the building changed roles so many times—a church, a pantheon, a church again—that it was hard to keep its function straight. After Hugo was buried here, it became a pantheon once again. Other notable men entombed within are Rousseau, Soufflot, Zola, and Braille. Only one woman has so far been deemed worthy of placement here: Marie Curie, who joined her husband, Pierre. Most recently, in 1996, the ashes of André Malraux were transferred to the Panthéon because, according to former French president Jacques Chirac, he "lived

The Panthéon.

[his] dreams and made them live in us." As Charles de Gaulle's culture minister, Malraux decreed the arts should be part of the lives of all French people, not just Paris's elite.

Before entering the crypt, note the striking frescoes: On the right wall are scenes from Geneviève's life, and on the left is the saint with a white-draped head looking out over medieval Paris, the city whose patron she became, as well as Geneviève relieving victims of famine with supplies.

Place du Panthéon, 5e. www.monum.fr. (*) 01-44-32-18-00. Admission 8.50€ adults, 5.50€ ages 18–25, free for children 17 and younger. Apr–Sept daily 10am–6:30pm; Oct–Mar daily 10am–6pm (last entrance 45 min. before closing). Métro: Cardinal Lemoine or Maubert-Mutualité.

St-Etienne-du-Mont ★★ CHURCH Once there was an abbey here, founded by Clovis and later dedicated to St. Geneviève, the patroness of Paris. Such was the fame of this popular saint that the abbey proved too small to accommodate the pilgrimage crowds. Now part of the Lycée Henri IV, the Tour de Clovis (Tower of Clovis) is all that remains of the ancient abbey—you can see the tower from rue Clovis. Today, the task of keeping St. Geneviève's cult alive has fallen on this church, practically adjoining the Panthéon. The interior is Gothic, an

The interior of St-Etienne-du-Mont.

unusual style for a 16th-century church. Building began in 1492 and was plagued by delays until the church was finally finished in 1626.

Besides the patroness of Paris, such men as Pascal and Racine were entombed here. Because of the destruction of church records during the French Revolution, church officials aren't sure of the exact locations in which they're buried. St. Geneviève's tomb was destroyed during the revolution, but the stone on which her coffin rested was discovered later, and her relics were gathered for a place of honor at St-Etienne. The church possesses a remarkable early-16th-century **rood screen:** Crossing the nave, it's unique in Paris—called spurious by some and a masterpiece by others. Another treasure is a wood **pulpit,** held up by Samson, clutching a bone in one hand, with a slain lion at his feet. The fourth chapel on the right when you enter contains impressive 16th-century stained glass.

1 place St-Geneviève, 5e. ℂ **01-43-54-11-79.** Free admission. With the exception of some of France's school holidays, when hours may vary slightly, the church is open year-round as follows: Mon noon–7:30pm; Tues–Fri 8:45am–7:30pm; Sat 8:45am–7:45pm; Sun 8:45am–12:15pm and 2:30–7:45pm. Métro: Cardinal Lemoine or Luxembourg.

St-Germain-des-Prés & Luxembourg (6e)

This neighborhood in the 6th arrondissement was the postwar home of existentialism, associated with great writers and philosophers Jean-Paul Sartre, Simone de Beauvoir, Albert Camus, and an intellectual bohemian crowd that gathered at **Café de Flore** or **Les Deux Magots** (p. 231). St-Germain-des-Prés still retains an intellectually stimulating bohemian street life, full of many interesting bookshops, art galleries, *caveau* (basement) clubs, bistros, and coffeehouses. But the stars of the area are two churches, **St-Germain-des-Prés** and **St-Sulpice,** and the **Musée National Eugène Delacroix.**

Institut de France HISTORIC SITE   Designed by Louis Le Vau, this dramatic baroque building with an enormous cupola is the seat of all five academies that dominate France's intellectual life—Française, Sciences, Inscriptions et Belles Lettres, Beaux Arts, and Sciences Morales et Politiques. The members of the Académie Française (limited to 40), guardians of the French language referred to as "the immortals," gather here. Many are unfamiliar figures (though Jacques Cousteau and Marshall Pétain were members), and the academy is remarkable for the great writers and philosophers who have *not* been invited to join—Balzac, Baudelaire, Diderot, Flaubert, Descartes, Proust, Molière, Pascal, Rousseau, and Zola, to name only a few. The cenotaph was designed by Coysevox for Mazarin.

23 quai de Conti, 6e. www.institut-de-france.fr. ℂ **01-44-41-44-47.** Free admission (guests can walk into courtyard only). Daily 9am–6pm. Métro: Louvre-Rivoli.

Jardin du Luxembourg ★★ ☺ GARDEN   Hemingway once told a friend that the Jardin du Luxembourg "kept us from starvation." He related that in his poverty-stricken days in Paris, he wheeled a baby carriage (the vehicle was considered luxurious) through the garden because it was known "for the classiness of its pigeons." When the gendarme went across the street for a glass of wine, the writer would eye his victim, preferably a plump one; lure him with corn; "snatch him, wring his neck"; and hide him under the blanket. "We got a little tired of pigeons that year," he confessed, "but they filled many a void."

The Luxembourg has always been associated with artists, though children, students, and tourists predominate nowadays. Watteau came this way, as did

Attractions in St-Germain-des-Prés, Luxembourg, Montparnasse & Southern Paris (6e, 14e & 15e)

Jardin du Luxembourg.

Verlaine. In 1905, Gertrude Stein would cross it to catch the Batignolles/Clichy/ Odéon omnibus, pulled by three gray mares, to meet Picasso in his studio at Montmartre, where he painted her portrait.

Marie de Medici, the wife of Henri IV, ordered the **Palais du Luxembourg** built on this site in 1612, shortly after she was widowed. A Florentine by birth, the regent wanted to create another Pitti Palace, where she could live with her "witch" friend, Leonora Galigal. Architect Salomon de Brossee wasn't entirely successful, though the overall effect is Italianate. Alas, the queen didn't get to enjoy the palace, as her son, Louis XIII, forced her into exile when he discovered she was plotting to overthrow him. She died in poverty in Cologne. For her palace, she'd commissioned 21 paintings from Rubens, which glorified her life, but they're now in the Louvre. It is extremely difficult to visit the palace, because it is the chamber of French senators. A few visits are organized throughout the year but there is no schedule. You can call © **01-44-54-19-49** and take a chance. Even so, when tours are offered only 30 tickets are available. The cost is 8€ per person.

You don't really come to the Luxembourg to visit the palace; the gardens are the attraction. For the most part, they're in the classic French tradition: well groomed and formally laid out, the trees planted in patterns. Urns and statuary on pedestals—one honoring Paris's patroness, St. Geneviève, with pigtails reaching to her thighs—encircle a central water basin. Kids can sail a toy boat, ride a pony, or attend an occasional Grand Guignol puppet show. And you can join a game of *boules* (lawn bowling) with a group of men who wear black berets and have Gauloises dangling from their mouths.

Place Edmond Rostand, place André Honnorat, rue Guynemer, rue de Vaugirard, 6e. 8am–dusk. Métro: Odéon; RER: Luxembourg.

Musée National Eugène Delacroix ★ MUSEUM   This museum is for Delacroix groupies. If you want to see where he lived, worked, and died, this is worth at least an hour. Delacroix (1798–1863) is something of an enigma to art historians. Even his parentage is a mystery. Many believe Talleyrand was his father. One biographer saw him "as an isolated and atypical individualist—one who respected traditional values, yet emerged as the embodiment of Romantic revolt." Baudelaire called him "a volcanic crater artistically concealed beneath bouquets of flowers." The museum is on one of the Left Bank's most charming squares, with a romantic garden. A large arch on a courtyard leads to Delacroix's studio—no poor artist's studio, but the creation of a solidly established man. Sketches, lithographs, watercolors, and oils are hung throughout. If you want to see more of Delacroix's work, head to the Chapelle des Anges in St-Sulpice (p. 132).

6 place de Furstenberg, 6e. www.musee-delacroix.fr. ☏ **01-44-41-86-50.** Admission 5€ adults, free for children 17 and younger. Wed–Mon 9:30am–5pm. Métro: St-Germain-des-Prés or Mabillon.

Musée Zadkine MUSEUM   This museum near the Jardin du Luxembourg was once the home of sculptor Ossip Zadkine (1890–1967), and his collection has been turned over to the city for public viewing. Included are some 300 pieces of sculpture, displayed in the museum and the garden. Some drawings and tapestries are also exhibited. At these headquarters, where he worked from 1928 until his death, you can see how he moved from "left wing" cubist extremism to a renewed appreciation of the classic era. You can visit his garden for free even if you don't want to go into the museum—in fact, it's one of the finest places to relax in Paris on a sunny day, sitting on a bench taking in the two-faced *Woman with the Bird*. The museum underwent significant renovations in 2012.

100 bis rue d'Assas, 6e. www.zadkine.paris.fr. ☏ **01-55-42-77-20.** Free admission to permanent collections. Tues–Sun 10am–6pm. Métro: Notre-Dame des Champs or Vavin.

St-Germain-des-Prés ★★ CHURCH   It's one of Paris's oldest churches, from the 6th century, when a Benedictine abbey was founded here by Childebert, son of Clovis. Alas, the marble columns in the triforium are all that remain from that period. The Normans nearly destroyed the abbey at least four times. The present building has a Romanesque nave and a Gothic choir with fine capitals. At one time, the abbey was a pantheon for Merovingian kings. Restoration of the site of their tombs, **Chapelle de St-Symphorien,** took place in 1981, when unknown Romanesque paintings were discovered on the triumphal arch. Among the others interred here are Descartes (his heart, at least) and Jean-Casimir, the king of Poland who abdicated his throne. The Romanesque tower,

St-Germain-des-Prés church.

Delacroix's famous frescoes in St-Sulpice.

topped by a 19th-century spire, is the most enduring landmark in St-Germain-des-Prés. Its church bells, however, are hardly noticed by the patrons of Les Deux Magots across the way.

3 place St-Germain-des-Prés, 6e. www. eglise-sgp.org. ℰ **01-55-42-81-33.** Free admission. Mon–Sat 8am–7:45pm; Sun 9am–8pm. Métro: St-Germain-des-Prés.

St-Sulpice ★★ CHURCH Pause first outside St-Sulpice. The 1844 fountain by Visconti displays the sculpted likenesses of four bishops of the Louis XIV era: Fenelon, Massillon, Bossuet, and Flechier. Work on the church, at one time Paris's largest, began in 1646. Though laborers built the body by 1745, work on the bell towers continued until 1780, when one was finished and the other left incomplete. One of the priceless treasures inside is Servandoni's rococo **Chapelle de la Madone (Chapel of the Madonna),** with a Pigalle statue of the Virgin. The church has one of the world's largest organs, comprising 6,700 pipes; it has been played by musicians such as Marcel Dupré and Charles-Marie Widor.

The real reason to come here is to see the Delacroix frescoes in the **Chapelle des Anges (Chapel of the Angels),** the first on your right as you enter. Look for his muscular Jacob wrestling (or dancing?) with an effete angel. On the ceiling, St. Michael is having some troubles with the Devil, and yet another mural depicts Heliodorus being driven from the temple. Painted in Delacroix's final years, the frescoes were a high point in his baffling career. If these impress you, pay the painter tribute by visiting the Musée National Eugène Delacroix (see above).

Rue St-Sulpice, 6e. ℰ **01-42-34-59-98.** Free admission. Daily 8:30am–8pm. Métro: St-Sulpice.

Eiffel Tower & Nearby (7e)

The **Eiffel Tower** has become a symbol for Paris itself. For years it remained the tallest man-made structure on earth, until skyscrapers such as the Empire State Building surpassed it. After admiring and climbing the elegant structure, stroll west along the river to two other important attractions: the **Musée du quai Branly** and the **Musée d'Orsay.**

Hôtel des Invalides/Napoleon's Tomb ★★ HISTORIC BUILDING In 1670, the Sun King decided to build this "hotel" to house soldiers with disabilities. It wasn't an entirely benevolent gesture, considering that the men had been injured, crippled, or blinded while fighting his battles. When the building was finally completed (Louis XIV had long been dead), a gilded dome by Jules Hardouin-Mansart crowned it, and its corridors stretched for miles. The best way to approach the Invalides is by crossing over the Right Bank via the early-1900s Pont Alexander-III and entering the cobblestone forecourt, where a display of massive cannons makes a formidable welcome.

Before rushing on to Napoleon's Tomb, you may want to visit the world's greatest military museum, the **Musée de l'Armée.** In 1794, a French inspector started collecting weapons, uniforms, and equipment, and with the accumulation of war material over time, the museum has become a documentary of man's

Eiffel Tower & Nearby Attractions (7e)

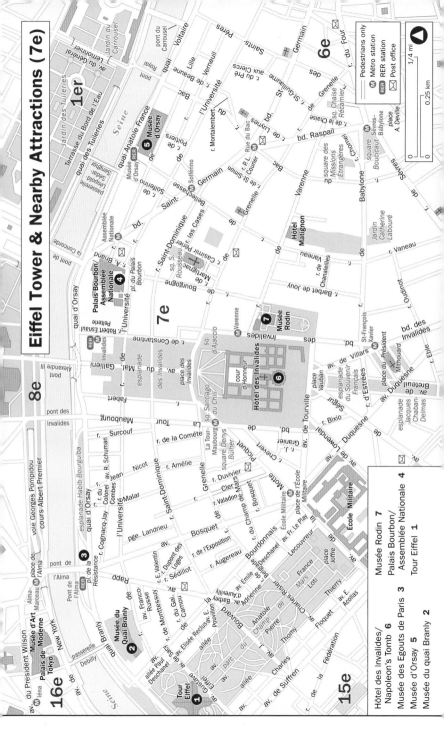

Hôtel des Invalides/
Napoleon's Tomb **6**
Musée des Egouts de Paris **3**
Musée d'Orsay **5**
Musée du quai Branly **2**

Musée Rodin **7**
Palais Bourbon/
Assemblée Nationale **4**
Tour Eiffel **1**

Pedestrians only
M Métro station
RER RER station
⊠ Post office

1/4 mi
0.25 km

self-destruction. Viking swords, Burgundian battle axes, 14th-century blunder-busses, Balkan *khandjars,* American Browning machine guns, war pitchforks, salamander-engraved Renaissance serpentines, a 1528 Griffon, musketoons, grenadiers—if it can kill, it's enshrined here. As a sardonic touch, there's even the wooden leg of General Daumesnil, the governor of Vincennes, who lost his leg in the battle of Wagram. Oblivious to the irony of committing a crime against a place that documents man's evil nature, the Nazis looted the museum in 1940.

Among the outstanding acquisitions are suits of armor worn by the kings and dignitaries of France, including Louis XIV. The best are in the new Arsenal. The most famous one, the "armor suit of the lion," was made for François I. Henri II ordered his suit engraved with the monogram of his mistress, Diane de Poitiers, and (perhaps reluctantly) that of his wife, Catherine de Medici. Particu-larly fine are the showcases of swords and the World War I mementos, including those of American and Canadian soldiers—seek out the Armistice Bugle, which sounded the cease-fire on November 7, 1918, before the general cease-fire on November 11. The west wing's Salle Orientale has arms of the Eastern world, including Asia and the Mideast Muslim countries, from the 16th century to the 19th century. Turkish armor (look for Bajazet's helmet) and weaponry, and Chi-nese and Japanese armor and swords are on display.

Then there's that little Corsican who became France's greatest soldier. Here you can see the death mask Antommarchi made of him, as well as an oil by Dela-roche painted at the time of Napoleon's first banishment (Apr 1814) and depict-ing him as he probably looked, paunch and all. The First Empire exhibit displays Napoleon's field bed with his tent; in the room devoted to the Restoration, the 100 Days, and Waterloo, you can see his bedroom as it was at the time of his death on St. Helena. The Turenne Salon contains other souvenirs, such as the hat Napoleon wore at Eylau; the sword from his Austerlitz victory; and his "Flag of Farewell," which he kissed before departing for Elba.

You can gain access to the **Musée des Plans-Reliefs** through the west wing. This collection shows French towns and monuments done in scale models (the model of Strasbourg fills an entire room), as well as models of military forti-fications since the days of the great Vauban.

A walk across the Cour d'Honneur (Court of Honor) delivers you to the **Eglise du Dôme,** designed by Hardouin-Mansart for Louis XIV. The architect began work on the church in 1677, though he died before its completion. The dome is the second-tallest monument in Paris (the Tour Eiffel is the tallest, of course). The hearse used at the emperor's funeral on May 9, 1821, is in the Napoleon Chapel.

To accommodate **Napoleon's Tomb ★★★**, the architect Visconti had to redesign the church's high altar in 1842. First buried on St. Helena, Napoleon's remains were exhumed and brought to Paris in 1840 on the orders of Louis-Philippe, who demanded that the English return the emperor to French soil. The remains were locked inside six coffins in this tomb made of red Finnish porphyry, with a green granite base. Surrounding it are a dozen Amazon-like figures repre-senting Napoleon's victories. Almost lampooning the smallness of the man, everything is done on a gargantuan scale. In his coronation robes, the statue of Napoleon stands 2.5m (8¼ ft.) high. The grave of the "King of Rome," his son by second wife, Marie-Louise, lies at his feet. Surrounding Napoleon's Tomb are those of his brother, Joseph Bonaparte; the great Vauban, who built many of France's fortifications; World War I Allied commander Foch; and the *vicomte* de Turenne, the republic's first grenadier (actually, only his heart is entombed here).

Napoleon's Tomb.

Place des Invalides, 7e. www.invalides.org. ℰ **01-44-42-37-72.** Admission to Musée de l'Armée, Napoleon's Tomb, and Musée des Plans-Reliefs 9€ adults, 7€ students, free for children 17 and younger. Oct 1–Mar 31 Mon–Sat 10am–5pm, Sun 10am–5:30pm; Apr 1–Sept 30 Mon, Wed–Sat 10am–6pm, Sun 10am–6:30pm, Tues 10am–9pm; June–Aug daily 10am–7pm. Closed Jan 1, May 1, Nov 1, and Dec 25. Métro: Latour-Maubourg, Varenne, Invalides, or St-Francois-Xavier.

Musée des Egouts de Paris ★ ☺ HISTORIC SITE   Some sociologists assert that the sophistication of a society can be judged by the way it disposes of waste. If so, Paris receives good marks for its mostly invisible sewer network. Victor Hugo is credited with making them famous in *Les Misérables:* Jean Valjean takes flight through them, "all dripping with slime, his soul filled with a strange light." Hugo also wrote, "Paris has beneath it another Paris, a Paris of sewers, which has its own streets, squares, lanes, arteries, and circulation."

In the early Middle Ages, drinking water was taken directly from the Seine, and wastewater poured onto fields or thrown onto the unpaved streets transformed the urban landscape into a sea of smelly mud. Around 1200, the streets were paved with cobblestones, and open sewers ran down the center of each. These open sewers helped spread the Black Death, which devastated the city. In 1370, a vaulted sewer was built on rue Montmartre, draining effluents into a Seine tributary. During Louis XIV's reign, improvements were made, but the state of waste disposal in Paris remained deplorable.

During Napoleon's reign, 31km (19 miles) of sewer were constructed beneath Paris. By 1850, as the Industrial Revolution made the manufacture of iron pipe and steam-digging equipment more practical, Baron Haussmann developed a system that used separate channels for drinking water and sewage. By 1878, it was 580km (360 miles) long. Beginning in 1894, the network was enlarged, and laws required that discharge of all waste and storm-water runoff be funneled into the sewers. Between 1914 and 1977, an additional 966km (600 miles) were added. Today, the network of sewers is 2,093km (1,300 miles) long.

The city's sewers are constructed around four principal tunnels, one 5.5m (18 ft.) wide and 4.5m (15 ft.) high. It's like an underground city, with the street names clearly labeled. Sewer tours begin at Pont de l'Alma on the Left Bank, where a stairway leads into the city's bowels. Visiting times might change during bad weather, as a storm can make the sewers dangerous. The tour consists of a film, a small museum visit, and then a short trip through the maze. *Warning:*

The smell is pretty bad, especially in summer, but kids should love the gross-out factor.

Pont de l'Alma, 7e. ℰ **01-53-68-27-81.** Admission 4.30€ adults; 3.50€ seniors, students, and children 5–16; free for children 4 and younger. May–Sept Sat–Wed 11am–5pm; Oct–Apr Sat–Wed 11am–4pm. Métro: Alma-Marceau. RER: Pont de l'Alma.

Musée d'Orsay ★★★ MUSEUM   Architects created one of the world's great museums from an old rail station, the neoclassical Gare d'Orsay, across the Seine from the Louvre and the Tuileries. Don't skip the Louvre, of course, but come here even if you have to miss all the other art museums in town. The Orsay boasts an astounding collection devoted to the watershed years 1848 to 1914, with a treasure-trove by the big names plus all the lesser-known groups (the symbolists, pointillists, nabis, realists, and late romantics). The 80 galleries also include Belle Époque furniture, photographs, objets d'art, and architectural models.

A monument to the Industrial Revolution, the Orsay is covered by an arching glass roof allowing in floods of light. It displays works ranging from the creations of academic and historic painters such as Ingres to romanticists such as Delacroix, to neorealists including Courbet and Daumier.

The museum's Impressionist and post-Impressionist galleries, as well as the four floors of the "Pavillon Amont," underwent a major renovation in 2011 which enlarged exhibition spaces and improved displays. The Impressionists still draw the crowds to this museum. Led by Manet, Renoir, and Monet, the Impressionists shunned ecclesiastical and mythological set pieces for a light-bathed Seine, faint figures strolling in the Tuileries, pale-faced women in hazy bars, and even vulgar rail stations such as the Gare St-Lazare. And the Impressionists were the first to paint that most characteristic feature of Parisian life: the sidewalk cafe, especially in the artists' quarter of Montmartre.

The most famous painting from this era is Manet's 1863 ***Déjeuner sur l'herbe (Picnic on the Grass),*** whose forest setting with a nude woman and

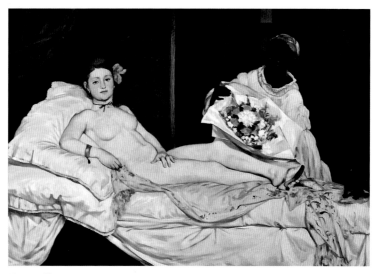

Manet's *Olympia.*

two fully clothed men sent shock waves through respectable society when it was first exhibited. Two years later, Manet's **Olympia** created another scandal by depicting a woman lounging on her bed and wearing nothing but a flower in her hair and high-heeled shoes; she's attended by an African maid in the background. Zola called Manet "a man among eunuchs."

One of Renoir's most joyous paintings is here: the **Moulin de la Galette** (1876). Degas is represented by his paintings of racehorses and dancers; his 1876 cafe scene, **Absinthe,** remains one of his most reproduced works. Paris-born Monet was fascinated by the effect of changing light on Rouen Cathédrale and brought its stone bubbles to life in a series of five paintings; our favorite is **Rouen Cathédrale: Full Sunlight.** Another celebrated work is by an American, Whistler's **Arrangement in Grey and Black: Portrait of the Painter's Mother,** better known as **Whistler's Mother.** It's said that this painting heralded modern art, though many critics denounced it at the time because of its funereal overtones. Whistler was content to claim he'd made "Mummy just as nice as possible."

You'll also see works by Matisse, the cubists, and the expressionists in a setting once used by Orson Welles to film a nightmarish scene in *The Trial,* based on Kafka's unfinished novel. You'll find Millet's sunny wheat fields, Barbizon landscapes, Corot's mists, and Tahitian Gauguins.

FROM TOP: **Musée d' Orsay; an exhibit from the Musée du quai Branly.**

1 rue de Bellechasse or 62 rue de Lille, 7e. www.musee-orsay.fr. ✆ **01-40-49-48-14.** Admission 9€ adults, 6.50€ ages 18–24, free ages 17 and younger. Joint ticket to this museum and the Musée de l'Orangerie (p. 80) 13€. Tues–Wed and Fri–Sun 9:30am–6pm; Thurs 9:30am–9:45pm. Closed Jan 1 and Dec 25. Métro: Solférino. RER: Musée d'Orsay.

Musée du quai Branly ★★★ ☺ MUSEUM   The architect Jean Nouvel said he wanted to create something "unique, poetic, and disturbing." And so he did with this $265-million museum, which opened in 2006. Set in a lush, rambling garden on the Left Bank in the shadow of the Eiffel Tower, this museum houses nearly 300,000 tribal artifacts from Africa, Asia, Oceania, and the Americas. Galleries stand on sculpted pillars that evoke totem poles.

Housed in four spectacular buildings with a garden walled off from the quai Branly are the art, sculpture, and cultural materials of a vast range of non-Western civilizations, separated into different sections that represent the traditional cultures of Africa, East and Southeast Asia, Oceania, Australia, the Americas, and New Zealand. The pieces here come from the now-defunct Musée des Arts Africains et Oceaniens, from the Louvre, and from the Musée de l'Homme. Temporary exhibits are shown off in boxes all along the 183m-long (600-ft.) exhibition hall.

Incredible masterpieces are on display made by some very advanced traditional civilizations; some of the most impressive exhibits present tribal masks of different cultures, some of which are so lifelike and emotional in their creation that you can feel the fear and elation involved in their use, which is well documented by descriptions in English. The exhibitions are very engaging for children. Allow 2 hours for a full visit; also take a stroll in the carefully manicured garden, or have a café au lait in the small cafeteria across from the main building. There are numerous entrances to the museum grounds from the area near the Eiffel Tower; the main entrance is on quai Branly.

27–37 quai Branly and 206–208 rue de Université, 7e. www.quaibranly.fr. ✆ **01-56-61-70-00.** Admission to permanent exhibitions 8.50€ adults, 6€ seniors and students 18–26, free for children 17 and younger; admission to temporary exhibitions 7€ adults, 5€ seniors and students 18–26 Tues–Wed and Sun 11am–7pm; Thurs–Sat 11am–9pm. Métro: Alma-Marceau. RER: Pont d'Alma.

Musée Rodin ★★ ☺ MUSEUM   Today Rodin is acclaimed as the father of modern sculpture, but in a different era, his work was labeled obscene. The world's artistic taste changed, and in due course, in 1911, the French government purchased Rodin's studio in this gray-stone, 18th-century mansion in the Faubourg St-Germain. The government restored the rose gardens to their 18th-century splendor, making them a perfect setting for Rodin's most memorable works.

In the courtyard are three world-famous creations. Rodin's first major public commission, *The Burghers of Calais,* commemorated the heroism of six citizens of Calais who in 1347 offered themselves as a ransom to Edward III in return for ending his siege of their port. Perhaps the single best-known work, *The Thinker,* in Rodin's own words, "thinks with every muscle of his arms, back, and legs, with his clenched fist and gripping toes." Not completed when Rodin died, *The Gate of Hell,* as he put it, is "where I lived for a whole year in Dante's *Inferno.*"

Inside, the recently renovated museum presents sculptures, plaster casts, reproductions, originals, and sketches that reveal the freshness and vitality of a remarkable artist. You can almost see his works emerging from

The Thinker, at the Musée Rodin.

Tour Eiffel Bargain

The least expensive way to see the Tour Eiffel (www.tour-eiffel.fr) is to walk up the first two floors at a cost of 4.50€ adults, or 3.50€ ages 25 and younger. That way, you also avoid the long lines waiting for the elevator—although the views are less spectacular from this platform. If you dine at the tower's own **58 Tour Eiffel** ((✆ **01-45-55-20-04**), an Eiffel restaurant on the first floor, management allows patrons to cut to the head of the line.

marble into life. Everybody is attracted to *Le Baiser* (*The Kiss*), of which one critic wrote, "The passion is timeless." Upstairs are two versions of the celebrated and condemned *Nude of Balzac,* his bulky torso rising from a tree trunk (Albert E. Elsen commented on the "glorious bulging" stomach). Included are many versions of his *Monument to Balzac* (a large one stands in the garden), Rodin's last major work. Other significant sculptures are the soaring *Prodigal Son; The Crouching Woman* (the "embodiment of despair"); and *The Age of Bronze,* an 1876 study of a nude man modeled after a Belgian soldier. (Rodin was falsely accused of making a cast from a living model.) Generally overlooked is a room devoted to Rodin's mistress, Camille Claudel, a towering artist in her own right. She was his pupil, model, and lover, and created such works as *Maturity, Clotho,* and the recently donated *The Waltz* and *The Gossips.* The little alley behind the Musée Rodin winds its way down to a pond with fountains, flower beds, and even sand pits for children. It's one of the most idyllic hidden spots in Paris.

In the Hôtel Biron, 79 rue de Varenne, 7e. www.musee-rodin.fr. (✆ **01-44-18-61-10.** Admission 7€ adults, 5€ ages 18–25, free for children 17 and younger. Apr–Sept Tues–Sun 9:30am–5:45pm; Oct–Mar Tues–Sun 10am–5:45pm. Métro: Varenne, Invalides, or St-Francois-Xavier.

Palais Bourbon/Assemblée Nationale ★ HISTORIC SITE   The French parliament's lower house, the Chamber of Deputies, meets at this 1722 mansion built by the duchesse de Bourbon, a daughter of Louis XIV. You can make reservations for one of two types of visits as early as 6 months in advance. Hour-long tours on art, architecture, and basic French government processes are given Monday, Friday, and Saturday. They're in French (in English with advance booking). You may also observe sessions of the National Assembly, held Tuesday afternoon and all day Wednesday and Thursday beginning at 9:30am. Remember, this is a working government building, and all visitors are subject to rigorous security checks.

33 quai d'Orsay, 7e. www.assemblee-nationale.fr. (✆ **01-40-63-64-08.** Free admission. Hours vary, so call ahead. Métro: Assemblée Nationale.

Tour Eiffel ★★★ ☺ MONUMENT   This is without doubt one of the most recognizable structures in the world. Weighing 7,000 tons, but exerting about the same pressure on the ground as an average-size person sitting in a chair, the wrought-iron tower wasn't meant to be permanent. Gustave-Alexandre Eiffel, the French engineer whose fame rested mainly on his iron bridges, built it for the 1889 Universal Exhibition. (Eiffel also designed the framework for the Statue of Liberty.) Praised by some and denounced by others (some called it a "giraffe," the "world's greatest lamppost," or the "iron monster"), the tower created as much controversy in the 1880s as I. M. Pei's glass pyramid at the Louvre did in the 1980s. What saved it from demolition was the advent of radio—as the tallest structure in Europe, it made a perfect spot to place a radio antenna.

The tower, including its antenna, is 317m (1,040 ft.) high. On a clear day you can see it from 65km (40 miles) away. An open-framework construction, the tower unlocked the almost unlimited possibilities of steel construction, paving the way for skyscrapers. Skeptics said it couldn't be built, and Eiffel actually wanted to make it soar higher. For years it remained the tallest man-made structure on earth, until skyscrapers like the Empire State Building surpassed it.

We could fill an entire page with tower statistics. (Its plans spanned 5,400 sq. m/58,000 sq. ft. of paper, and it contains 2.5 million rivets.) But forget the numbers. Just stand beneath the tower, and look straight up. It's like a rocket of steel lacework shooting into the sky.

Tour Eiffel.

After undergoing major renovations, the Eiffel Tower's first floor reopened in 2013 with entirely redeveloped public spaces including a new pavilion for visitor services, restaurants, and shops; a new entertaining and educational museum circuit; and two new attractions: a glass floor giving you a view plunging 57m (188 ft.) down to the ground, and an immersive, emotionally powerful film.

From December to February, it is possible to ice-skate inside the Eiffel Tower. Skating takes place on an observation deck 57m (188 ft.) above ground. The rectangular rink is a bit larger than an average tennis court, holding 80 skaters at once. Rink admission and skate rental are free, after you pay the initial entry fee below.

To get to **Le Jules Verne** (www.lejulesverne-paris.com; ✆ **01-45-55-61-44**), the Ducasse–owned fine dining restaurant on the second platform, take the private south foundation elevator. You can enjoy an aperitif in the piano bar and then take a seat at one of the dining room's tables, all of which provide an

TIME OUT AT the tower

To see the Eiffel Tower best, don't sprint—approach it gradually. We suggest taking the Métro to the Trocadéro stop and walking from the Palais de Chaillot to the Seine to get the full effect of the tower and its surroundings; then cross the Pont d'Iéna and head for the base, where you'll find elevators in two of the pillars—expect long lines. (When the tower is open, you can see the 1889 lift machinery in the east and west pillars.) You visit the tower in three stages: The first landing provides a view over the rooftops, as well as a cinema museum showing films, restaurants, and a bar. The second landing offers a panoramic look at the city. The third landing gives the most spectacular view; Eiffel's office has been re-created on this level, with wax figures depicting the engineer receiving Thomas Edison.

inspiring view. The menu changes seasonally, offering fish and meat dishes that range from filet of turbot with seaweed and buttered sea urchins to veal chops with truffled vegetables. Reservations are recommended.

Champ de Mars, 7e. www.tour-eiffel.fr. ℭ **01-44-11-23-23.** Admission to 2nd landing 8.20€ adults, 6.60€ ages 12–24, 4.10€ ages 4–11; admission to 3rd landing 13€ adults, 12€ ages 12–24, 9.30€ ages 4–11; admission for stairs to 2nd floor 4.70€ adults, 3.70€ ages 12–24, 3.20€ ages 4–11. Free admission for children 3 and under. Sept–May daily 9:30am–11:45pm; June–Aug daily 9am–12:45am. Sept–June stairs open only to 6:30pm. Métro: Trocadéro, Ecole Militaire, or Bir Hakeim. RER: Champ de Mars–Tour Eiffel.

Montparnasse & Southern Paris (14e & 15e)

For the "Lost Generation," life centered around the cafes of Montparnasse, at the border of the 6th and 14th arrondissements. Hangouts such as the **Dôme, Coupole, Rotonde,** and **Sélect** became legendary, as artists—especially American expats—turned their backs on touristy Montmartre. Picasso, Amedeo Modigliani, Man Ray, and Hemingway frequented this neighborhood, as did Fitzgerald when he was poor (when he was rich, you'd find him at the Ritz). William Faulkner, Archibald MacLeish, Joan Miró, James Joyce, Ford Madox Ford, and even Leon Trotsky spent time here. Today Montparnasse plays second fiddle to St-Germain-des-Prés, though the Jean Nouvel–designed **Fondation Cartier** remains a real stand out.

Cimetière du Montparnasse ★ CEMETERY In the shadow of the Tour Montparnasse, this debris-littered cemetery is a burial ground of yesterday's celebrities. A map to the left of the main gateway will direct you to the gravesite of its most famous couple, **Simone de Beauvoir** and **Jean-Paul Sartre.** Others resting here include **Samuel Beckett; Guy de Maupassant; Pierre Larousse** (famous for his dictionary); **Capt. Alfred Dreyfus;** auto tycoon **André Citroën;** sculptors **Ossip Zadkine** and **Constantin Brancusi;** actress **Jean Seberg;** composer **Camille Saint-Saëns;** photographer **Man Ray;** poet **Charles Baudelaire,** who wrote about "plunging into the abyss, Heaven or Hell;" and American intellectual and activist **Susan Sontag,** who was interred here in 2005.

3 bd. Edgar-Quinet, 14e. ℭ **01-44-10-86-50.** Mon–Fri 8am–6pm; Sat 8:30am–6pm; Sun 9am–6pm (closes at 5:30pm Nov–Mar). Métro: Edgar-Quinet.

Fondation Cartier ★★ MUSEUM This is a special place. The fine jeweler Cartier commissioned Pritzker Architecture Prize–winning architect Jean Nouvel to design a headquarters for its art foundation, and the result is an airy glass and steel structure. Once you enter the building—passing under a vertical plant wall—you will encounter a range of themed exhibitions from both French and international artists. The foundation is known for presenting art from stars better known for their success in other fields, like Patti Smith or David Lynch. There is also a wild-looking garden surrounding the building, which is a pleasure to walk though.

261 bd. Raspail, 14th. www.fondation.cartier.fr. ℭ **01-42-18-56-50.** Admission 9.50€ adults, 6.50€ students and seniors. Tues–Sun 11am–8pm (until 10pm Tues). Métro: Raspail

Les Catacombes ★ HISTORIC SITE Every year, about 50,000 visitors explore some 910m (2,986 ft.) of tunnel in these dank catacombs to look at 6 million ghoulishly arranged, skull-and-crossbones skeletons. First opened to the public in 1810, this "empire of the dead" is now illuminated with electric lights

KIKI DE MONTPARNASSE

One of the most notable characters in Montparnasse was **Kiki de Montparnasse** (born Alice Prin; 1901–1953). She was raised by her grandmother in Burgundy until her mother called her to Paris to work. Here she adopted her new name and iconic look (a bowl cut, black rimmed eyes, and red lips), and became a model and muse for the Montparnasse artists. She posed for artists including Amedeo Modigliani, Tsuguharu Foujita, and Alexander Calder. She was Man Ray's lover and favorite model in the early '20s—his famous "Violin d'Ingres" is, in fact, a photograph of Kiki, and you can see it at the Musée d'Art Moderne. (On display at the same museum is Calder's 1930 mobile named "Kiki de Montparnasse ou Masque.") She sang at the Jockey Club, and in 1936, she opened her own cabaret on rue Vavin known as *Chez Kiki* to locals. In her black hose and garters, she captivated dozens of men, among them Frederick Kohner, who went so far as to title his memoirs *Kiki of Montparnasse*. Kiki later wrote her own memoirs, with an introduction by Hemingway. Papa called her "a Queen," noting that it was "very different from being a lady."

over its entire length. In the Middle Ages, the catacombs were quarries, but by the end of the 18th century, overcrowded cemeteries were becoming a menace to public health. City officials decided to use the catacombs as a burial ground, and the bones of several million persons were transferred here. In 1830, the prefect of Paris closed the catacombs, considering them obscene and indecent. During World War II, the catacombs were the headquarters of the French Resistance.

1 place du Colonel Henri Rol-Tanguy, 14e. www.catacombes-de-paris.fr. (℃ **01-43-22-47-63.** Admission 8€ adults, 6€ seniors, 4€ ages 14–25, free for children 13 and younger. Tues–Sun 10am–5pm. Métro: Denfert-Rochereau.

Musée Bourdelle ★ 🏛 MUSEUM Here you can see works by Rodin's star pupil, Antoine Bourdelle (1861–1929), who became a celebrated artist in his own right. Along with changing exhibitions, the museum permanently displays the artist's drawings, paintings, and sculptures, and lets you wander through his studio, garden, and house. The original plaster casts of some of his greatest works are on display, but what's most notable here are the 21 studies of Beethoven. Though some of the exhibits are poorly captioned, you'll still feel the impact of his genius.

18 rue Antoine-Bourdelle, 15e. www.bourdelle. paris.fr. (℃ **01-49-54-73-73.** Free entry to the permanent collection; admission to the temporary exhibitions 7€ adults, 3.50€ ages 14–26, free for children 13 and younger. Tues–Sun 10am–6pm. Métro: Montparnasse-Bienvenüe.

Skulls in Les Catacombes.

Tour Montparnasse ☺ ARCHITECTURE   Completed in 1973 and rising 206m (676 ft.) above the skyline, the Tour Montparnasse was denounced by some as "bringing Manhattan to Paris." The city soon passed an ordinance outlawing any further structures of this size in the heart of Paris. Today, the modern tower houses an underground shopping mall, as well as much of the infrastructure for the Gare de Montparnasse rail station. You can ride an elevator up to the 56th floor (where you'll find a bar and restaurant) and then climb three flights to the roof terrace. The terrific view encompasses virtually every important Paris monument, including Sacré-Coeur, Notre-Dame, and La Défense.

33 av. de Maine, 15e. www.tourmontparnasse56.com. ✆ **01-45-38-52-56.** Admission 7€ adults, 4€ students, 3€ children 7–15. Free for children 6 and younger. Apr–Sept daily 9:30am–11:30pm, Oct–Mar daily 9:30am–10:30pm. Métro: Montparnasse-Bienvenüe.

BEYOND CENTRAL PARIS

With regular Métro, train, and bus service, it is easy to access the major attractions outside of Paris, like Basilique St-Denis and La Grande Arche de la Défense. For more attractions outside of Paris, see chapter 10.

Basilique St-Denis ★★ CHURCH   In the 12th century, Abbot Suger placed an inscription on the bronze doors here: "Marvel not at the gold and expense, but at the craftsmanship of the work." France's first Gothic building that can be precisely dated, St-Denis was constructed between 1137 and 1281 and was the "spiritual defender of the State" during the reign of Louis VI. The facade has a rose window and a crenellated parapet on the top similar to the fortifications of a castle. The stained-glass windows—in stunning mauve, purple, blue, and rose—were restored in the 19th century.

The first bishop of Paris, St. Denis became the patron saint of the monarchy, and royal burials began here in the 6th century and continued until the Revolution. The sculpture designed for the **tombs**—some two stories high—spans French artistic development from the Middle Ages to the Renaissance. (There are guided tours in French of the Carolingian-era crypt.) François I was entombed at St-Denis, and his funeral statue is nude, though he demurely covers himself with his hand. Other kings and queens here include Louis XII and Anne de Bretagne, as well as Henri II and Catherine de Medici. Revolutionaries

The Royal Heart of the Boy Who Would Be King

In a bizarre twist, following a Mass in 2004, the heart of the 10-year-old heir to the French throne, Louis XVII, was buried at **Saint-Denis Basilica,** near the graves of his parents, Marie Antoinette and Louis XVI. The heart was pickled, stolen, returned, and 2 centuries later, DNA tested. More than 2 centuries of rumor and legend surrounding the child's death were put to rest. Genetic testing has persuaded even the most cynical historians that the person who might have been the future Louis XVII never escaped prison. The boy died of tuberculosis in 1795, his body ravaged by tumors. The child's corpse was dumped into a common grave, but not before a doctor secretly carved out his heart and smuggled it out of prison in a handkerchief. The heart of the dead boy was compared with DNA of hair trimmed from Marie Antoinette during her childhood in Austria. It was a perfect match.

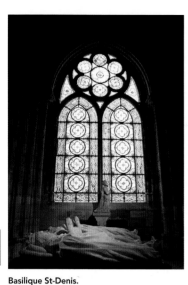

Basilique St-Denis.

La Grande Arche de La Défense.

stormed through the basilica during the Terror, smashing many marble faces and dumping royal remains in a lime-filled ditch in the garden. (These remains were reburied under the main altar during the 19th c.) Free organ concerts are given on Sundays at 11:15am.

1 rue de la Légion d'Honneur, St-Denis. http://saint-denis.monuments-nationaux.fr/en. ☎ **01-48-09-83-54.** Admission 7.50€ adults, 4.50€ seniors and students 18–25, free for children 17 and younger. Apr–Sept Mon–Sat 10am–6:15pm, Sun noon–6:15pm; Oct–Mar Mon–Sat 10am–5pm, Sun noon–5:15pm. Closed Jan 1, May 1, Dec 25. Métro: St-Denis.

An exhibit from Sèvres, Cité de la Céramique.

La Grande Arche de La Défense

MONUMENT The sprawling satellite suburb of La Défense was built as a dedicated business district over 3 decades from the late '50s, just outside Paris, across the river from the 16th arrondissement. La Grande Arche, a massive steel-and-masonry arch rising 35 stories, was designed as its architectural centerpiece and was inaugurated in 1989. It was built with the blessing of the late François Mitterrand and extends the magnificently engineered straight line linking the Louvre, the Arc de Triomphe du Carrousel (a monument between the Louvre and the Tuileries Gardens), the Champs-Élysées, the Arc de Triomphe, the Avenue de la Grande Armée, and the place du Porte Maillot. The arch is ringed with a circular avenue patterned after the one around the Arc de Triomphe. The monument is tall enough to shelter Notre-Dame beneath its heavily trussed canopy.

1 place du parvis de La Défense, Puteaux, 16e. www.grandearche.com. ✆ **01-49-07-27-27.** Métro: Grande Arche de la Défense.

Sèvres, Cité de la Céramique ★★ MUSEUM   Once endorsed and promoted by the mistresses of Louis XV, the historic French porcelain maker Sèvres continues to manufacture between 4,000 to 5,000 pieces every year. Of these, many are reserved as replacements for government and historical entities. As well as the porcelain factory (accessible by appointment only), this charming 19th-century site features a recently renovated museum displaying extraordinary collections of ceramic pieces sourced from all over the world and dating back as far as antiquity. The ceramics museum also demonstrates a serious commitment to contemporary design, with regular temporary exhibitions presenting the works of contemporary artists. The museum features a sales outlet for the porcelain manufactured inside. Located a short walk beyond the western edge of Paris's 16th arrondissement, in the suburb of Sèvres, the museum is just next door to one of Europe's most beautiful gardens, the Parc de Saint Cloud.

2 place de la Manufacture, 92310 Sévres. www.sevrescitederamique.fr. ✆ **01-46-29-22-10.** Admission 4.50€ adults, 3€ seniors, students and children; additional admission fee (varies) for temporary exhibitions. Mon–Sat 10am–5pm. Métro: Pont-de-Sèvres.

ESPECIALLY FOR KIDS

Paris is not always the easiest city to navigate with children, but kids will still love many of the museums, parks, and attractions the city has to offer. If you're staying on the Right Bank, take the children for a stroll through the **Jardin des Tuileries** (p. 78), where there are donkey rides, ice-cream stands, and a marionette show; at the circular pond, you can rent a toy boat. On the Left Bank, similar treats exist in the **Jardin du Luxembourg** (p. 128). After a visit to the Eiffel Tower, you can take the kids for a donkey ride in the **Champ de Mars.**

A Paris tradition, **puppet shows** are worth seeing for their colorful productions; they're a genuine French child's experience. At the Jardin du Luxembourg, or the Buttes Chaumont, puppets reenact plots set in Gothic castles and

Riding the carousel in the Jardin du Luxembourg.

A traditional puppet show.

The Montmartre *funiculaire*.

Oriental palaces; some critics say the best puppet shows are held in the Champ de Mars.

On Sunday afternoon, many French families head to the **Butte Montmartre** to bask in the fiesta atmosphere. You can join in: Take the Métro to Anvers, and walk to the *funiculaire* (the cable car that carries you up to Sacré-Coeur). When up top, follow the crowds to place du Tertre, where a Sergeant Pepper–style band will usually be blasting off-key and you can have the kids' pictures sketched by local artists. You can take in the views of Paris from the various vantage points and treat your children to ice cream. For a walking tour of Montmartre, see chapter 5.

Your kids may want to check out the Gallic versions of Mickey Mouse and his pals, so see chapter 10, "Side Trips from Paris," for **Disneyland Paris.**

Here is our list of top attractions that children will enjoy:

Basilique du Sacré-Coeur (p. 111)
Bois de Boulogne (p. 101)
Centre Pompidou (p. 90)
Cimetière du Père-Lachaise (p. 115)
Cité des Sciences et de l'Industrie (p. 117)
Gaîté Lyrique (p. 92)
Jardin d'Acclimatation (p. 103)
Jardin des Tuileries (p. 78)
Jardin du Luxembourg (p. 128)
La Promenade Plantée (p. 114)

The "Beach" of Paris

Relaxing under a palm tree on a chaise lounge sounds more Caribbean than Parisian, but a nearly 4.8km (3-mile) stretch of sandy shore opens along the Seine each summer. With the Eiffel Tower looming in the background, visitors and locals can enjoy the *plage* (beach), splash in fountains, swing in hammocks, play volleyball, or enjoy a picnic. Just don't go into the polluted water of the murky Seine.

Le 104 (p. 119)
Musée Carnavalet-Histoire de Paris (p. 93)
Musée de la Chasse et de la Nature (p. 95)
Musée des Arts et Métiers (p. 96)
Musée des Egouts de Paris (p. 135)
Musée du quai Branly (p. 137)
Musée National d'Histoire Naturelle (p. 125)
Musée Rodin (p. 138)
Palais de Tokyo (p. 108)
Parc de la Villette (p. 120)
Parc des Buttes Chaumont (p. 120)
Place des Vosges (p. 96)
Tour Eiffel (p. 139)
Tour Montparnasse (p. 143)

OUTDOOR PURSUITS

In addition to lazing about in a park or the terrace of your favorite cafe, there's actually quite a bit going on in outdoor Paris. Over the last decade, a somewhat more American approach to fitness has become popular, with more folks jogging and taking up gym memberships than ever before. Here are a few suggestions for getting out and exploring Paris's natural side.

Bicycling

Bicycling through the streets and parks of Paris, perhaps with a baguette tucked under your arm, might have become your fantasy after seeing your first Maurice Chevalier film. Luckily, in the last few years the city has become even more bike-friendly than ever before.

Biking in Paris.

In 2007 Mayor Bertrand Delanoë launched the **Vélib'** bicycle rental program, bringing 10,000 bikes into the city, placing them in specially built bike racks around high-pedestrian destinations. (The name Vélib' is a portmanteau of *vélo* for bicycle and *liberté* for freedom or liberty.) Today, there are more than 20,000 bicycles and more than 1,200 stations throughout Paris. Vélib' users have become ubiquitous around the city, biking at all hours of the day and night.

Buy a 1-day (1.70€) or 7-day (8€) short-term ticket *(abonnement courte durée)* at any Vélib' station. You will need a valid credit card with a microchip (in order to charge a temporary security deposit of 150€).

The bicycle can be used for free as long as it's returned to any of the Vélib' stations within 30 minutes of its rental. Afterward, you will be charged 1€ for every extra 30 minutes.

Bikes are one size fits all, with adjustable seats; children 13 and younger are not permitted to use the cycles. Maps showing the locations of Vélib' stations throughout Paris are available at the city hall in each of the 20 arrondissements. For more information, call ✆ **01-30-79-79-30,** or see www.velib.paris.fr.

Riding a bike around Paris is lovely, but for some well-informed commentary on what you're seeing, **Bike About Tours** (✆ **06-18-80-84-92;** www.bike abouttours.com) has a staff of friendly, knowledgeable, fluent-English speakers. The 3½-hour tours cost 30€ per person and includes helmet, bicycle, and insurance. All tours, which range from the big monuments to personalized "hidden Paris" adventures, leave from the statue of Charlemagne in front of Notre-Dame at 10am (and 3pm during the summer). You can also organize private tours and rent bikes at a reasonable 15€ per day rate. With small groups (12 people maximum) you won't get lost in the crowd, or worse, left behind in the often-confusing maze of boulevards.

Fitness Centers

You may be shocked to see Parisians taking cigarette breaks outside gym entrances, but the fitness trend has found a foot here and is moving toward a serious approach to *le gym.* Only the more expensive hotels usually offer onsite fitness centers, so hitting up the local gyms is a good way to get in your regular workout routine. The best options for short stays are local swimming pools, which often double as fitness centers *(espaces forme),* offering exercise bikes, cardio machines, and weights for 10€ per entry. **L'Espace Forme de la Butte aux Cailles,** 5 place Paul Vermaine, 13e (✆ **01-45-89-60-05;** Métro: Place d'Italie), is set inside one of the city's loveliest swimming pool centers (from the 1930s); here you'll find treadmills, exercise bikes, and other cardio machines. Another excellent option, off the tourist track, is **l'Espace Forme de Pailleron,** 32 rue Edouard Pailleron, 19e (✆ **01-40-40-27-70;** Métro: Bolivar or Jean-Jaurès). Aside from the standard gym offerings (bikes, treadmills, weights), there are also a sauna and an ice rink. **Club Med Gym** (www.clubmedgym.fr) is the largest and most popular chain of fitness centers in France. They have 21 clubs in Paris, which offer every conceivable kind of fitness, body-building, and cardio training machines, as well as squash courts. Two of their most central clubs are located at République (2 rue du Faubourg du Temple, 11e) and at Palais Royal (147 rue Saint-Honoré, 1er), and are open on Sundays. The rate to use the facilities is 26€ per day.

Ice-Skating

In the deep of winter (usually around Christmas to Feb), Paris officials always set up a free outdoor rink (not counting the 5€ for skate rental) in front of the **Hôtel de Ville** (see p. 92) in the 4th arrondissement (Métro: Hôtel-de-Ville). But you can don your blades the rest of the year too at two ice rinks *(patinoires):* The 800 sq. meter (8,611 sq. ft.) **Patinoire de Pailleron,** 32 rue Edouard Pailleron, 19e (ⓒ **01-40-40-27-70;** Métro: Bolivar or Jean-Jaurès); and the **Patinoire Sonia Henie,** entrance at Porte 28, 12e (ⓒ 01-40-02-60-60; www.bercy.fr/patinoire; Métro: Bercy), inside the behemoth Palais Omnisports Paris Bercy. Both rinks charge 4€–6€ entry, plus 4€ for skate rentals. Sonia Henie is open until 12:30am on Friday nights so also makes for a fun night out.

Jogging

The French say *le jogging,* and also *le footing,* although the latter is outmoded. Once pretty much ridiculed, the sport itself has gained quite a following in Paris recently. The most popular places for jogging include the **quays of the Seine** and **Jardin du Luxembourg.**

Some other lovely routes are the **Parc des Buttes Chaumont** and **Prom-enade Plantée ★**—the converted green rooftop of the old train trestle route. The entrance is just behind the opera house at Bastille along avenue Daumesnil, and continuing all the way to the Bois de Vincennes on the city's "green lung."

Other spots are the paths around the lakes in the **Bois de Boulogne** and the **Bois de Vincennes.**

Jogging in the Promenade Plantée.

Swimming

Paris offers some three dozen public swimming pools called *piscines.* They are found throughout the city, and a complete list of them is available at www.paris.fr/sport. Admission to any municipal pool is 3.10€; you can also purchase a *carnet* granting 10 visits for 25€.

Our favorite Right Bank pool is the vast 33m (108 ft.) **Piscine Edouard Pailleron ★★**, 32 rue Edouard Pailleron, 19e (ⓒ **01-40-40-27-70;** Métro: Bolivar or Jean-Jaurès). On the Left Bank, **St-Germain ★**, 12 rue Lobineau, 6e (ⓒ **01-56-81-25-40;** Métro: Mabillon or Odéon), in a modern underground space near Marché St-Germain, is a standout. The **Piscines de Pontoise,** 17 rue de Pontoise, 5e (ⓒ **01-55-42-77-88;** Métro: Maubert Mutualité), and **Butte aux Cailles,** 5 place Paul Verlaine, 13e (ⓒ **01-45-89-60-05;** Métro: Place d'Italie), both sport fabulous 1930s architecture. The **Piscine Josephine Baker** (ⓒ **01-56-61-96-50;** Métro: Quai de la

Gare) is a floating swimming pool docked on quai François Mauriac in the Seine (the water is not from the river)—you can actually watch the boats go by as you swim.

Tennis

There are 43 public tennis courts in Paris for recreational use. The courts in the **Jardin de Luxembourg** (6e; Métro: Saint-Placide) are particularly nice. There is also in the **Marais** at 5–7 rue Neuve-Saint-Pierre (4e; Métro: Saint Paul). The fee for an hour of play is 7.50€ in an open court, and 14€ for covered courts. *Note:* You will need to bring your own tennis equipment. More locations can be found at **www.paris.fr**.

SIGHTS & ATTRACTIONS BY THEME

Amusement Park

Jardin d'Acclimatation (p. 103)

Architecture

Tour Montparnasse (p. 143)

Cemetery

Cimetière de Montmartre (p. 112)
Cimetière de Passy (p. 102)
Cimetière du Montparnasse (p. 141)
Cimetière du Père-Lachaise (p. 115)
Cimetière St-Vincent (p. 113)

Cathedral

American Cathedral of the Holy Trinity (p. 97)
Cathédrale de Notre-Dame (p. 86)

Church

Basilique du Sacré-Coeur (p. 111)
Basilique St-Denis (p. 143)
La Madeleine (p. 104)
Panthéon (p. 126)
Sainte-Chapelle (p. 96)
St-Etienne-du-Mont (p. 127)
St-Eustache (p. 85)
St-Germain l'Auxerrois (p. 85)
St-Germain-des-Prés (p. 131)
St-Sulpice (p. 132)

Cultural Institution

Le 104 (p. 119)
Gaîté Lyrique (p. 92)

Garden

Jardin d'Acclimatation (p. 103)
Jardin des Tuileries (p. 78)
Jardin du Luxembourg (p. 128)
Palais Royal (p. 84)

Historic Site

Conciergerie (p. 91)
Grand Palais (p. 102)
Hôtel des Invalides/Napoleon's Tomb (p. 132)
Hôtel de Ville (p. 92)
Institut de France (p. 128)
Les Catacombes (p. 141)
Musée des Egouts de Paris (p. 135)
Palais Bourbon/Assemblée Nationale (p. 139)
Palais Royal (p. 84)
Petit Palais (p. 109)

Library

Bibliothèque Nationale de France, Site Tolbiac/François Mitterrand (p. 121)

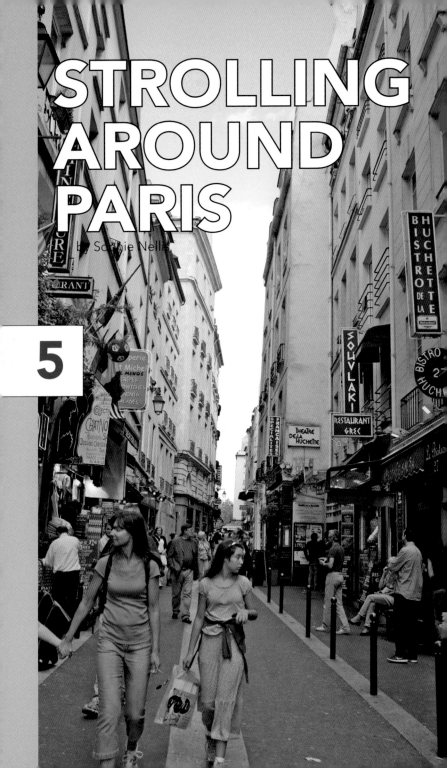

STROLLING AROUND PARIS

by Sophie Nellis

5

Aimlessly wandering around the city is an art in Paris—it's called *flânerie*. And those strollers who practice this art are known as *flâneurs*. The most famous Parisian *flâneur* was undoubtedly the 19th-century French poet Charles Baudelaire, and many of his poems were inspired by his aimless strolls through Paris. Despite vast improvements to public transport over the past 150 years, the best way to explore the city is still on foot. Walking will not only open your eyes to Paris's charm and beauty, but will enable you to discover the city's rich history. In this chapter we suggest three walking tours around different Parisian neighborhoods: Montmartre, the Marais, and the Latin Quarter.

For more walking tours see *Frommer's 24 Great Walks in Paris*.

WALKING TOUR 1: **MONTMARTRE**

START:	**Place des Abbesses (Métro: Abbesses).**
FINISH:	**Place Blanche (Métro: Blanche).**
TIME:	**2 hours (not including stops). It's a 3km (2-mile) trek.**
BEST TIME:	**During the day.**
WORST TIME:	**After dark.**

Known as much for its village-like atmosphere as for its monuments, Montmartre is one of the most picturesque areas in Paris. Its name has always been the subject of much disagreement. During the Gallo-Roman period, the hill (or *la butte* as the French like to call it) was known both as Mount Mercury and Mount Mars. However, it was Saint Denis, one of Paris's patron saints, who made the hill famous. Denis was the first bishop of Paris and he was beheaded by the Romans in Montmartre in A.D. 250. Legend has it that he miraculously picked up his head and carried it to the Paris suburb now known as Saint Denis. So another possible origin of the name is the Mount of Martyrs.

At the end of the 19th century, Montmartre was full of painters, writers, and musicians—all of whom were attracted by Montmartre's authentic atmosphere and cheap rents. The neighborhood soon gained a reputation for bohemia and creativity. Toulouse-Lautrec painted Montmartre as a district of cabarets, circus freaks, and prostitutes. This seedy side of Montmartre is still very much visible—the area between Place Blanche and Place Pigalle is full of sex shops, sex shows, and prostitutes.

Le Bateau-Lavoir.

1   Place des Abbesses

In 1134 King Louis *Le Gros* (the Fat) founded an abbey at the top of the hill. Place des Abbesses is named after the various abbesses who ran the abbey that was located in this square. They all came from wealthy, aristocratic families. During the French Revolution, the 46th abbess, Louise de Montmorency-Laval, who was 71 years old and both blind and deaf, was guillotined and the abbey was pillaged. Her crime? The elderly abbess was found guilty of "blindly and deafly plotting against the revolution."

Admire the beautiful Métro entrance at Abbesses. Designed by Hector Guimard in 1900, the Paris Métro is one of the rare examples of the Art Nouveau style found in the city. At 36m (118 ft.) underground, this is the deepest Métro station in Paris.

With your back to the Métro, turn right and cross place des Abbesses. Go along rue des Abbesses and turn up rue Ravignan, which leads to tree-studded place Emile-Goudeau. At no. 11bis–no. 13 is the:

2   Le Bateau-Lavoir (Boat Washhouse)

This building, known as the cradle of cubism, was given the nickname *Le Bateau-Lavoir* by the poet Max Jacob, who noticed a line of washing when he came here for the first time. The building was originally used to manufacture pianos but in 1889, 10 artists' studios were installed. Picasso lived at the Bateau-Lavoir from 1904 to 1912, and it was here that he painted *Les Demoiselles d'Avignon*, the painting that marked the beginning of Cubism. Other famous residents included Kees Van Dongen, Max Jacob, and Juan Gris. The city of Paris acquired the building in 1965 and it was classified as a historic monument, only to be destroyed by a fire in 1960. Reconstructed in 1978, it now houses 25 ateliers.

Continue up the hill along rue Ravignan. Turn left into place Jean-Baptiste Clément and go up the hill. Here rues Norvins, St-Rustique, and des Saules collide. Take rue Norvins and turn right down rue Poulbot. At no. 11 you come to:

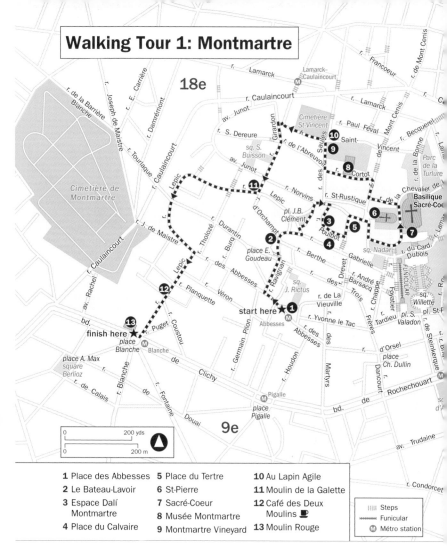

Walking Tour 1: Montmartre

18e

9e

1 Place des Abbesses	5 Place du Tertre	10 Au Lapin Agile
2 Le Bateau-Lavoir	6 St-Pierre	11 Moulin de la Galette
3 Espace Dalí Montmartre	7 Sacré-Coeur	12 Café des Deux Moulins
4 Place du Calvaire	8 Musée Montmartre	13 Moulin Rouge
	9 Montmartre Vineyard	

‖‖‖	Steps
⊪⊪⊪⊪	Funicular
Ⓜ	Métro station

3 Espace Dalí Montmartre

Salvador Dalí came to live in Montmartre in 1929. He was inspired by the windmills of Cervantes's *Don Quixote*, and he came to capture the windmills of Montmartre. In November 1956, Dalí undertook the first engraving of the Don Quixote series before the press in place Jean-Baptiste Clément. He used two rhino horns and some ink-dipped bread. The phantasmagoric world of **Espace Dalí Montmartre** (www.daliparis.com; ✆ **01-42-64-40-10**) features 300 original Dalí works, including this famous 1956 lithograph of Don Quixote. Open daily from 10am to 6pm.

An exhibit at Espace Dalí Montmartre.

Portrait artists on place du Tertre.

Rue Poulbot crosses the tiny:

4 Place du Calvaire

Place du Calvaire (Calvary Sq.) is believed to be named after a large cross that once stood here. This square offers a panoramic view of the rooftops of Paris, and the greenery on the steps of the rue du Calvaire is typical of the more rural side of Montmartre. The artist/painter/lithographer Maurice Neumont lived at no. 1 (a plaque is fixed to the door).

Turning your back on the view, walk along rue du Calvaire to:

5 Place du Tertre

The site of Montmartre's first town hall (built in 1890), this old square is always overflowing with tourists. Look out for **La Mère Catherine** at no. 6, one of the oldest restaurants in the square. It was here that the word *bistrot* was invented. On March 30, 1814, a group of Russian soldiers were eating here and demanded a drink, "bystro" (which means "quick" in Russian). Thus, *bistrot* came to refer to a restaurant where you could get a quick bite to eat. Since the late 19th century, place du Tertre has been associated with art and artists, and there are still a lot of street artists floating around. (You'll be asked countless times if you want your portrait sketched.) Despite its proximity to Sacré-Coeur, the square has lost a lot of its charm and can seem rather gaudy and inauthentic.

Turn right off the square on place Jean Marais to:

6 St-Pierre

Consecrated by Pope Eugène III in 1147, this church, along with St-Germain-des-Près, is one of Paris's oldest buildings. St-Pierre had two uses:

the eastern part was reserved for the Abbey of Montmartre, while the western part was a parish church. Thanks to this second, more community-oriented function, St-Pierre was spared destruction during the revolution. The current facade dates from 1775, and the three bronze doors that represent the three patron saints of the Church—Saint Pierre in the center, Our Lady on the right, and Saint Denis on the left—were added in 1980. The small cemetery next door is only open to the public on November 1.

Sacré-Coeur.

Leaving St-Pierre, turn left and then left again into rue Azaïs. Continue until:

7 Sacré-Coeur

The Roman-Byzantine style basilica marks the Paris skyline with its colossal proportions. Work began on the church in 1876 and it was finally consecrated in 1919. Despite pollution, the church remains white, thanks to the Souppes stone with which it was built. Resistant as granite, it exudes calcite when it comes into contact with rainwater. See p. 111.

Facing the basilica, take the street running along the left-hand side of the church (rue du Cardinal-Guibert); then turn left onto rue du Chevalier-de-la-Barre and right onto rue du Mont-Cenis. Continue along this street to rue Cortot, then turn left. At no. 12 is the:

8 Musée Montmartre

Musée Montmartre (© **01-49-25-89-37;** www.museedemontmartre.fr) presents a collection of mementos from the neighborhood, and retraces the history of the area from the Abbey through the Paris Commune and into the 20th century. Great artists such as Duffy, van Gogh, Renoir, and Suzanne Valadon and her son, Utrillo, occupied this house at the end of the 19th century, and it was here that Renoir put the final touches to his famous *Moulin de la Galette.* Open daily from 10am to 6pm.

From the museum turn right on rue Cortot. Make another right onto rue des Saules. On your right you'll see:

9 Montmartre Vineyard

The Benedictine Abbey that was founded in Montmartre in the 12th century encouraged the plantation of vines. Two centuries later they covered the hills of Montmartre, and wine remained one of this area's main sources of income until the 19th century. This vineyard was planted in 1933 to oppose construction that had been planned in the neighborhood. It produces gamay and pinot noir grape varieties and a grape-harvesting festival called *la Fête des Vendanges,* is held in Montmartre every October.

At the intersection of rue des Saules with rue St-Vincent is one of the most visited and photographed corners of **la butte.** Here, on one corner, sits the famous:

10 Au Lapin Agile

This village-like house opened as a cabaret in 1860. Owned by the Sals family, it was known as the Cabaret des Assassins. Madame Sals was an excellent cook, renowned for her *lapin gibelotte* (rabbit casserole). Around 1800, the satirical artist André Gill created a sign featuring a rabbit jumping out of a casserole dish,

A street performer in Montmartre.

brandishing a bottle of wine (you can see the original in the Musée Montmartre). The cabaret was given the name Le Lapin à Gill, after the artist, which gradually became **Au Lapin Agile.** All of the Montmartre artists used to come here to sing and play the guitar, including Picasso, Utrillo, Braque, Modigliani, Apollinaire, and Jacob.

Turn left on rue St-Vincent. At place Constantin-Pecqueur climb up the stairs. Go straight ahead along rue Girardon. At the junction with rue Lepic is the:

11 Moulin de la Galette

This windmill is known as the **Moulin Radet,** and is now part of a restaurant. Around the corner on rue Lepic is the **Moulin Blute Fin.** Built in the 17th century, these windmills were used to produce flour until the late 19th century, when they became dance halls. People came to sing, dance, and eat *galettes* (a type of crepe), and as a result each of the windmills became known as a Moulin de la Galette. It was the Blute-Fin that was immortalized in oil in Renoir's *Le Moulin de la Galette* (the painting is now in the Musée d'Orsay). Toulouse-Lautrec, van Gogh, Picasso, and Utrillo were also regulars at the dance halls.

Turn right onto rue Lepic (the Blute-Fin is opposite no. 88) and continue to no. 54. From 1886 to 1888, van Gogh lived here with his beloved brother, Theo. It was during this period that he first discovered Impressionism. Follow the street as it winds down the hill toward the boulevard.

12 Café des Deux Moulins

Most of the restaurants around place du Tertre are unabashed tourist traps. If you're looking for somewhere more authentic to eat and drink, head toward rue des Abbesses or rue Lepic, where there are a number of nice cafes and restaurants. Named after the two surviving windmills, the **Café des Deux Moulins,** 15 rue Lepic, 18e (✆ **01-42-54-90-50**), has charming 1950s decor, mirrored walls, and Art Deco details. It became a neighborhood icon when it featured in the 2001 film Amélie, starring Audrey Tautou. Serving traditional French food and open daily from 8am to 1am, this cafe is worth a visit.

Follow the street until it meets boulevard de Clichy. To the right is:

13 Moulin Rouge

Established in 1889, Le Moulin Rouge was named after the local windmills and the huge wooden windmill built above the entrance. The cabaret soon gained a reputation for highly provocative dancing, most notably the cancan. The Moulin Rouge was immortalized in the artwork of Toulouse-Lautrec, who painted the poster for opening of the season in 1891. It featured one of the cabaret's most famous dancers, Louise Weber, whose nickname was, strangely enough "La Goulue" ("The Glutton"). More recently the cabaret starred in Baz Luhrmann's 2001 film, Moulin Rouge. The windmill and the cancan are still here, but the rest has become an expensive, slick variety show with an emphasis on undraped women. See p. 275.

Moulin Rouge.

WALKING TOUR 2: **THE LATIN QUARTER**

START:	**Boulevard St-Michel (Métro: Cluny).**
FINISH:	**St-Étienne-du-Mont (nearest Métro: Cardinal Lemoine).**
TIME:	**1½ hours (not including stops). The distance is about 2km (1¼ miles).**
BEST TIME:	**Monday to Saturday from 11am to 11pm.**
WORST TIME:	**Sunday morning, when everybody else is asleep.**

One of the oldest areas of Paris, the 5th arrondissement was the heart of Roman Paris during the period in which France was under Roman control (from the 1st c. B.C. to the 5th c. A.D.). You can still see traces of this period as you walk around.

It became known as the Latin Quarter during the Middle Ages, when most of its residents were either students or clergymen who spoke Latin. Long associated with education and learning, it is here that you'll find the most famous branch of the Université de Paris, the Sorbonne, and the prestigious Collège de France. However, the revolutionary days of May '68 are long gone, and although the 5th has retained a certain degree of youthful charm and romance, parts of it have become very touristy.

1 Boulevard St-Michel

Nicknamed Boul' Mich by locals, this is the main street of the Latin Quarter. Opened in 1855, boulevard St-Michel was one of the first boulevards to be built under Baron Haussmann, the man responsible for the modernization and redevelopment of Paris in the 19th century. Haussmann wanted the city to be organized around a huge central crossroads, called *la grande croisée*, at the center of which was place du Châtelet. The rue de Rivoli was the east-west axis, boulevard Sebastopol the northern axis, and boulevard St-Michel achieved the southern leg. Just over a century later, the student uprisings of May '68 began here. The Latin Quarter was suddenly full of would-be revolutionaries, and residents witnessed violent clashes between protesters and police.

At the junction of boulevard St-Michel and boulevard St-Germain, head north, making sure you are on the left hand side of the boulevard, until you reach:

2 Place St-Michel

At the center of the place St-Michel is the huge fountain built by Gabriel Davioud in 1860, featuring a sculpture of Saint Michel slaying the dragon. Davioud, a contemporary of Haussmann, designed a great deal of street furniture and many landmark buildings in the 19th century, including the Théâtre du Châtelet and the Théâtre de la Ville just across the river at place du Châtelet. Since it was created, place St-Michel has witnessed several historic events. It was the scene of frequent skirmishes between the Germans and the Resistance in the summer of 1944, and there is a plaque dedicated to those who fought here in front of the fountain. Several decades later

Place St-Michel.

Walking Tour 2: The Latin Quarter

ÎLE DE LA CITÉ

LATIN QUARTER

5e

6e

4e

1e

1 Boulevard St-Michel
2 Place St-Michel
3 Rue de la Huchette
4 Rue du Chat-qui-Pêche
5 St-Séverin
6 St-Julien-le-Pauvre
7 La Fourmi Ailée ☕
8 Musée de Cluny
9 Sorbonne
10 Collège de France
11 Panthéon
12 St-Étienne-du-Mont

in 1988, the Espace Saint-Michel cinema (which you can see on the left of the square if you're facing the fountain) was burned down by Catholic extremists protesting the screening of Martin Scorsese's *The Last Temptation of Christ.* Today the square is a popular meeting place, and the square is often full of amateur breakdancers and street performers.

Cross boulevard St-Michel and go down:

3 Rue de la Huchette

This street is now one of the most touristy streets in Paris, and you should avoid the fast food and Greek-style restaurants down here. However, walking along this narrow street will give you an idea of what Paris looked like during the Middle Ages, when most Parisian streets were between 2 and 5m (6½–16 ft.) wide. Few streets like this one remain. At no. 23 is the tiny **Théâtre de la Huchette,** which is famous for having shown Eugène Ionesco's absurdist double bill of *The Lesson* and *The Bald Soprano* continuously since 1957. At no. 5 is the legendary jazz club **Caveau de la Huchette** (see p. 280). Established in 1946, this was the first club in Paris where jazz was played, and jazz legends such as Sidney Bechet and Lionel Hampton have played here.

Before you reach No. 5, branching off rue de la Huchette to your left is:

Rue de la Huchette.

4 Rue du Chat-qui-Pêche

This tiny alleyway is said to be the narrowest street in Paris, and also dates back to the Middle Ages. Before the *quai* was built, the Seine sometimes flooded the cellars of the houses, and legend has it that an enterprising cat took advantage of its good fortune and went fishing in the confines of the cellars—hence the street's name, which means "Street of the Cat Who Fishes."

Rue du Chat-qui-Pêche.

At the end of rue de la Huchette, turn right up rue du Petit Pont and continue to:

5 St-Séverin

Originally a hermits' cell (an isolated dwelling), the church of St-Séverin was built from 1210 to 1230 and reconstructed in 1448. Before entering, walk around the church to examine the gargoyles, birds of prey, and reptilian monsters projecting from its roof. These decorative features are typical characteristics of Flamboyant Gothic architecture. The bell tower is home to the oldest bell in Paris, which dates back to 1412, and next door is the city's only remaining charnel house, a place which houses the bones and bodies of the dead. Inside, you'll see an unusual pillar in the shape of a palm tree and seven modern stained-glass windows in the apse, designed by painter Jean Bazaine in 1966; these were inspired by the seven sacraments of the Catholic Church.

Where rue du Petit Pont becomes rue St-Jacques, cross over the street to rue Galande and look back over your shoulder at the spires of St-Séverin. Then turn back to the small church in front of you:

6 St-Julien-le-Pauvre

A chapel has stood on this spot since the 6th century, but the current church dates back to the 12th century. It was built a year after the birth of Gothic (1144), making it the oldest Gothic church in Paris. You can see remnants of an exterior wall, indicating that the church used to be larger than it is today. It's now owned by the followers of the Melchite Greek rite, a branch of the Byzantine church. St-Julien-le-Pauvre is known for putting on great classical concerts—if you're interested, there are posters near the door. The garden in front of the church has the best view of Notre-Dame and is home to the oldest tree in Paris; it's an acacia tree that was brought to Paris from Guyana in 1680 (it's fenced off and supported).

Continue along rue Galande and, if you fancy a break, turn left down rue du Fouarre to:

7 La Fourmi Ailée ☕

At no. 8 rue du Fouarre is **La Fourmi Ailée** (✆ **01-43-29-40-99**), a charming restaurant and tea room. Because it has clouds painted on the ceiling and books lining the walls, you're bound to leave here feeling calm, refreshed, and inspired. Open for lunch and dinner, and serving tea all day, La Fourmi Ailée serves typical French cuisine with a surprising number of good vegetarian options. Open daily noon to midnight.

As you leave the cafe, backtrack along rue du Fouarre, which turns into rue Danté. At the junction, turn right onto boulevard St-Germain (this means crossing over rue St-Jacques). Turn left on rue de Cluny until you come to place Paul Painlevé.

8 Musée de Cluny

Even if you're not particularly interested in medieval history and the origins of Paris, it's worth dropping into the Musée de Cluny to see the allegorical *The Lady and the Unicorn* tapestries and the remains of the Roman baths. See p. 125.

With the museum behind you, cross the square to rue des Écoles, where you'll see the main entrance to the Sorbonne. Don't forget to look back and admire the Musée de Cluny from afar.

9 Sorbonne

One of the most famous academic institutions in the world, the Sorbonne was founded in 1253 by Robert de Sorbon, St. Louis's confessor, as a theology college. By the next century it had become the most prestigious university in the West, attracting such professors as Thomas Aquinas and Roger

Bacon, and such students as Dante, Calvin, and Longfellow. Following May 1968, when the Sorbonne was occupied by rebellious students, the University of Paris was split up into different faculties located in different parts of Paris. The current building dates from the early 1900s, and if you look at the side of the building on rue St-Jacques, you can see the names of the different academic subjects inscribed above the windows.

The Chapel of the Sorbonne.

Turn left along rue des Écoles, then right up rue St-Jacques, which follows the line of an early Roman thoroughfare. On your left you'll pass:

10 Collège de France

In 1530, the humanist Guillaume Budé inspired Francois I to create a body of independent royal readers who were interested in subjects that were then ignored by the University of Paris, such as Hebrew, Greek, and mathematics. By the 18th century, the institution taught Sanskrit, Chinese, and Egyptology. In 1870 the Royal College became the Collège de France. Many eminent thinkers have taught there over the years, including Claude Lévi-Strauss, Roland Barthes, and Michel Foucault. Today, the college continues in the mission that inspired its creation in the 16th century: to disseminate emerging knowledge and remain independent of the university system.

Continue up rue St-Jacques. When you reach rue Soufflot, turn left. At the street's end is place du Panthéon:

11 Panthéon

Sitting atop Mont St-Geneviève, this former church is now a nonreligious mausoleum, and the final resting place of such distinguished figures as Hugo, Zola, Rousseau, Voltaire, and Curie. See p. 126.

Facing the Panthéon, walk around the left-hand side of the building until you come to place Ste-Geneviève. In front of you is:

12 St-Étienne-du-Mont

This church is home to a very elaborate shrine dedicated to Saint Geneviève, one of Paris's two patron saints. In 451, Attila the Hun was threatening

St-Étienne-du-Mont.

to enter Paris. The city's elders advised people to flee, but a young woman named Geneviève encouraged them to remain and fight. Miraculously, Attila chose not to come to Paris and Geneviève was credited with saving the city. This church also contains Paris's only rood screen (a fancy wooden screen that divides the chancel and the nave). The screen was used by priests to address the congregation but after the Council of Trent in 1563, priests were instructed to use the pulpit and most rood screens were removed. The church itself was built between 1518 and 1626, and is thus a curious mix of Gothic (the apse and the choir) and Renaissance architecture (the main portal with its columns and triangular pediment).

To get to Métro Cardinal Lemoine, go past the church along rue Clovis and turn left onto rue du Cardinal Lemoine.

WALKING TOUR 3: **THE MARAIS**

START:	**Hôtel de Ville (Métro: Hôtel de Ville).**
FINISH:	**Métro Saint Paul.**
TIME:	**2½ hours (not including stops). The walk is about 4km (2½ miles).**
BEST TIME:	**Every day, during the day. Sunday is a very popular day to visit the Marais.**
WORST TIME:	**Toward dusk, when shops and museums are closed and it's too dark to admire the architectural details. Also, Saturday is the Jewish Sabbath so the area around rue des Rosiers can be quite quiet.**

165

By the late 16th century, the marshy area east of the Louvre was the only part of central Paris that remained undeveloped. It was Henri IV who transformed the Marais (meaning marsh) into one of Paris's chicest neighborhoods. He commissioned the building of place des Vosges in 1605 and the success of the square made the Marais a fashionable area for the aristocracy and led to the construction of many *hôtels particuliers* (mansions) in the surrounding neighborhood. However, after Louis XIV moved his court to Versailles, and aristocrats fled France during the Revolution, the once-elegant *hôtels* fell into disrepair. In 1969, the Marais was the first district of Paris to be declared a historic district and this led to the restoration of its *hôtels*. They now house museums, archives, and libraries.

Today, the Marais (which covers the 3rd and 4th arrondissements) is home to great shops, bars and restaurants, and it's one of the few neighborhoods where shops are open on Sundays. It's long been a center for Paris's Jewish community and you'll find Jewish shops and businesses around rues des Rosiers, Pavée, and des Écouffes. More recently, it has become Paris's center of gay and lesbian life, particularly on rues St-Croix-de-la-Bretonnerie, des Archives, and Vieille-du-Temple.

1 Hôtel de Ville

In 1532, François I commissioned an Italian architect to build a prestigious town hall in the Renaissance style. However, due to the Wars of Religion the building wasn't finished until 1628. During the Paris Commune the Hôtel de Ville was set on fire and it burned for 8 days, destroying all the artworks, state registers, and archives inside. However, almost as soon as it

Hôtel de Ville.

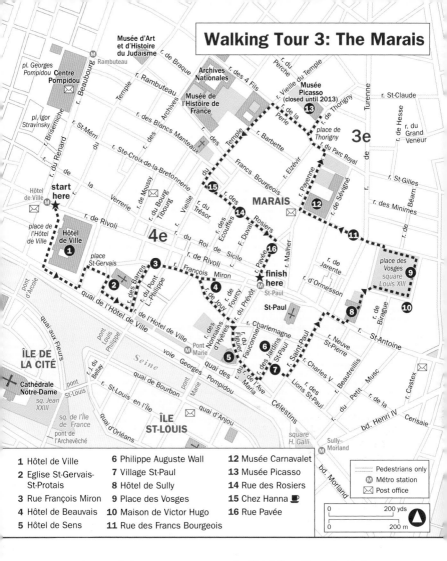

Walking Tour 3: The Marais

Musée d'Art et d'Histoire du Judaisme

pl. Georges Pompidou Centre Pompidou

pl. Igor Stravinsky

Archives Nationales

Musée de l'Histoire de France

Musée Picasso (closed until 2013)

place de Thorigny

3e

Hôtel de Ville
start here

place de l'Hôtel de Ville

Hôtel de Ville
1

MARAIS

4e

place St-Gervais

★ finish here

St-Paul

St-Paul

ÎLE DE LA CITÉ

Cathédrale Notre-Dame

place des Vosges square Louis XIII

ÎLE ST-LOUIS

1 Hôtel de Ville	**6** Philippe Auguste Wall	**12** Musée Carnavalet	
2 Eglise St-Gervais-St-Protais	**7** Village St-Paul	**13** Musée Picasso	
3 Rue François Miron	**8** Hôtel de Sully	**14** Rue des Rosiers	
4 Hôtel de Beauvais	**9** Place des Vosges	**15** Chez Hanna 🍽	
5 Hôtel de Sens	**10** Maison de Victor Hugo	**16** Rue Pavée	
	11 Rue des Francs Bourgeois		

Pedestrians only
Ⓜ Métro station
✉ Post office

0   200 yds
0   200 m

was destroyed, the new government—the Third Republic—decided to construct a newer, grander building with a reproduction of the Renaissance façade. The building you can see today was inaugurated on July 13, 1882, but it looks much the same as it would have in 1628. The facade is decorated with 378 works by 230 sculptors, including Rodin. During the summer there are often screenings of big sporting events in front of the Hôtel de Ville, and in the winter the square is home to Paris's most popular ice rink.

Facing Hôtel de Ville, go right. Turn left at the *quai* and walk along the river and then turn left again onto rue Lobau. On your right you'll come to place Saint Gervais:

2 Eglise St-Gervais-St-Protais

Named after the twins Gervais and Protais who were martyred in Milan under the rule of Emperor Nero, this is one of the oldest parishes on the Right Bank. The church was built in 1494 and typifies the late Gothic style. You'll see some of the Gothic features if you look at the windows and gargoyles on the right-hand side of the church. The facade, however, was added much later—in 1616—and is an example of early French classicism. On March 29, 1918, the church was hit by a German shell and 88 people were killed when the roof collapsed. This was the worst single incident involving a loss of civilian lives during the German bombardment of Paris in 1918.

To better admire the gothic parts of the St-Gervais, turn right down rue de Brosse and then left onto rue de l'Hôtel de Ville. When you reach rue des Barres turn left and you'll find yourself at the back of the church. Continue up the street until you reach rue François Miron. Turn right and walk along this street.

3 Rue François Miron

At **no. 11** and **no. 13** are two half-timbered houses that were built in the 14th century. No. 11 was known as the *Maison à l'enseigne du Faucheur* (the house with the sign of the reaper) and no. 13 was the *Maison à l'enseigne du Mouton* (the house with the sign of the sheep). These names refer to hand-painted signs, which would have been there in the 13th century, and were used to locate buildings before street signs and house numbers existed. Both buildings are perfect examples of gabled houses with their narrow facades, ground floors built from stone, and half-timbered upper stories, and they give us an insight into what Parisian houses would have looked like during the Middle Ages.

If you cross over to the other side of the street and continue until no. 68, you'll see the facade of the:

4 Hôtel de Beauvais

In the 13th century the Cistercian Abbey of Chaalis (Oise) used this building as a town house when the monks traveled to Paris. In 1654, Pierre de Beauvais and his wife Catherine-Henriette Bellier moved here, having commissioned an architect to build them a sumptuous *hôtel*. The *hôtel* was inaugurated on August 26, 1660, when Louis XIV and his new wife, Marie-Thérèse, entered Paris. Anne of Austria (Louis's mother), Cardinal Mazarin, and the Queen of England all stood on the balcony here to watch the procession as it came down rue François Miron. If the doors are open, go in and admire the courtyard.

From here you need to backtrack along the rue François Miron until you come to rue de Jouy. Turn left down this street and continue until you come to a junction. Cross over the street onto rue Charlemagne and turn right almost immediately onto rue du Figuier. At no.1 is:

Hôtel de Sens.

5 Hôtel de Sens

Now home to a public library, this building is one of only two civil buildings from the Middle Ages still standing in Paris (the other is the Hôtel de Cluny). Built between 1498 and 1507, it was here that the archbishops of Sens stayed when they came to Paris. One of the *hôtel's* most famous residents was Marguerite de Valois, whose life inspired Alexandre Dumas's 1845 novel *La Reine Margot*. Daughter of Henri II and Catherine de Medici, she married Henri de Navarre (who became Henri IV) in 1572. Their marriage was later annulled by the Pope and Henri IV married Marie de Medici in 1600. After a long exile, Marguerite de Valois returned to Paris in 1605 and lived in the Hôtel de Sens for a year. Known for her great beauty, she scandalized society by having numerous affairs with younger men. The gates of the **Bibliothèque Forney** (*©* **01-42-78-14-60**) are open Tuesday to Saturday 1 to 7pm.

At the junction of rue Figuier and rue du Fauconnier, cross rue du Fauconnier and go down rue de l'Ave Maria. Turn left onto rue des Jardins St-Paul. Behind the basketball courts is the:

6 Philippe Auguste Wall

An extraordinary piece of the Philippe Auguste Wall, which includes a small tower, has been conserved in the Marais. Before departing for the crusades in 1190, King Philippe Auguste wanted to assure that Paris was properly defended, so he ordered the construction of a wall around the city. Over the centuries the wall gradually expanded as Paris flourished. The old walls were torn down and new ones were constructed. The Philippe Auguste Wall was constructed with limestone dating from the Lutetian era (43–49 million years ago). At that time Paris had a tropical climate with palm trees, crocodiles, and exotic fish, and fossils of crustaceans and mollusks have been found in the stone.

Turn right into the courtyard at the green sign advertising the Village St-Paul:

7 Village St-Paul

Based around several adjoining courtyards, the Village St-Paul is a collection of small art galleries, quirky shops, and trendy cafes and restaurants. In the 1360s Charles V built himself a royal residence here, the Hôtel Saint-Pol. Charles believed that the *hôtel's* proximity to both the Bastille prison and the Philippe Auguste Wall would guarantee its security. This residence remained popular with the monarchy until the reign of François I, who couldn't bear the stench of the nearby sewers. The *hôtel* was abandoned in 1543. Today, this is one of the most peaceful corners of the Marais and a great place to wander around if you're looking for an unusual gift.

After you've explored, leave through the archway opposite to the one by which you entered. You'll come out onto rue St-Paul. Turn left up this street, admiring the variety of shops on your way. Look out for the English-language bookshop The Red Wheelbarrow at no. 22. Turn right onto rue Saint-Antoine. If you cross the road, at no.62 you'll see:

8 Hôtel de Sully

Designed by Jean Androuet du Cerceau in 1624, the Hôtel de Sully is typical of the late French Renaissance style. The Duc de Sully, Henri IV's minister of finance, bought the building in 1634. After a straight-laced life as the "accountant of France," Sully broke loose in his declining years, adorning himself with garish jewelry and a young bride who had a fondness for very young men. The *hôtel* was bought by the state in 1944 and is now home to the *Centre des Monuments Nationaux,* which preserves historic monuments across France. Open daily from 9am to 7pm.

The Hôtel de Sully has two courtyards. At the far-right corner of the second courtyard there is an arch (opening hours are the same as Hôtel de Sully) that leads to:

9 Place des Vosges

Commissioned by Henri IV in 1605, the square was unfinished when he died in 1610. It was inaugurated in 1612 for the double wedding of Louis XIII to Anne of Austria and Elisabeth of France (the king's sister) to the future Philippe IV of Spain—that's why there's a statue of Louis XIII hidden among the trees in the center of the square's formal garden. Place des Vosges was the first public square in Paris. Henri IV told his courtiers that they could come and build their houses around the square, but that they had to respect certain rules, such as using brick (which was, and still is, quite unusual in Paris). But the aristocrats wanted to cut corners and you'll notice that some of the arcaded pavilions are not made from brick but painted plaster. The square was named place Royale until the Revolution,

A room in the Maison de Victor Hugo.

when it became place d'Indivisibilité. In 1799 it was renamed place des Vosges after the *département* of Vosges that raised the most taxes for the revolutionary wars.

10 Maison de Victor Hugo

The square's most famous resident was undoubtedly Victor Hugo. Hugo lived at no. 6 from 1832 to 1848, when he went into voluntary exile on the Channel Islands after the rise of Napoleon III. It was here that he began his masterpiece *Les Misérables*. Hugo's former home is now a museum (www.musee-hugo.paris.fr; ℰ **01-42-72-10-16**) and literary shrine; see p. 93.

If you leave the place des Vosges by its northwest corner, you'll find yourself on:

11 Rue des Francs-Bourgeois

The rue des Francs-Bourgeois marks the border between the 3rd and 4th arrondissements. Jack Kerouac suggested that the name meant "street of the outspoken middle-classes" but it actually refers to the *francs bourgeois*— poor members of the bourgeoisie who were exempt from paying taxes. You won't find many poor people here today though, as the rue des Francs-Bourgeois is one of the chicest streets in the Marais, full of elegant boutiques and designer brands. Some of the shops have retained their original façades; check out the pretty "boulangerie" at no. 23.

After the junction with rue de Sévigné, continue along the rue des Francs-Bourgeois but peer through the gates of the building on the right and admire the gardens. This is the:

Musée Carnavalet.

12 Musée Carnavalet

This 16th-century mansion is the most important and well-known of all the Renaissance *hôtels* in the Marais. It is now a museum (http://carnavalet. paris.fr; *©* **01-44-59-58-58**) dedicated to the history of Paris and the French Revolution (p. 93). The entrance is on rue de Sévigné. Open Tuesday to Sunday from 10am to 6pm.

Turn right up rue Payenne and then left onto rue du Parc Royal. You'll come to place de Thorigny. If you turn right up rue Thorigny on your left you'll see:

13 Musée Picasso

The museum occupies the Hôtel Salé (*salé* means salty) and the name comes from the *hôtel's* first owner Pierre Aubert de Fontenay, who was responsible for collecting the salt tax. The museum is closed until summer 2013 for renovations so check on its status at the time of your visit (www. musee-picasso.fr; *©* **01-42-71-25-21**).

Backtrack along rue Thorigny, and turn right onto rue de la Perle. Turn left on rue Vieille du Temple. Cross the rue des Francs-Bourgeois, passing a covered market called the Marché des Blancs Manteaux on your left. Turn left into:

14 Rue des Rosiers

This street, which was named after the rosebushes planted in neighboring gardens, is one of the most popular streets of the Marais. It has been the historic heart of Jewish Paris since the 12th century, and you'll find an

Rue des Rosiers.

intriguing blend of Ashkenazi and Sephardic traditions. Here you'll see everything from Eastern European bakeries to North African falafel restaurants. Sephardic Jews from North Africa have sought refuge here since the end of WWII and the collapse of the French colonial empire. To a certain degree, they replenished Paris's Jewish population, a significant proportion of whom were rounded up by the Nazis and the French police and deported to concentration camps during WWII. Like many streets in the Marais, the rue des Rosiers has become quite a trendy place to shop in recent years and you'll find a number of nice boutiques here.

15 Falafel Break 🍽

The rue des Rosiers is famous for its delicious falafel. If it's summer, you can get falafel to go and continue your exploration of the Marais, pita bread in hand. But if you'd like to sit down, try **Chez Hanna** (54 rue des Rosiers; ☏ **01-42-74-74-99**). The menu is full of Jewish specialties, there's a friendly atmosphere, and the food is very reasonably priced. Open Tuesday to Sunday 11:30am to midnight.

At the end of rue des Rosiers, turn right onto rue Pavée.

16 Rue Pavée

This street dates from the Middle Ages. It got its current name in 1450 when it became one of the first streets to be paved over. At **no. 10** is the **Agoudas Hakehilos Synagogue,** built by Art Nouveau architect Hector Guimard (who was also responsible for designing the Paris Métro) in 1913. The building of this synagogue really tested Guimard's skills as an architect because he had to work with a piece of land measuring only 5m by 23m (16×75 ft.). To give the impression of a more ample facade, he built continuous pilasters (slightly projecting columns) and narrow windows.

Continue down the rue Pavée and you'll come to Métro St-Paul.

WHERE TO EAT

by Anna E. Brooke

Black-and-white–clad waiters dance around tables during service as glasses clink on zinc-topped bars, conversations rise to a gentle buzz, and fragrant air wafts from the kitchen into the noses of diners sipping chardonnay and fine bordeaux wines. This can only mean one thing: you're in Paris.

Whether you're looking for an opulent culinary experience or edgy, provocative cooking, Paris's culinary offerings are unmatched anywhere else in the world. The addition of French culinary traditions to UNESCO's world cultural heritage list in 2010 (celebrating France's talent for marrying food and wine, setting the table, and ordering the dishes from *apéritif* to *digéstif*), has given enduring impetus to many top chefs here too, encouraging them to experiment with new ideas and re-perfect the old ones. But you'll find far more than just French cuisine on the menus: France is a land of immigration and Paris the capital of that land, so influences from Asia, the Mediterranean, and North Africa are omnipresent, adding spice and exotic flavor to an already delicious national cuisine.

Although Paris has long been home to high-end gourmet restaurants, a growing number of affordable, high-end bistros serving gourmet food have entered Paris's culinary scene—this is the **bistronomy** movement. For more than a decade now, chefs who have trained under traditional three-star chefs have been leaving these "palace" restaurants to open more reasonably priced neo-bistrots, where you can get a three-course meal for about 30€ to 40€. Combining classic technique with an emphasis on fresh, seasonal ingredients, this new generation of chefs is revitalizing the culinary scene.

One important challenge remains, even at the informal bistro level: getting in. Paris's most coveted restaurants can be small in size, and they rarely offer multiple seatings during a lunch or dinner service, so to avoid disappointment, make sure you reserve in advance. You needn't worry about booking weeks ahead (except for a few we mention); the majority will have space the same day or a few days in advance. Ask your hotel concierge to help if you can't manage the telephone, but don't shy away from this step if you plan to release your inner foodie on your Paris visit. The quality of what you can "stumble in" and find, versus what you can experience when you reserve, can be radically different.

Finally, don't forget to sample the elixir of French cuisine: the wine. The pleasures of eating and drinking are rarely separated in France, and many Parisian establishments have world-class *cartes de vin* (wine lists), with waiters and sommeliers capable of matching the perfect wine with the dishes you have chosen. And be open-minded: the best wine for your cheese, for instance, might not be red, but white! Bon appétit!

best RESTAURANT BETS

○ **Best for Romance: Lasserre** (p. 193), with its over-the-top opulence and retractable ceiling, is an obvious setting for romance. A more affordable romantic option is **Nansouty** (p. 201), a modern bistro, tucked away in the 18th, with an open kitchen and an intimate atmosphere.

○ **Best for Families:** For kids who are tired of tasting new things, **Breakfast in America** (p. 213) and **Chibby's Diner** (p. 205) are havens of recognizable favorites like hamburgers, milkshakes, and all-day breakfast. Set inside the city's biggest park, **Rosa Bonheur** (p. 209) allows parents to sample various tapas on a large, outdoor terrace while their kids play in the park.

○ **Best Splurge: Passage 53** (p. 180), inside the city's oldest covered passage-way, is bursting with postcard charm—it also has delicious, yet modern, cuisine, and it just received its second Michelin star. Among the three-star Michelin splurges, we're most taken with **L'Arpège** (p. 220).

○ **Best Value:** Located just a few blocks from each other in the Marais, the **Breizh Café** (p. 188) and the **Café des Musées** (p. 186) are the places to go when you want to fill up on authentic French comfort food for under 20€ a head.

○ **Best Service:** Of all the lavish three-star restaurants in Paris, **Le Bristol** (p. 192) is widely thought to have the most warm and gracious service. On the other side of town, and the other end of the gastronomic spectrum, the res-taurant **Fish** (p. 216) is always a warm and friendly place to go, and the largely expatriate waitstaff are a great help for those who don't speak French.

○ **Best Classic Bistro:** In a city with so many excellent bistros, it's difficult to choose a favorite, but we'll narrow it down to **Le Regalade** (p. 223), **Le Bis-trot Paul Bert** (p. 204), and **Chez l'Ami Jean** (p. 221). Book in advance for any of these three.

○ **Best for Sunday Dinner:** Many restaurants in Paris are closed on Sundays, but **L'Atelier Saint-Germain de Joël Robuchon** (p. 220) is open every day of the year, and **Goumard** (p. 178), also open on Sundays, is a fun place to indulge in some fresh oysters.

○ **Best Steak Frites:** Run by a former butcher, **Le Severo** (p. 225) serves some of the city's best steak frites, along with *côtes de boeuf,* and other massive cuts of beef. **Le Relais de L'Entrecôte** (p. 217) is a fun dining option that serves multiple refills of steak and fries.

○ **Best for Young, Inventive Chefs:** The top restaurants for innovative and modern French cuisine are **Le Chateaubriand** (p. 203), **Frenchie** (p. 181), and **Septime** (p. 205). Book a few weeks in advance if you want a taste of what's new in Paris.

○ **Best for Wine Enthusiasts:** If what's in your glass is just as important as what's on the plate, we recommend a visit to **Le Verre Volé** (p. 208), **Les Papilles** (p. 212), **Vivant** (p. 209), **Le Chapeau Melon** (p. 208), or **Le Baratin** (p. 208)—all of these places take wine seriously.

PRICE CATEGORIES

Very Expensive	Main dishes 50€ and up
Expensive	Main dishes 30€–50€
Moderate	Main dishes 15€–30€
Inexpensive	Main dishes under 15€

THE RIGHT BANK

Les Halles, Louvre & Palais Royal (1er & 2e)

Les Halles takes its name from the soaring food pavilions that once stood on this spot as part of the city's largest outdoor market. That market, which writer Émile Zola famously nicknamed "the belly of Paris," has since moved to the suburbs, but Les Halles still has plenty of gourmet offerings today. Three of the city's most heralded newcomers—**Yam'Tcha, Spring,** and **La Régalade–St. Honoré**— have opened here in recent years. It's also the place to be for late-night dining opportunities (see p. 184). Just to the northwest, the 2nd arrondissement is another hotbed of restaurant activity. Sandwiched between the Louvre and Grands Boulevards you'll find Michelin stalwart **Le Grand Véfour** and the city's Japanese quarter along rue St-Anne. Here, foodies come from across the city to taste the freshly made gyoza and noodle soups—often even lining up in the street to get a table. You'll also find a sprinkling of excellent eateries, like **Passage 53,** inside the city's olde-worlde covered passages.

VERY EXPENSIVE

Le Grand Véfour TRADITIONAL FRENCH   Tucked inside the Palais Royal and boasting one of the most beautiful restaurant interiors in Paris, Le Grand Véfour remains a history-infused citadel of classic French cuisine. This restaurant has been around since the reign of Louis XV. Napoleon, Danton, Hugo, Colette, and Cocteau dined here—as the brass plaques on the tables testify—and it's still a gastronomic experience. Guy Martin, chef for the past decade, continues to serve the restaurant's signature dishes like Prince Rainier III pigeon and truffled oxtail parmentier alongside new dishes that feature more contemporary flavors like yuzu and tonka bean. Other specialties are noisettes of lamb with star anise, Breton lobster with fennel, and cabbage sorbet in dark-chocolate sauce. The desserts are always grand, such as the *gourmandises au chocolat* (medley of chocolate), served with chocolate sorbet.

17 rue de Beaujolais, 1er. www.grand-vefour.com. ℂ **01-42-96-56-27.** Reservations required far in advance. Main courses 75€–125€; fixed-price lunch 96€; fixed-price dinner 282€. AE, DC, MC, V. Mon–Fri 12:30–1:45pm and 8–9:30pm. Closed Aug 2–30. Métro: Louvre–Palais-Royal or Pyramides.

EXPENSIVE

Goumard SEAFOOD   Opened in 1872, this landmark is one of Paris's leading seafood restaurants, with much of its seafood arriving daily from Brittany. Seafood platters—laden with mussels, crabs, shrimp, and many different oysters— are a specialty here. Fresh fish, such as Dover sole with buttery potatoes, and roasted lobster with celery root purée and chestnut cream, are other delicious options. Meat has recently made it onto the menu too, notably succulent Black Angus steak and veal keftas (a type of meatball). The unusual restrooms, with commodes designed by Art Nouveau master cabinetmaker Majorelle, have been classified as a historic monument.

9 rue Duphot, 1er. www.goumard.com. ℂ **01-42-60-36-07.** Reservations required far in advance. Main courses 35€–56€; fixed-price menus 44€ and 54€. AE, DC, MC, V. Daily 11:30am–12:30am. Métro: Madeleine or Concorde.

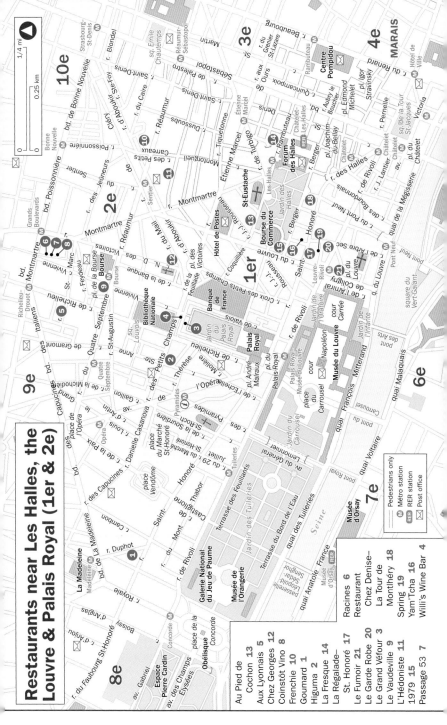

Restaurants near Les Halles, the Louvre & Palais Royal (1er & 2e)

8e

Au Pied de Cochon **13**
Aux Lyonnais **5**
Chez Georges **12**
Coinstôt Vino **8**
Frenchie **10**
Goumard **1**
Higuma **2**
La Fresque **14**
La Régalade–
    St. Honoré **17**
Le Fumoir **21**
Le Garde Robe **20**
Le Grand Véfour **3**
Le Vaudeville **9**
L'Hédoniste **11**
1979 **15**
Passage 53 **7**

Racines **6**
Restaurant
    Chez Denise–
    La Tour de
    Monthléry **18**
Spring **19**
Yam'Tcha **16**
Willi's Wine Bar **4**

179

Passage 53 ★★ MODERN FRENCH   After a stint at L'Astrance (p. 196), chef Shinichi Sato joined forces with famous butcher Hugo Desnoyer to open this petite restaurant inside the city's oldest covered passage. His cuisine has been so successful that it earned the restaurant two Michelin stars in 2011. Start with a splash of Champagne Jacquesson before diving into a tasting menu that might begin with pink cubes of raw veal topped with a bracing and briny raw oyster. Up next, you might be served some pristine fish or a *civet* (a type of stew) of wild hare served with chocolate sauce. Flavors are bold and clear, and the technical skill on display is impressive. End the meal with a delicious tart with the thinnest-possible pastry crust.

53 passage des Panoramas, 2e. www.passage53.com. ✆ **01-42-33-04-35.** Reservations recommended. Fixed-price lunch 60€; fixed-price dinner 110€. MC, V. Tues–Sat noon–2:30pm and 7–10pm. Métro: Grands Boulevards.

Spring ★★ MODERN FRENCH   This media-hyped restaurant was created by young American chef Daniel Rose. Spring initially opened in a remote Pigalle location, but after garnering rave reviews from French critics, Rose moved the restaurant to this space near the Louvre. Today, Spring has a 16th-century wine cave, an underground wine bar with vaulted ceilings, an open kitchen, and a sleek modern dining room. The fixed-price tasting menu is improvisational—it changes nearly every day—but it might begin with a little beignet of fried sole, followed by roasted pigeon or sweetbreads with wild mushrooms. Desserts might include a crustless lemon tart or berries floating in a tea made from the pit of a peach. The wine list is well chosen but it only offers a few moderately priced bottles. Spring also offers wine-tasting lessons on most Thursday afternoons (60€).

6 rue Bailleul, 1er. www.springparis.fr. ✆ **01-45-96-05-72.** Reservations required. Fixed-price dinner 58€–76€; fixed-price lunch 44€. MC, V. Wed–Fri noon–2pm and 7–10pm; Tues–Sat 7–10pm. Closed mid-Feb to early March. Métro: Louvre-Rivoli.

Yam'Tcha ★★★ MODERN FRENCH/CHINESE   A seat at this modern restaurant, on an ancient side street in Les Halles, is one of the city's most difficult to reserve. That has something to do with the small number of tables, but it is mostly due to the fact that Chef Adeline Grattard has received almost universal acclaim for her Franco-Chinese cooking. After spending time at the Michelin three-starred restaurant L'Astrance, Grattard set out on her own in 2009 and has been solidly booked ever since. The dishes on her prix-fixe menus reflect the seasons and change regularly; a recent menu included a flash-seared lobster with corn coulis, and a bouillon of beef with foie gras that one French critic called "the best dish of the year." Both wine and tea pairings (Yam'Tcha means "drink tea") are available. Reserve a month in advance for lunch and more than 3 months in advance for dinner.

4 rue Sauval, 1er. ✆ **01-40-26-08-07.** Reservations required far in advance. Fixed-price lunch 50€; fixed-price dinner 85€. AE, MC, V. Métro: Louvre-Rivoli.

MODERATE

Au Pied de Cochon TRADITIONAL FRENCH   Their famous onion soup and namesake specialty (grilled pigs' feet with béarnaise sauce) still lure visitors, and where else in Paris can you get such a good meal at 3am? Other specialties include a platter named after the medieval patron saint of sausage makers, *la* *temptation de St-Antoine,* which includes grilled pig's tail, pig's snout, and half a pig's foot, all served with béarnaise sauce, French fries and *andouillettes* (chitterling sausages). Two flavorful but less unusual dishes: a *jarret* (shin) of pork, caramelized in honey and served on a bed of sauerkraut, and grilled pork ribs with sage sauce. There are seafood platters too—packed with oysters, crab, and shrimp. And don't miss the Crêpes Suzettes, flamed with Grand Marnier.

6 rue Coquillière, 1er. www.pieddecochon.com. © **01-40-13-77-00.** Main courses 18€–50€. AE, DC, MC, V. Daily 24 hr. Métro: Les Halles or Louvre.

Aux Lyonnais LYONNAIS/TRADITIONAL FRENCH   The Belle Époque interior at this *bouchon* (a Lyon-style bistro) is undeniably charming and provides plenty of postcard appeal for the tourists who populate this restaurant. The kitchen, which is overseen but not frequented by star chef Alain Ducasse, does justice to Lyonnais classics like *quenelles de brochet* (fish dumplings with crayfish sauce), and *tablier de sapeur* (fried breaded tripe). Service, however, can be hurried and robotic—don't be surprised to see a bill slapped down before you've finished your first bite of soufflé.

32 rue St-Marc, 2e. www.auxlyonnais.com. © **01-42-96-65-04.** Reservations required. Main courses 20€–27€; fixed-price lunch menu 30€. AE, DC, MC, V. Tues–Fri noon–1:30pm and Tues–Sat 7:30–10pm. Métro: Grands-Boulevards.

Chez Georges TRADITIONAL FRENCH   This turn-of-the-century stalwart of traditional French cuisine used to be managed by three generations of the same family. It has recently changed ownership, but that hasn't dampened the restaurant's popularity, and it's still packed with businesspeople who come for their dose of *la cuisine bourgeoise* (comfort food) at lunchtime and after work. Waiters bring around bowls of appetizers, such as celery rémoulade, to get you started. You can follow with grilled turbot in a béarnaise sauce, cassoulet, or *pot-au-feu* (beef simmered with vegetables). The sweetbreads with morels and cream are always a delight.

1 rue du Mail, 2e. © **01-42-60-07-11.** Reservations required. Main courses 25€–37€. AE, MC, V. Mon–Fri noon–2pm and 7:30–10pm. Closed Aug. Métro: Bourse.

Coinstôt Vino WINE BAR   This cool wine bar occupies a corner spot in the historic passage des Panoramas—Paris's oldest covered passage, if not its prettiest. Stop here for a glass or bottle of "natural" wine—unfiltered and unsulfured—from Guillaume Duprés's eclectic wine list. The menu is made up mainly of small plates; you'll find everything from oysters in season to cheese and charcuterie. There are usually also a few hot dishes. There are tables and counter seats in the main room, as well as some seating out in the passage.

26 bis passage des Panoramas, 2e. http://coinstot-vino.com. © **01-44-82-08-54.** Reservations recommended. Main courses 15€–35€. MC, V. Mon noon–2pm; Tues–Fri 8.30am–midnight; Mon noon–midnight; Sat 6pm–midnight. Métro: Grands Boulevards.

Frenchie ★★ 🍽 MODERN FRENCH   Greg Marchand acquired the nickname Frenchie when he left his native France to work for Jamie Oliver in England and later at New York's Gramercy Tavern. In 2009, Marchand returned to Paris and opened up this tiny bistro in an unfashionable part of the Sentier. Word spread quickly about the delicious and wonderfully priced cuisine, and Frenchie began to win various "Best Bistro" awards and features in magazines. As a result, this simple place requires booking (at least) several months in advance. Marchand's cooking remains astonishingly good. Starters like house-smoked fish with pickled vegetables are bright and clean, and main dishes—like duck with blood orange and dandelion—manage to be both comforting and provocative. Desserts, like a cheesecake composed of *Brillat Savarin* (a delicious triple cream cheese), are never too sweet.

5 rue du Nil, 2e. www.frenchie-restaurant.com. ✆ **01-40-39-96-19.** Reservations required far in advance. Fixed-price dinner 34€–45€. MC, V. Mon–Fri 7–10:30pm. Métro: Sentier.

La Régalade–St. Honoré ★★ TRADITIONAL FRENCH/BISTRO It used to be that fans of the bistro La Régalade had to travel to the southern edge of the 14th arrondissement in order to enjoy the cooking of Bruno Doucet. Not anymore. In 2010, Doucet opened a second restaurant under the Régalade banner right on the rue Saint-Honoré. Now you can enjoy famously comforting dishes like sautéed morel mushrooms in cream with parsley and crispy croutons or farm-raised pork belly with a creamy interior and crispy skin. Just as at the restaurant down south, the same "help-yourself" crock of homemade pork terrine arrives with *cornichons* (gherkin pickles) and butter as you sit down to the table. Desserts, as you can imagine, are sometimes hard to face after all that pork fat, but they're included in the three-course prix fixe for a remarkable 32€—although note that some dishes come with supplementary charges.

123 rue Saint-Honoré, 1er. ✆ **01-42-21-92-40.** Reservations required. Fixed-price dinner 32€. MC, V. Mon–Wed noon–2:30pm and 7–10:30pm; Thurs–Fri noon–2:30pm and 7–11:30pm. Métro: Louvre-Rivoli.

Le Fumoir ★★ MODERN FRENCH With views onto the Louvre's eastern edge, this chic colonial-style restaurant, with a zinc bar and leather chesterfield armchairs, is a plum spot for escaping the tourists. Cocktails and coffee are served throughout the day, and at mealtimes inventive, affordable dishes are served to swarms of those in the know. The menu might include a starter of beef marinated in port wine, turnips, and salmon roe (an unusual combination, but it works); followed by pan-roasted cod with citrus and rosemary crust; and for dessert, blood-orange rice-pudding. The 22€ Sunday brunch menu is popular too: fruit juice, hot drinks, pancakes, poached eggs, and smoked ham or a juicy French steak with fries are on offer—and of course, there are those chesterfields for slumping into.

6 rue de l'Amiral Coligny, 1er. http://lefumoir.com. ✆ **01-42-92-00-24.** Reservations recommended. Main courses 20€–25€; 3-course fixed-price menu 35€. AE, DC, MC, V. Daily 11am-2am. Métro: Louvre-Rivoli.

Le Vaudeville BRASSERIE Adjacent to La Bourse (stock exchange), this brasserie retains its marble walls and Art Deco carvings from 1918. In summer, diners can eat on a terrace adorned with geraniums. The place is boisterous and informal, often welcoming groups of six or eight diners at a time. The roster of platters might include a salad of crayfish and asparagus points, grilled Dover sole, smoked salmon, sauerkraut, and grilled meats. Three dishes reign as enduring favorites: fresh grilled codfish with mashed potatoes and truffle juice, fresh *escalope* of warm foie gras with grapes or raspberries, and fresh pasta with morels. While the decor isn't quite as stunning as Bofinger (p. 186), Le Vaudeville is generally thought to have some of the best food among the surviving Paris brasseries.

29 rue Vivienne, 2e. www.vaudevilleparis.com. ☏ **01-40-20-04-62.** Reservations recommended in the evenings. Main courses 16€–30€; fixed-price menu 32€–50€. AE, DC, MC, V. Daily noon–3pm and 7pm–midnight. Métro: Bourse.

L'Hédoniste ★ 🎎 MODERN FRENCH   A French food writer and his wife opened this chic and gourmet address in 2010. The pair renovated a charming spot in the Sentier and brought in Sébastien Dubrulle to run the kitchen. Dubrulle's cooking can be both inventive (tandoori veal with gnocchi) and comforting (duck confit on a bed of whipped potatoes with toasted hazelnuts). The wine list is an important part of dining here, and although not extensive, it reflects the current demand among Parisians for natural (organic, unadulterated) wine and contains many reasonably priced bottles.

14 rue Léopold Bellan, 2e. www.lhedoniste.com. ☏ **01-40-26-87-33.** Reservations recommended. Main courses 23€–25€. Fixed-price lunch 24€. MC, V. Tues–Sat 12:30–2pm and 8–10pm. Métro: Sentier.

1979 MODERN FRENCH   In a gentrifying area between the Louvre and Etienne Marcel, 1979 (set in a former 1950's *cremerie*, or cream shop) draws a young crowd with the promise of innovative, tasty food and a laid-back atmosphere. Expect fusion dishes like beef laqué (sticky Asian-style beef) with oriental carrots and preserved lemons or succulent lamb with artichoke mash. This is also one of few Parisian restaurants to offer New World wines.

49 rue Berger, 1er. ☏ **01-40-41-08-78.** Main courses 17€–29€. MC, V. Mon–Fri noon–2pm, 8–11pm; Sat 8–11pm. Métro/RER: Les Halles.

Racines TRADITIONAL FRENCH   Fans of unadulterated wines come here to sip special bottles within the city's oldest covered passage and to enjoy the cooking of Nicolas Gauduin. This young chef, who has passed through the kitchens of l'Arpège and Laurent, selects fresh ingredients and cooks them with restraint. Be sure to book ahead, even at lunchtime, because its proximity to a lot of media headquarters makes Racines a popular hangout for journalists. Well, that, and the wine.

8 passage des Panoramas, 2e. ☏ **01-40-13-06-41.** Reservations recommended. Main courses 20€–35€. MC, V. Mon–Fri noon–2:30pm and 7–10:30pm. Métro: Grands Boulevards.

Restaurant Chez Denise, La Tour de Montlhéry ★★ TRADITIONAL FRENCH/BISTRO   Diners looking for the classic Paris bistro experience come to this raucous old dining room near Les Halles. Chez Denise (as the locals call it) stays open until the early hours of the morning and serves sturdy platters of *côte de boeuf* (a giant rib steak), grilled marrow bones, and brochettes of grilled meat so long they look like swords. The long-aproned waiters are used to encountering English speakers, but Chez Denise hasn't yet lost its bawdy, authentic local vibe. This might not be, however, the place to bring your vegetarian friend.

5 rue des Prouvaires, 1er. ☏ **01-42-36-21-82.** Reservations recommended. Main courses 22€–30€; fixed-price dinner 50€. MC, V. Mon–Fri noon–3pm and 7:30pm–4am. Closed July 15–Aug 15. Métro: Les Halles.

Willi's Wine Bar MODERN FRENCH/WINE BAR   With a name like Willi's Wine Bar and walls covered in wine posters by famous artists, you'd be forgiven for thinking that Willi's is all about the wine—but it isn't. While the wine list is outstanding, it's the food that takes center stage. Dishes, all prepared by Chef

François Yon, might include a starter of grouse filets with spiced nectarines, a main of Charolais beef in a parsley marinade, and a dessert of creamy panna cotta with raspberries. The cheeses come from Paris's acclaimed Fromagerie Quatrehomme, known for its pungent varieties, all married perfectly with Willi's wine, *bien sûr*. Make time after your meal for a stroll in the gardens of the Palais Royal.

13 rue des Petits Champs, 1er. http://williswinebar.com. *℗* **01-42-61-05-09.** Reservations recommended. Fixed-price lunch 21€–27€; fixed-price dinner 34€–37€. MC, V. Mon–Sat 7–11pm and Tues–Sat noon–3pm. Métro: Pyramide or Palais Royal.

INEXPENSIVE

Higuma ★ JAPANESE   This no-frills Japanese canteen in the Japanese quarter is always full, so get there early if you don't want to queue in the street at meal times. The reason behind its popularity is its quirky open kitchen, which fills the air with delicious-smelling steam, and the low prices—around 11€–13€ for a starter of gyoza (grilled dumplings filled with pork meat)—and its giant bowls of soup, rice, or noodles piled high with meat, seafood, of stir-fried vegetables. For some theater with your meal, arrive early and request a table at the bar surrounding the open kitchen. From your perch you can watch your food being cooked, and even dodge the steam and flames.

32bis rue St-Anne, 2e. *℗* **01-47-03-38-59.** Main courses 9€–14€. MC, V. Daily 11:30am–10pm. Métro: Pyramides.

La Fresque MODERN FRENCH   This cozy, atmospheric, centrally-located favorite is named for its frescoed walls, which have been restored despite a recent fire. The southwest French cuisine is served with a smile (and usually a cheeky joke) at unbeatable prices. While packed with business folk and shoppers at lunchtime, at night it draws a cooler crowd, ready to tuck into hearty dishes like rabbit pâté, duck leg in orange sauce, and chocolate mousse. There are vegetarian options too.

100 rue Rambuteau, 1er. *℗* **01-40-26-35-51.** Mains 17€; lunch menu 14€. MC, V. Lunch Mon–Sat; dinner daily. Métro: Les Halles. RER: Châtelet–Les Halles.

Le Garde Robe MODERN FRENCH/WINE BAR   In a quaint side street off rue de Rivoli in Châtelet, Le Garde Robe is a tiny wine bar with exposed stone walls and wine bottles lining the walls. Fans of French wine come for the large

---

Dining After Hours

When hunger strikes after hours try one of these restaurants in Les Halles. **Le Tambour,** 41 rue de Montmartre, 75002 (*℗* **01-42-33-06-90;** Metro: Les Halles), serves food like steak frites (mains 13€–18€) from noon to 4am every day in a dining room filled with kitschy Paris memorabilia. Nearby, **Au Pied de Cochon** (p. 180) is a lovely Belle Époque establishment open 24/7 with dishes for every budget. A full meal with fresh seafood or their famous pork dishes (practically every cut is used including the trotters) can cost up to 60€, but there are set menus for around 20€, and their piping hot French onion soup is legendarily restorative at 4am after a night on the town. For a late-night meat fix, head to **Chez Denise, La Tour de Montlhéry** (p. 183; open until 4am), where the steak is as juicy as it is huge.

selection of organic and biodynamic wines, which you can buy to take away; or if you decide to stay (which you will) corkage is 7€ extra. A laidback, suited crowd usually rolls up to the bar after work for a glass of red or white, accompanied by a *petit chèvre au pesto* (creamy goat cheese with pesto) or the excellent *croque robe* (a house take on traditional French *croque-monsieur*, with cheese, ham, and salad). For extra comfort (the bar stools can be awkward), reserve one of the tables in the back, then relax and enjoy the buzzy atmosphere.

41 rue de l'Arbre Sec, 1er. ✆ **01-49-26-90-60.** Reservations recommended. Main courses 10€–16€; MC, V. Mon–Sat 7:30–11pm; Métro: Louvre Rivoli or Châtelet.

Le Marais, Ile St Louis & Ile de la Cité (3e & 4e)

The Marais is packed with contemporary art galleries and cutting-edge fashion boutiques, but our favorite restaurants in this neighborhood are utterly traditional, whether they're serving the city's best roast chicken (**L'Ami Louis**) or classic dishes from the Basque region (**Au Bascou**), Brittany (**the Breizh Café**), or Provence (**Chez Janou**). Any stroll through the historic Jewish quarter around the rue des Rosiers requires a stop at **L'As du Fallafel** for the beloved (and messy) falafel sandwich.

VERY EXPENSIVE

L'Ami Louis ♨ TRADITIONAL FRENCH   L'Ami Louis was one of Paris's most famous brasseries in the 1930s, thanks to its legendary French staples, like foie gras and roast chicken, served in copious portions, and its charming "brown gravy" decor. In more recent years, thanks to regular visits from celebrities and politicians, L'Ami Louis has become a bastion of conspicuous consumption. Prices are high—Louis boasts the most expensive roast chicken in Paris (78€)—and reservations are hard to come by without the help of a five-star concierge, but an experience it is, with a wealthy, old-school clientele and food that you can't fault even if it costs a fortune. By Bacchus, there's even an 850 bottle-strong wine list.

32 rue du Vertbois, 3e. ✆ **01-48-87-77-48.** Reservations required far in advance. Main courses 43€–130€. AE, DC, MC, V. Wed–Sun noon–1:30pm and 8–11:30pm. Métro: Temple.

EXPENSIVE

Benoit TRADITIONAL FRENCH   There's something weighty about this historical monument, lined with mirrors, zinc, and tiles; every mayor of Paris has dined here since the restaurant was founded in 1912. Today Benoit is owned by the Alain Ducasse group, which adds extra pizzazz to the traditional bistro fare. Crowd-pleasers include cassoulet (home-made sausage, duck, and white bean hot-pot), filet of sole, and *tête de veau* (head cheese) with a *ravigote* sauce. The three-course lunch menu is particularly good value. It might include pork with pumpkin gratin, black pudding (sausage), or apple chocolate tart. There are over 350 types of wine to go with your meal, so ask the sommelier for a helping hand.

20 rue St-Martin, 4e. www.benoit-paris.com. ✆ **01-42-72-25-76.** Reservations required. Main courses 24€–44€; fixed-price lunch 36€. AE, DC, MC, V. Daily noon–2pm and 7:30–10pm. Métro: Hôtel-de-Ville.

MODERATE

Au Bascou BASQUE   The succulent cuisine of France's "deep southwest" is the specialty here, where art objects, paintings, and tones of ocher celebrate the beauty of the region, and hanging clusters of pimentos add spice to the air. Try *pipérade basquaise* (a spicy omelet loaded with peppers and onions), pimentos stuffed with purée of codfish, and *axoa* (a stew of veal shoulder, peppers, and onions). Also noteworthy are the *soupions* (baby squid) sautéed with chorizo and duck breast with pan-fried foie-gras.

38 rue Réaumur, 3e. www.au-bascou.fr. ✆ **01-42-72-69-25.** Reservations recommended. Main courses 17€; fixed-price lunch menu 18€. AE, DC, MC, V. Mon–Fri noon–2pm and 7:30–10:30pm. Métro: Arts-et-Métiers.

Bofinger 🍺 ALSATIAN/BRASSERIE   Opened in the 1860s, Bofinger is the oldest Alsatian brasserie in town and still very much a part of the city's culinary scene. Its Belle Époque interior, resplendent with brass and stained glass, is stunning. Affiliated with La Coupole, Julien, and Brasserie Flo, the restaurant has updated its menu but retained the most popular traditional dishes, such as *choucroute* (sauerkraut and sausages) and *sole meunière* (sole in lemon butter sauce). Other popular items include foie gras pressed with artichoke and celery and fresh oysters in season.

5–7 rue de la Bastille, 4e. www.bofingerparis.com. ✆ **01-42-72-87-82.** Reservations recommended. Main courses 15€–35€; fixed-price menu 29€–31€. AE, DC, MC, V. Mon–Fri noon–3pm and 6:30pm–12am; Sat 12pm–3:30pm, 6:30pm–12:30am; Sun noon–12am. Métro: Bastille.

Café des Musées 🍴 TRADITIONAL FRENCH/BISTRO   Close to both the Picasso museum and the Musée Carnavalet, Café des Musées boasts a good location, good food, and good prices—a rare combination in any part of Paris, but particularly in the Marais. The menu offers honest renderings of bistro classics, such as house-made terrines, steak frites, and a raspberry *dacquoise* (layer cake) for dessert. It also serves unpretentious wines in a bustling corner spot that expands to the sidewalk when the weather permits. The lunch menu is particularly good value.

49 rue de Turenne, 3e. ✆ **01-42-72-96-17.** Reservations recommended. Main courses 18€–35€; fixed-price lunch 14€. MC, V. Daily noon–3pm and 7–11pm. Métro: St. Paul.

Chez Janou PROVENÇAL/BISTRO   On one of the 17th-century streets behind place des Vosges, overlooked by magnolia trees, a pair of cramped but cozy dining rooms filled with memorabilia from Provence make up this loud and somewhat raucous bistro. The service is brusque and sometimes hectic, and chances are you'll be asked to wait for your table at the bar; but the sunny food, such as ratatouille and duck breast with rosemary, and boisterous clientele make for a fun and inexpensive night out. Start with a liquorice-flavored Pastis aperitif—there are over 80 to choose from, including a rather unusual violet–flavored Pastis.

2 rue Roger-Verlomme, 3e. www.chezjanou.com. ✆ **01-42-72-28-41.** Reservations recommended. Main courses 14€–20€; fixed-price lunch 16€. AE, MC, V. Daily noon–3pm and 7:30pm–midnight. Métro: Chemin Vert.

Jaja MODERN FRENCH/BISTRO   Tucked into a charming courtyard in the southern Marais, this bistro is coveted by the foodies and style hounds of the neighborhood. It's a place to be seen, sure, but also a place to eat well for not much money, especially at lunch. Jaja's take on the hot dog (an artisanal sausage topped with pungent cheese) and the croque-monsieur (ham and cheese grilled sandwich) are playful and delicious. Stick to the basics here, and wash them down with wine from Jaja's very well curated wine list.

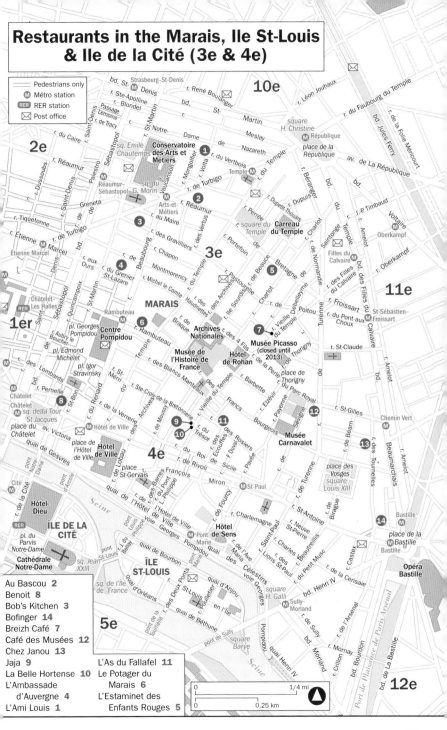

Restaurants in the Marais, Ile St-Louis & Ile de la Cité (3e & 4e)

Pedestrians only
Ⓜ Métro station
RER RER station
✉ Post office

Au Bascou **2**
Benoit **8**
Bob's Kitchen **3**
Bofinger **14**
Breizh Café **7**
Café des Musées **12**
Chez Janou **13**
Jaja **9**
La Belle Hortense **10**
L'Ambassade
    d'Auvergne **4**
L'Ami Louis **1**

L'As du Fallafel **11**
Le Potager du
    Marais **6**
L'Estaminet des
    Enfants Rouges **5**

3 rue Sainte-Croix-de-la-Bretonnerie, 4e. www.jaja-resto.com. ✆ **01-42-74-71-52.** Reservations recommended. Main courses 15€–23€; fixed-price lunch 16€. Mon–Sun noon–2:30pm and 8–11pm. Métro: Hotel de Ville.

L'Ambassade d'Auvergne AUVERGNAT/TRADITIONAL FRENCH   When you enter this rustic tavern through a bar that's heavy with oak beams, hanging hams, and ceramic plates, you feel immediately like you've been transported to the Auvergne. This homey restaurant showcases the culinary bounty of France's most isolated region, which produces some outstanding charcuterie and cheese. For mains, try the pork braised with cabbage, turnips, and white beans, or grilled tripe sausages with *aligot* (mashed potatoes and cantal cheese with garlic). Non-pork specialties might include pan-fried duck liver with gingerbread, perch steamed in verbena tea, or roasted rack of lamb with wild mushrooms.

22 rue de Grenier St-Lazare, 3e. www.ambassade-auvergne.com. ✆ **01-42-72-31-22.** Reservations recommended. Main courses 17€–23€; fixed-price menus at 28€. AE, MC, V. Daily noon–2pm and 7:30–10:30pm. Métro: Rambuteau.

INEXPENSIVE

Bob's Kitchen VEGETARIAN   Join the mix of *bobos*, fashion types, and Anglos at a communal table at this playful *bio* (organic) canteen for a refreshing, organic vegetarian lunch. Giant salads with greens and grains, a satisfyingly spicy veggie burger, curries, and soups are featured on the revolving menu. Pair it with a shot of wheatgrass or a freshly made smoothie. Go early on the weekends to avoid the brunch crunch.

74 rue des Gravilliers, 3e. www.bobsjuicebar.com. ✆ **09-52-55-11-66.** Reservations not required. Lunch 3.50€–8.50€. MC, V. Mon–Fri 8am–3pm; Sat–Sun 10am–4pm. Métro: Arts et Metiers.

Breizh Café ★ 🦋 CRÊPERIE   This popular spot in the Marais serves crepes like you've never had them before. Run by a Breton-Japanese couple, this warm and modern wood-paneled space that is decorated with funky Japanese art has friendly service and quality food. Start with oysters or go straight to a savory buckwheat *galette,* which is crisp and nutty and filled with high-quality organic ingredients, such as farm fresh eggs, Bordier butter, and seasonal produce. Sip on one of the artisanal ciders, and save room for a sweet crepe, drizzled with chocolate or salted butter caramel. Reservations highly recommended.

109 rue Vieille du Temple, 3e. www.breizhcafe.com. ✆ **01-42-72-13-77.** Reservations recommended. Main courses 5.50€–11€. MC, V. Wed–Sat noon–11pm; Sun noon–10pm. Métro: Filles du Calvaire.

L'As du Fallafel ★ FALAFEL/LIGHT FARE   You can distinguish the "king of falafel" from other pretenders on the street by the presence of a long line snaking away from the dark green shop front. Join the line (it moves fast) for a sandwich to go, or push through into one of two dining rooms and ask for a table. There are many options on the menu, including chicken shawarma and lamb kabobs, but you want the falafel sandwich. Stuffed with light and crispy balls of falafel (fried chickpeas) and topped with grilled eggplant and fresh salad, this really is one of the most delicious cheap bites in town. With a plate of fries to share and an Israeli beer, you can escape for less than 10€ per person. Note that L'As is closed Friday night and all day Saturday to honor the Jewish Sabbath.

34 rue des Rosiers, 4e. ✆ **01-48-87-63-60.** Reservations not accepted. Main courses 5€–16€. Sun–Thurs 11am–11:30pm; Fri 11am–5pm. Métro: St. Paul.

Paris's Gourmet Burger Food Truck: Le Camion Qui Fume

Pull out your smart phones and hook up to your Internet connection in order to find **Le Camion Qui Fume** ("the smoking truck"; www.lecamionquifume.com). This food truck drives to the rhythm of modern technology: The van's location is only disclosed via its website, Twitter, and Facebook, but when you find it, you're in for some of the best burgers in town, served on bread baked by a *boulanger* and accompanied by homemade fries and your choice of toppings, such as cheddar, mayo, BBQ sauce, or pickles; a burger and fries costs about 10€. For giant appetites, you can double your burger. There are vegetarian options too. **Tip:** During lunch time, the truck is frequently at Madeleine market on place de la Madeleine and at Porte Maillot.

Le Potager du Marais ★ VEGETARIAN   Arguably the best vegetarian restaurant in Paris, vegetarians flock to this place for its range of delicious organic offerings. Dishes are so tasty, even meat eaters won't complain. Many items are gluten-free. Your veggie meal might start with mushroom pâté, followed by tofu and pumpkin parmentier (pumpkin baked with mashed potato) seasoned with herbs and lentils, and finished with homemade apple compote. Just be prepared to get friendly with your neighbors: the restaurant is so narrow that the tables are packed in like sardines along just one wall.

22 rue Rambuteau, 3e. ℰ **01-42-74-24-66.** Entrees 9€–16€. MC, V. Daily noon–2pm and 7–10:30pm. Métro: Rambuteau.

L'Estaminet des Enfants Rouges TRADITIONAL FRENCH   Snuggled into a corner of the Marché des Enfants Rouge, Paris's oldest food market, this jovial joint makes for an atmospheric lunch, amid the hustle and bustle of stalls hawking hot Caribbean curries, sushi, and crêpes. Sidle up to the large *table d'hôte* (a single long wooden table to share with strangers) or grab a seat on the *terrasse*, which spills out into the market, and tuck into a lucious *tartine* (bread smothered in toppings like chicken, cheese, and caramelized onions), copious salads, or northern specialties like pigs trotters and black pudding—all from France's best butchers. Brunch is very popular on weekends; you can dine here too in the evening on weekdays if you opt for an early meal (L'Estaminet closes at 8pm). There's a wee boutique selling organic jams, honey, and mustards. *Parfait!*

39 rue de Bretagne, 3e. www.lestaminetdesenfantsrouges.com. ℰ **01-42-72-28-12.** Reservations not required. Tartines and salads 9€; fixed-price lunch 14€–19€; brunch 20€. MC, V. Tues–Sat 9am–8pm; Sun 9am–3pm. Closed Mon. Métro: Filles du Calvaire.

Champs-Élysées & Western Paris (8e, 16e & 17e)

The posh avenues that radiate from the Champs-Élysées are home to some of the most expensive and elegant dining in the city. If you're looking to splurge on a lavish gastronomic experience, this is the right neighborhood. Dress sharp and be ready to drop at least 100€ per head, unless you book a table at one of the few moderate tables like **Caïus, Le Hide,** or **La Fermette Marbeuf.**

Restaurants near the Champs-Élysées & Western Paris (8e, 16e & 17e)

17e

Palais des Congrès de Paris

place de la Porte Maillot

Porte Maillot

16e

← To Bois de Boulogne

CHAILLOT

Trocadéro

Palais de Chaillot

Jardins du Trocadéro

place de Varsovie

Cimetière de Passy

place de bd. Costa Rica

Champ de Mars-Tour Eiffel RER

Tour Eiffel

Arc de Triomphe

place Charles de Gaulle

Charles de Gaulle–Étoile RER

Charles de Gaulle–Étoile

place de la Porte Maillot

Ternes

place des Ternes

Courcelles

place Saint-Ferdinand

American Cathedral in Paris

Palais Galliera

Musée Guimet

Musée d'Art Moderne

Palais de Tokyo

Musée du Quai Branly

place de l'Alma

Pont de l'Alma RER

place de la Résistance

quai d'Orsay

7e

Seine

esplanade Habit

l'Université

190

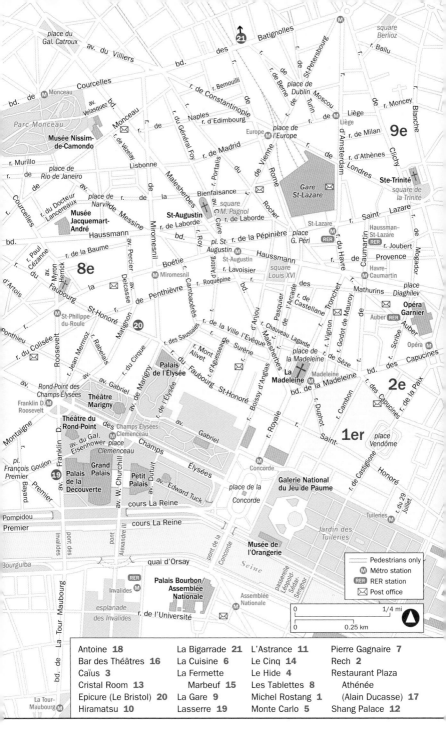

Antoine **18**	La Bigarrade **21**	L'Astrance **11**	Pierre Gagnaire **7**
Bar des Théâtres **16**	La Cuisine **6**	Le Cinq **14**	Rech **2**
Caïus **3**	La Fermette	Le Hide **4**	Restaurant Plaza
Cristal Room **13**	Marbeuf **15**	Les Tablettes **8**	Athénée
Epicure (Le Bristol) **20**	La Gare **9**	Michel Rostang **1**	(Alain Ducasse) **17**
Hiramatsu **10**	Lasserre **19**	Monte Carlo **5**	Shang Palace **12**

191

VERY EXPENSIVE

Antoine ★★ SEAFOOD   Seafood fans go wild for chef Mickaël Féval's perfect-every-time, innovative fish and shellfish dishes, which earned this restaurant its first Michelin star in 2011. The bouillabaisse is as good as any in Marseille, and the oysters come with tangy shallot vinegar and creamy salted butter for your bread. It's a handy address to have up your sleeve when you're exploring the Chaillot quarters, Champs-Élysées, and the Eiffel Tower. Come at night and you can just make out the Eiffel Tower sparkling through the trees on the other side of the river.

10 ave de New York, 16e. www.antoine-paris.fr. ℂ **01-40-70-19-28.** Main courses 50€–70€; fixed-price lunch 35€. MC, V. Daily noon–2pm and 7–10:30pm. Métro: Alma Marceau.

Epicure (Le Bristol) ★★ MODERN FRENCH   Inside one of the most lovely three-star dining rooms in Paris in the Bristol Hotel (p. 307), the cuisine of Chef Eric Frechon continues to delight even the most experienced gastronomes at Epicure. Frechon is particularly gifted with seafood, as evidenced by dishes such as sole stuffed with mushrooms and cooked in mussel jus, wild turbot served with a ravioli of pork lard and clams, and sea bass with oyster tartare. Another excellent dish is veal sweetbreads cooked in a tobacco leaf and served with a puree of anise-scented Jerusalem artichoke. Superb service and a strong wine list complete what is widely regarded as one of the best fine dining experiences in Paris.

112 rue Faubourg St. Honoré, 8e. www.lebristolparis.com. ℂ **01-53-43-43-40.** Reservations required. Main courses 65€–130€; fixed-price dinner 280€; fixed-price lunch 130€. AE, MC, V. Daily 12:30–2:30pm and 7–10:30pm. Métro: Miromesnil.

Hiramatsu TRADITIONAL FRENCH   Other than the fact that chef Hiroyuki Hiramatsu and most of his staff are Japanese, the only Asian touch at this restaurant is a hot, wet towel that arrives before the meal, in the Japanese style. Everything else is unabashedly French: the contemporary dining room, seating just 40, that's outfitted in mostly monochromatic tones of black and white; the rows of windows, each of which is set with shimmering panes of red-and-blue cut glass; and a polite staff wearing gray-and-white uniforms. Menu items change frequently, but are always artfully presented. Try pigeon breast with foie gras (flavored with strong coffee and cocoa), lobster with spinach wine sauce, or chops of veal with vegetables.

52 rue de Longchamps, 16e. www.hiramatsu.co.jp. ℂ **01-56-81-08-80.** Reservations required. Main courses 52€–112€; fixed-price lunch 45€ and fixed-price dinner 115€–130€. AE, DC, MC, V. Mon–Fri 12:30–1:30pm and 7:30–9:30pm. Métro: Trocadéro.

La Cuisine MODERN FRENCH   The latest addition to designer Philippe Starck's stable of dining rooms is La Cuisine, a restaurant inside the Royal Monceau-Raffles hotel (p. 307), one of the city's most talked-about palace hotels, and *très* popular with fashionistas. The room is eye-catching and busy, full of modern art and artful design touches like a "to-do" list scribbled on a lampshade. The cooking of Chef Laurent André is simple yet delicious and visually stunning—especially the "baroque" soft boiled egg with shrimp and porcini mushrooms and pan-fried scallops with celeriac and brown butter sauce. The consistently scrumptious desserts are all by Pierre Hermé, one of the most respected pastry chefs in Paris.

37 avenue Hoche, 8e. www.leroyalmonceau.com. ☎ **01-42-99-88-00.** Reservations recommended. Fixed-price dinner 90€–150€. Daily noon–10:30pm. Métro: Etoile.

Lasserre TRADITIONAL FRENCH   This elegant restaurant was a bistro
before World War II and has since become a legend. You have to take a lift to get
to the dining room, a tall, silk-draped, arch-windowed affair with tables set with
fine porcelain, silver knicknacks, and crystal candelabras. The ceiling is painted
with white clouds and a cerulean sky, but in good weather, the staff slides back
the roof to reveal the real sky. Audrey Hepburn and Marlene Dietrich once
graced these tables. Chef Christophe Moret, who previously worked under
Ducasse at the Plaza Athenée, is a master of taste and texture, and he's brought
renewed life to this swank citadel. Try the langoustines in a ginger-lime spiked
seafood bouillon, truffled sea bass, young pigeon stuffed with truffles and served
with turnips in lapsang-souchong tea, or the Brittany lobster with chestnut, salsify, and pumpkin. For dessert, try the roasted figs with olive oil and lime sorbet.
17 av. Franklin D. Roosevelt, 8e. www.restaurant-lasserre.com. ☎ **01-43-59-02-13.** Fax 01-45-63-
72-23. Reservations required in advance. Main courses 60€–95€; fixed-price lunch 80€; fixed-
price dinner 195€. AE, MC, V. Thurs–Fri noon–2pm; Mon–Sat 7:30–10pm. Closed Aug. Métro:
Franklin-D-Roosevelt.

Le Cinq ★★ MODERN FRENCH   Since it was established in 1928 in honor
of the king of England, there has always been a world-class dining venue associated with the Hotel George V. Today, the grand decor of this high-ceilinged room
evokes the Grand Trianon at Versailles. Critics have been lavishing Chef Eric
Briffard with praise, saying that he's a shoe-in to regain the restaurant's third
Michelin star. Briffard trained under both Joël Robuchon and Alain Ducasse and
cooks with precision and expertise. The menu changes frequently, but you may
start with something like abalone and razor clams with algae butter and fried
watercress, and move on to a main dish of venison with smoky bacon and a
chocolaty peppercorn sauce.
In the Four Seasons Hotel George V, 31 av. George V, 8e. www.fourseasons.com. ☎ **01-49-52-
71-54.** Reservations recommended 4 weeks in advance for dinner, 1 week in advance for lunch.
Main courses 80€–135€; fixed-price lunch 78€–160€; fixed-price dinner 160€–230€. AE, DC, MC,
V. Daily 12:30–2:30pm and 7–10:30pm. Métro: George V.

Les Tablettes ★ MODERN FRENCH/PROVENÇAL   Chef Jean-Louis
Nomicos left Lasserre (see above) to open Les Tablettes, a smart, modern restaurant where the menu is presented on an iPad (*tablette,* in French). Nomicos's
cooking has a modern edge, but is firmly based in the classic French tradition.
Loyalty to his Provençal roots is evident in dishes like sea scallops with bouillabaisse jus or filet of beef with black olives. The signature dish that has critics
raving, however, is a "royale" of sea urchin and fennel. The 58€ lunch menu,
which includes water, wine, and coffee, is a great introduction to fine dining in
Paris. It might include an entrée of poached egg with sweet-pumpkin soup and
truffle butter and Angus beef with pan-fried foie-gras that slices like butter.
16 av. Bugeaud, 16e. www.lestablettesjeanlouisnomicos.com. ☎ **01-56-28-16-16.** Reservations
recommended. Main courses 65€–165€; fixed-price dinner 140€; fixed-price lunch 58€. AE, MC,
V. Daily noon–2:30pm and 7:30–10:15pm. Métro: Victor Hugo.

Michel Rostang TRADITIONAL FRENCH   Michel Rostang is one of Paris's most renowned old-school chefs, the fifth generation of a distinguished

French "cooking family." His restaurant contains four dining rooms paneled in mahogany, cherrywood, or pearwood, some with frosted Lalique crystal panels. Changing every season, the menu offers modern improvements on *cuisine bourgeoise*. Truffles are the dish of choice in midwinter, and in spring you'll find racks of suckling lamb from the salt marshes of France's western coast; in autumn, look for pheasant, venison, and the infamous *lièvre* (wild hare)—Rostang is widely regarded as a master of wild game. Year-round staples include quail eggs with sea urchins, fricassee of sole, quenelles of whitefish with a lobster sauce, roasted scallops with chestnut gnocchi, or foie gras with roasted mandarins.

20 rue Rennequin, 17e. www.michelrostang.com. ✆ **01-47-63-40-77.** Reservations required 1 week in advance. Main courses 59€–98€; fixed-price lunch 78€; fixed-price dinner 169€. AE, DC, MC, V. Tues–Fri noon–2:30pm; Mon–Sat 7:30–10:30pm. Closed 3 weeks in Aug. Métro: Ternes.

Pierre Gagnaire ★★★ MODERN FRENCH Of all the three-star chefs working in Paris today, Gagnaire is by far the most playful and experimental. He spent years collaborating with molecular gastronomy pioneer Hervé This to create boundary-pushing dishes with unusual textures and forms. The menu changes regularly, but recent meals have featured lobster hidden under brightly colored blankets of vegetable gel, and raw clams on a bed of sweet and sour pumpkin. One tip if you plan to order a la carte: each *plat* is actually made up of four to five small dishes, so ordering both a starter and a main dish may yield more food than you could possibly eat. Perhaps it's not a bad thing that the desserts here are not as strong as you'll find at other three-star restaurants.

6 rue Balzac, 8e. www.pierre-gagnaire.com. ✆ **01-58-36-12-50.** Fax 01-58-36-12-51. Reservations required. Main courses 65€–165€; fixed-price lunch 105€; fixed-price dinner 265€. AE, DC, MC, V. Mon–Fri noon–1:30pm; Sun–Fri 7:30–10pm. Métro: George V.

Restaurant Plaza Athénée (Alain Ducasse) ★★ TRADITIONAL FRENCH This three-star restaurant bears the name of internationally renowned chef Alain Ducasse and serves as the flagship of his restaurant empire. The globe-trotting chef is rarely here himself, but he has left his kitchen in the capable hands of Christophe Saintagne. A special emphasis is placed on "rare and precious ingredients"; the chef whips up flavorful and very expensive combinations of caviar, lobster, crayfish, and truffles (both black and white). Dishes may include sea scallops with salsify and black truffles, duck liver "pot au feu," or sole meunière with Belgian endives. The wine list is superb, with selections deriving from the best vintages of France, Germany, Switzerland, Spain, California, and Italy. The dining room, designed by Patrick Jouin and featuring a jaw-dropping "deconstructed" chandelier, is among the most beautiful in Paris.

In the Hôtel Plaza Athénée, 25 av. Montaigne, 8e. www.alain-ducasse.com. ✆ **01-53-67-65-00.** Fax 01-53-67-65-12. Reservations required 4–6 weeks in advance. Main courses 90€–180€; fixed-price menu 260€–360€. AE, DC, MC, V. Thurs–Fri 12:45–2:15pm; Mon–Fri 7:45–10:15pm. Closed mid-July to Aug 25 and 10 days in late Dec. Métro: Alma-Marceau.

Shang Palace ★★★ CHINESE The palatial Hôtel Shangri-La (the former Palace of Roland Bonaparte, Napoleon's great nephew) is a veritable foodie heaven with no less than three fabulous, high-end eating opportunities. Our favorite is **Shang Palace,** the city's first-ever gourmet Cantonese restaurant serving the best dim sum and Peking duck in town in a beautiful dining room reminiscent of a 1930s Hong Kong gentleman's club. The 58€ lunch menu offers

Personalized Food Tours

Canadian Rosa Jackson is a self-declared foodie and an acclaimed food critic who shares her time between Paris and Nice. Through her company, **Edible Paris** (www.edible-paris.com), she concocts personalized food itineraries around the city. Whether you're into chocolate, cheese, bread, luxury restaurants, or all of these things, she provides you with routes to follow for a half-day, a whole day, or over 2 days. She can also set you up with your very own food guru— English-speaking restaurant critics, food writers, and professional cooks in Paris who spend their spare time sniffing out the very best food shops and restaurants to share with you during your break. These experiences cost 100€–350€.

a wide selection of gourmet dim sum and noodle dishes. The hotel's other restaurants—**L'Abeille,** which serves up French gastronomy in a magazine-perfect gray and yellow setting, and **La Bauhinia Brasserie,** which serves lip-smacking Chinese and French dishes—are both worth a visit if you have time (and money).

10 avenue Iéna, 16e. www.shangri-la.com. ℂ **01-53-67-19-98.** Reservations recommended. Main courses 22€–125€; fixed-price lunch from 58€; fixed-price dinner from 98€. AE, DC, MC, V. Daily 11:30am–2:30pm and 6:30–10:30pm. Métro: Iéna.

EXPENSIVE

Cristal Room MODERN FRENCH   The Taittinger family of champagne fame owns this Baccarat crystal–laden room in a former town house of the art patron Marie-Laure de Noailles. She was known as the benefactor of such artists as Man Ray and Salvador Dalí. For the new restaurant setting, Philippe Starck was called in to create the bling-bling decor (you climb a red carpet staircase encrusted with jewels to get to the restaurant), and the kitchen works under the direction of Guy Martin, who also oversees Le Grand Véfour (p. 178), putting out pleasing dishes such as crusty veal sweetbreads and filet of turbot with roasted fresh walnuts. After your meal visit the minuscule but lovely Baccarat museum in the former ballroom opposite the restaurant.

11 place des Etats-Unis, 16e. www.baccarat.com/en/the-world-of-baccarat/bars-restaurants/cristal-room.htm. ℂ **01-40-22-11-10.** Reservations required. Main courses 37€–45€; fixed-price lunch 29€–55€; fixed-price dinner 159€. AE, MC, V. Mon–Sat 12:15–2:15pm and 7:15–10:30pm. Métro: Boissière.

La Bigarrade MODERN FRENCH   The experimental cooking of Christophe Pelé has been described by some critics as "poetic" and "inspired." Your meal almost always starts with an amuse-bouche of *foccacia* made with fruity olive oil, then what comes next depends on the season and Pelé's mood. It might include juicy shrimp fried in whisky; duck with blackberries, almonds, and caviar; or a layered strawberry tart. The setting, out near the northern edge of the 17th, is inarguably pretty, and the service is kind and attentive. Book well in advance if you'd like to take a chance on one of the most challenging young chefs working in Paris today.

106 rue Nollet, 17e. www.bigarrade.fr. ℂ **01-42-26-01-02.** Reservations required. Fixed-price dinner 85€; fixed-price lunch 45€. Fixed seating times: Mon 8:30–9pm; Tues–Fri 12:30–1:30pm and 8:30–9pm. Métro: Brochant.

L'Astrance ★★★ MODERN FRENCH   This small and charming spot is owned by two former employees (some say "disciples") of megachef Alain Passard, scion of L'Arpège; Christophe Rohat supervises the dining room, while Pascal Barbot is a true culinary force in the kitchen. The menu changes seasonally, but might include an unusual form of "ravioli," wherein thin slices of avocado encase a filling of seasoned crabmeat, all of it accompanied by salted almonds and a splash of almond oil. Other delights to the palate include turbot flavored with lemon and ginger, or sautéed pigeon with potatoes au gratin. The signature dish is a galette of thinly sliced raw mushrooms and verjus-marinated foie gras with hazelnut oil and lemon confit.

4 rue Beethoven, 16e. ✆ **01-40-50-84-40.** Reservations required at least 1 month in advance. Main courses 24€–80€; fixed-price lunch 70€–120€; fixed-price dinner 125€–290€. AE, DC, MC, V. Fixed seating times: Tues–Fri 12:15–1:30pm and 8:15–9pm. Closed Aug. Métro: Passy.

Rech BRASSERIE/SEAFOOD   Chef Alain Ducasse has brought new life to this brasserie, founded in 1925, which today specializes in shellfish. The original Alsatian brasserie features have been retained, including the Art Deco furnishings—even the oyster shucker on the sidewalk. The previous owner, August Rech, believed in offering a limited but very select menu, and that tradition continues today. The specialty here is a gleaming platter of *fruits de mer*, but you can also order half a dozen different kinds of succulent fresh oysters. Poached skate wing appears with garlic and caper butter, and you can also order a grilled entrecôte with béarnaise sauce. For dessert, patrons order what might be the largest éclair served in Paris.

62 av. des Ternes, 17e. www.restaurant-rech.fr. ✆ **01-45-72-29-47.** Reservations required. Main courses 24€–45€; fixed-price lunch 32€; fixed-price dinner 54€. AE, DC, MC, V. Tues–Sat 12:30–2pm and 7:30–10pm. Closed Dec 24–Jan 5. Métro: Ternes.

MODERATE

Bar des Théâtres TRADITIONAL FRENCH   Its local patrons in the 8th arrondissement have long called this bar/restaurant "The Temple of the God Steak Tartare." It may have changed addresses (moving from avenue Montaigne to larger premises on rue Jean Goujon), but for those daring souls who still eat this blood-rare red meat specialty, this long-established restaurant is said to make the best dish. In the heart of the 8th arrondissement's theater district, many actors and musicians make this place their local haunt while working in the area. The chef also specializes in a delectable *magret de canard* (breast of duckling), and chateaubriand steak served with béarnaise sauce. You can also just pop in for snacks like cheese and cold meat platters.

44 rue Jean Goujon, 8e. http://bardestheatres.fr. ✆ **01-47-23-34-63.** Reservations recommended. Main courses 15€–23€. AE, DC, MC, V. Daily noon–1am. Closed Aug. Métro: Alma Marceau.

Caïus TRADITIONAL FRENCH   This chic place near the Arc de Triomphe, popular for business lunches and dinners, also draws well-heeled residents and visiting shoppers. The dining room is ringed with wood paneling, banquettes, and teakwood chairs and provides a showcase for Jean-Marc Notelet's comforting cuisine. Dishes like marinated and roasted sardines or sea bream with braised Belgian endives and root vegetables are evidence of Notelet's skill with seafood, but he's also good on dry land, serving a delicious confit of beef with fava beans and whipped celery root with almond milk. The 42€ tasting menu covers a wide selection from the menu and is a wonderful introduction to Notelet's cuisine.

6 rue d'Armaillé, 17e. www.caius-restaurant.fr. ☎ **01-42-27-19-20.** Reservations recommended. Main courses 19€–31€; fixed-price dinner 42€. AE, DC, MC, V. Mon–Fri noon–2pm and 7:30–10:30pm. Métro: Argentine.

La Fermette Marbeuf TRADITIONAL FRENCH   Just off the Champs-Élysées, there is something truly magical about this turn-of-the-century dining room famed for its splendid Art Nouveau conservatory, which was uncovered by accident during renovations in 1978. Families, business folk, and couples all come here to tuck into dishes like langoustine bisque perfumed with saffron, perfectly roasted lamb served with crunchy green beans and potato gratin, and an unsinkable Grand Marnier soufflé.

5 rue Marbeuf, 8e. www.fermettemarbeuf.com. ☎ **01-53-23-08-00.** Reservations recommended. Main courses 18€–39€; fixed-price lunch or dinner 48€. MC, V. Daily noon–3pm and 7–11:30pm. Métro: Alma Marceau.

La Gare MODERN FRENCH   Set in a former train station, La Gare is an über-trendy lounge, bar, and restaurant of monumental proportions: High ceilings, giant red brick walls, and a leafy terrace big enough for 185 people make this one of the biggest restaurants in Paris. An army of cooks creates tasty salads and traditional French dishes like *magret* (breast) of duck in mushroom sauce, and desserts like chocolate fondant (chocolate cake with a gooey center). The 300g (11 oz.) Angus steak is a house specialty, while the buffet brunch on Sundays reels in the locals. If you plan to make a night of it, stay for a drink after your meal. La Gare is open until 2am and the bartenders make superlative cocktails.

19 chaussée de la Muette, 16e. www.restaurantlagare.com. ☎ **01-42-15-15-31.** Fixed-price dinner 34€; fixed-price lunch 23€. MC, V. Daily 11am–2am. Métro: La Muette.

Le Hide ★ 👔 TRADITIONAL FRENCH   This bistro near the Eiffel Tower takes its name from chef Hide Kobayashi, who describes his food as French bistro cooking. The cuisine is certainly French, but a few of the recipes hint at his Japanese origins. Kobayashi perfected his craft in the kitchens of some of the world's greatest chefs, including Joël Robuchon. The menu changes regularly, and main courses, like fricassee of rabbit flavored with mustard or sweetbreads in cream with truffles, all carry the same price tag. In a neighborhood full of expensive and unmemorable restaurants, Le Hide is one of the best options for well-executed French bistro cuisine at an affordable price.

10 rue du General Lanrezac, 17e. www.lehide.fr. ☎ **01-45-74-15-81.** Reservations required. Main courses 16€; fixed-price menu 23€–30€. MC, V. Mon–Fri noon–3pm and Mon–Sat 7–10:30pm. Métro: Charles-de-Gaulle–Etoile.

INEXPENSIVE

Monte Carlo 👔 TRADITIONAL FRENCH   Local business types flock to this excellent self-service canteen at lunchtime for the quality 3-course menus—possibly the cheapest around the Champs-Élysées, starting at 11€. Being served over the counter probably isn't your dream dining experience for Paris, but the food is tasty, the staff friendly, and at these prices you simply can't complain. The dishes of the day (think *boeuf bourguignon* and *coq au vin*) are served with a choice of side dish—usually French fries, rice, or boiled vegetables. Desserts range from healthy yogurts to cream cakes. This is a top spot when you're on the run.

9 ave de Wagram, 17e. www.monte-carlo.fr. ℂ **01-43-80-02-20.** Reservations not accepted. Main courses 9€. MC, V. Daily 11am–11pm. Métro/RER: Charles-de-Gaulle Etoile.

Opéra & Grands Boulevards (9e)

This area, which stretches from the Opéra Garnier eastwards along the grand boulevards—Haussmann, Montmartre, and Bonne Nouvelle—is filled with good-value bistros and wine bars, often hidden down side streets. Recently, the Opéra Garnier saw the opening of its first-ever restaurant, the **Restaurant de l'Opéra,** a boldly modern affair nestled inside the former entrance for horse-drawn cariages.

EXPENSIVE

Restaurant de l'Opéra MODERN FRENCH   It took 5 years for director Pierre François Blanc to open the opera house's first ever restaurant—the building is so historically important that planning permission was almost impossible to obtain. However, it was worth the wait. Today's dining room is both edgy and beautiful. The bold, curvaceous red and white structure, designed by Odile Decq, fills the space without touching the Garnier's protected walls. Expect well-cooked, if not a little over-priced, dishes with prime ingredients like lobster, whiting, and sole, as well as guinea fowl and pata negra pork. End the night with a cocktail from the martini bar: Phantom (in reference to Leroux's 1910 Phantom of the Opera novel inspired by the Opéra Garnier) is the house special. You can also work your meal around a night at the ballet or opera in the adjoining opera house.

Palais Garnier, place Jacques-Rouché, 9e. www.opera-restaurant.fr. ℂ **01-42-68-86-80.** Reservations recommended. Main courses 26€–45€; fixed-price lunch 36€. MC, V. Daily noon–10pm. Métro: Opéra; RER Auber.

MODERATE

Casa Olympe PROVENÇAL/GREEK   Serious foodies make their way to the 9th to feast on the wares of an original cook. Olympe Versini earned a Michelin star at the age of 29 and dazzled some of the most discerning palates of *tout* Paris in Montparnasse before opening this unassuming 32-seat dining room. Critics love the earthiness of her cooking, which is evidenced in dishes such as duck ravioli bathed in a jus reduction or heavenly foie gras terrine brazenly studded with split vanilla beans. From head to hoof, Olympe serves most parts of the pig—and does so with gusto. Start your meal with an aperitif and some tapas, and then try her langoustine raviolio or her beef tenderloin with peppercorn sauce—one of the best versions of this time-honored dish.

48 rue St-Georges, 9e. www.casaolympe.com. ℂ **01-42-85-26-01.** Reservations required. Tapas 11€; fixed-price menu 45€. MC, V. Mon–Fri noon–2pm and 8–10:30pm; Sat 7:30–11pm. MC, V. Métro: St-Georges.

Chez Grenouille TRADITIONAL FRENCH   Chef Alexis Blanchard has won prizes for his terrines and boudins, so you'll find all manner of charcuterie on the menu here, plus dishes such as suckling pig with foie gras, duck parmentier, sweetbreads, oxtail, and pigs' feet, plus a fish dish or two for lighter eaters. It's true that the ambience leaves something to be desired; the main dining room

Restaurants near Opéra & Grands Boulevards (9e)

Casa Olympe **2**
Chartier **5**
Chez Grenouille **1**
Le Pantruche **3**
Restaurant de l'Opéra **6**
Wally Le Saharien **4**

is woefully outdated, and the room downstairs is even worse. But what's on the plate might be enough of a draw, at least for carnivores. Finish with the sinfully boozy baba au rhum for two.

52 rue Blanche, 9e. www.restaurant-chezgrenouille-paris.com. ✆ **01-42-81-34-07.** Reservations recommended. Main courses 20€–32€; fixed-price lunch Mon–Fri 25€. MC, V. Mon–Fri noon–3pm and 7–11pm; Sat 7–11pm. Métro: Trinité.

Le Pantruche ★ 🎫 TRADITIONAL FRENCH/BISTRO   From the moment it opened in early 2011, this modern bistro not far from Pigalle impressed critics with its friendly atmosphere, affordable prices, and better-than-average bistro fare. Dishes include a rich celery root soup, tender glazed beef cheeks, oyster tartare, and a classic Grand Marnier soufflé. Although it's dressed like a humble neighborhood joint, Franck Baranger's cooking puts Le Pantruche in another league altogether.

3 rue Victor Massé, 9e. http://lepantruche.com. ✆ **01-48-78-55-60.** Reservations recommended. Fixed-price dinner 32€; fixed-price lunch 17€. Mon–Fri noon–2:30pm and 7:15–10:30pm. Métro: Pigalle.

Wally Le Saharien MIDDLE EASTERN   Head to this dining room—lined with desert photos and tribal artifacts crafted from ceramics, wood, and weavings—for an insight into the spicy, slow-cooked cuisine that fueled the colonial expansion of France into North Africa. The prix-fixe dinner menu might begin with a trio of starters: spicy soup, stuffed and grilled sardines, and a savory pastilla of pigeon in puff pastry. Next comes any of several kinds of couscous or a *méchouia* (slow-cooked tart). Merguez, the cumin-laden spicy sausage of the North African world, factors importantly into any meal, as do homemade pastries.

36 rue Rodier, 9e. (☎) **01-42-85-51-90.** Reservations recommended. Main courses 20€–25€; fixed-price lunch 30€; fixed-price dinner 45€. MC, V. Tues–Sat noon–2pm and 7–10:30pm. Closed July. Métro: St-Georges or Anvers.

INEXPENSIVE

Chartier TRADITIONAL FRENCH/BRASSERIE   Opened in 1896, this unpretentious *fin-de-siècle* restaurant is now an official historic monument featuring a whimsical mural with trees, a flowering staircase, and an early depiction of an airplane (it was painted in 1929 by an artist who traded his work for food). The menu follows brasserie-style traditions, including items you might not dare to eat—beef tartare, chitterling sausages, tongue of beef with spicy sauce—as well as some classic temptations, like duck confit. The waiter will steer you through such dishes as *choucroute* (sauerkraut), *pavé* (a thick slice of rump steak), and at least five kinds of fish. High gastronomy this isn't, but you can't beat Chartier for a cheerful night on the cheap. Arrive early to avoid the queues.

7 rue du Faubourg Montmartre, 9e. www.restaurant-chartier.com. (☎) **01-47-70-86-29.** Main courses 9€–12€. AE, DC, MC, V. Daily 11:30am–10pm. Métro: Grands-Boulevards.

Pigalle & Montmartre (18e)

Montmartre today is home to a good number of reputable restaurants, including great finds like **Le Bal Café** and **La Table d'Eugène.** However, if you're looking for a good meal, avoid place du Tertre, where hopeful portrait artists sit waiting for tourists with their easels. Instead head to the northern side of the Butte around Lamarck-Caulincourt, where you'll find lovely low-key bistros like **Nansouty.**

MODERATE

Chéri Bibi ✦ TRADITIONAL FRENCH   Decorated with flea-market finds and featuring an affordable menu of classic French fare, Cheri Bibi has become the unofficial canteen for the young and artsy Montmartre crowd. The chalkboard menu includes rustic dishes like *boudin noir* (blood sausage), andouillette, head cheese, and steak frites. This might not be the place to bring a vegetarian friend. A crowd often gathers around the restaurant's zinc bar just to sip wine, sometimes spilling out onto the sidewalk that lies just below the eastern slope of the Sacre Coeur.

15 rue André del Sarte, 18e. (☎) **01-42-54-88-96.** Reservations recommended. Main courses 16€–35€; fixed-price dinner 22€–26€. MC, V. Mon–Sat 8pm–midnight (until 2am for the bar). Métro: Barbes-Rochechouart.

La Famille MODERN FRENCH   This Montmartre restaurant served as the launching pad for chef Inaki Aizpitarte, who has since moved on to Le Chateaubriand. The food at La Famille remains creative, but now relies more on gimmicks (dry ice, funny plating) than true gastronomic innovation. That doesn't

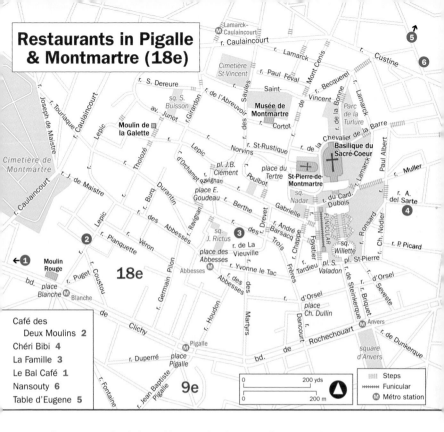

Restaurants in Pigalle & Montmartre (18e)

Café des Deux Moulins	**2**
Chéri Bibi	**4**
La Famille	**3**
Le Bal Café	**1**
Nansouty	**6**
Table d'Eugene	**5**

Steps ||||
Funicular
M Métro station

0   200 yds
0   200 m

much matter to the fashionable crowds who come for the cocktails (especially the mojitos) and sparkling scene. (They don't tend to eat much, anyway.) On the bright side, the short wine list is very solid and features small-scale organic producers like Foillard and Villemade.

41 rue des Trois Frères, 18e. ✆ **01-42-52-11-12.** Reservations required. Fixed-price menus at 30€ and 35€. MC, V. Tues–Sat 8–11:30pm. Métro: Abesses.

Nansouty ★ ▮ MODERN FRENCH   Just north of the Butte de Montmartre, Nansouty is an epicurean find, serving traditional French cuisine with a modern twist. Groups of friends tend to cluster at the large *table d'hôte* at the entrance, while couples make a beeline for the smaller tables nearest the semi-open kitchen at the back, where you can catch delicious odors wafting out of bubbling pots and sizzling frying pans. The menu changes with the seasons but a typical meal here might include pan-fried foie-gras with vegetable stew, côte de beouf, or a humongous rum baba (cake doused in rum and sugar) covered in cream. Nansouty is also about the wine, so tell the waiter your price range and he'll make suggestions to match your food.

35 rue Ramey, 18e. ✆ **01-42-52-58-87.** Reservations recommended. Main courses 16€–35€; fixed-price dinner 35€. MC, V. Mon–Sat noon–3pm and 7:30–11:30pm. Métro: Lamarck-Caulincourt or Château Rouge.

Table d'Eugene ★ 🎁🍴 TRADITIONAL FRENCH/BISTRO La Table d'Eugene opened in 2008 and has garnered a steady stream of praise, but the restaurant's location, far out in the untrendy part of northern Montmartre, ensures that it will continue to be overlooked by the tourist hordes. That's great news for anyone looking for an authentic bistro catering to a regular crowd of neighborhood locals. Expect slightly tweaked bistro fare such as crispy pigs' foot with shaved daikon radish and a balsamic reduction, risotto with wild mushrooms, and venison with red wine sauce and chestnuts.

18 rue Eugène Sue, 18e. ℂ **01-42-55-61-64.** Main courses 18€–30€; fixed-price dinner 35€; fixed-price lunch 18€. Tues–Sat noon–2:30pm and 7:30–10:30pm. Closed Aug. Métro: Marcadet-Poissonniers.

INEXPENSIVE

Le Bal Café ★ ENGLISH Brunch-loving Parisians have flipped for the traditional English breakfast that's served on the weekends here. Tucked inside a cultural center and photography museum near the place de Clichy, Le Bal Café is more than just eggs and bacon (and scones, kippers, and pancakes). The chef, who used to work at London's renowned Saint John restaurant, prepares an impressive array of modern British cuisine, with dishes like guinea hen with endives, lamb shoulder with carrots, and head cheese with prunes. The sturdy fare is complemented by a well-chosen and affordable wine list. Kill time waiting for your reservation by browsing the adjoining bookstore or taking in some of the wonderful photography exhibits at the center.

6 impasse de la Défense, 18e. www.le-bal.fr. ℂ **01-44-70-75-51.** Reservations not required. Main courses 5.50€–20€; brunch 12€. MC, V. Wed, Fri noon–8pm; Sat 11am–8pm; Sun 11am–7pm; Thurs 11am–10pm. Métro: Place de Clichy.

République, Bastille & Eastern Paris (11e & 12e)

With a mix of working-class families, hipsters, and *bobos*, the area between République and Nation is diverse, young, and fun. It's also one of the best food neighborhoods in the city, thanks to stand-out restaurants like **Le Chateaubriand, Le Bistrot Paul Bert,** and **La Gazzetta.** The atmosphere in these places is casual and buzzing, the waiters tend to be handsome and unshaved, and the wine is mostly natural. Don't let the informality trick you into believing that you don't need to book in advance or that prices will be low.

EXPENSIVE

Au Trou Gascon BISTRO Years ago, chef Alain Dutournier's parents mortgaged their Gascony inn to allow him to open a bistro in a lesser-known part of the 12th arrondissement. Word spread quickly about Dutournier's authentic cuisine moderne and his exciting cave containing several little-known wines along with a fabulous collection of Armagnacs. Foie gras and Gascony-cured ham make for great starters, and delicious main dishes include a hare stuffed with truffles and foie-gras, sautéed scallops with chestnuts, and cassoulet made with duck, pork, lamb, and sausage.

40 rue Taine, 12e. www.autrougascon.fr. ℂ **01-43-44-34-26.** Reservations recommended. Main courses 26€–42€; fixed-price lunch 40€; fixed-price dinner 60€. AE, DC, MC, V. Mon–Fri noon–2pm and 8–10pm. Closed Aug, and 6 days in Nov. Métro: Daumesnil.

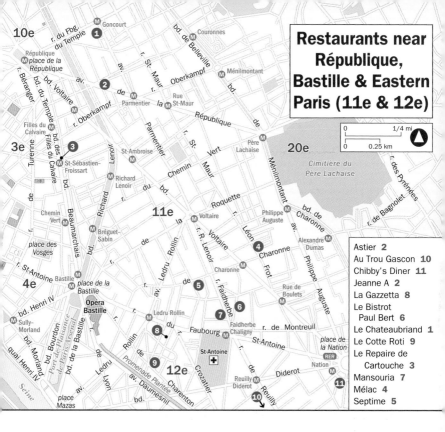

10e

r. du Fbg.
du Temple ① Goncourt Ⓜ

République
Ⓜ place de la
République

r. Béranger
bd. du Temple

av. ② Ⓜ
r. Oberkampf

bd. Voltaire

bd. de Belleville Ⓜ Couronnes

r. St. Maur

Oberkampf Ⓜ Ménilmontant

de Ⓜ
Parmentier la Ⓜ

Rue
St-Maur

République

Filles du
Calvaire

bd. des Filles du Calvaire

3e

r. Turenne

bd. des Filles du Calvaire

③ St-Sébastien-
Froissart

r. de

Chemin
Vert Ⓜ

place des
Vosges

r. St-Antoine Bastille Ⓜ

4e

bd. Henri IV

Ⓜ Sully-
Morland

bd. Bourdon

bd. Morland

quai Henri IV

Seine

place
Mazas

Ⓜ St-Ambroise

Richard
Lenoir Ⓜ

Beaumarchais

bd.

r. Richard Lenoir

Ⓜ Bréguet-
Sabin

place de la
Bastille

Opéra
Bastille

r. de la Bastille

Port de Plaisance
de Paris Arsenal

r. de Lyon

av. Daumesnil

Parmentier

r. St.
Maur

av. Parmentier

Chemin

r. du

Maur

r. Léon

bd.

Roquette

la Ⓜ Voltaire

de

av. Ledru Rollin

r. de la Roquette

r. R. Lenoir

r. de
Charonne Ⓜ

r. de Faidherbe

de

Ledru Rollin Ⓜ

du Faubourg

Rollin

de

Promenade Plantée

Charenton

Crozatier

Père
Lachaise Ⓜ

20e

Vert Ⓜ

Ménilmontant

Ⓜ Voltaire

Philippe
Auguste Ⓜ

④ Charonne

Léon Frot

Charonne Ⓜ

⑤

⑥

⑦ Faidherbe
Chaligny Ⓜ

St-Antoine

⑧ r. du Faubourg

St-Antoine
✚

⑨

12e

Reuilly Ⓜ
Diderot

⑩

Cimitière du
Père Lachaise

bd. de
Charonne

Alexandre
Dumas Ⓜ

av. Philippe Auguste

Rue de
Boulets Ⓜ

r. de Montreuil

St-Antoine

place de
la Nation

Nation Ⓜ

Diderot

Reuilly

Nation
RER

⑪

r. des Pyrénées

r. de Bagnolet

**Restaurants near
République,
Bastille & Eastern
Paris (11e & 12e)**

0		1/4 mi
0	0.25 km	

Astier **2**
Au Trou Gascon **10**
Chibby's Diner **11**
Jeanne A **2**
La Gazzetta **8**
Le Bistrot
  Paul Bert **6**
Le Chateaubriand **1**
Le Cotte Roti **9**
Le Repaire de
  Cartouche **3**
Mansouria **7**
Mélac **4**
Septime **5**

La Gazzetta ★★ MODERN FRENCH   Within one of the prettiest bistro settings in all of Paris, and just down the street from the bustling outdoor food market at Aligre, Chef Petter Nilsson is serving some of the city's most avant-garde cuisine. The beautiful Art Deco–inspired dining room, with its soft lighting, leafy palm trees, and dark polished wood, suggests a place serving classic bistro fare. But Nilsson's dishes are anything but traditional. A recent meal featured a soft poached egg floating in a broth of anise-scented cardoon that was spiked with briny mullet roe. That was followed by scallops roasted with beetroot and almonds, and seaweed scones served with Roquefort cheese and lemon caramel. For fans of experimental cooking, the seven-course tasting menu at 56€ is one the city's best values.

29 rue de Cotte, 12e. www.lagazzetta.fr. ✆ **01-43-47-47-05.** Reservations recommended. Fixed-price dinner 42€ and 56€; fixed-price lunch 17€. Tues–Sat noon–2pm and 8–11pm. Métro: Ledru-Rollin.

Le Chateaubriand ★★★ MODERN FRENCH   Chef Inaki Aizpitarte is the unofficial leader of France's neo-bistrot movement, and his restaurant, Le Chateaubriand, still receives superlative praise. Aizpitarte's regularly changing 55€ prix-fixe menu offers no choices, but open-minded diners are rewarded with some of the most innovative flavor pairings in Paris. You may try rare tuna slices in pink beet foam flavored with pomegranate seeds or eel flavored with orange juice and olive oil. Not every single plate is a winner, but usually at least three of four dishes tend to be brilliant. If you don't have a reservation, you can try to score a seat at the second seating, which begins around 10pm.

129 av. Parmentier, 11e. ℰ **01-43-57-45-95.** Reservations required. Fixed-price dinner 55€. AE, DC, MC, V. Tues–Sat 8–11:30pm. Métro: Goncourt.

MODERATE

Astier TRADITIONAL FRENCH/BISTRO   Open since 1956, old-fashioned Astier has managed to avoid becoming a relic thanks to Chef Christophe Kestler's thoughtful preparations of classics like wild boar terrine, rabbit rillettes, filet of sole, duck confit, roast chicken, and *tarte tatin* (apple tart), plus a legendary cheese tray. With red checked tablecloths, original woodwork and cafe curtains, it's a picture postcard version of a Paris bistro, without the surly waiters. The wine list is delectable too.

44 rue Jean-Pierre Timbaud, 11e. www.restaurant-astier.com. ℰ **01-43-57-16-35.** Reservations recommended. Fixed-price dinner 36€; fixed-price lunch 26€. MC, V. Daily 12:45–2:15pm and 7:30–10:30pm. Métro: Parmentier.

Le Bistrot Paul Bert ★★ BISTRO/TRADITIONAL FRENCH   Ask any local food writer to name his or her favorite classic bistros and there's a very good chance that you'll be directed here. The chalkboard menu is long and changes with the seasons, but a typical meal might begin with a plate of sunny-side up eggs with truffle cream and shaved black truffle, followed by one of the city's best steak frites (it's crowned with a glistening morsel of marrow), and ending with a generous slice of *tarte tatin* (apple tart) and its accompanying pitcher of thick crème fraîche. The decor is a jumble of wooden tables, cracked tile floors, flea market finds, and a polished zinc bar—exactly how you imagine a neighborhood bistro should be. The crowd is predominantly local, although the staff is used to dealing with the occasional food-minded traveler. The wine list features many unusual and affordable bottles from small wine producers.

18 rue Paul Bert, 11e. ℰ **01-43-72-24-01.** Reservations required. Mains 17€–25€; fixed-price dinner 34€. MC, V. Tues–Sat noon–2pm and 7:30–11pm. Métro: Faidherbe-Chaligny.

Le Cotte Roti BISTRO/MEDITERRANEAN   This neo-bistrot near the colorful marché Aligre is a great local's haunt with folk often popping in for a gourmet lunch, laden with shopping bags filled with Aligre's fresh market produce. There are some Mediterranean and Provençale dishes on the menu, such as an octopus salad or black risotto with clams, along with richer fare such as sweetbreads and pork belly on a bed of orzo. The mushroom lasagna is so delicious even die-hard meat-eaters might succumb. The name is a play on words between the address (on rue de Cotte) and the famous wine region (the Côte-Rôtie), which is well represented on the list.

1 rue de Cotte, 12e. ℰ **01-43-45-06-37.** Reservations recommended. Main courses 15€–35€. MC, V. Tues–Sat noon–2:30pm and 8–11pm. Métro: Ledru-Rollin.

Le Repaire de Cartouche TRADITIONAL FRENCH   Chef Rudolph Paquin is a towering red-cheeked man whose facility with game cookery is known far and wide. A stop here during an autumn visit is almost obligatory for fans of fowl and other wild forest animals. Paquin is also known for his impressive *carte des vins* (wine list), and wine enthusiasts come regularly to eat well while making their way through the chef's treasure-studded cave. Service can at times be a little gruff, which is a shame because it detracts from the often spectacular food and wine.

8 boulevard des Filles du Calvaire, 11e. ℂ **01-47-00-25-86.** Reservations recommended. Main courses 15€–28€. MC, V. Mon 7:30–11pm; Tues–Fri noon–2pm and 7:30–11pm; Sat noon–2pm and 7:30–11:30pm. Métro: St. Sebastian Froissart. Closed school holidays Aug, Feb.

Mansouria MOROCCAN   One of Paris's most charming Moroccan restaurants occupies a restored building midway between place de la Bastille and place de la Nation. The minimalist decor combines futuristic architecture with bare sand-colored walls, accented only with sets of antique doors and portals from the sub-Sahara. Look for eight different varieties of couscous and six different *tagines,* including versions with chicken, beef, lamb, and vegetables.

11 rue Faidherbe, 11e. www.mansouria.fr. ℂ **01-43-71-00-16.** Reservations recommended. Main courses 17€–26€; fixed-price dinner 28€–36€. AE, MC, V. Mon 7:30–11pm; Tues–Sat noon–2pm and 7:30–11pm. Métro: Faidherbe-Chaligny.

Septime MODERN FRENCH   This neo-bistrot is one of Paris's most exciting new restaurants. Here, Chef Bertrand Grébaut (who gave up a career in graphic design to become a cook) lets his imagination and culinary expertise run loose. Amid chic but understated decor, with light walls and old tiled flooring, the ever-changing menu might include a creamy tarragon and watercress risotto, veal tartare, roasted black pig with fennel, and a *p'tit suisse* (creamy fresh cheese tart). The 26€ lunch menu is a fine introduction to Grébaut's cuisine and includes a glass of wine. If you're curious, come in the evening for the 55€ tasting menu.

80 rue de Charonne, 11e. www.septime-charonne.fr. ℂ **01-43-67-38-29.** Reservations recommended. Main courses 18€–26€; fixed-price lunch 26€; fixed-price dinner 55€. MC, V. Mon 8–10:30pm; Tues–Fri 12:30–2pm, 8–10:30pm. Métro: Ledru Rollin or Charonne.

INEXPENSIVE

Chibby's Diner AMERICAN   Paris has numerous burger joints. The most famous place for burgers is Breakfast in America (p. 213), but Chibby's, set on an unlikely residential street off place de la Nation, makes burgers that rival even those of Breakfast's. Try the Three-in-One, a delicious, 15cm-tall (6-inch) stack of prime beef, bacon, mushrooms, and onions on a squishy bun. We usually start our meal with a plate of nachos, covered in guacamole and melted cheddar, or a platter of onion rings to share. The burgers are gut-busting, but if you've still got room, try the cheesecake.

9 rue Jaucourt, 12e. www.restaurant-chibbysdiner-paris.com. ℂ **01-44-73-98-18.** Reservations recommended. Tues–Sun 11am–11pm. Main courses 12€–16€. MC, V. Métro/RER: Nation.

Jeanne A ★ 🍴 TRADITIONAL FRENCH/WINE BAR   This restaurant/wine bar/takeout shop represents a new trend in Paris, providing an informal place to eat and drink well for not a lot of money. Run by the renowned Astier restaurant next door (p. 204), Jeanne A turns out spit-roasted meats (Challans duck or crispy-skinned chicken) served with salad and heaping portions of *potato gratin dauphinois.* These mains are bookended by delicious charcuterie and an impressive selection of artisanal cheeses, and complemented by high-quality wines that are well-priced. Order by the glass or the magnum (that's two bottles' worth), and take home what you're not able to drink.

42 rue Jean-Pierre Timbaud, 11e. ℰ **01-43-55-09-49.** Reservations recommended. Main courses 12€–17€; fixed-price lunch 15€. MC, V. Thurs–Mon 10:30am–10:30pm. Métro: Parmentier.

Mélac TRADITIONAL FRENCH/WINE BAR   This cramped and cozy wine bar was founded in 1938 and not much has changed here since. You still have to walk through the kitchen to get to the main dining room, and the hearty dishes of Jacques Mélac's Aveyron region are still served the way they were decades ago. Specialties include a confit of pig's liver, veal tripe bundles, fresh and cured sausages, and a *poêlon aveyronnais* (a cast-iron casserole of chicken liver and fried eggs in a sauce made with red wine and shallots). Water consumption is discouraged in favor of the robust red wines of Aveyron, one of which is made by Mélac himself.

42 rue Léon-Frot, 11e. www.melac.fr. ℰ **01-43-70-59-27.** Reservations recommended. Main courses 14€–20€; fixed-price lunch (Tues–Fri) 15€. DC, MC, V. Tues–Sat noon–4pm and 8–11pm. Closed Aug. Métro: Charonne.

Belleville, Canal St-Martin & Northeast Paris (10e, 19e and 20e)

Between the two parks of Belleville and Buttes Chaumont and along the Canal St-Martin lie some of the city's most quirky, delightful, and wine-centered restaurants. **Le Baratin** and **Le Chapeau Melon** are both widely acknowledged for having two of the most impressive wine cellars in town, with an emphasis on *vins naturels*. Belleville is also Paris's second Chinatown (after the 13th), and so there are several Chinese restaurants here, like Le President.

MODERATE

Brasserie Flo ★★ TRADITIONAL FRENCH/BRASSERIE   This well-known restaurant is tough to find, located down a discreet cobblestoned passage, but you'll be glad you tracked it down when you try the onion soup, sole meunière, or guinea hen with lentils. The 19th-century decor, reminiscent of a German beer tavern, is stunning, with rich wooden paneling and frescoes depicting little people making beer. As you tuck in, don't forget to watch the black-and-white–clad waiters at work; it's a veritable choreography of service as they wind in between tables carrying giant silver platters and hot pots.

7 cour des Petites-Ecuries, 10e. www.floparis.com. ℰ **01-47-70-13-59.** Reservations recommended. Main courses 16€–30€; price-fixed lunch 24€–40€, price-fixed dinner from 35€. AE, DC, MC, V. Métro: Château d'Eau or Strasbourg-St-Denis.

Chez Michel ★★ BRETON   Chef Thierry Breton prepares outstanding dishes from his native Brittany to diners who come from all over Paris and through the nearby Eurostar train hub at Gare du Nord. Breton recently ripped out a few tables and installed a massive oven in the dining room itself. He's now offering a four-course prix-fixe menu with comforting options like braised lamb, a chicken pot pie that's studded with foie gras, and other slow-baked specialties. For dessert, try the copious rice pudding or the awe-inspiring Paris-Brest (a choux pastry filled with praline cream).

10 rue de Belzunce, 10e. ℰ **01-44-53-06-20.** Reservations required. Fixed-price menu 33€. MC, V. Tues–Fri 11:45am–3pm and Mon–Fri 6:45pm–midnight. Métro: Gare du Nord.

Restaurants in Belleville, Canal St-Martin & Northeast Paris (10e, 19e & 20e)

Brasserie Flo **4**	Le President **8**
Chez Michel **1**	Le Verre Volé **5**
Hotel Du Nord **6**	Pink Flamingo **7**
La Grille **2**	Rosa
Le Baratin **9**	Bonheur **11**
Le Chapeau Melon **10**	Vivant **3**

Hôtel Du Nord TRADITIONAL FRENCH/BISTRO   At no. 102 quai de Jemmapes, on the edge of Canal St-Martin, stands the original facade of the Hôtel du Nord, made famous in director Marcel Carné's 1938 film of the same name. Today it's a bistro serving hearty French cuisine in a setting that evokes the 1930s. Expect hearty dishes like duck confit in a honey and ginger sauce; filet mignon of port with black linguine; sea bass with fig chutney; and an excellent vanilla crème-brûlée dessert. The wine list is like an armchair tour of France's wine-growing regions, with some particularly delicious bottles of St-Emilion grand cru.

102 quai de Jemmapes, 10e. www.hoteldunord.org. ✆ **01-40-40-78-78.** Main courses 14€–29€. MC, V. Daily noon–3pm, 8pm–midnight. Métro: Jacques-Bonsergent.

La Grille SEAFOOD/TRADITIONAL FRENCH   This tiny restaurant, with its historically classified 200-year-old wrought-iron grills, seems to be a holdover from another age. For at least a century after the French Revolution, fishermen from Dieppe used this place as a springboard for carousing and cabaret-watching after delivering their fish to Les Halles market. The holy grail at La Grille is an entire turbot prepared tableside with an emulsified white butter sauce. Other recommended dishes are seafood terrine, *boeuf bourguignon* (braised beef in red-wine sauce), and a brochette of scallops in white butter. The restaurant has a deal with the neighboring *caviste* (wine seller), so you can expect an excellent choice of wines too.

80 rue du Faubourg-Poissonnière, 10e. ✆ **01-47-70-89-73.** Reservations required. Main courses 18€–66€. AE, MC, V. Mon–Sat noon–2:15pm and 7:30–9:30pm. Métro: Poissonnière.

Le Baratin ★ 🍴 TRADITIONAL FRENCH/BISTRO   Argentina-born Chef Raquel Carena has created a neighborhood institution with Le Baratin, serving her imaginative bistro fare to both locals and foodies. Carena cooks from the heart, changing her menu regularly to reflect the seasons and her current inspiration. The value is most compelling at lunch, when one can enjoy a leisurely two-course affair for only 16€, to be followed by a stroll in the nearby Parc de Belleville. There is an impressive wine cellar here, managed by Raquel's famously grumpy husband, Philippe Pinoteau.

3 rue Jouye-Rouve, 20e. ✆ **01-43-49-39-70.** Reservations recommended. Fixed-price dinner 38€; fixed-price lunch 16€. MC, V. Tues–Fri noon–2:30pm and 8–11pm; Sat 8–11pm. Métro: Pyrénées.

Le Chapeau Melon ★ 🍴 MODERN FRENCH/WINE BAR   Olivier Camus, the cofounder of Le Baratin (see above), has created one of our favorite wine bars in the city. Perched high up on the Belleville hill, not far from the beautiful Parc des Buttes-Chaumont, Le Chapeau Melon serves a no-choice four-course tasting menu for 33€. Bright dishes such as langoustine carpaccio or vitello tonnato are often followed by slow-braised beef or lamb, signaling your move from white to red wine. The shelves that line the walls are stocked with bottles from some of the most renowned producers of natural wine, and you can buy them to go or drink them here for a modest corkage fee.

92 rue Rébeval, 19e. ✆ **01-42-02-68-60.** Reservations recommended. Prix-fixe dinner 33€. MC, V. Wed–Sun 8pm–1am. Métro: Pyrénées.

Le President CHINESE   The noisy President is a den of oriental kitsch with a monumental staircase that leads to a vast dining room frequently used by Chinese wedding parties. The waiters are somewhat robotic, but the food is decent with offerings like good Peking duck, dim sum, and the usual sweet and sour delights. Wine can sometimes be a downer: depending on how busy the restaurant is white and rosé might not be chilled. If that's the case, just ask for ice cubes (which is highly acceptable in France). This isn't the most gourmet Chinese restaurant in Paris, but it's a handy spot to have up your sleeve when you're in Belleville.

120-124 rue du Faubourg-du-Temple, 11e. ✆ **01-47-00-17-18.** Reservations not required. Main courses 9€–18€. MC, V. Daily noon–2:30pm, 7–10:30pm. Métro: Belleville.

Le Verre Volé ★★ WINE BAR/MODERN FRENCH   This wine bar, along the charming Canal Saint-Martin, has been open for more than 10 years, but it recently added a second dining room annex and brought in some real culinary talent in the form of Chef Delphine Zampetti. The sharable plates of charcuterie and cheese are still on the menu, but more inventive fare like octopus carpaccio, smoked swordfish, and pâté en croûte with pigeon and foie gras are also offered. Select a bottle of wine from the shelves that line the walls, and enjoy it (for a nominal corkage fee) in this informal and fun setting. It may be a casual place, but the popularity of the Verre Volé requires that you reserve in advance.

67 rue de Lancry, 10e. www.leverrevole.fr. ℰ **01-48-03-17-34.** Reservations recommended. Main courses 25€–30€; plate of the day 16€. MC, V. Daily 12:30–2pm and 7:30–10:30pm. Métro: Jacques Bonsergent.

Rosa Bonheur ★ 🍴 ☺ TAPAS   This restaurant inside the Parc des Buttes Chaumont boasts a sprawling terrace and one of the best panoramic views in town. A huge crowd gathers to drink and nibble tapas outside, but the menu also features main dishes such as stuffed and grilled shrimp, lamb and carrot stew, and monkfish with sage sauce. The real reason to visit is for the relaxed and friendly ambience, though—and the possibility of strolling through the city's largest and wildest park before or after your meal. That park, plus an indoor play area and kids' menu, makes Rosa Bonheur a great family option, too.

2 av. de la Cascade, 19e. www.rosabonheur.fr. ℰ **01-42-00-00-45.** Reservations not accepted. Tapas 5€–8€; fixed-price menus at 29€ and 35€; children's menu 14€. MC, V. Wed–Sun noon–midnight. Métro Botzaris.

Vivant ★ TRADITIONAL FRENCH/ITALIAN   Reflecting the mixed heritage of owner Pierre Jancou, this restaurant in an up-and-coming part of the 10th arrondissement serves French and Italian homey fare. Jancou has a gift for uncovering and restoring beautiful, historic spaces (one of his previous projects includes Racines in the 2nd, p. 183), and Vivant—dressed up in colorful tiles that date from 1903—is no exception. As soon as you enter the door, you hear the swish-swish of a Berkel slicing machine—cured Italian ham is a requisite beginning to any meal here. Jancou is a major figure in the natural wine movement and the wine list offers some of the most interesting, hard-to-find bottles in the country. Complete your visit with an espresso pulled from the most beautiful 1950s coffee machine you've ever seen.

43 rue des Petites Ecuries, 10e. ℰ **01-42-46-43-55.** Reservations recommended. Main courses 16€–28€. MC, V. Mon–Fri noon–2:30pm and 8–10:30pm. Métro: Château d'Eau.

INEXPENSIVE

Pink Flamingo PIZZA   Not only are the Pink's pizzas quirky (try the Poulidor: goat cheese and sliced duck breast), they're also put together with the best, freshest ingredients, and the crusts are made with organic flour. If you picnic by the canal, take a pink helium balloon, find your spot, and wait for the pizza delivery boy to cycle to you. There are other locations at 105 rue Vieille du Temple in the 3rd, 23 rue d'Aligre in the 12th, and 30 rue Muller in the 18th.

67 rue Bichat, 10th. www.pinkflamingopizza.com. ℰ **01-42-02-31-70.** Pizzas 11€–16€. MC, V. Sun noon–11:30pm; Mon 7–11:30pm; Tues–Sat noon–3pm and 7–11:30pm. Métro: Jacques Bonsergent.

THE LEFT BANK
Latin Quarter, Place d'Italie & Gobelins (5e & 13e)

This neighborhood, stretching south from the river near Notre Dame, past the market street of Mouffetard (one of the oldest and best preserved street markets in the city), leads to the area around place d'Italie and Paris's main Chinese quarter. The chefs who have set up shop here most recently are not content to merely perpetuate tradition. Some restaurants, such as **Le Pré Verre,** are using foreign flavors and techniques to update traditional French recipes, while others, like **Dans Les Landes** and **Les Papilles,** are trying to relax the rules and make restaurant dining a less formal experience.

VERY EXPENSIVE

La Tour d'Argent ♨ TRADITIONAL FRENCH   Although its reputation as the best in Paris has long been eclipsed, dining here remains an unsurpassed event—not because of the food (although the "Silver Tower" has one Michelin star), but because of its history and its view of the flying buttresses of Notre Dame. A restaurant of some sort has stood on this site since 1582: Mme de Sévigné refers to a cafe here in her letters, and Dumas used it in one of his novels. The fame of La Tour d'Argent spread during its ownership by Frédéric Delair, who in the 1890s started the practice of issuing certificates to diners who ordered *caneton* (pressed duckling). The birds are numbered: The first was served to Edward VII in 1890, and now the number has surpassed 1.2 million. For decades, the restaurant was owned by Claude Terrail, but after he died in 2006, his son, André, took over. A good part of the menu is devoted to duck, but the kitchen, of course, knows how to prepare other wonderful dishes.

15–17 quai de la Tournelle, 5e. www.latourdargent.com. ℂ **01-43-54-23-31.** Reservations required far in advance. Main courses 70€–140€; fixed-price dinner 170-190€; fixed-price lunch 65€. AE, DC, MC, V. Tues–Sat noon–1pm; Tues–Sat 7:30–9pm. Métro: St-Michel or Pont Marie.

EXPENSIVE

Itinéraires TRADITIONAL FRENCH   There's always a danger when a successful restaurant moves and expands. Often its original charm and patrons are lost. Not so with acclaimed chef Sylvain Sendra and his wife, Sarah, who closed their 26-seat Le Temps au Temps in the 11th arrondissement and opened this restaurant in the Latin Quarter. Their new place is twice as large, and the cuisine is just as good as it always was. Specialties include everything from Jerusalem artichoke soup to pheasant breast accompanied by dates, pistachios and fruit compote. One specialty is morchella mushrooms served with bacon chips and a soft-boiled egg. They have a distinctive strong taste and come in a creamy sauce. You might also order a delightful sea bass stuffed with white asparagus and served with a creamy Parmesan vanilla sauce. Many ingredients are organic.

5 rue de Pontoise, 5e. www.restaurantitineraires.com. ℂ **01-46-33-60-11.** Reservations required. Fixed-price lunch from 29€; fixed-price dinner at 59€ and 79€. AE, MC, V. Tues–Sat noon–2pm and 7:30–10:30pm (11:30pm Fri–Sat). Métro: Maubert-Mutualité.

MODERATE

Bouillon Racine ★ BISTRO/BRASSERIE   This jewel-box dining room is the best example of baroque Art Nouveau in Paris—a magnificent affair of swirling iron and woodwork, with twinkling stained glass, mirrors, and tiles. The excellent brasserie fare might include carpaccio of beef with basil, lemon, and Parmesan; scallop risotto; or chicken blanquette. If you've got a sweet tooth, the crème-brûlée flavored with maple syrup is delicious. The two-course lunch menu offered Monday to Friday is a steal at just 15€.

3 rue Racine, 6e. www.bouillon-racine.com. ℂ **01-44-32-15-60.** Mains 15€–23€; fixed-price dinner 30€ and 41€; fixed-price lunch 15€. MC, V. Daily noon–11pm. Métro: Odéon.

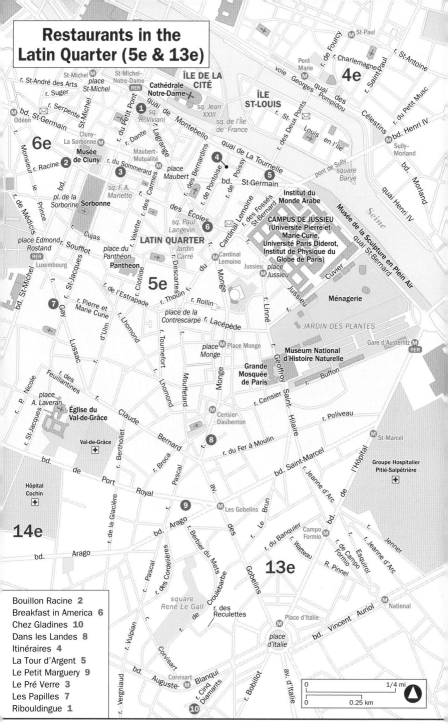

Restaurants in the Latin Quarter (5e & 13e)

Bouillon Racine **2**
Breakfast in America **6**
Chez Gladines **10**
Dans les Landes **8**
Itinéraires **4**
La Tour d'Argent **5**
Le Petit Marguery **9**
Le Pré Verre **3**
Les Papilles **7**
Ribouldingue **1**

Dans Les Landes ★ 🗡 SOUTHWESTERN FRENCH   Julien Duboué's modern eatery is named after the southwestern French region that inspired the chef's long list of tapas and small plates. Go for grilled quail breasts or the unmissable fried *chipirons* (small squid that are crisp, golden, and dusted with smoky pepper). Duboué's southwestern take on the spring roll—rice paper stuffed with foie gras, duck breast, and salad—is also compelling. Finish with an unusual dessert of warm anise-scented liquor with toasted crème anglaise.

119 bis rue Monge, 5e. 📞 **01-45-87-06-00.** Reservations recommended. Tapas 6€–15€; plat du jour 16€. MC, V. Mon–Sat noon–11pm. Métro: Censier-Daubenton.

Le Petit Marguery TRADITIONAL FRENCH/BISTRO   This place evokes the turn of the 20th century, with antique tile floors, banquettes, vested waiters, and a dark rose color scheme. The menu is also based in old-fashioned traditions, with an emphasis on game dishes in autumn and fresh produce in summer. Excellent dishes include duck and rosemary terrine with foie gras; a *petit salé* (family-style stew) of duckling that's served with braised cabbage and garlic-flavored cream sauce; a variety of homemade terrines, including an excellent version from blood sausage; and classic dishes including roasted pigeon with red cabbage and chestnuts or *coq* (rooster), which is deboned, marinated, roasted, and served in a sauce that combines red wine, some of the animal's blood, and foie gras. Top everything off with a classic soufflé au Grand Marnier.

9 bd. du Port-Royal, 13e. www.petitmarguery.com. 📞 **01-43-31-58-59.** Reservations recommended. 2- or 3-course lunch 23€–26€; 3-course dinner 30€–35€. AE, DC, MC, V. Daily noon–2:45pm and Mon–Sat 7:15–10:15pm. Closed Aug. Métro: Gobelins.

Le Pré Verre ★ 🗡 MODERN FRENCH/ASIAN FUSION   Around the corner from the Sorbonne in the heart of the Latin Quarter sits a refreshing restaurant where you can get seriously good food at an affordable price. The Delacourcelle brothers are firmly based in the French tradition but many of their chosen flavorings are inspired by Asia (they've got a second Pré Verre in Tokyo). In a welcoming, relaxed, and convivial atmosphere, tables are placed so close together that you're literally dining and rubbing elbows with your neighbors. For starters, dig into a well-flavored terrine—like the one made with layers of foie gras and mashed potatoes—or oysters marinated with ginger and poppy seeds or scallops with cinnamon. Main courses might include suckling pig with aromatic spices and crisp-cooked cabbage, or roasted codfish.

8 rue Thenard, 5e. www.lepreverre.com. 📞 **01-43-54-59-47.** Reservations required. Main courses 18€; fixed-price lunch 13€–29€; fixed-price dinner 39€. MC, V. Tues–Sat noon–2pm and 7:30–10:30pm. Closed Aug. Métro: Maubert-Mutualité.

Les Papilles ★ 🎁 TRADITIONAL FRENCH/BISTRO   One of the most exciting additions to Paris's culinary scene is this bustling combination bistro/wine shop run by Bertrand Bluy. The fixed price menu offers great value—four courses for 31€—but no choices. Dishes are comforting and often served family style from a cast-iron pot in the center of the table. Wine is available by the glass, but patrons are encouraged to choose a bottle from the nearby shelves and pay just a small corkage fee (7€) above retail price—a great way to try a good bottle without the usual substantial restaurant markup on the wine.

30 rue Gay-Lussac, 5e. www.lespapillesparis.fr. 📞 **01-43-25-20-79.** Reservations not needed. Market menu 31€. AE, MC, V. Mon–Sat noon–3pm and 7–11pm. Métro: Luxembourg.

Chinatown Paris Style

Although it's not widely known, Paris does, in fact, have a Chinatown (Quartier Chinois). In fact, it has two Chinatowns: The smallest is in Belleville, while the largest lies a 5-minute walk from Place d'Italie around avenues d'Ivry and de Choisy in the 13th arrondissement. (To get there, take the Métro to Porte d'Ivry or Place d'Italie in the 13e.) About 250,000 Asian people live in the Quartier Chinois, and a slew of Asian food stores, restaurants, and markets cater to the growing population. **Tang Frères,** 44 avenue d'Ivry, 13e (✆ **01-44-06-61-86**), is the largest Asian-food market in Paris—here you'll find rows of teas and spices from China. Spend a morning exploring here and stick around for lunch at **Le Mer de Chine,** 159 des Rentiers, 13e (✆ **01-45-84-22-49**), serving the best Cantonese cuisine in Paris; or grab a snack at **Pho 14,** 129 av. de Choisy, 13e. (✆ **01-45-83-61-15**), where the noodle soups with fresh herbs, soya shoots, and meatballs are some of the best in town, even if service is usually with a frown rather than a smile.

Ribouldingue TRADITIONAL FRENCH   Offal lovers flock to this bistro near St-Julien-le-Pauvre church to enjoy such old-fashioned fare as the tip of a pig's snout or thinly breaded and sautéed slices of a cow's udder. If those are unappealing, how about lamb's brain meunière, tripe cooked in white wine, or even veal kidneys in garlic sauce? For the offal timid, there are many other dishes, including veal rib with fried potatoes, pollock with eggplant caviar and crispy lardons (bacon cubes), or even a blanquette of monkfish. This Latin Quarter bistro is the creation of Nadège Varigny, who grew up without any fear of the sight of blood as the daughter of an Alpine butcher.

10 rue Saint-Julien-le-Pauvre, 5e. www.restaurant-ribouldingue.com. ✆ **01-46-33-98-80.** Reservations required. Main courses 17€–26€; fixed-price lunch 29€; fixed-price dinner 29€. MC, V. Tues–Fri noon–2:30pm and Tues–Sat 7:30–10:30pm. Closed 3 weeks in Aug. Métro: Cluny La Sorbonne or St-Michel.

INEXPENSIVE

Breakfast in America ☺ AMERICAN   Connecticut-born Hollywood screenwriter Craig Carlson opened this replica of a down-home U.S.-based diner in 2003, building it with funds from members of the California film community who donated memorabilia from their films. Its self-proclaimed mission involves dispensing proper, rib-sticking American breakfasts and diner food to Parisians. The setting replicates a 1950s-era railway car, replete with scarlet-and-black Naugahyde banquettes, faux windows with mirrored insets, and an unabashedly Americanized staff. Breakfast (heaping portions of the egg-and-waffle-and-bacon combinations, as well as omelets) is served throughout the day and evening. Also available are half a dozen variations of burgers, tacos, club sandwiches, and BLTs.

17 rue des Ecoles, 5e. ✆ **01-43-54-50-28.** Reservations not accepted. Breakfast platters 7€–11€; lunch and dinner platters and "blue-plate specials" 8€–12€; fixed-price Sun brunch 16€. MC, V. Daily 8:30am–10:30pm. Métro: Cardinal Lemoine or Jussieu.

Chez Gladines ⚑ BASQUE   Penny pinchers climb the cobblestone hill of the Butte aux Cailles to dine on the large portions at this dive. The setting is laid back (actually a bit grimy), but the food is hearty and authentic. This may not be the place to go to impress a date, but you can gorge on Gladines' giant "salads" (which consist of meat, cheese, garlic potatoes, and a few leaves of lettuce) and main dishes such as *pipérade* (Basque-style scrambled eggs with vegetables), cassoulet, potatoes with ham and Cantal cheese, and our favorite, ham in a creamy sauce with layers of gratin style potatoes that have been fried in duck fat. It's a bit leaden, but devotees love it.

30 rue des Cinq Diamants, 13e. ✆ **01-45-80-70-10.** Reservations not accepted. Main courses 8€–15€; fixed-price lunch 10€. No credit cards. Daily noon–3pm and 7pm–midnight; Sun noon–4pm. Closed 3 weeks in July. Métro: Corvisart or Place d'Italie.

St-Germain-des-Près & Luxembourg (6e)

Our favorite restaurants in Saint-Germain are classic bistros, serving traditional French fare with a few modern accents. **Le Comptoir du Relais, Le Relais Louis XIII,** and **Ze Kitchen Galerie** are run by notable chefs and require advance reservations, but the rest of our restaurant recommendations here are more casual and accept walk-ins and same-day bookings.

VERY EXPENSIVE

Hélène Darroze SOUTHWESTERN FRENCH   Chef Hélène Darroze is carving a name for herself on both sides of the Channel, with her successful venture in London's Connaught Hotel and this splendid little restaurant on rue d'Assas, specialized in Southwestern French cooking, renowned for game meats and foie gras. The elegant, contemporary dining room provides a sleek backdrop for the simple, yet delicious food. A typical meal might start with amuse-bouche of ham from the Landes region, then be followed with foie gras, seafood from Saint-Jean-de-Luz, game meats, cheese, and two desserts (one fruit, the other chocolate). The menu varies according to Darroze's mood and the season. The 65€ lunch menu, which includes two glasses of wine, is well worth the splurge and is a fine introduction to the chef's cooking.

4 rue d'Assas, 6e. www.helenedarroze.com. ✆ **01-42-22-00-11.** Reservations recommended. Fixed price dinner 85€–250€ (during truffle season); fixed-price lunch 28€–65€. AE, DC, MC, V. Tues–Sat noon–2:30pm, 7:30–10:30pm. Métro: Sèvres-Babylone or Rennes.

Le Relais Louis XIII ★ TRADITIONAL FRENCH   Chef Manuel Martinez upholds French traditions in this atmospheric, two-Michelin starred dining room, an old world space with dark wooden beams that wouldn't look amiss in an Alexandre Dumas novel. The key to Martinez's success is his mastery of traditional French cuisine, which he revisits with modern flair. Among his signature dishes you'll find lobster ravioli with foie gras, a Madame Burgaud challandais duckling basted in vinegar and orange juice (to create a tangy, citrussy crunch), and one of the best millefeuille with Bourbon vanilla cream in town. For a treat, order the canard au sang (literally "bloody duck"), made with cognac and madeira wines and prepared at your table with much pomp and circumstance (upon advance request). The impeccable wine list offers bottles from the Champagne, Bordeaux, Rhône Valley, and Burgundy regions.

8 rue des Grands-Augustins, 6e. www.relaislouis13.fr. ✆ **01-43-26-75-96.** Reservations recommended. Main courses 58€–60€; fixed-price lunch 50€; fixed price dinner 80€–130€. AE, DC, MC, V. Tues–Sat noon–2:30pm, 7:30–10:30pm.

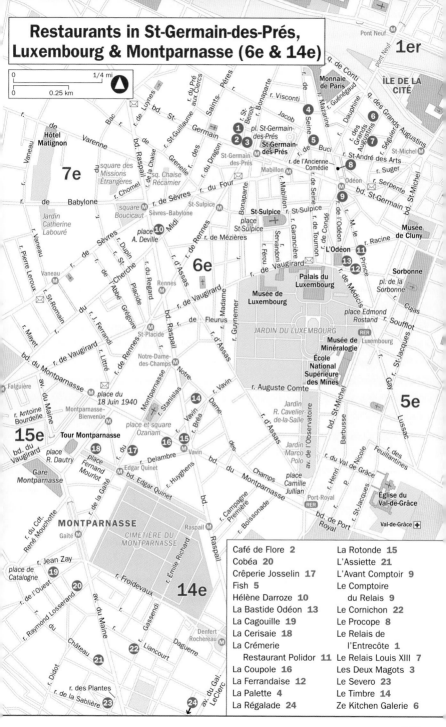

Restaurants in St-Germain-des-Prés, Luxembourg & Montparnasse (6e & 14e)

Café de Flore **2**
Cobéa **20**
Crêperie Josselin **17**
Fish **5**
Hélène Darroze **10**
La Bastide Odéon **13**
La Cagouille **19**
La Cerisaie **18**
La Crémerie
   Restaurant Polidor **11**
La Coupole **16**
La Ferrandaise **12**
La Palette **4**
La Régalade **24**

La Rotonde **15**
L'Assiette **21**
L'Avant Comptoir **9**
Le Comptoire
   du Relais **9**
Le Cornichon **22**
Le Procope **8**
Le Relais de
   l'Entrecôte **1**
Le Relais Louis XIII **7**
Les Deux Magots **3**
Le Severo **23**
Le Timbre **14**
Ze Kitchen Galerie **6**

EXPENSIVE

Le Comptoir du Relais ★★ TRADITIONAL FRENCH/BISTRO   Le Comptoir is the domain of Yves Camdeborde, the pioneering chef who kicked off the bistronomy movement, serving high-caliber food in a casual bistro setting, when he left a three-star kitchen to open his own bistro at the edge of the city. He sold La Régalade (which remains good) years ago to open this "counter," serving guests of the attached hotel and foodies who book dinner months and months in advance. Lunch is an easier table to score because reservations are not accepted—just line up before the doors open at noon and you're likely to get a table. All this fuss can be attributed to Camdeborde's well-executed bistro cuisine that reflects his southwestern roots and is made from high-quality ingredients. The menu changes regularly, but dishes might include creamy slices of foie gras with chunky prune sauce or a juicy rack of pork. It's comfort food with a touch of luxury, and it will spoil you for all subsequent bistros.

9 carrefour de l'Odéon, 6e. www.hotel-paris-relais-saint-germain.com. ✆ **01-44-27-07-97.** Reservations required several weeks in advance. Main courses weekends 27€–35€; fixed-price dinner weeknights 50€. MC, V. Daily noon–2am. Métro: Odéon.

Ze Kitchen Galerie ★ INTERNATIONAL/MODERN FRENCH   At this colorful loft space in an antique building with an open showcase kitchen, most of the paintings on display are for sale (the place doubles as an art gallery). Chef William Ledeuil oversees the innovative cuisine, which fuses Asian influences with French dishes. The menu changes about every 5 weeks. For starters, you might try the octopus with lemongrass and kalamenji. A pasta dish might feature homemade linguine with Bouchot mussels and dried fish eggs. Other mains might include grilled mackerel with miso or Challans duck with mostarda and plums. Dessert could be the restaurant's "cappuccino of the month," a frothy dessert concoction with ingredients that change with the seasons.

4 rue des Grands-Augustins, 6e. www.zekitchengalerie.fr. ✆ **01-44-32-00-32.** Reservations recommended. Main courses 24€–42€; fixed-price lunch with water and coffee 27€–70€; fixed-price dinner 82€. AE, DC, MC, V. Mon–Fri noon–2:30pm; Mon–Sat 7–11pm. Métro: St-Michel or Pont-Neuf.

MODERATE

Fish MODERN FRENCH/MEDITERRANEAN/SEAFOOD   This restaurant, run by Drew Harré, is the unofficial Anglo headquarters of the 6th arrondissement. Regulars fill the seats at the bar (a good spot for solo dining), where they drink wines from Juan Sanchez's La Derniere Goutte. The menu is slightly Mediterranean, offering solid if not revelatory cooking with an accent on seafood. But the service is friendly and multilingual, and the wine list is superb, if not a little expensive.

69 rue de Seine, 6e. ✆ **01-43-54-34-69.** Reservations recommended. Fixed-price dinner 32€ and 36€; fixed-price lunch 25€. M. Daily noon–3pm and 7pm–12:30am. Métro: Mabillon.

La Bastide Odéon PROVENÇAL   The sunny climes of Provence come through in the pale yellow walls, oak tables, and bouquets of wheat and dried roses. Chef Gilles Ajuelos prepares market-based cuisine for a dining room that's packed with both Anglophones and French locals. His simplest first courses are the most satisfying, such as scallop risotto with Parmesan, and eggplant-stuffed roasted rabbit with olive toast and balsamic vinegar. Main courses might include a warm napoleon of grilled eggplant served "in the style of the Riviera," and roasted chicken with a confit of Provençal garlic and fried potatoes.

7 rue Corneille, 6e. www.bastide-odeon.com. ☎ **01-43-26-03-65.** Reservations recommended. Fixed-price lunch menu 19€–30€; fixed price dinner menu 30€–36€. AE, MC, V. Tues–Sat 2:15–2pm and 7:30–10:30pm. Métro: Odéon. RER: Luxembourg.

La Ferrandaise TRADITIONAL FRENCH This restaurant near the Luxembourg Gardens is the place for anyone in search of meat-and-potatoes cooking done right. In celebration of a certain tasty cow from the Auvergne region, La Ferrandaise is decorated with photos of the namesake breed. Beef dishes are in the spotlight here, presented in various forms from steak to *pot au feu,* but heirloom pork and seasonal game offer some variety, too. Don't leave without trying the cheese plate—it includes many raw-milk varieties from central France that you won't find anywhere else.

8 rue de Vaugirard, 6e. www.laferrandaise.com. ☎ **01-43-26-36-36.** Reservations recommended. Fixed-price dinner 34€ and 46€; fixed-price lunch 16€ and 34€. MC, V. Mon–Thurs noon–3pm and 7–11:30pm; Fri–Sat 7pm–12am. Métro: Odéon.

Le Relais de l'Entrecôte ☺ TRADITIONAL FRENCH/STEAK For those who are tired of making decisions, Le Relais de l'Entrecôte has only one question for you: "La cuisson?" Tell them how you like your steak done (*bien cuit* for medium-well, *à point* medium rare, or *saignant* for rare) and then sit back and let the show begin. You'll start with a fresh green salad and then proceed to the main event: a giant silver platter of steak, doused in an addictive "secret sauce," and served with crispy golden fries. That platter is refillable, by the way—you can expect to see your server return with a second helping once you've finished. Desserts, if you can find the strength, are classic and delicious, including profiteroles and crème brûlée. The crowd that gathers inside the pretty-postcard dining room includes tourists, locals, and chefs; it also includes plenty of families with kids.

20 rue St. Benoît, 6e. www.relaisentrecote.fr. ☎ **01-45-49-16-00.** Reservations not required. Daily noon–3pm and 7–11pm. Fixed-price lunch and dinner 25€. MC, V. Métro: St. Germain des Prés.

Le Timbre TRADITIONAL FRENCH British Chef Chris Wright opened the tiniest restaurant on the tiniest street in Paris near the Luxembourg gardens. The Manchester-born chef shops for only the finest of French regional products, including truffles and foie gras, and he gets by with no microwave or freezer. Wright prepares faultless dishes, including trout stuffed with fresh fava beans and country ham, andouillette sausages with lentils from Puy, or a filet of white fish with olives. In spite of all these *à la française* dishes, he likes to put English cheddar on his cheeseboard. If not the cheese, you might end your meal with the ruby-red strawberry soup.

3 rue Sainte Beuve, 6e. www.restaurantletimbre.com. ☎ **01-45-49-10-40.** Reservations required. Main courses 16€–25€; fixed-price lunch 24€–32€. MC, V. Tues–Sat noon–2pm and 7:30–10:30pm. Closed 3 weeks in Aug. Métro: Notre-Dame-des-Champs or Vavin.

INEXPENSIVE

La Crèmerie Restaurant Polidor ☺ TRADITIONAL FRENCH/BISTRO Crèmerie Polidor is the most traditional (and heavily touristed) bistro in the Odéon area, serving *cuisine familiale.* Its name dates from the early 1900s, when

A Secret Dining Club: Lunch in the Loft

For a unique dining experience, with the added excitement of not knowing who you'll be sitting next to, try a clandestine meal at **Lunch in the Loft** (www.lunch intheloft.com), a secret luncheon club run by Miss Lunch (aka Claude Cabri), a food-loving artist who opens her private home to those looking for new flavors and culinary experiences. The meal kicks off at 1pm sharp (Wed, Sat, and Sun) and continues for hours of scrumptious home-cooking accompanied by excellent wines and Claude's friendly conversation. Miss Lunch also runs cooking lessons, often accompanied by Sommelier Sam, who teaches you how to pair wine with the dishes you've prepared. Meals are from 150€. The address, in central Paris, is divulged upon reservation only; for reservations, email reservations@ lunchintheloft.com.

it specialized in frosted cream desserts, but the restaurant can trace its history from 1845. The Crèmerie was André Gide's favorite, and Joyce, Hemingway, Valéry, Artaud, and Kerouac also dined here. Peer beyond the lace curtains and brass hat racks to see drawers where, in olden days, regular customers used to lock up their cloth napkins. Try the day's soup followed by kidneys in Madeira sauce, *boeuf bourguignon* (beef braised in red wine), *confit de canard* (leg of duck), or *blanquette de veau* (veal ragout in cream sauce). For dessert, order a chocolate, raspberry, or lemon tart.

39 rue Monsieur-le-Prince, 6e. www.polidor.com. ℃ **01-43-26-95-34.** Main courses 12€–20€; fixed-price menu 22€–32€. No credit cards. Daily noon–2:30pm; Mon–Sat 7pm–12:30am; Sun 7–11pm. Métro: Odéon.

L'Avant Comptoir ★ WINE BAR/SOUTHWESTERN FRENCH This shoebox-size wine bar is just steps from the Odéon and run by bistro maestro Yves Camdeborde. Next door to his seminal restaurant Le Comptoir, this place sells crepes and sandwiches during the day and hors d'oeuvres to a raucous crowd at night. Basque and Béarnais-inspired nibbles include fried croquettes stuffed with Iberian ham, a filling cod brandade, oxtail canapés with horseradish cream, and chicken hearts grilled with garlic and parsley. Plates of charcuterie are meant to be eaten (and shared) with the crocks of Bordier butter and gherkins that line the counter. No more than a dozen people can crowd into this place at a time and there are no chairs.

3 carrefour de l'Odéon, 6e. No phone and no reservations accepted. Main courses 3.50€–8€. MC, V. Daily 9am–1am. Métro: Odéon.

Eiffel Tower & Nearby (7e)

The chic 7th arrondissement is home to some of the city's most respected and innovative chefs, including Alain Passard (**L'Arpège**), **Jean-François Piège**, and **Joël Robuchon.** A table at one of their celebrated tables doesn't come cheap, but you'll never forget the experience. There are several *bistronomique* restaurants here too, including **Les Cocottes** and **Chez l'Ami Jean**, where gastronomes can go for a memorable meal at more modest prices.

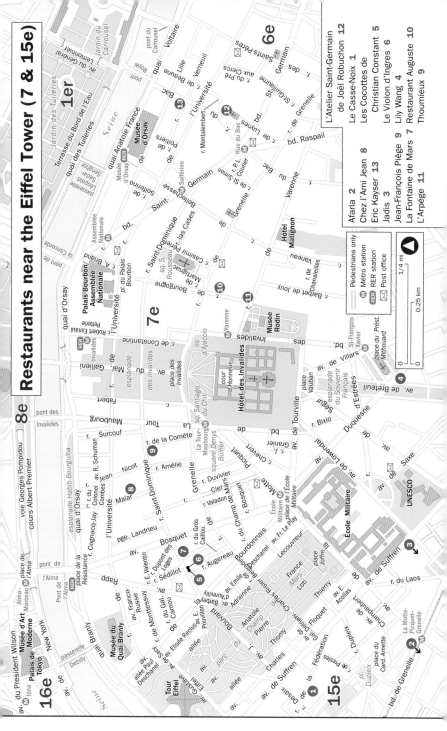

Restaurants near the Eiffel Tower (7 & 15e)

L'Atelier Saint-Germain de Joël Robuchon **12**
Le Casse-Noix **1**
Les Cocottes de Christian Constant **5**
Le Violon d'Ingres **6**
Lily Wang **4**
Restaurant Auguste **10**
Thoumieux **9**

Afaria **2**
Chez l'Ami Jean **8**
Eric Kayser **13**
Jadis **3**
Jean-François Piège **9**
La Fontaine de Mars **7**
L'Arpège **11**

Pedestrians only
M Métro station
RER RER station
⊠ Post office

0   0.25 km
0   1/4 mi

219

VERY EXPENSIVE

Jean-François Piège ★ MODERN FRENCH   This new restaurant, above the bustling brasserie Thoumieux, is the newest stage for star chef Jean-François Piège. After leaving the palatial kitchens of Les Ambassadeurs, Piège partnered with Thierry Costes to open a hotel and restaurant complex near Invalides. His namesake restaurant is an intimate 20-seat showcase, which has been enthusiastically welcomed by the critics, receiving two Michelin stars in 2011, just a year after opening. Dishes are creative and whimsical; you might try a mussel with a heap of fried frizzled potatoes—his version of *moules frites*. For dessert, the *tarte tatin* (apple tart)—a puff of sweet pizza dough topped with sliced apples and cream—is excellent. Piège's cooking has been called witty and precise, and the funky decor by India Mahdavi—featuring brightly colored sofas with black and white accents—has garnered almost as much attention as the food.

79 rue St. Dominique, 7e. www.jfpiege.com. ✆ **01-47-05-49-75.** Reservations recommended. Main courses 37€–75€; fixed-price menus 70€–165€. MC, V, Daily noon–midnight. Métro: La Tour Maubourg.

L'Arpège ★★★ MODERN FRENCH   Chef Alain Passard made waves years ago when he decided to put vegetables, not meat, in the spotlight at his three-star restaurant L'Arpège. Although meat is still featured on the menu, his dedication to carrots and turnips was something previously unseen. This pristine produce, which he raises on a farm near Le Mans, is often picked in the morning and served the same day in Paris. Uneaten food from his restaurant makes the return journey to become compost. Food politics aside, the flavors that Passard coaxes from these vegetables (often with the welcome addition of butter and cream) are truly remarkable. Service is discreet, as one expects at a restaurant frequented by diplomats and executives, and the dining room, with etched glass, burnished steel, and pearwood paneling, is beautiful, if a bit dated. Don't miss the cheese course, served on a giant polished plank of wood, or the *tarte aux pommes bouquet de roses* (a tart composed of apple ribbons rolled into tiny rosettes).

84 rue de Varenne, 7e. www.alain-passard.com. ✆ **01-47-05-09-06.** Fax 01-44-18-98-39. Reservations required 2 weeks in advance. Main courses 48€–180€; fixed-price lunch 125€; fixed-price dinner 420€. AE, DC, MC, V. Mon–Fri 12:30–2:30pm and 8–10:30pm. Métro: Varenne.

EXPENSIVE

L'Atelier Saint-Germain de Joël Robuchon ★★ MODERN FRENCH   World-renowned Chef Joël Robuchon came out of a short-lived retirement in 2003 in order to open this ground-breaking culinary workshop on the left bank. He recently added the words "Saint-Germain" when he opened a second Atelier near the Arc de Triomphe. This original location remains packed with gastronomes who want to eat well without the fuss implied by a three-star restaurant. Sitting informally upon high stools at a U-shaped bar, you can order the tasting menu or a series of sharable small plates including sea bream carpaccio, caviar with smoked eel and horseradish, grilled marrow bones, and the famous Robuchon mashed potatoes. Reservations are accepted for the extremely early and late seatings only (at 11:30am and 2pm for lunch, and 6:30pm for dinner); these spots are booked well in advance. Otherwise, it's first come, first served.

5 rue Montalembert, 7e. www.joel-robuchon.net. © **01-42-22-56-56.** Reservations required. Main courses 28€–75€; dinner tasting menu 150€. AE, MC, V. Daily 11:30am–3:30pm, 6:30pm–midnight. Métro: Rue du Bac.

Le Violon d'Ingres MODERN FRENCH   Christian Constant has built a sort of culinary empire in the 7th with three restaurants along the rue Saint-Dominique. Le Violon d'Ingres is his most refined restaurant, and a recent makeover has left it looking more sophisticated in tones of mushroom and red wine. Chef Stéphane Schmidt executes Constant's vision with dishes like the signature grilled wood pigeon served with a fricassee of wild mushrooms and sweet garlic, rock crab with fennel cream and herring caviar, and a spit roast turbot with baby potatoes and a mousseline sauce.

135 rue St-Dominique, 7e. www.leviolondingres.com. © **01-45-55-15-05.** Fax 01-45-55-48-42. Reservations required. Main courses 27€; fixed-price menu 49€. AE, DC, MC, V. Tues–Sat noon–2:30pm and 7–10:30pm. Métro: Invalides or Ecole-Militaire.

Restaurant Auguste ★★ TRADITIONAL FRENCH/SEAFOOD   Right by the Assemblée Nationale (the seat of French government along with the Sénat), chef Gael Orieux's red and white contemporary eatery is coveted by politicians—a handy clientele for this young chef, whose love of the sea has led him to represent "Mr. Good Fish," a European association dedicated to protecting the oceans. Serving some of the best seafood in town, Orieux's meals might include red mullet with Thai condiments; scallops with creamy risotto; and oysters in horseradish mousse. But there are also meat dishes, with fabulous preparations like Celtic duck with caramelized citrus fruits, and *ris de veau* (veal sweetbreads) with oyster mushrooms and apricots. For dessert, delicacies like pistachio soufflé, finish everything off perfectly.

54 rue de Bourgogne, 7e. www.restaurantauguste.fr. © **01-45-51-61-09.** Reservations required. Main courses 30€–48€; fixed-price lunch 35€; fixed-price dinner 80€. MC, V. Daily noon–2:30pm and 7–10:30pm. Métro: Assemblée Nationale.

Thoumieux MODERN FRENCH/BRASSERIE   After leaving the palatial kitchens of Les Ambassadeurs, Chef Jean-François Piège partnered with hotel scion Thierry Costes to reinvent the Paris brasserie. Critics have loved certain dishes, such as the squid carbonara and the juicy hamburger covered in Parmesan cheese, but have generally found the cooking to be uneven and unworthy of Piège. That hasn't stopped the trend-seeking set from packing the beautifully restored dining room every night. It's definitely a scene, and a very enjoyable one at that if you're more interested in gabbing than gastronomy. The chef's newer namesake restaurant (Jean-François Piège, p. 220) on the same site is pricier, but critics have rightly raved about the exceptional food.

79 rue St. Dominique, 7e. www.thoumieux.fr. © **01-47-05-49-75.** Reservations recommended. Main courses 37€–69€. MC, V. Daily noon–midnight. Métro: La Tour Maubourg.

MODERATE

Chez l'Ami Jean ★ BASQUE/SOUTHWESTERN FRENCH   This restaurant was originally opened by a Basque nationalist in 1931, but it was Chef Stéphane Jego who really put the bistro on the map. Jego maintained the original decor (if one can call wood panels and sports memorabilia a decor) but turned

L'Ami Jean into a destination for *cuisine bistronomique*—high-caliber cooking served in a homey neighborhood setting. Reserve in advance and arrive hungry because the Basque dishes served here are anything but light—even the fish dishes here are accented by foie gras and chorizo. However much you may have already eaten, say yes to the cheese plate with Basque brebis (sheep's milk cheese) and black cherry preserves, and finish with a heaping bowl of *riz au lait* (rice pudding).

27 rue Malar, 7e. www.amijean.eu. ✆ **01-47-05-86-89.** Reservations required. Main courses 20€–40€; fixed-price dinner at 35€, 42€, and 60€. MC, V. Tues–Sat noon–2pm and 7pm–midnight. Closed Aug. Métro: Invalides.

La Fontaine de Mars BISTRO/SOUTHWESTERN FRENCH   Visiting Americans began rushing to book tables here shortly after President Obama and the first lady dined at this classic French bistro. One of the old-school bistros of Paris, it's a venerable institution since it first opened in 1908, but it's never had this kind of business before. The cooking leans toward the southwest with dishes like cassoulet, foie gras, and duck breast figuring prominently on the menu. Starters include *escargots* (snails) and *oeufs au Madiran* (eggs baked with red wine and bacon), and the dessert list is full of classics such as *île flottante*, crème brûlée, and dark chocolate mousse.

129 rue St.-Dominique, 7e. www.fontainedemars.com. ✆ **01-47-05-46-44.** Reservations required. Main courses 17€–42€. AE, MC, V. Daily noon–3pm and 7:30–11pm. Métro: Ecole Militaire.

Les Cocottes de Christian Constant ★ TRADITIONAL FRENCH   Take a seat at the long counter or a high table for Christian Constant's updated comfort food—almost all of it served in cast iron *cocottes* (casseroles). Begin with a plate of sliced Ospital ham, then move on to scallops with endive and orange butter sauce, potato-stuffed pigs' feet, or a seasonal vegetable cocotte. Desserts include an oversized waffle with Chantilly cream and Constant's signature chocolate tarte. Reservations are not accepted, which can actually be an advantage in Paris.

135 rue St.-Dominique, 7e. www.maisonconstant.com. No phone. Reservations not accepted. Main courses 20€–35€. MC, V. Daily noon–3pm and 7–10.30pm. Métro: École Militaire.

Lily Wang CHINESE   This audacious Chinese restaurant is backed by the notorious Costes family and reflects the current obsession in Paris with anything Asian. The stylishly kitsch and dimly-lit dining room features velvet curtains, glowing lanterns, and lacquered furniture in shades of red and black. One French critic compared Lily's looks to that of a Chinese escort working in Saint-Tropez. Dishes including fried pork ravioli, pork tenderloin marinated in fish sauce, and smoky jian-jiao (pork dumplings) are indisputably delicious, but the steep prices put Lily's charms out of reach for budget-minded diners.

40 av. Duquesne, 7e. ✆ **01-53-86-09-09.** Reservations recommended. Main courses 23€–39€. MC, V. Daily noon–3pm and 7–11pm. Métro: Saint-François-Xavier.

INEXPENSIVE

Eric Kayser ★★ BAKERY/LIGHT FARE   If you're in the 7th arrondissement for breakfast or lunch, a good refueling stop is this bakery, bar, and cafe. Kayser's forte is bread making—he is known for the long fermentation of his dough.

He's always coming up with new ideas for his breads, including one made with apricots and pistachios and another with chorizo. This Alsatian baker offers many luxe breads and pastries, and breakfast is a delight here. At lunch you have a choice of 20 different combinations of *tartines* (open-faced sandwiches), and teatime features gourmet snacks such as a sweet tartine with meringue and chestnuts.

18 rue du Bac, 7e. © **01-42-61-27-63.** Sandwiches and savory tartes 4€–8.50€. MC, V. Tues–Sun 7am–8pm. Métro: Bac or Musée d'Orsay.

Montparnasse & Southern Paris (14e & 15e)

The largely residential 15th arrondissement has exploded with restaurants in recent years. Although this area may seem remote, those who venture here are rewarded with a large selection of fabulous and affordable bistros. **Afaria** and **Jadis** are the standouts, but relative newcomers **Le Cornichon** and **Le Casse-Noix** are well worth a visit, too. The 14th has long been a bastion of bistronomy, home to the wonderfully classic bistros **La Régalade** and **La Cerisaie,** as well as exciting newcomer **Cobéa,** which opened in late 2011.

EXPENSIVE

Cobéa ★ CONTEMPORARY FRENCH   Chef Philippe Bélissent and restaurant manager Jérôme Cobour left L'Hôtel in St-Germain-des-Prés (where they had gained a Michelin star) to open this new place at the end of 2011. In a pretty little house (a throw-back to when southern Montparnasse was part of the countryside), the dining room is smart and contemporary, decorated in steely grays and whites. Bélissent prepares expertly concocted dishes like St-Jacques scallops with Jerusalem artichokes, poached foie gras with beetroot, and pineapple meringue. The concept is as follows: there is one menu, from which you decide whether you'd like to try four (55€), six (75€), or eight (95€) courses. Service is impeccable.

11 rue Raymond Losserand, 14e. © **01-43-20-21-39.** Reservations required. Fixed-price lunch 38€; fixed-price dinner 55€–95€. MC, V. Tues–Sat noon–1:45pm, 7:15–9:15pm. Métro: Gaîté or Pernety.

La Régalade ★★ TRADITIONAL FRENCH/BISTRO   The *bistronomique* movement started here, under Chef Yves Camdeborde (who now works at Le Comptoir du Relais, p. 216), when people flocked to this sweet little bistro, with its cracked tile floors, polished wood, and burgundy banquettes, to taste excellent food in a low-key setting. In 2006, Camdeborde sold La Régalade to Bruno Doucet, who has maintained the tradition and become a respected chef in his own right. Meals here begin with a help-yourself crock of homemade terrine, served with bread and gherkins, and continue with starters such as foie gras in asparagus bouillon or marinated sea scallops with basil and Parmesan. Mains are comforting, such as caramelized pork belly with mashed potatoes or sea bream with caramelized fennel and black olives. Dessert could be a stinky Reblochon cheese, a molten Guanaja chocolate cake, or rice pudding.

14 av. Jean-Moulin, 14e. © **01-45-45-68-58.** Reservations recommended. Fixed-price menus 34€–50€. MC, V. Tues–Fri noon–2:30pm; Mon–Fri 7–11:30pm. Closed Aug. Métro: Alésia.

MODERATE

Afaria ★ BASQUE/BISTRO   Many visitors skip the 15th arrondissement, but Afaria is a good reason to go there. Chef Julien Duboué lures eaters from all over town to this dull corner of the 15th with his bright Basque cooking. The bistro, which he runs with his wife, Céline, includes a bar where locals nibble on tapas at a communal table, and a dining room with wooden tables decked in cheerful red and white tablecloths. Traditional recipes are revisited with an imaginative twist, including spicy pumpkin soup with scallops and artichokes; terrine of venison with fig chutney; and rosy charred duck breast on the bone served over smoking grapevines.

15 rue Desnouettes, 15e. ℭ **01-48-56-15-36.** Reservations required. Main courses 17€–19€; fixed-price lunch 22€–26€. MC, V. Tues–Sat noon–2:30pm and Mon–Sat 7–11pm. Métro: Convention.

Jadis ★ TRADITIONAL FRENCH/BISTRO   In the up-and-coming 15th arrondissement, Chef Guillaume Délage uses fresh seasonal ingredients to resuscitate "forgotten" bistro dishes from the past; start with an egg poached in red wine sauce and move on to beef stroganoff or stuffed breast of veal. Délage's nose-to-tail approach to cooking makes use of the whole animal, so don't be surprised to see cock's comb or kidney on the menu. The cheese course (if you've got room) is generally so ripe that it still smells like the farm, and desserts, like the bittersweet chocolate soufflé and coffee-flavored *pot de crème*, are pure comfort.

208 rue de la Croix Nivert, 15e. www.bistrot-jadis.com. ℭ **01-45-57-73-20.** Reservations required. Main courses 21€; fixed-price lunch 29€; fixed-price dinner 36€. AE, MC, V. Mon–Fri 12:15–2:30pm and 7:15–10:30pm. Métro: Convention.

La Cagouille SEAFOOD   Don't expect to find meat at this temple of seafood—owner Gérard Allamandou refuses to feature it. Everything about La Cagouille (except its unattractive 1970s setting) is a testimonial to a modern version of the culinary arts of La Charente, the flat sandy district on the Atlantic south of Bordeaux. In a trio of oak-sheathed dining rooms, you'll sample seafood prepared as naturally as possible, with no fancy sauces or elaborate techniques. Try such dishes as fried filet of sole, grilled John Dory, or warm cockles. Red mullet might be sautéed in oil or baked in rock salt. The name derives from the regional symbol of La Charente, the sea snail, whose preparation elevates its namesake to a fine culinary art. Look for a vast list of wines and cognacs.

10–12 place Constantin-Brancusi, 14e. www.la-cagouille.fr. ℭ **01-43-22-09-01.** Reservations recommended. Main courses 16€–45€; fixed-price lunch 26€; fixed-price dinner 42€. MC, V. Daily noon–2:30pm and 7:30–10:30pm. Métro: Gaîté.

La Cerisaie ★ 🎒SOUTHWESTERN FRENCH/BISTRO   This shoebox-size dining room near the Tour Montparnasse serves the soul-warming cuisine of southwestern France. Depending on the season, you might start with chestnut soup or an egg baked in porcini cream sauce, and foie gras is always on the menu. In autumn and winter, Chef Cyrill Lalanne does amazing things with wild game and his menu features every animal in the forest from hare to partridge to boar. Finish with the southwestern take on the classic *baba*, made with the region's Armagnac instead of rum. The atmosphere at La Cerisaie is informal and unpretentious, but the restaurant's popularity means that you'll need to reserve a few days in advance.

70 bd. Edgar-Quinet, 14e. www.restaurantlacerisaie.com. ⓒ **01-43-20-98-98.** Reservation recommended. Main courses 15€–35€. MC, V. Mon–Fri noon–2pm and 7–9pm. Métro: Montparnasse-Bienvenüe or Edgar Quinet.

L'Assiette MODERN FRENCH L'Assiette appeals to a nostalgic crowd seeking down-to-earth prices and flavorful food. The place was a *charcuterie* (pork butcher's shop) in the 1930s and still maintains some of its old accessories. The new chef and owner David Rathgeber was once a student of master chef Alain Ducasse. His twist on the bistro cooking tradition includes starters like shrimp tartare and a substantial terrine of pork and foie gras. His version of the classic steak frites dish uses beef from renowned butcher Hugo Desnoyer and features hand-cut fries. For dessert, don't miss the vanilla-flecked rice pudding with *confiture de lait* (milk jam).

181 rue du Château, 14e. www.restaurant-lassiette.com. ⓒ **01-43-22-64-86.** Reservations recommended. Main courses 24€–30€; fixed-price lunch 23€. AE, MC, V. Wed–Sun noon–2:30pm and 7:30–10:30pm. Closed Aug. Métro: Gaité.

Le Casse Noix ★ 🍴 TRADITIONAL FRENCH/BISTRO After cooking for 6 years at La Régalade (p. 223), Chef Pierre-Olivier Lenormand opened his own bistro—a place that serves high-caliber food in a casual setting—in 2010. The decor is nostalgic and the traditional French cooking is sincere and generous. Dishes like smoked chestnut soup, Iberian pork belly with choucroute of turnips, and the classic *petit salé aux lentilles* (lentils with smoky ham) are followed by crowd-pleasing desserts such as *île flottante* ("floating island," a meringue floating on custard). The wine list includes a good selection by the glass as well as many moderately priced bottles. This is a good option if you're looking for an affordable, traditional bistro that's not yet overrun with tourists.

56 rue de la Fédération, 15e. www.le-cassenoix.fr. ⓒ **01-45-66-09-01.** Reservations recommended. Fixed-price dinner 32€; fixed-price lunch 25€. Mon–Fri noon–2:30pm and 7:30–10:30pm. Métro: Dupleix.

Le Cornichon TRADITIONAL FRENCH/BISTRO Chef Matthieu Nadjar worked for years under Stéphane Jego at Chez l'Ami Jean (p. 221) before opening his own bistro in 2011. Le Cornichon (which means "The Pickle") was named by Nadjar's son, Elliot, and it serves southwest-inflected dishes, like monkfish with chorizo, alongside more globally inspired dishes such as skate wing with yuzu butter. Since prices are moderate and it's still relatively easy to get in, this is a great bistro option near the Montparnasse cemetery and the Fondation Cartier.

34 rue Gassendi, 14e. www.lecornichon.fr. ⓒ **01-43-20-40-19.** Reservations recommended. Mains 20€; fixed-price lunch 32€; fixed-price dinner 34€. MC, V. Mon–Fri noon–3pm and 7:30–11pm. Métro: Denfert-Rochereau.

Le Severo TRADITIONAL FRENCH Run by former butcher William Bernet, Le Severo is a carnivore's delight. Crispy fried pigs' feet, farmhouse *boudin noir* (blood pudding), steak tartare, and massive *côte de boeuf* (rib-eye steaks) are just some of the meaty offerings at this joint. The accompanying fries are hand-cut, and the desserts—if you still have room—are the sort that people were eating 100 years ago. One word of advice: don't ask the kitchen to cook your carefully aged steak beyond *à point* (medium rare). The majority of meat lovers here demand their meat *saingant* (rare) or even *bleu* (practically raw).

IN PURSUIT OF THE PERFECT
parisian pastry

Could it be true, as rumor has it, that more eggs, sugar, cream, and butter per capita are consumed in Paris than in any other city? From a modern-day Proust sampling a *madeleine* to a child munching a *pain au chocolat* (chocolate-filled croissant), everyone in Paris seems to be looking for two things: the perfect lover and the perfect pastry—and not necessarily in that order. As a Parisian food critic once said, "A day without a pastry is a day in hell!"

Who'd think of beginning a morning in Paris without a **croissant**—freshly baked, flaky, light, and made with real butter, preferably from Norman cows. The Greeks may have invented pastry making, but the French perfected it. Some French pastries have made a greater impact than others. The croissant and the **brioche**, a sweet and yeasty breakfast bread, are baked around the world today, as is the fabled **éclair au chocolat** (chocolate éclair), a pastry filled with whipped cream or pastry cream and topped with chocolate. Another pastry you should sample is the **mille-feuille** ("thousand leaves"), made by arranging thin layers of flaky pastry on top of one another, along with layers of cream or fruit purée or jam; the American version is called a napoleon.

Here are some of our favorite patisseries:

o **Dalloyau,** 101 rue du Faubourg St-Honoré, 8e (📞 **01-42-99-90-00;** www.dalloyau.fr; Métro: St-Philippe du Roule), has been in business since Napoleon was in power, and has a name instantly recognizable throughout Paris. Dalloyau supplies pastries to the Élysée Palace (the French White House) and many Rothschild mansions nearby. Its specialties are **Le Dalloyau,** praline cake filled with almond meringue that's marvelously light-textured; the **Opéra,** composed of an almond-flavored cookie layered with butter cream, chocolate, and coffee. Unlike Stohrer, Dalloyau has a tearoom (open daily 8:30am–7:30pm) one floor above street level, where ladies who lunch can drop in for a slice of pastry that Dalloyau warns is "too fragile to transport, or to mail, over long distances."

o **Fauchon,** 26–30 place de la Madeleine, 8e (📞 **01-70-39-38-00;** www.fauchon.com; Métro: Madeleine). As readers of French literature know, the taste of the **madeleine** (a scalloped tea cake) triggered the memory of the narrator in Marcel Proust's *Remembrance of Things Past.* Known since the 18th century, the madeleine also inspired chef Christophe Adam at Fauchon to tinker with the classic cookie recipe. Today he prepares madeleines in

8 rue des Plantes, 14e. 📞 **01-40-44-73-09.** Reservations required. Main courses 20€–32€. MC, V. Mon–Sat noon–2pm and Tues–Fri 7:30–10pm. Closed Aug. Métro: Mouton-Duvernet or Alésia.

INEXPENSIVE
Crêperie Josselin ★ 🍴 ☺ CRÊPERIE   Josselin is just 1 of maybe 20 crêperies that are concentrated around the "gateway to Brittany" Montparnasse train station, but it stands above all others as the city's best. The Breton working the

such flavors as orange, coffee-sesame, and pistachio.

o **Ladurée Royale,** 16 rue Royale, 8e (✆ **01-42-60-21-79;** www.laduree. fr; Métro: Concorde or Madeleine), is Paris's dowager tearoom, opened in 1862, and just a few steps from La Madeleine. Its pastry chefs are known for the **macaron,** a pastry for which this place is celebrated. Karl Lagerfeld comes here and raves about them. This isn't the sticky coconut-version macaroon known to many, but two almond meringue cookies, flavored with chocolate, vanilla, pistachio, coffee, or other flavors, stuck together with butter cream. You may also want to try **Le Faubourg,** a lusciously dense chocolate cake with layers of caramel and apricots, and the Pain au Chocolat à la Pistache, a pastry filled with delicious pistachio paste and dark chocolate.

o **Pierre Hermé,** 72 rue Bonaparte, 6e (✆ **01-43-54-47-77;** www. pierreherme.com; Métro: St-Sulpice). While Ladurée makes our favorite classic macaroons in recognizable flavors, we head to Pierre Hermé for unfamiliar combinations like olive oil and vanilla, white truffle, and foie gras. Anything pastry featuring the Ispahan flavor combination (litchi, rose, and raspberry) is also delicious;

and Hermé's vanilla millefeuille (pastry layered with vanilla cream) is the best in the city.

o **Sadaharu Aoki,** 56 bd. Port Royale, 5e (✆ **01-45-35-34-19;** www. sadaharuaoki.com; Métro: Les Gobelins). Parisians started eating éclairs, that cream-filled chocolate-covered shell of choux pastry, in the 1800s. Surprisingly it is a Japanese chef who makes the best éclairs in today's Paris. He even does a mâcha green tea version.

o **Stohrer,** 51 rue Montorgueil, 2e (✆ **01-42-33-38-20;** www.stohrer.fr; Métro: Sentier or Les Halles), has been going strong ever since it was opened by Louis XV's pastry chef in 1730. A pastry always associated with this place is *puits d'amour* (well of love), which consists of caramelized puff pastry filled with vanilla ice cream. Available at any time is one of the most luscious desserts in Paris: **baba au rhum,** made with rum-soaked sponge cake, or its even richer cousin, **un Ali Baba,** which also incorporates cream-based rum-and-raisin filling. Stohrer boasts an interior decor classified as a national historic treasure, with frescoes of damsels in 18th-century costume bearing flowers and (what else?) pastries.

griddle knows exactly how to achieve the lacy, golden edges of a perfect galette, and he's not shy with the butter. Our idea of a perfect lunch (especially after too much wine the night before) is Josselin's *complete*—a buckwheat galette stuffed with egg, cheese, and ham—paired with a ceramic bowl of hard cider and followed by a salted butter caramel crepe. The easy prices, continuous service and wide range of flavor combinations make this a great option for children as well.

67 rue du Montparnasse, 14e. ☎ **01-43-20-93-50.** Reservations not required. Crepes 6€–15€; fixed-price menu 11€. MC, V. Tues–Sun noon–11pm. Métro: Montparnasse-Bienvenüe.

FAMILY-FRIENDLY RESTAURANTS

Dining with children in Paris can be tricky, especially at night. Dinner service in most restaurants begins at 7:30pm, which requires keeping kids awake later than they might be used to, and only some restaurants offer kids' menus. But if you ask when you reserve (or even when you arrive), the chef will usually whip up something the kids will like. And if all else fails, order a *plat du jour* or *plat garni* (a garnished main-course platter), which will be suitable for most children, particularly if a dessert is to follow.

If you'd like to introduce your children to a real French restaurant, consider bringing them for **lunch.** Prices are often half of what you might pay at dinner, and daytime dishes tend to be less intricate (and potentially off-putting for a child). **Hotel dining rooms** can also be a good choice for family dining. They usually have children's menus or at least one or two *plats du jour* cooked for children, such as spaghetti with meat sauce.

In addition to the restaurants we recommend below, **cafes** are a great option for traveling families because they're cheaper, they often serve simpler food, and they welcome children during the day and early evening. At a cafe, children seem to like the sandwiches (try a croque-monsieur, or toasted ham and cheese), the omelets, and the *pommes frites* (French fries). Kids will also enjoy eating crepes at a **crêperie.**

Here is our list of top restaurants that children will enjoy:

Breakfast in America (p. 213)   This American restaurant in the Latin Quarter serves breakfast all day, hamburgers and fries, milkshakes, and other familiar kid favorites.

Crèmerie-Restaurant Polidor (p. 217)   This reasonably priced restaurant is so family friendly, it calls its food *cuisine familiale.* This might be a good place to introduce your child to bistro food.

Crêperie Josselin (p. 226)   This local favorite (a sit-down restaurant, not a stand on the street) is a great option for kids because they offer early dinner seating and easy prices. What kid doesn't love a crepe?

Le Relais de l'Entrecôte (p. 217)   This affordable restaurant offers unlimited servings of steak and fries, and desserts such as profiteroles never fail to make kids happy.

Rosa Bonheur (p. 209)   Located inside the city's biggest park, Parc des Buttes-Chaumont, Rosa Bonheur boasts a beautiful outdoor terrace where parents can nibble on tapas while watching their kids roll down the hill. There's also an indoor play area and kids' menu.

THE TOP CAFES

As surely everyone knows, the cafe is a Parisian institution. Parisians use cafes as combination club/tavern/snack bars, almost as extensions of their living rooms. They're spots where you can sit alone and read your newspaper, do your homework or write your memoirs; meet a friend or lover; nibble on a hard-boiled egg; or drink yourself into oblivion. At cafes, you meet your dates, and then go on to a show or stay and talk. Above all, cafes are for people-watching.

Coffee (*un café*), of course, is the chief drink. It comes black, in a small cup, unless you specifically order it with milk (*un café crème*) or with extra hot water (*un café allongé*), which is more like an americano. *Thé* (tea, pronounced *tay*) is also fairly popular but usually more expensive than coffee, hovering around the 4€ mark. You can also order fruit juice (*jus de fruits*), sparkling water (*un Perrier*), or soft drinks (*un Coca, un Coca Light*), but be warned that these are normally double the price of a glass of wine and may arrive without any ice. If you need ice, ask for your drink "*avec glacons*" (pronounced *glasson*). From the early afternoon onward, and especially during the *apéro* hour (the before dinner period when friends often meet for a drink), patrons order beer (*bière*) and wine (*vin*) by the glass—either a glass of white wine (*un verre de vin blanc*) or red wine (*un verre de vin rouge*).

Now, just a few words on cafe etiquette: Your bill will probably arrive with your order, but you're not expected to pay until you leave. *Service compris* means the tip is included in your bill, so it isn't necessary to tip extra. Still, tips are appreciated, but keep them small—a tip of small change (1€) is more than enough if you're only having a few drinks.

Café de Flore   This is perhaps the most famous cafe in the world, still fighting to maintain a Left Bank aura despite hordes of visitors from around the world. Jean-Paul Sartre—the granddaddy of existentialism, a key figure in the Resistance, and a renowned cafe-sitter—often came here during World War II. Wearing a leather jacket and beret, he sat and wrote his trilogy *Les Chemins de la Liberté (The Roads to Freedom)*. Camus, Picasso, and Apollinaire also frequented the Flore. The cafe is still going strong, although the existentialists have been replaced by tourists and sometimes fashionistas.

Did You Know?

You'll pay substantially less in a cafe if you stand at the counter rather than sit at a table, partly because there's no service charge, and partly because diners tend to linger at tables.

172 bd. St-Germain, 6e. www.cafe deflore.fr. (*©* **01-45-48-55-26.** Cafe espresso 4.10€; glass of beer 9€; snacks from 9€; full meal 25€–50€. AE, DC, MC, V. Daily 7:30am–1:30am. Métro: St-Germain-des-Prés.

Café de la Musique   Attached to one of the grandest of Mitterrand's *grands travaux*, a concert hall within the Parc de la Villette, this cafe's location guarantees a crowd that's passionately devoted to music. The recorded sounds that play in the background are likely to be more diverse and more eclectic than those in any other cafe in Paris. The red-and-green velour setting might remind you of a modern opera house. The main attraction, however, is the sprawling outdoor terrace with 30 tables that face a bubbling lion-shaped fountain and perfectly catch the afternoon light.

In the Cité de la Musique, place Fontaine aux Lions, 213 av. Jean-Jaurès, 19e. www.citedela musique.fr. (*©* **01-48-03-15-91.** Main courses 12€–24€; tapas 6€–9€. AE, DC, MC, V. Daily 8am–2am. Métro: Porte de Pantin.

Café des Deux Moulins *Amélie* was a quirky low-budget film that was nominated for five Oscars and was seen by more than 25 million people around the world following its release in 2001. The film was set in Montmartre, and the cafe featured in the film has developed into a mandatory stopping-off place for the constantly arriving "cult of Amélie." In the film, Amélie worked as a waitress at the Café des Deux Moulins. The musty atmosphere, with its 1950s decor, mustard-colored ceiling, and lace curtains, has been preserved—even the wall lamps and unisex toilet. The menu has retained classic, hearty dishes such as calf's liver, green frisée salad with bacon bits and warm goat cheese, and pigs' brains with lentils. They also serve hamburgers, with or without a fried egg on top.

15 rue Lepic, 18e. ✆ **01-42-54-90-50.** Main courses 11€–18€. MC, V. Daily 7am–2am. Métro: Blanche.

La Belle Hortense This is the most literary cafe in the Marais, loaded with literary antecedents and references. It contains an erudite and accessible staff; an inventory of French literary classics as well as modern tomes about art, psychoanalysis, history, and culture; and two high-ceilinged, 19th-century rooms, little changed since the days of Baudelaire and Balzac. Near the entrance is a zinc-covered bar that sells glasses of wine. If you're fluent in French, you might be interested in attending a reading, a book signing, or a lecture (check the website for information).

31 rue Vieille du Temple, 4e. http://cafeine.com. ✆ **01-48-04-71-60.** Glass of wine 4€–10€; coffee 2.10€; *plats du jour* 12€–24€. MC, V. Daily 5pm–2am. Métro: Hôtel-de-Ville or St-Paul.

La Coupole Born in 1927 and once a leading center of artistic life, La Coupole is now the epitome of the grand Paris brasserie in Montparnasse. Former patrons include Josephine Baker, Henry Miller, Dalí, Calder, Hemingway, Fitzgerald, and Picasso. At one of its sidewalk tables, you can sit and watch the passing scene and order a coffee or a cognac VSOP. The food is quite good, despite the fact that the dining room resembles an enormous rail-station waiting room. Try main dishes such as sole meunière, a very good rump steak, fresh oysters, shellfish, grilled lobster with flambéed whisky sauce, or curried lamb. The waiters are as rude and inattentive as ever, and the patrons would have it no other way.

102 bd. du Montparnasse, 14e. www.lacoupole-paris.com. ✆ **01-43-20-14-20.** Main courses 20€–40€; breakfast buffet 14€–19€; fixed-price lunch and dinner 28€–34€. AE, DC, MC, V. Daily 8am–1am (breakfast buffet Mon–Fri 8:30–10:30am). Métro: Vavin.

La Palette ★ The interior of this desperately romantic cafe, inhabited by amiably crotchety waiters and formerly frequented by Picasso and Braque, consists of tiled murals installed around 1935 advertising the virtues of a brand of liqueur that's no longer manufactured. If you happen to drop in during mealtime, you'll have a limited selection of salads and croque-monsieur (toasted ham and cheese), plus one *plat du jour*, always priced at 15€, which may include roast beef, lamb stew, fish, or lamb. The real reason to come, though, is the terrace, a beautiful outdoor space not far from the river where you can get a real sense of the village life in Saint-Germain.

43 rue de Seine, 6e. www.cafelapaletteparis.com. ✆ **01-43-26-68-15.** Sandwiches, omelets, and *plats du jour* 6€–15€. MC, V. Cafe and bar daily 8am–2am. Restaurant daily noon–3pm. Métro: Mabillon or St-Germain-des-Prés.

La Rotonde   Once patronized by Hemingway, the original Rotonde faded into history but is immortalized in the pages of *The Sun Also Rises,* in which Papa wrote, "No matter what cafe in Montparnasse you ask a taxi driver to bring you to from the right bank of the river, they always take you to the Rotonde." Having since been lavishly upgraded, its reincarnation has a paneled Art Deco elegance and shares the site with a cinema. The menu includes such hearty fare as pepper steak with French fries, shellfish in season, a superb and succulent version of sole meunière, and sea bass filets with herb-flavored lemon sauce.

105 bd. du Montparnasse, 6e. www.rotondemontparnasse.com. ℭ **01-43-26-48-26.** Glass of wine 4€–11€; main courses 10€–38€; fixed-price lunch 18€–35€; fixed-price dinner 39€. AE, MC, V. Cafe daily 7:15am–2am; food service daily noon–1am. Métro: Vavin.

Le Procope   To fans of French history, this is the holy grail of Parisian cafes. Opened in 1686, it occupies a three-story town house categorized as a historic monument. Inside, nine salons and dining rooms, each of whose 300-year-old walls have been carefully preserved and painted a deep red, are available for languorous afternoon coffee breaks or old-fashioned meals. Menu items include platters of shellfish, onion soup *au gratin*, *coq au vin* (chicken stewed in wine), duck breast in honey sauce, and grilled versions of various meats and fish. Every day between 3 and 6pm, the place makes itself available to sightseers who come to look but not necessarily eat and drink at the site that welcomed such movers and shakers as Diderot, Voltaire, George Sand, Victor Hugo, and Oscar Wilde. Especially charming is the ground-floor room outfitted like an antique library.

13 rue de l'Ancienne-Comédie, 6e. www.procope.com. ℭ **01-40-46-79-00.** Reservations recommended. Coffee 3€; glass of beer 5€–7€; main courses 20€–29€. AE, DC, MC, V. Daily 11:30am–1am. Métro: Odéon.

Les Deux Magots ♨   Among the two famous "philosopher cafes" of Saint-Germain, only the Café de Flore has retained any cachet among the locals. Les Deux Magots may have once provided a haven for struggling writers, but the only tomes you'll see on the tables today are of the guidebook variety. The terrace is a good place for people-watching, but you can expect to pay outlandish prices for the privilege.

6 place St-Germain-des-Prés, 6e. www.lesdeuxmagots.fr. ℭ **01-45-48-55-25.** Café crème 5€; whisky soda 12€–16€; main courses 22€–36€. AE, DC, V. Daily 7:30am–1am. Métro: St-Germain-des-Prés.

RESTAURANTS BY CUISINE

ALSATIAN
Bofinger (**$$**, p. 186)

AMERICAN
Breakfast in America (**$**, p. 213)
Chibby's Diner (**$**, p. 205)
Le Camion Qui Fume (**$**, p. 189)

ASIAN FUSION
Le Pré Verre ★ (**$$**, p. 212)

AUVERGNAT
L'Ambassade d'Auvergne (**$$**, p. 188)

BAKERY
Eric Kayser ★★ (**$**, p. 222)

KEY TO ABBREVIATIONS:
$$$$** = Very Expensive   **$$$** = Expensive   **$$** = Moderate   **$ = Inexpensive

BASQUE

Afaria ★ (**$$**, p. 224)
Au Bascou (**$$**, p. 185)
Chez Gladines (**$**, p. 213)
Chez l'Ami Jean ★ (**$$**, p. 221)

BISTRO

Afaria ★ (**$$**, p. 224)
Astier (**$$**, p. 204)
Au Trou Gascon (**$$$**, p. 202)
Bouillon Racine ★ (**$$**, p. 210)
Café des Musées (**$$**, p. 186)
Chez Janou (**$**, p. 186)
Hôtel du Nord (**$$**, p. 207)
Jadis ★ (**$$**, p. 224)
Jaja (**$$**, p. 186)
La Cerisaie ★ (**$$**, p. 224)
La Crèmerie Restaurant Polidor
   (**$**, p. 217)
La Fontaine de Mars (**$$**, p. 222)
La Régalade ★★ (**$$**, p. 223)
La Régalade–St. Honoré ★★
   (**$$**, p. 182)
Le Baratin ★ (**$$**, p. 208)
Le Bistrot Paul Bert ★★ (**$$**, p. 204)
Le Casse Noix ★ (**$$**, p. 225)
Le Comptoir du Relais ★★
   (**$$$**, p. 216)
Le Cornichon (**$$**, p. 225)
Le Cotte Roti (**$$**, p. 204)
Le Pantruche ★ (**$$**, p. 199)
Le Petit Marguery (**$$**, p. 212)
Les Papilles ★ (**$$**, p. 212)
Restaurant Chez Denise ★★
   (**$$**, p. 183)
Table d'Eugène ★ (**$$**, p. 202)

BRASSERIE

Bofinger (**$$**, p. 186)
Bouillon Racine ★ (**$$**, p. 210)
Brasserie Flo ★★ (**$$**, p. 206)
Chartier (**$**, p. 200)
Le Vaudeville (**$$**, p. 182)
Rech (**$$$**, p. 196)
Thoumieux (**$$$**, p. 221)

BRETON

Chez Michel ★★ (**$$**, p. 206)

CAFE

Café de Flore (**$**, p. 229)

Café de la Musique (**$**, p. 229)
Café des Deux Moulins (**$**, p. 230)
La Belle Hortense (**$**, p. 230)
La Coupole (**$**, p. 230)
La Palette ★ (**$**, p. 230)
La Rotonde (**$**, p. 231)
Le Procope (**$**, p. 231)
Les Deux Magots (**$**, p. 231)

CHINESE

Le President (**$$**, p. 208)
Lily Wang (**$$**, p. 222)
Shang Palace, Hôtel Shangri-la
   Paris ★★★ (**$$$$**, p. 194)
Yam'Tcha ★★★ (**$$$**, p. 180)

CRÊPERIE

Breizh Café ★ (**$$**, p. 188)
Crêperie Josselin ★ (**$**, p. 226)

ENGLISH

Le Bal Café ★ (**$**, p. 202)

FALAFEL

L'As du Fallafel ★ (**$**, p. 188)

FRENCH (MODERN)

Cobéa ★ (**$$$**, p. 223)
Cristal Room (**$$$**, p. 195)
Epicure (Le Bristol) ★★
   (**$$$$**, p. 192)
Fish (**$$**, p. 216)
Frenchie ★★ (**$$**, p. 181)
Jaja (**$$**, p. 186)
Jean-François Piège ★ (**$$$$**, p. 220)
La Bigarrade (**$$$**, p. 195)
La Cuisine (**$$$$**, p. 192)
La Famille (**$$**, p. 200)
La Fresque (**$**, p. 184)
La Gare (**$$**, p. 197)
La Gazzetta ★★ (**$$$**, p. 203)
L'Arpège ★★★ (**$$$$**, p. 220)
L'Assiette (**$$**, p. 225)
L'Astrance ★★★ (**$$$**, p. 196)
L'Atelier Saint-Germain de Joël
   Robuchon ★★ (**$$$**, p. 220)
Le Chapeau Melon ★ (**$$**, p. 208)
Le Chateaubriand ★★★
   (**$$$**, p. 203)
Le Cinq ★★ (**$$$$**, p. 193)
Le Fumoir ★★ (**$$**, p. 182)

Le Garde Robe (**$**, p. 184)
Le Pré Verre ★ (**$$**, p. 212)
Les Tablettes ★ (**$$$$**, p. 193)
Le Tambour (**$**, p. 184)
Le Verre Volé ★★ (**$$**, p. 208)
Le Violon d'Ingres (**$$$**, p. 221)
L'Hédoniste ★ (**$$**, p. 183)
Nansouty ★ (**$$**, p. 201)
1979 (**$$**, p. 183)
Passage 53 ★★ (**$$$**, p. 180)
Pierre Gagnaire ★★★
   (**$$$$**, p. 194)
Restaurant de l'Opéra (**$$$$**, p. 198)
Septime (**$$**, p. 205)
Spring ★★ (**$$$**, p. 180)
Thoumieux (**$$$**, p. 221)
Willi's Wine Bar (**$$$**, p.183)
Yam'Tcha ★★★ (**$$$**, p. 180)
Ze Kitchen Galerie ★ (**$$$**, p. 216)

FRENCH (TRADITIONAL)

Astier (**$$**, p. 204)
Au Pied de Cochon (**$$**, p. 180)
Aux Lyonnais (**$$**, p. 181)
Bar des Théâtres (**$$**, p. 196)
Benoit (**$$$**, p. 185)
Brasserie Flo ★★ (**$$**, p. 206)
Café des Musées (**$$**, p. 186)
Caïus (**$$**, p. 196)
Chartier (**$**, p. 200)
Chéri Bibi (**$$**, p. 200)
Chez Georges (**$$**, p. 181)
Chez Grenouille (**$$**, p. 198)
Hiramatsu (**$$$$**, p. 192)
Hôtel du Nord (**$$**, p. 207)
Itinéraires (**$$$**, p. 210)
Jadis ★ (**$$**, p. 224)
Jeanne A ★ (**$**, p. 205)
La Crèmerie Restaurant Polidor
   (**$**, p. 217)
La Fermette Marbeuf (**$$$**, p. 197)
La Ferrandaise (**$$**, p. 217)
La Grille (**$$**, p. 207)
L'Ambassade d'Auvergne (**$$**, p. 188)
L'Ami Louis (**$$$$**, p. 185)
La Régalade ★★ (**$$**, p. 223)
La Régalade–St. Honoré ★★
   (**$$**, p. 182)
Lasserre (**$$$$**, p. 193)
La Tour d'Argent (**$$$$**, p. 210)
Le Baratin ★ (**$$**, p. 208)

Le Bistrot Paul Bert ★★ (**$$**, p. 204)
Le Casse Noix ★ (**$$**, p. 225)
Le Comptoir du Relais ★★
   (**$$$**, p. 216)
Le Cornichon (**$$**, p. 225)
Le Grand Véfour (**$$$$**, p. 178)
Le Hide ★ (**$$**, p. 197)
Le Pantruche ★ (**$$**, p. 199)
Le Petit Marguery (**$$**, p. 212)
Le Relais de l'Entrecôte (**$$**, p. 217)
Le Relais Louis XIII ★ (**$$$$**, p. 214)
Le Repaire de Cartouche (**$$**, p. 204)
L'Estaminet des Enfants Rouge
   (**$$**, p. 189)
Le Timbre (**$$**, p. 217)
Les Cocottes de Christian
   Constant ★ (**$$**, p. 222)
Les Papilles ★ (**$$**, p. 212)
Le Severo (**$$**, p. 225)
Mélac (**$**, p. 206)
Michel Rostang (**$$$$**, p. 193)
Monte Carlo (**$**, p. 197)
Racines (**$$**, p. 183)
Restaurant Auguste ★★
   (**$$$**, p. 221)
Restaurant Chez Denise ★★ (**$$**,
   p. 183)
Restaurant Plaza Athénée (Alain
   Ducasse) ★★ (**$$$$**, p. 194)
Ribouldingue (**$$**, p. 213)
Table d'Eugene ★ (**$$**, p. 202)
Vivant ★ (**$$**, p. 209)

GREEK

Casa Olympe (**$$**, p. 198)

INTERNATIONAL

Ze Kitchen Galerie ★ (**$$$**, p. 216)

ITALIAN

Vivant ★ (**$$**, p. 209)

JAPANESE

Higuma ★ (**$**, p. 184)

LIGHT FARE

Eric Kayser ★★ (**$**, p. 222)
L'As du Fallafel ★ (**$**, p. 188)

LYONNAIS

Aux Lyonnais (**$$**, p. 181)

MEDITERRANEAN
Fish (**$$**, p. 216)
Le Cotte Roti (**$$**, p. 204)

MIDDLE EASTERN
Wally Le Saharien (**$$$**, p. 199)

MOROCCAN
Mansouria (**$$**, p. 205)

PIZZA
Pink Flamingo (**$**, p. 209)

PROVENÇAL
Casa Olympe (**$$**, p. 198)
Chez Janou (**$**, p. 186)
La Bastide Odéon (**$$**, p. 216)
Les Tablettes ★ (**$$$$**, p. 193)

SEAFOOD
Antoine ★★ (**$$$**, p. 192)
Fish (**$$**, p. 216)
Goumard (**$$$**, p. 178)
La Cagouille (**$$**, p. 224)
La Grille (**$$**, p. 207)
Rech (**$$$**, p. 196)
Restaurant Auguste ★★
   (**$$$**, p. 221)

SOUTHWESTERN FRENCH
Chez l'Ami Jean ★ (**$$**, p. 221)
Dans Les Landes ★ (**$$**, p. 212)
Hélène Darroze (**$$$$**, p. 214)
La Fontaine de Mars (**$$**, p. 222)
La Cerisaie ★ (**$$**, p. 224)
L'Avant Comptoir ★ (**$**, p. 218)

STEAK
Le Relais de l'Entrecôte (**$$**, p. 217)

TAPAS
Rosa Bonheur ★ (**$$**, p. 209)

VEGETARIAN
Bob's Kitchen (**$**, p. 188)
Le Potager du Marais (**$$**, p. 189)

WINE BAR
Coinstôt Vino (**$$**, p. 181)
Jeanne A ★ (**$**, p. 205)
L'Avant Comptoir ★ (**$**, p. 218)
Le Chapeau Melon ★ (**$$**, p. 208)
Le Garde Robe (**$**, p. 184)
Le Verre Volé ★★ (**$$**, p. 208)
Mélac (**$**, p. 206)
Willi's Wine Bar (**$$$**, p. 183)

PRACTICAL MATTERS: THE RESTAURANT SCENE

Hours

Unless otherwise indicated (by a sign that reads *service continu,* which means that food is served all day), Paris restaurants are usually open for lunch from noon to 2:30pm and dinner from 7:30 to 10:30pm. Cafes and brasseries are a good option if you need to eat a later lunch or earlier dinner. Some brasseries even serve until late at night. For late-night dining options see p. 184.

Prices, Taxes & Tipping

Many visitors often experience sticker shock in Parisian restaurants. **Three-star dining** remains quite expensive, with appetizers sometimes priced at 60€ and dinners easily costing 185€ to 250€ per person in the top dining rooms of celebrated chefs. Paris now boasts a large number of **neo-bistrots,** places that combine bistro ambience and prices with excellent culinary skills and

> ### 📎 Mystifying Menu?
>
> If you need help distinguishing a *coq au vin* from a *blanquette de veau,* see "Basic Menu Terms" in chapter 12.

Useful Foodie websites

- **Paris by Mouth** (www.parisbymouth.com) provides insider information (in English) on dining in the capital.

- **The Fork** (www.thefork.com) allows you to reserve restaurants online for free (according to area and type of food), and supplies a list of restaurant promotions—sometimes up to 50% off (check restrictions before you book).

- **Simon Says** (http://francoissimon.typepad.fr/english) is the English version of acclaimed French food critic François Simon's blog.

ingredients. The influx of high-quality neo-bistros has meant that there are many more affordable dining options in Paris today: The standard price for a very good bistro meal is 30€ to 40€ for three courses. **Cafes** offer sandwiches, soup, and salads in a relaxed setting. In a cafe, if you sit at the bar for a drink, coffee, or sandwich, prices are less than they would be if you were seated at a table.

However, you can get around these high price tags in many places by **dining at lunch** (when prices are always cheaper, especially in top-end restaurants) or ordering a prix-fixe meal at lunch or dinner. In France, lunch (as well as dinner) tends to be a full-course meal with meat, vegetables, salad, bread, cheese, dessert, wine, and coffee—lunch meals can be half the price of dinner, so we strongly recommend that you splurge at lunch. The **prix-fixe (fixed-price) menu** or *le menu* is a set meal that the chef prepares that day. It is most often fresh and promptly served, and represents a greater bargain than dining a la carte. Of course, it's limited, so you'll have to like the choices provided. Sometimes there are one to three menus, beginning with the least expensive and going up for a more elaborate meal. A lot depends on your pocketbook and appetite.

Remember that the price you see on the menu is the full price that you'll pay at the end of the meal, as tax and service are already included. But it is customary to leave a tip (about 50 cents for drinks, a euro or two in cafes where you have eaten; up to 10% in a restaurant) for excellent service. If you've had bad service (still too omnipresent in the French capital) make sure you leave nothing at all.

Reservations

Reservations are a necessary hurdle to overcome if you want to eat in the city's best restaurants. Travelers used to a more spontaneous approach are often surprised and disappointed when they show up without booking and are turned away. This has nothing to do with being a foreigner. It's simply that the restaurants here don't offer multiple seatings throughout the night, and there's rarely a bar where you can hang out and wait. If you haven't booked ahead, there may not be room at the table. Ask your hotel concierge to help if you're not comfortable making the call, or gather your courage and say "*Bonjour. Je voudrais faire une reservation pour dîner* (dinner) *or dejeuner* (lunch). *Vous parlez anglais?*" At this point, they may switch to English if you are polite and they are capable. If not, have the French translation for your desired date and time ready and be ready to give your name (*votre nom?*) and the number of people (*combien de personnes?*) in your party. Having a reservation is crucial, and it will open up a world of authentic and memorable dining experiences.

Restaurant Deals

Open Table doesn't operate in Paris, but a local version called **The Fork** (www. thefork.com) offers online booking for some restaurants, and you can select to view the site in English. Not all of the restaurants we recommend in this chapter are listed on this site, but a few very good ones are, including the Plaza Athenée, Les Ambassadeurs, Goumard, Michel Rostang, The Cristal Room, Caïus, Fish, and La Régalade. A few restaurants offer discounts or a free drink if you book through this site.

SHOPPING

By Kate van den Boogert

Paris is, of course, a world-famous shopping destination—and for good reason. The city marries art and commerce, elevating an afternoon of window shopping into a high-culture experience. Parisian department stores sell everything you could ever want under one elegant roof, while specialty shops hold countless small treasures, from jeweled safety pins to handcrafted candles. But true shoppers come to Paris for the fashion—Chanel, Dior, Hermès, and Louis Vuitton call Paris home. The city is also home to iconic cosmetic and perfume houses, as well as endless gourmet food shops. But you don't have to buy anything to appreciate shopping in Paris: Peer in the *vitrines* (window displays), keep an eye out for new trends, and return home with a whole new interpretation of style.

LES HALLES, LOUVRE & PALAIS ROYAL (1ER & 2E)

Subterranean shopping mall **Les Halles** (under renovation until 2016) is a short stroll from major shopping strip the **rue de Rivoli.** Both these destinations are a who's-who of the major international fashion chains, including H&M, Zara, Sephora, Etam, and Gap. At another end of the 1st is the **Palais Royal,** just north of the Louvre and one of the city's best shopping secrets. The 18th-century arcade of boutiques flanks the garden of a former palace and includes some of the hottest names in fashion and accessories, such as Marc Jacobs, Stella McCartney, and Pierre Hardy. It signals the beginning of the busy part of the rue St-Honoré, to the south, and to the north, behind the Palais Royal, is another sophisticated shopping destination, the **place des Victoires,** which to the east joins with the **Etienne-Marcel** shopping neighborhood, known for its jeans and street wear. In the 19th century, this area became known for its *passages,* glass-enclosed shopping streets—in fact, the world's first shopping malls. They were also the city's first buildings to be illuminated by gaslight. Many have been torn down, but a dozen or so have survived. The **Passage de Grand Cerf,** between 145 rue St-Denis and 10 rue Dussoubs (Métro: Etienne-Marcel), is filled with everything from ethnic-chic to jewelry and accessory shops. The **Place Vendome** is the city's fine jewelry quarter, where fine jewelers sit like gems in a crown around the Vendome column in the center of the square.

PREVIOUS PAGE: **Window shopping in Paris.**

Didier Ludot (p. 256)

Dior Joaillerie (p. 258)

Francis Kurkdjian (p. 248)

Galignani (p. 249)

Goyard (p. 255)

JC de Castelbajac (p. 253)

Jean-Paul Hévin (p. 261)

Kiliwatch (p. 256)

Lavinia (p. 263)

Le Louvre des Antiquaires (p. 245)

Les Halles (p. 243)

Maison Fabre (p. 255)

Manufacture Nationale de Sèvres (p. 145)

Morabito (p. 255)

107 Rivoli (p. 246)

Pierre Hardy (p. 255)

Salons du Palais Royal, Shiseido (p. 248)

Van Cleef & Arpels (p. 258)

Ventilo (p. 253)

White Bird (p. 258)

WH Smith (p. 250)

LE MARAIS, ILE ST-LOUIS & ILE DE LA CITÉ (3E & 4E)

The Marais provides two dramatically different shopping experiences. The Lower Marais is concentrated around the **rue des Francs-Bourgeois,** where you'll find a succession of charming fashion, accessories, and beauty stores. But don't be afraid to strike off into the neighborhood's medieval warren of twisting streets chockablock with up-to-the-minute fashions and trends. The Northern Marais, concentrated around the **rue de Bretagne,** is a hotbed of independent French designers. Some in-the-know shoppers are skipping St-Germain or St-Honoré and heading here instead, for guaranteed cutting-edge fashion and design.

Azzedine Alaïa (p. 250)

Bensimon (p. 251)

Bijoux Blues (p. 257)

Bonton (p. 254)

The Different Company (p. 247)

L'Eclaireur (p. 253)

L'Habilleur (p. 256)

Les Mots à la Bouche (p. 249)

Marché aux Fleurs et aux Oiseaux (p. 243)

Marché des Enfants Rouge (p. 245)

Merci (p. 259)

Sandro Homme (p. 254)

Village St-Paul (p. 246)

CHAMPS-ÉLYSÉES & WESTERN PARIS (8E, 16E & 17E)

The heart of the international designer parade is here on the Right Bank. **Rue du Faubourg St-Honoré** was the traditional miracle mile until recent years, when many of the exclusive shops shunned it for the even more deluxe **avenue Montaigne** at the other end of the arrondissement. (It's a long but pleasant walk from one fashion strip to the other.) Paris's most glamorous shopping street is lined with almost unspeakably fancy shops, where you float from big name to big name and in a few hours can see Dior, Chanel, and everything in between. The neighboring **Champs-Élysées** shouts "teen scene" with hot mass-market flagships. The zone around the **Madeleine** hosts many fine specialty food shops.

Avenue Montaigne.

OPÉRA & GRANDS BOULEVARDS (9E)

Opéra has at its beating heart the "other" two department stores: Le Printemps and Les Galeries Lafayette, built in a row along **boulevard Haussmann.** Their commercial energy draws many other big names and chains.

PIGALLE & MONTMARTRE (18E)

Villagey Montmartre's charming winding streets, fanning out around Abbesses, are filled with small shops specializing in design, fashion, jewelry, and food. Wander along the rue des Abbesses, down the rue Houdon, up the rue des Martyrs for a sweet afternoon of discovery.

RÉPUBLIQUE, BASTILLE & EASTERN PARIS (11E & 12E)

Shopping in Bastille is concentrated on and around the **rue du Faubourg St-Antoine,** which heads east from the place de la Bastille and counts big names and chains, and winding streets nearby, like the **rue de Charonne.** The **Viaduc des Arts** running parallel to avenue Daumesnil is a collection of about 30 specialist craft stores occupying a series of narrow vaulted niches under what used to be railroad tracks.

French Trotters (p. 252)

Isabel Marant (p. 252)

La Plaque Emaillées et Gravée Jacquin (p. 263)

Les Fleurs (p. 265)

Marché d'Aligre (p. 245)

Viaduc des Arts (p. 247)

BELLEVILLE, CANAL ST-MARTIN & NORTHEAST PARIS (10E, 19E & 20E)

Not a major shopping zone, this is where tourists come to soak up the cosmopolitan atmosphere and explore specialty shops from the city's various immigrant communities. The Canal St-Martin especially offers local bohemian charm along little streets like rue de Marseille, rue Beaurepaire, the quai de Valmy, and quai de Jemmapes.

agnès b (p. 250)

Antoine & Lili (p. 258)

Centre Commercial (p. 258)

LATIN QUARTER (5E & 13E)

More of a residential neighborhood, the Latin Quarter is better known for its major sights—the Luxembourg Gardens and the Sorbonne university—than for its shopping strips. However a host of specialist bookshops, which feed the local student population, remain a real draw.

Diptyque (p. 248)

La Quincaillerie (p. 265)

La Tuile à Loup (p. 264)

Librairie le Bail-Weissert (p. 249)

Shakespeare & Company (p. 249)

ST-GERMAIN-DES-PRÉS & LUXEMBOURG (6E)

This area is the soul of the Left Bank and is one of the most famous shopping districts in Paris. Traditionally a more literary neighborhood, high fashion addresses are gradually taking over the bookshops, and the Left Bank now rivals with classic Right Bank shopping zones such as St-Honoré and Avenue

Montaigne. Wander the avenue St-Germain, rue St Sulpice, rue du Cherche Midi, and rue du Vieux Colombier, the rue Bonapart and rue Jacob down to the Seine, or gourmet paradise rue de Buci, for some elevated shopping experiences.

Bonpoint (p. 254)

Christian Constant (p. 261)

Cire Trudon (p. 263)

Erès (p. 257)

Hermès (p. 252)

La Maison Ivre (p. 264)

Marché Buci (p. 245)

Pierre Hermé (p. 260)

Poîlane (p. 261)

Robert Clergerie (p. 255)

Sonia Rykiel (p. 253)

Souleiado (p. 265)

Taschen (p. 250)

Tea & Tattered Pages (p. 250)

Village Voice Bookshop (p. 250)

Yves Saint Laurent (p. 253)

Zadig & Voltaire (p. 254)

EIFFEL TOWER & NEARBY (7E)

The city's most glamorous department store Le Bon Marché sets the scene for a high-voltage shopping experience. If much of this neighborhood is more dedicated to culture and architecture than fashion, along its eastern edge, some of the glamour of adjacent St-Germain rubs off, around the **rue du Bac** and **rue du Grenelle,** for example, where you'll find all that wealth can buy.

Au Nom de la Rose (p. 263)

Barthelemy (p. 261)

Conran Shop (p. 265)

Defilé des Marques (p. 256)

Editions de Parfums Fréderic Malle (p. 248)

Le Bon Marché (p. 257)

Sennelier (p. 246)

7L (p. 249)

MONTPARNASSE & SOUTHERN PARIS (14E & 15E)

Located behind St-Germain, this neighborhood is dominated both by Paris's only skyscraper and France's tallest building, the Montparnasse tower, and a major railway station. Montparnasse might be worth a trip for the major shopping center located under the tower, and the shopping along adjacent **rue de Rennes.**

FNAC (p. 266)

Marché aux Puces de la Porte de Vanves (p. 243)

Montparnasse Shopping Centre (p. 243)

MALLS & MARKETS

Carrousel du Louvre ★★   If you want to combine an accessible location, a fun food court, boutiques, and plenty of museum gift shops with a touch of culture, don't miss the Carrousel. Always mobbed, this is one of the few venues allowed to open on Sunday. There's an Apple Store, Starbucks, Virgin Megastore,

Food Markets

Outdoor markets are plentiful in Paris. Some of the better known are the **Marché Buci** (see below); the **rue Mouffetard market,** open Tuesday to Sunday from 9:30am to 1pm and Tuesday to Saturday from 4 to 7pm (6e; Métro: Monge or Censier-Daubenton); and the **rue Montorgueil market,** behind the St-Eustache church, open Monday to Saturday from 9am to 7pm (1er; Métro: Les Halles). The covered **Marché d'Aligre** in the 12e dates back to the 18th century and boasts a lovely family atmosphere (see below). The trendiest market is **Marché Biologique,** along boulevard Raspail, a tree-lined stretch lying between rue de Rennes and rue du Cherche-Midi, 6e. It's open Sunday from 8:30am to 6:30pm (Métro: Montparnasse).

a branch of L'Occitane, and several other emporiums for conspicuous consumption. Check out Fragonard or Pylones for original souvenir ideas. Open daily, 10am to 8pm. 99 rue de Rivoli, 1er. www.carrouseldulouvre.com. © **01-43-16-47-10.** Métro: Palais-Royal or Musée du Louvre.

Le Forum des Halles   This major transport and shopping hub draws suburban Parisians to its subterranean labyrinth of chain stores, including H&M, FNAC, Zara, or Muji, as well as a heated swimming pool, and the UGC cinema multiplex. The complex is undergoing major renovations until 2016, but the shopping mall remains open throughout. Open Monday to Saturday 10am to 8pm. 101 Porte Berger, 1er. www.forumdeshalles.com. Métro: Châtelet-Les Halles.

Montparnasse Shopping Centre   This shopping center is sort of a quick-fix mini-mall in a business center and hotel (Le Méridien) complex, with a small branch of Galeries Lafayette, a Habitat for chic home ware, and some inexpensive fashion chains. The vibe continues up neighboring commercial strip rue de Rennes. Open Monday to Saturday 10am to 7pm. Btw. rue de l'Arrivée and 22 rue du Départ, 14e. No phone. Métro: Montparnasse-Bienvenüe.

Marché aux Fleurs et aux Oiseaux ★   Artists and photographers love to capture the Flower Market on canvas and film. Most of the time, the stalls are ablaze with color, and each is a showcase of flowers, most of which escaped the perfume factories of Grasse on the French Riviera. The Flower Market is along the Seine, behind the Tribunal de Commerce. But on Sunday, it becomes the poetic Bird Market. Open daily 8:30am to 4pm. Place Louis-Lépine, Ile de la Cité, 4e. No phone. Métro: Cité.

Marché aux Puces de la Porte de Vanves ★★ 🏠   This weekend event sprawls along two streets and is the best flea market in Paris—dealers swear by it. There's little in terms of formal antiques and furniture. It's better for old linens, vintage Hermès scarves, toys, ephemera, costume jewelry, perfume bottles, and bad art. Asking prices tend to be high, as dealers prefer to sell to nontourists. On Sunday, there's a food market one street over. Open Tuesday to Sunday 7am to 5pm. Av. Georges-Lafenestre, 14e. No phone. Métro: Porte de Vanves.

Marché aux Puces St-Ouen de Clignancourt ★ Paris's most famous flea market is a grouping of more than a dozen flea markets—a complex of 2,500 to 3,000 open stalls and shops on the northern fringe of the city, selling everything from antiques to junk, from new to vintage clothing. The market begins with stalls of cheap clothing along avenue de la Porte de Clignancourt. As you proceed, various streets will tempt you. Hold on until you get to rue des Rosiers; then turn left. Vendors

Wares at the Marché aux Puces St-Ouen de Clignancourt.

start bringing out their offerings around 9am Saturday to Monday and take them in around 6pm. Hours are a tad flexible, depending on weather and crowds. Monday is traditionally the best day for bargain seekers—attendance is smaller and merchants demonstrate a greater desire to sell.

First-timers always want to know two things: "Will I get any real bargains?" and "Will I get fleeced?" It's all relative. Obviously, dealers (who often have a prearrangement to have items held for them) have already skimmed the best buys. And it's true that the same merchandise displayed here will sell for less in the provinces. But for the visitor who has only a few days to spend in Paris—and only half a day for shopping—the flea market is worth the experience.

Dress casually and show your knowledge if you're a collector. Most dealers are serious and get into the spirit of things only if you speak French or make it clear you know what you're doing. The longer you stay, the more you chat and show your respect for the goods, the more room you'll have for negotiating. Most of the markets have restroom facilities; some have central offices to arrange shipping. Cafes, pizza joints, and even a few restaurants are scattered around. **Note:** Beware of pickpockets and teenage troublemakers while shopping the market. Open Saturday to Monday 9am to 7pm. Av. de la Porte de Clignancourt, 18e. No phone. www.marchesauxpuces.fr. Métro: Porte de Clignancourt (turn left, cross bd. Ney, and then walk north on av. de la Porte Montmartre). Métro: Porte de Clignancourt.

Marché Ave du Président Wilson ★ Even if you don't buy anything, browsing this market is a city attraction. Parisians flock to this open-air market to purchase some of the most exotic kinds of vegetables sold in the city; everything from purple cauliflower to sunflower yellow zucchini. One stallmaster even sells a type of heirloom pea, "Kelvedon Marvel," that was a particular favorite of Louis

---

> ### 🏷 A Discount Shopping Village Outside Paris
>
> Just 35 minutes from the center of Paris, **La Vallée Village,** 3 cours de la Garonne, 77700 Serris ((📞 **01-60-42-35-00;** www.lavalleevillage.com), is home to some 75 outlets in a chic, purpose-built shopping village. So, it might lack some of the charm of the avenue Montaigne, but you'll find hot French brands like agnès b, Robert Clergerie, Sandro, Maje, or Givenchy selling last season's collections at up to 70% off. From the center of Paris you can take RER to the Val d'Europe station; by car, follow the A4 motorway out of Paris to exit 12.1 (signposted from there).

XIV, who preferred eating them to bedding one of his mistresses. A major attraction here is a vegetable stall operated by **Joël Thiébault** ((📞 **01-44-24-05-77;** www.joelthiebault.fr), who supplies the city's best restaurants. Open Wednesday and Saturday from 7am to 2:30pm. On av. du Président Wilson btw. place d'Iena and rue Debrousse, 16e. No phone. Métro: Iena or Alma-Marceau.

Marché Buci This traditional French food market is set up at the intersection of two streets and is only a block long, but what a block it is! Seasonal fruits and vegetables cover tabletops, and chickens spin on the rotisserie. One stall is entirely devoted to big bouquets of fresh flowers. Monday mornings are light; Sunday is best. Open daily 9am to 7pm. Rue de Buci, 6e. No phone. Métro: St-Germain-des-Prés or Mabillon.

Marché d'Aligre ★ One of the most popular and affordable of the city's markets, this bustling daily affair has been stocking Parisian pantries since the 18th century. The charming Beauveau Covered Market stands at the center of the Aligre square, and running along the Rue Aligre are open-air stands loaded with everything from apples to zucchini. The neighborhood's long-standing North African immigrant community has added a fragrant influence to the produce on offer. Squashed along the eastern edge of the square are stands selling vintage clothes, furniture, and knick-knacks. Open Tuesday to Sunday, 7:30am to 2:30pm. Rue d'Aligre & place d'Aligre, 12e. http://marchedaligre.free.fr. Métro:Ledru-Rollin.

Marché des Enfants Rouges ★ This charming covered fresh food market is the oldest in Paris and dates from 1777. In the heart of the rapidly gentrifying Northern Marais neighborhood, it's a lively place for stocking up on picnic supplies (organic if you like), including wine and flowers, or for sitting down for a bite at any of the food stands. We recommend traditional French dishes at L'Estaminet in the western corner, or the excellent Japanese canteen Taeko on the eastern edge. Open Monday to Saturday, 8:30am to 7:30pm, Sunday 8:30am to 2pm. 39 Rue de Bretagne, 3e. (📞 **01-42-72-28-12.** Métro: Filles du Calvaire.

SHOPPING A TO Z
Antiques, Collectibles & Vintage

Le Louvre des Antiquaires ★★ Across from the Louvre, this store offers three levels of fancy knickknacks and 250 vendors. It's just the place if you're looking for 30 matching Baccarat-crystal champagne flutes from the 1930s, a Sèvres tea service from 1773, or a signed Jean Fouquet gold-and-diamond pin.

Too stuffy? No problem. There's always the 1940 Rolex with the eggplant crocodile strap. Prices can be high, but a few reasonable items are hidden here. What's more, the Sunday scene is fabulous, and there's a cafe with a variety of lunch menus. Pick up a free map and brochure of the premises from the information desk. Open Tuesday to Sunday 9am to 7pm. Closed Sunday. 2 place du Palais Royal, 1er. www.louvre-antiquaires.com. ✆ **01-42-97-27-27.** Métro: Palais-Royal.

L'Objet qui Parle ★★ This almost ridiculously charming shop sells a perfectly curated jumble of vintage finds, including Art Deco sunburst mirrors, teapots, kitchen canisters and crockery, hunting trophies, religious paraphernalia, and old lace. Great for souvenir shopping! Open Monday to Saturday 1pm to 7:30pm. 86 rue des Martyrs, 18e. ✆ **06-09-67-05-30.** Métro: Abbesses.

Village St-Paul This isn't an antiques center, but a cluster of dealers in their own hole-in-the-wall hideout. It really hops on Sunday. Bring your camera, because inside the courtyards and alleys is a dream vision of hidden Paris: dealers in a courtyard selling furniture and other decorative items in French-country and formal styles. The rest of the street, stretching from the river to the Marais, is also lined with dealers. Open Thursday to Monday 11am to 7pm. 23–27 rue St-Paul, 4e. www.village-saint-paul.com. No phone. Métro: St-Paul.

Art & Crafts

Artcurial ★ Set within minimalist showrooms in one of the most spectacular 19th-century mansions in Paris, this is one of the best outlets in Europe for contemporary art. Since it was established in 1975, it has represented megastars such as Man Ray and the "enfant terrible" of France's postwar intelligentsia, Jean Cocteau. Today, the names of showcased artists read like a who's who of contemporary art: Arman, Sonia Delaunay, and Niki de Saint Phalle for painting and sculpture; Claude Lalanne for jewelry design; and Matta for contemporary carpets. Technically, it's an auction house, similar in some ways to Sotheby's and Christie's, albeit with a specialization in modern and contemporary art, vintage photographs by "important" photographers, antique books and posters, and sculpture. Despite an address that might be among the most expensive in the world (the intersection of av. Montaigne and Champs-Élysées), the place is more welcoming than its location implies. A great arts bookshop, and a recently renovated daytime cafe, provide respite from the shops. Open Monday to Friday 10am to 7pm; Saturday 11am to 7pm. 7 rond-point des Champs-Élysées, 8e. www.artcurial.com. ✆ **01-42-99-20-20.** Métro: Franklin-D-Roosevelt.

107 Rivoli ★★ Inside the city's Decorative Arts Museum, itself located within a wing of the Louvre, this ground floor store presents a wonderful selection of contemporary ceramic, textile, glass, and design pieces, plus a great collection of books dedicated to the arts, architecture, fashion, and design, as well as take-home pieces inspired by the current exhibitions. Great for inspired souvenir shopping. Open Monday to Sunday 10am to 7pm. 107 rue de Rivoli, 1er. www.lesartsdecoratifs.fr. ✆ **01-42-60-64-94.** Métro: Palais-Royal.

Sennelier ★ This historic address has been keeping the city stocked in quality art supplies for over 120 years. Three generations of Senneliers have been providing students from the neighboring art school with the best pigments, from this rickety shop on the quays overlooking the river. Patron Gustave developed a range of oil pastels praised by artists such as Cézanne, Degas, and Chagall, and

Shops at the Viaduc des Arts.

still famous in the art world today. Open Monday, 2 to 6:30pm, Tuesday to Saturday 10am to 12:45pm and 2 to 6:30pm. Closed Sunday. 3 quai Voltaire, 7e. www. magasinsennelier.com. ℂ **01-42-60-72-15.** Métro: St Germain des Près.

Viaduc des Arts   This complex of boutiques and crafts workshops occupies the vaulted spaces beneath one of the 19th-century railway access routes into the Gare de Lyon. Around 1990, crafts artists, including furniture makers, potters, glassblowers, and weavers, began renting the niches beneath the viaduct, selling their wares to homeowners and members of Paris's decorating trades. Several trendsetting home-furnishing outfits have rented additional spaces. Stretching for more than 2 blocks between the Opéra Bastille and the Gare de Lyon, it allows one to see what Parisians consider chic in terms of home decorating. Open Monday to Saturday 11am to 7pm. 119 av. Daumesnil, 12e. www.viaduc-des-arts. com. ℂ **01-44-75-80-66.** Métro: Bastille, Ledru-Rollin, Reuilly-Diderot, or Gare-de-Lyon.

Beauty, Cosmetics & Perfume

Annick Goutal ★   Although there are other branches, and you can test Goutal bathroom amenities at many upscale hotels, the sidewalk mosaic tile and the gold accented boudoir vibe of this central flagship make it worth stopping by. Try their bestseller Eau d'Hadrien for a unisex splash of citrus and summer. Store hours are Monday to Saturday from 10am to 7pm. 14 rue Castiglione, 1er. www. annickgoutal.com. ℂ **01-42-60-52-82.** Métro: Concorde.

The Different Company ★ 🎒   Many fashionistas are deserting the fabled houses of scent and heading for this corner of counterculture chic in the Marais. The perfume shop is run by the father-daughter team of Jean-Claude and Céline Ellena. Dad is perfumer for Hermès and continues here a commitment to exceptional quality. They design scents including Osmanthus, Sel de Vétiver, and Rose Poivrée, which have been called "fragrances for the 21st century." Their perfumes include a high concentration of natural components and have received the "Green Label" by Greenpeace. Open Tuesday to Saturday noon to 7:30 or 8pm. 10 rue Ferdinand Duval, 4e. www.thedifferentcompany.com. ℂ **01-47-83-65-88.** Métro: Saint-Paul.

Diptyque ★★ This contemporary Parisian perfumery and candle maker has a truly unique range of aromatic plant–based scents, including bestsellers Philosykos, a woody blend of fig tree leaves and white cedar, or Tubéreuse, an intoxicating blend based on the heady tuberose flower. Open Monday to Saturday 10am to 7pm. 34 bd. St Germain, 5e. www.diptyqueparis.com. ℰ **01-43-26-77-44.** Métro: Maubert-Mutualité.

Editions de Parfums Fréderic Malle ★ 🎁 If the big brand-name perfumes that are sold at every duty-free airport in Europe bore you, consider a visit to this boutique. Founded in 2000 by master perfumer Fréderic Malle, whose nose is as sensitive as that of any wine expert, this brand curates a selection of unisex scents which come in varying intensities of floral, spice, or Oriental motifs; and carry evocative names like Iris Poudre, Noir Epices, En Passant, and one of the bestsellers, Musc Ravageur. There's a lot of elegant chichi about this place (the paneled decor was designed by superdecorators Andrée Putnam and Olivier Lempereur), and one of the things we like best about the place is the display of framed photographic portraits of each of the men and women who created the original scents sold here. Open Monday 1pm to 7pm; Tuesday to Saturday 11am to 7pm. 37 rue de Grenelle, 7e. www.editionsdeparfums.com. ℰ **01-42-22-76-40.** Métro: Rue du Bac.

Francis Kurkdjian ★★ 🎁 Francis Kurkdjian has created scents for many of the most famous French perfumers, including Guerlain, Dior, and Gaultier, over the past 15 years. In 2009 he set up his own *maison* and here sells an elegant range of scents for men and women, but also for the home, your laundry (!), and even perfumed bubble blowers for the kids. The store itself is a delightful homage to the city of Paris, inspired by its zinc roofs and gilded monuments. Open Monday to Saturday 11am to 7pm. 5 rue d'Alger, 1er. www.franciskurkdjian.com. ℰ **01-42-60-07-07.** Métro: Tuileries.

Parfums Caron Although you can buy scents in any duty-free or discount *parfumerie*, it's worth visiting the source of some of the world's most famous perfumes in this tiny shop boasting old-fashioned glass beakers filled with fragrances and a hint of yesteryear. Fleur de Rocaille, a Caron scent, was the featured perfume in the movie *Scent of a Woman*. Store hours are Monday to Saturday from 10am to 6:30pm. Also at 90 rue du Faubourg St-Honoré, 8e. 34 av. Montaigne, 8e. www.parfumscaron.com. ℰ **01-47-23-40-82.** Métro: Franklin-D-Roosevelt.

Salons du Palais Royal, Shiseido ★★ 🎁 Shiseido, the world's fourth-largest maker of cosmetics and skincare goods, has become more prominent thanks to the efforts of its star perfumer, Serge Lutens. This special, secret place stocks more than 20 exclusive unisex fragrances created by Lutens, including Jeux de Peau, a nostalgic spicy scent inspired by the odor of hot bread and butter. Don't be afraid to wander in and ask for some scent strips. Open Monday to Saturday from 10am to 7pm. 142 Galerie de Valois, Palais Royal, 1er. www.salons-shiseido.com. ℰ **01-49-27-09-09.** Métro: Palais-Royal.

Sephora ★ The buzzing, late-night Champs-Élysées flagship of this international chain dedicated to cosmetics, skin care, and beauty is a great place to try many of the exclusive products you've admired in shop windows. Much of the staff speaks English. Open daily 10am to midnight daily, and the weekend till 1am. 70 avenue des Champs-Élysées, 8e. www.sephora.fr. ℰ **01-53-93-22-50.** Métro: Franklin-D-Roosevelt.

Books, Maps & Stationery

If you like rare and unusual books, there's not only the choice of the city's exceptional bookshops, you also have the choice to patronize one of the *bouquinistes*, the owners of those army-green stalls that line the Seine (on the Left Bank between the quai de la Tournelle and quai Malaquais, and on the Right Bank between Pont Marie and the quai du Louvre). This is where tourists in the 1920s and 1930s went to buy "dirty" French postcards. You might get lucky and come across some treasured book, such as an original edition of Henry Miller's *Tropic of Cancer*, which was banned for decades in the United States.

Cassegrain ★   Nothing says elegance more than thick French stationery and notecards. Cassegrain, originally an engraver in 1919, offers beautifully engraved stationery, most often in traditional patterns, and business cards engraved to order. Several other items for the desk, many suitable for gifts, are for sale as well; there are even affordable pencils and pens, leather wallets, and small desktop accessories. Open Monday to Saturday 10am to 7pm. 422 rue St-Honoré, 8e. www. cassegrain.fr. ℂ **01-42-60-20-08.** Métro: Concorde.

Galignani   Sprawling over a large street level and supplemented by a mezzanine, this venerable wood-paneled bookstore has thrived since 1810. Enormous numbers of books are available in French and English, with a special emphasis on French classics, modern fiction, sociology, and fine arts. Looking for English-language translations of works by Balzac, Flaubert, Zola, or Colette? Most of them are here; if not, they can be ordered. Open Monday to Saturday 10am to 7pm. 224 rue de Rivoli, 1er. www.galignani.com. ℂ **01-42-60-76-07.** Métro: Tuileries.

Les Mots à la Bouche   This is Paris's largest, best-stocked gay bookstore. You can find French- and English-language books as well as gay-info magazines such as *Illico, Blue, e.m@le, Carol's Girlfriends,* and *Lesbia.* You'll also find lots of free pamphlets advertising gay/lesbian venues and events. Open Monday to Saturday 11am to 11pm; Sunday 1 to 9pm. 6 rue Ste-Croix-la-Bretonnerie, 4e. www.motsbouche. com. ℂ **01-42-78-88-30.** Métro: Hôtel-de-Ville.

Librairie le Bail-Weissert   Paris is filled with rare book shops, but this one has the best collection of atlases, rare maps, and engravings from the 15th century to the 19th century. The shop sells original topographical maps of European and world cities, along with various regions of Europe. There's also a superb collection of architectural engravings. Open Monday to Friday 10am to 12:30pm and 2 to 7pm; Saturday 2 to 6pm. 13 rue Frederic Sauton, 5e. www.librairie-lebail.fr. ℂ **01-43-29-72-59.** Métro: Cluny–La Sorbonne.

7L ★   Monsieur Karl Lagerfeld is not only the creative director of Chanel, the city's emblematic fashion label, but also a prolific photographer and publisher. Here is where he sells his coffee table tomes on art, architecture, photography, and design, in an elegant space designed by Japanese architect Tadao Ando. Open Tuesday to Saturday 10:30am to 6:45pm. Closed Sunday and Monday. 7 rue de Lille, 7e. www.steidlville.com/bookshops. ℂ **01-42-92-03-58.** Métro: St-Germain-des-Prés.

Shakespeare and Company ★   The most famous bookstore on the Left Bank is Shakespeare and Company, on rue de l'Odéon, home to Sylvia Beach, "mother confessor to the Lost Generation." Hemingway, Fitzgerald, and Stein were frequent patrons, as was Anaïs Nin, the diarist noted for her description of struggling American artists in 1930s Paris. Nin helped her companion Henry

Miller publish *Tropic of Cancer,* a book so notorious in its day that returning Americans who tried to slip copies through Customs often had them confiscated as pornography. (When times were hard, Nin herself wrote pornography for a dollar a page.) Long ago, the shop moved to rue de la Bûcherie, a rickety old place where expatriates still swap books and literary gossip and foreign students work in exchange for modest lodgings. Monday nights host free readings; check the program on their site. Open daily 10am to midnight. 37 rue de la Bûcherie, 5e. www.shakespeareandcompany.com. ✆ **01-43-25-40-93.** Métro: St-Michel.

Taschen   Taschen is a German-based publishing house known for its collection of delicious mass-market coffee-table books. Erudite, high-profile, and glossy, most of them focus on architecture, art, photography, or eroticism. Flick through their latest international releases, in this sleek space designed by local design hero Philippe Starck. Open Tuesday to Saturday 11am to 7pm. 2 rue de Buci, 6e. www.taschen.com. ✆ **01-40-51-79-22.** Métro: Odéon.

Tea & Tattered Pages   At this largely English-language paperback bookshop, you can take a break from browsing to have tea. Though it's out of the way, an extra dose of charm makes it worth the trip. Open Monday to Saturday 11am to 7pm; Sunday noon to 6pm. 24 rue Mayet, 6e. ✆ **01-40-65-94-35.** Métro: Duroc.

Village Voice Bookshop   This favorite of expatriate Yankees is on a side street in the heart of the best Left Bank shopping district, near some of the gathering places described in Gertrude Stein's *The Autobiography of Alice B. Toklas.* Opened in 1981, the shop is a hangout for literati. Its name has nothing to do with the New York weekly. Regular author events are publicized on their website. Open Monday 2 to 8pm; Tuesday to Saturday 10am to 8pm; Sunday 2 to 7pm. 6 rue Princesse, 6e. www.villagevoicebookshop.com. ✆ **01-46-33-36-47.** Métro: Mabillon.

WH Smith   This three-story Paris outpost of the U.K. chain store provides books, magazines, and newspapers published in English (most titles are from Britain). You can get the *Times* of London, of course, and the Sunday *New York Times* is available every Monday. There's a fine selection of maps and travel guides, plus a special children's section that includes comics. Upstairs, there's an English grocery selling foodstuffs like cheddar cheese and Colman's Mustard. Open Monday to Saturday 9am to 7:30pm; Sunday 1 to 7:30pm. 248 rue de Rivoli, 1er. www.whsmith.fr. ✆ **01-44-77-88-99.** Métro: Concorde.

Clothing & Accessories

WOMEN'S

agnès b ★   Agnès b's take on relaxed but elegant urban fashion has been winning over Parisians, and the rest of the planet, since the '70s. She produces collections for the whole family; note that you will find her menswear collections on sale around the corner at agnès b. homme (1 rue Dieu, 10e). There are numerous other addresses scattered around the city. Open Monday 1 to 7pm, Tuesday to Saturday 11am to 7pm. Closed Sunday. 13 rue de Marseille, 10e. www.agnesb.com. ✆ **01-42-06-66-58.** Métro: Jacques Bonsergent.

Azzedine Alaïa   Alaïa, who became the darling of French fashion in the 1970s, is the man who put body consciousness back into Paris chic. If you can't afford the current collection, try the **stock shop** around the corner at 18 rue de la Verrerie, 4e (✆ **01-42-72-54-97;** Métro: Hôtel-de-Ville), where last season's

A women's clothing store.

leftovers are sold at serious discounts. Both outlets sell leather trench coats, knit dresses, pleated skirts, cigarette pants, belts, purses, and fashion accessories. Open Monday to Saturday 10am to 7pm. 18 rue Verrerie, 4e. ℭ **01-42-72-19-19.** Métro: Hôtel-de-Ville.

Balenciaga ★ Creative director Nicolas Ghesquière took control of this floundering but mythical *maison* in 1997 and immediately brought the label bang up to date. For the last 15 years his visionary designs have been splashed across the pages of fashion magazines from Milan to Tokyo. His taste for futuristic chic is visible right down to the boutique's decor, a kind of moonscape developed in collaboration with French artist Dominique Gonzalez-Foerster. **Note:** A dedicated menswear store is located on the Left Bank at 5 rue de Varenne, 7e. Open Monday to Saturday 10am to 7pm. 10 avenue George V 8e. www.balenciaga.com. ℭ **01-47-20-21-11.** Métro: Alma-Marceau.

Bensimon ★ This popular French label designs wearable fashion and sportswear for the whole family. They also produce an important range of accessories, including a model of canvas sneaker that has become a cult summer classic. Just down the street at no. 8 rue des Francs-Bourgeois you'll find Home Autour du Monde, stocking their ethnic-chic interiors range. Open Monday to Saturday 11am to 7pm, Sunday 1:30 to 7pm. 12 rue des Francs-Bourgeois, 3e. www.bensimon.com. ℭ **01-42-77-06-08.** Métro: St-Paul.

Chanel ★ If you can't have the sun, the moon, and the stars, at least buy something with Coco Chanel's initials on it—either a serious fashion statement or something fun and playful. Karl Lagerfeld's designs come in all flavors and have added a subtle twist to Chanel's classicism. This mythical flagship store is located just behind the Ritz, where Mlle Chanel once lived. Check out the beautiful staircase of the *maison* before you shop the two-floor boutique—where a series of rooms display Chanel fashion, accessories, beauty, and perfumes, including store exclusives. It's well worth a peek. Open Monday to Saturday 10am to 7pm. 31 rue Cambon, 1er. www.chanel.fr. ℭ **01-42-86-28-00.** Métro: Tuileries or Madeleine.

Dior ★ This exquisite flagship on the Avenue Montaigne is set up like a small department store, selling men's, women's, and children's clothing, as well as affordable gift items, makeup, and perfume, throughout a seemingly never-ending suite of signature Dior grey rooms. Avant-garde Brit designer John Galliano built the house's reputation with a flamboyant vision of women's wear that wowed the international fashion pack. After making some inflammatory remarks, Galliano stepped down as head designer in 2011, and Riccardo Tisci from Givenchy filled the role. Unlike some of the other big-name fashion houses, Dior is very approachable. Open Monday to Saturday 10am to 7pm. 30 av. Montaigne, 8e. www.dior.fr. ℭ **01-40-73-73-73**. Métro: Franklin-D-Roosevelt.

French Trotters　A temple to urban chic, this store sells hot international fashion and accessories for men and women, from brands including local talents Jerome Dreyfuss, Le Mont Saint Michel, Les Prairies de Paris, Martin Margiela, Tila March, A.P.C., Comme des Garçons, and Maison Fabre. French Trotters also develops collaborations on limited-edition pieces available exclusively in store. *Note:* Little French Trotters selling designer children's wear is open next door at no. 28. Open Monday 2:30 to 7.30pm, Tuesday to Saturday 11:30am to 7:30pm. 30 rue Charonne, 11e. http://frenchtrotters.fr. ✆ **01-47-00-84-35.** Métro: Bastille or Ledru-Rollin.

Givenchy ★　Hubert de Givenchy made fashion news around the world with his establishment, in 1962, of his couture company for elegant women. Today, the Italian designer Riccardo Tisci continues the Givenchy traditions, but with a distinctly contemporary take on ready-to-wear. This flagship, overseen by Tisci himself in partnership with Brit architect Jamie Fobert, presents the brand's range of women's and menswear and accessories, in an exquisite gallery-like space, where five pods display the cutting-edge collections. Open Monday to Saturday 10am to 7pm. 28 rue Fbg-St-Honoré, 8e. www.givenchy.fr. ✆ **01-42-68-31-00.** Métro: Concorde. Other locations: 3 av. George V, 8e. ✆ **01-44-31-50-00.** Métro: George V. Givenchy Hommes: 56 rue François Premier, 8e. ✆ **01-40-76-07-27.** Métro: Alma-Marceau.

Hermès ★★　France's single most important status item is a scarf or tie from Hermès. Patterns on these illustrious scarves, retailing from about 220€, have recently included the galaxies, Africa, the sea, the sun, and horse racing and breeding. But the choices don't stop there—this large flagship store sells everything from beach towels and accessories, dinner plates, *prêt-à-porter* for men and women, the complete collection of Hermès fragrances (including their "24 Faubourg," named after this mythic address), to saddles; a package of postcards could be the least expensive item sold. Outside, note the horseman on the roof with his scarf-flag flying. The illustrious brand opened a magnificent new flagship on the Left Bank in late 2010, which concentrates more on homeware than on the fashion lines, and features a bookshop, florist, and pricey cafe (17 rue de Sèvres, 6e; ✆ **01-42-22-80-83;** Mon–Sat 10:30am–7pm). Open Monday to Saturday 10:30am to 7pm. 24 rue du Faubourg St-Honoré, 8e. www.hermes.com. ✆ **01-40-17-46-00.** Métro: Concorde.

Isabel Marant ★★　With her elegant but wearable urban fashion, Isabel Marant has defined this generation of Parisian chic, and now exports to all the fashion capitals. This is her original store, opened in 1996 when the Bastille neighborhood was where it was at. Here you'll find her signature range of trendy looks, sporting ethnic and vintage details, for women and children. Open Monday to Saturday 10:30am to 7:30pm. Closed Sunday. Also at 47 rue Saintonge, 3e, and 1 Rue Jacob, 6e. 16 rue Charonne, 11e. www.isabelmarant.tm.fr. ✆ **01-49 29-71-55.** Métro: Bastille or Ledru-Rollin.

Jean-Paul Gaultier　Supporters of this high-camp, high-fashion mogul describe him as an avant-garde classicist without allegiance to any of the aesthetic restrictions of the bourgeoisie. Detractors call him a glorified punk rocker with a gimmicky allegiance to futurist models as interpreted by *Star Trek*. Whatever your opinion, it's always refreshing and insightful, especially for fashion buffs, to check out one of France's most emblematic designers. Open Monday and Saturday 10:30am to 7pm; Tuesday to Friday 10am to 7pm. 44 av. George V,

8e. www.jeanpaulgaultier.com. ☏ **01-44-43-00-44.** Métro: George V. Other locations: 6 rue Vivienne, 2e. ☏ **01-42-86-05-05.** Métro: Bourse.

JC de Castelbajac JC/DC's vivid, multicolored world borrows from different cultural universes, like pop music and pop art. He's been working on transforming the cultural zeitgeist into fun and wearable fashion since the '70s, and he's still on the map. Open Monday to Saturday 11am to 7pm. 10 rue Vauvilliers, 1er. http://jc-de-castelbajac.com. ☏ **01-40-41-00-30.** Métro: Châtelet-Les Halles. Other locations: 61 rue des Saint Pères, 6e. ☏ **09-64-48-48-54.**

L'Eclaireur ★ You might feel as if you're stepping into an art gallery when you enter this, the latest address in this prestige string of multibrand emporiums created by the pioneering Madame and Monsieur Hadida. Their beautifully curated selection of high-end fashion is available in five exceptional stores around Paris. This Marais address was designed by Belgian artist Arne Quinze, and conceived of as a multimedia experience, or a sculpture, rather than a simple store. You'll discover women's wear from designers like Rick Owens, Maison Martin Margiela, Lanvin, Dries Van Noten, and Balenciaga. Open Monday to Saturday 11am to 7pm. 40 rue Sévigné, 3e. www.leclaireur.com. ☏ **01-48-87-10-22.** Métro: St-Paul.

Sonia Rykiel ★★ The emblematic Left Bank fashion designer has been dressing the independent and audacious women of St-Germain-des-Prés since 1968. Her modern wardrobe of elegant, comfortable clothes is instantly recognizable by its bestselling signature range of stripey knits. So you'll find a piece of the city's fashion history in this glamorous two-floor flagship. Open Monday to Saturday 10:30am to 7pm. 175 boulevard St Germain, 6e. www.soniarykiel.fr. ☏ **01-45-49-13-10.** Métro: St-Germain-des-Prés.

Uniqlo All of Paris seems to worship at this temple to the low-cost basic. The cult Japanese brand sells menswear and women's wear over three floors and is particularly revered for its range of well-cut jeans, plus their winter collection of cut-price cashmere and down jackets. The colorful, upbeat designs appeal to teenagers, but the premium range–designed guest designers, such as Jil Sander, targets their mothers. Open Monday to Saturday 10am to 8pm (9pm Thurs). 17 rue Scribe, 9e. www.uniqlo.com. ☏ **01-58-18-30-55.** Métro: Havre-Caumartin or Chaussée d'Antin-La Fayette.

Ventilo ★ The biggest of this Paris designer brand's eight stores, this flagship covers four floors and features a gallery, bookshop, and cafe. It's a wonderful setting for browsing the wearable and feminine collections. For nearly 40 years, Ventilo has been offering a perfect hybrid of ethnic chic and Parisian cool styles, with lots of bright silks and edgy cuts. Open Monday to Saturday 10:30am to 7pm. 27 bis rue du Louvre, 1e. www.ventilo.fr. ☏ **01-44-76-82-95.** Métro: Etienne-Marcel.

Yves Saint Laurent It's easy to forget the days, in the '70s and '80s, when anything the late, great Yves Saint Laurent did was touted by the international press as a sign of his genius, and the fashionable French dressed up in his luxurious versions of Cossack costumes, replete with boleros, riding boots, and copies of antique jewelry from the Russian steppes. But the master's genius continues to be conjured for today's forward-looking fashionista, and we recommend this historic place St-Sulpice boutique for getting in touch with his spirit. Monday 11am to 7pm; Tuesday to Saturday 10:30am to 7pm. 6 place St-Sulpice, 6e. www.ysl. com. ☏ **01-43-29-43-00** or 01-43-26-84-40. Métro: St-Sulpice. Other locations at 32 (men) and

38 (women) rue du Faubourg St-Honoré, 8e. ☎ **01-53-05-80-80.** Métro: Madeleine or Concorde; and 9 Rue Grenelle, 7e. ☎ **01-45-44-39-01.** Métro; St-Sulpice.

Zadig & Voltaire This trendy young French brand is doing well at capturing a contemporary European rock 'n' roll spirit. This spacious first-floor store, overlooking the place St-Sulpice in the heart of the Left Bank, displays their popular collections of up-to-date luxury: perfectly worn jeans, comfortable cashmeres, biker boots, and more, for men, women, and children. Open Monday to Saturday 10:30am to 7:30pm. 1 rue du Vieux Colombier, 6e. www.zadig-et-voltaire.com. ☎ **01-43-54-72-56.** Métro: St-Sulpice.

MEN'S

Citadium A whole department store over four floors dedicated to streetwear and "lifestyle" for men. You'll find all the usual, international, suspects like North Face, Adidas, and Diesel, but also quality local brands including Petit Bateau, Veja, or The Kooples. The Beaubourg branch is smaller, but more central. Monday to Saturday 10am to 8pm (9pm Thurs). 50/56 rue Caumartin, 9e. www.citadium.fr. ☎ **01-55-31-74-00.** Métro: Havre-Caumartin. Other location at 33 rue Quincampoix, 4e. ☎ **01-70-06-99-89.** Métro: Rambuteau.

Sandro Homme If you're wanting to resemble the nonchalantly elegant gentlemen you see lounging around Parisian cafes, this Paris label is for you, with flannel pants in tones of charcoal or chocolate, merino turtlenecks, leather biker jackets, woolen suits, silk scarves, and more. There's no compromising on style, but prices remain reasonable. The brand has a string of stores dedicated to its equally appealing women's wear. Open Monday to Saturday 10:30am to 7pm. 11 rue des Francs Bourgeois, 4e. www.sandro-paris.com. ☎ **01-44-59-84-51.** Métro: St-Paul.

CHILDREN'S

Bonpoint ★★ 👜 This stylish brand helps parents transform their darlings into models of well-tailored conspicuous consumption. Though you'll find some garments for real life, the primary allure of the place lies in its tailored, fairly traditional—and expensive—garments. This breathtaking flagship is located inside a mansion set around an interior courtyard, and includes a secret cafe with chairs outside under the trees. Open Monday to Saturday 10am to 7pm. 6 rue de Tournon, 6e. www.bonpoint.com. ☎ **01-41-51-98-20.** Métro: Odéon.

Bonton ★ This fun three-floor emporium includes a candy counter, a hairdresser, a retro photo booth, toys, books, a basement knickknack and interiors department, plus the French label's signature collections of trendy clothing for boys and girls, from birth to age 16. It's hard to walk out empty-handed. Open Monday to Saturday 10am to 7pm. 5 boulevard des Filles du Calvaire, 3e. www.bonton. fr. ☎ **01-42-72-34-69.** Métro: Filles du Calvaire.

SHOES & ACCESSORIES

Christian Louboutin A pair of iconic red-soled Louboutins are all any party girl needs on her pretty, pedicured feet. Sarah Jessica Parker helped launch the brand in the English-speaking market. The brand's deliciously romantic Paris flagship, inside a 19th-century covered passage, is the perfect context to admire the iconic towering stilettos. In 2011 the brand opened a store dedicated to its men's collection on the other side of the passageway. Open Monday to Saturday 10:30am to 7pm. 233 rue St-Honoré, 1er. www.christianlouboutin.com. ☎ **01-42-60-57-04.** Métro: Louvre-Rivoli.

Goyard ★ Like its rival Louis Vuitton, this luxury trunk maker was established in France in the mid-19th century. But while Louis Vuitton went on to international stardom and a listing on the stock market, Goyard has remained a relatively modest family business. However, the brand's range of totes and trunks have been quietly picking up a cult following. Goyard also has a store dedicated to luxury pet accessories, or "le chic de chien," across the street at number 352. Open Monday to Saturday 10:30am to 7pm. 233 rue Saint-Honoré, 1er. www.goyard. fr. ✆ **01-42-60-57-04.** Métro: Tuileries.

Louis Vuitton ★★ Its luggage is among the most famous and prestigious in the world, a standard accessory aboard the first-class cabins of aircraft flying transatlantic and transpacific. Not content to cover the world's luggage with his initials, Vuitton also creates breathtaking ready-to-wear lines for men and women, as well as bags and other leather accessories, writing instruments, travel products, and more. The Champs-Élysées flagship rivals the Eiffel Tower as a destination for jet loads of flushed Japanese tourists, and note that the building includes a quality exhibition space (free entry) on its top floor (entry via rue Bassano). Open Monday to Saturday 10am to 8pm, Sunday 11am to 7pm. 101 avenue Champs-Élysées, 8e. www.louisvuitton.com. ✆ **01-53-57-52-00.** Métro: George V. Other location 6 place St-Germain-des-Prés, 6e. ✆ **01-45-49-62-32.** Métro: St-Germain-des-Prés.

Maison Fabre ★ Three generations of the Fabre family have taken this family-owned glove factory in rural France to the pages of the world's finest fashion magazines. The brand sells an exquisite range of gloves, for day and night, summer or winter, that will wow your friends back home. Open Monday to Saturday 10am to 7pm. 128-129 Galerie de Valois, 1er. www.maisonfabre.com. ✆ **01-42-60-75-88.** Métro: Palais-Royal. Other location: 60 Rue des Saints Pères, 7e. ✆ **01-42-22-44-86.**

Morabito This glamorous leather purveyor was originally established by an Italian entrepreneur on the place Vendôme in 1905. In the 1990s, it was partially acquired by an organization in Tokyo. Today, from a site on the glamorous rue François-Premier, it sells chicer-than-thou handbags. Morabito also has suitcases—some of the best in Paris—for men and women. Open Monday to Saturday 10am to 7pm. 259 rue St-Honoré, 1er. www.morabitoparis.com. ✆ **01-53-23-90-40.** Métro: George V.

Pierre Hardy ★ Another of the city's iconic cobblers. Pierre Hardy presents his cutting-edge, urban footwear collections from within sleek, black-lacquered spaces. You'll find shoes for men and women, as well as a range of leather accessories. Hardy was one of the first to propose luxury trainers. Open Monday to Saturday 11am to 7pm. 156 galerie de Valois, 1er. www.pierrehardy.com. ✆ **01-42-60-59-75.** Métro: Palais-Royal. Other location: 9 place du Palais Bourbon, 7e. ✆ **01-45-55-00-67.** Métro: Assemblée Nationale.

Robert Clergerie ★ This beautiful luxury French shoe brand combines tradition and modernity with originality and passion. Led by shoe designer Robert Clergerie, the brand is associated with elegant simplicity, purity of design, and exceptional "Made in France" quality. Of his philosophy, Clergerie said, "In my creations, I always respect the basic principle, learned from the famous boot maker André Perugia, that you carry a garment, but a shoe is different: the shoe carries you, and all the difficulty is here." Open Monday to Saturday 11am to 7pm. 5 rue du Cherche-Midi, 6e. www.robertclergerie.com. ✆ **01-45-48-75-47.** Métro: Saint-Sulpice. Other location: 18 avenue Victor Hugo, 16e. ✆ **01-45-01-81-30.** Métro: Charles de Gaulle-Etoile.

7

SHOPPING | Shopping A to Z

VINTAGE CLOTHING

Chine Machine   This trendy store in the heart of Montmartre provides an opportunity for a pleasurable afternoon sifting through fashion from yesteryear. Open noon to 8pm daily. 100 rue des Martyrs, 18e. www.chinemachinevintage.com. © **08-73-75-50-50.** Métro: Abbesses.

Didier Ludot ★   Fashion historians salivate when they're confronted with an inventory of vintage haute couture. In this frenetically stylish shop, albeit at prices that rival what you'd expect to pay for a serious antique, you'll find a selection of gowns and dresses created between 1900 and 1980 for designing women who looked *faaabulous* at Maxim's, at chic cocktail parties on the avenue Foch, in Deauville, or wherever. Open Monday to Saturday 11am to 7pm. 24 galerie de Montpensier, in the arcades surrounding the courtyard of the Palais Royal, 1er. www.didier ludot.fr. © **01-42-96-06-56.** Métro: Palais-Royal.

Kiliwatch ★   The city's biggest central vintage emporium will not disappoint. It has everything from second-hand jeans and military wear to Hermès scarves and couture pieces. Plus there's a great arts book corner. Open Tuesday to Sunday 11am to 7pm, Monday 2 to 7pm. 64 rue Tiquetonne, 1er. http://espacekiliwatch.fr. © **01-42-21-17-37.** Métro: Etienne-Marcel.

DISCOUNT STORES

Défilé des Marques   French TV stars often shop here, picking up Saint Laurent, Dior, Lacroix, Prada, Chanel, Versace, Hermès, and others at a fraction of the price. Yes, it sells discounted Hermès scarves as well. Low prices here derive from the owners' skill at picking up used clothing from last year's collections in good condition and, in some cases, retro-chic clothing from collections of many years ago, sometimes from estate sales. Open Tuesday to Saturday 11am to 8pm. 171 rue de Grenelle, 7e. © **01-45-55-63-47.** Métro: Latour-Maubourg.

L'Habilleur ★   This northern Marais institution discounts last season's collections of quality brands including the Italian knit brand Roberto Collina or French fashion for men and women by Paul and Joe and Antik Batik. The garments are impeccably maintained and most aesthetically organized by their color, creating a rainbow of fashion opportunities. Open Tuesday to Saturday 11am to 7pm. 44 Rue du Poitou, 3e. © **01-48-87-77-12.** Métro: St-Sébastien Froissart.

Réciproque ★   Forget about serious bargains, but celebrate what could be your only opportunity to own designer clothing of this caliber. Within a series of six storefronts side by side along the same avenue, you'll find used clothing from every major name in fashion, along with shoes, accessories, menswear, and wedding gifts. Everything has been worn, but some items were worn only on fashion runways or during photo shoots. Open Tuesday to Saturday 11am to 7pm. 89–101 rue de la Pompe, 16e. www.reciproque.fr. © **01-47-04-30-28.** Métro: Pompe.

LINGERIE

Cadolle   Herminie Cadolle invented the brassiere in 1889. Today, her family manages the store she founded, and they still make specialty brassieres for the Crazy Horse cabaret. This is the place to go if you want made-to-order items or are hard to fit. Open Monday to Saturday 9:30am to 1pm and 2 to 6:30pm. 4 rue Cambon, 1er. www.cadolle.com. © **01-42-60-94-22.** Métro: Concorde.

Chantal Thomass ★★   This lingerie brand sells luxury French underwear for the contemporary pin-up with a penchant for suspenders and corsets. The boutique is a delicious burlesque boudoir lined in pink satin. Open Monday to Saturday 10am to 7pm. 211 rue St-Honoré, 1er. www.chantalthomass.fr. *℃* **01-42-60-40-56.** Métro: Tuileries.

Erès ★★   Minimal collections of luxury French lingerie and swimwear flaunt a subtle palette and high prices. Open Monday to Saturday 10am to 7pm. 4 bis rue du Cherche Midi, 6e. www.eresparis.com. *℃* **01-45-44-95-54.** Métro: St-Sulpice.

Princesse Tam-Tam ★   This quality lingerie chain sells seasonal collections of sexy French underthings, for all ages and budgets. Open Monday to Saturday 10am to 7pm. 31 rue des Abbesses, 18e. www.princessetamtam.com. *℃* **01-42-52-34-99.** Métro: Abbesses.

JEWELRY

Bijoux Blues ★ 📋   This Marais boutique offers unique jewelry handmade in Paris with a variety of different materials, including Austrian and bohemian crystals, natural and semiprecious stones, pearls, coral, and mother-of-pearl. Custom requests are welcomed for individually-designed pieces. The store offers jewelry at what the staff calls "atelier prices." Open Tuesday to Saturday noon to 7pm, Sunday 2 to 6pm. 30 rue St-Paul, 4e. www.bijouxblues.com. *℃* **01-48-04-00-64.** Métro: St. Paul.

Bijoux Burma   If you can't afford any of the spectacular and expensive bijoux at the city's world-famous jewelers, come here to console yourself with some of the best fakes anywhere. This quality costume jewelry is the secret weapon of many a Parisian woman. Open Monday to Saturday 10:30am to 6:45pm. 50 rue François-Premier, 8e. www.bijouxburma.com. *℃* **01-47-23-79-93.** Métro: Franklin-D-Roosevelt.

Cartier ★   One of the most famous jewelers in the world, Cartier has prohibitive prices to match its glamorous image. Go to gawk, and if your pockets are deep enough, pick up an expensive trinket. Open Monday to Saturday

The Cartier store.

10:30am to 7pm. 23 place Vendôme, 1er. www.cartier.com. 𝄞 **01-44-55-32-20.** Métro: Opéra or Tuileries.

Dior Joaillerie ★★   The talented Parisian aristocrat with the dreamy name Victoire de Castellane launched Dior's fine jewelry department in 1998. Colored stones, bright enamels, and flower and insect motifs, are some of the signature elements. Discover her astounding, dreamy collections displayed within a jewel box of a store installed on the magnificent place Vendome. Open Monday to Saturday 11am to 7pm. 8 place Vendôme, 1er. www.diorjoaillerie.com. 𝄞 **01-42-96-30-84.** Métro: Tuileries.

Van Cleef & Arpels ★   Years ago, Van Cleef's designers came up with an intricate technique that remains a vital part of its allure—the invisible setting, wherein a band of sparkling gemstones, each cut to interlock with its neighbor, creates an uninterrupted flash of brilliance. Come browse with the rich and famous. Open Monday to Friday 10:30am to 7pm; Saturday 11am to 7pm. 22 place Vendôme, 1er. www.vancleef-arpels.com. 𝄞 **01-53-45-35-50.** Métro: Opéra or Tuileries.

White Bird ★   This new multi-brand shop offers a fine selection of jewelry, including limited edition pieces by a unique selection of international craftsmen. Store owner Stephanie Roger carefully curates the collection by selecting independent-minded international jewelry designers with a unique aesthetic. The boutique manages to exude neither the coolness of a contemporary art gallery nor the hushed and stifling atmosphere of the classic jewelry store. It's a stone's throw from the place Vendôme, but a world away from the trade jewelry scene. Open Monday to Saturday 11:30am to 7pm. 38 rue du Mont Thabor, 1er. www.white birdjewellery.com. 𝄞 **01-58-62-25-86.** Métro: Concorde.

Concept Stores

Antoine & Lili ★   This brightly-colored string of stores sells the Paris brand's range of ethnic-inspired ready to wear for women, plus children's collections, toys, and home goods. There's a bright canteen to refuel. The spirit of the cosmopolitan Canal St-Martin might reside here. Open daily 11am to 7pm. 95 quai de Valmy, 10e. www.antoineetlili.com. 𝄞 **01-40-37-41-55**. Métro: Jacques-Bonsergent.

Colette ★★   Colette is a swank citadel for a la mode fashion. It buzzes with excitement, stocking fashion by some of the city's most promising young talent, from Comme des Garçons to Carven. This is for the sophisticated international shopper who'd never be caught dead shopping at Galeries Lafayette and the like. A pioneering concept store, it also curates home furnishings by designers such as Tom Dixon, books, music, DVDs and even zany Japanese accessories. If you're not in the mood for shopping, head straight for the basement "water bar," with its fresh quiches, salads, and cakes, plus three dozen brands of bottled water. Open Monday to Saturday 11am to 7pm. 213 rue St-Honoré, 1er. www.colette.fr. 𝄞 **01-55-35-33-90.** Métro: Tuileries or Pyramides.

Centre Commercial ★   This innovative, collaborative, fair-trade concept store set up by the ethical French trainer brand Véja sells fashion for men and women from like-minded brands including Gloverall, Grenson, Saint-James, and Leaf, plus vintage furniture, secondhand bicycles, and a book and music corner. Open Monday 2 to 7:30pm. Tuesday to Saturday 11am to 7:30pm. 2 rue de Marseille, 10e. www.centrecommercial.cc. 𝄞 **01-42-02-26-08.** Métro: Jacques Bonsergent.

Les Galeries Lafayette.

Le 66 ★★   This appealing labyrinthine space in an arcade off the Champs-Élysées provides some welcome relief from the hysteria on the avenue. Explore the considered selection of edgy fashion and accessories for men and women at your leisure. Discover the latest pieces from an impressive list of local and international brands such as Le Mont St Michel, Thomsen, JC de Castelbajac, and Vivienne Westwood. Plus there's a satellite Kiliwatch vintage bazaar on site. Open Monday to Saturday 11am to 8pm, Sunday 2 to 8pm. 66 ave des Champs-Élysées, 8e. www.le66.fr. ✆ **01-53-53-33-80.** Métro: George V or Franklin-D-Roosevelt.

Merci ★★   This airy, three-floor superstore brings together a carefully selected selection of furniture, home goods, fashion, and beauty. There's a delicious and healthy basement canteen overlooking a courtyard herb garden, and a literary cafe on the ground level for further refreshments. This imposing address in the northern Marais exemplifies the neighborhood's panache and creativeness, and you don't know who you might run into. Open Monday to Saturday 10am to 7pm. 11 boulevard Beaumarchais, 3e. www.merci-merci.com. ✆ **01-42-77-00-33.** Métro: Saint Sébastien-Froissart.

Spree ★ 🎁   Possibly the best store in Montmartre, Spree has been doing its bohemian thing since 2000, and slowly drawing other quality retail to the vicinity. This relaxed concept store presents an inspiring fusion of fashion and accessories, art and design, with pieces from talents including Isabel Marant, Tsumori Chisato, Vanessa Bruno, Jerome Dreyfuss, Acne, and APC. The staff is warm and helpful. Open Monday to Saturday 11am to 7:30pm, Sunday 3 to 7pm. 16 rue Vieuville, 18e. www.spree.fr. ✆ **01-42-23-41-40.** Métro: Abbesses.

Department Stores

Le Bon Marché ★★   This Left Bank landmark has worked hard positioning itself as the most exclusive of the city's department stores. Its modest size makes it manageable to wander the exclusive selection of fashion for men, women, and children; cosmetics and perfumes; furniture; upscale gifts; and housewares. It also boasts one of the largest food halls in Paris which should not be missed. The magnificent displays of the finest fresh and preserved produce from France and around the world is a feast for the senses. Open Monday to Wednesday and Saturday 10am to 8pm; Thursday and Friday 10am to 9pm. 22–24 rue de Sèvres, 7e. www.lebonmarche.fr. ✆ **01-44-39-80-00.** Métro: Sèvres-Babylone.

Les Galeries Lafayette ★   Opened in 1896, with a lobby capped by an early-1900s stained-glass cupola classified as a historic monument, the family-owned Galeries Lafayette remains Paris's most popular department store. This store could provision a small city with its thousands of racks of clothing for men, women, and children, and a staggering array of cosmetics and perfumes. Also in the complex is **Lafayette Gourmet,** one of the fanciest grocery stores in Paris, selling culinary exotica at prices usually lower than those at Fauchon (see "Food & Drink," below); **Lafayette Sports; Galeries Lafayette Mariage** (for wedding accessories); and two other general-merchandise stores, both known simply as **"GL."** The floor above street level has a concentration of high-end, corners, including Cartier, Vuitton, and Prada. The **Galerie des Galeries** is located within this Luxury department and presents regular quality contemporary art exhibitions (free entry). At the street-level Welcome Desk, a multilingual staff will tell you where to find various items in the store, where to get a taxi back to your hotel, and so on. Across the street at 35 boulevard Haussmann you'll find the 3-story **Lafayette Maison,** dedicated to everything you might need for the home. Open Monday to Wednesday and Friday to Saturday 9:30am to 8pm; Thursday 9:30am to 9pm. 40 bd. Haussmann, 9e. www.galerieslafayette.com. ☎ **01-42-82-34-56.** Métro: Chaussée d'Antin. RER: Auber.

Printemps ★   Take a look at the elaborate facade of this store for a reminder of the Gilded Age. Inside, the merchandise is divided into housewares (**Printemps Maison**), women's fashion (**Printemps de la Mode**), and men's clothes (**Le Printemps de l'Homme**). Since a change in ownership in 2006, the Printemps has been chasing a serious luxury market, and now displays a cavalcade of high-end brands across its selection. Inside is a magnificent stained-glass dome, through which turquoise light cascades into the sixth-floor **La Brasserie Printemps;** you can have a coffee or a full meal here. Interpreters at the Welcome Service in Printemps de la Mode will help you find what you're looking for, claim your VAT refund, and so on. Printemps also has a tourist discount card, offering a flat 10% discount. Open Monday to Wednesday and Friday to Saturday 9:35am to 7pm; Thursday 9:35am to 9pm. 64 bd. Haussmann, 9e. www.printemps.com. ☎ **01-42-82-50-00.** Métro: Havre-Caumartin. RER: Auber or Haussmann–St-Lazare.

Food & Drink
BREAD & CAKES

Ladurée ★★   Japanese tourists have been known to faint when reaching the celadon and gilt entry to this mythical French patisserie. Sofia Coppola even called on the *maison* to prepare their famous macaroons for her 2006 film *Marie Antoinette.* Although the branch on the Champs-Élysées is the most spacious, the one on rue Royale is the original store, which opened back in 1862 and where the modern day macaroon is credited with actually being invented. But you can expect queues at all three Parisian outposts. As well as their exquisite macaroons available in classic flavors like chocolate, raspberry, and rose petal, Ladurée makes all the traditional French cakes, and includes an onsite tea room cum restaurant where you can enjoy the desserts. Open Monday to Friday from 7:30am to 11pm, Saturday from 7:30am to midnight, Sunday 7:30am to 10pm. 75 avenue des Champs-Elysées, 8e. www.laduree.fr. ☎ **01-40-75-08-75.** Métro: George V. Other locations at 16-18 rue Royale, 8e. ☎ **01-42-60-21-79.** Métro: Madeleine; 21 rue Bonaparte, 6e. ☎ **01-44-07-64-87.** Métro: St-Germain-dès-Prés.

Pierre Hermé ★★   The cult of the macaroon, a delicate sweet biscuit, has swept the city over the last few years, and Monsieur Hermé is one of its pioneers.

From this elegant Left Bank flagship you will find Pierre Hermé's full range, with original flavor combinations like passion fruit and chocolate, or wasabi and strawberry. There is also an incomparable selection of cakes, to eat in, take out or simply admire. Open daily 10am to 7pm. 72 rue Bonaparte, 6e. www.pierreherme.com. 𝄐 **01-43-54-47-77.** Métro: St-Sulpice.

Poilâne ★★   One of Paris's best-loved bakeries, Poilâne hasn't changed much since it opened in 1932. Come here to taste and admire the beautiful loaves of bread decorated with simple designs of leaves and flowers that'll make you yearn for an all-but-vanished Paris. Specialties include apple tarts, butter cookies, and a chewy sourdough loaf cooked in a wood-fired oven. Breads can be specially wrapped to stay fresh during your journey home. Cherche-Midi location open Monday to Saturday 7:15am to 8:15pm; Grenelle location Tuesday to Sunday 7:15am to 8:15pm. 8 rue du Cherche-Midi, 6e. www.poilane.fr. 𝄐 **01-45-48-42-59.** Métro: St-Sulpice. Also: 49 bd. de Grenelle, 15e. 𝄐 **01-45-79-11-49.** Métro: Dupleix.

CHOCOLATE

Christian Constant ★★   Opened in 1970, Christian Constant sells some of Paris's most delectable chocolates by the kilo. Each is a blend of ingredients from Ecuador, Colombia, or Venezuela, usually mingled with scents of spices and flowers such as orange blossoms, jasmine, the Asian blossom ylang-ylang, and vetiver and *verveine* (herbs more usually used to brew tea). Open daily 9am to 8pm. 37 rue d'Assas, 6e. www.christianconstant.fr. 𝄐 **01-53-63-15-15.** Métro: St-Placide.

Jadis et Gourmande   This chain of chocolatiers has a less lofty reputation than Christian Constant and more reasonable prices. Across five centrally located stores, you'll find their famous alphabetical chocolate blocks, which allow you to spell out any message (well . . . almost), in any language. *"Merci"* comes prepackaged. Specialties that are even more delectable are *pralines fondants*, a mixture of praline, nuts, and chocolate that begins to melt the moment it hits your taste buds. Open Monday 1 to 7pm; Tuesday through Saturday 10am to 7pm. 27 rue Boissy d'Anglais, 8e. www.jadisetgourmande.fr. 𝄐 **01-42-65-23-23.** Métro: Madeleine. An even larger premises, with greater quantities of the same inventories, is at 88 bd. du Port-Royal, 5e. 𝄐 **01-43-26-17-75.** Métro: Gobelins. RER: Port-Royal.

Jean-Paul Hévin ★★   One of the great chocolatiers of Paris, its owner has mastered the fusion of *chocolat* with *fromage* (cheese, of course). Sweet luscious chocolates with tart cheeses such as Camembert or Roquefort are infused to satisfy both the cheese fan and the chocolate lover's sweet tooth. Savory chocolates are also served without cheese. New offerings—unique in Paris—have caused this place to become one of the most acclaimed in Europe for chocolate devotees. Open Monday to Saturday 10am to 7:30pm. 231 rue St-Honoré, 1er. www.jphevin.com. 𝄐 **01-55-35-35-96.** Métro: Tuileries or Concorde.

CHEESE

Barthélémy ★   This historic cheese monger has been supplying the country's presidents since 1973 with an incredible range of specialty produce from the four corners of France. Their specialty? The Mont d'Or, a creamy cow's milk cheese from the Alps available between September and May. Open Tuesday to Saturday 7:30am to 7:30pm. 51 rue de Grenelle, 7e. 𝄐 **01-42-22-82-24.** Métro: Rue du Bac.

SPECIALTY

Fauchon ★★★   At place de la Madeleine stands one of the city's most popular sights—not the church, but Fauchon, a hyper-upscale mega-delicatessen that thrives within a city famous for its finicky eaters. In the original store (26 place de la Madeleine) you'll find a *pâtissier* and *boulangerie,* for breads and pastries, and a *traiteur,* for fresh produce including cheeses, terrines, pâtés, caviar, and fruits. Prices are steep, but the inventories—at least to serious foodies—are without equal. The selection of cakes is mouth-watering; try one of their famous *éclairs,* with new flavor combinations each season. Or a *Paris-Brest,* a ring in the shape of a bicycle wheel that's loaded with pastry cream, almond praline, butter cream, and hazelnut paste capped with almonds. At the second, neighboring address (30 place de la Madeleine), you'll discover an *épicerie* (for jams, crackers, pastas, and exotic canned goods), a *confiserie* selling chocolates and confectionary, a wine cellar, plus two dining areas (a casual basement lunch space La Cantine and upstairs more formal dining at Le Café). At some of the counters, you'll indicate to attendants what you want from behind glass display cases and get an electronic ticket, which you'll carry to a *caisse* (cash register). Surrender your tickets, pay the bill, and then return to the counter to pick up your groceries. In other cases, you simply load up a shopping basket with whatever you want and pay for your purchases at a cash register, just as you would at any grocery store. Open Monday to Saturday 9:30am to 7pm. 26 and 30 place de la Madeleine, 8e. www.fauchon.com. ✆ **01-70-39-38-00.** Métro: Madeleine.

Hédiard ★★   Another fine Parisian delicatessen, this 1850 temple of *haute gastronomie* has a more traditional style than its neighbor Fauchon. The old-fashioned decor is a series of red and black salons filled with towering displays of exotic and specialty foodstuffs, giving the store the look of an early-1900s spice emporium. Hédiard is rich in coffees, teas, jams, and spices. They have a quality wine cellar, and the fresh produce department displays exotic fruit and vegetables from the four corners of the planet, in all seasons. Open Monday to Friday 8am to 10pm, Saturday noon to 10:30pm. 21 place de la Madeleine, 8e. www.hediard.fr. ✆ **01-43-12-88-99.** Métro: Madeleine.

Le Maison du Miel   Running "The House of Honey" has been a family tradition since before World War I. The entire store is devoted to products derived from honey: honey oil, honey soap, and various honeys to eat, including one made from heather. This store owes a great debt to the busy bee. Monday to Saturday 9:30am to 7pm. 24 rue Vignon, 9e. www.lamaisondumiel.com. ✆ **01-47-42-26-70.** Métro: Madeleine, Havre-Caumartin, or Opéra.

Maison de la Truffe ★ 🎁   Cramped and convivial, the layout of this shop was modeled after a Parisian's fantasy of an affable, cluttered, old-fashioned butcher shop in Lyon. It's *the* source for foie gras, caviar, black and white truffles, and other high-end foodstuffs. Artfully assembled gift baskets are a house specialty. One corner is devoted to a restaurant where many (but not all) of the dishes contain the costly items (especially truffles) sold in the shop. Examples include noodles or risottos with truffles and caviar with all the fixings. The restaurant is open Monday to Saturday noon to 6pm and 7 to 11pm. The store is open Monday to Saturday 10am to 9pm. 19 place de la Madeleine, 8e. www.maison-de-la-truffe.com. ✆ **01-42-65-53-22.** Métro: Madeleine or Auber.

WINES

Lavinia ★   This is the largest wine-and-spirits store in Europe, opened in 2002 to great acclaim in Paris. Spread over three floors near place de la Madeleine, it stocks more than 3,000 brands of French wine and spirits, along with more than 2,000 brands from other parts of the world. A simple lunch-only restaurant is on-site, as well as a tasting bar. Wine sales here are big business and reflective of France's marketing ideas that regard wine as a part of life. This is the only place in Paris where you can buy a good bottle of South Dakota wine. But who would want to? Open Monday to Saturday 10am to 8pm. 3–5 bd. de la Madeleine, 1er. www.lavinia.fr. ℂ **01-42-97-20-20.** Métro: Madeleine.

Les Caves Taillevent   This is a temple to the art of making fine French wine. Associated with one of Paris's grandest restaurants, Taillevent, it occupies the street level and cellar of an antique building. Stored here are more than 25,000 bottles of wine, with easy access in nearby warehouses to almost a million more. Open Monday 2 to 7:30pm; Tuesday to Saturday 9am to 7:30pm. 199 rue du Faubourg St-Honoré, 8e. www.taillevent.com. ℂ **01-45-61-14-09.** Métro: Charles-de-Gaulle–Etoile.

Nicolas ♟   This is the flagship store of this chain of wine boutiques, and as such, its vintages are likely to be more esoteric and rare than what you'd find in any of the other 400 or so members of its chain. Scattered over three floors of a large space near La Madeleine are fairly priced bottles of mainstream wines such as Alsatian Gewürztraminers and Collioures from Languedoc-Roussillon. Nicolas also stocks some exceptionally rare vintages, such as a Romanée-Conti from Burgundy. Open Monday to Saturday 9:30am to 8pm. 31 place de la Madeleine, 8e. www.nicolas.com. ℂ **01-42-68-00-16.** Métro: Madeleine.

Gifts & Souvenirs

Au Nom de la Rose   Tasteful and frilly, this flower shop and gift boutique sells many of the floral arrangements that decorate local hotels and restaurants, as well as gift objects that are scented, emblazoned, or permeated with "the spirit or scent of the rose." Expect an overwhelming mass of flowers, many of them temporarily resting in glassed-in coolers, as well as rose-hip jams and marmalades, scented soaps and candles, rosewater-based perfumes, and decorative items for the home and kitchen. A "refinement" (their word) that you might consider either hopelessly decadent or whimsical and charming, depending on your point of view, is a perfume that's specifically designed to enhance the allure of your bedsheets. Open Monday to Saturday 9am to 9pm; Sunday 9am to 2pm. 46 rue du Bac, 7e. www.aunomdelarose.fr. ℂ **01-42-22-22-12.** Métro: Rue du Bac.

Cire Trudon ★★ ♟   Originally the royal wax and candle makers, this historic brand dates from 1643. Still in operation, it manufactures a delicious selection of contemporary perfumed candles, and the more classic variety too, in an exquisite rainbow of colors. This charming, rickety, two-floor store is a delight. Open Monday to Saturday 10am to 7pm. 78 rue de Seine, 6e. www.ciretrudon.com. ℂ **01-43-26-46-50.** Métro: Odéon.

La Plaque Emaillées et Gravée Jacquin   Established in 1908, when the Art Nouveau craze swept Paris, the outfit has done a respectable business promoting turn-of-the-20th-century Parisian charm ever since. Its specialty is the custom manufacture of cast-iron plaques, enameled and baked, commemorating virtually any event, person (including yourself), or piece of real estate that appeals to you. Phillippe Jacquin, the owner, offers a variety of shapes, sizes, and colors for the finished product. It will take 3 to 4 weeks for your plaque to be manufactured, after which it can be shipped. Much smaller plaques, some ready-made, are also available. Open Monday to Friday 9am to 1pm and 2 to 6pm. 18 bd. des Filles-du-Calvaire, 11e. www.la-plaque-emaillee.com. ✆ **01-47-00-50-95.** Métro: St-Sébastien.

La Tuile à Loup   This emporium has been selling authentic examples of all-French handicrafts since around 1975, making a name through its concentration of hand-produced woven baskets, cutlery, and woodcarvings. Especially appealing are the hand-painted crockery and charming stoneware from such traditional manufacturers as Quimper and Malicorne and from small-scale producers in the Savoy Alps and Alsace. Open Monday 1 to 7pm; Tuesday to Saturday 10:30am to 7pm. 35 rue Daubenton, 5e. www.latuilealoup.com. ✆ **01-47-07-28-90.** Métro: Censier-Daubenton.

Home Design, Furnishings & Housewares

CERAMICS, CHINA & PORCELAIN

Astier de Villatte ★★   This impossibly charming two-story shop sells a range of white, uncompromisingly handmade earthenware in a range of designs inspired by 18th-century styles. There are regular special collections in collaboration with other Paris creatives, and a corner devoted to all sorts of other objects that appeal to the owners, from postcards to scented candles. Astier de Villatte also produce a cult range of annual diaries and notebooks. Everything they do radiates good taste. Open Monday to Saturday 11am to 7:30pm. 173 rue Saint-Honoré, 1er. www.astierdevillatte.com. ✆ **01-42-60-74-13.** Métro: Palais Royal.

La Maison Ivre   This quaint shop is perfect for country-style ceramics that add authenticity to French-country decor. It carries an excellent selection of handmade pottery from all over France, with an emphasis on Provençal and southern French ceramics, including ovenware, bowls, platters, plates, pitchers, mugs, and vases. Open Monday to Saturday 10:30am to 7pm. 38 rue Jacob, 6e. www.maison-ivre.com. ✆ **01-42-60-01-85.** Métro: St-Germain-des-Prés.

CRYSTAL

Baccarat ★★   Opened in 1764, Baccarat is one of Europe's leading purveyors of full-lead crystal. They sell luxury jewelry pieces based on colored crystal and precious gems, tableware, glassware, and contemporary chandeliers and other crystal light fittings. The most prestigious outlet is on place de la Madeleine, but the exquisite, Philippe Starck–designed **Maison Baccarat** at 11 place des Etats-Unis, 16e, is larger and includes the **Musée Baccarat** (p. 104). Branches are open Tuesday to Friday 10am to 7pm; Monday and Saturday 10am to 7:30pm. 11 place de la Madeleine, 8e. www.baccarat.fr. ✆ **01-42-65-36-26.** Métro: Madeleine. Also: 11 place des Etats-Unis, 16e. ✆ **01-40-22-11-22.** Métro: Boissière.

Lalique ★★   This historic crystal manufacturer is known for its smoky frosted-glass sculpture, Art Deco crystal, and unique perfume bottles. The shop sells a wide range of merchandise, including leather belts with Lalique buckles and silk scarves, designed to compete directly with those sold by Hermès. You'll also find a branch inside the Carrousel du Louvre. Open Monday to Saturday 10am to 7pm. 11 rue Royale, 8e. www.cristallalique.fr. ✆ **01-53-05-12-81.** Métro: Concorde.

FABRICS

Marché Saint-Pierre   At the foot of the Sacré Coeur sits this 5-story fabric emporium that draws in designers and tailors from all over the city. Every type of textile imaginable is on sale, plus bed linens, curtains, and other soft home accessories. The Marché Saint-Pierre is at the heart of the city's traditional fabric district, a bustling neighborhood crammed with all sorts of stores, each with their own specialty, from fake fur to prints. Open Monday to Friday 10:30am to 6:30pm; Saturday 10am to 7pm. 2 rue Charles Nodier, 18e. www.marchesaintpierre.com. ℭ **01-46-06-92-25.** Métro: Barbès-Rochechouart.

Souleiado   This is the only Paris branch of Souleiado, one of Provence's most successful purveyors of the iconic bright fabrics and thick pottery from southern France. Fabrics are measured out by scissors-wielding saleswomen and then sold by the meter for seamstresses to whip into curtains, tablecloths, or whatever. In a separate shop just around the corner, at 78 rue de Seine (same phone), there are displays of table settings, housewares, and gift items, each reflecting the bright sunshine and colors (usually ocher, cerulean blue, and a strong medium green) of the Midi. Open Monday to Saturday 10:30am to 7pm. 3 rue Lobineau, 6e. www.souleiado.com. ℭ **01-43-54-62-25.** Métro: Odéon or Mabillon.

HOME DESIGN & FURNISHINGS

Conran Shop   This shop might remind you of an outpost of the British Empire, valiantly imposing Brit aesthetics and standards on the French-speaking world. Inside, you'll find the latest contemporary furniture; articles for the kitchen and dining room; glass and crystal vases; fountain pens and stationery; reading material and postcards; and even a selection of chocolates, teas, and coffees to help warm up a foggy English day. Open Monday to Friday 10am to 7pm; Saturday 10am to 7:30pm. 117 rue du Bac, 7e. www.conranshop.fr. ℭ **01-42-84-10-01.** Métro: Sèvres-Babylone.

Dehillerin ★   Established in 1820, Dehillerin is Paris's most famous cookware shop, in the "kitchen corridor" around Les Halles, where all the city's chefs once came to stock up on provisions at the central fresh food market. The shop has a professional, though dusty, feel to it, but don't be intimidated. Equipped with the right tools from Dehillerin, you too can learn to cook like a master chef. Open Monday 9am to 12:30pm and 2 to 6pm; Tuesday to Saturday 9am to 6pm. 18–20 rue Coquillière, 1er. www.e-dehillerin.fr. ℭ **01-42-36-53-13.** Métro: Les Halles.

La Quincaillerie   This is one of those shopping oddities that seem to exist only in Paris. The owners specialize in doorknobs for front doors, windows, and cupboards. There are knobs for almost any piece of furniture, and dozens of accessories, often by top designers such as Philippe Starck. The wares in their stores at no. 3 and no. 4 are modern and designed by some of Europe's top names, including the Italian legend Gio Ponti or Portuguese architect Alvaro Siza. Open Monday to Friday 10am to 1pm and 2 to 7pm; Saturday 10am to 1pm and 2 to 6pm. 3–4 bd. St-Germain-des-Prés, 5e. www.laquincaillerie.com. ℭ **01-46-33-66-71.** Métro: St-Germain-des-Prés.

Les Fleurs ★   Tucked down a little alleyway in Bastille, this is a charming clutter of curated accessories for the home or for you. Unique products by young designers are piled together; expect to find everything from leather bags to coffee mugs, but always with a twist. Great for gifts. Open Monday to Saturday Noon to 7:30pm; closed Sunday. 6 passage Josset, 11e. http://lesfleurs.canalblog.com. ✆ **06-64-35-75-54.** Métro: Ledru-Rollin.

Music

FNAC ★   This is a large chain of music, books, and electronics stores known for their wide selection and discounted prices. Great for the traveler, it offers everything you need for your computer, iPod, or digital camera. Most branches include digital photo development services. Stock up on French music in the CD department, or browse the bookshelves. Seven branches are in Paris, with the largest being at 136 rue de Rennes, Montparnasse. Other locations include rue St-Lazare, avenue des Champs-Élysées, Forum des Halles, avenue des Ternes, and avenue d'Italie. All are open Monday to Saturday 10am to 7:30pm except Champs-Élysées, which is open daily noon to midnight. 136 rue de Rennes, 6e. www. fnac.com. ✆ **08-25-02-00-20.** Métro: St-Placide.

Virgin Megastore   Paris has three branches of Europe's biggest, most widely publicized CD and record store. The Champs-Élysées branch is the city's largest music store, with a bookstore and cafe downstairs. The store's opening in a landmark building helped to rejuvenate the avenue. You'll also find a Virgin Megastore at each airport. Open Monday to Saturday 10am to midnight; Sunday noon to midnight (other locations: Carrousel du Louvre, Sun–Tues 10am–8pm, Wed–Sat 10am–10pm; Gare Montparnasse, Mon–Thurs 7am–8pm, Fri 7am–9pm; Sat 7am–8pm). 52–60 av. des Champs-Élysées, 8e. www.virginmegastore.fr. ✆ **01-49-53-50-00.** Métro: Franklin-D-Roosevelt.

Technology

Apple Store ★   This Paris temple to the world of Apple is spread out over three stores, just steps from the Opéra Garnier and the department stores. Open Monday to Wednesday 9am to 8pm; Thursday to Saturday 9am to 9pm. Note, there's a second outlet inside the Carrousel du Louvre. 12 rue Halévy, 9e. www.apple. com. ✆ **01-44-83-42-00.** Métro: Opéra.

Toys & Games

Au Nain Bleu ★   This is the largest, oldest, and most centrally-located toy store in Paris. More important, it's probably the fanciest toy store in the world. But don't panic—in addition to the expensive stuff, you'll find rows of cheaper items on the first floor. Open Monday 2 to 7pm; Tuesday to Saturday 10am to 7pm. 5 bd. Malesherbes, 8e. www.aunainbleu.com. ✆ **01-42-65-20-00.** Métro: Concorde or Madeleine.

PRACTICAL MATTERS: THE SHOPPING SCENE

Business Hours

Usual shop hours are Monday to Saturday from 10am to 7pm, but hours vary, with some fashion boutiques not opening until 11am or even later, and Monday mornings don't run at full throttle. Small shops sometimes close for a 2-hour lunch break and some do not open at all until after lunch on Monday. Thursday is the best day for late-night shopping, with stores open to 9 or 10pm.

Sunday shopping is limited to tourist areas and flea markets, though there's growing demand for full-scale Sunday hours. The department stores are now open on the five Sundays before Christmas. The **Carrousel du Louvre** (www.carrouseldulouvre.com; ☏ **01-43-16-47-10**), a mall adjacent to the Louvre, is open daily 10am to 8pm. The tourist shops lining rue de Rivoli across from the Louvre are open on Sunday, as are the antiques villages, flea markets, and specialty events. Several food markets enliven the streets on Sunday. For our favorites, see the box "Food Markets" (p. 243). Most of the shops along the Champs-Élysées stay open on Sunday.

Note: Many independent stores close for about a month at the height of summer, from late July to late August.

Getting a VAT Refund

The French **value-added tax** (**VAT—TVA** in French) is generally 19.6%, but you can get most of that back if you spend a minimum of 175€ on the same day, in the same, participating, store. All department and luxury stores participate in the VAT refund program. However, some people find the trouble isn't worth the refund.

When you meet your required minimum purchase amount, you qualify for a tax refund. The amount of the refund varies with the way the refund is handled and the fee some stores charge you for processing it. So the refund at a department store may be 13%, whereas at a small shop it may be 15% or 18%.

You'll receive the **Retail Export Form** in the shop; some stores, such as Hermès, have their own, while others provide a government form. Make sure you have the form stamped before leaving the store.

All refunds are processed at the point of departure from the **European Union (E.U.),** so if you're going to another E.U. country, don't apply for the refund in France. At the airport of your last stop in the E.U. look for the Detaxe counter at the airport. Then expect to stand in line for as long as half an hour. You must show your ticket, your passport, the forms you collected on the day you bought the goods, and the goods themselves, so have them on you or visit the Customs office before you check your luggage. After Customs has checked everything, keep a copy of the form for your records then drop the original in the envelope provided and in the mail. After the papers are mailed, a credit will appear, often months later, on your credit card bill.

Be sure to mark the paperwork to request that your refund be applied to your credit card so you aren't stuck with a check in euros, which may be hard to cash.

To avoid refund hassles, ask for a Global Refund form (Shopping Cheque) at a store where you make a purchase. When leaving an E.U. country, have it stamped by Customs, after which you take it to a Global Refund counter at one of more than 700 airports and border crossings in France. Your money is refunded on the spot. For information, contact **Global Blue,** 18 rue de Calais, 75009 Paris (www.global-blue.com; ☏ **01-41-61-51-51**).

Duty-Free Boutiques

The advantage of duty-free shops is that you don't have to pay the VAT, so you avoid the red tape of getting a refund. Both Charles de Gaulle and Orly airports have shopping galore (de Gaulle has a virtual mall with crystal, cutlery, chocolates, luggage, wine, pipes and lighters, lingerie, silk scarves, perfume, knitwear, jewelry, cameras, cheeses, and even antiques). You'll also find duty-free shops on the avenues branching out from the Opéra Garnier, in the 1st and 9th arrondissements. Sometimes bargains can be found, but most often not.

Sales & Bargains

The French sales take place twice a year, over 5 weeks, beginning at the end of June for the summer collections and the beginning of January for winter. Remember, the first in are the best dressed.

ENTERTAINMENT & NIGHTLIFE

By Anna E. Brooke

8

While the stereotype of the French may suggest a nation of hard-playing, work-adverse people, Parisians are as hardworking as the rest of us. Work ethics aside, it seems that every resident of this luminous city has a higher education in pleasure. With the workday behind them, locals head for a cafe or wine bar to meet with friends over a drink and perhaps a meal (see "The Top Cafes," in chapter 6). Whatever your diversional whim, Paris can answer it. Stadiums, racetracks, and city parks cater to sports enthusiasts, while theaters and concert halls captivate audiences with performances ranging from classical to postmodern. As its moniker indicates, Parisian streets and monuments remain illuminated until late at night. Restaurants won't expect you before 7:30pm, and by midnight the party is only just getting started at hundreds of bars and dance clubs throughout the city.

In this chapter, we highlight the best leisure and entertainment options in Paris: the top performance spaces for live entertainment, the best bars for whistle-wetting, and the hottest clubs for dancing off all that foie gras. From a jog along the city's "green lung" to outlandish floor shows and everything in between, if it's about having fun, then you'll find it here.

THE PERFORMING ARTS

Home to a broad range of performing arts, Paris showcases everything from world-renowned opera and contemporary dance to classical music, slap-stick comedy and edgy and modern theater. The **Opéra Garnier** and **Opéra Bastille** are the stalwart venues of world-class opera and ballet, kicking out classics by the likes of Puccini and Mozart (often with cutting-edge mise-en-scènes), or hosting performances from foreign ballet powerhouses as well as their own Opéra de Paris corps. Theater in Paris is generally in French, but check the programs of theaters such as **Odéon, Théâtre de L'Europe,** and **Les Bouffes du Nord** for the occasional play in English.

LISTINGS Announcements of shows, concerts, and operas are plastered on kiosks all over town and in the Métro. You'll find listings in the weekly *Pariscope,* an entertainment guide with an English-language section, or in *L'Officiel des Spectacles,* available at newsstands. Also check out **en.parisinfo.com**, the city's official English-language tourism website. The "What's On" section has detailed listings for every concert and show in town. *Note:* Performances tend to start later in Paris than in London or New York—from 8 to 9pm—and Parisians tend to dine after the theater.

PREVIOUS PAGE: **A jazz band playing in a** *caveaux.*

GETTING TICKETS   Your best bet for cheap tickets is to try the theater's box office at the last minute. Or head for a discount agencies such as the **Kiosque-Théâtre,** 15 place de la Madeleine, 8e (✆ **01-42-65-35-64;** www.kiosque theatre.com; Métro: Madeleine), offering leftover tickets for up to 50% off on the day of performance. Tickets for evening shows sell Tuesday to Saturday from 12:30 to 8pm, for matinees, Sunday 12:30 to 4pm. Other branches are in front of Gare Montparnasse and at the exit of Ternes Métro station.

Another option is **FNAC.** There are several branches across the city, but two handy ones are at 136 rue de Rennes, 6e (✆ **08-25-02-00-02;** Métro: St. Placide); and 1–7 rue Pierre-Lescot, in the Forum des Halles, 1er (✆ **08-25-02-00-20;** Métro: Châtelet–Les Halles). The chain sells music, movies, electronics, and books, as well as tickets for festivals, concerts, and the theater. You can pick up your tickets at the *billetterie* (ticket booth) of any of these locations, or online at www.fnacspectacles.com. Two other great websites for reduced-price tickets is www.ticketnet.fr and **www.billetreduc.fr.**

Tip: Students with ID can get great last-minute deals by applying for the lottery at box offices an hour before curtain time.

The easiest (and most expensive) way to get tickets is to ask your concierge to arrange for them. A service fee is added, but it's a lot easier if you don't want to waste precious hours in Paris trying to secure often hard-to-get tickets.

Theater

Comédie-Française ★★   Those with an understanding of French can delight in a sparkling production of Molière at this national theater, established to keep the classics alive and to promote important contemporary authors. Nowhere else will you see the works of Molière and Racine so beautifully staged. In 1993 a Left Bank annex was launched, the **Comédie Française-Théâtre du Vieux-Colombier,** 21 rue du Vieux-Colombier, 4e (✆ **01-44-39-87-00**). Though its repertoire varies, it's known for presenting serious French dramas and the occasional foreign adaptation. The troupe's contemporary plays are usually shown in the **Studio Théâtre** (just opposite in the Carrousel du Louvre, 99 rue de Rivoli, 1er). 2 rue de Richelieu, 1er. www.comedie-francaise.fr. ✆ **08-25-10-16-80.** Tickets range from 12€–40€. Métro: Palais-Royal or Musée du Louvre.

Odéon, Théâtre de l'Europe   More than a theater, the Odéon hosts debates on literature, philosophy, and European politics—a Euro-enthusiasm that is translated on stage with quality plays in different European languages (including English), such as Shakespeare's *Romeo and Juliet* and Tennessee Williams' *A Streetcar Named Desire.* As it's one of France's five national theaters, prices start as low as 10€ a seat, with discounts for students and job-seekers. Place de l'Odéon, 75006. www. theatre-odeon.fr. ✆ **01-44-85-40-00.** Tickets range from 10€–32€. Métro: Odéon.

Théâtre du Châtelet ★★   The Châtelet's Belle Époque interior makes a stunning setting for some the best musical theater in Paris. Troupes from the West End and Broadway, as well as the best French companies, frequently perform classic musicals like *Sweeney Todd, West Side Story,* and *The Sound of Music,* in English, with full orchestras. Check the website for up-to-the-minute details. 1 place du Châtelet, 1er. www.chatelet-theatre.com. ✆ **01-40-28-28-40.** Tickets range from 12€–130€. Métro: Palais-Royal or Musée du Louvre.

ENTERTAINMENT & NIGHTLIFE

The Performing Arts

Belly Laughs in English

There comes a time when a little humor from the homeland soothes the soul. For those moments, head to promoter Karel Beer's **Laughing & Music Matters** nights at **La Java,** 105 rue du Faubourg du Temple, 75010 (📞 **01-53-19-98-88;** www.anythingmatters.com; Metro: République), where mirth merchants from the U.K., U.S., and Australia cross the seas to play to needy Anglophone audiences. Tickets vary but are usually around 20€; check website for show dates, which tend to be confirmed at last minute.

Théâtre de la Ville The performances held at this theater are consistently inventive and often ground-breaking, with avant-garde spectacles by both French and international directors. Full-price tickets vary according to the production, but rarely exceed 25€ for the top seats and 17€ for the lower category. 2 place du Châtelet, 75004. www.theatredelaville-paris.com. 📞 **01-42-74-22-77.** Tickets 17€–25€. Metro: Châtelet.

Opera, Dance & Classical Concerts

Cité de la Musique ★★★ This testimony to the power of music has been the most widely applauded of the late François Mitterrand's *grands projets*. At the city's northeastern edge in what used to be a run-down neighborhood, this $120-million stone-and-glass structure incorporates a network of concert halls, a library and research center for the study of all kinds of music, and a museum (see the Musée de la Musique, p. 119). The complex hosts a rich variety of concerts, ranging from Renaissance music through 19th- and 20th-century works, including jazz and traditional music from nations around the world. There's a great cafe on site if you'd like to sip some wine on the sunny terrace before your concert. 221 av. Jean-Jaurès, 19e. www.cite-musique. fr. 📞 **01-44-84-44-84.** Tickets 8€–39€. Métro: Porte de Pantin.

Opéra Bastille ★★ This controversial building—it has been called a "beached whale"—was designed by Canadian architect Carlos Ott, with curtains by Japanese designer Issey Miyake. Since the house's grand opening in July 1989, the Opéra National de Paris has presented works such as Mozart's *Marriage of Figaro* and Tchaikovsky's *Queen of Spades*. The main hall is the largest of any French opera house, with 2,700 seats, but the building also contains two smaller concert halls, including an intimate 250-seat room that usually hosts chamber music. Both traditional opera performances and symphony concerts are

Opéra Garnier.

presented here, as well as classical and modern dance. 2 place de la Bastille, 4e. www. operadeparis.fr. ☏ **08-92-89-90-90.** Tickets 5€–180€ opera, 8€–100€ dance. Métro: Bastille.

Opéra Garnier ★★★   With its grand decor, underground lake and cellars, and haunted history—a falling chandelier killed a man here in 1896—this place served as the inspiration for Gaston Leroux's 1910 novel (and later a musical hit), *The Phantom of the Opera.* Today, this is once again the premier venue for dance and opera. Charles Garnier designed this 1875 rococo wonder during the heyday of the French Empire under Napoleon III; the facade is adorned with marble and sculpture, including *The Dance* by Carpeaux. You can see the original gilded busts and statues, the rainbow-hued marble pillars, the mosaics, and inside, the ceiling painted by Chagall. The Opéra Garnier combines ballet and opera, and provides one of the most elegant evenings you can spend in the City of Light. The box office is open Monday to Saturday from 10:30am to 6:30pm. You can also visit the building outside performance times. Place de l'Opéra, 9e. www.operadeparis.fr. ☏ **08-92-89-90-90** or 01-40-01-18-50. Tickets 5€–180€ opera, 8€–89€ dance. Métro: Opéra.

Salle Pleyel ★★★   New York has Carnegie Hall, but for years Paris lacked a permanent home for its orchestra. That is, until several years ago when the restored Salle Pleyel opened once again. Built in 1927 by the piano-making firm of the same name, Pleyel was the world's first concert hall designed exclusively for a symphony orchestra. Ravel, Debussy, and Stravinsky performed their masterpieces here, only to see the hall devastated by fire less than 9 months after its opening. In 1998, real estate developer Hubert Martigny purchased the concert hall and pumped $38 million into it, restoring the Art Deco spirit of the original and also refining the acoustics it once knew. Nearly 500 seats were removed to make those that remained more comfortable. The Orchestre Philarmonique de Radio France and the Orchestre de Paris now have a home worthy of their reputations, and the London Symphony Orchestra makes Pleyel its venue in Paris. The box office is open Monday to Friday 10am to 6pm. You'll also find jazz and high-brow pop on the agenda. 252 rue du Faubourg-St-Honoré, 8e. www.sallepleyel.fr. ☏ **01-42-56-13-13.** Tickets 10€–160€. Métro: Miromesnil.

◎ The Music of Angels

Some of the most moving music in Paris echoes through its churches, with sounds that can take you back to the Middle Ages. At **Eglise de St-Eustache,** 2 impasse St-Eustache, 1er (☏ **01-42-36-31-05;** www.saint-eustache.org; Métro: Rambuteau), High Mass with the organ playing and the choir singing is at 11am on Sunday. In summer, concerts are played on the organ, marking the church's role in holding the premiere of Berlioz's *Te Deum* and Liszt's *Messiah.* Tickets to these special concerts range from 12€ to 40€. The church is open daily 9:30am to 7pm (from 10am Sat).

The **American Church in Paris,** 65 quai d'Orsay, 7e (☏ **01-40-62-05-00;** www.acparis.org; Métro: Invalides or Alma-Marceau), sponsors concerts from September to June on Sundays at 5pm. You can also attend free concerts at **Eglise St-Merri,** 76 rue de la Verrerie, 4e (☏ **01-42-71-93-93;** Métro: Hôtel-de-Ville). These performances are staged with variable musicians based on their availability, from September to July on Saturdays at 8:30pm, and again on Sundays at 4pm.

Théâtre des Champs-Élysées   This Art Deco theater, constructed in 1913, attracts a very haute couture crowd and hosts both national and international orchestras (such as the Vienna Philharmonic) as well as opera and dance. The box office is open Monday to Saturday from 11am to 6pm (from 2pm on Saturday). There are no performances in August. 15 av. Montaigne, 8e. www.theatrechampselysees. fr. (✆ **01-49-52-52-52** for box office. Tickets 5€–140€. Métro: Alma-Marceau.

Théâtre National de Chaillot   Part of the Palais de Chaillot architectural complex facing the Eiffel Tower (built for the 1937 World Fair), this is one of the city's largest concert halls. In addition to music, you might see a dance performance here or a brilliantly performed play by Marguerite Duras. The box office is open Monday to Saturday from 11am to 7pm, Sunday 1 to 5pm. 1 place du Trocadéro, 16e. www.theatre-chaillot.fr. (✆ **01-53-65-30-00.** Tickets 8€–60€. Métro: Trocadéro.

Cabaret

Decidedly expensive and wholly kitsch cabarets give you your money's worth by providing lavishly spectacular floor shows with bare-breasted ladies in feathers and sequins, and fun acts by ice-skaters and ventriloquists. The dancing is beautiful—the music less so—but Paris just wouldn't be Paris without its cabarets.

The Crazy Horse   Since 1951, this sophisticated strip joint has thrived, thanks to good choreography and an avant-garde, coquettish celebration of the female form. The Crazy Horse has been getting more attention in recent years ever since the famous burlesque performer Dita Von Teese decided to make it her home away from home in Paris. Shows last less than 2 hours. You'll find a small number of women among the audience of mainly businessmen. Shows Sunday to Friday 8:15 and 10:45pm; Saturday at 7, 9:30, and 11:45pm. The Crazy doesn't have a restaurant but you can buy a combined show-dining ticket and eat at affiliated restaurants like La Fermette Marbeuf (p. 197). 12 av. George V, 8e. www.lecrazyhorseparis.com.

Moulin Rouge.

The Reel World in Paris

Paris loves the cinema. It was invented here, thanks to the Lumière brothers, Louis and Auguste, who are credited with the world's first public movie screening in 1895 on the boulevard des Capucines. And *le cinéma* loves Paris too; no matter where you point the camera, you get a compelling result, which is why so many production companies merrily ignore the traffic jams and cordon off whole roads for days at a time. Paris's cinemas are often as much an event as the films themselves. For the best experiences in French and English film, try **Le Grand Rex,** 1 bd. Poissonnière, 75002

((℡ **08-92-68-05-96;** www.legrandrex. com), an Art Deco theater with three tiers and a starlit ceiling; and **La Géode,** 26 av. Corentin-Cariou, 75019 (℡ **08-92-68-45-40;** www.lageode.fr), a futuristic silver ball at Parc de la Villette, inside which you'll find an IMAX screen that hosts 3D films, including nature documentaries and animated adventures. The most beautiful cinema however, has to be **La Pagode,** 57 bis rue de Babylone, 75007 (℡ **01-45-55-48-48**), a glorious 19th-century replica of a pagoda where the former silk-clad ballroom has been turned into one of the world's most beautiful screening rooms.

℡ **01-47-23-32-32.** Reservations recommended. Entry from 100€ for the show and champagne; show plus dinner packages 180€–240€. Métro: George V or Alma Marceau.

Lido de Paris   The Lido competes with the best that Las Vegas has to offer. In explaining the concept of *Bonheur,* the Lido's current production, artistic director Pierre Rambert invites us to imagine "a bird-woman arriving on her cloud of feathers from a shore where happiness does not exist." She then discovers joy through Paris, India, and the cinema. Don't worry if that doesn't make any sense, because you're really there just to see the topless Bluebell Girls anyway. There are several lunchtime shows a year too (check the site for dates). Lunch and the show costs 140€. 16 av. des Champs-Élysées, 8e. www.lido.fr. ℡ **01-40-76-56-10.** Tickets for the show alone from 95€ and dinner plus show packages range from 160€–300€. Price includes half-bottle of champagne per person. Métro: George V.

Moulin Rouge   This place is a camp classic. The establishment that Toulouse-Lautrec immortalized is still here, but the artist would probably have a hard time recognizing it today, surrounded as it is by so many tour buses. Colette once created a scandal here by offering an on-stage kiss to Mme de Morny, but shows today have a harder time shocking audiences. Try to get a table—the view is much better on the main floor than from the bar. What's the theme? Synchronized dancing by handsome men and girls, girls, girls, virtually all topless. Dance finales usually include two dozen of the belles doing a topless cancan. Revues begin nightly at 9 and 11pm. 82 bd. Clichy, place Blanche, 18e. www.moulinrouge.fr. ℡ **01-53-09-82-82.** Tickets for the show alone range from 95€–105€ and packages including dinner range from 175€–200€. Métro: Blanche.

THE BAR SCENE

Rather than go home to often-cramped apartments, Parisians socialize in the bars and cafes throughout the city. Besides focusing on wine, wine bars *(bars à vin)* also serve small plates, usually of meat and cheese, so that you don't have to drink on an empty stomach. Some like **Po-Za-Da** and **Rouge Passion** even serve excellent food to accompany your wine choices. Anglo- and Irish-style pubs are also scattered throughout the city; these bars serve cocktails and beer, and can be more boisterous than the intimate settings of cafes. Paris's bars, especially in the city's northern and eastern stretches where districts like Bastille, Oberkampf, Pigalle, Montmartre, and Batignolles (just west of place de Clichy), tend to attract trendy crowds for late night partying and sometimes even free live music concerts.

Along with hot drinks and alcohol, cafes also serve meals, making the experience a night out in itself. For our selection of the best cafes, see "The Top Cafes" in chapter 6.

Bars & Pubs

You will find Parisians enjoying their drinks at any of the ubiquitous cafes and bars throughout town (many of which often double as an extension of personal living rooms). What follows are among the best places to enjoy a beer or cocktail, in part because of the interesting crowds they draw. Paris is also home to quite a few luxurious, world-class bars, including those at the **Plaza Athénée** and the **Ritz**—imbibing at these bars is a uniquely Parisian experience. Just dress up for the occasion. As a general rule, bars and pubs are open daily from 11am to 2am.

Andy Wahloo ★ This bar has a 1970s Moroccan vibe, with colorful rugs and other North African collectables. The cocktails are expensive, but people-watching among the youthful and *branché* (hip) Parisians perched on the stools makes up for the prices, and DJs play into the wee hours most nights. Open Tuesday to Saturday 6pm to 2am. 69 rue des Gravilliers, 3e. http://andywahloo-bar.com. ✆ **01-42-71-20-38.** Métro: Arts et Métiers.

Café Charbon In many ways the social center of trendy Oberkampf, this former Belle Époque dance hall has big wooden banquettes, distressed mirrors, and pleasantly vaulted ceilings. Spacious but often crowded, it's a great place to start off your evening bar crawl along rue Oberkampf. It's also adjoined to the Nouveau Casino concert hall and club so it's perfect for a pre- or post-concert tipple.

The swanky Hemingway Bar at the Ritz.

Open daily 9am to 2am (until 4am Fri–Sat with live DJ sets). 109 rue Oberkampf, 11e. www.lecafecharbon.com. 📞 **01-43-57-55-13.** Métro: Parmentier or Ménilmontant.

Chez Jeannette   When Chez Jeanette was taken over by a young hip crowd, everyone thought it would incite the surrounding bars to clean themselves up. But Jeanette remains a lone-rider in this part of town, which makes it all the more attractive. Crowds of trendy 30-somethings lap up the cheap wine and concentrate on being cool, while the occasional older regular sweeps in, seemingly oblivious to the change of clientele. Hot meals are served at lunchtime, but at night, you have to make do with cheese and ham platters. Open daily 8am–2am. 47 rue du Faubourg Saint-Denis, 75010. www.chezjeannette.com. 📞 **01-47-70-30-89.** Metro: Château d'Eau.

Dédé La Frite   Suits from the surrounding banks head here after work, when the cocktails are just 7.50€ and the beer 4€. When the alcohol has flowed for an hour or two, most punters give in to the aroma of juicy burgers and frites (from 9€) wafting from the kitchen. Open daily 8am–2am. 135 rue de Montmartre, 75002. 📞 **01-40-41-99-90.** Metro: Bourse.

Experimental Cocktail Club   This cosmopolitan lounge has the feel of a retro speakeasy. The cocktails here are spot-on and the crowd is fashionable—starchitect Philippe Starck and actor Adrian Grenier have been spotted sipping drinks here late into the evening. Drinks start at 12.50€. Open daily from 6pm to 2am, until 5am Friday and Saturday. 37 rue St-Sauveur, 2e. www.experimental cocktailclub.com. 📞 **01-45-08-88-09.** Métdo: Sentier.

Le Bar (Hôtel Plaza Athénée)   This classy, historic joint is all glamour and fabulousness with a shockingly 21st-century decor. It will cost you a small fortune to drink a glass of champagne (24€), but for some it's definitely worth it. The specialty Love Mojito (a mix of vodka, litchi, pink champagne, and rose petals) is as delicious as it is decadent (28€). Dress to the nines if you're going—but if you're planning on making the trip, you already knew that. Drinks start at 20€. Open daily from 6 to 2am. Hotel Plaza-Athénée, 25 av. Montaigne, 8e. www.plaza-athenee-paris.fr. 📞 **01-53-67-66-65.** Métro: Alma-Marceau.

Le China   This site has been home to various clubs stretching back decades. In the 1930s, it was an opium den and jazz club. Today, in its latest incarnation, it is all dark colors, candles, soft lights, and intimacy. The onsite restaurant evokes 1930s Shanghai with red-painted walls and Asian cuisine. There is a long zinc bar (the longest in Paris) on the ground floor, and the basement bar hosts regular jazz concerts. Cocktails cost from 10€. The Chinatown (gin, fresh mint, lemon, and soda) was invented here in the 1990s. Open Monday to Friday noon to 2am and Saturday and Sunday from 5pm to 2am. 50 rue de Charenton, 12e. www.lechina.eu. 📞 **01-43-46-08-09.** Métro: Ledru Rollin.

Le Forum   The polished oak paneling, ornate stucco, and selection of single-malt whiskeys on offer here recall a posh English gentleman's club. The Forum however is all about cocktails. You can sample from among 180 of them, including many that haven't been popular since the Jazz Age. Champagne by the glass is common, as is that social lubricant, the martini. Open Monday to Thursday noon to 1am, Friday noon to 2am, Saturday 5:30pm to 2am. 4 bd. Malesherbes, 8e. www.bar-le-forum.com. 📞 **01-42-65-37-86.** Métro: Madeleine.

Le Merle Moqueur   This student institution is so well loved, it still draws nostalgic 30-somethings looking for frivolous fun just like in the old days. Its main appeal is the rum (more than 20 types) and the long list of cheap cocktails.

For real fun, get here after 10pm, when the crowds get animated. It's open daily 5pm to 2am. 11 rue de la Butte aux Cailles, 75013. No phone. Métro: Place d'Italie.

La Palette   For a hint of sophistication in surroundings that are part of the Left Bank's artistic history (Jim Morrison, Hemingway, and Picasso all drank here) choose La Palette. The leafy terrace is a godsend on a hot day, but for true romance head to the fresco-clad back room where you can steal a kiss undisturbed. Cheese, pâté, and cold meat platters are good to share (14€). It's open Monday to Saturday 9am to 2am. 43 rue de Seine, 75006. ℂ **01-43-26-68-15.** Métro: Odéon.

The Frog and the Princess   It's loud and crowded in this English-style pub. You'll be surrounded by students and sports enthusiasts, most of whom will speak English. It's so un-Parisian that it has become an especially Parisian place to go, especially if you're an Anglophile or enjoy a good pint. A definite place to try and catch a game, match, or whatever your countrymen consider the sporting event of the day. This is also a great place for weekend brunches. Open Monday to Friday from 5:30pm to 2am, and Saturday to Sunday noon to 2am. 9 rue Princesse, 6e. www.frogpubs.com. ℂ **01-40-51-77-38.** Métro: St Germain des Prés/Mabillon.

The Quiet Man   Named after a famous John Wayne movie set in Ireland, this is one of the best Irish pubs in Paris. Naturally, it's the watering hole for all Irish expats who gravitate to their Guinness, Irish music, and of course, darts. Open daily 5pm to 2am. 5 rue des Haudriettes, 3e. www.thequietman.eu. ℂ **01-48-04-02-77.** Métro: Rambuteau.

Wine Bars

The wine bar, or *bar à vin,* is a welcome departure from sitting down at a typical cafe or restaurant. They are often calm and warmly decorated, and many have regional themes. All offer diverse and interesting selections of wines and serve simple small dishes and platters—perfect for those in the mood for a delectable snack with their drinks.

Enjoying wine and company at Le Baron Rouge.

5e Cru ★ 🍴 This shabby-chic spot, with only three pine tables as well as a few barrels converted to dining stations, is a favorite of foodies. Jean de Toalier boasts that he's got "every *terroir* of France covered" in his kitchen, offering more than 150 different French wines. He may well be right. You can get a simple menu, or daily small plate special, for 15€; a glass of wine for 4€ to 8€, with bottles priced as low as 8€ and rarely more than 60€. Open Tuesday to Friday 10:30am to midnight, Saturday 3pm to 1am. 7 rue du Cardinal Lemoine, 5e. www.5ecru. com. 📞 **01-40-46-86-34.** Métro: Jussieu.

Le Baron Rouge ★★ This immensely popular Bacchanalian temple only has four tables, so get here before the pre-dinner crowds sweep in if you want to sit. If not, be prepared to slurp any one of its 50 or so labels standing, or resting on a giant wine barrel outside. Snacks of cheese, charcuterie, and (when in season) oysters add to the attraction. Being in the middle of the Marché Aligre, it's also a coveted bar with the Sunday market crowds. It's open Tuesday to Thursday 10am to 3pm and 5 to 10pm; Friday to Saturday 10am to 10pm; and Sunday 10am to 3pm. 1 rue Théophile Roussel, 75012. 📞 **01-43-43-14-32.** Metro: Ledru-Rollin.

Le Sancerre Enter this rustic place in the center of the chic and moneyed 7th arrondissement and—with its aging furniture and wooden bar—you'll think you've been transported somewhere in the countryside of the Loire Valley. Lovingly cared for by friendly proprietors, this place specializes in—what else—Sancerre wine. There are other vintages as well, include chinon and saumur wine (both from the Loire Valley) among many others. The plates are as countryside as the decor: *andouillettes* (chitterling sausages), Loire cheeses, fresh oysters, and fresh quiches galore. Glasses of wine cost 4€ to 7€; simple platters of food cost 8€ to 18€ each. Open Monday to Friday 8am to 4pm and 6:30 to 11pm, Saturday 8:30am to 4pm. 22 av. Rapp, 7e. 📞 **01-45-51-75-91.** Métro: Alma-Marceau.

Les Bacchantes This place prides itself on offering more wines by the glass—at least 90—than any other wine bar in Paris; prices range from 3€ to 6€ per glass. It also does a hefty restaurant trade in well-prepared *cuisine bourgeoise*, with main courses costing 10€ to 28€. Its cozy, rustic setting—with paneling, and chalkboards announcing vintages and platters—attracts theatergoers before and after performances at the nearby Olympia concert hall (p. 282). Wines are mainly from France, but you'll also find examples from neighboring countries. Open Monday to Saturday noon to 3pm and 6:30pm to midnight. 21 rue Caumartin, 9e. www.lesbacchantes.fr. 📞 **01-42-65-25-35.** Métro: Havre-Caumartin.

Les Caves Populaires The name says it all: This is a hugely popular wine bar with friendly waiters, rustic decor, cheap platters of cheese and meat, and even cheaper wine, starting at just 2.50€ a glass. It's a real local's joint in the heart of the Batignolle's district and a place to mix with 30-something artsy types and students. It's open Monday to Saturday 8am to 2am, and Sunday 11am to 2am. 22 rue des Dames, 75017. 📞 **01-53-04-08-32.** Metro: Place de Clichy.

Po-za-da This small contemporary joint, located off the beaten tourist track near Nation, does triple duty as a restaurant, bar, and wine shop (next door). From the kitchen come hearty Southwestern French–influenced cuisine, platters of ham, and cheeses so ripe they almost walk off your plate. There are over 100 wines on offer, many of which are available by the glass. If you're not sure what to choose, the friendly manager Beedoo will advise you according to what you like and what you're eating. Open Monday to Saturday 10am to 2am. 2 rue Guénot, 11e. www.pozada.com. 📞 **01-43-70-63-24.** Métro: Rue des Boulets or Nation.

ENTERTAINMENT & NIGHTLIFE

The Bar Scene

Rouge Passion   Anne and Sébastien's wine bar is a hip, romantic joint where lovers and wine-lovers alike share giant platters of cheese and cold meats (15€) over a glass of Bacchus's finest from the downstairs cellar (glasses from 4€). This place also serves bistro fare, and lunch is a steal, at 16€ for two consistently excellent courses of French cuisine. You can also eat dinner here; food is served Monday to Friday noon to 2:30pm and 7 to 10:30pm and Saturday 7 to 10:30pm. 14 rue Jean-Baptiste Pigalle, 75009. www.rouge-passion.fr. *©* **01-42-85-07-62.** Metro: Pigalle.

THE CLUB & MUSIC SCENE

The live music and club scene in Paris is legendary. The City of Light is home to everything from the swankiest of chic nightclubs—with thousand-euro bottle service and models—to the smallest and sweatiest dive bars and glitzy cabarets. There is also a world-class jazz scene here, as well as a varied live music scene; clubs and concert halls host everything from cutting-edge electronica music to hip-hop to the soft glamour of indie rock, and just about everything else in between. Paris is a moveable dance floor.

Live Music

JAZZ CLUBS

The great jazz revival that long ago swept America is still going strong here, with Dixieland, Chicago, bop, and free-jazz rhythms being pounded out in dozens of cellars, mostly called *caveaux*, where music-lovers of all ages gather to listen to jazz.

Baiser Salé   This appealing club is housed in a cellar lined with jazz-related paintings, a large bar, and videos that show jazz greats of the past (Charlie Parker, Miles Davis). Everything is mellow and laid-back, with an emphasis on the music. Genres include Afro-Caribbean, Afro-Latino, salsa, merengue, rhythm and blues, and sometimes fusion. Open daily 5:30pm to 6am. 58 rue des Lombards, 1er. www. lebaisersale.com. *©* **01-42-33-37-71.** Cover free to 20€ depending on the act. Métro: Châtelet.

Caveau de la Huchette   This celebrated jazz *caveau*, reached by a winding staircase, draws a young crowd, mostly students, who dance to the music of

Musicians at New Morning jazz club.

well-known jazz combos. In prejazz days, Robespierre and [...] place. It's open Sunday to Wednesday 9:30pm to 2:30am; [...] and holidays 9:30pm to 4am. 5 rue de la Huchette, 5e. ww[...] © **01-43-26-65-05.** Cover 12€ Sun–Thurs, 14€ Fri–Sat; students 24[...] RER: St-Michel.

Caveau des Oubliettes ★ It's hard to say which is [...] entertainment and drinking or the setting. An oubliette is [...] door at the top as its only opening, and the name is accurate. Located in the Latin Quarter, just across the river from Notre-Dame, this night spot is housed in a genuine 12th-century prison, complete with dungeons and spine-tingling passages, where prisoners were tortured and sometimes pushed through portholes to drown in the Seine. The *caveau* is beneath the subterranean vaults that many centuries ago linked it with the fortress prison of Petit Châtelet. Today patrons laugh, drink, talk, and flirt in the narrow *caveau* or else retreat to the jazz lounge. There's a free jam session every night, which might be funk, jazz, or rock. At some point on Friday and Saturday nights concerts are staged, sometimes with a cover charge. Open daily 5pm to 4am. 52 rue Galande, 5e. www.caveaudesoubliettes. fr. © **01-46-34-23-09.** Métro: St-Michel.

Le Duc des Lombards Comfortable and appealing, this low-key jazz club is renowned for its exciting, high quality jazz by international artists. Performances usually begin nightly at 9pm and continue (with breaks) for 5 hours, touching on everything from free jazz to more traditional forms such as hard bop. Entry is free on Fridays and Saturdays after midnight. 42 rue des Lombards, 1er. www.ducdes lombards.com. © **01-42-33-22-88.** Cover free–30€. Métro: Châtelet.

Le Sunset/Le Sunside ★ This is a dual temple of jazz, one of the hottest addresses on the after-dark scene in Paris, lying between the Forum des Halles and the Centre Georges Pompidou. Le Sunset Jazz, created in 1983, is dedicated to electric jazz and international music, whereas le Sunside, launched in 2001, is devoted to acoustic jazz for the most part. Some of the most innovative names in European jazz appear here regularly, along with jazz legends, many from abroad. Both clubs form a single complex with two concerts every night. Open Monday to Saturday 9:30pm to 1am. 60 rue des Lombards, 1er. www.sunset-sunside.com. © **01-40-26-46-60.** Tickets 20€–30€. Métro: Châtelet.

New Morning ★ Jazz maniacs come to drink, talk, and dance at this enduring club. It's sometimes a scene, attracting such guests as Spike Lee and Prince. Recent bookings have included Robin McKelle, The Klezmatics, Patricia Barber, and folk rock acts such as Steve Earle. It opens nightly at 8pm, with concerts beginning at 9pm. 7 rue des Petites-Ecuries, 10e. www.newmorning.com. © **01-45-23-51-41.** Cover 18€–26€. Métro: Château-d'Eau.

MODERN CONCERT HALLS

La Boule Noire The Black Ball is one of those intimate, divey Parisian haunts that attract biggies such as the Dandy Warhols, Metallica, Cat Power, Franz Ferdinand, and Jamie Cullum. Despite the star-studded line up, prices tend to hover around the 20€ mark, making this one of the cheapest venues around. 120 bd. Rochechouart, 75018. www.laboule-noire.fr. © **01-49-25-81-75.** Métro: Anvers or Pigalle.

La Cigale ★ This 19th-century music hall, next door to the Boule Noire, draws some of the biggest artists working in music today—everything from indie rock to hip-hop and jazz. Recent bookings include Band of Horses, Cee Lo

...d the Eric Truffaz Quartet. Balcony seating is available for those who ...arly, and there's plenty of open floor space for those who want to dance. ...oulevard de Rochechouart, 18e. www.lacigale.fr. ✆ **01-49-25-81-75.** Tickets 8€–55€. ...étro: Pigalle or Anvers.

La Flèche d'Or   Set inside a converted train station and boasting beautiful windows that look out over the tracks below, this concert hall books both unknown and major label bands. Recent performances have included England's Razorlight, Band of Horses, and the Walkmen. Tickets tend to be cheap here, but beers are expensive. 102 bis rue de Bagnolet, 20e. www.flechedor.fr. ✆ **01-44-64-01-02.** Tickets 8€–20€. Métro: Alexandre Dumas or Gambetta.

La Maroquinerie ★   This little club atop the Ménilmontant hill is the place to catch local and international music artists before they blow up big and start playing La Cigale. The roster leans heavily toward the indie rock genre but there are electro and folk acts in the mix, too. An attached restaurant and bar with a pretty outdoor courtyard are good places to hang before and after the show. 23 rue Boyer, 20e. www.lamaroquinerie.fr. ✆ **01-40-33-64-85.** Tickets 10€–20€. Métro: Ménilmontant.

Le Bataclan   You'll never have trouble finding this place, considering its colorful exterior inspired by Chinese architecture. Inside is an equally awe-inspiring and massive space, perfect for big dance parties or concerts. Le Bataclan hosts an eclectic bevy of shows, from Swedish trip-hop star Jay-Jay Johanson to indie-leaning rock groups like Three Doors Down and Morcheeba. 50 bd. Voltaire, 11e. ✆ **01-49-23-96-33.** Cover varies depending on the show. Métro: Oberkampf.

Les Trois Baudets   Between 1947 and 1966 this small theater launched more musical careers than anywhere else (Serge Gainsbourg, Jacques Brel, and Brigitte Fontaine to name but a few), but that didn't stop it from becoming an erotic cabaret, before falling into total disrepair in 1996. After much lobbying by songmaster Charles Aznavour, it was finally decided that Paris lacked a theater for Francophone music, and that the cradle of *chanson* should be brought back to launch up-and-coming artists. Today, thanks to an enviable sound-system, two bars, a restaurant overlooking Pigalle, and a jam-packed program of *chanson* and slam, it draws visitors in by the coachload. Open Tuesday to Saturday 6pm to 1:30am and Sunday 10:30am to 5pm. 64 bd. de Clichy, 75018. www.lestroisbaudets.com. ✆ **01-42-62-33-33.** Admission varies (usually 6€–15€). Métro: Pigalle.

Olympia   Charles Aznavour and other big French names appear in this cavernous hall near the Opéra Garnier. The late Yves Montand performed once, and the show was sold out 4 months in advance. Today, you're more likely to catch Chris Rea or PJ Harvey. Performances usually begin at 8:30pm Tuesday to Saturday, with Sunday matinees at 5pm. 28 bd. des Capucines, 9e. www.olympiahall.com. ✆ **01-55-27-10-00** or 08-92-68-33-68. Tickets 25€–100€. Métro: Opéra or Madeleine.

LIVE MUSIC BARS

L'Alimentation Générale   This ode to all things kitsch has oodles of unusual beers (Flag, Sagres, and Orval) for 3€ to 5€, and inventive cocktails from 8€. But that's not the only reason to visit: DJs or live bands (often world music) play here practically every night, and only the biggest names tend to have a cover charge (10€ including one free drink). Open Wednesday and Sunday 7pm to 2am and Thursday to Saturday 7pm to 4am. 64 rue Jean-Pierre Timbaud, 75011. www.alimentation-generale.net. ✆ **01-43-55-42-50.** Métro: Parmentier.

L'International   The already cool 11th arrondissement got a little cooler when this joint opened—a breath of fresh air for music lovers with its free entry and a string of on-the-up bands playing to hip indie crowds. Beer is a steal at 3€, and once a month there's an after-show party until 4am. 5/7 rue Moret, 75011. www.linternational. fr. ⓒ **01-49-29-76-45.** Métro: Ménilmontant.

OPA   Industrial-chic OPA is like a live MySpace music joint: it's free, and Paris's up-and-coming bands play from 9pm until late, before DJs take over and play into the wee hours. Tuesday is rock or folk, Wednesday pop or French *chanson,* Thursday varies, and Friday and Saturday nights are electro rock and pop. 9 rue Biscornet, 75012. www.opa-paris.com. ⓒ **01-46-28-12-90.** Métro: Bastille.

Nightclubs

From the dance halls of the cancan and raucous and energetic jazz clubs of the 1920s, Parisians have historically made it a point to get out at night and go dancing. Stepping into a Parisian club today (known as *les boîtes de nuit,* or just *une boîte*) with the locals is one of the best ways to experience a night on the town in the City of Lights. Like in any big city, Parisian clubs are divided into different scenes: some places more "see and be seen," while others tend to focus less on what you're wearing and more on the music being played—not to suggest that the glitz and glam spots don't have great music. Certain locations stay popular for years, but most will wax and wane in their level of "coolness." Also, the French love their fashion, so dressing to impress is obligatory—sneakers will rarely get you past the line outside. Check **Time Out: Paris** (www.timeout.fr/paris/en) or **Pariscope** to get a sense of current trends. Most of these clubs don't really get going until at least 11pm, if not later.

Batofar ★   While most clubs would never last more than a few years before the crowds moved on, somehow Batofar remains fresh and consistently full. The fact that it sits on a converted barge floating on the Seine must have something to do

Partying at Cab nightclub.

with it. It has also opened a restaurant so hungry clubbers can fill up without leaving the boat. On good nights you'll see hundreds of gyrating dancers moving in rhythm to house, garage, techno, and live jazz music. Beer costs about 10€ a bottle, while cover runs from free to 15€, depending on the band or DJ. Open Tuesday to Saturday from 6pm to 4am (restaurant open Tues–Sat noon–2pm and 7:30–11pm). Facing 11 quai François Mauriac, 13e. www.batofar.org. Métro: Quai de la Gare.

Cab ★★   Although it's not as glamorous as it once was, the former cabaret still sees crowds of rich international types, young bourgeois Parisians, and impossibly skinny fashion models. Located in an underground restaurant/lounge right next to the Louvre, after 11pm the space converts into a dimly lit, classy affair. Cozy up in a nook behind the red velvet ropes or hit the expertly–lit dance floor. You'll hear the latest dance and electro-lounge hits, as well as trendy American sounds, even the occasional hip-hop. Open Wednesday to Saturday 11:30pm to 6am. 2 place du Palais Royal, 1er. www.cabaret.fr. *C* **01-58-62-56-25.** Cover 20€–30€, including 1 drink. Métro: Palais Royal-Musée du Louvre.

Chez Moune   This former lesbian cabaret in Pigalle is now known as a premier spot for young *branché* (hip) Parisians and debaucherous dancing. With low ceilings and walls covered in mirrored tiles, it's all about the crowd and the music—electro, neodisco, and house—and not so much the 1930s decor. If you want to stomp around in your best dancing shoes while pumping your fist in the air, Chez Moune is the place to do it. The club generally opens at 11pm but the crowd usually swarms to the bar of Le Sans Souci across the street to start off the evening. Open Tuesday to Saturday 11pm to 5am. 54 rue Jean-Baptiste Pigalle, 9e. *C* **01-45-26-64-64.** Métro: Pigalle.

Machine du Moulin Rouge   This expansive space next door to the Moulin Rouge Cabaret serves the dual function of disco and concert hall. The music savvy crowds come for electronic everything: rock, funk, pop, dubstep, and live music by rising stars. The regular "We are the 90s" revival nights are particularly coveted by the under–30 crowds. Trendy Parisian radio station, Radio Nova, also programs soirées here. 90 bd. de Clichy, 18. www.lamachinedumoulinrouge.com. *C* **01-53-41-88-89.** Cover varies (free–35€ depending on who's playing). Métro: Blanche.

Favela Chic   The saunalike dance floor of this Brazilian *festa* is always packed with cool crowds grinding to bossa jazz, samba rap, and tropical electro. They make some of the best mojitos in town here, and the already decent onsite restaurant (perfect for a pre-clubbing dinner) just got a lot better with the arrival of young star chef Benjamin Darnaud. Open Tuesday to Thursday 8pm to 2am. 18 rue du Faubourg du Temple, 11e. www.favelachic.com. *C* **01-40-21-38-14.** Cover 10€ Fri–Sat 8pm–4am. Métro: République.

La Bellevilloise   This club/art space/restaurant is right at the top of hilly rue de Menilmontant, but it's worth the climb for its two levels of dance space. The club regularly hosts live DJs or bands playing rock, reggae, and every indie-scene in between. Crowd-surfing has been known to occur on the basement dance floor, while the upstairs is an unpretentious bar including a gorgeous outdoor terrace for a little fresh air. Art exhibitions are also held in the top floor loft space. If you're peckish, sample the French fusion cuisine at the attached Halle des Oliviers restaurant. Open from Wednesday to Sunday 7pm to 1am (until 2am Fridays and Saturdays). 19-21 rue Boyer, 20e. www.labellevilloise.com. *C* **01-46-36-07-07.** Cover free to 15€. Métro: Ménilmontant or Gambetta.

Le Baron ★ Once the most expensive brothel in Paris, much of Le Baron's original decor remains, including the 1920s-era tile of frolicking nude ladies, sexy red walls, and tasseled lamps. It's long been regarded as the playground of the rich and bored, or sometimes just fabulous and occasionally androgynous. The dance floor is regularly packed with some of the world's most beautiful people. Drinks are costly but so is being trendy. It's open daily 11pm to 6am, although hours can vary. 6 av. Marceau, 8e. www.clublebaron.com. ✆ **01-47-20-04-01.** Cover free– 15€ depending on the event and the night of the week. Métro: Champs-Élysées.

Le Gibus One of the original venues for the French punk-rock scene, this place pulls in the under-40s and remains one of the best-known rock clubs in Paris. It opens late every night, entertaining its diverse medley of counterculture Parisians and visitors. The themes are constantly rotating; there might be a live rock band or even a gay clubbing night presented as part of the evening's rhythms. Other nights of the week this place tends to be the venue for private parties or for loosely scheduled rock or pop concerts. 18 rue du Faubourg du Temple, 11e. www.gibus. fr. ✆ **01-47-00-78-88.** Cover 15€–20€. Métro: République.

Le Silencio Arrive after midnight if you want to try and get into movie director David Lynch's private club: it's members only until midnight, at which point the doors open to the public (although the bouncers can be rather picky). If you do make it inside, order a cocktail and watch the fauna slink around. 142 rue Montmartre, 2e. http://silencio-club.com. No phone. No cover after midnight (members only before midnight). Métro: Bourse.

Nouveau Casino Rue Oberkampf is still hyper-hip and in this former movie theater adjacent to the Café Charbon (a drafty space centered on a dance floor and an enormous bar crafted to resemble an iceberg) you can listen to live concerts most nights of the week. On Friday and Saturday, the party continues from 1am till dawn, with a DJ who spins some of the most avant-garde dance music in Paris. Celebrity spotters have picked out Prince Albert of Monaco, British pop star Jarvis Cocker, and such French-language film stars as Vincent Cassel and Mathieu Kassovitz. 109 rue Oberkampf, 9e. www.nouveaucasino.net. ✆ **01-43-57-57-40.** Cover free–30€. Métro: St-Maur, Parmentier, or Ménilmontant.

Rex Club With its sunken dance floors and angular nonfigurative designs gracing the walls, this space recalls the big techno-grunge clubs of London, complete with an international mood-altered crowd. The music here is usually deep and dark, bass-heavy house, and other electronica. Recent luminaries to make an appearance here include rap superstar Grandmaster Flash and popular Russian electronic music-maker Nina Kraviz. Open Thursday to Saturday 11:30pm to 6am. 5 bd. Poissonnière, 2e. www.rexclub.com. ✆ **01-42-36-10-96.** Entry ranges from free to 15€. Métro: Bonne Nouvelle.

Showcase Set almost unbelievably beneath the Pont Alexandre III, with incredible views of the Seine, this may be the only club you'll ever enter that's literally under a bridge. Unique location aside, they have DJs and live bands and gorgeous lighting along the endlessly long bar. Expect a BCBG crowd dressed in Gucci blazers and impossibly high heels. While the live bands are all over the map, the DJs play mostly electro, house, and disco beats. Open Friday and Saturday nights from 11pm until 7am. Port des Champs-Élysées under the Pont Alexandre III. www.showcase.fr. ✆ **01-45-61-25-43.** Entry ranges from free–20€. Métro: Invalides.

ENTERTAINMENT & NIGHTLIFE

The Club & Music Scene

Social Club   If you're the type who likes to say "I saw him/her before he/she was really famous" and rub shoulders with Paris's music savvy it crowds, take a trip to the oh-so-alternative Social Club, where many trend-setting DJs and bands are tried and tested by their record labels. The well-dressed *branché* (hip) crowd comes to dig the live hip-hop, jazz, funk, drum 'n' bass, and all-night electro parties. Open Tuesday to Saturday 11pm to 6am. 142 rue de Montmartre, 75002. www.parissocialclub.com. ✆ **01-40-28-05-55.** Cover free–15€ (depending on who's playing). Métro: Bourse, or Grands Boulevards.

THE GAY & LESBIAN SCENE

Paris has a vibrant gay nightlife scene, centered around **le Marais, les Halles,** and to some extent, **Bastille.** The area with the greatest concentration of gay and lesbian clubs, restaurants, bars, and shops is the area surrounding the Hôtel de Ville and Rambuteau Métro stops. Gay dance clubs come and go so fast that even the magazines devoted to them, such as *2x*—distributed free in the gay bars and bookstores—have a hard time keeping up. For lesbians, there is *Lesbia Magazine.* Also look for *Têtu* magazine, sold at most newsstands—it has special nightlife inserts for gay bars and clubs. Also see Le Gibus (p. 285).

Gay & Lesbian Bars & Clubs

Banana Café   This party central is a popular all-night bar for gays looking for a wild night of cocktails, dancing, and flirting with strangers. It has been known to provide go-go dancers and every now and again there are fortune-telling nights. 13 rue de la Ferronnerie, 1e. www.bananacafeparis.com. ✆ **01-42-33-35-31.** Métro Châtelet.

Chez Michou   The setting is blue, the incredibly tan master of ceremonies wears blue, and the spotlights bathe performers in yet another shade of blue. Cross-dressing belles bear names such as Hortensia and DuDuche and lip-sync

The scene in le Marais.

in costumes from haute couture to haute concierge, paying tribute to such Americans as Tina Turner and to French stars such as Mireille Mathieu, Sylvie Vartan, and Brigitte Bardot. If you don't want dinner, you'll have to stand at the bar, paying a compulsory 35€. Dinner is served nightly at 8:30pm (reservations required); shows begin nightly at 11pm. 80 rue des Martyrs, 18e. ☏ **01-46-06-16-04.** www.michou. com. Cover (including dinner, aperitif, wine, coffee, and show) 135€. Métro: Pigalle.

La Bôite à Frissons   Although still referred to by its former name, Tango, this old classic has music ranging from accordion (the thrill box) to disco and an emphasis on couples dancing. (No techno gets played here!) Everything is unbelievably adorable; club nights are Friday and Saturday, tea dances (tea is served while you boogie) start in the late afternoon Sundays. Interested in a singles dance? Consult the website for more information. It's open Monday to Saturday 11pm to 5am, and Sunday 6 to 11pm. 13 rue au Maire, 4e. www.boite-a-frissons.fr. ☏ **01-42-72-17-78.** Métro: Arts et Métiers.

Le Cox   This place gets so busy early in the evening that the muscled, tank-top-wearing crowd overflows out onto the sidewalk. This is where you'll find a dependably mixed gay crowd in Paris—from hunky American tourists to sexy Parisians. 15 rue des Archives, 4e. www.cox.fr. ☏ **01-42-72-08-00.** Métro: Hôtel de Ville.

Le Duplex   This welcoming bar is a good choice if loud club music isn't your cup of tea. Usually piping in jazz and some hip rock, actual conversation can take place and the clientele is mostly local and quite friendly. Open daily 8pm to 2am (until 4am Friday and Saturday). 25 rue Michel Le Comte, 3e. www.duplex-bar.com. ☏ **01-42-72-80-86.** Métro: Rambuteau.

Le Raidd ★   The bartenders here may be hunks and so are most of the patrons. Be prepared for attitude galore. A special feature is a plexiglass shower box where nude shower boys flaunt their assets throughout the night. It's shoulder-to-shoulder action here with pickup possibilities at every turn. Only the best dressed can expect to get invited in at the door. Open daily 5pm to 5am. 23 rue du Temple, 4e. www. raiddbar.com. ☏ **01-92-77-09-88.** Métro: Hôtel-de-Ville or Rambuteau.

Le Rive Gauche   This swanky joint hosts a regular lesbian party on Saturday nights for a young, stylish crowd. Men are welcome when accompanied by women. 1 rue du Sabot, 6e. www.lerivegauche.com. ☏ **01-40-20-43-23.** Métro: St-Germain-des-Prés.

Le 3w Kafe   The 3w means "Woman with Woman." This is the best-known lesbian bar in the Marais, where an unattached woman usually will have little trouble finding a drinking buddy. On weekends there's dancing downstairs with a DJ in control of the sounds. Straight men are welcome too, if accompanied by a woman. Gay men are admitted without problem. Open Wednesday to Sunday 5pm to 2am, Friday and Saturday 5pm to 4am. 8 rue des Ecouffes, 4e. ☏ **01-48-87-39-26.** Métro: St. Paul.

Open Café   Although this bar is side-by-side with Le Cox, each place has an independent feel, even if their clientele is not. Both places define themselves as bars rather than dance clubs, but on particularly busy nights, someone will inevitably begin to dance. Simple cafe-style food is served from noon to around 5pm. Patrons include just about every type of man that roams the streets of gay Europe today. Open daily from 11am to 2am, Friday and Saturday to 3am. 17 rue des Archives, 4e. ☏ **01-42-72-26-18.** Métro: Hôtel-de-Ville.

Randos Île-de-France   Gays and lesbians from across France get together for Randos Île-de-France's free hikes in and around Île de France. Whether you're a seasoned walker or just fancy getting back to nature and meeting new people, there's a walk for you. Just choose your level (the difficulty for each walk is always indicated), and then turn up at the location at the time indicated. The walks take you into the countryside surrounding Paris, like Fontainebleau forest and the along the river Marne, and usually take place on weekends. All walks are free. For more information and to enroll check the website. 181 avenue Daumesnil, 12e. www. randos-idf.fr. No phone.

ALTERNATIVE ENTERTAINMENT
Comedy Clubs
Laughing Matters   For some belly laughs in the Bard's tongue, head to promoter Karel Beer's Laughing Matters nights at the Java, where mirth-merchants from the U.K., U.S., and Australia cross the seas to play to needy Anglophone audiences. Big names who have previously played include Rich Hall and Greg Proops. Check website for show dates which tend to be confirmed at the last minute. 105 rue du Faubourg du Temple, 10e. ℰ **01-53-19-98-88.** www.anythingmatters. com. Tickets vary (usually around 25€). Metro: République.

Literary Readings
Centre Culturel Irlandais   The Irish Cultural Centre is a hub of English-language activities from free art exhibitions and poetry readings to story-telling for the wee ones, free films by Irish directors (or on Ireland), and cheap music concerts by Irish groups. There's even a Bibliothèque Patrimonial (heritage library). The website has a comprehensive list of dates and activities. 5 rue des Irlandais, 5e. www.centreculturelirlandais.com. ℰ **01-58-52-10-30.** Metro: Place Monge or RER Luxembourg.

Shakespeare & Co.   Paris's stalwart English and American bookstore reels in the crowds with regular readings and workshops, usually in the atmospheric upstairs library, surrounded by owner George Whitman's personal book collection. Readings (usually free) range from poetry to fiction, plus the occasional autobiography (read of course by the authors). Check the web for the up-to-date schedule. Daily 10am to 11pm (from 11am Sun). 37 rue de la Bûcherie, 5e. ℰ **01-43-25-40-93.** www.shakespeareandcompany.com. Métro: St-Michel or Cité.

SPECTATOR SPORTS
Aside from watching octogenarians playing *pétanques*—the lawn bowling game that's always played in parks and always seems to draw spectators—the French love to watch sports. Paris's biggest stadium, **le Stade de France,** is in the northern suburb of St-Denis, while several smaller stadiums are within the city limits. Rugby and soccer games (known as *le foot*) are the most popular to watch alongside Parisians, and the city also plays host to one of the biggest tennis events in the world, the French Open, known as Roland Garros. You can also join the locals at the races, as Paris's horse tracks are a big pull with a large number of very dedicated fans. For additional spectator events and dates, see the "Paris Calendar of Events" on p. 49.

Racing at the Hippodrome d'Auteuil.

Horse Racing

Paris boasts an army of avid horse-racing fans who get to the city's eight race-tracks whenever possible. Information on current races is available in newspapers like **L'Equipe,** sold at kiosks throughout the city, and online at www.france-galop.com.

The epicenter of Paris horse racing is the **Hippodrome de Long-champ ★★★**, in the Bois de Boulogne, 16e (✆ **01-44-30-75-00;** RER or Métro: Porte Maillot and then a free shuttle bus on race days only). Established in 1855, during the autocratic and pleasure-loving reign of Napoleon III, it's the most prestigious track, boasts the greatest number of promising thoroughbreds, and awards the largest purse in France. The most important events at Longchamp are the **Grand Prix de Paris** in late June and the **Prix de l'Arc de Triomphe** in early October.

Another racing venue is the **Hippodrome d'Auteuil,** also in the Bois de Boulogne (✆ **01-40-71-47-47;** Métro: Porte Auteuil). Known for its steeple-chases and obstacle courses, it sometimes attracts more than 50,000 Parisians at a time. Spectators appreciate the park's promenades as much as they do the equestrian events. Races are conducted from early March to late November.

Rugby

A popular national sport is rugby, the rough-and-tumble precursor to American football. The high-profile matches are played at either the **Parc des Princes,** 24 rue du Commandant Guilbau, 16e (✆ **01-47-43-71-71;** www.leparcdesprinces.fr, Métro: porte de Saint-Cloud), or in the **Stade de France** (✆ **08-92-70-09-00;** www.stadefrance.fr), the 81,000-person-capacity stadium in St-Denis, Paris's northern suburb. The rugby season generally runs from August to April. If you're adventurous, check out the *Dieux du Stade,* a calendar and book of the French rugby stars in various states of, well, undress.

Soccer (Football)

Known throughout France as *le football,* or just *le foot,* soccer is one of France's most popular national sports. Paris is home to several football clubs—another term for a team organization—including the one professional club, the ***Paris Saint-Germain Football Club,*** also known as ***Paris SG.*** They play their home matches at the **Parc des Princes,** 24 rue du Commandant Guilbau, 16e (✆ **01-47-43-71-71;** www.leparcdesprinces.fr; Métro: Porte de Saint-Cloud), a stadium with a capacity of almost 49,000 spectators. Their season runs from January to May; tickets start at 12€ and can be purchased on their website, **www.psg.fr**.

Tennis

Much like Wimbledon or the U.S. Open, France dominates the tennis world with the **French Open,** or as it's known here, **Roland Garros** (www.roland garros.com). Matches take place over 2 weeks between late May and early June in the Roland Garros Stadium in the 16e (Métro: Porte d'Auteuil). Tickets should be purchased well in advance, as this is a world-scale tennis event; tickets can be purchased online.

WHERE TO STAY

by Kate van den Boogert

aturally, the most visited city in the world boasts an overwhelming number of hotels, which range from mythical palaces, like the Meurice and the Crillon, to dives so repellent that even George Orwell, author of *Down and Out in Paris and London*, wouldn't have considered checking in. (Of course, you won't find those in this guide!) We include deluxe places for those who can afford to live like the sultan of Brunei, as well as a wide range of moderate and budget choices for the rest of us.

best PARIS HOTEL BETS

- **Best for a Romantic Getaway:** Who doesn't take a deep sigh then murmur yes when he first pushes open this hotel's heavy wooden gate and lays his eyes on the **Pavillon de la Reine,** an enchanting ivy-covered mansion opposite the Marais' place des Vosges? See p. 301.

- **Best for Families:** You'll find all the comfort of home at the stylish **Hôtel Arvor St Georges.** Three suites include an extra single bed, and rooms can also take an extra cot. Kids will also appreciate the homemade cake in the relaxed downstairs lobby. See p. 312.

- **Best Splurge:** This new Philippe Starck–designed gem has the whole city talking. The **Le Royal Monceau–Raffles Paris** offers absolute luxury for contemporary jet-setters, including a Clarins spa, an indoor pool, a state-of-the-art cinema, edgy fashion, and a mobile sound studio that can be set up in any of the soundproofed rooms. See p. 307.

- **Best Value:** The **Mama Shelter** might be off the beaten track, but this Starck-designed hotel nonetheless attracts the in-crowd with its buzzing downstairs restaurant/bar space, high-tech setup, and low rates. See p. 318.

- **Best-Kept Secret:** The **Villa Mazarin** provides elegant and spacious rooms in the thick of the lovely lower Marais, just minutes from the Centre Pompidou, the river, and Notre-Dame. See p. 302.

- **Best Service:** Of all the palace hotels in Paris, the **Hôtel Le Meurice** has perhaps the most warmth and contemporary style. The service here is welcoming, and not at all stuffy. See p. 296.

- **Most Eco-Friendly:** The delightful Canal St-Martin hotspot **Le Citizen** recycles all waste, stocks locally-sourced filtered tap water, serves organic breakfasts, and its rooms tout bedding made from organic fair-trade cotton and water-conserving toilets and showers. See p. 318.

PRICE CATEGORIES

Very Expensive	Moderate
500€ and up	150€–300€
Expensive	Inexpensive
300€–500€	Under 150€

PREVIOUS PAGE: **The entrance to Le Royal Monceau-Raffles Paris.**

- **Most Trendy:** The one-of-a-kind **Hotel Amour** is run by a couple of the city's nightlife barons. Each of the 24 rooms boasts a unique, edgy, contemporary design, and you'll run into many of the city's trendsetters at the raucous downstairs bar and restaurant. See p. 311.

- **Best Boutique Hotel:** Decorated by India Mahdavi, the **Hôtel Thoumieux's** delightful 15 rooms boast high style and top amenities, like marble bathrooms, iPads, the iHome system, an espresso machine, and a complimentary minibar. The hotel also hosts a Michelin–starred restaurant by chef Jean-François Piège and a buzzing downstairs brasserie. See p. 332.

- **Most Charming:** In the heart of the Latin Quarter, and set within a luxuriant and peaceful little garden, the delightful **Hôtel des Grandes Ecoles** is a budget option boasting a unique, provincial charm. See p. 323.

THE RIGHT BANK
Les Halles, Louvre & Palais Royal (1er & 2e)

Located on the right bank, this area is the *très chic* center of Paris. This part of Paris—by the Seine river and clustered around the Louvre—boasts exquisite monuments, boulevards, gardens, and shopping.

Best For: Travelers who like to be in the thick of the action. The trendy area is also great for epic shopping sessions.
Drawbacks: Tourists galore!

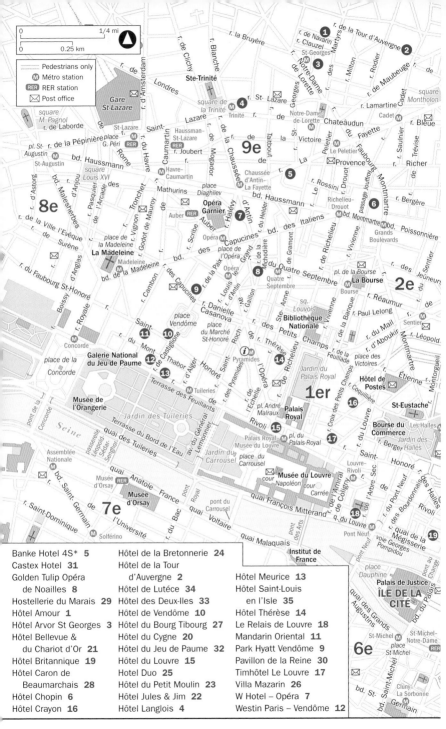

Hotels near Les Halles, the Louvre, Palais Royal, Marais, Ile St-Louis, Ile de la Cité, Opéra & Grands Boulevards (1er–4e & 9e)

FRANCE'S PALACE HOTELS

After adding a fifth star to their official hotel rating system back in 2009, putting France more in line with international standards, in 2011 the French tourism authorities launched a new hotel label called "Distinction Palace." Criteria for this new label include the hotel's location, historical significance, room comfort, personalized service, multilingual staff, and health and spa facilities. France counts a total of 127 five-star hotels, but at launch of the new category, only 8 hotels earned the distinction immediately, and this restricted selection is as notable for who it included as for who it left out. The four hotels in Paris to go straight to the top are the Bristol (p. 307), the Meurice (below), Park Hyatt Paris-Vendôme (p. 297), and the Plaza Athenée (p. 307). Certainly in response to the snub, the majestic George V is undertaking a major renovation program until the end of 2013 (though it remains open to the public throughout), and the place Vendôme's legendary Ritz Hotel closed for at least 2 years of renovations in mid-2012.

VERY EXPENSIVE

Hôtel de Vendôme ★★   This luxury boutique hotel sits on one of Paris's most prestigious addresses, the place Vendôme, surrounded by the city's finest jewelers. The soundproof rooms are opulent and designed in classic Second Empire style, with prestige beds and well-upholstered, hand-carved furnishings. Suites have generous space and such extras as blackout draperies and quadruple-glazed windows. The security is fantastic, with TV intercoms, and the service is warm and professional. This hotel is a short walk from the Louvre and Tuileries gardens.

1 place Vendôme, 75001 Paris. www.hoteldevendome.com. ☎ **01-55-04-55-00.** Fax 01-49-27-97-89. 29 units. 535€–865€ double; 835€–1,525€ suite. AE, DC, MC, V. Parking 27€. Métro: Concorde or Opéra. **Amenities:** Restaurant; piano bar; babysitting; concierge; room service. *In room:* A/C, TV, hair dryer, minibar, MP3 docking station, Wi-Fi (free).

Hôtel Meurice ★★★   This landmark hotel, which lies between the place de la Concorde and the Grand Louvre, facing the Tuileries Gardens, is media-hip and style-conscious. Since the 1800s, it has welcomed the royal, the rich, and even the radical. The mad genius Salvador Dalí made the Meurice his headquarters, and in 2008 that other mad genius, Philippe Starck, overhauled the hotel's public areas, bringing an exquisite contemporary touch of the surreal to the lobby and downstairs bar and restaurant. Each room is individually decorated with period pieces, fine carpets, Italian and French fabrics, marble bathrooms, and modern features. Our favorites and the least expensive are the sixth-floor rooms. Some have painted ceilings of puffy clouds and blue skies, along with canopy beds. Suites are among the most lavish in France.

228 rue de Rivoli, 75001 Paris. www.meuricehotel.com. ☎ **01-44-58-10-10.** Fax 01-44-58-10-15. 160 units. 790€–1,070€ double; 1,300€–1,900€ junior suite; from 2,100€ suite. AE, DC, MC, V. Parking 45€. Métro: Tuileries or Concorde. **Amenities:** 2 restaurants; bar; babysitting; concierge; health club and spa; room service. *In room:* A/C, TV, TV/DVD player, fax, hair dryer, minibar, Wi-Fi (24€ per day).

Mandarin Oriental ★★   Located in a chic Art Deco building on fashionable rue Saint-Honoré, the Mandarin Oriental opened with much acclaim in mid-2011.

This outpost of the modern luxury Asian hotel chain integrates Asian-inspired elements into its design, such as bright Oriental silks and lacquer details. The rooms offer all the opulence and comfort you'd expect from a hotel of this caliber, with soundproofed windows, LCD TVs, high-quality linens, and Nespresso coffee machines. Two of the hotel's four restaurants are directed by Michelin–starred chef Thierry Marx. The spa and health center are exquisite, featuring a 15 meter (50 ft.) pool, a technologically advanced gym, treatment suites with steam showers, and an Oriental herbal steam room; spa treatments integrate traditional Chinese holistic methods.

251 rue Saint-Honoré, 75001 Paris. www.mandarinoriental.com/paris. ✆ **01-70-98-78-88.** Fax 01-70-98-73-05. 138 units. 795€–985€ double; 1,750€–20,000€ suite. AE, DC, MC, V. Parking 35€. Métro: Concorde. **Amenities:** 4 restaurants; bar; babysitting; concierge; health club; pool (indoor); room service; spa. *In room:* A/C, TV, DVD, hair dryer, minibar, MP3 docking station, Wi-Fi (15€ per day or free in the suites).

Park Hyatt Vendôme ★★★ American interior designer Ed Tuttle took five separate Haussmann-era buildings and wove them into a seamless entity to create this citadel of 21st-century luxury living. High ceilings, colonnades, and interior courtyards speak of the buildings' former lives, but other than the facades, all is completely modern and luxurious inside. The third Hyatt in Paris, this palace enjoys the greatest and most prestigious location in "Ritz Hotel country." Graced with modern art, it is filled with elegant fabrics, huge mirrors, walk-in closets, mahogany doors, and Jim Thompson silk. Bedrooms and bathrooms are spacious and state-of-the-art, with elegant furnishings and glamorous bathrooms with "rain showers," plus separate tubs.

5 rue de la Paix, 75002 Paris. www.paris.vendome.hyatt.com. ✆ **800/492-8804** in the U.S. and Canada, or 01-58-71-12-34. Fax 01-58-71-12-35. 168 units. 800€–910€ double; from 1,010€ suite. AE, DC, DISC, MC, V. Métro: Tuileries or Opéra. Free parking. **Amenities:** 2 restaurants; bar; babysitting; concierge; health club and spa; room service. *In room:* A/C, TV, DVD, CD player, hair dryer, minibar, Wi-Fi (19€ per day).

EXPENSIVE

Hôtel du Louvre ★ When Napoleon III inaugurated this hotel in 1855, it was described as "a palace of the people, rising adjacent to the palace of kings." In 1897, Camille Pissarro moved into a room with a view that inspired many of his landscapes; its decor features marble, bronze, and gilt. The guest rooms are filled with souvenirs of the Belle Époque, along with elegant fabrics, carpeting, double-glazed windows, comfortable beds, and wood furniture. Suites provide greater dimensions and better exposures, as well as such upgrades as antiques, trouser presses, and robes.

Place André-Malraux, 75001 Paris. www.hoteldulouvre.com. ✆ **800/888-4747** in the U.S. and Canada, or 01-44-58-38-38. Fax 01-44-58-38-01. 177 units. 200€–700€ double; 300€–750€ junior suite. AE, DC, MC, V. Parking 20€. Métro: Palais-Royal-Louvre or Louvre-Rivoli. **Amenities:** Restaurant; bar; babysitting; concierge; exercise room. *In room:* A/C, TV, minibar, Wi-Fi (free).

Westin Paris - Vendôme ★ ☺ At this hotel it's location, location, location: you're 30 seconds from the Tuileries Gardens, 3 minutes from the place Vendôme, 5 minutes from the place de la Concorde, and 7 minutes from the Louvre. The guest rooms are elegantly decorated, comfortable, and well-maintained, and they feature Westin's Signature "Heavenly Beds." Two connecting rooms can be blocked off for families, and family rates are available. Many of the units overlook an inner courtyard, but others have panoramic views over the Eiffel Tower, the Louvre, the Tuileries gardens, and the place de la Concorde.

3 rue de Castiglione, Paris 75001. www.thewestinparis.fr. ℂ **800/454-6835** in the U.S., or 01-44-77-11-11. Fax 01-44-77-14-60. 428 units. 350€–430€ double; from 600€ suite. AE, DC, MC, V. Métro: Tuileries. **Amenities:** 2 restaurants; bar; babysitting; concierge; exercise room; room service, spa. *In room:* A/C, TV, DVD player, hair dryer, minibar, Wi-Fi (19€ per day).

MODERATE

Golden Tulip Opéra de Noailles If you're looking for a choice address in the style of Putman and Starck, this place is worth a look, in a great location. The refined Art Deco choice offers bold colors and cutting-edge style. The guest rooms come in various shapes and sizes, but all are comfortable and some have small terraces and patios. A favorite is no. 601, which has its own indoor Japanese garden.

9 rue de la Michodière, 75002 Paris. www.paris-hotel-noailles.com. ℂ **800/344-1212** in the U.S., or 01-47-42-92-90. Fax 01-49-24-92-71. 57 units. 200€–350€ double; 495€ suite. AE, DC, MC, V. Métro: 4 Septembre or Opéra. RER: Opéra. **Amenities:** Bar; babysitting; concierge; small health club; room service. *In room:* A/C, TV, hair dryer, Wi-Fi (free).

Hôtel Britannique ✦ Conservatively modern and plush, this renovated 19th-century hotel near Les Halles and Notre-Dame is not only British in name, but it seems to cultivate English graciousness. The guest rooms are small but immaculate and soundproof, with comfortable beds. A satellite receiver gets U.S. and U.K. television shows. The reading room is a cozy retreat. Its exceptional location in the center of Paris makes this a good-value choice.

20 av. Victoria, 75001 Paris. www.hotel-britannique.com. ℂ **01-42-33-74-59.** Fax 01-42-33-82-65. 39 units. 190€–230€ double; from 279€ suite. AE, DC, MC, V. Métro: Châtelet. **Amenities:** Bar; room service. *In room:* A/C, TV, hair dryer, minibar, Wi-Fi (free).

Hôtel Crayon The colorful quirky style of this new boutique hotel, which opened in 2011, might not appeal to all tastes, but its great central location within walking distance of the Louvre should. Each of the small but comfortable rooms is individually decorated with a jumble of vintage furniture, original artworks, and nice touches like your own perfume diffuser. The lobby is bright and airy and decorated in a chic contemporary style, and features a 24-hour honesty bar (there are no minibars in the rooms). It's worth noting that the hotel usually offers good discounts on their website.

25 rue du Bouloi, 75001 Paris. www.hotelcrayon.com. ℂ **01-42-36-54-19.** Fax 01-42-33-66-31. 27 units. 299€ double; 468€ suite. AE, MC, V. Métro: Les Halles. **Amenities:** Bar, breakfast room. *In room:* A/C, TV, hair dryer, safe, Wi-Fi (free).

Hôtel Thérèse ★★ Close to the Louvre, place Vendôme, and the Tuileries Gardens, this hotel combines French charm with English classicism. For example, the library and bar evoke a London club with wood-paneled walls and plush armchairs, but the lounge is adorned with Parisian art. Owner Sylvia de Lattre, who likes shades of pistachio and royal blue, trolled the flea markets for paintings and prints to personalize each bedroom. The rooms are unpretentious but filled with quality furnishings, from the soft, efficient lighting by Philippe Starck to the natural wool quilts. The hotel's public areas were redecorated in late 2011.

5–7 rue Thérèse, Paris 75001. www.hoteltherese.com. ℭ **01-42-96-10-01.** Fax 01-42-96-15-22. 43 units. 165€–295€ double. AE, MC, V. Métro: Musée du Louvre. **Amenities:** Library/bar; room service; smoke-free rooms. *In room:* A/C, TV, hair dryer, Wi-Fi (free).

Le Relais du Louvre   Centrally located, Relais du Louvre overlooks the neo-classical colonnade at the eastern end of the Louvre. Between 1800 and 1941, its upper floors contained the printing presses that recorded the goings-on in Paris's House of Representatives. Its street level held the Café Momus, favored by Voltaire, Hugo, and intellectuals of the day, and where Puccini set one of the pivotal scenes of *La Bohème.* Bedrooms are outfitted in monochromatic schemes of blue, yellow, pink, or soft reds, usually with copies of Directoire-style (French 1830s) furniture. Most rooms are a bit small, but some contain roomy sitting areas.

19 rue des Prêtres-St-Germain-l'Auxerrois, 75001 Paris. www.relaisdulouvre.com. ℭ **01-40-41-96-42.** Fax 01-40-41-96-44. 21 units. 175€–260€ double; 255€–350€ suite. AE, DC, MC, V. Parking 26€. Métro: Louvre or Pont Neuf. **Amenities:** Babysitting; room service. *In room:* A/C, TV, hair dryer, minibar, Wi-Fi (free).

INEXPENSIVE

Hôtel du Cygne   This centrally located hotel is within walking distance of the charming gourmand–friendly rue Montorgueil, the place des Victoires, the Marais, and the Louvre. In a restored 17th-century building, the hotel combines the old with touches of the new; much of the eclectic decor has been handpicked by the hotel's friendly owner, Isabelle. The staff is helpful, but there is no elevator, so be prepared to carry your luggage up the narrow, winding stairs. Avoid the rooms overlooking the street, as they can be noisy. Room 35 is the largest.

3–5 rue du Cygne, 75001 Paris. www.cygne-hotel-paris.com. ℭ **01-42-60-14-16.** Fax 01-42-21-37-02. 18 units. 122€–132€ double; 147€ suite. MC, V. Métro: Etienne Marcel. **Amenities:** Breakfast room. *In room:* TV, hair dryer, Wi-Fi (free).

Timhôtel Le Louvre ☺   This hotel and its sibling in the 2nd arrondissement, the Timhôtel Palais-Royal, are part of a new breed of two-star, family-friendly hotels cropping up in France. Though the rooms at the Palais-Royal branch are a bit larger than the ones here, this branch is so close to the Louvre that it's almost irresistible. In both, the ambience is modern, with monochromatic rooms and wall-to-wall carpeting.

4 rue Croix des Petits-Champs, 75001 Paris. www.timhotel.fr. ℭ **01-42-60-34-86.** Fax 01-42-60-10-39. 56 units. 99€–170€ double. AE, DC, MC, V. Métro: Palais-Royal. The 46-room **Timhôtel Palais-Royal** is at 3 rue de la Banque, 75002 Paris (ℭ **01-42-61-53-90;** fax 01-42-60-05-39; Métro: Bourse). **Amenities** (at both branches): Restaurant (breakfast only). *In room:* A/C (in some), TV, Wi-Fi (free).

Le Marais, Ile St-Louis & Ile de la Cité (3e & 4e)

This busy neighborhood includes the city's gay and Jewish quarters. Most of the important contemporary galleries are here too. You'll find a concentration of great stores from independent local labels in the northern Marais, around the rue de Bretagne. But it's the architecture that really sets this area apart, as it conserves buildings dating back to the Renaissance.

Best For: Trendsetters with no time to lose.

Drawbacks: Expats from all over the world have made the lower Marais their own, so if you want to feel like you've actually left home, try a different neighborhood.

EXPENSIVE

Hôtel du Jeu de Paume ★ This small-scale hotel encompasses a pair of 17th-century town houses accessible through a timbered passageway from the street outside. The hotel is located on the incredibly quaint and charming Ile St-Louis in the Seine, and is just a 5-minute walk from Notre-Dame. Originally, the hotel was a clubhouse used by members of the court of Louis XIII, who amused themselves with *les jeux de paume* (an early form of tennis) nearby. Public areas are outfitted in a simple version of Art Deco. Renovated in 2010, guest rooms have a sleek contemporary style, with elegant materials such as oak floors and fine craftsmanship. Some have wooden-beamed ceilings. The rooms are a bit larger than those of some nearby competitors. The most luxurious units are the five duplexes and two junior suites, each individually decorated and opening onto an indoor courtyard.

54 rue St-Louis-en-l'Ile, 75004 Paris. www.jeudepaumehotel.com. © **01-43-26-14-18.** Fax 01-40-46-02-76. 30 units. 285€–360€ double; 360€–560€ suite. AE, DC, MC, V. Métro: Pont Marie. **Amenities:** Bar; babysitting; concierge; exercise room; room service. *In room:* A/C, TV, hair dryer, minibar, Wi-Fi (free).

Hôtel Duo ★ 🏨 Fashionistas flock to this restored hotel in the Marais, which is one of the cutting-edge places to stay in Paris. The location is convenient to the Centre Pompidou, Notre-Dame, and the Louvre. The building has been in the family of Veronique Turmel since 1918. In 2002, she decided to completely convert the interior while retaining the facade. She hired Jean-Philippe Nuel, who kept many of the original architectural features, including exposed beams, old stones, and hardwood floors. He created a modern and stylish look graced with Wenge-wood furnishings, white walls, and bronzed sconces—old-world charm in a tasteful and refined setting. The midsize bedrooms are completely up-to-date, with beautiful and comfortable furnishings. The so-called breakfast "cave" is a charming room with slipcovered chairs and sea-grass matting.

11 rue du Temple, 75004 Paris. www.duo-paris.com. © **01-42-72-72-22.** Fax 01-42-72-03-53. 58 units. 200€–380€ double; 400€–550€ suite. AE, DC, MC, V. Métro: Hôtel de Ville. **Amenities:** Exercise room; room service. *In room:* A/C, TV, hair dryer, Wi-Fi (free).

Hôtel du Petit Moulin In the heart of the Northern Marais, this hotel, an enclave of bohemian chic, used to be a *boulangerie* where Victor Hugo came every morning to buy freshly baked baguettes. No more. Designer Christian Lacroix has gone behind the unpretentious facade and turned it into an idiosyncratic hotel with bold, daring designs in the bedrooms, which range in price from the Comfort Rooms to the Superior or Executive Rooms. We think room 204 is the most elegant. A well-heeled array of international guests meets in the quiet, downstairs bar or can be seen making their way through the lounge decorated with period tapestries and Flemish frescoes.

29–31 rue du Poitou, Paris 75003. www.hoteldupetitmoulin.com. © **01-42-74-10-10.** 17 units. 190€–350€ double. AE, MC, V. Métro: Bastille or Filles du Calvaire. **Amenities:** Bar. *In room:* TV, minibar, Wi-Fi (free).

Pavillon de la Reine ★★ 🎁   This is a hidden gem that opens onto the most romantic square in Paris: the place des Vosges. You enter through an arcade that opens onto a small formal garden. In days of yore the 1612 mansion was a gathering place for the likes of Racine, La Fontaine, Molière, and the Madame de Sévigné. Today, the Louis XIII decor evokes the heyday of the square itself, and iron-banded Spanish antiques create a rustic aura. Each guest room is individually furnished in a historic or modern style—take your pick. Some units are duplexes with sleeping lofts above cozy salons.

28 place des Vosges, 75003 Paris. www.pavillon-de-la-reine.com. 𝄞 **01-40-29-19-19.** Fax 01-40-29-19-20. 56 units. 330€–450€ double; 600€–800€ suite. AE, MC, V. Métro: Bastille. **Amenities:** Bar; concierge; room service. *In room:* A/C, TV, minibar, Wi-Fi (free).

MODERATE

Hôtel Caron de Beaumarchais ★ 🍴   Built in the 18th century, this good-value choice features floors of artfully worn gray stone, antique reproductions, and elaborate fabrics based on antique patterns. Hotelier Alain Bigeard intends his primrose-colored guest rooms to evoke the taste of the French gentry in the 18th century, when the Marais was the scene of high-society dances and even duels. Most rooms retain their original ceiling beams. The smallest units overlook the courtyard, and the top-floor rooms are tiny, but have panoramic balcony views across the Right Bank.

12 rue Vieille-du-Temple, 75004 Paris. www.carondebeaumarchais.com. 𝄞 **01-42-72-34-12.** Fax 01-42-72-34-63. 19 units. 145€–195€ double. AE, MC, V. Métro: St-Paul or Hôtel de Ville. **Amenities:** Breakfast room; babysitting. *In room:* A/C, TV, hair dryer, minibar, Wi-Fi (free).

Hôtel de Lutèce   This 19th-century hotel feels like a country house in Brittany. The lounge, with its old fireplace, is furnished with antiques and contemporary paintings. Each of the guest rooms boasts antiques. The tastefully-furnished suites, though larger than the doubles, are often similar to doubles with extended sitting areas. Located on pretty Ile St-Louis, the hotel is comparable in style and amenities to the Deux-Iles (see below), under the same ownership.

65 rue St-Louis-en-l'Ile, 75004 Paris. www.paris-hotel-lutece.com. 𝄞 **01-43-26-23-52.** Fax 01-43-29-60-25. 23 units. 205€ double; 245€ triple. AE, MC, V. Métro: Pont Marie or Cité. **Amenities:** Babysitting; concierge. *In room:* A/C, TV, hair dryer, minibar, Wi-Fi (free).

Hôtel des Deux-Iles ★   This is an unpretentious but charming choice in a great location. In a restored 18th-century town house, the hotel has elaborate decor, with bamboo and reed furniture and French provincial touches. The guest rooms are on the small side, but the beds are very comfortable and the bathrooms well maintained. A garden off the lobby leads to a basement breakfast room that has a fireplace.

59 rue St-Louis-en-l'Ile, 75004 Paris. www.deuxiles-paris-hotel.com. 𝄞 **01-43-26-13-35.** Fax 01-43-29-60-25. 17 units. 205€ double. AE, MC, V. Métro: Pont Marie. **Amenities:** Room service. *In room:* A/C, TV, hair dryer, Wi-Fi (free).

Hôtel du Bourg Tibourg ★   What you get here is a sophisticated and super-charged color palette, a sense of high-profile design, and a deliberately cluttered venue that looks like an Edwardian town house decorated by an individual on psychedelic drugs. It is set behind an uncomplicated, cream-colored facade in the Marais and marked only with a discreet brass plaque and a pair of carriage lamps. Bedrooms are genuinely tiny, but rich with romantic, neo-Gothic, and in some cases neo-Venetian swirls and curlicues. Decorated by Jacques Garcia, each room is quirky, idiosyncratic, richly upholstered, and supercharged with tassels, faux leopard skin, contrasting stripes, fringes, and lavish window treatments. Rooms facing the front get more sunlight; rooms facing the courtyard tend to be quieter.

19 rue du Bourg-Tibourg, 75004 Paris. www.bourgtibourg.com. ✆ **01-42-78-47-39.** Fax 01-40-29-07-00. 30 units. 250€–270€ double; 370€ suite. AE, DC, MC, V. Métro: Hôtel de Ville. **Amenities:** Room service. *In room:* A/C, TV, hair dryer, minibar, Wi-Fi (free).

Hôtel Jules & Jim ★★   Proudly gay friendly, this new boutique hotel opened in late 2011. Spread across three buildings, it's a little urban oasis arranged around two beautiful, paved courtyards. The rooms either look out at the rooftops of Paris or into the lush vertical garden in the courtyard. Guest rooms are sleek and designed with durable materials, like glass, wood, stone, and concrete; they are soundproofed and equipped with sophisticated amenities, like luxury linens and an iPod docking station. The bar is a great place to wind down your day, with a working outdoor fireplace (in winter) and live music (in summer).

11 rue des Gravilliers, 75003 Paris. www.hoteljulesetjim.com. ✆ **01-44-54-13-13.** Fax 01-42-78-10-01. 23 units. 180€–310€ double; 390€–550€ suite. AE, MC, V. Métro: Arts-et-Métiers. **Amenities:** Bar; concierge; room service. *In room:* AC, TV, hair dryer, iPod Dock, Wi-Fi (free).

Hôtel Saint-Louis en l'Isle ★ 🥂   Proprietors Guy and Andrée Record maintain a charming family atmosphere at this antiques-filled hotel in a 17th-century town house. The hotel represents an incredible value, considering its prime location on Ile St-Louis. Expect cozy, slightly cramped rooms, each with a small bathroom. With mansard roofs and old-fashioned moldings, the top-floor units sport tiny balconies that afford sweeping views. The breakfast room is in the cellar, which has 17th-century stone vaulting.

75 rue St-Louis-en-l'Ile, 75004 Paris. www.saintlouisenlisle.com. ✆ **01-46-34-04-80.** Fax 01-46-34-02-13. 19 units. 169€–239€ double. MC, V. Métro: Pont Marie or St-Michel-Notre-Dame. **Amenities:** Babysitting; concierge; smoke-free rooms. *In room:* A/C, TV, hair dryer, Wi-Fi (free).

Villa Mazarin ★ 🎁   This is a special under-the-radar hotel in a great lower Marais location, across from the Hôtel de Ville. The large and bright rooms are decorated in an elegant Napoleon III style and offer a comfort that you normally only enjoy in a superior category and price range. The beds are large and comfortable with quality linens, and there are Clarins toiletries in the bathrooms. The duplex suites on the fifth floor have balconies. Open the windows and listen to the buzz of the city waft in over the rooftops; just outside is great shopping and dining.

6 rue des Archives, 75004 Paris. www.villamazarin.com. ✆ **01-53-01-90-90.** 29 units. 220€–300€ double. AE, MC, V. Métro: Hôtel de Ville. **Amenities:** Bar; restaurant; room service. *In room:* A/C, TV, minibar, Wi-Fi (free).

INEXPENSIVE

Castex Hotel 🥂   Long known to thrifty travelers, the Castex lies on the fringe of both the Bastille sector and the Marais. Bedrooms are small and somewhat simple, decorated in a 17th-century style with Louis XIII furnishings and wrought iron features. There's a complimentary bottle of wine in every room. Several of the units open onto a courtyard patio that bursts into full bloom in the spring.

5 rue Castex, 75004 Paris. www.castexhotelparis.com. ✆ **01-42-72-31-52.** 30 units. 155€ double; 220€ triple. AE, MC, V. Métro: Bastille. **Amenities:** Breakfast room. *In room:* A/C, TV, hair dryer, Wi-Fi (free).

Hostellerie du Marais Half a block from the place des Vosges, this hotel occupies a corner building whose 17th-century vestiges have been preserved—this includes the remnants of a well in the cellar. Although the building facade evokes an earlier time, its interior feels quite modern. Though small, the guest rooms are comfortable, decorated in neutral gray and beige tones. Rooms on the upper floors and facing the street have great views over the gray roofs of Paris—but note that they can be noisy.

30 rue de Turenne, Paris 75003. www.hostelleriedumarais.com. ✆ **01-42-72-73-47.** Fax 01-42-72-54-10. 24 units. 112€–230€ double. AE, MC, V. Métro: Chemin Vert or St-Paul. **Amenities:** Bar. *In room:* A/C, TV, hair dryer, minibar, Wi-Fi (free).

Hôtel Bellevue & du Chariot d'Or Originally built in 1860 as part of the majestic redevelopment of central Paris by Baron Haussmann, this hotel has a grand facade and inexpensive, relatively comfortable and cozy, simple bedrooms. The hotel has become more desirable because of its location in the once-neglected Arts et Métiers district north of the Pompidou Center. The second part of its name—"Chariot d'Or" (Golden Carriage)—derives from the medieval custom of placing brides-to-be (along with their dowries) in a flower-draped ceremonial carriage. During the occupation of Paris during World War II, the site was commandeered as a garrison for rank-and-file Nazi troops.

39 rue de Turbigo, 75003 Paris. www.hotelbellevue75.com. ✆ **01-48-87-45-60.** Fax 01-48-87-95-04. 59 units. 72€–75€ double; 87€ triple; 98€ quad. AE, DC, MC, V. Métro: Châtelet–Les Halles or Réaumur-Sebastopol. **Amenities:** Bar; babysitting. *In room:* TV, Wi-Fi (free).

Hôtel de la Bretonnerie This popular and good-value hotel has plenty of character. Decorated with heavy wooden antiques and old-fashioned wallpapers and curtains, the charming 17th-century hotel also boasts exposed beams, high ceilings, and four-poster beds. Large windows look onto either the surrounding streets or a quiet inner courtyard. The hotel has an excellent location, near the atmospheric Jewish quarter and the busy Marais shopping district. It's not fancy, but it is a comfortable and clean hotel with friendly staff.

22 rue Sainte Croix de la Bretonnerie, 75004 Paris. www.hotelbretonnerie.com. ✆ **01-48-87-77-63.** Fax 01-42-77-26-78. 29 units. 145€–175€ double; 200€ suite. MC, V. Métro: Hôtel de Ville. **Amenities:** Breakfast room. *In room:* TV, hair dryer, minibar, Wi-Fi (free).

Champs-Élysées & Western Paris (8e, 16e & 17e)

This is where most of the city's money and power is concentrated. The "Golden Triangle" (avenue Montaigne, George V, and the Champs-Élysées) is bling-bling heaven, with all the major fashion labels jostling for position. It's also a business neighborhood, so get ready to navigate the suits.

Best For: Travelers who have deep pockets, or those who want to pretend they do.
Drawbacks: Not really a residential area, this area lacks some of the authentic local charm of other neighborhoods.

Hotels near the Champs-Élysées & Western Paris (8e, 16e & 17e)

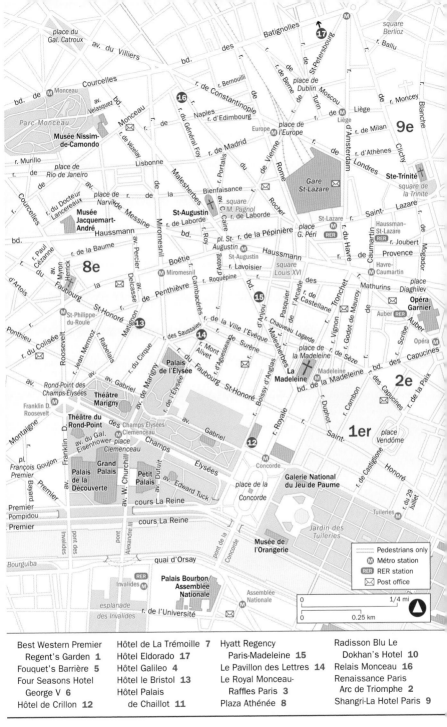

Best Western Premier
  Regent's Garden **1**
Fouquet's Barrière **5**
Four Seasons Hotel
  George V **6**
Hôtel de Crillon **12**

Hôtel de La Trémoille **7**
Hôtel Eldorado **17**
Hôtel Galileo **4**
Hôtel le Bristol **13**
Hôtel Palais
  de Chaillot **11**

Hyatt Regency
  Paris-Madeleine **15**
Le Pavillon des Lettres **14**
Le Royal Monceau-
  Raffles Paris **3**
Plaza Athénée **8**

Radisson Blu Le
  Dokhan's Hotel **10**
Relais Monceau **16**
Renaissance Paris
  Arc de Triomphe **2**
Shangri-La Hotel Paris **9**

VERY EXPENSIVE

Fouquet's Barrière ★★★   This deluxe boutique hotel on the corner of the Champs-Élysées may lack the historic cachet of the neighboring George V or Plaza Athénée, but it's a more contemporary brand of glitz and glamour. Standing alongside its namesake, the legendary restaurant Fouquet's, it offers some of the most luxurious and spacious bedrooms in Paris, its decor dominated by ceiling-high padded headboards in shiny gold. The hotel contains such novel features as waterproof floating TV remotes in the bathtub, and a bedside button that, when pressed, will summon your butler. There's one butler to every eight guests, and the service is the best in Paris. That butler even arrives to unpack your luggage and serve you champagne.

46 av. George V, 75008 Paris. www.fouquets-barriere.com. ℡ **01-40-69-60-00.** Fax 01-40-69-60-05. 107 units. 750€–1,300€ double; 1,100€–1,700€ junior suite; 1,700€–3,600€ suite. AE, MC, V. Métro: George V. Parking 45€. **Amenities:** 2 restaurants; 2 bars; concierge; health club and spa; pool (indoor); room service. *In room:* A/C, TV, TV/DVD, hair dryer, minibar, Wi-Fi (free).

Four Seasons Hotel George V ★★★ ☺   In its latest reincarnation, with all its glitz and glamour, this hotel is a favorite with the international jet-set. The George V opened in 1928 in honor of George V of England, grandfather of Queen Elizabeth. During the liberation of Paris, it housed Dwight D. Eisenhower. The guest rooms are about as close as you'll come to residency in a well-upholstered private home where teams of decorators have lavished vast amounts of attention and money. The beds rival those at the Plaza Athénée and the Bristol in comfort. The largest units are magnificent; the smallest are, in the words of a spokesperson, *"très agréable."* Security is tight—a fact appreciated by sometimes-notorious guests. The staff pampers children with bathrobes, bedtime milk and cookies, and even special menus. *Note:* The hotel is undergoing a makeover throughout 2013, but it remains open to the public.

31 av. George V, 75008 Paris. www.fourseasons.com. ℡ **800/332-3442** in the U.S. and Canada, or 01-49-52-70-00. Fax 01-49-52-70-10. 245 units. 750€–1,095€ double; from 1,795€ suite. Parking 40€. AE, DC, MC, V. Métro: George V. **Amenities:** 2 restaurants; 2 bars; babysitting; concierge; health club and spa; room service. *In room:* A/C, TV, TV/DVD, CD player, hair dryer, minibar, Wi-Fi (15€).

Hôtel de Crillon ★★   The Crillon, one of Europe's grand hotels, sits across from the U.S. Embassy on the place de la Concorde. Although some international CEOs and diplomats treat it as a shrine, those seeking something more up-to-date might prefer the adjacent Bristol or the Meurice. The 200-plus-year-old building, once the palace of the Comte de Crillon, is now in the hands of Saudi royalty. The salons boast 17th- and 18th-century tapestries, gilt-and-brocade furniture, chandeliers, fine sculpture, and Louis XVI chests and chairs. The guest rooms are luxurious. Think Madame Pompadour meets Louis XV. Some are spectacular, such as the Leonard Bernstein Suite, which has one of the maestro's pianos. The third floor suites all boast views over the wonderful place de la Concorde, and the hotel bar was sculpted by French New Realist sculptor César.

10 place de la Concorde, 75008 Paris. www.crillon.com. ℡ **01-44-71-15-00.** Fax 01-44-71-15-02. 147 units. From 950€ double; from 1,400€ junior suite; from 1,800€ suite. AE, MC, V. Free parking. **Amenities:** 2 restaurants; bar; babysitting; concierge; state-of-the-art health club; room service; Wi-Fi (free). *In room:* A/C, TV, TV/DVD, CD player, hair dryer, minibar.

Hôtel de La Trémoille ★★ In the heart of Paris and a 2-minute walk from the Champs-Élysées, this is a preferred Right Bank address for fashionistas, as it lies in the heart of the haute couture district. Built in the 19th century, the hotel preserves the building's original elegance and charm, while still incorporating modern elements. Originally a private residence, the hotel is outfitted in a Louis XV style, all in woodwork and tapestries. Rooms are cozy and comfortable, each decorated in harmonies of tawny, ocher, gray, and white, with much use of silks, synthetic furs, and mohair.

14 rue de la Trémoille, 75008 Paris. www.hotel-tremoille.com. ℰ **01-56-52-14-00.** Fax 01-40-70-01-08. 93 units. 555€–725€ double; 815€–1,220€ suite. AE, DC, MC, V. Métro: Alma-Marceau. **Amenities:** Restaurant; bar; concierge; exercise room; room service. *In room:* A/C, TV, hair dryer, iPod dock, minibar, Wi-Fi (free).

Hôtel le Bristol ★★★ This palace is near the Palais d'Élysée (home of the French president), on the shopping street parallel to the Champs-Élysées. The 18th-century Parisian facade has a glass-and-wrought-iron entryway, where uniformed English-speaking attendants greet you. Hippolyte Jammet founded the Bristol in 1924, installing many antiques and Louis XV and XVI furnishings. The guest rooms are opulent, with antiques or well-made reproductions, inlaid wood, bronze, crystal, Oriental carpets, and original oil paintings. Their restaurant, Epicure, serves contemporary French cuisine by Eric Frechon and has earned 3 Michelin stars. In 2011 the hotel launched their magnificent new spa, by La Prairie.

112 rue du Faubourg St-Honoré, 75008 Paris. www.lebristolparis.com. ℰ **01-53-43-43-00.** Fax 01-53-43-43-01. 187 units. 800€–1,020€ double; 1,150€–1,660€ junior suite; from 2,000€ suite. AE, DC, MC, V. Free parking. Métro: Miromesnil or Champs-Élysées. **Amenities:** 2 restaurants; bar; babysitting; children's programs; concierge; health club and spa; pool (indoor); room service. *In room:* A/C, TV, TV/DVD, CD player, hair dryer, minibar, Wi-Fi (21€ per day).

Le Royal Monceau – Raffles Paris ★★★ 🛎 This five-star Raffles hotel opened in late 2010 and immediately wowed Paris with its luxurious chic interiors designed by Philippe Starck. The decor is contemporary, but is still in tune with the Art Deco heritage of the building. The spacious rooms offer all the comfort and amenities that you would expect from a hotel of this caliber, but maintain a relaxed vibe. There's even an electric guitar in each room, if you feel like expressing your inner rock star. The hotel has a unique commitment to contemporary art: it regularly hosts art exhibitions, has a fully-stocked art bookstore, and it publishes a sophisticated website (www.artforbreakfast.com), which gives an insider's perspective on the Paris art scene. The hotel offers cutting-edge fashion in its satellite L'Éclaireur store. The icing on the cake? Star *pâtissier* Pierre Hermé is responsible for the desserts.

37 av. Hoche, 75008 Paris. www.leroyalmonceau.com. ℰ **01-42-99-88-00.** Fax 01-42-99-89-00. 160 units. 780€–930€ double; from 1,200€–10,000€ suite. AE, DC, MC, V. Métro: Ternes. **Amenities:** 2 restaurants; bar; children's programs; cigar lounge; concierge; health club; movie theater; pool (indoor); room service; spa. *In room:* A/C, TV/DVD, hair dryer, iPod dock, minibar, Wi-Fi (free).

Plaza Athénée ★★★ The Plaza Athénée, an 1889 Art Nouveau marvel, is a landmark of discretion and style and one of the city's most emblematic hotels. About half the celebrities visiting Paris have been pampered here; in the old days, Mata Hari used to frequent the place. The **Salon Gobelins** (with tapestries against rich paneling) and the **Salon Marie Antoinette,** a richly paneled and grand room, are two public rooms that add to the ambience of this lavish hotel. There's also a calm, quiet interior courtyard draped with vines and dotted with geraniums. The quietest guest rooms overlook a courtyard with awnings and parasol-shaded tables. Some rooms overlooking avenue Montaigne have views of the Eiffel Tower. The hotel is also home to **Alain Ducasse au Plaza Athénée,** where Alain Ducasse presents a gourmet French menu. The spa is by Dior. During Paris Fashion Week, the bar becomes the event's nonofficial HQ.

25 av. Montaigne, 75008 Paris. www.plaza-athenee-paris.com. © **866/732-1106** in the U.S. and Canada, or 01-53-67-66-65. Fax 01-53-67-66-66. 191 units. 865€–965€ double; 1,160€–1,800€ junior suite; 1,900€–22,000€ suite. AE, MC, V. Parking 28€. Métro: Franklin-D.-Roosevelt or Alma-Marceau. **Amenities:** 5 restaurants; bar; babysitting; concierge; state-of-the-art health club; room service; smoke-free rooms; spa. In room: A/C, TV, TV/DVD, CD player, hair dryer, minibar, Wi-Fi (24€ per day).

Shangri-La Hotel, Paris ★ The luxury Hong Kong hotelier opened its first Paris address at the end of 2010 inside a beautifully restored national monument, the former home of Prince Roland Bonaparte (Napoleon Bonaparte's grandnephew), dating from 1896. This new palace hotel is located near some of the city's best museums, including the Musée d'Art Moderne and the Palais de Tokyo, and has exceptional views sweeping across the Seine river to the Eiffel Tower. Grand, traditional interiors in tones of beige with gilt highlights transport you to a purely Parisian heritage setting. The rooms are exceptionally large, even for this caliber of hotel—they average 47 sq. m (506 sq. ft.). The marble bathrooms feel extra luxurious, with heated floors, rainfall shower heads and separate tubs, flatscreen TVs, and Bvlgari toiletries. The hotel is planning to open a wellness area, with spa services and an indoor pool, by 2013.

10 avenue d'Iéna, 75016 Paris. www.shangri-la.com. © **01-53-67-19-98.** Fax 01-53-67-19-19. 81 units. From 760€ double; from 1,565€ suite. AE, DC, MC, V. Métro: Iéna. **Amenities:** 3 restaurants; bar; babysitting; concierge; exercise room; pool (indoor); room service; smoke-free rooms; Wi-Fi in public areas (free). In room: A/C, TV, hair dryer, minibar, Wi-Fi (free).

EXPENSIVE

Best Western Premier Regent's Garden ★★ Near the convention center (Palais des Congrès) and the Arc de Triomphe, the Regent's Garden boasts a proud heritage: Napoleon III built this château for his physician. The hotel prides itself on its sustainability; it was awarded a prestigious European Eco-Label for its efforts in preserving the environment by reducing the consumption of water, gas, electricity, and waste. The smart guest rooms feature tall soundproof windows, traditional French furniture, and modern textiles—the environmental approach extends to the guest rooms, as the duvets in each room are made from fair-trade cotton. Even breakfast is composed of organic ingredients. Guests have access to a neighboring fitness center and spa, Eclipse & Vous. A garden with ivy-covered walls and umbrella-shaded tables makes for a perfect place to meet other guests. The hotel is smoke-free throughout.

6 rue Pierre-Demours, 75017 Paris. www.hotel-regents-paris.com. © **800/528-1234** in the U.S., or 01-45-74-07-30. Fax 01-40-55-01-42. 40 units. 290€–440€ double; from 490€ suite. AE, DC, MC, V. Parking 20€. Métro: Ternes or Charles-de-Gaulle–Etoile. **Amenities:** Babysitting; spa. In room: A/C, TV, hair dryer, minibar, Wi-Fi (free).

Hyatt Regency Paris–Madeleine ★★ In the heart of the financial district, this is our top recommendation for those visiting Paris on business, as rooms are designed not only for rest, but also for work, with large writing desks, three phones, modem sockets, voice mail, individual fax machines, wireless Internet, you name it. As you enter, the hotel evokes a noble, romantic private home with a lavish use of quality materials such as sycamore wood. Some of the units boast exceptional views over the rooftops of Paris.

24 bd. Malesherbes, 75008 Paris. www.paris.madeleine.hyatt.com. ℂ **01-55-27-12-34.** Fax 01-55-27-12-35. 86 units. 400€–600€ double; from 885€ suite. AE, DC, MC, V. Métro: Madeleine. **Amenities:** 2 restaurants; bar; babysitting; concierge; health club and spa; room service. *In room:* A/C, TV, TV/DVD, CD player, fax, hair dryer, minibar, Wi-Fi (free).

Le Pavillon des Lettres ★ If you're a literature fan, this hotel—Paris's first literary-themed hotel—might just be the place for you. Located in the 8th arrondissement, this charming boutique hotel opened in 2010, and is owned by the same owners of the Pavillon de la Reine. It features 26 rooms—one for each letter of the alphabet. Each room is dedicated to the life and work of great writers, from Anderson to Proust to Zola, and you'll find excerpted texts from these writers printed on the bedroom walls. There's also an iPad in each room loaded with a rich digital library. The comfortable rooms are designed to encourage relaxation and are decorated in metallic tones. Lounge in the hotel's library over a well-thumbed classic, and when you're tired of reading, just step outside to reach the many nearby shops and restaurants in the thick of Right Bank.

12 rue des Saussaies, 75008 Paris. www.pavillondeslettres.com. ℂ **01-49-24-26-26.** Fax 01-49-24-26-27. 26 units. From 300€–340€ double; 460€ suite. AE, DC, MC, V. Métro: Madeleine. **Amenities:** Restaurant; bar; library; room service. *In room:* A/C, TV, iPad, iPod docking stations, minibar, Wi-Fi (free).

Renaissance Paris Arc de Triomphe ★★ On the site of the once-famous Theatre de l'Empire, this cutting-edge hotel with its intriguing modern interiors lies only steps from the Arc de Triomphe and the Champs-Élysées. The top-floor rooms and suites open onto large terraces with panoramic views over the heart of Paris. The upscale hotel rooms and suites are spacious, tastefully decorated, and outfitted with the latest in-room technology. Its all-glass exterior has made this a distinctive landmark, even though it opened only in 2009. This is definitely a trendy and hip hotel, so probably not the best for kids. The on-site Makassar Lounge & Restaurant blends French bistro flavors with authentic Indonesian dishes. The hotel is smoke-free.

39 av. de Wagram, 75017 Paris. www.marriott.com. ℂ **01-55-37-55-37.** Fax 01-55-37-55-38. 108 units. 289€–599€ double; from 429€ suite. Parking 35€. Métro: Charles-de-Gaulle–Etoile. **Amenities:** Restaurant; bar; concierge; exercise room; room service. *In room:* A/C, TV/DVD, hair dryer, minibar, Wi-Fi (19.95€ per day).

MODERATE

Hôtel Palais de Chaillot ✦ Located between the Champs-Élysées and Trocadéro, the town house was restored from top to bottom in 2010, and the result is a contemporary yet informal variation on Parisian chic. The guest rooms are soundproofed, come in various shapes and sizes, and are furnished in pastel shades. Rooms 61, 62, and 63 afford partial views of the Eiffel Tower.

9

WHERE TO STAY | The Right Bank

35 av. Raymond-Poincaré, 75016 Paris. www.hotelpalaisdechaillot.com. ✆ **01-53-70-09-09.** Fax 01-53-70-09-08. 31 units. 189€–200€ double; 20€ extra bed. AE, DC, MC, V. Métro: Victor Hugo or Trocadéro. **Amenities:** Room service. *In room:* A/C, TV, hair dryer, Wi-Fi (free).

Radisson Blu Le Dokhan's Hotel ★★   If not for the porters walking through its public areas carrying luggage, you might suspect that this well-accessorized hotel was a private home. It's in a stately 19th-century Haussmann-styled building vaguely inspired by Palladio, and it contains accessories such as antique paneling, Regency-era armchairs, and chandeliers. Each guest room has a different decorative style, with antiques or good reproductions, lots of personalized touches, and triple-glazed windows. Beds are often antique reproductions with maximum comfort. Suites have a larger living space and spacious bathrooms with such extras as makeup mirrors and luxe toiletries.

117 rue Lauriston, 75116 Paris. www.radissonblu.com/dokhanhotel-paristrocadero. ✆ **01-53-65-66-99.** Fax 01-53-65-66-88. 45 units. 250€–350€ double; from 470€ suite. AE, DC, MC, V. Parking 30€. Métro: Trocadéro. **Amenities:** Babysitting; champagne bar; concierge; room service. *In room:* A/C, TV, fax, hair dryer, minibar, Wi-Fi (free).

INEXPENSIVE

Hôtel Eldorado ✦   If you're looking for something to criticize, you might well find it here. But if you're an intrepid bargain hunter, and don't mind living in an offbeat neighborhood on the border of Montmartre, this is one of the best cheap hotels in an overpriced city. Of course, don't expect an elevator to take you to a room with a TV, phone, or air-conditioning. But the price is right. The manager, Anne Gratacos, continually decorates the hotel with flea market finds, including Buddha busts and Art Deco armoires. The most spacious and evocative units are in a separate pavilion separated from the main structure by a garden patio with a restaurant, Bistrot des Dames.

18 rue des Dames, 75017 Paris. www.eldoradohotel.fr. ✆ **01-45-22-35-21.** Fax 01-43-87-25-97. 33 units, 23 with private bathroom. 70€–80€ double with bathroom; 80€–90€ triple with bathroom. AE, MC, V. Parking 25€. Métro: Place de Clichy. **Amenities:** Restaurant. *In room:* No phone, Wi-Fi (free).

Hôtel Galileo ★ ∎∎   This is one of the 8th's most charming hotels. Proprietors Roland and Elisabeth Buffat have won friends from all over with their Hôtel des Deux-Iles and Hôtel de Lutèce on St-Louis-en-l'Ile (see earlier in this chapter). A short walk from the Champs-Élysées, this town house is the epitome of French elegance and charm. The medium-size rooms are a study in understated taste. Within this hotel, rooms with numbers ending in 3 (specifically 103, 203, 303, 403, and 503) are more spacious than the others. Rooms 501 and 502 have private glassed-in verandas that you can use even in winter.

54 rue Galilée, 75008 Paris. www.galileo-paris-hotel.com. ✆ **01-47-20-66-06.** Fax 01-47-20-67-17. 27 units. 105€–335€ double. AE, DC, MC, V. Métro: Charles-de-Gaulle–Etoile or George V. *In room:* A/C, TV, hair dryer, minibar, Wi-Fi (free).

Relais Monceau ★ ✦   Finding an elegant but affordable hotel in the over-priced 8th is always a challenge, but Relais Monceau is an inviting choice. This former 19th-century town house with two private courtyards has become a lovely government-rated three-star hotel, which pays tribute to its past while integrating modern amenities. It takes its name from the nearby Parc Monceau. The midsize bedrooms are furnished with elegance and taste and are spread over three floors. There are also several large public guest areas as well.

85 rue du Rocher, Paris 75008. www.relais-monceau.com. ☎ **01-45-22-75-11.** Fax: 01-45-22-30-88. 51 units. 110€–198€ double; 195€–264€ suite. AE, MC, V. Métro: Champs-Élysées. **Amenities:** Bar. *In room:* A/C, TV, hair dryer, minibar, Wi-Fi (free).

Opéra & Grands Boulevards (9e)

Two of Paris's major department stores are located just above Opéra, and they set the tone for this dynamic shopping district which extends west along the tree-lined boulevard Haussmann and east up to the "Grands Boulevards" Metro station.

Best For: Travelers looking for some retail therapy and proximity to monuments (Opéra).

Drawbacks: Can be high-voltage.

VERY EXPENSIVE

Banke Hotel 4S* In the tradition of Derby Hotels Collection, this luxurious boutique hotel is art oriented. Works of art adorn both the public rooms and the accommodations. The building dates from the Belle Époque–era and contains a majestic hall from that time, which is embellished with a great mosaic. Bedrooms are midsize to spacious and decorated with antique art and an avant-garde design. The on-site spa focuses on a self-styled "purification and regeneration of your internal ecology." Bathrooms, for the most part, are very spacious. The staff is also extremely friendly, a rarity in Paris. The terrace opens onto a panoramic view of Sacré-Coeur and the Opéra.

20 rue Lafayette, 75009 Paris. www.derbyhotels.com/Banke-Hotel-Paris. ☎ **01-55-33-22-22.** Fax 01-55-33-22-28. 94 units. 630€ double; 1,265€ suite. AE, DC, MC, V. Métro: Opéra. **Amenities:** 2 restaurants; bar; exercise room; room service; smoke-free rooms; spa w/steam room and sauna. *In room:* A/C, TV, hair dryer, minibar, Wi-Fi (free).

EXPENSIVE

W Hotel–Opéra ★ Opened in 2012, this is the first outpost in Paris of the trendy W Hotel chain, flaunting vivid design, cutting-edge technology, and modern amenities. A stone's throw from the Opéra Garnier, and the two major department stores Galeries Lafayette and Printemps, the hotel is located in a historic 19th-century building above one of the city's two Apple Stores. The neighborhood is a shopper's delight and the smoke-free hotel offers a flirty, fun, and fresh experience, focusing on fashion, music, and entertainment. Guest rooms have plush pillow-top beds with 350-thread count sheets, and Bliss bath products.

4 rue Meyerbeer, Paris 75009. www.wparisopera.com. ☎ **01-77-48-94-94.** Fax 01-42-60-38-95. 91 units. 340€–550€ double; 700€–2,300€ suite. AE, DC, MC, V. Métro: Opéra. **Amenities:** Restaurant; bar; fitness center; room service. *In room:* A/C, TV, mini-bar, iPod docking station, Wi-Fi (17€).

MODERATE

Hôtel Amour ★★ 🎁 This hotel oozes streetwise chic and attitude. One critic claimed that thanks to the hotel bar being frequented by young European fashionistas, each flaunting his or her respective allure and neurosis, "waiting in a queue for the toilets has never been so entertaining." Each bedroom is decorated by a celebrity friend of the owner (like Sophie Calle, Marc Newson), so the trendy decor varies widely, from minimalist white-on-white with touches of faux baroque to disco balls to graffiti written directly on the walls. The relaxed downstairs bar and restaurant are a great destination at any time for seeing and being seen. And the ivy-covered courtyard is perfect for sipping champagne on warm days or nights.

8 rue Navarin, 75009 Paris. www.hotelamourparis.fr. (© **01-48-78-31-80.** 20 units. 155€–215€ double; 285€ duplex. AE, MC, V. Métro: St-Georges. **Amenities:** Restaurant; bar; room service. *In room:* A/C, minibar, no phone, Wi-Fi (free).

Hôtel Arvor St Georges ★★ 🛍 This fresh, contemporary hotel is located in the charming "New Athens" neighborhood, off the tourist beat and nestled below Montmartre. In the 19th century, this neighborhood was frequented by Romantic artists such as Victor Hugo, George Sand, and Frédéric Chopin, but today the neighborhood is a gourmand's paradise, with the restaurant-lined rue des Martyrs nearby. The hotel is relaxed and comfortable, and you'll feel like a guest in a chic Parisian's private home as you flip through some of the art and photography titles over a cup of coffee in the airy downstairs lobby. The tasty breakfast (14€) is served here or outside in the flower-filled patio when the weather is nice. The rooms have a clean, designer style, and the six suites boast views over Paris to the Eiffel Tower. Service is friendly and professional.

8 rue Laferrière, 75009 Paris. www.arvor-hotel-paris.com. (© **01-48-78-60-92.** Fax 01-48-78-16-52. 30 units. 125€–190€ double. AE, DC, MC, V. Métro: St-Georges. **Amenities:** Bar; room service. *In room:* TV, hair dryer, Wi-Fi (free).

INEXPENSIVE

Hôtel Chopin 🗝 Enter this intimate, offbeat hotel through a passageway that includes a toy store, a bookstore, the exit from the Musée Grevin, and the architectural trappings of its original construction in 1846. Just off the Grands Boulevards, this old-fashioned hotel evokes the charm of yesteryear. In honor of its namesake, the Chopin has a piano in its reception area. The inviting lobby welcomes you behind its 1850s facade of elegant woodwork and Victorian-era glass. In the style of the Paris of long ago, the comfortably furnished bedrooms open onto a glass-topped arcade instead of the hysterically busy street, so they are rather tranquil. We prefer the bedrooms on the top floor, as they are larger and quieter, with views over the rooftops of Paris. The least expensive bedrooms lie behind the elevator bank and get less light.

10 bd. Montmartre or 46 passage Jouffroy, 75009 Paris. www.hotel-chopin.com. (© **01-47-70-58-10.** Fax 01-42-47-00-70. 36 units. 98€–114€ double; 136€ triple. AE, MC, V. Métro: Grands Boulevards. **Amenities:** Wi-Fi (free). *In room:* TV, hair dryer.

Hôtel de la Tour d'Auvergne ★ Here's a good bet for those who want to be near the Opéra or the Gare du Nord. This building was erected before Baron Haussmann reconfigured Paris's avenues around 1870. Later, Modigliani rented a room here for 6 months, and Victor Hugo and Auguste Rodin lived on this street. The interior has been recently redecorated in a chic international style. The guest rooms are meticulously coordinated, yet the small decorative canopies over the headboards can make them feel cluttered. Though the views over the back courtyard are uninspired, some guests prefer the quiet of the rear rooms.

10 rue de la Tour d'Auvergne, 75009 Paris. www.hoteltourdauvergne.com. (© **01-48-78-61-60.** Fax 01-49-95-99-00. 24 units. 115€–135€ double. AE, DC, MC, V. Métro: Cadet. **Amenities:** Bar; room service. *In room:* A/C, TV, hair dryer, minibar, Wi-Fi (free).

Hôtel Langlois ★ ⬛ This hotel used to be known as Hôtel des Croises, but when it was used as a setting for the Jonathan Demme film *The Truth About Charlie* (2002), the hotel owners changed the name to match the one used in the film. It's a well-proportioned, restored town house with a main stairwell and a spacious landing. An antique wrought-iron elevator running up the center of the building adds an old-fashioned Parisian touch. The rooms are well proportioned and spacious; those in the front get the most light. Units in the rear are darker but quieter. Rooms, with their aura of *Ecole de Nancy* (a florid Art Nouveau style), have well-chosen antiques, tasteful rugs and fabrics, even an occasional fireplace.

63 rue St-Lazare, 75009 Paris. www.hotel-langlois.com. ℂ **01-48-74-78-24.** Fax 01-49-95-04-43. 27 units. 140€–150€ double; 190€ suite. AE, DC, MC, V. Métro: Trinité. **Amenities:** Breakfast room; room service. *In room:* A/C, TV, hair dryer, minibar, Wi-Fi (free).

Pigalle & Montmartre (18e)

The wedding cake Sacré-Coeur basilica crowns the city's highest point, on the summit of Montmartre. A neighborhood apart in Paris, with a rich artistic history and all the charm of a village, Montmartre runs into Pigalle below, a harmless red-light district with a high concentration of concert and club venues.

Best For: Dynamic travelers who want to take advantage of the nightlife.
Drawbacks: Climbing up and down the hill requires a good level of fitness.

EXPENSIVE

Hôtel Particulier ★★ No hotel in Paris seems quite as special as this one, lying between avenue Junot and rue Lepic and nestled in a "secret" passageway called le passage du Rocher de la Sorcière, or the Witch's Rock Passage. Modern Paris meets Old Montmartre in this Directoire mansion from the 18th century, and the marriage is harmonious. Louis Bénech, one of the landscape architects who renovated the Tuileries, created the intimate gardens of the hotel. Each of the five suites has a different personality, the work of various artists that range in decor from an erotic window by Philippe Mayaux to poems and hats by Olivier Saillard. The most unusual is the suite "Curtain of Hair," a loft created in the attic with images of the long hair of photographer Natacha Lesueur. The downstairs bar has exceptional cocktails. Service may not be on a par with hotels in a similar price range.

23 av. Junot, 75018 Paris. www.hotel-particulier-montmartre.com. ℂ **01-53-41-81-40.** Fax 01-42-58-00-87. 5 units. 390€–590€ suite. MC, V. Métro: Blanche. **Amenities:** Bar; garden. *In room:* A/C, TV, hair dryer, Wi-Fi (free).

MODERATE

Le Chat Noir Design Hotel ★ Located two steps from the Moulin Rouge cabaret in the heart of Paris's red light district, this stylish hotel takes its name from another 19th-century cabaret just next door; Le Chat Noir was one of the favorite haunts of painter Henri de Toulouse-Lautrec. Making reference to the cabaret's glory days, the hotel is decorated in red and black throughout, with black motifs making reference to the shadow plays once so popular at the cabaret. Guest rooms are contemporary and spotlessly clean, and some rooms on the 8th floor boast Eiffel Tower views. The generous buffet breakfast (15€) is served

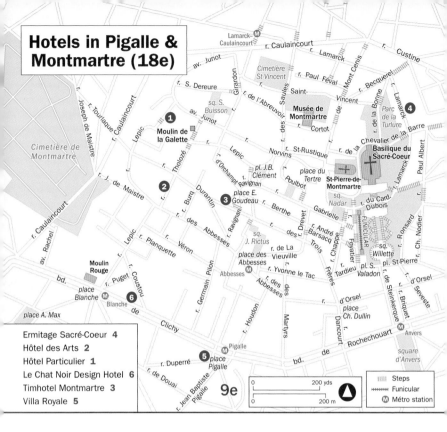

Hotels in Pigalle & Montmartre (18e)

on the ground floor (beware: rooms 101 and 102 are just outside the breakfast room so they can be noisy). The staff is very friendly and helpful.

68 bd. de Clichy, Paris 75018. www.hotel-chatnoir-paris.com. ℂ **01-42-64-15-26.** Fax 01-46-06-35-03. 38 units. 210€ double. AE, DC MC, V. Métro: Blanche. *In room:* A/C, TV, DVD player, hair dryer, Wi-Fi (free).

Villa Royale ★ 🛎   Paris can be many things to many people, and if your vision of the city involves the scarlet-toned settings once associated with the Moulin Rouge and the paintings of Toulouse-Lautrec, this designer hotel might be for you. It does a flourishing business renting small but carefully decorated rooms, each of which evokes Paris's sometimes kitschy world of glitzy and risqué night-life entertainment. Expect rooms outfitted Liberace-style, with rococo gewgaws, velvet and velour upholsteries, jewel-toned walls, and TV screens that are sometimes encased in gilded frames. Each is named after someone from the world of French entertainment, including namesakes inspired by La Bardot, La Deneuve—even Claude Debussy.

2 rue Duperré, 75009 Paris. www.villa-royale.com. ℂ **01-55-31-78-78.** Fax 01-55-31-78-70. 31 units. 239€–299€ double; 289€–449€ suite. AE, DC, MC, V. Métro: Pigalle. Bus: 30 or 54. **Amenities:** Room service. *In room:* A/C, TV, hair dryer, minibar, Wi-Fi (10€).

INEXPENSIVE

Ermitage Sacré-Coeur Built in 1870 of chiseled limestone in the Napoleon III style, this hotel's facade evokes a perfectly proportioned small villa. Family run, it's set in a calm area, a brief downhill stroll from Sacré-Coeur. Views extend over Paris, and there's a garden in the back courtyard. The small guest rooms are similar to those in a countryside *auberge* (inn), with exposed ceiling beams, flowered wallpaper, and casement windows opening onto the garden or a street seemingly airlifted from the provinces.

24 rue Lamarck, 75018 Paris. www.ermitagesacrecoeur.fr. ℰ **01-42-64-79-22.** Fax 01-42-64-10-33. 12 units. 110€–115€ double; 160€–180€ quad. Rates include breakfast. No credit cards. Métro: Lamarck-Caulaincourt. Parking 15€. **Amenities:** Babysitting; room service; smoke-free rooms. *In room:* Hair dryer, Wi-Fi (free).

Hôtel des Arts ★ In the center of Montmartre between place du Tertre and the Moulin Rouge, this hotel lies in a delightful quarter of Paris once made famous by poets and painters. It has a warm, welcoming atmosphere, and in a former life it was a dormitory for the dancers of the Moulin Rouge. As you might expect, the rooms are small yet comfortable, with country-style curtains and bedspreads. Opt for one of the four bedrooms on the sixth floor for a panoramic view of Paris. Keeping up with the zeitgeist, the hotel now offers iPads on loan to hotel guests.

5 rue Tholozé, Paris 75018. www.arts-hotel-paris.com. ℰ **01-46-06-30-52.** Fax 01-46-06-10-83. 50 units. 85€–160€ double. AE, MC, V. Métro: Blanche. **Amenities:** Breakfast room. *In room:* TV, Wi-Fi (free).

Timhotel Montmartre ★ This two-star hotel is located in a charming square in Montmartre, and is located next door to the historical Bateau-Lavoir building, where Picasso had a studio for many years and painted his masterpiece *Les Demoiselles d'Avignon*. The compact hotel rooms are decorated in a fairly basic and impersonal style, but they're clean. Rooms on the fourth and fifth floors offer excellent views over the rooftops of Paris and the Sacré-Coeur. Note that the hilltop location means that it can be a steep climb up from the closest public transport stops.

11 place Émile Goudeau, 75018 Paris. www.timhotel.com. ℰ **01-42-55-74-79.** Fax 01-42-55-71-01. 59 units. 85€–180€ double. AE, DC, MC, V. Métro: Abbesses. **Amenities:** Breakfast room; concierge. *In room:* A/C (in some rooms), TV, hair dryer, Wi-Fi (free).

République, Bastille & Eastern Paris (11e & 12e)

Paris's former industrial heart has been converted into a string of cosmopolitan neighborhoods with a bohemian vibe.

Best For: Travelers wanting to look backstage, behind the glittering Paris grandeur.

Drawbacks: You might feel like you're missing out on some of the Paris mythology.

MODERATE

Gabriel Paris Marais ★ 🎁 This chic boutique hotel calls itself Paris's first "detox hotel." The hotel takes an active approach to purifying the bodies of its guests, with an emphasis on restful sleep and healthy food. One example of this is that some accommodations are outfitted with "NightCove," a system that uses sound and light to encourage natural sleeping patterns; the rooms are also sound-proofed to ensure a restful night. You can continue to detox with an organic breakfast and spa treatments in their Bioo Detox Room. Located close to place de la République and the Canal St-Martin, this hotel offers comfortably furnished rooms with modern amenities and stylish lighting that range from small to midsize. In the surrealist but harmoniously decorated "detox bar," guests can order a large choice of antioxidant drinks and teas.

25 rue du Grand-Prieuré, 75011 Paris. www.gabrielparismarais.com. ✆ **01-47-00-13-38.** 41 units. 155€–280€ double. AE, DC, MC, V. Métro: République. **Amenities:** Cafeteria; room service; small spa. *In room:* A/C, TV/DVD, hair dryer, minibar, MP3 docking station, Wi-Fi (free).

Le Général Hotel ★ As the neighborhood around place de la République, Canal St-Martin, and rue Oberkampf becomes increasingly tuned to Paris's sense of counterculture chic, this is a good example of that neighborhood's improving fortunes. Opened within the premises of a run-down hotel that was radically renovated and decorated by noted designer Jean-Philippe Nuel, the hotel's upbeat interior revolves around prominent rectilinear lines, spartan-looking decors, and an intelligent distribution of spaces. The result is a seven-story hotel with floors linked by two separate elevator banks and pale, monochromatic beige-and-off-white color schemes, and with furniture that is either dark (specifically, rosewood-toned) or pale (specifically, birch- or maple-toned). Bathrooms include L'Occitane products.

5–7 rue Rampon, 75011 Paris. www.legeneralhotel.com. ✆ **01-47-00-41-57.** Fax 01-47-00-21-56. 46 units. 167€–260€ double; 290€–320€ suite. AE, MC, V. Métro: République. **Amenities:** Bar; exercise room; room service; sauna. *In room:* A/C, TV, hair dryer, iPod dock, Wi-Fi (free).

Le Pavillon Bastille ★ ☺ This is an unpretentious hotel in a town house across from the Opéra Bastille, a block south of place de la Bastille. A 17th-century fountain graces the pretty, sun-filled courtyard. The contemporary but neutral rooms are soundproofed, and have twin or double beds, partially mirrored walls, and contemporary built-in furniture. In just a few minutes' walk, you can discover the Marais district, the Faubourg Saint-Antoine, and the Opéra Bastille. Rooms can be connected easily, making this a good option for families.

65 rue de Lyon, 75012 Paris. www.paris-hotel-pavillonbastille.com. ✆ **01-43-43-65-65.** Fax 01-43-43-96-52. 25 units. 195€–215€ double; 400€ suite. AE, DC, MC, V. Métro: Bastille. **Amenities:** Bar; babysitting; concierge; room service. *In room:* A/C, TV, hair dryer, minibar, Wi-Fi (free).

INEXPENSIVE

Cosmos Hotel 🎀 This no-frills option in the heart of the animated Oberkampf neighborhood has got to be one of the best deals in town. The simply furnished rooms are clean and have fresh towels provided on a daily basis. The staff is helpful, and the hotel is also home to a little furry feline mascot. The only downside is that the hotel can be noisy on the weekends as people spill out of the busy local bars and restaurants.

35 rue Jean-Pierre Timbaud, 75011 Paris. www.cosmos-hotel-paris.com. ✆ **01-43-57-25-88.** Fax 01-43-57-25-88. 36 units. 62€–70€ double; 78€ triple. AE, MC, V. Métro: Parmentier. *In room:* TV, hair dryer, Wi-Fi (free).

Grand Hôtel Doré Deep in the heart of the Daumesnil area, this venerated old hotel has been a Paris tradition since the early 20th century. Today it's been brought

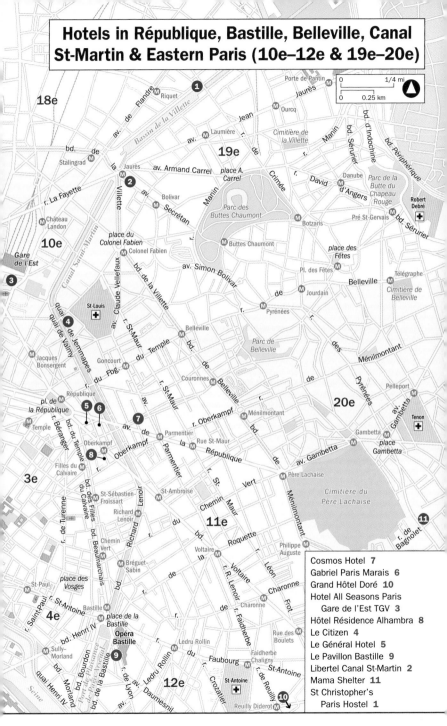

Hotels in République, Bastille, Belleville, Canal St-Martin & Eastern Paris (10e–12e & 19e–20e)

Cosmos Hotel **7**
Gabriel Paris Marais **6**
Grand Hôtel Doré **10**
Hotel All Seasons Paris
  Gare de l'Est TGV **3**
Hôtel Résidence Alhambra **8**
Le Citizen **4**
Le Général Hotel **5**
Le Pavillon Bastille **9**
Libertel Canal St-Martin **2**
Mama Shelter **11**
St Christopher's
  Paris Hostel **1**

into the 21st century with a major restoration and vast improvements, so that once again it is a hotel of charm and character. Some of the past remains visible here, architecturally, but the hotel has been completely modernized. The bedrooms are small to midsize, but each is comfortably furnished and well maintained.

201 av. Daumesnil, 75012 Paris. www.grand-hotel-dore.com. (℡) **01-43-43-66-89.** Fax 01-43-43-65-20. 40 units. 120€–155€ double. AE, MC, V. Métro: Daumesnil. **Amenities:** Babysitting; concierge. *In room:* A/C, TV, minibar, Wi-Fi (free).

Hôtel Résidence Alhambra   Named for the famous cabaret/vaudeville theater that once stood nearby, the Alhambra dates from the 1800s, and it was last renovated in 2006. It is a budget option located just north of the trendy northern Marais district. In the rear garden, where breakfast is served, its two-story chalet offers eight additional guest rooms. The small accommodations are bland but comfortable, each in a dull pastel scheme with white and ocher.

13 rue de Malte, 75011 Paris. www.hotelalhambra.fr. (℡) **01-47-00-35-52.** Fax 01-43-57-98-75. 58 units. 87€–129€ double; 107€–176€ triple. AE, DC, MC, V. Métro: Oberkampf. **Amenities:** Smoke-free rooms; Wi-Fi (free) in lobby. *In room:* TV.

Belleville, Canal St-Martin & Northeast Paris (10e, 19e & 20e)

Not as many tourists venture to these cosmopolitan areas, located in the city's old industrial heartland. But up-and-coming Belleville includes one of the city's Chinatowns, a new wave of contemporary art galleries, and the must-see Buttes Chaumont park, while on the charming and leafy Canal St-Martin, you can linger over coffee with bohemian locals.

Best For: Travelers looking for budget accommodations and those who want to experience a different dimension of the city.

Drawbacks: The Eiffel Tower is quite a hike!

MODERATE

Le Citizen ★★   This chic 12-room boutique hotel on the Canal St-Martin opened in 2011. Designed by Christophe Delcourt and Stéphane Lanchon, the hotel has a low-key, contemporary vibe, with a minimalist Swedish look featuring natural wood accents throughout. The soundproofed rooms include top-of-the-line bedding, flatscreen TVs with a variety of international channels, free Wi-Fi access, an iPad, and a complimentary minibar. The hotel is eco-friendly, and strives to conserve water, paper, and energy; it's also entirely smoke-free.

96 quai de Jemmapes, 75010 Paris. www.lecitizenhotel.com. (℡) **01-83-62-55-50.** Fax 01-83-62-55-71. 69 units. 175€–235€ double, 275€–450€ suite. Rates include breakfast. AE, MC, V. Métro: Jaques Bonsergent. **Amenities:** Room service; smoke-free rooms. *In room:* A/C, TV, minibar (free), hairdryer iPad, Wi-Fi (free).

Mama Shelter ★★ ✦   Even though it's located off the beaten track, this Philippe Starck–designed hotel nevertheless attracts the in-crowd with its buzzing downstairs restaurant-bar space, sleek design, and high-tech features. The stylish yet simple rooms are equipped with iMac computers, offering on-demand movies, Internet access, and television programs. Plus, the low rates make the rooms a great value. This is a place for the young and hip, and the in-house bar and restaurant are local hot spots.

109 rue de Bagnolet, 75020 Paris. www.mamashelter.com. ☏ **01-43-48-48-48.** Fax 01-43-48-48-49. 170 units. 89€–209€ double. Rates include breakfast. MC, V. Free parking. Métro: Gambetta. **Amenities:** Restaurant; bar; babysitting; bicycle rental; concierge. *In room:* A/C, iMac, microwave, minibar, Wi-Fi (free).

INEXPENSIVE
Hotel All Seasons Paris Gare de l'Est TGV 🔥   Opposite the Gare de l'Est railway station, this hotel lives up to its name. It is truly a hotel for all seasons and a great convenience for passengers disembarking at Gare de l'Est, which has good taxi, bus, and Métro links to all of Paris. All Seasons is the budget chain link of the famous French hotel group, Accor, and as such, it's aimed at both vacationers and business travelers who seek affordable rates. The bedroom furnishings are fairly standard, except for the bedding, which emphasizes "antistress" quilts and pillows made with carbon threads said to channel the body's electricity. Breakfast is called "as much as you wish," and there is unlimited tea, coffee, and mineral water. Magazines and games for children are available. The hotel is smoke-free.

87 bd. de Strasbourg, 75010 Paris. www.accorhotels.com. ☏ **01-42-09-12-28.** Fax 01-42-09-48-12. 32 units. 95€–115€ double. Rates include breakfast. MC, V. Métro: Gare de l'Est. **Amenities:** Room service. *In room:* A/C, TV, hair dryer, Wi-Fi (free).

Libertel Canal St-Martin ★   This hotel consists of three small typical Parisian buildings that are connected by a charming courtyard and a small garden. Though small, guest rooms are clean and contemporary, with flatscreen TVs and Wi-Fi access. Located in the Canal St-Martin neighborhood, the hotel is near some charming shops and restaurants, as well as the beautiful Buttes-Chaumont Park; it is also very close to the Jaurés Métro stop. The hotel is entirely non-smoking.

5 avenue Secrétan, 75019 Paris. www.hotel-canal-st-martin.com. ☏ **01-42-06-62-00.** Fax 01-42-40-64-51. 69 units. 105€–145€ double. Rates include breakfast. MC, V. Métro: Jaurès. **Amenities:** Smoke-free rooms. *In room:* A/C (in most rooms), TV, Wi-Fi (free).

St Christopher's Paris Hostel ★ 🔥   Located on the picturesque Bassin de la Villette, which connects the Canal St-Martin to the Seine, this massive purpose-built hostel, opened in 2008, is close to some great bars, cinemas, restaurants, and clubs, and is particularly lovely in summer, when the banks of the canal come to life. The hostel is home to an animated bar called Belushi's.

159 rue Crimée, 75019 Paris. www.st-christophers.co.uk/paris-hostels. ☏ **01-40-34-34-40.** Fax 01-40-34-31-38. www.st-christophers.co.uk. 70 units. 75€–100€ double. Rates include breakfast. MC, V. Métro: Crimée or Laumière. **Amenities:** Restaurant; bar; bicycle rental. *In room:* Wi-Fi (free).

THE LEFT BANK
Latin Quarter (5e & 13e)

The Sorbonne University is at the heart of this Left Bank neighborhood, which gets its name from the Latin the students and professors spoke there until the end of the 18th century. To feed those minds, the 5th arrondissement boasts some of the city's best specialty bookshops. This neighborhood dates from the time when the Romans ruled—Paris was conquered by the Romans in 52

B.C.—and the area still conserves Roman ruins, which you can explore at the Cluny Museum. Nearby, the 13th arrondissement is a former industrial zone in the process of gentrification; it's home to the capital's newest national library.

Best For: Travelers interested in tracing the city's rich history and families grateful for some quiet close to the Luxembourg gardens.

Drawbacks: The vibe might be too bookish for some.

EXPENSIVE

Grand Hôtel Saint-Michel ★   Built in the 19th century, this hotel is larger and more businesslike than many town house–style inns nearby. It basks in the reflected glow of Brazilian dissident Georges Amado, whose memoirs recorded his 2-year sojourn in one of the rooms. The public areas are tasteful, with portraits and rich upholsteries. Improvements have enlarged some rooms, lowering their ceilings and adding amenities, but retained old-fashioned touches such as wrought-iron balconies (on the fifth floor). Triple rooms have an extra bed and are suitable for families, who share a private bathroom with tub and shower. Sixth-floor rooms have views over the rooftops.

19 rue Cujas, 75005 Paris. www.grand-hotel-st-michel.com. ℰ **01-46-33-33-02.** Fax 01-40-46-96-33. 47 units. 320€–400€ double; 450€ suite. AE, DC, MC, V. Métro: Cluny–La Sorbonne. RER: Luxembourg or St-Michel. **Amenities:** Bar; babysitting; exercise room; room service. *In room:* A/C, TV, hair dryer, minibar, Wi-Fi (free).

Hotel Seven   Run by the same team as the Five Hotel (see below), this luxury concept hotel is not for the fainthearted, taking the commitment to exceptional interiors a step beyond. Each room and suite is totally unique, with evocative names like Marie Antoinette, The Black Diamond, and On/Off; in the Levitation rooms, the bed is actually suspended off the floor. Each room is well appointed, and might include a complimentary bottle of champagne, an iPod docking base, an espresso machine, a large flatscreen TV, luxurious beds and linens, and designer bath products. Couples looking for a romantic setting will enjoy this hotel. The only downside is the slightly off-the-beaten path location.

20 rue Berthollet, 75005 Paris. www.sevenhotelparis.com. ℰ **01-43-31-47-52.** Fax 01-43-36-41-40. 37 units. 327€–397€ double; 737€–1,107€ suite. AE, DC, MC, V. Métro: Les Gobelins. **Amenities:** Bar, breakfast room, room service. *In room:* A/C, TV, iPod dock, hair dryer, minibar, Wi-Fi (free).

MODERATE

Best Western La Tour Notre-Dame ★   In the heart of the Sorbonne district, this restored Latin Quarter hotel rises seven floors over a 17th-century vaulted cellar where breakfast is served. A hotel of Rive Gauche character, it is ideally situated for Left Bank living, lying between St-Germain-des-Prés and the cathedral of Notre-Dame, opposite the Sorbonne and the Cluny Museum. Bedrooms, many with exposed beams, are adorned with romantic accents, like liberty prints and Empire-era furniture. A Vélib' bike rental station is located just outside the front door. The hotel is entirely smoke-free.

20 rue du Sommerard, 75005 Paris. www.bestwestern-latour-notredame.com. ℰ **01-43-54-47-60.** Fax 01-43-26-42-34. 48 units. 125€–230€ double. AE, DC, MC, V. Métro: Cluny–Sorbonne. RER: Saint-Michel or Notre-Dame. **Amenities:** Bar; smoke-free rooms. *In room:* A/C, TV, hair dryer, minibar, Wi-Fi (free).

Hotels in the Latin Quarter & Southern Paris (5e & 13e)

Best Western La Tour
Notre-Dame **1**

The Five Hotel **12**

Grand Hôtel Saint-Michel **3**

Hôtel Agora St-Germain **5**

Hôtel des Grandes Ecoles **9**

Hôtel Design De
La Sorbonne **2**

Hôtel des Jardins du
Luxembourg **8**

Hôtel La Manufacture **14**

Hôtel Le Vert Galant **13**

Hôtel Quartier Latin **7**

Hôtel Saint-Christophe **10**

Hotel Seven **11**

Hôtel St-Jacques **4**

Minerve Hôtel **6**

Hôtel Design De La Sorbonne ★★   Located near the Sorbonne University and a short walk from the Luxembourg Gardens, this boutique hotel is stylish and comfortable. Though small, guest rooms are sleek and trendy, and are decorated in bold colors and patterns; rooms feature new bathrooms and modern amenities such as Apple iMac computers. The owners, who manage several other quality hotels in Paris, demonstrate inventiveness through the hotel design—look down at the floor to read excerpts from French literary classics woven into the hotel's carpets. The hotel is smoke-free.

6 rue Victor Cousin, 75005 Paris. www.hotelsorbonne.com. ✆ **01-43-54-58-08.** Fax 01-40-51-05-18. 38 units. 250€–340€ double. AE, DC, MC, V. Métro: Cluny–La Sorbonne. RER: Luxembourg. **Amenities:** Smoke-free rooms. *In room:* A/C, TV, iMac, hair dryer, minibar, Wi-Fi (free).

The Five Hotel ★★ 🏨   A charmer among Left Bank boutique hotels, the Five is named for the 5th arrondissement and lies in a restored 1800s town house on a U-shaped street off boulevard de Port-Royal. The funky interior design is not to everyone's taste, including a red leather paneled hall or a red-painted gas fireplace. The rooms are individually designed in various colors (blood red or Halloween orange, for example), and tiny white lights evoke a planetarium. Of course, if you want a room the color of a prune, that too is available. A Chinese lacquer artist, Isabelle Emmerique, has certainly been busy here. Some rooms are small, but all the beds are exceedingly comfortable.

3 rue Flatters, Paris 75005. www.thefivehotel.com. ✆ **01-43-31-74-21.** Fax 01-43-31-61-96. 24 units. 245€–315€ double. AE, MC, V. Métro: Bastilel or Gobelins. **Amenities:** Bar; room service. *In room:* A/C, TV, hair dryer, Wi-Fi (free).

Hôtel Agora St-Germain   This unpretentious hotel occupies a building constructed in the early 1600s to house a group of guardsmen protecting the brother of the king at his lodgings nearby. It's in the heart of artistic/historic Paris and offers compact, soundproof guest rooms that have been sensitively renovated. All but seven of the bedrooms have tub/shower combinations; the rest have only showers.

42 rue des Bernardins, 75005 Paris. www.agorasaintgermain.com. ✆ **01-46-34-13-00.** Fax 01-46-34-75-05. 39 units. 240€–350€ double. AE, DC, MC, V. Parking 25€. Métro: Maubert-Mutualité. **Amenities:** Room service. *In room:* A/C, TV, hair dryer, minibar, Wi-Fi (free).

Hôtel des Jardins du Luxembourg   Built during Baron Haussmann's 19th-century overhaul of Paris, this hotel boasts an imposing facade of honey-colored stone accented with ornate iron balconies. Sigmund Freud stayed here in 1885. The interior is outfitted in strong, clean lines, often with groupings of Art Deco furnishings. The high-ceilinged guest rooms, some with Provençal tiles and ornate moldings, are well maintained, the sizes ranging from small to medium. Best of all, they overlook a quiet dead-end alley, ensuring relatively peaceful nights. Some have balconies overlooking the rooftops.

5 impasse Royer-Collard, 75005 Paris. www.les-jardins-du-luxembourg.com. ✆ **01-40-46-08-88.** Fax 01-40-46-02-28. 26 units. 171€–181€ double. AE, DC, MC, V. Métro: Cluny–La Sorbonne. RER: Luxembourg. **Amenities:** Bar; babysitting; room service. *In room:* A/C, TV, hair dryer, minibar, Wi-Fi (10€ per day).

Hôtel La Manufacture ★ 🏨   With good rooms and decent prices, this place is a real find. Lying on a small street near place d'Italie in the 13th arrondissement, it is only 10 minutes by Métro from the stations at Montparnasse and Gare de Lyon. Small to midsize bedrooms are decorated in printed fabrics and soothing pastels. The most desirable room is no. 74 because of its distant views of the Eiffel Tower. This restored 19th-century building has a wrought-iron door and is graced with iron lamps, wicker chairs, oak floors, and bright paintings. It contains a number of old-fashioned armoires called *chapeau de gendarme* (police hat).

8 rue Philippe de Champagne (av. des Gobelins), 75013 Paris. www.hotel-la-manufacture.com. ℂ **01-45-35-45-25.** Fax 01-45-35-45-40. 56 units. 175€–195€ double; 310€ triple. AE, DC, MC, V. Métro: Place d'Italie. **Amenities:** Bar; room service. *In room:* A/C, TV, hair dryer, Wi-Fi (free).

Hôtel Quartier Latin   Between the Sorbonne and the Musée de Cluny, this hotel captures the flavor of the Paris literati better than any other in Paris. Its original decor was conceived in 1997 by Didier Gomez, who referred to it as "contemporary with cultural references." That means walls stenciled with passages from Victor Hugo or photographs of Colette and André Gide. Even the breakfast room is stocked with bookshelves and its ceiling inscribed with quotes from Baudelaire. Bibliomania continues in the lobby, which is filled with floor-to-ceiling bookcases. Bedrooms are decorated comfortably and tastefully in blue and white, with such delicacies as linen curtains, along with fine wood furnishings, plus white-tiled bathrooms. In all, this is a "novel" hotel and ideal for bookworms.

9 rue des Ecoles, 75005 Paris. www.hotelquartierlatin.com. ℂ **01-44-27-06-45.** Fax 01-43-25-36-70. 29 units. 187€–248€ double; 242€–310€ junior suite. AE, MC, V. Métro: Cardinal Lemoine. Parking nearby: 20€. **Amenities:** Babysitting; room service. *In room:* A/C, TV, hair dryer, minibar, Wi-Fi (free).

Hôtel St-Jacques ★ 👥   Try for a room with a balcony view of Notre-Dame and the Panthéon. The Belle Époque atmosphere of the hotel was made famous in the movie *Charade* (1963), which starred Cary Grant and Audrey Hepburn. Jean-Paul and Martine Rousseau, the owners, welcome you to this old-fashioned Latin Quarter gem, filled with Second Empire overtones, including frescoes in the breakfast room and lounge, 18th-century ceiling murals in some of the bedrooms, wedding cake plasterwork, and corridors painted with *trompe l'oeil* marble. Bedrooms are generally spacious and have been attractively and comfortably restored. Street-side rooms can be a bit noisy.

35 rue des Ecoles, 75005 Paris. www.paris-hotel-stjacques.com. ℂ **01-44-07-45-45.** Fax 01-43-25-65-50. 26 units. 168€–290€ double; 278€ triple. AE, DC, MC, V. Métro: Maubert-Mutualité. **Amenities:** Babysitting. *In room:* A/C, TV, hair dryer, Wi-Fi (free).

INEXPENSIVE

Hôtel des Grandes Ecoles ★★ ✎   Few hotels in the neighborhood offer so much low-key charm at such reasonable prices. It's composed of a trio of high-ceilinged buildings, interconnected via a sheltered courtyard, where in warm weather, singing birds provide a worthy substitute for the TVs deliberately missing from the rooms. Accommodations, as reflected by the price, range from snug, cozy doubles to more spacious chambers. Each room is comfortable, but with a lot of luggage, the very smallest would be cramped. The decor is old-fashioned, with feminine touches such as flowered upholsteries and ruffles. Many have views of a garden where trellises and flower beds evoke the countryside.

75 rue de Cardinal-Lemoine, 75005 Paris. www.hotel-grandes-ecoles.com. ℂ **01-43-26-79-23.** Fax 01-47-47-65-48. 51 units. 118€–145€ double. Extra bed 20€. MC, V. Parking 30€. Métro: Cardinal Lemoine, Jussieu, or Place Monge. RER: Port-Royal, Luxembourg. **Amenities:** Babysitting; room service. *In room:* Hair dryer, Wi-Fi (free).

Hôtel Le Vert Galant ★   Verdant climbing plants and shrubs make this family-run hotel feel like an *auberge* (inn) deep in the French countryside. The smallish guest rooms have tiled or carpeted floors, unfussy furniture, and (in most cases) views of the private garden or the public park across the street. One of the hotel's best aspects is the Basque restaurant next door, the Auberge Etchegorry, sharing the same management; hotel guests receive a discount.

41 rue Croulebarbe, 75013 Paris. www.vertgalant.com. *℅* **01-44-08-83-50.** Fax 01-44-08-83-69. 15 units. 90€–130€ double. AE, MC, V. Parking 15€. Métro: Corvisart or Gobelins. RER: Gare d'Austerlitz. **Amenities:** Restaurant; room service; smoke-free rooms. *In room:* TV, hair dryer, minibar, Wi-Fi (free).

Hôtel Saint-Christophe   This hotel, in one of the Latin Quarter's undiscovered areas, offers a gracious English-speaking staff. It was created in 1987, when an older hotel was connected to a butcher shop. All the small- to medium-size rooms have Louis XV–style furniture.

17 rue Lacépède, 75005 Paris. www.charm-hotel-paris.com. *℅* **01-43-31-81-54.** Fax 01-43-31-12-54. 31 units. 130€ double. AE, DC, MC, V. Parking 24€. Métro: Place Monge. **Amenities:** Breakfast room. *In room:* TV, hair dryer, minibar, Wi-Fi (free).

Minerve Hôtel   This is a well-managed three-star hotel in the heart of the Latin Quarter, with good-size, comfortable rooms and a staff with a sense of humor. The comfortable bedrooms have old-fashioned mahogany furniture and walls covered in fabric. Try for 1 of 10 rooms with balconies where you can look out over Notre-Dame. Depending on your room assignment, bathrooms range in dimension from cramped to midsize. Street-side rooms have sweet wrought-iron decorations in front of the window, hung with geranium-filled garden boxes.

13 rue des Ecoles, 75005 Paris. www.hotel-paris-minerve.com. *℅* **01-43-26-26-04.** Fax 01-44-07-01-96. 54 units. 132€–168€ double; 165€ triple. AE, DC, MC, V. Métro: Cardinal Lemoine. Parking 20€. **Amenities:** Breakfast room, room service, Wi-Fi (in lobby). *In room:* A/C, TV, hair dryer, Wi-Fi (6€ per day).

St-Germain-des-Prés & Luxembourg (6e)

This glamorous neighborhood is home to great shops and cafes. Intellectuals such as Simone de Beauvoir and Jean-Paul Sartre put St-Germain on the map postwar, when they and their friends had high-minded conversations at such cafes as Les Deux Magots and Café de Flore. The area still draws many of the city's artists and thinkers, and most of the modern art galleries are here too.

Best For: Travelers hoping to bump into Catherine Deneuve.
Drawbacks: The lack of budget accommodations and the competition for sidewalk space between the tourists and fanatical shoppers.

EXPENSIVE

Hotel Bel-Ami ★★ 🛏   This four-star hotel was designed expressly to appeal to fashion-conscious patrons in the heart of the Left Bank cafe district. Its name translates as "handsome (male) friend." You'll get the feeling that this is an arts-conscious hotel whose minimalist public areas were built only after months of careful design by a team of trend-following architects. Expect color schemes of lilac walls, acid-green sofas, copper-colored tiles, bleached ash, and industrial-style lighting fixtures. Bedrooms contain a palette of earth tones, such as pistachio ice cream or pumpkin pie, and an almost aggressively minimalist, even

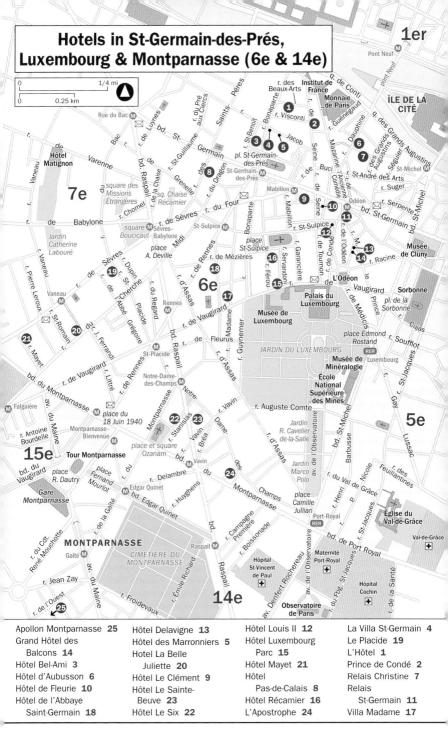

Hotels in St-Germain-des-Prés, Luxembourg & Montparnasse (6e & 14e)

cubist, design. Bathrooms are artfully spartan. The suites and first-floor rooms have all been recently renovated and the hotel is entirely non-smoking.

7–11 rue St. Benoît, 75006 Paris. www.hotel-bel-ami.com. ✆ **01-42-61-53-53.** Fax 01-49-27-09-33. 112 units. 410€–690€ double; 990€ suite. AE, DC, MC, V. Métro: St-Germain-des-Prés. **Amenities:** Bar; concierge; espresso bar; exercise room. *In room:* TV, minibar, Wi-Fi (free).

Hôtel d'Aubusson ★★   This mansion in the heart of St-Germain-des-Prés was the site of the city's first literary salon. Fully restored, it is today one of the best luxe boutique hotels in Paris. Lying 2 blocks south of Pont Neuf and the Seine, the hotel has taken over a former private residence from the 1600s, to which is attached a 1950s building. You enter a grand hall under a beamed ceiling with a baronial fireplace, original Aubusson tapestries, and furnishings in the style of Louis XV. There are also a number of smaller, more intimate lounges. The bedrooms are midsize to large, each attractively and comfortably furnished, often in a Directoire style and sometimes with exposed ceiling beams. Antiques are often placed in front of the original stone walls. For the most traditional flair, ask for one of the rooms on the top two floors. Bathrooms are stocked with Hermès toiletries.

33 rue Dauphine, Paris 75006. www.hoteldaubusson.com. ✆ **01-43-29-43-43.** Fax 01-43-29-12-62. 49 units. 315€–480€ double; 625€ suite. AE, DC, MC, V. Parking 25€. Métro: Odéon. **Amenities:** Bar; cafe; babysitting; room service. *In room:* A/C, TV, hair dryer, minibar, Wi-Fi (free).

Hotel La Belle Juliette ★★ 🎁   This luxury hotel, which opened in Saint-Germain-des-Prés in 2011, stands out for its chic interior design by local textile designer Anne Gelbard. The hotel is inspired by the life of Juliette Récamier, a 19th-century French socialite whose Parisian salon drew intellectuals and artists. Guest rooms feel very contemporary while still paying homage to the 19th century and Madame Récamier, with sophisticated color combinations, luxurious fabrics, original engravings, and restored antiques. Yet the rooms are also completely modern, with Apple iMac computers for entertainment.

92 rue du Cherche Midi, 75006 Paris. www.hotel-belle-juliette-paris.com. ✆ **01-42-22-97-40.** Fax 01-45-44-89-97. 34 units. 400€–500€ double; 600€–750€ suite. AE, DC, MC, V. Métro: St-Germain-des-Prés. **Amenities:** Bar; restaurant, room service, spa. *In room:* A/C, iMac, hair dryer, minibar, Wi-Fi (free).

Hôtel Le Six ★ 🎁   This boutique hotel is a bastion of restrained charm and low-key luxury with harmonious tones and soft lighting. Its major feature is an elegant spa offering the same products as the swanky Ritz Hotel. The staff promises to leave you "gorgeous." Sturdy oak furnishings and autumnal colors fill the hotel; the best accommodations are the upper suites, opening onto views of the skyline of Paris. But all the accommodations are imbued with a high comfort level, made all the more so by the soundproofing. Guests gather in the library and lounge, sheltered under a glass roof and evoking a winter garden.

14 rue Stanislas, 75006 Paris. www.hotel-le-six.com. ✆ **01-42-22-00-75.** Fax 01-42-22-00-95. 41 units. 300€–450€ double; 402€–600€ junior suite; 700€ suite. AE, DC, MC, V. Métro: Notre-Dame-des-Champs or Vavin. **Amenities:** Room service; spa. *In room:* A/C, TV, minibar, Wi-Fi (free).

Hôtel Luxembourg Parc ★★   Near the Luxembourg Gardens for those lovely strolls, this elegant bastion of fine living has been called a small-scale version of the swank Hôtel de Crillon. In one of the Left Bank's most charming and historic districts, a 17th-century palace has been beautifully restored and decorated. The bedrooms are decorated in the styles of Louis XV, Louis XVI, and Napoleon III. The bar is an elegant rendezvous point and the library is relaxing. The around-the-clock room service is actually takeout from nearby restaurants. The breakfast room on the ground floor overlooks the Luxembourg Gardens.

42 rue de Vaugirard, 75006 Paris. www.luxembourg-paris-hotel.com. ℰ **01-53-10-36-50.** Fax 01-53-10-36-59. 23 units. 325€–400€ double; 495€ suite. AE, DC, MC, V. Métro: Luxembourg. **Amenities:** Bar; exercise room; room service. *In room:* A/C, TV, hair dryer, minibar, Wi-Fi (free).

L'Hôtel ★   Ranking just a notch below the Relais Christine (see below), this is one of the Left Bank's most charming boutique hotels. It was once a 19th-century fleabag whose major distinction was that Oscar Wilde died in one of its bedrooms, but today's guests aren't anywhere near destitution. Guest rooms vary in size, style, and price; all have decorative fireplaces and fabric-covered walls. All the sumptuous beds have tasteful fabrics and crisp linens. About half the bathrooms are small, tubless nooks. Room themes reflect China, Russia, Japan, India, or high-camp Victorian. The Cardinal room is all scarlet, the Viollet-le-Duc room is neo-Gothic, and the room where Wilde died is Victorian.

13 rue des Beaux-Arts, 75006 Paris. www.l-hotel.com. ℰ **01-44-41-99-00.** Fax 01-43-25-64-81. 20 units. 290€–385€ double; 660€–800€ suite. AE, DC, MC, V. Métro: St-Germain-des-Prés. **Amenities:** Restaurant; bar; babysitting; room service. *In room:* A/C, TV, TV/DVD, hair dryer, minibar, Wi-Fi (free).

Relais Christine ★★   This hotel welcomes you into a former 16th-century Augustinian cloister. From a cobblestone street, you enter a symmetrical courtyard and find an elegant reception area with sculpture and Renaissance antiques. Each room is uniquely decorated with wooden beams and Louis XIII–style furnishings; the rooms come in a range of styles and shapes. Some are among the Left Bank's largest, with extras such as mirrored closets, plush carpets, and some balconies facing the courtyard. The least attractive rooms are in the interior. Bed configurations vary, but all mattresses are on the soft side, offering comfort with quality linens.

3 rue Christine, 75006 Paris. www.relais-christine.com. ℰ **01-40-51-60-80.** Fax 01-40-51-60-81. 51 units. 300€–510€ double; 450€–930€ duplex or suite. AE, DC, MC, V. Free parking. Métro: Odéon or St-Michel. **Amenities:** Bar; babysitting; concierge; exercise room; room service; spa. *In room:* A/C, TV, TV/DVD, hair dryer, minibar, Wi-Fi (free).

Relais St-Germain ★★ 🏩   It's difficult to exaggerate the charm of this deeply personalized and intimate hotel created from side-by-side 17th-century town houses. You'll navigate your way through a labyrinth of narrow and winding hallways to soundproofed bedrooms that are spacious, and artfully and individually decorated in a style that evokes late-19th-century Paris at its most sensual. Two of the rooms have terraces. Come here for a discreet escape from the anonymity of larger, less personalized hotels, and for an injection of boutique-style Parisian charm. Even *Vogue* magazine referred to this place as "an oasis of Left Bank charm." We heartily agree. The owner of the hotel is one of the city's best chefs; hotel guests have priority booking at the attached restaurant, Le Comptoir (p. 216), where Parisians often wait 6 months for a reservation.

9 carrefour de l'Odéon, 75006 Paris. www.hotelrsg.com. ℰ **01-43-29-12-05.** Fax 01-46-33-45-30. 22 units. 285€–370€ double; 395€ suite. Rates include breakfast. AE, DC, MC, V. **Amenities:** Restaurant. *In room:* A/C, TV, TV/DVD, hair dryer, minibar, Wi-Fi (free).

MODERATE

Hôtel de Fleurie ★ ☺ Off the boulevard St-Germain on a colorful little street, the Fleurie is one of the best of the city's updated old hotels; its statuary-studded facade recaptures 17th-century elegance, and the stone walls in the salon have been exposed. Many of the guest rooms have elaborate draperies and antique reproductions. Because some rooms are larger than others and contain an extra bed for one or two children, the hotel has long been a family favorite.

32–34 rue Grégoire-de-Tours, 75006 Paris. www.fleurie-hotel-paris.com. ✆ **01-53-73-70-00.** Fax 01-53-73-70-20. 29 units. 250€–320€ double; 465€ family room. Children 12 and under stay free in parent's room. AE, DC, MC, V. Métro: Odéon or Mabillon. **Amenities:** Bar; babysitting; room service; Wi-Fi (free). *In room:* A/C, TV, hair dryer, minibar, Wi-Fi (free).

Hôtel de l'Abbaye Saint-Germain ★ This is one of the district's most charming boutique hotels, built as a convent in the early 18th century. Its brightly colored rooms have traditional furniture, plus touches of sophisticated flair. In front is a small garden and in back is a verdant courtyard with a fountain, raised flower beds, and masses of ivy and climbing vines. If you don't mind the expense, one of the most charming rooms has a terrace overlooking the upper floors of neighboring buildings. Guest rooms are midsize to large and are continually maintained. Suites are large and full of Left Bank charm, often with antique reproductions.

10 rue Cassette, 75006 Paris. www.hotelabbayeparis.com. ✆ **01-45-44-38-11.** Fax 01-45-48-07-86. 44 units. 240€–352€ double; 442€–498€ suite. Rates include breakfast. AE, MC, V. Métro: St-Sulpice. **Amenities:** Bar; room service. *In room:* A/C, TV, hair dryer, Wi-Fi (free).

Hôtel Delavigne Despite modernization, you still get a sense of the 18th-century origins of the building, which is next to the Luxembourg Gardens. The public areas reveal a rustic use of chiseled stone, some of it original. The high-ceilinged guest rooms are tasteful, sometimes with wooden furniture, Spanish-style wrought iron, and upholstered headboards.

1 rue Casimir Delavigne, 75006 Paris. www.hoteldelavigne.com. ✆ **01-43-29-31-50.** Fax 01-43-29-78-56. 34 units. 160€–230€ double; 270€ triple. AE (accepted for Internet reservations only), MC, V. Métro: Odéon. **Amenities:** Babysitting; concierge; room service. *In room:* TV, hair dryer, Wi-Fi (free).

Hôtel des Marronniers ☺ In the heart of St-Germain-des-Prés, this is one of those hidden gems that is nestled in the back of a courtyard on a street lined with antiques stores. At the rear of this "secret" address is a small garden with a veranda, where you can linger over afternoon tea. Some of the rooms open onto views of the steeple of the church of St-Germain-des-Prés. The midsize bedrooms were renovated in 2012, and have a contemporary style. Three- and four-person bedrooms are available for families.

21 rue Jacob, 75006 Paris. www.paris-hotel-marronniers.com. ✆ **01-43-25-30-60.** Fax 01-40-46-83-56. 37 units. 180€–195€ double. MC, V. Métro: St-Germain-des-Prés. *In room:* A/C, TV, hair dryer, Wi-Fi (free).

Hôtel Le Sainte-Beuve ★ 🎁 Lying off the tree-lined boulevard Raspail, this quiet and charming choice is close to the "Lost Generation" cafes made famous in the pages of Ernest Hemingway's *The Sun Also Rises*. If you stay here, you're just 3 minutes from the Luxembourg Gardens. You enter a small reception area opening into a Georgian parlor with plush sofas, armchairs, columns, and even a marble fireplace for those nippy Paris nights. Bedrooms are often furnished in part with antiques, but have all the modern comforts. The cheaper rooms are small. If you can afford it, ask for one of the deluxe units that also has love seats and safes.

9 rue St-Beuve, 75006 Paris. www.hotel-sainte-beuve.fr. ☏ **01-45-48-20-07.** Fax 01-45-48-67-52. 22 units. 159€–332€ double; 282€–372€ junior suite. AE, DC, MC, V. Métro: Notre-Dame-des-Champs or Vavin. **Amenities:** Bar; babysitting; room service. *In room:* A/C, TV, hair dryer, minibar, Wi-Fi (free).

Hôtel Louis II ★   In an 18th-century building on the rue St-Sulpice, this elegant boutique hotel offers guest rooms decorated in modern French tones. Afternoon drinks and morning coffee are served in the reception salon, where gilt-framed mirrors, fresh flowers, and antiques radiate a provincial aura, as though something out of Proust. The generally small, soundproof rooms with exposed beams and lace bedding complete the impression. Many visitors ask for the romantic attic rooms.

2 rue St-Sulpice, 75006 Paris. www.hotel-louis2.com. ☏ **01-46-33-13-80.** Fax 01-46-33-17-29. 22 units. 195€–220€ double; 310€ junior suite. AE, DC, MC, V. Métro: Odéon. **Amenities:** Bar; room service. *In room:* A/C, TV, hair dryer, minibar, Wi-Fi (free).

Hôtel Pas-de-Calais   The Pas-de-Calais dates from the 17th century. It retains its elegant facade, with wooden doors. Novelist Chateaubriand lived here from 1811 to 1814, but its most famous guest was Jean-Paul Sartre, who struggled with the play *Les Mains Sales (Dirty Hands)* in room no. 41. The hotel was renovated recently. Rooms are small; inner units surround a courtyard with two garden tables and several trellises. From January until the end of March, the hotel often grants substantial discounts.

59 rue des Sts-Pères, 75006 Paris. www.hotelpasdecalais.com. ☏ **01-45-48-78-74.** Fax 01-45-44-94-57. 38 units. 180€–260€ double; 315€ suite. AE, DC, MC, V. Parking 25€. Métro: St-Germain-des-Prés or Sèvres-Babylone. **Amenities:** Bar; babysitting; room service. *In room:* A/C, TV, hair dryer, Wi-Fi (free).

Hôtel Récamier ★★   Sitting on the picturesque place St-Sulpice, this intimate little hotel resembles a charming private home. Its 24 individually decorated rooms offer elegant calm and comfort, with quality textiles and linens spiced up with original art works and unexpected details. The deluxe rooms have views over the square and its 17th-century church. The quality of the service is excellent, there's a complimentary tea time in the salon every day between 4 and 6pm, and room service is available until 11pm (the home-made soups are especially popular). If you do make it out, all St-Germain is at your feet.

3 bis place St.-Sulpice, Paris 75006. www.hotelrecamier.com. ☏ **01-43-26-04-89.** Fax 01-43-26-35-76. 24 units. 260€–450€ double. AE, DC, MC, V. Métro: St-Sulpice. **Amenities:** Bar; room service. *In room:* A/C, TV, hair dryer, minibar, Wi-Fi (free).

L'Apostrophe ★ 🛏   This Rive Gauche boutique hotel lies near the Café de Flore and Café des Deux-Magots, once the favorite literary haunts of some of France's most celebrated writers. This hotel pays homage to that tradition, becoming the first Parisian "poem hotel," an establishment devoted to the aesthetic, beauty, and mystery of writing. On the ground floor is painted the story of *One Thousand and One Nights*. The first floor is devoted to the markings that predate writing. On the second floor are signs indicating the alphabet, calligraphy, and music. The third floor is devoted to books and posters. A stay here is like no other in Paris. Bedrooms are beautifully decorated and comfortable, though a bit small. Be aware that the shower and water basin are actually in the room—the shower is visible through a glass door, but the toilet is in its own room.

3 rue de Chevreuse, 75006 Paris. www.apostrophe-hotel.com. ℂ **01-56-54-31-31.** 16 units. 149€–290€ standard double; 199€–350€ double with a Jacuzzi. Métro: Vavin. **Amenities:** Bar. *In room:* A/C, TV/DVD, CD player, hair dryer, Wi-Fi (free).

La Villa St-Germain ★ This hotel's facade resembles those of many of the other buildings in the neighborhood. Inside, however, the decor is a minimalist ultramodern creation rejecting traditional French aesthetics. The public areas and guest rooms contain Bauhaus-like furniture; the lobby's angular lines are softened with bouquets of leaves and flowers. Most unusual are the tubs, with decidedly postmodern stainless steel and pink, black, or beige marble.

29 rue Jacob, 75006 Paris. www.villa-saintgermain.com. ℂ **01-43-26-60-00.** Fax 01-46-34-63-63. 31 units. 280€–390€ double; from 480€ suite. AE, DC, MC, V. Métro: St-Germain-des-Prés. **Amenities:** Bar; babysitting; room service. *In room:* A/C, TV, hair dryer, minibar, Wi-Fi (free).

Le Placide ★★ 🏠 Converted from a former family home in the 19th century, Le Placide has the aura of a private club. This small boutique hotel—there are only two rooms per floor—lies just steps from the chic Bon Marché department store. It was designed by a member of Philippe Starck's firm, who brought a 21st-century style of luxury and comfort to the interior, featuring white Moroccan leather, lots of glass, a bit of chrome, and a crystal pedestal table. Fresh flowers adorn each room, and rose petals are placed on your bed at night. The spacious bathrooms provide natural light.

6 rue St-Placide, 75006 Paris. www.leplacidehotel.com. ℂ **01-42-84-34-60.** 11 units. 153€–530€ double. AE, MC, V. Métro: St-Placide. **Amenities:** Bar. *In room:* A/C, TV/DVD, CD player, hair dryer, minibar, MP3 docking station, Wi-Fi (free).

Prince de Condé In the heart of St-Germain-des-Prés, with all its art galleries, this 18th-century building has been restored and turned into the epitome of Left Bank charm. Guests gather in the elegant lounge with its cozy ambience, carved stone walls, and arches. The wallpapered bedrooms, small to midsize, are comfortably furnished and intimate, each tidily maintained with double-glazed windows.

39 rue de Seine, 75006 Paris. www.prince-de-conde.com. ℂ **01-43-26-71-56.** Fax 01-46-34-27-95. 11 units. 234€ double; 280€ suite. AE, MC, V. Métro: St-Germain-des-Prés. *In room:* A/C, TV, hair dryer, minibar, Wi-Fi (free).

Villa Madame ★ In the heart of St-Germain-des-Prés, this hotel is a smart Left Bank address in a neighborhood of tiny boutiques and fashionable hair salons, just a short walk from Jardin du Luxembourg. The bedrooms are sleek and modern with the latest gadgets. We prefer the accommodations on the top floor, with their balconies overlooking the rooftops of Paris. There is an inside courtyard, where you can order breakfast or else drinks in the evening. The Big Salon is actually a tearoom with a fireplace.

44 rue Madame, 75006 Paris. www.hotelvillamadameparis.com. ℂ **01-45-48-02-81.** Fax 01-45-44-85-73. 28 units. 225€–325€ double; 505€ suite. AE, DC, MC. Métro: Rennes or St-Sulpice. RER: Luxembourg. *In room:* A/C, TV, minibar, Wi-Fi (free).

WHERE TO STAY | The Left Bank

INEXPENSIVE

Grand Hôtel des Balcons   The Corroyer-André family welcome you to this restored 19th-century building, once patronized by Baudelaire and the poets Henri Michaux and Endre Ady. You enter an Art Nouveau setting with stained-glass windows and tulip-shaped molten glass lamps and chandeliers. The hotel lies behind a restored façade studded with small balconies—hence, its name. Bedrooms are not only affordable, but also harmonious in decor and comfort. Close to the gardens of Luxembourg, the rooms are not large but ample enough for big closets and full-length dressing mirrors.

3 rue Casimir Delavigne, 75006 Paris. www.balcons.com. ✆ **01-46-34-78-50.** Fax 01-46-34-06-27. 50 units. 125€ double; 220€ triple or quad. AE, MC, V. Métro: Odéon. RER: Luxembourg. *In room:* TV, hair dryer, Wi-Fi (free).

Hôtel Le Clément   This charming two-star hotel sits on a narrow street within sight of the towers of St-Sulpice church. The building dates from the 1700s, but was renovated several years ago. Rooms are comfortably furnished, with elegant upholstered walls, but many are small.

6 rue Clément, 75006 Paris. www.hotelclementparis.com. ✆ **01-43-26-53-60.** Fax 01-44-07-06-83. 28 units. 126€–148€ double; 165€ suite. AE, DC, MC, V. Métro: Mabillon. **Amenities:** Bar; room service. *In room:* A/C, TV, fax, hair dryer, Wi-Fi (free).

Hotel Mayet ★ 🎒   This affordable hotel has a great location close to shopping heaven Le Bon Marché and St-Germain. The compact rooms are clean, comfortable, and contemporary, designed in a bordeaux and gray color scheme. The low-key lobby sets the scene: deep, comfortable sofas are set against a brightly painted wall with some original graffiti by Parisian artist André. There's an iMac computer in the lobby with Internet access. Service goes the extra mile.

3 rue Mayet, 75006 Paris. www.mayet.com. ✆ **01-47-83-21-35.** Fax 01-40-65-95-78. 23 units. 140€–175€ double. Rates include breakfast. AE, DC, MC, V. Métro: Duroc. **Amenities:** Bar, breakfast room. *In room:* A/C, minibar, TV, Wi-Fi (free).

Eiffel Tower & Nearby (7e)

Running along the Seine on the Left Bank, from the Musée d'Orsay to the Eiffel Tower and opposite the Louvre, this elegant residential neighborhood counts Monsieur Karl Lagerfeld as one of its well-heeled inhabitants.

Best For: Its proximity to major monuments and museums.
Drawbacks: Can be a touch bourgeois for some.

EXPENSIVE

Hôtel Montalembert ★   The elegant Montalembert dates from 1926, when it was built in the Beaux-Arts style. Its beige, cream, and gold decor borrows elements of Bauhaus and postmodern design. The guest rooms are spacious except for some standard doubles that are small unless you're a very thin model. Frette linens decorate roomy beds topped with cabana-stripe duvets that crown deluxe French mattresses, and bathrooms are stocked with L'Occitane products.

3 rue de Montalembert, 75007 Paris. www.hotel-montalembert.fr. ✆ **800/786-6397** in the U.S. and Canada, or 01-45-49-68-68. Fax 01-45-49-69-49. 56 units. 300€–520€ double; 650€–900€ suite. AE, DC, MC, V. Parking 33€. Métro: Rue du Bac. **Amenities:** Restaurant; bar; concierge; access to nearby health club; room service. *In room:* A/C, TV, DVD, hair dryer, iPod Dock, minibar, Wi-Fi (free).

Hôtel Thoumieux ★★ ✍ This hotel-cum-dining destination is a collaboration between Chef Jean-François Piège and Paris dining baron Thierry Costes. Parisians and visitors flock here to eat in either the buzzing brasserie downstairs or the fine dining restaurant, with two Michelin stars, upstairs. The restaurants are so successful that in 2011, the owners opened up this boutique hotel in the rest of the building. Decorated by celebrated interior designer India Mahdavi, the rooms evoke the 1950s, and are colorful yet elegant, adorned with loud prints on the wallpaper, carpet, and upholstery. Though the hotel lacks an elevator, each room is an oasis, with an iPad, an iHome system, a coffee machine, and a complimentary (alcohol-free) minibar. This place oozes contemporary Parisian extravagance.

79 rue St-Dominique, 75007 Paris. www.thoumieux.fr. ✆ **01-47-05-79-00.** Fax 01-47-05-36-96. 15 units. 200€–400€ double. AE, DC, MC, V. Métro: Rue du Bac. **Amenities:** 2 restaurants; bar; room service. *In room:* A/C, TV, hair dryer, iHome, iPad, minibar, Wi-Fi (free).

MODERATE

Bourgogne & Montana Across from the Palais Bourbon and just 2 blocks from the Seine, this boutique hotel dates from 1791. A 1924 cage elevator takes visitors to the accommodations, which are midsize for the most part, although some are small and have no view whatsoever. Two of the bedrooms open onto the Grand Palais or the Assemblée Nationale. Each room is individually decorated, often in Empire style or with Empire reproductions. *Note:* The hotel is slated to close for about 3 months at the beginning of 2013 for a complete make-over.

3 rue de Bourgogne, 75007 Paris. www.bourgogne-montana.com. ✆ **01-45-51-20-22.** Fax 01-45-56-11-98. 32 units. 230€–305€ double; 410€ junior suite. Rates include breakfast. AE, DC, MC, V. Métro: Invalides. **Amenities:** Bar; babysitting; room service. *In room:* A/C, TV, hair dryer, minibar, Wi-Fi (free).

Derby Eiffel This hotel faces the Ecole Militaire and contains airy public areas. Our favorite is a glass-roofed conservatory in back, filled with plants and used as a breakfast area. The soundproof and modern guest rooms are fairly basic, but employ thick fabrics and soothing neutral colors. Most front-facing rooms have balconies with views of the Eiffel Tower.

5 av. Duquesne, 75007 Paris. www.hotelsderby.com. ✆ **01-47-05-12-05.** Fax 01-47-05-43-43. 43 units. 155€–196€ double. AE, DC, MC, V. Métro: Ecole Militaire. **Amenities:** Bar; babysitting; concierge; room service. *In room:* A/C, TV, hair dryer, minibar, Wi-Fi (5€ per day).

Hôtel de l'Académie The exterior walls and old ceiling beams are all that remain of this 18th-century residence of the duc de Rohan's private guards. Other than its associations with the duc de Rohan, this place is locally famous for having housed poet and novelist Antonio Marchado, "the Victor Hugo of Spain," between 1909 and 1914. Guest rooms have a lush Ile-de-France decor and views over the neighborhood's 18th- and 19th-century buildings. Rooms are smallish.

32 rue des Sts-Pères, 75007 Paris. www.academiehotel.com. ✆ **800/246-0041** in the U.S. and Canada, or 01-45-49-80-00. Fax 01-45-44-75-24. 34 units. 199€–229€ double; from 299€ junior suite. AE, DC, MC, V. Parking 23€. Métro: St-Germain-des-Prés. **Amenities:** Babysitting; room service. *In room:* A/C, TV, hair dryer, minibar, Wi-Fi (free).

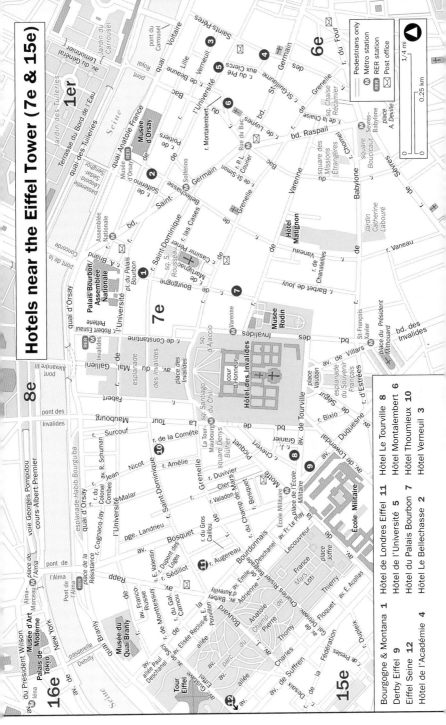

Hotels near the Eiffel Tower (7e & 15e)

Bourgogne & Montana 1
Derby Eiffel 9
Eiffel Seine 12
Hôtel de l'Académie 4
Hôtel de Londres Eiffel 11
Hôtel de l'Université 5
Hôtel du Palais Bourbon 7
Hôtel Le Bellechasse 2
Hôtel Le Tourville 8
Hôtel Montalembert 6
Hôtel Thoumieux 10
Hôtel Verneuil 3

Pedestrians only
Ⓜ Metro station
RER RER station
☒ Post office

0   0.25 km
0   1/4 mi

Hôtel de Londres Eiffel ★★ Small and charming, this independently-run hotel is just a 2-minute walk from the Eiffel Tower. Completely renovated, it is "dressed" in colors of yellow and raspberry, which is far more harmonious and elegant than the combination sounds. In a residential district (one of the best in Paris), the bedrooms are midsize and tastefully decorated, each with an individual decor. The top floors open onto views of the illuminated Eiffel Tower at night.

1 rue Augereau, 75007 Paris. www.londres-eiffel.com. © 01-45-51-63-02. Fax 01-47-05-28-96. 30 units. 190€–230€ double; 390€ suite. AE, DC, MC. Parking 34€. Métro: Ecole Militaire. **Amenities:** Concierge. *In room:* A/C, TV, hair dryer, minibar, Wi-Fi (free).

Hôtel de l'Université This 300-year-old, antiques-filled town house enjoys a location in a discreetly upscale neighborhood. Room no. 54 is a favorite, containing a rattan bed, period pieces, and a terrace. Another charmer is room no. 35, which has a nonworking fireplace and opens onto a courtyard with a fountain. Beds have plush comfort and discreet French styling. You'll sleep well here. A complete renovation in 2011 improved the comfort and modernity of all the rooms and public areas.

22 rue de l'Université, 75007 Paris. www.hoteluniversite.com. © **01-42-61-09-39.** Fax 01-42-60-40-84. 27 units. 190€–350€ double. AE, DC, MC, V. Métro: St-Germain-des-Prés. **Amenities:** Room service. *In room:* A/C, TV, hair dryer, minibar, Wi-Fi (free).

Hôtel du Palais Bourbon ★ The solid stone walls of this 18th-century building aren't as grand as those of the embassies and stately homes nearby. But don't be put off by the tight entranceway and rather dark halls: Though the guest rooms on the upper floors are larger, all the rooms are comfortable and pleasantly decorated, with carefully crafted built-in furniture.

49 rue de Bourgogne, 75007 Paris. www.hotel-palais-bourbon.com. © **01-44-11-30-70.** Fax 01-45-55-20-21. 29 units. 195€–220€ double. Rates include breakfast. MC, V. Métro: Varenne. **Amenities:** Room service. *In room:* A/C, TV, hair dryer, minibar, Wi-Fi (free).

Hôtel Le Bellechasse ★★ 🏆 This gem of a hotel, seconds on foot from the Musée d'Orsay, is still one of the city's most fanciful designer hotels. It's the creation of couturier Christian Lacroix, who let his imagination go wild. A stay here is like wandering into a psychedelic garden. Each guest room is different in a pastiche of colors with baroque overtones. One French critic called Lacroix's designs "magpie sensibility," perhaps a reference to one room where top-hatted, frock-coated Paris dandies with butterfly wings wrap around both walls and ceilings. The helpful staff is part of the fun—that and taking a bath in a fiberglass tub.

8 rue de Bellechasse, 75007 Paris. www.lebellechasse.com. © **01-45-50-22-31.** Fax 01-45-51-52-36. 34 units. 160€–245€ double. MC, V. Métro: Solferino. RER: Musée d'Orsay. **Amenities:** Dining room (breakfast). *In room:* A/C, TV, TV/DVD, CD player, hair dryer, minibar, MP3 docking station, Wi-Fi (free).

Hôtel Le Tourville This town house between the Eiffel Tower and Les Invalides originated in the 1930s as a hotel and was revitalized much later into the charmer it is today. Bedrooms offer original art, antique furnishings or reproductions, and wooden furniture covered in modern, sometimes bold, upholsteries. Four of the rooms, including the suite, have private terraces. Beds are queens or twins, each of which was recently replaced. The staff is well trained, with the kinds of personalities that make you want to linger at the reception desk. Breakfast is the only meal served, but you can get a drink in the lobby.

16 av. de Tourville, 75007 Paris. www.hoteltourville.com. ✆ **01-47-05-62-62.** Fax 01-47-05-43-90. 30 units. 210€–300€ double; 380€–470€ suite. AE, MC, V. Métro: Ecole Militaire. **Amenities:** Bar; concierge; room service. *In room:* A/C, TV, hair dryer, Wi-Fi (free).

Hôtel Verneuil ★ 🏨   Small-scale and personal, this hotel feels modern, while still evoking nostalgia for *la vieille France* (old-fashioned France). Built in the 1600s as a town house, it is a creative and intimate jumble of charm and coziness inside. All the rooms were renovated in 2012. Expect a mixture of antique and contemporary furniture; lots of books; and, in the bedrooms, *trompe l'oeil* ceilings, antique beams, quilts, and walls covered in fabric that comes in a rainbow of colors.

8 rue de Verneuil, 75007 Paris. www.hotelverneuil.com. ✆ **01-42-60-82-14.** Fax 01-42-61-40-38. 26 units. 185€–276€ double. AE, DC, MC, V. Métro: St-Germain-des-Prés. **Amenities:** Bar; babysitting; room service. *In room:* A/C (in some), TV, hair dryer, minibar, Wi-Fi (free).

Montparnasse & Southern Paris (14e & 15e)

Back in the early days of the 20th century, Montparnasse was a hotbed of creativity. Between the two World Wars, artists, expats, and extravagant figures such as Kiki de Montparnasse and Gertrude Stein reinvented the world in the bars and cafes of the area.

Best For: Travelers looking for a quiet residential zone with a rich history.
Drawbacks: Much of the area shuts down early in the evening.

MODERATE

Eiffel Seine ★   Rising on the banks of the Seine, this Art Nouveau–style hotel lies only 5 minutes by foot from the Eiffel Tower. That style pervades the hotel from the reception lounge to the personalized doubles and family rooms. Two ground floor rooms, opening onto an interior garden, are suited for persons with disabilities. Each room has its own special decoration, and the decor is harmonious from the tiles to the wallpaper to the mirrors and wall lamps. The quiet rooms are filled with modern technology as well as comfy beds.

3 bd. De Grenelle, 75015 Paris. www.paris-hotel-eiffelseine.com. ✆ **01-45-78-14-81.** Fax 01-45-79-46-95. 45 units. 162€–230€ double. MC, V. Métro: Bir Hakeim. **Amenities:** Exercise room. *In room:* A/C, TV, TV/DVD, room service, Wi-Fi (free).

INEXPENSIVE

Apollon Montparnasse   This privately owned hotel lies in Montparnasse, former home of such famous Left Bank residents as Gertrude Stein and Alice B. Toklas. People come here for the hotel's good rates and very comfortable bedrooms, which are midsize and furnished with flower spreads and draperies. The building was originally constructed in the 1930s as private apartments, and was completely renovated in 2009. The clean and simple rooms are decorated with pale wood and gray-and-white-striped wall paper.

91 rue de l'Ouest, 75014 Paris. www.apollon-montparnasse.com. ✆ **01-43-95-62-00.** Fax 01-43-95-62-10. 33 units. 130€–142€ double. AE, DC, MC, V. Métro: Pernety. Parking 18€. **Amenities:** Room service. *In room:* A/C, TV, hair dryer, minibar, Wi-Fi (free).

NEAR THE AIRPORTS

Orly

Air Plus This hotel offers standard rooms that are comfortable, insulated against airport noise, and a bit larger than you might expect. The location is in an out-of-the-way, leafy residential zone. It is connected with Orly by 10-minute complimentary shuttle-bus rides, which can be irregular, so it's worth checking the timetable with the hotel directly.

58 voie Nouvelle (near the Parc Georges Mélliès), 94310 Orly. www.hotelairplus.com. ☎ **01-41-80-75-75.** Fax 01-41-80-12-12. 72 units. 110€ double; 125€ triple. AE, DC, MC, V. Free parking. Transit to and from airport by complimentary shuttle bus. **Amenities:** Restaurant; room service. *In room:* A/C, TV, hair dryer, Wi-Fi (free).

Hilton Paris Orly Airport ★ Boxy and bland, the Hilton at Orly is a well-maintained and convenient business hotel. Noise from incoming planes can't penetrate the guest rooms' sound barriers, giving you a decent shot at a night's sleep. (Unlike the 24-hr. Charles de Gaulle Airport, Orly is closed to arriving flights from midnight–6am.) The midsize rooms are standard for a chain hotel; each has been renovated.

Aéroport Orly, 267 Orly Sud, 94544 Orly Aérogare Cedex. www.hilton.com. ☎ **800/445-8667** in the U.S. and Canada, or 01-45-12-45-12. Fax 01-45-12-45-00. 351 units. 90€–250€ double; 300€ suite. AE, DC, MC, V. Parking 14€. Transit to and from airport by complimentary shuttle bus. **Amenities:** Restaurant; bar; babysitting; concierge; exercise room; room service. *In room:* A/C, TV, TV/DVD player, hair dryer, Wi-Fi (13€ per day).

Charles De Gaulle

Hyatt Regency Paris–Charles de Gaulle ★ This property is adjacent to the Charles de Gaulle Airport. Lying only a 25-minute drive from Disneyland Paris and a half-hour from the attractions of central Paris, the Roissy property was designed by the renowned architect Helmut Jahn. He created a stunning five-story structure of sleek design and tech-smart features. Jet-lagged passengers find comfort in the elegantly furnished and soundproof guest rooms, which meld modern convenience with European style.

351 av. du Bois de la Pie, 95912 Roissy. www.paris.charlesdegaulle.hyatt.fr. ☎ **01-48-17-12-34.** Fax 01-48-17-17-17. 388 units. 155€–255€ double; 265€–400€ suite. AE, DC, MC, V. RER-B train to its final destination (Aéroport Charles de Gaulle-Terminal Two). From there, take the hotel's shuttle bus (departures every 20 min.) directly to the hotel. Parking 29€. Free shuttle to and from airport. **Amenities:** Restaurant; bar; babysitting; concierge; exercise room; pool (indoor); room service; 2 tennis courts. *In room:* A/C, TV, TV/DVD, hair dryer, minibar, Wi-Fi (12€ per day).

ibis Paris CDG Terminal Roissy ★ Conveniently located near CDG's Terminal 3, this two-star hotel is the cheapest option near the airport. Recently renovated, the hotel rooms are clean and comfortable, though they are decorated in that bland aesthetic common to airports.

Roissy Aéroport, 95701 Roissy en France. www.ibishotel.com. ☎ **01-49-19-19-19.** Fax 01-49-19-19-21. 556 units. 79€–139€ double. AE, DC, MC, V. Parking 16€ per day. Transit to and from airport by complimentary shuttle bus. **Amenities:** 2 restaurants; bar; room service. *In room:* A/C, TV, hair dryer, minibar, Wi-Fi (free).

Novotel Convention & Wellness Roissy CDG ★ ☺ This comfortable four-star hotel located on the airport grounds is ideal for business travelers, families, or for people who need to be near the airport to make a flight. The hotel offers a Wellness Club, with a heated pool, hammam, sauna, gym, and beauty treatments to help exhausted travelers unwind. There are regular free shuttles that go between the hotel and the airport.

Allée des Vergers, 95700 Roissy. www.novotel.com. ℂ **01-30-18-20-00.** Fax 01-34-29-95-60. 289 units. 129€–295€ double. AE, DC, MC, V. Free shuttles 5:15am–12:30am btw. the RER/TGV train stations at Paris CDG airport and the hotel. Transit to and from airport terminals by free shuttle. Parking 21€ per day. **Amenities:** Restaurant; bar; babysitting; concierge; exercise room; pool (indoor); room service. *In room:* A/C, TV, hair dryer, minibar, Wi-Fi (free).

Pullman Paris Aéroport CDG Many travelers pass through this bustling, somewhat anonymous member of the French chain. It employs a multilingual staff accustomed to accommodating international business travelers. The conservatively furnished guest rooms are soundproof havens against the all-night roar of jets. Suites are larger and more comfortable, although they are not especially elegant.

Aéroport Charles de Gaulle, Zone Central, 20248, 95713 Roissy. www.pullmanhotels.com. ℂ **800/221-4542** in the U.S. and Canada, or 01-49-19-29-29. Fax 01-49-19-29-00. 350 units. 140€–370€ double; 450€–1,100€ suite. AE, DC, MC, V. Parking 12€. Free shuttle to and from airport. **Amenities:** Restaurant; bar; concierge; exercise room; room service. *In room:* A/C, TV, hair dryer, minibar, Wi-Fi (free).

PRACTICAL MATTERS: THE HOTEL SCENE

As in most large cities, accommodation choices in Paris vary widely. France rates its hotels by an official government star system, which is based on a complex formula of room sizes, facilities, plumbing, elevators, dining options, renovations, and so on. Hotels range from one star (for a simple inn) to five stars (for a luxury hotel), and since 2012 a reduced number of hotels boast the extra label "Palace Distinction." In one-star hotels, the bathrooms can be shared, the facilities are extremely limited (such as no elevator), the rooms may not have phones or TVs, and breakfast is often the only meal served. Despite limited amenities, they may be perfectly clean and decent places. Two- or three-star hotels usually have elevators, and rooms will likely have bathrooms, phones, and TVs. In four- and five-star establishments, you'll get all the amenities plus facilities and services such as room service, concierges, elevators, and perhaps even health clubs. Do remember that the system can be deceptive, and a charming two-star hotel in a historic building can be more appealing than a brand-new three-star hotel with all the amenities.

Because hot weather rarely lasts long in Paris, air-conditioning is not a standard feature in the city's hotels. If you're trapped in a garret on a hot summer night, you'll have to sweat it out. Noise can be an issue too, particularly in those rooms facing the street. Check if a room has double-glazed windows or ask for a room off the street. Expect rooms to be small unless you pay for a suite. Some hotel websites explain the differences between different room categories by including average room surface area. Beds are usually standard doubles, or queen size for superior rooms and the pricier hotels; it's rare to find a king-size bed. Be warned that you'll have to carry your bags to and from your room in most hotels—don't expect to find bellboys unless you're staying at a luxury hotel. Free Wi-Fi in rooms has become a standard offer for most hotels.

Getting the Best Deal

If you're looking for budget options, Paris has some good-value places in the lower price ranges, and we've included reviews for the best of these properties in this chapter.

Prices dip during Paris's low season over winter from November to February. The height of summer, during July and August, can be quiet too. Most visitors, at least those from North America, come to Paris at this time, but many French people are on vacation, and trade fairs and conventions come to a halt, so there are usually plenty of rooms available. Peak periods are from March to July and September to November, the major trade show season in September and October, and seasonal events like Fashion Week in early March and late September. Book ahead if you come during these times. If you arrive without a reservation, you may have to take what you can get, often at a much higher price than you'd like. It's true that you can almost always get a room at a deluxe hotel if you're willing to pay the price.

Online travel booking sites offer considerable discounts off of room rates. Check sites like Expedia, Priceline, ebookers.com, hotels.com, venere.com, france-hotel-guide.com, or booking.com to find discount rates on hotel rooms.

Reservation Services

Most hotels require a credit card number to confirm a reservation. You can usually cancel a room reservation 1 week ahead of time without paying a deposit. A few hotel keepers will return your money up to 3 days before the reservation date, but some will keep a deposit, even if you cancel far in advance. To secure special Internet deals, you often must pay up-front. If you'd prefer someone to take care of the details for you, check out **Mondiale Tourisme** (✆ **01-42-46-83-29;** www.mondialfrance.com), a Paris-based travel agency with an international team and 15 years of experience booking vacations both in Paris and throughout France.

Alternative Accommodations

More intimate than a hotel, a bed-and-breakfast within a private home can be an affordable and interesting option. The **Hôtes Qualité Paris** (www.hotesqualite paris.fr) is the city's official agency for professional B&Bs in selected private homes; it offers rooms for about 50€ to 140€ per person per night, based on double occupancy. **Alcôve & Agapes** (✆ **01-44-85-06-05;** www.bed-and-breakfast-in-paris. com) is a reliable private agency that promotes upmarket B&B accommodations in Paris. These services provide a bridge between travelers who seek rooms in private homes and Parisians who wish to welcome visitors. Most hosts speak at least some English, range in age from 30 to 75, and have at least some points of view about entertainment and dining options within the neighborhood. Available options include individual bedrooms, usually within large, old-fashioned private apartments, as well as "unhosted" accommodations where the apartment is otherwise empty and without the benefit (or restrictions) of a live-in host.

If you'd prefer to live like an expat, it is also possible to rent an apartment in Paris. A number of agencies lease apartments that are centrally located, furnished, and well-equipped; short- or long-term rentals are available. To rent an apartment in Paris, contact one of the following agencies: **Paris Attitude** (✆ **01-42-96-31-46;** www.parisattitude.com); **Parisian Home** (✆ **01-45-08-03-37;** www.parisianhome.com); **France Lodge** (✆ **01-56-33-85-85;** www.francelodge.fr); **Paris Appartements Services** (✆ **01-56-33-85-85;** www.paris-appartements-services.com); **Appartement de Ville** (✆ **01-40-28-01-28;** www.appartementdeville.com); or **Flip Key** (www.flipkey.com). Through these organizations, you will likely deal with the agency (not the owners), and the minimum stay is usually 1 week. Another option is **Airbnb** (www.airbnb.com), a network of accommodations offered directly by local owners.

It is possible to get a good deal at an *aparthotel,* a cross between a hotel and an apartment. Short on charm, these rentals are good on convenience, each with a kitchenette. Although rates are more than short-term studios, you get more of the services of a hotel, including fresh towels and a reception desk. The best known agency renting *aparthotels* is **Citadines** (✆ **08-25-33-33-32;** www.citadines.com). The cheapest rentals are the studios with pull-out beds; a studio for two might range from 140€ to 250€ a night—or even more in such highly prized locations as the Louvre area or St-Germain-des-Prés.

9

Practical Matters: The Hotel Scene

SIDE TRIPS FROM PARIS

By Lily Heise

10

P arisians generally feel that their capital is the center of the universe. They may be correct, if only geographically speaking. Paris is at the heart of the region of *Ile-de-France* (the Island of France) and is encircled by seven suburban *départements* commonly and regally referred to as the *petite* and *grande couronnes*. These "crowns" are dotted with cultural and historic treasures, from majestic palaces to picturesque artistic villages, and are only a short journey from the city center.

Bask in the glory of the French royals and nobles at the magnificent **Chateau de Versailles** or the more discrete **Châteaux de Fontainebleau** or **Vaux-le-Vicomte.** Step into the paintings of Monet and van Gogh at the picturesque villages of **Giverny** and **Auvers-sur-Oise.** Travel back to medieval France while wandering the narrow laneways of **Chartres** and marveling at the amazing stained glass of its cathedral. Kids of all ages can get their thrills at **Disneyland Paris.** In this chapter, we offer only a handful of the possibilities for day jaunts. For a more extensive list, see *Frommer's France.*

For pretrip planning, abundant visitor information can be found on the various websites listed in the details of our side trip destinations or on the office website for **Ile-de-France tourism** (www.new-paris-ile-de-france.co.uk). Once in Paris, you can also obtain more information at the main **Tourist Information Office,** 25 rue des Pyramides, 75001 Paris (📞 **01-49-52-42-63**). You can reach all of these destinations by train from Paris. Train tickets do not require reservations and can be bought the day of an excursion at the departing train or subway station. You can find more information about the train schedule of suburban trains at **www.transilien. com**; for national trains (only required for Chartres and Vernon/Giverny), check **www.voyages-sncf.com.** You can also inquire directly at any Paris train station (most have an information desk with staff who speak English).

VERSAILLES ★★★

21km (13 miles) SW of Paris, 71km (44 miles) NE of Chartres

Just 45 minutes southwest of Paris, Le Château de Versailles is the most sumptuous castle in Europe and forever associated with the Sun King, Louis XIV, and the doomed Queen Marie Antoinette. The palace's regal gardens were designed by the famous landscape architect, Le Nôtre, to create a French Eden. But the town of Versailles—practically synonymous with its decadent royal palace—has its pleasures too, with stately streets ringing the Cathédrale St-Louis, colorful markets, and antiques shops.

THINGS TO DO   Walk in the footsteps of the Sun King down the majestic **Hall of Mirrors** or imagine the daily rituals of court life while strolling through the **Petits & Grands Appartements.** The gardens contain a line-up of noble statuary, hidden *bosquets* (groves), and fountains adorned with frolicking Greek gods.

Trek across the park to see the royals' getaway retreat at the **Trianon Palaces** and **Marie Antoinette Hamlet.**

RESTAURANTS & DINING   The Trianon Palace Hotel is home to the wonderfully decadent **Gordon Ramsay au Trianon,** which offers a Michelin-starred English take on French classics. Sample royal veggies at **Le Potager du Roy** or head to affordable **rue de Satory,** where crêperies, Thai, and Lebanese restaurants line the street.

NIGHTLIFE & ENTERTAINMENT   Try to catch the famous *Grands Eaux Musicales,* when the fountains dance majestically to the rhythm of classical music. During the summer, the gardens are also the setting for nighttime spectacles of opera, theater, fireworks, and music, which capture the pomp of the celebrations the Sun King once hosted. If you're lucky, you can also catch "Les Fêtes de Nuit de Versailles," an impressive fireworks display around late August.

Essentials

GETTING THERE   To get to Versailles, catch the **RER** line C1 to Versailles–Rive Gauche at the Gare d'Austerlitz, St-Michel, Musée d'Orsay, Invalides, Ponte de l'Alma, Champ de Mars, or Javel stop, and take it to the Versailles–Rive Gauche station. The trip takes 35 to 40 minutes. Do not get off at Versailles Chantier, which will leave you on the other end of town, a long walk from the château. The round-trip fare is 6.50€; Eurailpass holders travel free on the RER but need to show the pass at the ticket kiosk to receive an RER ticket. A section of the RER C line within Paris (often a stretch of key stations from Gare d'Austerlitz to Invalides) may be closed from mid-July to mid-August for renovation work, scheduled to continue every summer until 2017. Ask any Métro ticket agent for re-routing assistance. **SNCF trains** (Société Nationale des Chemins de Fer) make frequent runs from Gare St-Lazare and Gare Montparnasse in Paris to Versailles: Trains departing from Gare St-Lazare arrive at the Versailles Rive Droite railway station; trains departing from Gare Montparnasse arrive at Versailles Chantiers station, a long walk as mentioned.

The Versailles–Rive Gauche station is within a 10-minute walk of the château, and we recommend the walk as a means of orienting yourself to the town, its geography, its scale, and its architecture. If you can't or don't want to walk, you can take bus B, or (in midsummer) a shuttle bus marked CHATEAU from either station to the château for either a cash payment of around 2€ (drop the coins directly into the coin box near the driver) or the insertion of a valid ticket for the Paris Métro. Because of the vagaries of the bus schedules, we highly recommend the walk. Directions to the château are clearly signposted from each railway station.

If you're **driving,** exit the *périphérique* (the ring road around Paris) on N10 (av. du Général-Leclerc), which will take you to Versailles; park on place d'Armes in front of the château.

TICKETS   You can purchase individual entrance tickets to the various sights, but the easiest option is an all-inclusive **Château Passeport,** which grants you access to the main chateau, the gardens (on special entrance days), the Trianon Palaces, and the Marie Antoinette Hamlet. From April to October the passport costs 18€ Monday to Friday, rising to 25€ on Saturday and Sunday. From November to March it costs 18€ per day. You can avoid the long lines

Île-de-France

at the château by purchasing the pass online at www.chateauversailles.fr or at the tourist office in Versailles. If you hold the **Paris Museum Pass,** admission is free to the château (but does not include the gardens on Tuesdays and the weekends in high season or the evening spectacles; supplementary garden tickets available onsite), and the pass also allows you to enter via the shorter advance ticket-holders' entrance.

VISITOR INFORMATION   The **Office de Tourisme** is at 2 bis av. de Paris (www. versailles-tourisme.com; ☏ **01-39-24-88-88;** fax 01-39-24-88-89;). Open April to October Tuesday to Sunday 9am to 7pm, Monday 10am to 6pm; November to March Tuesday to Saturday 9 to 6pm, Sunday and Monday 11am to 5pm.

EVENING SPECTACLES   Aiming to capitalize on its full potential, Versailles features a program of fireworks and illuminated fountains, "Les Fêtes de Nuit de Versailles," on about 7 to 10 widely publicized dates between late August and early September, usually beginning at 9:30pm. Observers, who sit in bleachers near the palace's boulevard de la Reine entrance, close to the Fountain (*Bassin*) of Neptune, are treated to a display of fireworks, prerecorded classical music, and up to 200 players in period costume, portraying the glories of France as symbolized by Louis XIV and the courtiers of the *Ancien Régime.* Shows are big on pomp and visuals, and last about 90 minutes. Tickets range from 15€ to 85€. Gates open around 90 minutes prior to showtime.

Since it reopened after an extensive restoration, big names in classical music, theater, and dance are filling the stage at the magnificent **Opéra Royal;** reserve well in advance and expect royal ticket prices (45€–100€). Tickets can be purchased online at www.chateauversailles-spectacles.fr or by phone at ✆ **01-30-83-78-89.**

DAYTIME SPECTACLES   *Les Grandes Eaux Musicales* are held Saturdays and Sundays from April to early October, between 11:30am and noon and 3:30 and 5pm. The spectacles showcase the landscaping vision of the palace's designers and encourage participants to walk, promenade, or meander the vast park, enjoying the juxtaposition of supremely grand architecture with lavish waterworks. On Tuesdays music is broadcast in the gardens; however, the fountains are only occasionally running. Admission to any part of the park during these spectacles can vary from 6€ to 10€. For information and a full schedule, see www.chateauversailles-spectacles.fr or call ✆ **01-30-83-78-89.**

You can purchase tickets to all spectacles at Versailles up until about a half-hour prior to the day or night of any performance from the ticket office in the *Accueil-Billeterie* on place d'Armes, immediately across from the main facade of the palace, online at www.chateauversailles-spectacles.fr or from any French branch of the FNAC department store (www.fnacspectacles. com; ✆ **01-55-21-57-93**).

Exploring Versailles

In 1661, Louis XIV set out to build a palace that would be the envy of Europe and created a symbol of opulence copied, yet never duplicated, the world over. Less than 40 years and more than 40,000 workmen later, the Château de Versailles was transformed from Louis XIII's humble hunting lodge into an extravagant palace and century-long base of the French court.

Wishing (with good reason) to keep an eye on the nobles of France, Louis XIV summoned them to live at his court. Here he amused them with constant entertainment and lavish banquets. To some he awarded such tasks as holding the hem of his robe. While the aristocrats played at often-silly intrigues and games, the peasants on the estates sowed the seeds of the revolution.

Le Château de Versailles.

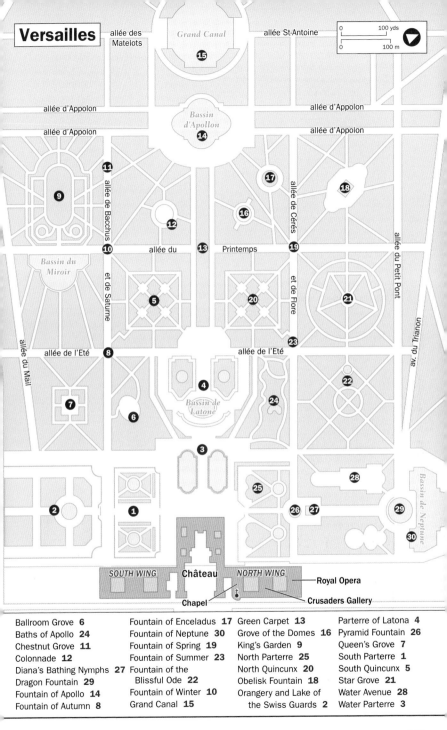

Versailles

allée des Matelots

Grand Canal **15**

allée St-Antoine

| 0 | 100 yds |
| 0 | 100 m |

allée d'Appolon

allée d'Appolon

Bassin d'Apollon **14**

allée d'Appolon

allée d'Appolon

11

9

allée de Bacchus

17

18

allée de Cérès

12

16

10

allée du

13

Printemps

19

Bassin du Miroir

et de Saturne

5

20

et de Flore

21

allée du Petit Pont

allée de l'Eté

8

allée de l'Eté

23

allée du Mail

7

6

4

Bassin de Latone

24

22

av. du Trianon

3

28

Bassin de Neptune

2

1

25

26 **27**

29

30

SOUTH WING

Château

NORTH WING

Royal Opera

Chapel

Crusaders Gallery

Ballroom Grove **6**
Baths of Apollo **24**
Chestnut Grove **11**
Colonnade **12**
Diana's Bathing Nymphs **27**
Dragon Fountain **29**
Fountain of Apollo **14**
Fountain of Autumn **8**

Fountain of Enceladus **17**
Fountain of Neptune **30**
Fountain of Spring **19**
Fountain of Summer **23**
Fountain of the Blissful Ode **22**
Fountain of Winter **10**
Grand Canal **15**

Green Carpet **13**
Grove of the Domes **16**
King's Garden **9**
North Parterre **25**
North Quincunx **20**
Obelisk Fountain **18**
Orangery and Lake of the Swiss Guards **2**

Parterre of Latona **4**
Pyramid Fountain **26**
Queen's Grove **7**
South Parterre **1**
South Quincunx **5**
Star Grove **21**
Water Avenue **28**
Water Parterre **3**

Contemporary Versailles

Even though it is one of France's most visited sights, Versailles still attempts to attract regular visitors through a program of controversial temporary exhibits by international contemporary artists such as Jeff Koons and Takashi Murakami. The Sun King might be rolling in his grave, but the shows have drawn in huge crowds of new admirers to the Château.

When Louis XIV died in 1715, his great-grandson Louis XV succeeded him and continued the outrageous pomp, though he is said to have predicted the outcome: *"Après moi, le déluge"* ("After me, the deluge"). His Polish wife, Marie Leszczynska, was shocked by the blatant immorality at Versailles.

The next monarch, Louis XVI, found his grandfather's behavior scandalous—in fact, on gaining the throne, he ordered that the "stairway of indiscretion" (secret stairs leading to the king's bedchamber) be removed. The well-intentioned but weak king and his queen, Marie Antoinette, were well liked at first, but the queen's frivolity and spending led to her downfall. Louis and Marie Antoinette were at Versailles on October 6, 1789, when they were notified that mobs were marching on the palace. As predicted, *le déluge* had arrived.

Château de Versailles ★★★
PALACE/MUSEUM/GARDEN
Upon entering the grand palace of Versailles, before going up to the second floor which houses most of the highlights, have a quick glance at the **Chapel**. Designed by Hardouin-Mansart, it was the fifth chapel to be built at Versailles. This was where the Sun King attended Mass every morning and where Louis XVI married Marie Antoinette in 1770, while he was the Dauphin.

Upstairs, step into the magnificent **Grands Appartements ★★★**. In the Louis XIV style, each bears the name of the allegorical painting on the ceiling. The best-known and largest is the **Hercules Salon ★★**, with a ceiling painted by François Lemoine depicting the Apotheosis of Hercules. In the **Mercury Salon** (with a ceiling by Jean-Baptiste Champaigne), the body of Louis XIV was put on display in 1715; his 72-year reign was one of the longest in history.

The most famous room at Versailles is the 71m-long (233-ft.) **Hall of Mirrors ★★★**. Begun by Mansart in 1678 in the Louis XIV style, it was decorated by Le Brun with 17 arched windows faced by beveled mirrors in simulated arcades. In 2007, a

Grands Appartements.

Hall of Mirrors.

Gardens of Versailles.

$16-million makeover was completed, returning the Hall of Mirrors to its original appearance during the reign of the Sun King. Several important events took place here, including the proclamation of the German Empire in 1871, and the Treaty of Versailles was signed here on June 28, 1919, officially ending World War I.

The royal apartments were for the public life of the kings, but Louis XV and Louis XVI retired to the **Petits Appartements ★★** to escape the demands of court etiquette. Louis XV died in his bedchamber in 1774, a victim of smallpox. In a second-floor apartment, which you can visit only with a guide, he stashed away his mistresses, first Mme de Pompadour and then Mme du Barry. Despite being pillaged in the revolution, the **Queen's Apartments** have been restored to their appearance in the days of Marie Antoinette, when she played her harpsichord in front of special guests. Her **bathroom** underwent a renovation in late 2011.

Louis XVI had a sumptuous **Library,** designed by Jacques-Ange Gabriel, the designer of place de la Concorde in Paris. Its panels are delicately carved, and the room has been restored and refurnished. The **Clock Room** contains Passement's astronomical clock, encased in gilded bronze. Twenty years in the making, it was completed in 1753. The clock is supposed to keep time until the year 9999. At age 7, Mozart played for the court in this room. Gabriel also designed the **Opéra ★★** for Louis XV in 1748, though it wasn't completed until 1770. In its heyday, it took 3,000 candles to light the place.

In 2005, previously off-limits sections of the palace were opened to the public including the mammoth **Battle Gallery,** which, at 119m (390 ft.), is the longest hall at Versailles. The gallery displays monumental paintings depicting all of France's great battles, ranging from the founding of the monarchy by Clovis, who reigned in the 5th and 6th centuries, through the Napoleonic wars in the early 19th century.

Spread across 100 hectares (247 acres), the **Gardens of Versailles ★★★** were laid out by landscape artist André Le Nôtre. He created a Garden of Eden

Versailles' *Jardins Secrets*

Tucked away in the wooded areas of the gardens are various *bosquets* (groves). These hidden gardens each have a specific theme, and several have significant links to certain royals. The **Apollo Baths,** surrounded by a mix of English and Chinese gardens, were constructed on the request of Louis XIV's mistress Mme de Montespan. The **Queen's Grove** was the setting of the infamous 1785 Affair of the Diamond Necklace (when Marie Antoinette was wrongly accused of arranging the purchase of an exorbitantly priced diamond necklace), which forever tarnished Marie Antoinette's image—despite her innocence. Today they offer visitors a quiet escape from the masses marching along the Grand Canal.

using ornamental lakes and canals, geometrically designed flower beds, and avenues bordered with statuary. At the peak of their glory, 1,400 fountains spewed forth. One of the most famous fountains, located at the base of the Grand Canal, where Louis XV used to take gondola rides with his favorite mistress of the moment, depicts Apollo in his chariot pulled by four horses, surrounded by Tritons rising from the water.

Equestrians and horse lovers shouldn't miss **Les Grandes Ecuries** (the Stables), situated immediately opposite the château's main front facade, where the horses and carriages of the kings were housed. Today the **Académie de Spectacle Equestre** is housed here, directed by Bartabas, whose equestrian theater company, Zingaro, has garnered world fame. Visitors can watch a team of up to a dozen riding school students, with their mounts, strut their stuff during hour-long riding demonstrations within the covered, 17th-century amphitheater of the historic stables. Demonstrations are conducted Thursday, and Saturday and Sunday at 11:15am; tickets cost 6.50€ to 12€. On some weekend afternoons, a more elaborate "equestrian ballet" is on offer; tickets to those shows are 25€. After the shows visitors are able to tour the stables. For additional information see www.bartabas.fr/Academie-du-spectacle-equestre.

Place d'Armes. www.chateauversailles.fr. ⓒ **01-30-83-78-00.** Palace 15€ adults; free for 18 and under. Both Trianons and Le Hameau (see below) 10€ adults; everything free for children 17 and younger. Palace Apr–Oct Tues–Sun 9am–6:30pm; Nov–Mar Tues–Sun 9am–5:30pm. Trianons and Le Hameau Tues–Sun noon–6pm. Grounds daily dawn–dusk.

The Trianons & The Hamlet ROYAL BUILDING/GARDEN   A long walk across the garden (or a short ride on the park's little train), will take you to the pink-and-white-marble **Grand Trianon ★★**, the first building of what would become the royals' escape from the formalities (and lack of privacy) of court life. Louis XIV had Le Vau build a Porcelain Trianon here in 1670, covered with blue-and-white china tiles, but its fragile construction was short-lived. So, in 1687, the king commissioned Hardouin-Mansart to build the Grand Trianon. Traditionally, it has been a place where France has lodged important guests, though de Gaulle wanted to turn it into a weekend retreat. Nixon once slept here in the room where Mme de Pompadour died. The original furnishings are gone, of course, with mostly Empire pieces there today.

Opened to the public in 2006, **Le Petit Trianon ★★** was designed in 1768 by Gabriel for Louis XV. It served as a discrete venue for the King's trysts with Mme du Barry. When he died, Louis XVI presented it to his wife, and Marie

Le Hameau (Hamlet).

Antoinette adopted it as her favorite residence, a place to escape the rigid life and oppressive scrutiny at the main palace. Many of the current furnishings, including a few in her rather modest bedchamber, belonged to the ill-fated queen.

Also opened in 2006 is the nearby **Hameau** (Hamlet), commissioned in 1783 by Marie Antoinette, compelled by Rousseau's theories about recapturing the natural beauty and noble simplicity of life, much in favor in the late 18th century. Here, she experienced the simplicity of peasant life—or at least peasant life as seen through the eyes of a frivolous queen. Dressed as a shepherdess, she would watch sheep being tended and cows being milked, men fishing and washerwomen beating their laundry in the lake. The interiors of the hamlet buildings cannot be visited, but the surrounding informal landscaping—in obvious contrast to the formality of the other gardens at Versailles—and bizarre origins make views of their exteriors one of the most popular attractions

Follow the signs from the place d'Armes (to the immediate right after entering the Palace of Versailles). See previous entries for admission times and hours to visit.

> ## Impressions
>
> When Louis XIV finished the Grand Trianon (Grand Pavilion), he told [Mme de] Maintenon he had created a paradise for her, and asked if she could think of anything now to wish for . . . She said she could think of but one thing—it was summer, and it was balmy France—yet she would like well to sleigh ride in the leafy avenues of Versailles! The next morning found miles and miles of grassy avenues spread thick with snowy salt and sugar, and a procession of those quaint sleighs waiting to receive the chief concubine of the gaiest and most unprincipled court that France has ever seen!
> —Mark Twain, *The Innocents Abroad* (1869)

Exploring the Town

If you have some extra time, or want to escape the hoards of tourists at the château, take a stroll through the center of Versailles, and you'll see the real life of this elegant Parisian suburb. The heart of the town is the **Saint-Louis Cathedral.** To make room for the burgeoning palace, the village church of Saint-Julien of Brioude was demolished in 1679. With Versailles' rising importance, Louis XIV commissioned a new church, not surprisingly in honor of his namesake, St-Louis. Finished almost a century later in the Rococo style, it was converted into a "temple of Abundance" during the revolution and, with the revival of religion, consecrated a cathedral in 1843.

A short distance from the cathedral is the vibrant **Notre-Dame market,** a gastronomic paradise held in the 1841 covered market building Tuesday to Sunday mornings and overflowing into the neighboring streets on Tuesdays, Fridays, and Sundays. Antiques fans will be in heaven perusing the dozens of shops in the **Passage de la Geôle,** occupying the former royal jail. More shops can be found in the picturesque **Les Carrés Saint-Louis.** Built by Louis XV in 1755, these square blocks of low slate-roofed houses make up one of the first-ever shopping malls. Even if you're not looking to buy, it's entertaining to imagine what could fill the gorgeous 18th-century mansions scattered around Versailles, constructed by aristocrats during the city's heyday as seat of the French government.

Where to Eat

Gordon Ramsay au Trianon ★★★ FRENCH/INTERNATIONAL   One of the kings of cuisine reigns over this Art Deco restaurant in the swanky **Trianon Palace Hotel**—and he's not French. Scottish-born and Michelin laureate Gordon Ramsay, the *enfant terrible* of chefs, offers up a seasonal traditional French menu with modern flair. Treat yourself to the exceptional tasting menu or choose a la carte from the bubbly wild roasted sea bass with mussels; baby squid and champagne; rich pressed foie gras; Scottish venison; or Périgord truffle, fig, and raspberries. Finish with the delicate roasted apple with spices and iced almond mousse. The service, the setting, and the cuisine are a delight. The food is of the highest order—and so are the prices. For more relaxed dining, opt for its little sister **La Veranda** in the terrace of the hotel, perfect in summer.

In the Hotel Trianon Palace, 1 bd. de la Reine. www.gordonramsay.com ✆ **01-30-84-50-18.** Reservations required. Main courses 55€–72€; fixed-price menu 160€. AE, DC, MC, V. Fri–Sat 12:30–2:30pm and Tues–Sat 7–10:30pm. Closed first 2 weeks of Jan and 1 week in Mar.

L'Angélique MODERN FRENCH   Chef Régis Douysset's creative menu has earned him one Michelin star. In a renovated 17th-century *hôtel particulier* a few minutes' walk from the château, you will find *bistronomie* at its best—and it won't break the bank. Tantalize your taste buds with the creamy pumpkin soup with chestnuts or the sautéed chanterelle mushrooms with baked artichokes before moving on to the roasted monkfish paired with celery root and fresh algae or the local hare with glazed grapes and foie gras. If the *fermier* cheese plate doesn't tempt you, try the delicious layered praline meringue and Ecuadorian Guayaquil chocolate cake with rosemary ice cream.

27 av. de Saint-Cloud. www.langelique.fr ✆ **01-30-84-98-85.** Main courses 25€; fixed-price menu 44€–61€. MC, V. Tues–Sat noon–2:30pm and 7:30–10pm.

Le Resto du Roy FRENCH   This informal bistro lies in an 18th-century building overlooking the western facade of the palace at Versailles. The chef prepares an appetizing array of dishes, starting with cassolette of scallops with leek fondue or salmon smoked with birch branches. For a main course, we recommend such dishes as poached tuna steak poached in coconut milk and lime sauce or the regal Sun King's Charolais steak tartare. There are also large *salades* including the vegetarian Estivale with hot goat cheese on toast and melon. For dessert, try the divine profiterole *royale* with grilled almonds.

1 av. de St-Cloud. www.lerestoduroy-versailles.fr. © **01-39-50-42-26.** Reservations recommended. Main courses 15€–16€; fixed-price menu 20€–38€ lunch menu 13€. AE, MC, V. Daily 11:45am–2:30pm and 7–10:30pm.

Nuance MODERN FRENCH   This restaurant serves up creative plays on traditional French bourgeois cuisine. Located close to the main château, the decor is modern yet the ambience and service remain friendly and welcoming. The good-value menu may feature scallop cassolette with spinach fondue and anise seed cream, "opera" of foie gras with chestnuts candied in port and fig chutney, or roasted duck accompanied by potatoes and spicy honey sauce. The creativity carries over into the desserts with such delicacies as poached pear with tonka bean chocolate sauce and coconut ice cream. Junior gastronomes can delight on a special children's menu.

10 bd. du Roi. www.restaurant-nuance.com. © **01-39-49-58-35.** Main courses 13€–20€. MC, V. Tues–Fri noon–2:30pm and 7:30–10pm, Sat 7:30–10:30pm.

CHARTRES ★★★

97km (60 miles) SW of Paris, 76km (47 miles) NW of Orléans

An hour south of Paris, amid a sea of wheat fields, rises the city of Chartres. Crowned with one of the world's most breathtaking cathedrals, Chartres, with its quaint historic center, is a quintessential French town. In a half-day excursion you'll be captivated by the splendid Notre-Dame. Spend the rest of the day exploring the local farmers market, enjoying a lunch of *pâté de Chartres*, wandering along its medieval laneways, or visiting its lovely Fine Arts Museum.

Essentials

GETTING THERE   From Paris's Gare Montparnasse, **trains** run directly to Chartres, taking about an hour. Tickets cost 29€ round-trip; for more information, see www.voyages-sncf.com or call © 3635. If **driving,** take A10/A11 southwest from the *périphérique* and follow signs to Le Mans and Chartres. (The Chartres exit is clearly marked.)

VISITOR INFORMATION   The **Office de Tourisme** is on place de la Cathédrale (www.chartres-tourisme.com; © **02-37-18-26-26;** fax 02-37-21-51-91).

Music of the Spheres

If you're visiting Chartres on a Sunday afternoon in July or August, the cathedral has a free 1-hour organ concert at 4:45pm, when the filtered light of the setting sun makes the western windows come thrillingly alive.

Exploring the Cathedral

Cathédrale Notre-Dame de Chartres ★★★ CATHEDRAL It's not hard to understand why visitors flock to see the awe-inspiring Cathédrale de Chartres, a UNESCO World Heritage Site since 1979. With its mixed-and-matched bell towers, its weather-worn, revolution-damaged exterior, and above all, its shimmering stained-glass windows, the phenomenal church seduces the eyes and the spirit. Reportedly, Rodin once sat for hours on the sidewalk, admiring the sculptures on the facade. His opinion: Chartres is the French Acropolis. If you take the time to absorb the cathedral's intricacies, you will most certainly come to the same conclusion.

The cathedral's origins are uncertain; some have suggested it grew up over an ancient Druid site that later became a Roman temple. As early as the 4th century, there was a Christian basilica here. An 1194 fire destroyed most of what had by then become a Romanesque cathedral but spared the western facade and crypt. The cathedral you see today dates principally from the 13th century, when it was rebuilt with the efforts and contributions of kings, princes, churchmen, and pilgrims from all over Europe. One of the world's greatest high Gothic cathedrals, it was one of the first to use flying buttresses to support the soaring dimensions within.

As you approach the building, stop to admire the beautiful 12th-century sculptures on the **Royal Portal ★★★**. A landmark in Romanesque art, the sculptured bodies are elongated, often stylized, in their long, flowing robes. But the faces are amazingly (for the time) lifelike, occasionally winking or smiling. In the central tympanum, Christ is shown at the Second Coming, with his descent depicted on the right and his ascent on the left. Before entering, walk around to both the **North Portal** and the **South Portal,** each from the 13th century. Look carefully and you can read some of the biblical scenes depicted such as the expulsion of Adam and Eve from the Garden of Eden.

Upon entering the cathedral visitors are immediately overcome by the amazing light from the **stained glass ★★★**. Covering an expanse of

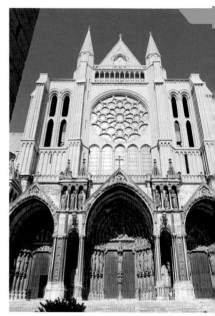

Chartres Cathedral.

Stained-glass windows at the Chartres Cathedral.

more than 2,500 sq. m. (26,910 sq. ft.), the glass is unlike anything else in the world. The stained glass, most of which dates from the 12th and 13th centuries, was spared in both world wars by being painstakingly removed, piece by piece, and stored away. See the windows in the morning, at noon, in the afternoon, at sunset—as often as you can. Like the petals of a kaleidoscope, they constantly change. It's difficult to single out one panel or window above the others, but an exceptional one is the 12th-century *Vierge de la Belle Verrière* **(Our Lady of the Beautiful Window)** on the south side. Of course, there are the three fiery rose windows, but you couldn't miss those if you tried.

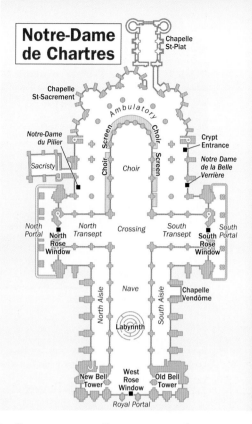

Though you might be too transfixed by the heavenly light, don't neglect to take in the celebrated **choir screen;** work on it began in the 16th century and lasted until 1714. The niches, 40 in all, contain statues illustrating scenes from the life of the Madonna and Christ—everything from the *Massacre of the Innocents* to the *Coronation of the Virgin.* Before exiting, have a look at the floor of the **nave,** which still contains its ancient floor labyrinth, a 262m-long (858 ft.) pilgrimage path that used to be walked by pilgrims in prayer or often traveled on one's knees as an act of repentance. The wooden *Notre-Dame du Piller* **(Virgin of the Pillar),** to the left of the choir, dates from the 14th century. The crypt was built over 2 centuries, beginning in the 9th century. Enshrined within is *Our Lady of the Crypt,* a 1976 Madonna that replaced one destroyed during the revolution.

Try to take a tour conducted by Malcolm Miller (millerchartres@aol.com; *C* **02-37-28-15-58;** fax 02-37-28-33-03), an Englishman who has spent 3 decades studying the cathedral and giving tours in English. His rare blend of scholarship, enthusiasm, and humor will help you understand and appreciate the cathedral. He usually conducts 75-minute tours at noon and 2:45pm Monday to Saturday for 10€ for adults or 5€ students. Tours may be fewer in winter and are canceled during pilgrimages, religious celebrations, and large funerals.

If you're fit enough, don't miss the opportunity, especially in summer, to climb to the top of the tower.

After your visit, stroll through the **Episcopal Gardens** and enjoy yet another view of this remarkable cathedral.

Vieux Quartier (Old Town), Chartres.

16 Cloître Notre-Dame. www.cathedrale-chartres.monuments-nationaux.fr. ✆ **02-37-21-22-07.** General admission to the cathedral is free, admission to the treasury and towers 7€ adults; 4.50€ adults 18–25; free for children 17 and under. Cathedral open daily 8:30am–7:30pm.

Exploring the Old Town

If time remains, you may want to explore the medieval cobbled streets of the **Vieux Quartier (Old Town)** ★. Wandering around the narrow lanes near the cathedral, you will find many gabled houses, including the colorful facades of **rue Chantault,** one of which is 8 centuries old. Seek out rue du Bourg, where you'll find the famous **Salmon House,** and some lovely medieval sculptures (including a certain fish). In the lower town, you can stroll along the picturesque Eure River with its stone bridges and ancient wash-houses. From the Pont de Bouju, you can see the lofty spires in the background. If you go on a Saturday morning you can enjoy the atmosphere of a local farmers market held in **place Billard** (until 1pm), the perfect place to grab some supplies for a casual lunch in the park behind the cathedral or along the river.

Musée des Beaux-Arts de Chartres ★   Located next to the cathedral, a stop here will be a highlight of your visit. A former Episcopal palace, the building at times competes with its exhibitions—one part dates from the 15th century and encompasses a courtyard. This museum of fine arts boasts a collection covering the 16th to the 20th centuries, including the work of masters such as Zurbarán, Watteau, and Soutine. Of particular interest is David Ténier's painting *Le Concert.* Allot about 1 hour for your visit.

29 Cloître Notre-Dame. ✆ **02-37-90-45-80.** May 3–Oct 30 Mon, Wed–Sun 10am–noon and 2–6pm (closed Sun mornings); the rest of the year, until 5pm. Admission 3.20€ adults, 1.60€ 18 and under, extra fee for temporary exhibits.

Where to Eat

La Vieille Maison ★★ MODERN FRENCH   Even if the food here wasn't superb, the 14th-century building would still be worth visiting for its historic value. The dining room, outfitted in the Louis XIII style, is centered on a narrow ceiling vault, less than 2m (6½ ft.) across, crafted of chiseled white stone blocks during the 9th century. Bruno Letartre, the only *maître cuisinier de France* (master French chef) in Chartres, supervises the cuisine. The menu changes four or five times a year, reflecting the seasonality of the region and its produce. Some good examples include cream of green-and-white asparagus soup topped with shellfish; grilled sea bass with potato mousse, fennel, and oranges; and roasted lamb with a Basque-style omelet with pepper and crushed olives. For dessert, opt for the "prisoner" mango and passion-fruit lava cake with Ivory Coast chocolate ganache.

5 rue au Lait. www.lavieillemaison.fr. ℂ **02-37-34-10-67.** Reservations recommended. Main courses 28€–32€; fixed-price menu 30€–58€. MC, V. Tues–Sun noon–2:15pm; Tues–Sat 7–10pm. Closed 1 week in Aug.

Le Georges ★★ FRENCH   The best food with the most upscale dining ambience in Chartres is not surprisingly found at the town's best hotel (see below). The friendly staff makes you feel comfortable in its elegant dining room, which expands in summer to the courtyard terrace. Its excellent gastronomic menu changes with the seasons, but usually includes savory portions of *pâté de Chartres* (made with a combination of minced meats baked in a giant puff pastry), a superb version of roasted veal "Grand Monarque," served with a casserole of mushrooms and cheese as well as dishes highlighting local products such as the *escargots fricassées*, or the Eure and Loire raised saddle of lamb with mint pistou. Desserts are sumptuous, especially the Grand Marnier Soufflé, and the cheese cart will warm the heart of any Francophile.

In the Grand Monarque Best Western, 22 place des Epars. www.bw-grand-monarque.com. ℂ **02-37-18-15-15.** Reservations recommended. Main courses 18€–36€; fixed-price menu 51€–90€. AE, DC, MC, V. Tues–Sun noon–2:45pm; Tues–Sat 7–10pm.

Where to Stay

Grand Monarque Best Western   Located in the town center, this is certainly the most appealing and desirable hotel in Chartres. Functioning as an inn since its original construction in the 15th century, it has been expanded and improved many times since then. Today it's a grand hotel that remains under the direction of the Jallerat family. It attracts guests who enjoy its old-world charm—such as Art Nouveau stained glass and Louis XV chairs in the dining room. The 55 guest rooms are decorated with reproductions of antiques; many have sitting areas in addition to the five more spacious suites. Request a room facing the courtyard for a peaceful night's sleep or one facing the main square for a nice view of the city. Its spa complex provides a relaxing break after a day's touring.

22 place des Epars, 28005 Chartres. www.bw-grand-monarque.com. ℂ **800/528-1234** in the U.S., or 02-37-18-15-15. Fax 02-37-36-34-18. 55 units. 130€–180€ double; 250€ suite. AE, DC, MC, V. Parking 8€. **Amenities:** 2 restaurants; bar; room service, spa. *In room:* A/C (in some), TV, hair dryer, minibar, Wi-Fi (free).

GIVERNY ★

80km (50 miles) NW of Paris

When artist Claude Monet moved to Giverny in 1883, looking for some peace and quiet, little did he know he would forever change the fate of this sleepy Norman village. Soon after his arrival, the town was invaded by eager young artists who'd come from all over the world in search of the Impressionist master. Today, artists and art lovers alike still trek out to Giverny to tour his restored home and gardens. If you fall in love with the amazing Monet paintings at the Orsay, Orangerie, or Marmottan museums in Paris, Giverny should be next on your list.

Essentials

GETTING THERE   It takes a half day to get to Giverny and see its sights or a full day to take your time, have a nice lunch, and then amble through the village. It's best to visit in the morning on a weekday to avoid the crowds. Take the Paris-Rouen train from Paris's Gare St-Lazare to the Vernon station (45-min. ride; 13.20€ each way), where you can either take a taxi (around 15€) or local bus (4€), located just outside the station) the 5km (3 miles) to Giverny. Vernon itself lies 40km (25 miles) southeast of Rouen. Another option is to take a 5-hour bus tour from Paris, for 75€ per person, that focuses on Monet's house and garden. For ages 3 to 11, the fare is 38€. Tours depart at 1:45pm Monday to Saturday and 8:15am on Sunday between April and October. These tours can be booked through **Cityrama,** 149 rue St-Honoré, 1er (www.pariscityrama.com; ✆ **01-44-55-61-00;** Métro: Palais-Royal–Musée du Louvre) in summer, or year-round through **American Express,** 11 rue Scribe, 9e (✆ **01-47-14-50-00;** Métro: Opéra). **Context Travel** (www.contexttravel.com) runs small group excursions with art historians regularly from April to October from 85€ per person.

If you're **driving,** take the Autoroute de l'Ouest (Port de St-Cloud) toward Rouen. Leave the highway at Bonnières, and then cross the Seine on the Bonnières Bridge. From here, a direct road with signs leads to Giverny. Expect it to take about an hour; try to avoid weekends. Another approach is to leave the highway at the Bonnières exit and go toward Vernon. Once there, cross the bridge over the Seine and follow signs to Giverny or Gasny (Giverny is before Gasny). This is easier than going through Bonnières, where there aren't many signs.

VISITOR INFORMATION   The **Office de Tourisme des Portes de l'Eure** has a branch in Giverny located close to the Fondation Monet at 70 rue Claude Monet (www.cape-tourisme.fr; ✆ **02-32-51-39-60**). Open daily April to August 9:30am to 5:30pm, September and October 10am to 5pm.

Exploring Giverny

Claude Monet Foundation ★★★ HISTORIC HOME/GARDEN   Monet is certainly one of France's most renowned artists. One of the founders of Impressionism, it was his painting titled *Impression, Sunrise* (at the **Musée Marmottan,** p. 106) that gave the movement its name. A brilliant innovator, he excelled at presenting the effects of light at different times of the day. His paintings of the Rouen cathedral and of water lilies are just a few of his masterpieces.

Claude Monet Foundation.

Monet was born in Le Havre in 1840. His career flowed along the path of the Seine River—as a young man, he lived in Paris before leaving the bustling city for the suburbs, then the town of Vernon before finally settling in Giverny. Once here, Monet barely left, preferring to stay in his peaceful gardens. However, many of his friends came to visit him here at *Le Pressoir,* including Clemenceau, Cézanne, Rodin, Renoir, Degas, and Sisley. When Monet died in 1926, his son, Michel, inherited the house, but left it abandoned until it decayed. The gardens became almost a jungle, inhabited by river rats. In 1966, Michel died and left the property to the Académie des Beaux Arts. It wasn't until 1977 that Gerald van der Kemp, who restored Versailles, decided to work on Giverny.

Unfortunately, you won't find any original Monet paintings at the foundation; however, his house and famous gardens are open to the public. The house contains Monet's collection of 18th- and 19th-century Japanese prints, as well as antique (though not original) furnishings. You can stroll the garden and view the thousands of flowers, including the *nymphéas.* The Japanese bridge, hung with wisteria, leads to a setting of weeping willows and rhododendrons. Monet's studio barge was installed on the pond.

84 rue Claude-Monet Parc Gasny. www.fondation-monet.com. ✆ **02-32-51-28-21.** Admission 9€ adults, 5€ students, 3.50€ children 7–12, free for children 6 and under. Apr–Oct daily 9:30am–6pm. Closed Nov–Mar.

Where to Eat

Baudy FRENCH   While the hotel Baudy might be overrun with tourists, it's still well worth dining at this legendary *auberge* (inn), especially for true art fans. In Monet's time, it was an *epicerie-buvette* (casual hangout) run by the painter's friends Angelina and Gaston Baudy. During the town's 19th-century heyday, the American painters used the pink villa as their lodging. Classic French standards are offered, such as chicken liver terrine with Armagnac liquor, the Baudy omelet

The gardens and lily pond at Giverny.

with *confit de canard* and sautéed potatoes, or deluxe "wine merchant" *faux filet*. Grab a table on the terrace to escape the crowds and be sure to pop your head into the back gardens before leaving to experience a second Giverny garden wonder.

81 rue Claude-Monet. www.restaurantbaudy.com. (✆ **02-32-21-10-03.** Reservations recommended. Main courses 14€–25€; fixed-price menu 24€. MC, V. daily 10am–9:30pm; Sun 10am–3pm. Closed Nov–Mar.

L'Esquisse Gourmande FRENCH   Located at the far end of town near the church, this is a refreshing alternative to the tourist traps near le Fondation Monet. This combined tea salon and restaurant is perfect for a relaxing summer lunch. Service is friendly, yet tends to be a little slow on busy days. The seasonal menu is inspired by regional specialties and the apple reigns. Start with a *kir-normand*, local cider with crème de cassis, followed by the Camembert crumble, or daily specials such as lamb brochettes or quail with caramelized baby vegetables and apples. Save room for their tasty desserts, which include *crème brûlée normand* with cooked apples or apple cheesecake.

73 bis rue Claude-Monet. www.lesquissegourmande.fr. (✆ **02-32-51-86-95.** Main courses 8€–20€. AE, MC, V. Wed–Sun noon–2pm; Tues–Sat 7:30–10pm.

> ### Giverny's Other Sights
>
> After you've explored the Claude Monet Foundation, take a stroll along the main street up the cemetery to visit the Monet family tomb. The **Musée des Impressionismes,** 99 rue Claude Monet; www. museedesimpressionnismesgiverny.com; (✆ **02-32-51-94-65**), the former American museum, also has notable temporary exhibits that occasionally feature some Monet works.

AUVERS-SUR-OISE

30km (18 miles) N of Paris

"Here we are far from Paris, far enough for it to be the real country . . . Auvers is truly beautiful," was how post-Impressionist master Vincent van Gogh described scenic Auvers-sur-Oise. While the town itself has not changed much since the artist's brief stay in 1890, his 70-day sojourn here and his tragic death immortalized this country nook both on canvas and in history. Terribly poor his whole adult life, financially supported by his brother Theo, Vincent van Gogh has since become an artistic icon. Ironically, a century after his death, **van Gogh's *Portrait of Dr. Gachet***—the reason he came to Auvers—fetched a record sale price of $82.5 million. Come pay homage to van Gogh in his last resting place and tour the town that so inspired him.

Essentials

GETTING THERE BY TRAIN: The easiest way to get here is by taking the direct train to Auvers-sur-Oise that runs every Saturday, Sunday, and public holidays April to October departing from Gare du Nord at 9:56am, with a direct return train to Paris at 6:15pm (approx. 35 min. each way). Alternatively, take a suburban train at Saint-Lazare or Gare du Nord toward Pontoise. Change at St-Ouen L'Aumone. Note that it's the second St-Ouen stop, not the first (approx. 1 hr.). Switch to the Persan Beaumont Creil line (walk downstairs and change to opposite platform; consult screens for departures) and get off at Gare d'Auvers-sur-Oise (approx. 15 min.) 11€ round-trip.

   BY CAR: From Porte Maillot or la Porte de Clignancourt take the A15 highway direction Cergy-Pontoise. After 5km (3 miles) take the A115, in the direction of Amiens-Beauvais. Exit at Méry-Auvers-sur-Oise, follow signs to "Maison de Van Gogh" (30 min.). If you are driving you may want to combine Auvers with Giverny to make a full day art-themed trip.

   There are also full day **bus tours** from Paris visiting both Auvers and Giverny, for 173€ per person, 86€ for children aged 3 to 11. Tours depart at 8:30am Wednesday and Saturday April to October. You can arrange these through **Cityrama,** 149 rue St-Honoré, 1er (www.pariscityrama.com; ✆ **01-44-55-61-00**). Private or group tours of Auvers are also available through the Office du Tourisme.

VISITOR INFORMATION The Office du Tourisme is located in the Manoir des Colombières, rue de la Sansonne, across from the entrance to the Maison de Van Gogh (www.lavalleedeloise.com; ✆ **01-30-36-10-06**). Open April to October Tuesday to Sunday 9:30am to 12:30pm and 2 to 6pm and November to March Tuesday to Sunday 2 to 5pm (5:30pm on weekends).

SPECIAL EVENTS Auvers is far from a sleepy town in summers, with an annual international music festival (www.festival-auvers.com), frequent jazz concerts (www.auversjazz.com), a contemporary art festival called the "Festival des Peintres," and mini-cruises along the Oise River on Sundays. For information on all special events in town, see "Events'" at www.lavalleedeloise.com.

Exploring La Maison de Van Gogh

Auberge Ravoux MUSEUM/HISTORIC BUILDING An inn and restaurant since 1876, l'Auberge Ravoux is often referred to as the Maison de van Gogh, as the artist lodged here, in a tiny 7 sq. m (75 sq. ft.) room for 3.5 francs a day. Vincent had been encouraged to come to Auvers by fellow painter **Paul Cézanne** to be treated by his friend **Dr. Gachet.** From the moment he arrived at the end of May 1890, Dr. Gachet pushed van Gogh to paint to help overcome his psychological problems. And paint he did, with frenetic energy, creating virtually a painting a day. The room at the Auberge also acted as his studio, and after a day of painting in the village he would stack his works in his room or outside on the landing.

At first the country proved beneficial to Vincent; however, as the weeks went on his mood, along with his palette, darkened. He remained forever tormented and overwhelmed by the feeling he was a burden to his art-dealer brother, Theo.

On July 27, 1890, the artist headed out to the fields armed with his brushes, easel, and apparently a pistol. At the end of the day, he came crawling back to the Auberge with a fatal gunshot wound to the chest. As he lay dying for almost 2 days in his bed, with Theo by his side, it is hoped they reconciled any disputes. "Sadness goes on forever," are his supposed last words. You can't stay at the Auberge today, and there's really not much to see here besides Vincent's room (no. 5), but it remains exactly as it was in 1890. Visiting it can be a deeply moving experience.

52 rue du Général de Gaulle. www.maisondevangogh.fr. ℂ **01-30-36-60-63.** Admission 6€ adults, 4€ ages 12–17 and under, free for children 11 and under. Mar–Oct Wed–Sun 10am–6pm. Closed Nov–Feb.

Van Gogh's *L'Eglise d'Auvers-sur-Oise.*

Auberge Ravoux (Maison de Van Gogh).

Auvers-sur-Oise

ATTRACTIONS

Absinthe Museum **3**
Auberge Ravoux **8**
Auvers Cemetery **7**
Château d'Auvers **2**
L'Atelier de Daubigny **4**
Maison du Docteur
  Gachet (Doctor
  Gachet's Home) **1**
Manoir des
  Colombières **5**
Notre-Dame church **6**

RESTAURANTS

Auberge Ravoux **8**
Chemin des Peintres **9**

Exploring the Town

After visiting the Auberge, amble along the *Chemin des Peintres* to visit the various intriguing sights around Auvers (all well signposted). Hike up the gentle hill to visit the **Notre-Dame church,** which features in one of van Gogh's tableaux (now at the Musée d'Orsay). A little further up the hill is the **Auvers Cemetery,** the final resting place of both Vincent and Theo, who died 6 months after Vincent. You'll find their ivy-covered graves side-by-side against the far left cemetery wall.

Van Gogh wasn't the first artist to come to Auvers. Like Monet, in the mid–19th century many artists started to break out of their Parisian studios and travel to towns in and around Ile-de-France to paint *en plein air*. One day, **Charles Daubigny,** an early open-air painter, docked his floating studio on the banks of the Oise and instantly fell in love with Auvers. Today you can visit two sights dedicated to this artist: the **Manoir des Colombières,** rue de la Sansonne (www.musee-daubigny.com; ☎ **01-30-36-80-20**), a museum in his honor, and **L'Atelier de Daubigny,** his home and studio just down the road at 61 rue Daubigny (www.atelier-daubigny.com; ☎ **01-30-36-60-60**).

If you have enough energy, keep walking along the rue Flery and you'll reach the 17th-century **Château d'Auvers,** rue de Léry (www.chateau-auvers.fr; ☎ **01-34-48-48-48**), which has a multimedia display on Impressionist artists.

Another 10 minutes along the road, which turns into rue du Docteur Gachet, you'll come to **Maison du Docteur Gachet** (Dr. Gachet's home), 78 rue du Docteur Gachet (☎ **01-30-36-81-27**), which also has thematic exhibits. However, his wonderful art collection was donated to the Louvre by his son in the 1950s.

To end your visit with a little fun, head to the **Absinthe Museum,** 44 rue Alphonse Callé (www.musee-absinthe.com; ☎ **01-30-36-83-26**), where you'll learn about the strong liquor which was much enjoyed by the Impressionist artists. The museums of Auvers are only open from spring to late autumn.

Where to Eat

Auberge Ravoux 🎁 FRENCH We can wholeheartedly recommend the Auberge Ravoux, which distinguishes itself with its unique, historically accurate approach to cuisine. The restaurant aims, with great success, to re-create the ambience of the van Gogh era, right down to the use of historic recipes and 19th-century furniture and tableware. Chef Laurent Gattuso's menus feature seasonal local ingredients in both traditional working-class and bourgeois dishes. Start off with the homemade Ravoux pâté or rabbit loaf with lentil salad and onions marmalade, before savoring the veal blanquette or perhaps in honor of van Gogh, the *waterzooï du pêcheur* (a type of fish stew). Tempt yourself with the rich *mousse au chocolat*, or, if you're coming from the Absinthe Museum, you may want to try the Muse Ravoux—anise ice cream.

52 rue du Général de Gaulle. www.maisondevangogh.fr. ☎ **01-30-36-60-63.** Reservations recommended. Main courses 18€–32€; fixed-price menu 29€–38€. MC, V. Restaurant open early Mar to end of Nov. Wed–Fri lunch 12–2:30pm, tea and coffee from 3pm Sat, Sun, and public holidays: 1st sitting at noon, 2nd sitting at 2:15pm, tea and coffee from 4pm. Fri–Sat: dinner 7:30–9:30pm.

Chemin des Peintres FRENCH Like the Auberge Ravoux, various other restaurants in Auvers are returning to authentic gastronomic philosophies and recipes, and the Chemin des Peintres is among the best. Set in a restored 19th-century barn, it serves tasty traditional dishes with a dash of creativity using local organic and farm products. The atmosphere is friendly and relaxed, fitting its country locale. Some mouthwatering dishes include warm Chauvy goat-cheese salads, local Commency rabbit seasoned with prunes, and free-range Sagy chicken with a red wine reduction. It's also a teahouse, so you can stop in after hiking up to the cemetery for a coffee and pear tart draped with chocolate and almond slivers.

3 bis, rue de Paris. ☎ **01-30-36-14-15.** Main courses 12€–25€; fixed-price menu 18€–24€. MC, V. Mon–Fri 11am–4pm; Sat 11am–11pm; Sun 11am–7pm.

DISNEYLAND PARIS

32km (20 miles) E of Paris

It might be an ocean away from the other Disney parks, but Disneyland Paris looks, tastes, and feels like the ones in California and Florida—except this fairy-tale château belongs to *Belle au Bois Dormant* instead of Cinderella, and Mickey might greet you with a friendly *bonjour!* The controversy over the opening of Disneyland Paris in 1992 has long been forgotten, and the resort has surpassed the Eiffel Tower and the Louvre to become France's number-one tourist attraction—drawing a whopping 50 million visitors annually. Take a day to get your fill of thrills at the main park or two to enjoy the full Disney atmosphere and movie action at the Walt Disney Studios.

Essentials

GETTING THERE The RER commuter express **rail** network (Line A) stops within walking distance of the park. Board the RER in Paris at Charles-de-Gaulle–Etoile, Châtelet–Les Halles, or Nation. Get off at Line A's last stop, Marne-la-Vallée/Chessy, 45 minutes from central Paris. The round-trip fare is 14€. Trains run daily, every 10 to 20 minutes from 5:30am to midnight.

    Shuttle buses connect Orly and Charles de Gaulle airports with each hotel in the resort. Buses depart the airports every 30 to 45 minutes. One-way transport to the park from either airport is 17€ for adults, 14€ for children 3 to 11.

    If you're **driving,** take A4 east from Paris and get off at exit 14, DISNEYLAND PARIS. Parking begins at 15€ per day, but is free if you stay at one of the park hotels. A series of moving sidewalks speeds up pedestrian transit from parking areas to the park entrance.

VISITOR INFORMATION All the hotels we recommend offer general information on the theme park. For details and reservations at any of its hotels, contact the **Disneyland Paris Guest Relations Office,** located in City Hall on Main Street, U.S.A. (www.disneylandparis.com; ☎ **01-60-30-60-53** in English, or 08-25-30-60-30 in French). For information on Disneyland Paris and specific details on the many other attractions and monuments in the Ile-de-France and the rest of the country, contact the **Maison du Tourisme,** Disney Village (B.P. 77705), Marne-la-Vallée (☎ **01-60-43-33-33**).

> ### ✎ Fast Pass Those Long Lines
>
> Disneyland Paris has instituted a program that's done well at the other parks. With the **Fast Pass** system, visitors reserve a 1-hour time block at various rides, by printing a fast pass from the machine at the entrance to the attraction. Within that block, the wait is usually no more than 8 minutes.

ADMISSION Admission varies depending on the season. In peak season, a 1-day park ticket (for either the main park or Walt Disney Studios) costs 57€ for adults, 51€ for children 3 to 12, and is free for children 2 and younger; a 2-day park-hopper ticket is 122€ for adults, 109€ for kids; and a 3-day park-hopper ticket is 151€ for adults, 130€ for kids. See the official Disneyland website (www.disneylandparis.com) for ticket specials, especially in low season. Peak season is from mid-June to mid-September as well as Halloween, Christmas, and Easter weeks. Entrance to Disney Village is free, though there's usually a cover charge at the dance clubs.

HOURS Hours vary throughout the year, but most frequently they are 10am to 7pm. Be warned that autumn and winter hours vary the most; it depends on the weather and national holidays. It's a good idea to phone ahead if you're contemplating a visit at this time.

Exploring Disney

Disneyland Paris ★★★ THEME PARK Situated on a 2,000-hectare (4,942-acre) site (about one-fifth the size of Paris) in the suburb of Marne-la-Vallée, the resort was designed as a total vacation destination: In one enormous unit, the park includes five "lands" of entertainment, a dozen hotels, a campground, an entertainment center, a 27-hole golf course, and dozens of restaurants, shows, and shops. **Disney Village** contains dance clubs, shops, restaurants (one of which offers a dinner spectacle based on the original *Buffalo Bill's Wild West Show*), bars for adults trying to escape their children, a French Government Tourist Office, a post office, and a marina.

Visitors stroll among flower beds, trees, reflecting ponds, fountains, and a large artificial lake flanked with hotels. An army of smiling employees and Disney characters—many of whom are multilingual, including Buffalo Bill, Mickey and Minnie Mouse, and of course, the French-born Caribbean pirate Jean Laffite—are on hand to greet the thousands of *enfants*.

Disneyland Paris's Sleeping Beauty Castle.

Main Street, U.S.A. abounds with horse-drawn carriages and barbershop quartets. Steam-powered railway cars embark from the Main Street Station for a trip through a Grand Canyon diorama to **Frontierland,** with its paddlewheel steamers reminiscent of Mark Twain's Mississippi River. Other attractions are the **Big Thunder Mountain** roller coaster and the ghosts and ghouls of **Phantom Manor.** Parents can take a break in the Lucky Nugget Saloon, its cancan show inspired from the cabarets of turn-of-the-20th-century Paris.

The park's steam trains chug past **Adventureland**—with its swashbuckling pirates, Swiss Family Robinson treehouse, and re-enacted Arabian Nights legends—to **Fantasyland.** Here you'll find the **Sleeping Beauty Castle (*Le Château de la Belle au Bois Dormant*),** whose pinnacles and turrets are an idealized (and spectacular) interpretation of French châteaux. In its shadow are Europeanized versions of *Blanche Neige et Les Sept Nains* (Snow White and the Seven Dwarfs), Peter Pan, Dumbo, Alice (from Wonderland), the Mad Hatter's Teacups, and Sir Lancelot's Magic Carousel. Fairy tale dreams come true for young visitors at the recently opened **Princess Pavilion,** featuring Cinderella, Aurora, Jasmine, and other Disney princesses.

Visions of the future can be found in **Discoveryland,** where tributes to invention and imagination draw from the works of Leonardo da Vinci, Jules Verne, H. G. Wells, the modern masters of science fiction, and the *Star Wars* series. Favorites here include hyperfast **Space Mountain** and **Buzz Light-year's Laser Blast.**

Throughout the park or during the daily parades you'll see characters from *Aladdin, The Lion King, Pocahontas, Toy Story,* and *Monsters, Inc.* As Disney continues to churn out animated blockbusters, look for the newest stars to appear in the theme park.

Where to Eat

Disneyland Paris offers a gamut of cuisine in more than 45 restaurants and snack bars. You can live on burgers and fries, or you can experiment at the following upscale restaurants.

California Grill ★★ ☺ CALIFORNIAN/FRENCH   The resort's showcase restaurant serves cuisine that's equal to the fare at a one-Michelin-star restaurant. The elegant restaurant accommodates both adults and children gracefully. The cuisine mixes light Californian fare with various French inspirations; their wonderful range of dishes includes skewer of scallops, mango and lime vinaigrette; pan-fried skate wing with lemon flavored butter and capers; or beef fillet with melegueta peppers and baby vegetables. Many items are specifically for children. If you want a quiet, mostly adult venue, go here as late as your hunger pangs will allow.

In the Disneyland Hotel. ☎ **01-60-45-65-76.** Reservations required. Fixed-price menu 57€–79€; children's menu 21€. AE, DC, MC, V. Daily 6:30–10:30pm.

Inventions ⚑ INTERNATIONAL   This may be the only buffet restaurant in Europe where animated characters from the Disney films (including Mickey and Minnie) go table-hopping. With views over a park, Sleeping Beauty's Castle, and

A pirate ship in Adventureland.

Walt Disney Studios

You don't need to go all the way to Hollywood to experience movie magic—**Walt Disney Studios** takes guests on a behind-the-scenes interactive discovery of film, animation, and television through four thematic Studio Lots.

The main entrance to the studios, called the **Front Lot,** consists of "Sunset Boulevard," an elaborate sound stage complete with hundreds of film props. The **Toon Studio** reveals some of the trade secrets of Disney animators; here families can have gigantic fun in the oversized **Toy Story Playland,** speed around on the **RC Racer,** get dizzy on the **Slinky Dog Zigzag Spin,** or soar through the skies on the **Toy Soldiers Parachute Drop.** The **Production Courtyard** lets guests take a look behind the scenes of film and TV production; bigger and braver kids enter the spooky Hollywood Tower Hotel at their own risk. The abandoned hotel's rickety elevator sends you flying 13 floors to the depths of the **Twilight Zone Tower of Terror.** Finally, the **Back Lot** is home to special-effects and stunt workshops. A live stunt show features cars, motorbikes, and jet skis.

Big thrill seekers turn up the volume on the **Rock 'n' Roller Coaster,** a roller-coaster featuring the music of Aerosmith that combines a state-of-the-art rock video with high-speed scary twists and turns.

Admission is 57€ for adults, 51€ for children. Hours are daily from 10am to 7pm.

Space Mountain, the restaurant contains four enormous buffet tables. Selections are wide, portions can be copious, and no one leaves hungry. Don't expect *grande cuisine*—however, the quality is much better than your average buffet, topped with a mix of French and international delicacies such as chilled asparagus, Italian prosciutto, or even escargot and bouillabaisse, plus lots of kid-friendly dishes from spaghetti with meatballs to Buzz Lightyear éclairs.

In the Disneyland Hotel. (✆ **01-60-45-65-83.** Buffet 52€ adults, 26€ children 7–11, 20€ children 3–6. Fixed-price lunch menu 36€ adults, 18€ children 6–11, 16€ children 3–6. Brunch (Sun only) 58€ adults, 27€. AE, DC, MC, V. Daily 12:30–3pm and 6–10:30pm.

Disneyland After Dark

The fun doesn't stop after the park gates close. Head to the Disney Village to continue your magical day. Experience the world in 3-D at the **Gaumont Disney Village IMAX cinema,** grab a drink at the sophisticated **New York City Bar** (located in the Hotel New York) or dance the night away to the hottest international hits at the **Hurricanes nightclub.** The whole family will enjoy **Le Legende de Buffalo Bill** in Disney Village (✆ **01-60-45-71-00**). The twice-per-night stampede of entertainment recalls the show that once traveled the

West with Buffalo Bill and Annie Oakley. You'll dine at tables arranged amphithe-ater-style around a rink where sharpshooters, runaway stagecoaches, and dozens of horses and Indians ride fast and perform alarmingly realistic acrobatics. Don't be surprised if you see a few special cowboys, or rather cow-mice. A Texas-style barbecue adds to the lively far West atmosphere served in an assembly line by waiters in 10-gallon hats. Shows start at 6:30 and 9:30pm; the cost (dinner included) is 59€ for adults, 45€ for children 3 to 11.

Where to Stay

You can easily make Disneyland a day trip from Paris—the transportation links are excellent—or spend the night. The resort's seven theme hotels share a reser-vation service. In North America, call ☏ **011-33-1-60-30-60-53.** In France, contact the **Central Reservations Office,** Euro Disney Resort, S.C.A., B.P. 105, F-77777 Marne-la-Vallée Cedex 4 (☏ **08-25-30-60-30;** for more informa-tion and specials and packages, see www.disneylandparis.com).

Disneyland Hotel ★★   Mouseketeers who have rich daddies and mommies frequent Disney's poshest resort. Located right at the park entrance, this flagship four-story hotel is Victorian, with red-tile turrets and jutting balconies. The spa-cious guest rooms are plushly furnished but evoke the image of Disney, with car-toon depictions and candy-stripe decor. The beds are king-size, double, or twin; in some rooms armchairs convert to beds. Accommodations in the rear overlook Sleeping Beauty Castle and Big Thunder Mountain; however, some less desirable units open onto a parking lot. The luxurious bathrooms have marble vanities, show-ers and tubs, and twin basins. The exclusive Castle Club on the third floor pampers guests with a separate elevator, reception desk, and additional perks like free news-papers, all-day beverages, and access to a well-equipped private lounge.

Disneyland Paris, B.P. 111, F-77777 Marne-la-Vallée Cedex 4. www.disneylandparis.com. ☏ **01-60-45-65-89.** Fax 01-60-45-65-33. 495 units. 530€–860€ double; from 775€ suite. Rates include bre-akfast. AE, DC, MC, V. **Amenities:** 2 restaurants; bar; babysitting; health club and spa; pool (indoor); room service. In room: A/C, TV, TV/DVD player, hair dryer, minibar, Wi-Fi (10€ for 3 hr.).

Hotel Cheyenne/Hotel Santa Fe ☺   Head to the far West for the best hotel bargains at the resort. These two Old West–style lodgings stand side-by-side near a re-creation of Texas's Rio Grande. The Cheyenne consists of 14 two-story buildings along Desperado Street; the desert-themed Santa Fe encompasses four "nature trails" winding among 42 adobe-style pueblos. The Cheyenne is a favorite among families, offering a double bed and bunk beds. Children have an array of activities, including a play area in a log cabin with a lookout tower and a section where you can explore the "ruins" of an ancient Anasazi village. The only disadvantage is the absence of a pool.

Whenever the Cheyenne and the Santa Fe are full, Disney usually directs the overflow to the nearby **Kyriad Hotel,** a government-rated two-star hotel designed for families that evokes the aesthetics and layout of a French country inn.

Disneyland Paris, B.P. 115, F-77777 Marne-la-Vallée Cedex 4. www.disneylandparis.com. ☏ **01-60-45-63-12** (Cheyenne), or 01-60-45-79-22 (Santa Fe). Fax 01-60-45-62-33 (Cheyenne), or 01-60-45-78-33 (Santa Fe). 2,000 units. Hotel Cheyenne 140€–310€ double; Hotel Santa Fe 120€–274€ double. Rates include breakfast. AE, DC, MC, V. **Amenities:** Restaurant; bar; babysitting. In room: A/C, TV, Wi-Fi (15€ per 100 min.).

Newport Bay Club ★★   The Disney lake might not be the Atlantic, but with its central cupola, balconies, awnings, and pergolas, the Newport Bay mirrors a harborfront New England hotel (ca. 1900). The yacht club atmosphere carries over to the nautically decorated blue and cream rooms, arranged in various shapes and sizes. Try to book a corner unit, which is the most spacious; in one of these you'll hardly realize you are staying in the biggest hotel in France. The hotel is a good balance for everyone with such distractions as the **Sea Horse Club Game Arcade** for the little ones and the **Fisherman's Wharf bar** for tired parents.

Disneyland Paris, B.P. 105, F-77777 Marne-la-Vallée Cedex 4. www.disneylandparis.com. *(℃)* **01-60-45-55-00.** Fax 01-60-45-55-33. 1,093 units. 245€–460€ double; from 370€suite. Rates include breakfast. AE, DC, MC, V. **Amenities:** 2 restaurants; 2 bars; state-of-the-art health club; 2 pools (indoor and outdoor); room service. *In room:* A/C, TV/DVD player, minibar, Wi-Fi (15€ per day).

FONTAINEBLEAU ★★

60km (37 miles) S of Paris, 74km (46 miles) NE of Orléans

From the elegant Renaissance castle of François I to 19th century Napoleonic stronghold, the hallways and vast forest of Fontainebleau have played host to some of the most important figures and events in French history. Far from the overwhelming glitz and pomp of Versailles, Fontainebleau, which Napoleon referred to as "the house of the centuries," offers visitors a more intimate look at the real lives of French monarchs, and its immense forest provides a great getaway from hectic Paris for lovers of the great outdoors.

GETTING THERE   Allow for a half day with lunch or a full day with a visit to the gardens and forest. **Trains** to Fontainebleau depart from the Gare de Lyon in Paris. The trip takes 45 minutes each way and costs 8.50€ oneway. Fontainebleau's railway station lies 3km (1¾ miles) north of the château, in the suburb of Avon. A local bus (marked simply CHATEAU and part

Château de Fontainebleau.

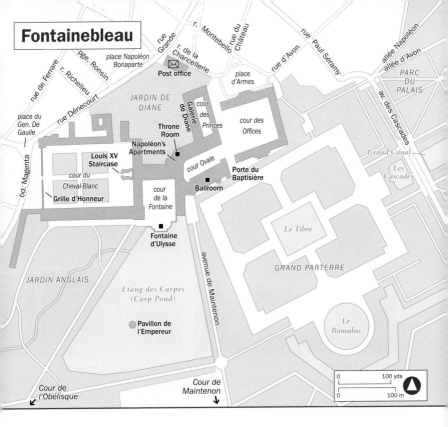

Fontainebleau

of line A) makes the trip to the château at 15-minute intervals Monday through Saturday and at 30-minute intervals on Sunday; the fare is 1.80€ each way. If you're **driving,** take A6 south from Paris, exit onto N191, and follow the signs.

VISITOR INFORMATION The **Office de Tourisme** is at 4 rue Royale, Fontainebleau (www.fontainebleau-tourisme.com; *📞* **01-60-74-99-99**), opposite the main entrance to the château.

Exploring Fontainebleau

Musée National du Château de Fontainebleau ★★★ CASTLE/ MUSEUM/GARDEN Napoleon's affection for this palace is understandable. He followed the pattern of a succession of French kings who used Fontainebleau as a resort and hunted in its forests. François I converted the hunting lodge into a royal palace in the Italian Renaissance style, bringing artists, including Benvenuto Cellini, there to work for him. Under this patronage, the School of Fontainebleau gained prestige, led by painters Rosso Fiorentino and Primaticcio. The artists adorned the 63m-long (207-ft.) **Gallery of François I ★★★**, where stucco-framed panels depict such scenes as *The Rape of Europa* and the monarch holding a pomegranate, a symbol of unity. The salamander, the symbol of the Chevalier king, is everywhere.

Gallery of François I.

The Ballroom at the Château de Fontainebleau.

If it's true that François I built Fontainebleau for his mistress, then Henri II, his successor, left a memorial to the woman he loved, Diane de Poitiers. Sometimes called the Gallery of Henri II, the **Ballroom** ★★★ displays the interlaced initials "H&D," referring to Henri and his mistress Diane. Competing with this illicit tandem are the initials "H&C," symbolizing Henri and his dowdy wife, Catherine de Medici. At one end of the room is a monumental fireplace supported by two bronze satyrs, made in 1966 (the originals were melted down during the Revolution). At the other side is the **Balcony of the Musicians,** with sculptured garlands. Looking up, you can see a wonderful example of a Renaissance ceiling displaying octagonal coffering adorned with rosettes. Above the wainscoting is a series of frescoes, painted between 1550 and 1558, that depict subjects such as *The Feast of Bacchus.* An architectural curiosity is the richly adorned **Louis XV Staircase** ★★. To make room for the monumental stairway, the floor was removed from the upper level bedroom of the duchesse d'Etampes, but luckily the beautiful sculpture and paintings by artist Primaticcio, which decorated the duchesse's suite, were incorporated into the final staircase design. Of the Italian frescoes that were preserved, one depicts the queen of the Amazons climbing into Alexander the Great's bed.

When Louis XIV ascended to the throne, Fontainebleau was all but forgotten due to the Sun King's preoccupation with Versailles. Though Louis XV and Marie Antoinette took an interest in Fontainebleau, the château only found its renewed glory under Napoleon, who used it as one of his bases. Imperial influences include the **throne room** where he abdicated rule of France, his **offices,** his monumental **bedroom,** and his **bathroom.** Second Empire decor can be observed in the **Papal Apartment,** where Pope Pius VII lodged for Napoleon's coronation in 1804 and was later held as the emperor's hostage in 1812–14. The ceilings date from the 16th century when the suite was the Queen Mother's Apartment.

You will leave the chateau via the horseshoe-shaped stairway where Napoleon stood to bid farewell to his shattered army before departing for Elba.

After your trek through the palace, visit the **gardens** and especially the **carp pond;** the gardens, however, are only a prelude to the Forest of Fontainebleau.

Place du Général-de-Gaulle. www.musee-chateau-fontainebleau.fr. © **01-60-71-50-70.** *Grands appartements* 10€ adults, 8€ students 18–25 (includes audio-guide); ticket to *petits appartements* and Napoleonic rooms 6.50€ adults, 5€ students 18–25; combination ticket including the *grands appartements* plus another section 15€ adults, free 17 and under. Apr–Sept Wed–Mon 9:30am–6pm; Oct–Mar Wed–Mon 9:30am–5pm.

Where to Eat

Chez Bernard ★ TRADITIONAL FRENCH   The premier dining choice in Fontainebleau has a covered terrace overlooking the château and the cour des Adieux. Chef Bernard Crogiez's cuisine is meticulous; he serves such dishes as oysters from the Bay of Quiberon or Aubrac regional steak with Roquefort sauce and home fries. Cheese lovers should save room for some local Brie de Meaux.

3 rue Royale. www.chez-bernard.fr © **01-64-22-24-68.** Reservations required. Main courses 23€–45€; fixed-price lunch Mon–Fri only 15€; fixed-price dinner daily 20€–25€. AE, MC, V. Tues–Sun noon–2pm; Mon–Sat 7:30–10pm. Closed 2 weeks in Aug and 1 week in Dec.

La Table des Marechaux FRENCH   Located close to the château in the Hotel Napoleon, this is a great value gastronomic restaurant, especially at lunch. Its modern sophisticated decor mirrors its traditional beautifully presented dishes. Start with the light vegetable mousse with scallop petals or splurge on the marbled foie gras with fig chutney. Main courses include scallops with endives and saffron cream, émincé of venison with five pepper sauce, and filet of beef Rossini. Service is friendly and professional. In the summer, try to get a table on the terrace in the private garden.

9 rue Grande. www.naposite.com. © **01-60-39-50-50.** Reservations recommended. Main courses 20€–32€; fixed-price menu 28€–40€. AE, MC, V. Daily noon–2pm and 7–10:30pm.

○ Hiking Along Trails Left by French Kings

The Forest of Fontainebleau is riddled with *sentiers* (hiking trails) made by French kings and their entourages who went hunting in the forest. A *Guide des Sentiers* is available at the tourist information center (see above). Bike paths also cut through the forest. You can rent bikes at **A La Petite Reine,** 4 rue de la Paroisse, located in the center of town, a few blocks from the chateau (www.ala petitereine.com; © **01-60-74-57-57**). The cost of a bike is 5€ per hour, 15€ for a half or full day. The shop is open Tuesday to Saturday from 9am to 7:30pm, and Sunday from 9am to 6pm.

Where to Stay

Grand Hôtel de l'Aigle-Noir (The Black Eagle) ★   This 17th-century mansion, once the home of Cardinal de Retz, has been a hotel since 1764 and is certainly the finest lodging in Fontainebleau. Conveniently situated opposite the château, it fits into this regal setting with its formal courtyard entrance surrounded by a high iron grill-gate and pillars crowned by black eagles. The rooms are decorated with Louis XVI, Empire, or Regency-era antiques or reproductions, with plush beds and elegant bathroom amenities. Enjoy a drink in the Napoleon III–style piano bar before dinner.

27 place Napoleon-Bonaparte, 77300 Fontainebleau. www.hotelaiglenoir.fr. ℂ **01-60-74-60-00.** Fax 01-60-74-60-01. 51 units. 170€–240€ double; 380€ suite. AE, DC, MC, V. Parking 10€. Closed 2 last weeks of Dec. **Amenities:** Restaurant; bar; exercise room; pool (indoor); room service. *In room:* A/C, hair dryer, minibar, Wi-Fi (free).

VAUX-LE-VICOMTE

55km (34 miles) SE of Paris

Ambition, jealousy, and treachery underlie the troubled history of the Château de Vaux-le-Vicomte, the most influential baroque castle in all of Europe. For the first time, a château's architectural plan, its interior and grounds, were designed in unison by the era's top artistic minds, creating a perfectly harmonious effect. However, the lavish château would become the theater of the tragic downfall of its owner, Nicolas Fouquet, and would lead to the birth of an even more extravagant palace: the Château de Versailles.

Essentials

GETTING THERE   Vaux might not be the easiest place to get to, but it's well worth the effort. Take the RER line D to Melun at Châtelet-Les Halles, Gare de Lyon, or Gare du Nord (30 min.–1hr.; round-trip 16€). In Melun take the shuttle bus to the château (6€–8€ round-trip, weekends and public holidays only) or take a taxi (around 15€ each way). If you don't take the shuttle back to the station, the château staff can call you a taxi, or call ℂ **01-64-52-51-50.** You can arrange bus tours through **ParisVision** (www.parisvision.com; ℂ **01-42-60-30-01**) or **Cityrama,** 149 rue St-Honoré, 1er (www.pariscityrama.com; ℂ **01-44-55-61-00;** from 55€– 175€). Cityrama also offers a tour with dinner and a visit to candlelight shows Saturdays at 6pm May to October (154€). If you're driving, take Autoroute A4 or A6 at Porte de Charenton or Ivry and follow the direction of Troyes-Nancy via the A5. Take the first exit at Saint-Germain-Laxis and follow the signs 1km (½ mile) to the château.

VISITOR INFORMATION   Tourist help can be obtained at the **Service Jeunesse et Citoyenneté,** 2 av. Gallieni (www.ville-melun.fr; ℂ **01-60-56-55-10**), located next to the train station in Melun. Open Tuesday to Saturday 10am to noon and 2 to 6pm. For information on the chateau, visit www.vaux-le-vicomte.com.

EVENING SPECTACLES   Candlelight evenings in the Vaux gardens take place on Saturdays from May through October. On the first and third Saturday of the month you can enjoy an extra special show including a fireworks display around 10:30pm. More information about tickets can be found at www.vaux-le-vicomte.com; excursions on these special evenings are also available through **Cityrama** and **ParisVision** (see contact details above).

Exploring Vaux-le-Vicomte

Le Château de Vaux le Vicomte ★★ CASTLE/GARDEN   Nicolas Fouquet, an aristocrat from an important noble family, acquired the estate of Vaux, well located between the royal castles Vincennes and Fontainebleau, in 1641 at the age of 26. Ambitious and clever, he quickly rose in the political ranks, soon reaching the prestigious position of superintendent of finance. In 1757, to create a stunning dwelling worthy of his status, Fouquet assembled an artistic dream team comprised of the architect Louis Le Vau, the landscape architect André Le Nôtre, and the painter-decorator Charles Le Brun.

To inaugurate his spectacular residence, Fouquet organized a celebration on August 17, 1661, which would outshine any previously held at the court of Louis XIV. The king and several hundred courtiers were treated to a sumptuous banquet served on solid silver and gold tableware, followed by a new comedy by Molière. To top everything off, a phenomenal fireworks display showered the night sky. However, Fouquet had gone too far with his opulent fete, inciting the young king's jealousy. Voltaire wrote, "On August 17, at 6 in the evening, Nicolas Fouquet was the King of France; at two in the morning, he was nobody." Within 2 weeks, poor Fouquet was arrested on trumped up charges of embezzlement,

Le Château de Vaux le Vicomte.

Experience a classic 17th-century *grande fête* (lavish party) during one of its **Chandelle evenings,** when the gardens and the castle are illuminated with 2,000 candles and costumed actors help re-create the ambience of the extravagant feasts in honor of the Sun King. For more information, see "Evening Spectacles," above.

and spent the rest of his days, not in the beautiful new château, but in a decrepit prison cell. The king seized the castle, confiscated its contents, and hired its artists and architects to work on Versailles.

Vaux-le-Vicomte was eventually released to Fouquet's widow, and the castle has remained in private hands ever since. Members of the Sommier family, who have owned it since 1875, have done an excellent job restoring Vaux to its original splendor.

The symmetrical château is flanked on either side by service buildings and is surrounded by a three-quarter rectangular moat. The front facade is rather simple; however, the south facade facing the gardens is where the grandeur is displayed, with an Italian-inspired central oval salon that soars up two stories and is crowned with an oval dome. Look carefully at the rear walls and you will also find "F" motifs and squirrels (Fouquet means squirrel), as well as images of the sun, a symbol that would be adopted by Louis XIV. The interior is beautifully decorated and has a much more intimate feel than Versailles. Many rooms feature allegorical Le Brun wall and ceiling paintings; some of the finest are in the **King's Apartments** and **Fouquet's bedroom,** known as the *Chambre des Muses.* The kitchens add insight into the life of the era and it's also interesting to have a look at the vast cellars where there is usually a temporary exhibit. If you have enough energy, climb up to the top of the dome for the best views of the impressive gardens.

The true highlight of Vaux is the famed **Le Nôtre gardens.** Here, Le Nôtre fused various new landscaping principles developed in the first half of the 17th century, creating what would become the model *jardin à la française.* Le Nôtre designed the perspective so that the composition is balanced from every point of view, creating an optical illusion with widening canals, water basins, and patterned parterres (mirror motifs that Le Brun also used indoors), which extend nearly 3km (1½ miles) along the central axis. If you can make it all the way to the end to where the Farnese Hercules statue is perched, you will be rewarded with the vista of the whole grounds and the château.

Vaux Le Vicomte 77950 Maincy. www.vaux-le-vicomte.com. ✆ **01-64-14-41-90.** Admission day pass 16€ adults, 13€ students and children 6–16. Candlelight visit pass 19€ adults, 17€ students and children 6–16, free for children under 6. Gardens only ticket 8€ adults and students. Mid-Mar to Oct and some public holidays such as Christmas Thurs–Tues 10am–6pm; July–Aug daily 10am–6pm. Candlelight evenings until midnight. Closed Nov to mid-Mar.

Where to Eat

In addition to the selections below, The **Ecureuil** restaurant (www.vaux-le-vicomte.com), located in a wing of the château's outbuildings, is a good option for casual dining; it's open daily from 11:30am to 6pm.

Le Nôtre gardens at le Château de Vaux-le-Vicomte.

Le Pouilly FRENCH   A 15-minute drive from Vaux is one of the region's best restaurants. Set in an old farmhouse, the dining room's stone-walls covered with antique tapestries, the high ceiling with wooden beams, and the large fire-place add to its ageless charm. Michelin-starred Chef Anthony Vallette prepares traditional French cuisine with a dash of innovation. Taste the freshness of his daily "from the market" specials or try the "from the past to today" gastronomic menu, which could include grilled tuna marinade with ginger, citrus fruit peels and endive salad, or cocotte of wild game with heirloom vegetables drizzled with carrot and beet concentrate. For dessert, treat yourself to the rich Guanaja chocolate cake with glazed bananas and caramel ice cream.

> ### Vaux on the Silver Screen
>
> You may recognize Vaux-le-Vicomte even if you haven't been there yet. The château is a popular location for French and Hollywood movie shoots. It has been featured in *The Man in the Iron Mask* with Leonardo DiCaprio and Sophia Coppola's *Marie Antoinette*.

1 rue de la fontaine, Pouilly le For, 77240 Vert Saint Denis. www.restaurant-lepouilly.com. © **01-64-09-56-64.** Main courses 25€–45€; fixed-price menu 45€ and 78€. MC, V. Tues–Sun 12:15–1:30pm and 7:30–930pm. Closed Sun for dinner.

Les Charmilles MODERN FRENCH   Located on the Diane parterre, facing the south facade of the château and the gardens, Les Charmilles' menu changes seasonally, offering a wide array of dishes. Take a break from the summer heat with the cool langoustine and salmon tartare served with cucumber and mint before savoring the medallion of veal with bacon cream or grilled suckling pig with Mogette beans. Finish your meal with pineapple soup with vanilla essence and mango sorbet. The restaurant is also open on the candlelight evenings, making it ideal for a romantic *dîner-à-deux* under the stars before the fireworks begin.

Located in the Vaux Gardens. ✆ **01-60-66-95-66.** Reservations recommended for candlelight evenings; ask about their special packages for these evenings. Main courses 10€–18€; fixed-price menu 35€. MC, V. Daily 11:30am–6pm and 11pm on candlelight evenings. Closed Nov–Mar.

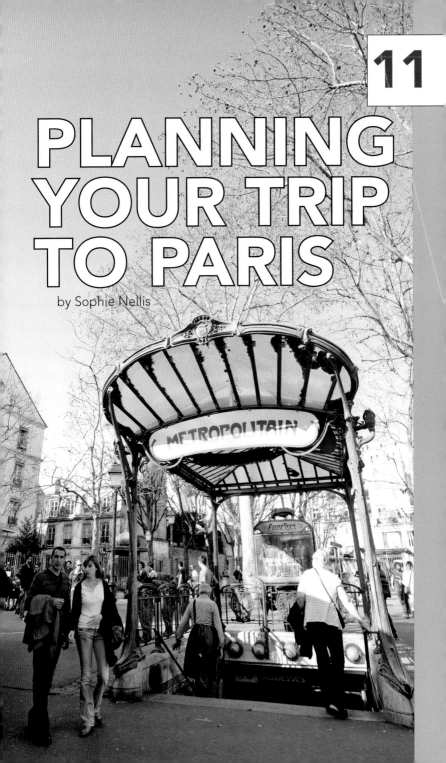

PLANNING YOUR TRIP TO PARIS

by Sophie Nellis

Paris is a relatively small capital city with a well-developed public transportation network, making it very easy to navigate. Although the Métro is probably the easiest way to get around, many people choose to get around by bus or bicycle. And if you're arriving by plane, consider how you will get into Paris from the airport before you arrive, as the major airports have several terminals and are quite far away from the city center.

GETTING THERE
By Plane

Paris has two international airports: **Aéroport d'Orly,** 18km (11 miles) south of the city, and **Aéroport Roissy-Charles-de-Gaulle,** 30km (19 miles) northeast. An Air France bus (Line 3; 19€ for a single journey) makes the 50- to 75-minute journey between the two airports every 30 to 45 minutes. A budget airport, **Beauvais,** is located about 70km (40m) from Paris.

ROISSY-CHARLES-DE-GAULLE AIRPORT There are three terminals at Roissy-Charles-De-Gaulle Airport (www.aeroportsdeparis.fr; ✆ **00-33-1-70-36-39-50** from abroad, or **39-50** from France only), which are some distance apart from each other. A free train called the CDGVAL connects all three of them to the two train stations.

The quickest way into central Paris is the fast **RER B** (Réseau Express Régional; www.ratp.fr), local trains that leave every 10 to 15 minutes between 5am and 11pm (midnight at weekends). It takes about 40 minutes to get to Paris, and RER B stops at several Métro stations including Gare du Nord (sometimes referred to as Paris Nord), Châtelet-Les-Halles, Saint-Michel-Notre-Dame, Luxembourg, Port-Royal, and Denfert-Rochereau. A single ticket costs 9.10€ and you can buy it from the machines located in the stations at both terminals.

Air France operates two buses from the airport to the center of Paris. **Air France bus Line 2** (www.cars-airfrance.com; ✆ **08-92-35-08-20**) costs 15€ one-way; children 2 to 11 pay 7.50€. It stops at the Palais des Congrès (Porte Maillot) and continues to place Charles de Gaulle–Etoile, where you can take the Métro to anywhere in Paris. The journey, depending on the traffic, takes 45 to 55 minutes. The bus leaves every 20 minutes between 6am and 10pm and there are two additional buses that leave the airport at 10:30pm and 11pm.

Air France bus Line 4 (www.cars-airfrance.com; ✆ **08-92-35-08-20**) is slightly more expensive, charging 16.50€ one-way; children 2 to 11 pay 7.50€, because it takes you to the south of Paris. It stops at Gare de Lyon and continues onto Gare Montparnasse, both of which are connected to several Métro lines. The journey, depending on the traffic, takes about 60 minutes. The bus leaves every 30 minutes between 6am and 9:30pm. Bear

PREVIOUS PAGE: **A Métro stop entrance.**

in mind that the Air France buses may be affected by strike action within Air France.

The **Roissybus** (www.ratp.fr/en/ratp/r_28065/roissybus; ✆ **32-46** from France only) departs from the airport daily from 6am to 11pm and costs 10€ for the 60-minute ride. Departures are every 15 to 20 minutes between 5:45am and 10pm and every 30 minutes between 10pm and 11pm. The bus leaves you in the center of Paris, at the corner of rue Scribe and rue Auber, near the Opera House.

A **taxi** from Roissy into the city will cost at least 50€, not including 1€ per item of luggage, and the fare is 15% higher from 5pm to 10am, as well as on Sundays and Bank Holidays. Long, orderly lines for taxis form outside each of the airport's terminals.

ORLY AIRPORT   Orly (www.aeroportsdeparis.fr; ✆ **00-33-1-70-36-39-50** from abroad, or **39-50** from France) has two terminals—Orly Sud (south) for international flights and Orly Ouest (west) for both domestic and international flights.

There are no direct trains from Orly to the center of Paris; however, you can take the 8-minute monorail **OrlyVal** to the RER station "Anthony" to get **RER B** into the center. Combined travel time is about 45 to 55 minutes, and the train stops at several Métro stations including Denfert-Rochereau, Port-Royal, Luxembourg, Saint-Michel-Notre-Dame, Châtelet-Les-Halles, and Gare du Nord (sometimes referred to as Paris Nord). Trains run between 5am and midnight and the one-way fare for the OrlyVal plus the RER B is 11€.

Alternatively, you can take the **Paris par le Train bus** from Orly Ouest and Orly Sud to station "Pont de Rungis" and then get **RER C** to Paris. Buses leave every 15 minutes between 5:33am and 10:18pm and then every 30 minutes from 10:18pm to 12:49am. RER C stops at several Métro stations in Paris, including Invalides, Saint-Michel-Notre-Dame, and Gare Austerlitz, and trains run between 5am and midnight. Combined travel time is about 30 minutes and the one-way fare for the Paris par le Train bus and the RER C is 6.10€.

Air France bus Line 1 (www.cars-airfrance.com; ✆ **08-92-35-08-20**) leaves from Exit L of Orly Sud and from Exit D of Orly Ouest every 20 minutes between 6am and 11:30pm, stopping at Gare Montparnasse, Invalides, and Charles de Gaulle-Etoile. The fare is 11.50€ one-way, 18.50€ round-trip, and 5.50€ for children ages 2 to 11. Depending on the traffic, the journey takes between 30 and 50 minutes.

A **taxi** from Orly to central Paris will cost at least 50€, not including 1€ per item of luggage, and the fare is 15% higher from 5pm to 10am, as well as on Sundays and Bank Holidays. Lines for taxis form outside Exit L of Orly Sud and Gate B on the arrivals level of Orly Ouest.

BEAUVAIS AIRPORT   Beauvais airport (www.aeroportbeauvais.com; ✆ **08-92-68-20-66**) is located 70km (40 miles) from Paris and is served by budget airlines such as Ryanair, Wizzair, and Blue Air. Buses leave 15 to 20 minutes after each flight has landed, and, depending on the traffic, take about 1 hour and 15 minutes to get to Paris. The bus drops you at Porte Maillot (Métro: Porte Maillot). To return to Beauvais, you need to be at the bus station 3 hours and 15 minutes before the departure of your flight. A one-way ticket costs 15€.

By Train

Paris has six major stations: **Gare d'Austerlitz** (55 quai d'Austerlitz, 13e), serving the center of France, with trains to and from the Loire Valley and Limousin, as well as night trains to Nice and Spain; **Gare de Lyon** (place Louis-Armand, 12e), serving the center and southeast, with trains to and from Burgundy, the Alps, Provence, the Côte d'Azur (Nice, Cannes, St-Tropez), and beyond, to Geneva and Italy; **Gare Montparnasse** (17 bd. Vaugirard, 15e), serving the west and southwest with trains to and from Brittany, Normandy, Bordeaux, as well as trains to the northwest of Spain; **Gare St-Lazare** (13 rue d'Amsterdam, 8e), serving the northwest, with trains to and from Normandy; **Gare de l'Est** (place du 11-Novembre-1918, 10e), serving the east, with trains to and from Strasbourg, Reims, and beyond to Germany, Switzerland, and Austria; and **Gare du Nord** (18 rue de Dunkerque, 10e), serving the north, with trains to and from Picardy, and beyond to the U.K., Holland, Denmark, and Germany. Each station can be reached by bus or Métro; further information on each station can be obtained from **SNCF** (La Société Nationale des Chemins de Fer Français; www.gares-connexions.com/en).

Eurostar trains arrive at and depart from the Gare du Nord (www.eurostar.com). Thanks to the new high-speed track, the journey between Paris and London St. Pancras now only takes 2 hour and 15 minutes (it's a little longer if the train goes via Ashford or Lille). Cheap return tickets to London are available for 88€ if you are flexible about the times and dates of your trip.

For information about train travel from Paris to other parts of France or other destinations in Europe, and to make reservations, use SNCF (www.voyages-sncf.com). Prices depend on the distance of the journey, when you make the reservation, and the type of train you book (for example, the **TGV,** France's high-speed train service, is usually more expensive than regional trains). For further information about international train travel try **Rail Europe** (www.raileurope.com). *Warning:* As in most major cities, the stations and surrounding areas are rather seedy and frequented by pickpockets. Be alert, especially at night.

By Bus

Most coaches arrive at the **Eurolines France** station, 28 av. du Général-de-Gaulle, Bagnolet (www.eurolines.fr; ✆ **08-92-89-90-91;** Métro: Gallieni). Eurolines has recently expanded its national network and now operates between Paris and various cities in France, including Bordeaux, Lille, and Lyon. Although the journey time is longer than if you took the train, prices are a lot cheaper than SNCF.

By Car

Driving in Paris is *not* recommended. Parking is difficult and the traffic dense. If you drive, remember that Paris is encircled by a ring road, the *périphérique.* Always obtain detailed directions to your destination, including the name of the exit (called *portes*) on the *périphérique* as exits aren't numbered. Avoid rush hours.

The major highways into Paris are A1 from the north; A13 from Rouen, Normandy, and other points northwest; A10 from Spain and the southwest; A6 and A7 from the French Alps, the Riviera, and Italy; and A4 from eastern France.

The Channel Tunnel—the undersea rail tunnel that connects France and the U.K.—accommodates not only trains but cars, buses, taxis, and motorcycles.

The Chunnel, as it is informally known, is home to the Eurostar and the **Eurotunnel,** a train that carries vehicles under the English Channel (www.euro tunnel.com; ℭ **08-10-63-03-04** in France, or **08443-35-35-35** in the U.K.), connecting Calais, France, with Folkestone, England; the journey takes a mere 35 minutes. It operates up to four shuttles an hour and prices start at 30€ per car.

Rental cars are available at all the major airports and train stations in Paris. You must be over 25 and have held a driving license for at least a year. The major car rental companies are **Hertz** (www.hertz.fr; ℭ **08-25-86-18-61**), **Europcar** (www.europcar.fr; ℭ **08-25-35-83-58**), and **Avis** (www.avis.fr; ℭ **08-21-23-07-60**).

By Ferry from England or Ireland

Ferry travel to France appears to be in its waning days, since more and more travelers are opting for low-cost flights or a much speedier passage through the Channel Tunnel. In England the two leading operators of ferries are **P&O Ferries** (ℭ **08716 64 21 21** in the U.K.; www.poferries.com), which runs ferries from Dover to Calais, and **Britanny Ferries** (ℭ **08712 44 07 44** in the U.K.; www.britanny-ferries.com), which runs ferries from Portsmouth to Le Havre. **Irish Ferries** (ℭ **0818 300 400** in Ireland; www.irishferries.com) operates an overnight ferry from Cherbourg to Rosslare. Call or check websites for specific times, prices, and points of departure/arrival.

SPECIAL-INTEREST TRIPS & TOURS

An organized tour can provide good background information on the city and help you get your bearings. There are a number of different tour options on offer in Paris, including boat tours, bus tours, and walking tours. Many visitors are looking for more and more creative ways of getting to know Paris. Whether you dream of learning to speak French or perfecting your French culinary skills, here are several ideas for exploring Paris in a different, more innovative, way.

Boat Tours

Whether you choose to explore the Seine or Paris's canals, a boat tour is a lovely way to see Paris. **Bateaux-Mouches** (www.bateaux-mouches.fr; ℭ **01-42-25-96-10;** Métro: Alma-Marceau) cruises depart from Pont de l'Alma on the Right Bank of the Seine, and last for a little over 1 hour; cruises run regularly from 10:15am to 11pm from April to September, and from 11am to 9pm from October to March. Tickets cost 11€ and the commentary is in French and English.

On the other side of the river, in front of the Eiffel Tower, the **Bateaux Parisiens** (www.bateauxparisiens.com; ℭ **01-76-64-14-45;** Métro: Bir Kakeim; RER Champ de Mars Tour Eiffel) offers smaller boats that run every half hour from 10:30am to 10:30pm from April to September, and every hour from 10:30am to 10pm from October to March. The tour lasts for an hour, the commentary is available in 13 languages, and tickets cost 12€. Bateaux Parisiens also runs a tour departing from Notre-Dame but the service is a lot less regular.

Vedettes du Pont Neuf (www.vedettesdupontneuf.com; ℭ **01-46-33-98-38;** Métro: Pont Neuf) runs hour-long cruises from the Square du Vert

Galant at the tip of the Ile de la Cité. Tickets cost 13€ and boats depart roughly every 30 minutes from 10:30am to 10:30pm from mid-March to October, and less regularly from November to mid-March. Cheaper tickets can be bought on the Internet.

The best canal cruise is **Canauxrama** (www.canauxrama.com; ℂ **01-42-39-15-00**; Métro: Jaurés or Bastille), which tours the picturesque Canal St-Martin. Boats leave from Bassin de la Villette at 9:45am and 2:45pm, and from Bastille at 9:45am and 2:30pm; tickets cost 16€ (13.50€ if you buy them on the Internet), and the cruise takes about 2½ hours. The service runs daily from May to September and a less regular service is run during the rest of the year.

Bus Tours

A bus tour is a good way to get orientated and see the major sites. **L'Open Tour** (www.parislopentour.com; ℂ **01-42-66-56-56**) offers four bus route tours—Paris Grand Tour, Montmartre–Grands Boulevards, Montparnasse–St-Germain, and Bastille–Bercy—which run from around 9am to 7:30pm. A 1-day pass costs 29€, and a 2-day pass 32€. **Les Cars Rouge** (www.carsrouges.com; ℂ **01-53-95-39-53**) offers a hop-on, hop-off trip that stops at nine sites, including the Eiffel Tower, the Louvre, Notre-Dame, and the Champs-Élysées. Buses leave every 10 minutes in summer and every 20 minutes in winter. A multilingual commentary is available and a 2-day ticket is 26€.

Cooking Schools

Le Cordon Bleu (www.cordonbleu.edu; ℂ **01-53-68-22-50**; Métro: Vaugirard) is one of the most famous French cooking schools—this is where Julia Child mastered the art of French cooking. The school is well-known for its longer cooking courses, which last several months and offer would-be professionals a diploma at the end of the course; prices for one level start at 8,500€. If this sounds like too much of a commitment, short courses are on offer for all food enthusiasts, with prices starting at 45€ for a 1-hour class. Classes are translated into English.

Less formal but equally enjoyable are the cooking classes offered by **La Cuisine Paris** (www.lacuisineparis.com; ℂ **01-40-51-78-18**; Métro: Hôtel de Ville), a friendly school set up by a Franco-American team. They offer French cooking classes by professional chefs in both French and English, including the popular French Macaron Class. The calendar of classes is updated every month and class sizes are small (max. 12 people, depending on the class). Prices range from 65€ for 2 hours to 150€ for 4 hours.

Similarly, **Cook'n with Class** (www.cooknwithclass.com; ℂ **01-42-55-70-59**; Métro: Château Rouge, Lamarck-Caulaincourt) offers a range of individual and small-group classes, the most popular of which is the Morning Market Class which includes a walk to a local market. Set up by a French chef, all classes are taught in English by professionals and prices range from 125€ for 3-hour classes to 185€ for 5-hour classes.

Cycling & Running Tours

Fat Tire Bike Tours (www.fattirebiketours.com/paris; ℂ **01-56-58-10-54**; Métro: RER Champ de Mars Tour Eiffel) offers a 4-hour day- and night-tour of Paris by bike; tickets cost 28€, including the bike rental. Tours leave from the south leg of the Eiffel Tower daily at 11am and 3pm from April to October and daily at 11am from November to March. This company also offers bike tours of Versailles and Monet's gardens in Giverny.

Paris à Vélo, C'est Sympa (www.parisvelosympa.com; ☎ **01-48-87-60-01;** Métro: Richard Lenoir) offers four 3-hour bike tours in French and English: Heart of Paris, Unusual Paris, Paris Contrasts, and for the early birds, Paris at Dawn. The tour schedule varies, so check the website for departure times. Tickets cost 34€, which includes bike rental and insurance.

Paris Running Tours (www.parisrunningtours.com; Métro: Alma-Marceau) offers jogging tours of the city. The standard tours—Paris West, Paris East, Paris North, and the popular Da Vinci Code tour—take participants on a 10km (6-mile) jog, and cost 50€. (Each additional runner costs 25€.) All tours start and end at Alma, except Paris North, which ends at Abbesses.

Guided Tours

4 Roues Sous 1 Parapluie (www.4roues-sous-1parapluie.com; ☎ **08-00-80-06-31**) offers chauffeur-driven themed rides around Paris in its colorful fleet of Citroën 2CV, the legendary French car described as *"4 roues sous 1 parapluie"* ("4 wheels under 1 umbrella") by the director of Citroën in 1935. It is a fun and stylish way to discover the city, particularly if it's your first visit to Paris. Tours include Romantic Paris and Unknown Paris; it is also possible to customize your own tour. Prices start at 20€ per person if there are 3 people in the car (the fewer people there are in the car, the more expensive it is).

Paris is a dream-come-true for shopaholics. **Chic Shopping Paris** (www. chicshoppingparis.com; ☎ **06-77-65-08-01**) offers tours that are designed to give visitors a behind-the-scenes shopping experience. Focusing on new shops and discovering new trends, tours include a Chic and Cheap tour, a Sunday Shopping tour, and an Arts and Antiques tour of a flea market. All of the standard tours last for 4 to 4½ hours and cost 100€ per person, and custom tours are available.

Created by professional travel writer Heather Stimmler-Hall, **Secrets of Paris** (www.secretsofparis.com; ☎ **01-43-36-69-85**) offers private, customized tours of Paris. All tours are designed with the client, and each unique tour aims to reveal a previously unseen side of the city. Suggested themes include Multicultural Paris, Graffiti Art tours, and Paris After Dark. Prices range from 150€ to 600€, depending on the length of the tour.

Hot Air Balloon Tours

A unique way to see the city from above is by a hot air balloon. Located in the Parc André Citroën in the 15e, **Ballon de Paris** (www.ballondeparis.com; ☎ **01-44-26-20-00;** Métro Javel or Balard) has a hot air balloon that reaches an altitude of 150m (492 ft.) but remains tethered to the ground. Tickets cost 12€ Saturday and Sunday, 10€ Monday through Friday.

Language Classes

The **Alliance Française** (www.alliancefr.org; ☎ **01-42-84-90-00**), a highly reputable nonprofit organization, offers French language classes at its Paris school. Prices are calculated per week and the price decreases per week the longer you stay. Evening courses (4 hr. per week) start at 55€, general French classes

(9 hr. per week) start at 95€, and the intensive course starts at 216€. Reservations can be made 2 to 6 weeks in advance.

Les Cours de Civilisation Française de la Sorbonne (www.ccfs-sorbonne.fr; ☏ **01-44-10-77-00**) offers French-language classes for students of all levels. There are four semesters per year, and within each semester a range of different classes are offered. Prices vary depending on the course and the semester; a 2-week conversation class costs 260€, while the 12-week intensive summer session costs 2,800€.

Walking Tours

Paris was made for walking and the best way to discover the city is on foot. **Context** (www.contexttravel.com; ☏ **01-72-81-36-35**) organizes small group and private walking tours led by scholars and experts. Tours range from general 2-hour orientation strolls to longer, more focused themed walks, such as an in-depth tour of the Louvre or a gastronomic stroll. Prices range from 40€ to 85€ per person, depending on the walk. **Sight Seeker's Delight** (www.sightseekers delight.com; ☏ **06-65-98-01-66**) offers a range of walking tours, including Paris along the Seine, and a Whirlwind Jump-out tour. Tours last from 2½ to 4 hours and prices vary between 25€ and 40€. **Paris Walks** (www.paris-walks. com; ☏ **01-48-09-21-40**) organizes 2-hour walks of the city, based on either a theme or a neighborhood. Most of the walks cost 12€ and do not require a reservation, but some of the walks, such as the Chocolate Tour, are a little more expensive and need to be booked in advance.

GETTING AROUND
Finding an Address

The river Seine divides Paris into the **Rive Droite (Right Bank)** to the north and the **Rive Gauche (Left Bank)** to the south. Paris is divided into 20 municipal districts called arrondissements. Arrondissements spiral out clockwise from the 1st, which is the geographical center of the city. The 2nd through the 8th form a ring around the 1st, and the 9th through the 17th form an outer ring around the inner ring. The 18th, 19th, and 20th are at the far northern and eastern reaches of the Right Bank. Arrondissements 5, 6, 7, 13, 14, and 15 are on the Left Bank.

Most city maps are divided by arrondissement, and addresses include the arrondissement number (in Roman or Arabic numerals and followed by "ème" or "e," for example 10e or 10ème). Paris also has its own version of a zip code. For example, the mailing address for a hotel is written as "Paris 75014." The last two digits, 14, indicate that the address is in the 14th arrondissement—in this case, Montparnasse.

Numbers on buildings running parallel to the Seine usually follow the course of the river—east to west. On perpendicular streets, the lowest building numbers are closest to the river.

MAPS

If you're staying more than 2 or 3 days, purchase an inexpensive pocket-size book called *Paris Pratique par arrondissement,* available at newsstands and bookshops for around 8€. This guide provides you with a Métro map and maps of each arrondissement, with all streets listed and keyed. Free maps of the Paris Métro and bus and RER networks are available at all Métro stations.

By Public Transport

The majority of Paris's public transport is run by **RATP** (Régie Autonome des Transports Parisiens; www.ratp.fr; ✆ **08-92-69-32-46,** or 32-46 in France). Paris and its suburbs are divided into six travel zones, and the city itself is covered by zones 1 and 2.

RATP tickets are valid on the Métro, bus, and RER. You can buy tickets over the counter or from machines at most Métro entrances. A **single ticket** costs 1.70€ and a *carnet* of 10 tickets costs 12.70€. Tourists can benefit from a **Paris Visite** pass, which offers unlimited travel in zones on bus, Métro, and RER, and discounts on some attractions. A 1-day pass for zones 1 to 3 costs 9.75€, 2-day pass 16€, a 3-day pass 22€, and a 5-day pass 31€. Each day begins at 5:30am and finishes at 5:30am the following day. It is also possible to buy more expensive passes for zones 1 to 6. Slightly cheaper is the 1-day **Mobilis** ticket, which offers unlimited travel in zones 1 and 2 and costs 6.40€. For travelers under 26, look out for the **Ticket Jeunes,** a 1-day ticket which can be used on a Saturday, Sunday, or bank holiday, and provides unlimited travel in zones 1 to 3 for 3.55€. The day begins at 5:30am and finishes at 2:30am the following day.

If you're staying for a while, it's worth getting the **Navigo Découverte,** a swipe card that you can buy at most stations for 5€. You must provide a passport photo, but once you have the card it offers unlimited travel in the relevant zones. The weekly tariff (which runs Mon–Sun) for zones 1 and 2 is 19€, and the monthly tariff (which runs from the first to the last day of the month) is 63€.

BY MÉTRO (SUBWAY)

The Métro is the fastest and most efficient way to get around Paris. All lines have a different number and color, and the final destination of each line, which will tell you which direction the train is going in, is clearly marked on subway maps, and in the system's underground passageways. The Métro runs daily from 5:30am to 12:40am (last departure at 1:30am Fri–Sat). It's reasonably safe at any hour but beware of pickpockets.

To familiarize yourself with the Métro, check out the color map on the inside back cover of this book. Most stations display a map of the Métro at the entrance. To locate your train on a map, find your destination, follow the line to the end of its route, and note the name of the final stop, which is that line's direction. In the station, follow the signs for your direction in the passageways until you come to the right platform.

To change lines follow the signs saying *Correspondances,* which usually indicate the numbers of the other Métro lines. Some stations such as Châtelet-Les-Halles, République, and Montparnasse-Bienvenüe require long walks. Don't follow a *Sortie* (exit) sign, or you'll have to pay again to get back on the train.

At the turnstile entrances to the Métro, insert your ticket and pass through. Hold onto your ticket as you occasionally need it to change trains or exit a station. There are also occasional ticket checks on trains in Métro stations.

BY RER

A suburban train system, **RER** (Réseau Express Regional), passes through the heart of Paris, traveling faster than the Métro and running daily from 5am to 1am. This system works like the Métro and requires the same tickets (if you stay within zones 1 and 2). If you go further afield, for example to Versailles, you will need a more expensive ticket available from Métro stations. The major stops on Paris's Right Bank, linking the RER to the Métro, are Nation, Gare de Lyon, St-Lazare, Charles-de-Gaulle–Etoile, Gare de l'Est, Gare du Nord, as well as Châtelet-Les-Halles. On the Left Bank, RER stops include Denfert-Rochereau, St-Michel, Invalides, and Champ de Mars Tour Eiffel. The five RER lines are marked A through E, and each line corresponds to a different color. Different branches are labeled by a number, for example the C5 Line serving Versailles–Rive Gauche. Electric signboards next to each track outline all the possible stops along the way. Make sure that the little square next to your intended stop is lit up.

BY BUS

Buses are obviously slower than the Métro. The majority run from 6:30am to 9:30pm (a few operate until 12:30am) and service is limited on Sundays and holidays. You can use Métro tickets on the buses or you can buy tickets directly from the driver (1.90€). Tickets need to be validated in the machine next to the driver's cabin.

There is usually a map of the bus route at the bus stop, which lists all of the stops, highlights which stop you are currently at, and indicates the direction of travel. Each bus route has a different number and a corresponding color. Inside the bus, the next stop is usually written on an electronic panel on the ceiling of the bus. Press the red button when you want to get off.

At night, after the bus and Métro services stop running, there are a number of night bus lines called **Noctilien** (www.noctilien.fr). Most of the lines leave from place du Châtelet and pass by the main train stations, crossing the city's major streets before leaving Paris for the suburbs (Mon–Thurs every hour 12:30am–5:30am; Fri–Sat every 30 min.). Although often a little rowdy, the night buses are usually quite safe. Tickets cost 1.90€ if bought from the driver but travel passes are valid.

BY TRAM

Paris has three tramway lines, but these lines are currently being extended and four new lines are being added. The extensions are due to be completed by the end of 2012 and the new lines between 2013 and 2015. Line 1 runs from Saint-Denis RER station to Noisy-le-Sec; Line 2 runs from La Défense to Porte de Versailles–Parc des Expositions; and Line 3 from Pont du Garigliano to Porte d'Ivry. All three lines connect to bus stops and both Métro and RER stations, and tickets are the same price as the Métro. However, because they run along the outskirts of Paris, most visitors are not likely to take them.

By Bicycle

Cycling in Paris has been revolutionized by the hugely successful **Vélib'** scheme (the name comes from *vélo* meaning bicycle and *liberté* meaning freedom) launched in 2007 (www.velib.paris.fr). There are now more than 20,000 bicycles available at 1,500 stations—that's one every 300m (186 ft.)—around Paris. The service can be accessed at any time of day and to get a bike you need to have an account. Creating one is reasonably easy to do on the machines located at every Vélib' stand, but make sure you select the English-language option before you read the instructions. You can choose either a 1-day (1.70€) or 7-day (8€) account (which you have to pay for using a credit card) and you will be asked to choose a PIN code. This will give you unlimited access to the Vélib' service. You then use the PIN to select a bike from those available at your stand. Journeys under 30 minutes are free, and after that the price goes up by 1€ every half an hour. If you arrive at a Vélib' station to return a bike and discover it is full, you can enter your code in the machine and have 15 minutes to find another terminal. To use the services you will be asked to pay a 150€ *caution* (deposit), which freezes the money in your account until the bike is returned. With foreign credit cards this can sometimes take a couple of days. **Note:** It is preferable to cycle in bike lanes—there are 400km (250 miles) of green bike paths in Paris—and it's illegal to cycle on footpaths or down one-way streets. Remember to cycle on the right-hand side of the street and to give way to your right. Remember that the bikes do not come with helmets.

Alternatively, you can rent a bike from **Paris à vélo, c'est sympa!,** 22 rue Alphonse Baudin (www.parisvelosympa.com; ✆ **01-48-87-60-01;** Métro: St-Sébastien-Froissart or Richard Lenoir). Rentals cost 12€ for half a day and 15€ for a full day, but they do require 250€ or a passport as a deposit. Open Monday to Friday from 9:30am to 1pm and 2 to 6pm (until 5:30pm in winter), Saturday and Sunday 9am to 7pm (9:30 am to 6:30pm in winter). Closed Tuesday.

Vintage Vespas are available for rent from **Left Bank Scooters** (www.left bankscooters.com; ✆ **06-78-12-04-24**) from 70€ per day, and the company will deliver the scooters to your hotel or apartment. A credit card deposit of 1,200€ is required, but this can be reduced to 500€ for an additional fee. This amount is held rather than charged on a credit card.

Note that bicycles are not allowed on buses or the Métro, except on Line 1 on Sundays and public holidays, until 4:30pm. Bikes can be taken aboard all RER trains except during rush hours (Mon–Fri 6:30–9am and 4:30–7pm).

By Car

Although Paris is a stressful and difficult city to drive in, there is a new concept in Paris that looks to revolutionize our relationship with the car. Named after the highly successful, Vélib', the **Autolib'** (www.autolib.eu; ✆ **08-00-94-20-00**) scheme offers the public a short-term, self-service rental service with electric cars. The 100% electric Bluecars mean no noise or air pollution, and if it leads to a reduction in the number of privately-owned cars, there will hopefully be fewer traffic jams. There are currently 250 Bluecars and 250 rental stations in Paris and the surrounding area, but this is due to increase throughout 2012. To register you must go to one of the Autolib' parking spaces or to the Autolib' information center (5 rue Edouard, 5e) with your driving license, a valid form of ID, and a credit card. Here you choose a subscription which enables you to use the service. A 24-hour subscription costs 10€, 7 days costs 15€, and a year costs 144€. You are given a badge that you then pass over the sensor at a rental station to unlock the car. Unplug it from the charger and drive away. To return it, you must select an

Autolib' station and plug in the Bluecar. The first 30 minutes costs 7€, the second 30 minutes 6€, and every additional 30 minutes is charged at 8€. For information about other car rental companies, please refer to the "By Car" section of "Getting There," earlier in this chapter.

By Boat

The **Batobus** (www.batobus.com; ☎ **08-25-05-01-01**) is a 150-passenger boat that operates along the Seine, stopping at such points of interest as the Eiffel Tower, Musée d'Orsay, the Louvre, Notre-Dame, and the Hôtel de Ville. Unlike the Bateaux-Mouches (p. 381), the Batobus does not provide a recorded commentary. The only fare option available is a day pass valid for either 1, 2, or 5 days, each allowing as many entrances and exits as you want. A 1-day pass costs 15€ for adults, and 7€ for children 16 and under. From November to mid-April boats operate daily every 25 to 35 minutes, between 10am and 6pm (closed most of January). From mid-April to October boats operate daily every 17 to 25 minutes between 10am and 9:30pm. The timetable changes slightly every year so it's always worth double-checking on the website.

By Taxi

Taxi drivers are organized into a union that limits their number to around 15,000, which can make it difficult to find a taxi in Paris. It's virtually impossible to get a taxi at rush hour, and your best option for finding a taxi is often to wait at a *station de taxi*. Located across the city, you'll find a *station de taxi* by looking for a blue sign saying TAXI above a turquoise column.

You can hail regular cabs on the street when their signs are lit with a white light. An orange light means a taxi is occupied. Some taxis are now changing to a new system where green means unoccupied and red occupied. Taxis are easier to find at the many stands near Métro stations. The flag drops at 2.20€ and the rates are then based on time and zone. From 10am to 5pm you pay .89€ per kilometer, from 5pm to 10am you pay 1.14€ to 1.38€ per kilometer. Journeys within Paris usually cost between 10€ and 20€, and there is a minimum fee of 6.10€.

You're allowed several pieces of luggage free if they're transported inside and are less than 5 kilograms (11 lb.). Heavier suitcases carried in the trunk cost 1€ to 2€ apiece. For radio cabs, contact **Les Taxis Bleus** (www.taxis-bleus.com; ☎ **01-49-36-29-48**) or **Taxi G7** (www.taxisg7.fr, ☎ **01-47-39-47-39**). Avoid minicabs or unlicensed taxis and make sure the meter is at 2.20€ when you first get in.

On Foot

Paris is made for walking; this is the only real way to explore the city in any depth. Stroll the streets and absorb the sights and smells. On almost every block you will find something of interest—a Belle Époque shopping arcade, a Renaissance square, a medieval rampart. After walking through an arrondissement, stop in a cafe for coffee and some people-watching. If you'd like more guidance instead of an aimless stroll, you can always refer to chapter 5, "Strolling Around Paris."

FAST FACTS

Area Codes   The country code for France is 33 and the area code for Paris is 01. See "Telephones," later in this section, for further information.

Business Hours   Opening hours in Paris are erratic. Most museums close 1 day a week (usually Mon or Tues) and some national holidays. Museum hours tend to be from 9:30am to 6pm. Some museums, particularly the smaller ones, close for lunch from noon to 2pm. Generally, **offices** are open Monday to Friday from 9am to 6pm, but don't count on it—always call first. **Banks** tend to be open from 9am to 5pm Monday to Friday, but some branches are also open on Saturday. **Large stores** are open from around 10am to 6 or 7pm. Some **small stores** have a lunch break that can last for up to 2 hours, from noon onward, but this is becoming increasingly rare. Most shops, except those in the Marais or on the Champs-Élysées, are closed on Sunday. Restaurants are typically closed on Mondays and many businesses across the city are closed in August.

Car Rental   See "By Car" under "Getting There" and "By Car" under "Getting Around," earlier in this chapter.

Cellphones   See "Mobile Phones," later in this section.

Crime   See "Safety," later in this section.

Customs   What you can bring into France: Citizens of E.U. countries can bring in any amount of goods as long as the goods are intended for their personal use and not for resale. Non-E.U. citizens are entitled to 200 cigarettes, 100 small cigars, 50 cigars, or 250g of tobacco duty-free. You can also bring in 2 liters of wine or beer and 1 liter of spirits (more than 22% alcohol). In addition, you can bring in 50g (1.76oz) of perfume.

What you can take out of France:

AUSTRALIAN CITIZENS   A helpful brochure is available from the Australian Customs and Border Protection Service *Know Before You Go*, online under "Guide for Travelers." For more information, call the **Australian Customs Service** (www.customs.gov.au; ✆ **1300/363-263** in Australia, or 612/9313-3010 if you're abroad). The duty-free allowance in Australia is A$900 or, for those 17 or younger, A$450. If you're returning with valuables you already own, you should file the "Goods Exported in Passenger Baggage" form.

CANADIAN CITIZENS   For a clear summary of Canadian rules, ask for the booklet *I Declare* issued by the **Canada Border Services Agency** (www.cbsa-asfc.gc.ca; ✆ **800/461-9999** in Canada, or 204/983-3500 from abroad, under "Travel Tips"). Canada allows its citizens a C$750 exemption and you're allowed to mail gifts to Canada from abroad valued at less than C$60 a day, provided they're unsolicited and don't contain alcohol or tobacco (write on the package "Unsolicited gift, under C$60 value"). All valuables, including serial numbers of valuables you already own, should be declared on the Y38 form before departure from Canada.

NEW ZEALAND CITIZENS   The answers to most questions regarding customs can be found on the website of the **New Zealand Customs Service** under "Customs charges, duties and allowances" (www.customs.govt.nz; ✆ **0800/4-CUSTOMS,** 0800/428-786, or 649/927-8036 from outside New Zealand).The duty-free allowance for New Zealand is NZ$700. Fill out a certificate of export, listing the valuables you are taking out of the country, so that you can bring them back without paying duty.

U.K. CITIZENS   When returning to the U.K. from an E.U. country such as France, you can bring in an unlimited amount of most goods. There is no limit on what you can bring back from an E.U. country, as long as the items are for personal use (this includes gifts) and you have already paid the duty and tax. However, you may be asked to prove that the goods are for your own use. For information, contact **HM Revenue Customs** (✆ **0845 010 9000;** www.hmrc.gov.uk).

U.S. CITIZENS   For specifics on what you can bring back and the corresponding fees, download the invaluable free pamphlet *Know Before You Go* online at **www.cbp. gov**. Or, contact the **U.S. Customs & Border Protection (CBP)** (✆ **877/CBP-5511** [877/227-5511] in the U.S. or 703/526-4200 from outside the U.S). Returning U.S. citizens who have been away for 48 hours or more are allowed to bring back, once every 30 days, $800 worth of merchandise duty-free. On mailed gifts, the duty-free limit is $100. To avoid having to pay duty on foreign-made personal items you owned before your trip, bring along a bill of sale, insurance policy, jeweler's appraisal, or receipt of purchase or request a Certificate of Registration for Personal Effects Taken Abroad before you leave. You cannot bring fresh foodstuffs into the U.S.

Disabled Travelers   Paris is an old city and therefore not particularly well equipped to welcome travelers with disabilities. However, this is changing, and if you visit the tourist office's website (www.parisinfo.com) and click on "Paris Pratique," you'll find links to a number of guides and websites dedicated to travelers with disabilities. This includes a link to *Paris, An Accessible City*, a guidebook that can also be downloaded in PDF format. With the exception of Line 14 and several other stations, most Métro lines do not have access for those with disabilities and are not always equipped with either escalators or elevators. Buses are a much better option for visitors with disabilities, as many lines are now equipped with lowering floors and space for wheelchairs. RER lines and some SNCF services are wheelchair-accessible (call ✆ **08-10-64-64-64,** or see www.infomobi.com for a useful disabled-access version of the Paris Métro map). Paris taxis are legally obliged to take passengers in wheelchairs at no extra charge.

Doctors   Doctors are listed in the **Pages Jaunes** (French equivalent of the Yellow Pages, www.pagesjaunes.fr) under Médecins: Médecine Générale. If you're using the web-site, you can search for a doctor in your neighborhood by typing your post code (for example, 75006 if you're staying in the 6th arrondissement) in the "Où" box. The mini-mum fee for a consultation is about 23€—for this rate look for a doctor who is described as "conventionée secteur 1." The higher the "secteur," the higher the fee. **SOS Médecins** (✆ **36-24** or 01-47-07-77-77) makes house calls that cost 33€ during the week and 90€ at weekends or on holidays (prices quoted are for people without French social security). The **Urgences Médicales de Paris** (✆ **01-53-94-94-94**) also makes house calls and some doc-tors speak English. During the day it costs 60€, until midnight 80€, and after midnight 90€ (if you don't have French social security). See also "Emergencies" and "Health," below in this section.

Drinking Laws   Supermarkets, grocery stores, and cafes sell alcoholic beverages. The legal drinking age is 18, but persons under that age can be served alcohol in a bar or restaurant if accompanied by a parent or legal guardian. Wine and liquor are sold every day of the week, year-round. Hours of cafes vary. Some open at 6am, serving drinks to 3am; others are open 24 hours. Bars and nightclubs may stay open as late as they wish.

The law regarding drunk driving is tough. A motorist is considered "legally intoxi-cated" if his or her blood-alcohol limit exceeds .05%. If it is under .08% (the limit in the U.K., Ireland, and some U.S. states) the driver faces a fine of 135€. Over .08% and it could cost 4,500€ or up to 2 years in jail. If you cause an accident while drunk driving the fine could be increased to 30,000€, and if you cause serious injury or death, you face 10 years in jail and a fine of up to 150,000€.

Driving Rules   The French drive on the right side of the road. At junctions where there are no signposts indicating the right of way, cars coming from the right have priority. Many roundabouts now give priority to those on the roundabout. If this is not indicated, priority is for those coming from the right.

Drugstores   You'll spot French *pharmacies* by looking for the green neon cross above the door. If your local pharmacy is closed, there should be a sign on the door indicating the nearest one open. *Parapharmacies* sell medical products and toiletries, but they don't dispense prescriptions. Both the **Pharmacie des Champs-Élysées** (84 av. des Champs-Élysées; Métro: George V; ✆ **01-45-62-02-41**) and the **Pharmacie Européene de la Place de Clichy** (6 place de Clichy; Métro: Place de Clichy; ✆ **01-48-74-65-18**) are open 24 hours daily. See also "Emergencies" and "Health," below.

Electricity   Electricity in France runs on 220 volts AC (60 cycles). Adapters or transformers are needed to fit sockets, which you can buy in branches of Darty, FNAC, or BHV. Many hotels have two-pin (in some cases, three-pin) sockets for electric razors.

Embassies & Consulates   If you have a passport, immigration, legal, or other problem, contact your consulate. Call before you go—they often keep odd hours and observe both French and home-country holidays.

The Embassy of **Australia** is at 4 rue Jean-Rey, 15e (www.france.embassy.gov.au; ✆ **01-40-59-33-00;** Métro: Bir Hakeim), open Monday to Friday 9am to 5pm except public holidays. The Consular section is open Monday to Friday from 9am to noon and 2 to 4pm.

The Embassy of **Canada** is at 35 av. Montaigne, 8e (www.amb-canada.fr; ✆ **01-44-43-29-00;** Métro: Franklin-D-Roosevelt or Alma-Marceau), open Monday to Friday 9am to 5pm.

The Embassy of **Ireland** is at 4 rue Rude, 16e (www.embassyofireland.fr; ✆ **01-44-17-67-00;** Métro: Etoile), open Monday to Friday 9:30am to noon.

The Embassy of **New Zealand** is at 7ter rue Léonard-de-Vinci, 16e (www.nzembassy.com/france; ✆ **01-45-01-43-43;** Métro: Victor Hugo), open Monday to Thursday 9am to 1pm and 2 to 5:30pm, Friday 9am to 1pm and 2 to 5pm.

The Embassy of the **United Kingdom** is at 35 rue du Faubourg St-Honoré, 8e (http://ukinfrance.fco.gov.uk; ✆ **01-44-51-31-00;** Métro: Concorde or Madeleine), open Monday to Friday 9:30am to 1pm and 2:30 to 6pm.

The Embassy of the **United States,** 2 av. Gabriel, 8e (http://france.usembassy.gov; ✆ **01-43-12-22-22;** Métro: Concorde), is open Monday to Friday 9am to 6pm.

Emergencies   In an emergency, call ✆ 112 from a mobile phone, or the fire brigade *(Sapeurs-Pompiers)* (✆ 18), who are trained to deal with all kinds of medical emergencies, not just fires. For an ambulance, call ✆ **15.** For the police, call ✆ **17.**

Etiquette & Customs   Parisians like pleasantries and take manners seriously: Say *bonjour, madame/monsieur,* when entering an establishment and *au revoir* when you depart. Always say *pardon* when you accidentally bump into someone. With strangers, people who are older than you, and professional contacts, use *vous* rather than *tu* (*vous* is the polite form of the pronoun you).

Family Travel   To locate accommodations, restaurants, and attractions that are particularly kid-friendly, look for the "Kids" icon throughout this guide.

Health   For travel abroad, non-E.U. nationals should consider buying medical travel insurance. For U.S. citizens, Medicare and Medicaid do not provide coverage for medical costs incurred abroad, so check what medical services your health insurance covers before leaving home. U.K. nationals will need a **European Health Insurance Card (EHIC)** to receive free or reduced-cost medical care during a visit to a European Union (EU) country, Iceland, Liechtenstein, Norway, or Switzerland (go to www.ehic.org.uk for further information).

If you suffer from a chronic illness, consult your doctor before your departure. Pack prescription medications in your carry-on luggage and carry them in their original containers, with pharmacy labels—otherwise they won't make it through airport security. Carry the generic name of prescription medicines, in case a local pharmacist is unfamiliar with the brand name.

For further tips on travel and health concerns, and a list of local English-speaking doctors, contact the **International Association for Medical Assistance to Travelers (IAMAT;** www.iamat.org; ☎ **716/754-4883** in the U.S., or 416/652-0137 in Canada). You can also find listings of reliable medical clinics overseas at the **International Society of Travel Medicine** (www.istm.org). See also "Doctors," "Drugstores," "Emergencies," and "Hospitals."

Holidays Major holidays are New Year's Day (January 1), Easter Sunday and Monday (Late Mar/Apr), May Day (May 1), VE Day (May 8), Ascension Thursday (40 days after Easter), Pentecost/Whit Sunday and Whit Monday (7th Sun and Mon after Easter), Bastille Day (July 14), Assumption Day (Aug 15), All Saints Day (Nov 1), Armistice Day (Nov 11), and Christmas Day (Dec 25). For more information on holidays, see "Paris Calendar of Events," p. 49.

Hospitals Open Monday to Saturday from 8am to 7pm (until 6pm on Saturdays), **Centre Médical Europe,** 44 rue d'Amsterdam, 9e (www.centre-medical-europe.com; ☎ **01-42-81-93-33;** Métro: Liège or St-Lazare), maintains contacts with medical and dental practitioners in all fields. It's best to call in advance for an appointment.

The following hospitals have 24-hour accident and emergency services: **Hôpital Hôtel Dieu** (1 place du Parvis Notre-Dame, 4e; ☎ **01-42-34-82-34**), **Hôpital St-Louis** (1 av. Claude-Vellefaux, 10e; ☎ **01-42-49-49-49**), **Hôpital St-Antoine** (184 rue du Faubourg St-Antoine, 12e; ☎ **01-49-28-20-00**), **Hôpital de la Pitié-Salpêtrière** (47-83 Bd. de l'Hôpital, 13e; ☎ **01-42-16-00-00**), **Hôpital Cochin** (27 rue du Faubourg St-Jacques, 14e; ☎ **01-58-41-41-41**), **Hôpital Européen Georges Pompidou** (20 rue Leblanc, 15e; ☎ **01-56-09-20-00**), **Hôpital Bichat-Claude Bernard** (46 rue Henri-Huchard, 18e; ☎ **01-40-25-80-80**), and **Hôpital Tenon** (4 rue de la Chine, 20e; ☎ **01-56-01-70-00**). These hospitals, as well as other hospitals, are all listed on www.aphp.fr.

There are two private hospitals with English-speaking staff that operate 24 hours daily: the **American Hospital of Paris** (63 bd. Victor Hugo, 92200 Neuilly-sur-Seine; www.american-hospital.org; ☎ **01-46-41-25-25;** Métro: Pont de Levallois or Pont de Neuilly; bus: 82) and **Hertford British Hospital, Hôpital Franco-Britannique** (3 rue Barbès, 92300 Levallois; www.ihfb.org/en; ☎ **01-47-59-59-59;** Métro: Anatole-France).

Hot Lines S.O.S. Help is a hot line for English-speaking callers in crisis at ☎ **01-46-21-46-46;** www.soshelpline.org. Open daily 3 to 11pm.

Internet & Wi-Fi Many Parisian hotels and cafes have Internet access, and Wi-Fi (pronounced *wee-fee*) is becoming increasingly common in cafes and public spaces. To find cybercafes in Paris, check **www.cybercafe.com.** Cybercafes tend to be pretty pricey, but a reasonably priced option in the center of Paris is **Luxembourg Micro,** 81 bd. Saint-Michel, 5e (www.luxembourg-micro.com; ☎ **01-46-33-27-98;** RER: Luxembourg). For 15 minutes, you pay .90€, for 30 minutes 1.80€, and for an hour 2.50€. It's open daily from 9am (10am on Sunday) to 10pm.

Language   English is widely understood in Paris, and is common in all the tourist areas—museums, hotels, restaurants, cafes, and nightclubs. For handy French words and phrases, as well as food and menu terms, refer to chapter 12, "Useful Terms & Phrases." A good phrasebook is *Frommer's French PhraseFinder & Dictionary*.

Legal Aid   In an emergency, especially if you get into trouble with the law, your country's embassy or consulate will provide legal advice. See "Embassies & Consulates," above.

LGBT Travelers   France is one of the world's most tolerant countries toward gays and lesbians. "Gay Paree" boasts a large gay population, and an openly gay mayor, Bertrand Delanoë. The center of gay and lesbian life is Le Marais, particularly on rues St-Croix-de-la-Bretonnerie, des Archives, and Vieille-du-Temple. The annual Gay Pride March takes place on the last Sunday in June. Information and resources can be found in Paris's largest, best-stocked gay bookstore, **Les Mots à la Bouche,** 6 rue Ste-Croix de la Bretonnerie, 4e (www.motsbouche.com; ✆ **01-42-78-88-30;** Métro: Hôtel-de-Ville), which carries publications in both French and English. *Têtu* (www.tetu.com) and *Préf* are two magazines dedicated to gay life that have texts in English. *La Dixième Muse* (www.ladixiememuse.com) is the lesbian equivalent. In addition, both www.paris-gay.com and www.gayvox.fr have updated listings about the gay and lesbian scene and events.

Lost & Found   All lost objects—except those found in train stations or on trains—are taken to the **Bureau des Objets Trouvés** (36 rue des Morillons, 15e; www.prefecturede police.interieur.gouv.fr/Vos-demarches/Autres-demarches/Objets-trouves; ✆ **08-21-00-25-25**). It's better to visit in person than to call, but be warned that there are huge delays in processing claims. It's open from Monday to Thursday 8:30am to 5pm and Friday 8:30am to 4:30pm. Objects lost on the Métro are held by the station agents before being sent onto the Bureau des Objets Trouvés. If you lose something on a train or in a train station, go to the Lost Property office of the SNCF station in question.

Mail   Most post offices in Paris are open Monday to Friday from 8am to 5pm and every Saturday from 8am to noon. The main post office (52 rue du Louvre Métro: Louvre-Rivoli) is open 24 hours daily. Stamps are also sold in *tabacs* (tobacconists). Tariffs depend on the weight and size of the letter or package but more information can be found on www.laposte.fr.

Medical Requirements   Unless you are arriving from an area of the world known to be suffering from an epidemic, especially cholera or yellow fever, inoculations or vaccinations are not required for entry in France.

Mobile Phones   The three letters that define much of the world's wireless capabilities are **GSM** (Global System for Mobile Communications), a big, seamless network that makes for easy cross-border mobile phone use throughout Europe and dozens of other countries worldwide. You can use your mobile phone in France provided it is GSM and tri-band or quad-band; just confirm this with your operator before you leave.

Using your phone abroad can be expensive, and you usually have to pay to receive calls, so it's a good idea to get it "unlocked" before you leave. This means you can buy a SIM card from one of the four main French providers: **Bouygues Télécom** (www.bouygues telecom.fr), **Orange** (www.orange.fr), **SFR** (www.sfr.fr), or **Virgin Mobile** (www.virgin mobile.fr). A SIM card with a 5€ call credit costs about 10€. Alternatively, if your phone isn't unlocked, you could buy a cheap mobile phone. To top-up your phone credit, buy a Mobicarte from *tabacs*, supermarkets, and mobile phone outlets. Prices range from 5€ to 100€.

THE VALUE OF THE EURO VS. OTHER POPULAR CURRENCIES

Euro (€)	US$	C$	UK£	A$	NZ$
1	1.27	1.31	0.82	1.24	1.63

Frommer's lists exact prices in the local currency. The currency conversions quoted above were correct at press time. However, rates fluctuate, so before departing consult a currency exchange website such as www.oanda.com/convert/classic to check up-to-the-minute rates.

For decades Paris was known as one of the most expensive cities on earth. It still is a pricey destination, but London has not only caught up with Paris, it has surpassed it. Paris is not as expensive as Tokyo or Oslo, but it's increasingly difficult to find even an average hotel for less than 150€.

ATMs are widely available in Paris, but if you're venturing into rural France, it's always good to have cash in your pocket. Be sure you know your personal identification number (PIN) and daily withdrawal limit before you depart. Many banks impose a fee when you withdraw money abroad, and that fee can be higher for international transactions than for domestic ones. In addition, the bank from which you withdraw cash may charge its own fee. Currency exchange is available at Paris airports, train stations, and along most of the major boulevards—just look out for a sign saying *Bureau de Change*. They charge a small commission.

Visa (known as Carte Bleue in French) is the most common credit card in France but most international credit cards are widely used. In an attempt to reduce credit card fraud, French credit cards are issued with an embedded chip and a PIN to authorize transactions. Non-French cards (which don't have a chip) do work but they print a slip that requires a signature. This does mean, however, that they cannot be used in automated machines, such as those in Métro stations. Check for hidden fees when using your card abroad—some bank charges can be up to 3% of the purchase price. The following number can be used to report any lost or stolen credit card: **08-92-70-57-05. American Express (℃ 01-47-77-72-00;** www.americanexpress.com) and **MasterCard (℃ 08-00-90-13-87;** www.mastercard.com) have their own emergency numbers. **Visa ℃ 08-92-70-57-05;** www.visaeurope.com) lists the standard one for all cards. It may be difficult to get a new card until you get home, so carrying two cards is better than one. There are still shops, restaurants, and bars, often family run, that don't accept credit or debit cards, so it's always good to both check in advance and have cash on you. The minimum amount you have to spend to use a credit or debit card is slowly decreasing, but in some shops and bars, again often smaller businesses, it can be as high as 15€.

You can buy traveler's checks at most banks, and they are widely accepted in France, although frankly, merchants prefer cash. Because of difficulties with credit cards (see above) or ATMs that can reject your card for no apparent reason, travelers are once again buying traveler's checks for security in case something goes wrong with their plastic. They are offered in denominations of $20, $50, $100, $500, and sometimes $1,000. Generally, you'll pay a service charge ranging from 1% to 4%. The most popular traveler's checks are offered by **American Express, Visa,** and **MasterCard.** You can change traveler's checks at most post offices. If you carry traveler's checks, keep a record of their serial numbers

WHAT THINGS COST IN PARIS	EURO
Taxi from the airport to downtown Paris (Orly or CDG)	50.00–70.00
Métro ticket	1.90
Double room, expensive	350.00–800.00
Double room, moderate	150.00–350.00
Double room, inexpensive	90.00–150.00
Three-course dinner for one without wine, moderate	25.00–30.00
Bottle of beer	3.00–5.00
Espresso	1.00–2.50
1 liter of premium gas	1.40–1.50
Admission to most museums	7.00–10.00

separate from your checks in the event that they are stolen or lost—you'll get your refund faster.

For help with currency conversions, tip calculations, and more, download Frommer's convenient Travel Tools app for your mobile device. Go to www.frommers.com/go/mobile and click on the "Travel Tools" icon.

Newspapers & Magazines   Only 20% of French people read a national paper. The most famous is the serious, center-left **Le Monde** (www.lemonde.fr), which is strong on both politics and economic issues. **Le Figaro** (www.lefigaro.fr) is more conservative and tends to favor lifestyle features over controversial issues. **Libération** (www.liberation.fr), founded in the late 1960s by Jean-Paul Sartre and Simone de Beauvoir, has good news and arts coverage and is considered more left-wing. For more local news, try **Le Parisien** (www.leparisien.fr).

English-language newspapers are available at kiosks across the city. Published Monday to Saturday, the Paris-based *International Herald-Tribune* is the most widely available English-language newspaper. The most popular British and American papers and magazines can be found at kiosks. **WH Smith** (248 rue de Rivoli; www.whsmith.fr; ℂ **01-44-77-88-99**) has a good selection of English-language press.

Passports   Citizens of the U.K., New Zealand, Australia, Canada, and the United States need a valid passport to enter France. The passport is valid for a stay of 90 days. To prevent international child abduction, E.U. governments have initiated procedures at entry and exit points. These often (but not always) include requiring documentary evidence of relationship and permission for the child's travel from the parent or legal guardian not present. Having such documentation on hand, even if not required, facilitates entries and exits. All children must have their own passports.

Allow plenty of time before your trip to apply for a passport; processing normally takes 3 weeks but can take longer during busy periods (especially spring). Keep in mind that if you need a passport in a hurry, you'll pay a higher processing fee.

For Residents of Australia: You can pick up an application from your local post office or any branch of Passports Australia. Visit the government website at www.passports.gov.au for more details.

For **Residents of Canada:** Passport applications are available at Passport Canada agencies throughout Canada. Forms and further information can be found at www.ppt.gc.ca.

For Residents of Ireland: You can apply for a passport using the Passport Express service at most post offices. Further information can be found at www.foreignaffairs.gov.ie.

For Residents of New Zealand: You can pick up a passport application at any New Zealand Passports Office or download it from their website www.passports.govt.nz.

For Residents of the United Kingdom: To pick up an application for a passport visit your nearest passport office, major post office, or download the forms from the website www.direct.gov.uk/en/index.htm.

For **Residents of the United States:** Whether you're applying in person or by mail, you can download passport applications from the U.S. State Department website at http://travel.state.gov.

Police   In an emergency, call ℂ **17** or **112** from a mobile. The Préfecture de Police has 94 stations in Paris. To find the nearest police station, call ℂ **08-91-01-22-22** or go to www.prefecturedepolice.interieur.gouv.fr. See also "Emergencies," earlier in this section.

Safety   In general, Paris is a safe city and it is safe to use the Métro late at night. However, certain Métro stations (and the areas around them) are best avoided at night: Châtelet-Les Halles, Gare du Nord, Barbès Rochechouart, and Strasbourg St-Denis. Violent incidents and robberies have been known on the RER, particularly RER B, so it is best find alternative transport to and from the airport (such as buses or taxis) late at night or early in the morning.

The most common crime in Paris is the plague of pickpockets. They prey on tourists around popular attractions such as the Louvre, the Eiffel Tower, Notre-Dame, St-Michel, Centre Pompidou, and Sacré-Coeur, in the major department stores, and on the Métro. Take precautions and be vigilant at all times: don't take more money with you than necessary, keep your passport in a concealed pouch or leave it at your hotel, and ensure that your bag is firmly closed at all times. Also, around the major sites it is quite common to be approached by a young Roma girl and asked if you speak English. It's best to avoid these situations, and any incident that might occur, by shaking your head and walking away.

In cafes, bars, and restaurants, it's best not to leave your bag under the table or on the back of your chair. Keep it between your legs or on your lap to avoid it being stolen. Never leave valuables in a car, and never travel with your car unlocked.

The government of France maintains a national antiterrorism plan; in times of heightened security concerns, the government mobilizes police and armed forces, and installs them at airports, train and Métro stations, and high-profile locations such as schools, embassies, and government installations.

Paris is a cosmopolitan city and most nonwhite travelers won't experience any problems. Although there is a significant level of discrimination against West and North African immigrants, there has been almost no harassment of African-American tourists to Paris or France itself. In fact, many expatriate Americans, including such cultural figures as Josephine Baker and author James Baldwin, fled to Paris in decades past to escape the racism of America. **S.O.S. Racisme** (51 av. de Flandre, 19e; www.sos-racisme.org; ℂ **01-40-35-36-55**) offers legal advice to victims of prejudice and will even intervene to help with the police.

Female travelers should not expect any more hassle than in other major cities and the same precautions apply. Avoid walking around the less safe neighborhoods (Barbès Rochechouart, Strasbourg St-Denis, Châtelet-Les-Halles) alone at night and never get into an unmarked taxi. If you are approached in the street or on the Métro, it's best to avoid entering into conversation and walk away.

Senior Travel Many discounts are available to seniors—men and women over 60. Although they often seem to apply to residents of E.U. countries, it pays to announce at the ticket window of a museum or monument that you are 60 years old or more. You may not receive a discount, but it doesn't hurt to ask. "Senior," incidentally, is pronounced *seenyore* in France. Senior citizens do not get a discount for traveling on public transport in Paris, but there are senior discounts on national trains. Check out www.voyages-sncf. com for further information. Frommers.com offers more information and resources on travel for seniors.

Smoking Smoking is now banned in all public places, including cafes, restaurants, bars, and nightclubs.

Student Travel Student discounts are less common in France than other countries, but simply because young people under 26 are usually offered reduced rates. Some discounts only apply to residents of E.U. countries, who will need to prove this with a passport or driver's license, but if you're not from the E.U. it's worth carrying ID to prove your age and announcing it when buying tickets. Look out for the **Ticket Jeunes** when using the Métro. It can be used on a Saturday, Sunday, or bank holiday, and provides unlimited travel in zones 1 to 3 for 3.55€ (see "By Public Transport," earlier). SNCF also offer discounts for under-26-year-olds traveling on national trains (www.voyages-sncf.com).

Taxes As a member of the European Union, France routinely imposes a value-added tax (VAT in English; *TVA* in French) on most goods. The standard VAT is 19.6% and prices that include it are often marked TTC (*toutes taxes comprises,* "all taxes included"). If you're not an E.U. resident, you can get a VAT refund if you're spending less than 6 months in France, you purchase goods worth at least 175€ at a single shop on the same day, the goods fit into your luggage, and the shop offers *vente en détaxe* (duty-free sales or tax-free shopping). Give them your passport and ask for a *bordereau de vente à l'exportation* (export sales invoice). This is then signed by the retailer and yourself. When you leave the country, you need to get all three pages of this invoice validated by France's customs officials. They'll keep one sheet and you must post the pink one back to the shop. Once the shop receives its stamped copy, it will send you a *virement* (fund transfer) using the payment method you requested. It may take several months.

Telephones Public phones can still be found in France. They all require a phone card (known as a *télécarte*), which can be purchased at post offices, tabacs, supermarkets, SNCF ticket windows, Métro stations, and anywhere you see a blue sticker reading *télécarte en vente ici* ("phone card for sale here"). They cost 7.50€ for 50 calling units and 15€ for 120 units.

The country code for France is 33. To make a local or long distance call within France, dial the 10-digit number of the person or place you're calling. Mobile numbers begin with 06. Numbers beginning with 0 800, 0 804, 0 805, and 0 809 are free in France, other numbers beginning with 8 are not. Most four-digit numbers starting with 10, 30, or 31 are free of charge.

To make international calls from Paris, first dial 00 and then the country code (U.S. and Canada 1, U.K. 44, Ireland 353, Australia 61, New Zealand 64). Next you dial the area code and number. For example, if you want to call the British Embassy in Washington, D.C., you would dial ✆ **001 202/588-7800.**

For operator assistance and French directory enquiries dial ✆ **12.**

Time   France is on Central European Time, which is 1 hour ahead of Greenwich Mean Time. French daylight saving time lasts from the last Sunday in March to the last Sunday in October, when clocks are set 1 hour ahead of the standard time. France uses the 24-hour clock. So 13h is 1pm, 14h15 is 2:15pm, etc. For help with time translations and more, download our convenient Travel Tools app for your mobile device. Go to www.frommers.com/go/mobile and click on the "Travel Tools" icon.

Tipping   By law, all bills in **cafes, bars, and restaurants** say *service compris,* which means the service charge is included. However, it is customary to leave 1€ or 2€ depending on the quality of the service. **Taxi drivers** usually expect a 5% to 10% tip, or for the fare to be rounded up to the next euro. The French give their **hairdressers** a tip of about 15%, and if you go to the theater, you're expected to tip the **usher** 2€ or 3€. For help with tip calculations, currency conversions, and more, download our convenient Travel Tools app for your mobile device. Go to www.frommers.com/go/mobile and click on the "Travel Tools" icon.

Toilets   Paris is full of gray-colored, automatic street toilets, which are free to use and are washed and disinfected after each use. If you're in dire need, duck into a cafe or brasserie to use the toilet but expect to make a small purchase if you do so. In older establishments, you can still find Turkish toilets, otherwise known as squat toilets.

VAT   See "Taxes," above.

Visas   E.U. nationals don't need a visa to enter France. Nor do U.S., Canadian, Australian, New Zealand, or South African citizens for trips of up to 3 months. Nationals of other countries should make inquiries at the nearest French embassy or consulate before they travel to France. If non-E.U. citizens wish to stay for longer than 3 months, they must apply to a French embassy or consulate for a long-term visa.

Visitor Information   The **Office du Tourisme et des Congrès** (25 rue des Pyramides, 1er; www.parisinfo.com; ℓ **08-92-68-30-00**) has information on hotels, restaurants, monuments, shopping, excursions, events, and transport. From May to October it is open every day from 9am to 7pm (except May 1st); from November to April it's open from 10am to 7pm. There are several other offices around Paris: **Montmartre** (21 place du Tertre, 18e; daily 10am–7pm); **Anvers** (72 bd. Rochechouart, 9e; daily 10am–6pm except major holidays); **Gare du Nord** (18 rue de Dunkerque, 10e; daily 8am–6pm except major holidays); **Gare de l'Est** (place du 11-novembre-1918, 10e; Mon–Sat 8am–7pm except major holidays); **Gare de Lyon** (20 bd. Diderot, 12e; Mon–Sat 8am–6pm except bank holidays); and **Porte de Versailles** (1 place de la Porte de Versailles, 15e; daily 11am–7pm during trade fairs).

There are lots of interesting blogs written in English about Paris, but some of the best are **GoGo Paris** (www.gogoparis.com), an insider guide to Paris's fashion, food, art, and gigs; and **Chocolate & Zucchini** (http://chocolateandzucchini.com), the hugely successful food blog written by a 30-something Parisian called Clotilde.

Water   Drinking water is generally safe. To order tap water in a restaurant ask for *une carafe d'eau.*

Wi-Fi   See "Internet & Wi-Fi," earlier in this section.

Women Travelers   See "Safety," above.

USEFUL TERMS & PHRASES

FRENCH-LANGUAGE TERMS

If Parisians have a reputation for seeming aloof and uninterested in foreigners and tourists, it's amazing how a word or two of uncertain French can change their dispositions. At the very least, try to learn the basic greetings, a few numbers, and—above all—the life raft, *"Parlez-vous anglais?"* You'll discover that many Parisians speak passable English and will use it liberally if you initiate the courtesy by greeting them in their language. Go out, try a few phrases from this chapter, and don't be bashful. *Bonne chance!*

BASICS

English	French	Pronunciation
Yes/No	Oui/Non	**Wee/Nohn**
Okay	D'accord	**Dah-*core***
Please	S'il vous plaît	**seel voo *play***
Thank you	Merci	**Mair-*see***
You're welcome	De rien	**duh ree-*ehn***
Hello (during daylight)	Bonjour	**Bohn-*jhoor***
Hi	Salut	**sal-*oo***
Good evening	Bonsoir	**bohn-*swahr***
Good-bye	Au revoir	**O ruh-*vwahr***
What's your name?	Comment vous appellez-vous?	**Ko-*mahn* voo za-pell-ay-*voo*?**
My name is . . .	Je m'appelle . . .	**Jhuh ma-*pell* . . .**
Happy to meet you	Enchanté(e)	**Ohn-shahn-tay**

English	French	Pronunciation
Miss	Mademoiselle	**Mad-mwa-*zel***
Mr.	Monsieur	**muh-*syuh***
Mrs.	Madame	**Ma-*dam***
How are you?	Comment allez-vous?	**Kuh-*mahn* tahl-ay-*voo*?**
Fine, thank you, and you?	Très bien, merci, et vous?	**Tray bee-*ehn*, mare-*ci*, ay *voo*?**
Very well, thank you	Très bien, merci	**tray bee-ehn, mair-*see***
So-so	Comme ci, comme ça	**Kom-*see*, kom-*sah***
I'm sorry/excuse me	Pardon	**pahr-*dohn***
I'm so very sorry	Désolé(e)	**Day-zoh-*lay***
That's all right	Il n'y a pas de quoi	**Eel nee ah pah duh kwah**

GETTING AROUND/STREET SMARTS

English	French	Pronunciation
Do you speak English?	Parlez-vous Anglais?	**Par-lay-*voo* ahn-*glay*?**
I don't speak French.	Je ne parle pas Français	**Jhuh ne parl pah frahn-*say***
I don't understand.	Je ne comprends pas	**Jhuh ne kohm-*prahn* pas**
Could you speak . . .	Pouvez-vous parler un peu . . .	**Poo-vay-*voo* par-*lay* un puh**
. . . more loudly?	. . . plus fort?	**. . . ploo for?**
. . . more slowly?	. . . plus lentement?	**. . . ploo lan-te-*ment*?**
Could you repeat that?	Répetez, s'il vous plaît?	**Ray-pay-*tay*, seel voo *play***
What is it?	Qu'est-ce que c'est?	**Kess kuh *say*?**
What time is it?	Quelle heure est-il?	**Kel uhr eh-*teel*?**
What?	Quoi?	**Kwah?**
How?/What did you say?	Comment?	**Ko-*mahn*?**
When?	Quand?	**Kahn?**
Where is . . . ?	Où est . . . ?	**Ooh eh . . . ?**
Who?	Qui?	**Kee?**
Why?	Pourquoi?	**Poor-*kwah*?**
I'm American.	Je suis Américain(e).	**Jhe sweez a-may-ree-*kehn***
. . . British.	. . . Anglais(e).	**ahn-glay (*glaise*)**
. . . Canadian.	. . . Canadien(e).	**can-ah-dee-*en***
I'm sick.	Je suis malade	**Jhuh swee mal-*ahd***
Fill the (gas) tank, please.	Le plein, s'il vous plaît	**Luh plan, seel voo play**

English	French	Pronunciation
I'm going to . . .	Je vais à . . .	**Jhe vay ah . . .**
I want to get off at . . .	Je voudrais descendre à . . .	**Jhe voo-*dray* day-*son-drah* ah**
. . . the airport	. . . l'aéroport	**lair-o-*por***
. . . the bank	. . . la banque	**lah bahnk**
. . . the bridge	. . . le pont	**luh pohn**
. . . the bus station	. . . la gare routière	**lah gar roo-tee-*air***
. . . the bus stop	. . . l'arrêt de bus	**lah-*ray* duh boohss**
by bicycle	en vélo/par bicyclette	**ahn *vay-low*/par bee-see-*clet***
by car	en voiture	**ahn vwa-*toor***
cashier	la caisse	**lah *kess***
castle/palace	un château	**uh sha-*tow***
cathedral	la cathédrale	**lah ka-tay-*dral***
church	l'église	**lay-*gleez***
dead end	une impasse	**ewn am-*pass***
driver's license	un permis de conduire	**uh per-*mee* duh con-*dweer***
elevator	l'ascenseur	**lah-sahn-*seuhr***
entrance	une entrée	**ewn ohn-*tray***
exit (from building/freeway)	une sortie	**ewn sor-*tee***
garden	un jardin	**uh jhar-*dehn***
gasoline	du pétrol/de l'essence	**doo pet-*role*/de lay-*sahns***
ground floor	rez-de-chaussée	**ray-de-show-*say***
here/there	ici/là	**ee-*see*/lah**
highway to . . .	la route pour . . .	**la root por**
hospital	l'hôpital	**low-pee-t*ahl***
insurance	les assurances	**lez ah-sur-*ahns***
left/right	à gauche/à droite	**a goash/a drwaht**
luggage storage	la consigne	**lah kohn-*seen*-yuh**
museum	le musée	**luh mew-*zay***
no entry	sens interdit	**sehns ahn-ter-*dee***
no smoking	défense de fumer	**day-*fahns* de fu-may**
on foot	à pied	**ah pee-*ay***
one-day pass	ticket journalier	**tee-kay jhoor-nall-ee-*ay***
one-way ticket	aller simple	**ah-*lay* sam-pluh**
police	la police	**lah po-*lees***

English	French	Pronunciation
rental car	une voiture de location	ewn vwa-*toor* de low-ka-see-*on*
round-trip ticket	aller-retour	ah-*lay*-re-*toor*
second floor	premier étage	prem-ee-*ehr* ay-*taj*
slow down	ralentir	rah-lahn-*teer*
store	un magasin	uh luh ma-ga-*zehn*
straight ahead	tout droit	too drwah
street	la rue	lah roo
suburb	banlieu/environs	bahn-*liew*/en-veer-*ohns*
subway	le Métro	luh *May*-tro
telephone	le téléphone	luh tay-lay-*phone*
ticket	un billet	uh *bee*-yay
ticket office	vente de billets	vahnt duh bee-*yay*
toilets	les toilettes/les WC	lay twa-*lets*/les Vay-*Say*

NECESSITIES

English	French	Pronunciation
How much does it cost?	C'est combien?/Ça coûte combien?	Say comb-bee-*ehn?*/Sah coot comb-bee-*ehn?*
That's expensive.	C'est cher/chère	Say share
That's inexpensive.	C'est raisonnable/C'est bon marché	Say ray-son-*ahb*-bluh/Say bohn mar-*shay*
Do you take credit cards?	Est-ce que vous acceptez les cartes de credit?	Es-*kuh* voo zak-sep-*tay* lay kart duh creh-*dee?*
I'd like . . .	Je voudrais . . .	Jhe voo-*dray*
I'd like to buy . . .	Je voudrais acheter . . .	Jhe voo-dray ahsh-*tay*
. . . an aspirin	. . . des aspirines/des aspros	dayz ahs-peer-*eens*/deyz ahs-*prohs*
. . . cigarettes	. . . des cigarettes	day see-ga-*ret*
. . . condoms	. . . des préservatifs	day pray-ser-va-*teefs*
. . . a dictionary	. . . un dictionnaire	uh deek-see-oh-*nare*
. . . a dress	. . . une robe	ewn robe
. . . envelopes	. . . des envelopes	days ahn-veh-*lope*
. . . a gift (for someone)	. . . un cadeau	uh kah-*doe*
. . . a handbag	. . . un sac à main	uh *sahk* uh muhn
. . . a magazine	. . . une revue	ewn reh-*vu*
. . . a map of the city	. . . un plan de ville	unh plahn de *veel*
. . . a computer	. . . un ordinateur	unh ord-ee-nat-*uhr*
. . . a laptop	. . . un laptop	unh lap-top

English	French	Pronunciation
. . . a charger (telephone/computer)	. . . un chargeur	**unh charg-uhr**
. . . a cell phone	. . . un téléphone portable	**uh tay-lay-*phone* port-*ahble***
. . . matches	. . . des allumettes	**dayz a-loo-*met***
. . . a newspaper	. . . un journal	**uh zhoor-*nahl***
. . . a phone card	. . . une carte téléphonique	**uh cart tay-lay-fone-*eek***
. . . a postcard	. . . une carte postale	**ewn carte pos-*tahl***
. . . a road map	. . . une carte routière	**ewn cart roo-tee-*air***
. . . a shirt	. . . une chemise	**ewn che-*meez***
. . . shoes	. . . des chaussures	**day show-*suhr***
. . . a skirt	. . . une jupe	**ewn jhoop**
. . . soap	. . . du savon	**dew sah-*vohn***
. . . socks	. . . des chaussettes	**day show-*set***
. . . a stamp	. . . un timbre	**uh *tam*-bruh**
. . . trousers	. . . un pantalon	**uh pan-tah-*lohn***

IN YOUR HOTEL

English	French	Pronunciation
Are taxes included?	Est-ce que les taxes sont comprises?	***Ess*-keh lay taks son com-*preez*?**
Is breakfast included?	Petit déjeuner inclus?	**Peh-*tee* day-jheun-ay ehn-*klu*?**
We're staying for . . . days.	On reste pour . . . jours.	**Ohn rest poor . . . jhoor.**
balcony	un balcon	**uh bahl-*cohn***
bathtub	une baignoire	**ewn bayn-*nwar***
Internet	l'Internet	**luhn-tair-*net***
key	la clé (la clef)	**lah *clay***
room	une chambre	**ewn *shahm*-bruh**
shower	une douche	**ewn dooch**
sink	un lavabo	**uh la-va-*bow***
suite	une suite	**ewn sweet**
two occupants	pour deux personnes	**poor duh pair-*sunn***
cold water	l'eau froide	**low fwad**
hot water	l'eau chaude	**low showed**
Wi-Fi	avec une connexion Wi-Fi	**ah-*vek* ewn con-neks-*iohn* wee-*fee***
with air-conditioning	avec climatisation	**ah-*vek* clee-mah-tee-zah-see-*on***

English	French	Pronunciation
without	sans	**sahn**
youth hostel	une auberge de jeunesse	**oon oh-*bayrhj* duh jhe-*ness***

IN THE RESTAURANT

English	French	Pronunciation
Is the tip/service included?	Est-ce que le service est compris?	***Ess*-ke luh ser-*vees* eh com-*pree*?**
I would like . . .	Je voudrais	**Jhe voo-*dray***
. . . to eat	. . . manger	**mahn-*jhay***
. . . to order	. . . commander	**ko-mahn-*day***
. . . to reserve a table	. . . réserver une table	**rez-er-vay ewn tar-*bluh***
Please give me . . .	Donnez-moi, s'il vous plaît . . .	**Doe-nay-*mwah*, seel voo play . . .**
. . . a bottle of . . .	. . . une bouteille de . . .	**ewn boo-tay duh . . .**
. . . an ashtray	. . . un cendrier	**uh sahn-dree-ay**
. . . a cup of . . .	. . . une tasse de . . .	**ewn tass duh . . .**
. . . a glass of . . .	. . . un verre de . . .	**uh vair duh . . .**
. . . a plate of . . .	. . . une assiette de . . .	**ewn ass-ee-et duh . . .**
Can I buy you . . .	Puis-je vous offrir . . .	***Pwee*-jhe vooz-off-*reer***
. . . a drink?	. . . un verre?	**uh *vaihr*?**
. . . a cocktail?	. . . un aperitif?	**uh ah-pay-ree-*teef*?**
appetizer	une entrée	**ewn en-*traymain***
breakfast	le petit déjeuner	**luh puh-*tee* day-zhuh-*nay***
check/bill	l'addition/la note	**la-dee-see-*ohn*/la noat**
Cheers!	à votre santé	***ah* vo-truh sahn-*tay***
cheese tray	le plâteau de fromage	**luh plah-*tow* duh fro-*mahj***
course	un plat principal	**uh plah pran-see-*pahl***
for dinner	pour dîner	**poor dee-*nay***
dish of the day	le plat du jour	**luh plah dew jhoor**
drinks not included	boissons non comprises	**bwa-*sons* no com-*preez***
fixed-price menu	un menu	**uh may-new**
fork	une fourchette	**ewn four-*shet***
knife	un couteau	**uh koo-*toe***
napkin	une serviette	**ewn sair-vee-*et***
salt	du sel	**dew sell**
soup	une soupe/un potage	**ewn soop/uh poh-*tahj***
spoon	une cuillère	**ewn kwee-*air***

English	French	Pronunciation
sugar	du sucre	**dew sook-ruh**
tasting menu	menu dégustation	**may-new day-gus-ta-see-on**
tip included	service compris	**sehr-vees cohm-pree**
Waiter!/Waitress!	Monsieur!/Mademoiselle!	**Mun-syuh/Mad-mwa-zel**
wine list	la carte des vins	**lah cart day van**

SHOPPING

English	French	Pronunciation
antiques store	un magasin d'antiquités	**uh maga-zan don-tee kee-tay**
bakery	une boulangerie	**ewn boo-lon-zhur-ree**
bank	une banque	**ewn bonk**
bookstore	une librairie	**ewn lee-brehr-ree**
butcher	une boucherie	**ewn boo-shehr-ree**
cheese shop	une fromagerie	**ewn fro-mazh-ree**
dairy shop	une crèmerie	**ewn krem-ree**
delicatessen	une charcuterie	**ewn shar-koot-ree**
department store	un grand magasin	**uh grah maga-zan**
drugstore	une pharmacie	**ewn far-mah-see**
fishmonger	une poissonerie	**ewn pwas-son-ree**
gift shop	un magasin de cadeaux	**uh maga-zan duh ka-doh**
greengrocer	un marchand de légumes	**uh mar-shon duh lay-goom**
hairdresser	un coiffeur	**uh kwa-fuhr**
market	un marché	**uh mar-shay**
pastry shop	une pâtisserie	**ewn pa-tee-sree**
supermarket	un supermarché	**uh soo-pehr-mar-shay**
tobacconist	un tabac	**uh ta-bah**
travel agency	une agence de voyages	**ewn azh-ahns duh vwa-yazh**

COLORS, SHAPES, SIZES & ATTRIBUTES

English	French	Pronunciation
black	noir	**nwahr**
blue	bleu	**bleuh**
brown	marron/brun	**mar-rohn/bruhn**
green	vert	**vaihr**

English	French	Pronunciation
orange	orange	**o-*rahnj***
pink	rose	**rose**
purple	violet	**vee-o-*lay***
red	rouge	**rooj**
white	blanc	**blahnk**
yellow	jaune	**jhone**
bad	mauvais(e)	**moh-*veh*/moh-*vayz***
big	grand(e)	**gron/gronde**
closed	fermé(e)	**fer-*meh***
down/below	en bas	**on *bah***
early	de bonne heure	**duh bon *urr***
enough	assez	**as-*say***
far	loin	**lwan**
free, unoccupied	libre	***lee*-bruh**
free, without charge	gratuit(e)	**grah-*twee*/grah-*tweet***
good	bon/bonne	**bon/bun**
hot	chaud(e)	**show/shoad**
near	près	**preh**
open (as in "museum")	ouvert(e)	**oo-*ver*/oo-*vert***
small	petit(e)	**puh-*tee*/puh-*teet***
up	en haut	**on *oh***
well	bien	**byehn**

NUMBERS & ORDINALS

English	French	Pronunciation
zero	zéro	**zare-*oh***
one	un	**uh**
two	deux	**duh**
three	trois	**twah**
four	quatre	***kaht*-ruh**
five	cinq	**sank**
six	six	**seess**
seven	sept	**set**
eight	huit	**wheat**
nine	neuf	**nuf**
ten	dix	**deess**
eleven	onze	**ohnz**

English	French	Pronunciation
twelve	douze	**dooz**
thirteen	treize	**trehz**
fourteen	quatorze	**kah-torz**
fifteen	quinze	**kanz**
sixteen	seize	**sez**
seventeen	dix-sept	**deez-set**
eighteen	dix-huit	**deez-wheat**
nineteen	dix-neuf	**deez-nuf**
twenty	vingt	**vehn**
twenty-one	vingt-et-un	**vehnt-ay-uh**
twenty-two	vingt-deux	**vehnt-duh**
thirty	trente	**trahnt**
forty	quarante	**ka-rahnt**
fifty	cinquante	**sang-kahnt**
sixty	soixante	**swa-sahnt**
sixty-one	soixante-et-un	**swa-sahnt-et-uh**
seventy	soixante-dix	**swa-sahnt-deess**
seventy-one	soixante-et-onze	**swa-sahnt-et-ohnze**
eighty	quatre-vingts	**kaht-ruh-vehn**
eighty-one	quatre-vingt-un	**kaht-ruh-vehn-uh**
ninety	quatre-vingt-dix	**kaht-ruh-venh-deess**
ninety-one	quatre-vingt-onze	**kaht-ruh-venh-ohnze**
one hundred	cent	**sahn**
one thousand	mille	**meel**
one hundred thousand	cent mille	**sahn meel**
first	premier	**preh-mee-ay**
second	deuxième	**duhz-zee-em**
third	troisième	**twa-zee-em**
fourth	quatrième	**kaht-ree-em**
fifth	cinquième	**sank-ee-em**
sixth	sixième	**sees-ee-em**
seventh	septième	**set-ee-em**
eighth	huitième	**wheat-ee-em**
ninth	neuvième	**neuv-ee-em**
tenth	dixième	**dees-ee-em**

English	French	Pronunciation
January	Janvier	*jhan*-vee-ay
February	Février	*feh*-vree-ay
March	Mars	marce
April	Avril	a-*vreel*
May	Mai	meh
June	Juin	jhwehn
July	Juillet	*jhwee*-ay
August	Août	oot
September	Septembre	sep-*tahm*-bruh
October	Octobre	ok-*toh*-bruh
November	Novembre	no-*vahm*-bruh
December	Decembre	day-*sahm*-bruh
Sunday	Dimanche	dee-*mahnsh*
Monday	Lundi	*luhn*-dee
Tuesday	Mardi	*mahr*-dee
Wednesday	Mercredi	*mair*-kruh-dee
Thursday	Jeudi	*jheu*-dee
Friday	Vendredi	*vawn*-druh-dee
Saturday	Samedi	*sahm*-dee
yesterday	hier	ee-*air*
today	aujourd'hui	o-jhord-*dwee*
this morning/this afternoon	ce matin/cet après-midi	suh ma-*tan*/set ah-preh-mee-*dee*
tonight	ce soir	suh *swahr*
tomorrow	demain	de-*man*
summer	l'été	lett-*ay*
fall	l'automne	law-*tonne*
winter	l'hiver	liv-*erre*
spring	le printemps	le prun-*tawm*

BASIC MENU TERMS

Note: No need to get intimidated when ordering in French. Simply preface the French-language menu item with the phrase *"Je voudrais"* (jhe voo-*dray*), which means, "I would like . . ." *Bon appétit!*

MEATS

English	French	Pronunciation
beef stew	du pot au feu	**dew poht o *fhe***
brains	de la cervelle	**duh lah ser-*vel***
chicken	du poulet	***dew poo*-lay**
warm dumplings of creamed chicken, veal, or fish (often pike)	des quenelles	**day ke-*nelle***
chicken with mushrooms and wine	du coq au vin	**dew cock o vhin**
gooseliver	du foie gras	**dew fwah grah**
ham	du jambon	**dew jham-bohn**
haunch or leg of an animal, especially that of a lamb or sheep	du gigot	**dew *jhi*-goh**
kidneys	des rognons	**day *row*-nyon**
lamb	de l'agneau	**duh lahn-*nyo***
lamb chop	une cotelette de l'agneau	**ewn koh-te-*let* duh lahn-*nyo***
liver	du foie	**dew fwah**
pork	du porc	**dew poor**
potted and shredded pork	des rillettes	**day ree-yet**
rabbit	du lapin	**dew lah-*pan***
sirloin	de l'aloyau	**duh lahl-why-*yo***
steak	du bifteck	**dew beef-*tek***
filet steak, served with a pepper sauce	un steak au poivre	**uh stake o *pwah*-vruh**
thick filet steak from the tenderloin, usually serves two	du chateaubriand	**dew *sha*-tow-bree-ahn**
snails	des escargots	**dayz ess-car-*goh***
stewed meat with white sauce	de la blanquette	**duh lah blon-*ket***
sweetbreads	des ris de veau	**day *ree* duh voh**
veal	du veau	**dew *voh***

FISH

English	French	Pronunciation
fish	du poisson	**dew pwoiss-*ohn***
herring	du hareng	**dew ahr-*rahn***

English	French	Pronunciation
lobster	du homard	**dew oh-***mahr*
mussels	des moules	**day** *moohl*
mussels in white wine and shallots	des moules marinières	**day moohl mar-ee-nee-***air*
oysters	des huîtres	**dayz hoo-***ee*-**truhs**
pike	du brochet	**dew broh-***chay*
shrimp	des crevettes	**day kreh-***vette*
smoked salmon	du saumon fumé	**dew sow-***mohn* **fu-may**
trout	de la truite	**duh lah tru-eet**
tuna	du thon	**dew tohn**
wolffish (Mediterranean sea bass)	du loup de mer	**dew loo duh** *mehr*

SIDES/APPETIZERS

English	French	Pronunciation
bread	du pain	**dew pan**
butter	du beurre	**dew bhuhr**
fries	des frites	**day freet**
rice	du riz	**dew ree**
salad	de la salade	**duh lah sa-***lahd*
vegetables	des légumes	**day lay-***goom*

BEVERAGES

English	French	Pronunciation
beer	de la bière	**duh lah bee-***aire*
coffee	un café	**uh ka-***fay*
coffee (black)	un café allongé	**uh ka-***fay* **all-on-***jay*
coffee (decaf)	un café décaféiné (slang: un déca)	**uh ka-***fay* **day-kah-fay-***nay*
coffee (espresso)	un café express	**uh ka-***fay* **ek-***sprehss*
coffee (with milk)	un café crème	**uh ka-***fay* **krem**
coffee (with milk)	un café au lait	**uh ka-***fay* **o** *lay*
milk	du lait	**dew** *lay*
orange juice	du jus d'orange	**dew joo d'or-***ahn*-**jhe**
tea	un thé	**uh** *tay*
tea (herbal)	une tisane	**ewn tee-***zahn*
tea (w/lemon)	du thé au citron	**uh tay o see-***tran*

English	French	Pronunciation
water	de l'eau	**duh lo**
wine (red)	du vin rouge	**dew vhin *rooj***
wine (white)	du vin blanc	**dew vhin *blahn***
soda	soda	**so-*da***
tap water	l'eau du robinet	**low du rob-in-*ay***

SPICES/CONDIMENTS

English	French	Pronunciation
mayonnaise	de la mayonnaise	**duh lah may-o-nayse**
mustard	de la moutarde	**duh lah moo-*tard*-uh**
ketchup	du ketchup	**dew ketch-up**
pepper	du poivre	**dew *pwah*-vruh**
salt	du sel	**dew *sel***
sour heavy cream	de la crème fraîche	**duh lah krem *fresh***
sugar	du sucre	**dew *sook*-ruh**
vinegar	vinaigre	**vin-*aigre***
olive oil	huile d'olive	**weele dol-*eeve***

Index

RESTAURANT INDEX

PHOTO CREDITS

p. i: © Elisabeth Blanchet; p. iii: © Nicholas MacInnes; p. iv: © Markel Redondo; p. v: © Markel Redondo; p. 1: © Nicholas MacInnes; p. 3: © Alden Gewirtz; p. 4: © Nicholas MacInnes; p. 5, top: © Nicholas MacInnes; p. 5, bottom: © Nicholas MacInnes; p. 6, top left: © Markel Redondo; p. 6, top right: © Markel Redondo; p. 6, bottom: © Nicholas MacInnes; p. 7: © Markel Redondo; p. 8, top: © Markel Redondo; p. 8, bottom: © Jessica Hauf; p. 9: © Markel Redondo; p. 10: © David Adamson/Alamy; p. 11: © Markel Redondo; p. 12, left: © Markel Redondo; p. 12, right: © Markel Redondo; p. 13: © Markel Redondo; p. 14: © Markel Redondo; p. 15: © Elisabeth Blanchet; 16, top: © Alden Gewirtz; p. 16, bottom: © Markel Redondo; p. 17: © Markel Redondo; p. 18: © Markel Redondo; p. 19: © Nicholas MacInnes; p. 21: © Markel Redondo; p. 22: © Markel Redondo; p. 23: © Stephanie Lamy; p. 27: © Markel Redondo; p. 29: © Nicholas MacInnes; p. 32: © Markel Redondo; p. 33: © Alden Gewirtz; p. 34: © Markel Redondo; p. 35: © North Wind Picture Archives/Alamy; p. 36: © Markel Redondo; p. 37: © Elisabeth Blanchet; p. 39, left: © Markel Redondo; p. 39, right: © The Print Collector/Alamy; p. 40: © CSU Archives/Everett Collection/Alamy; p. 43: © INTERFOTO/Alamy; p. 44: © Nicholas MacInnes; p. 56: © Fridmar Damm/Corbis Bridge/Alamy; p. 59, top left: © Nicholas MacInnes; p. 59, top right: © Markel Redondo; p. 59, bottom: © Markel Redondo; p. 63: © Markel Redondo; p. 66: © Markel Redondo; p. 68, top: © Elisabeth Blanchet; p. 68, bottom left: © Markel Redondo; p. 68, bottom right: © Alden Gewirtz; p. 70, left: © Markel Redondo; p. 70, right: © Markel Redondo; p. 71, top: © Markel Redondo; p. 71, middle: © Markel Redondo; p. 71, bottom: © Markel Redondo; p. 72, top left: © Markel Redondo; p. 72, top right: © Stephanie Lamy; p. 72, bottom: © Stephanie Lamy; p. 75, top: © Elisabeth Blanchet; p. 75, bottom left: © Elisabeth Blanchet; p. 75, bottom right: © Elisabeth Blanchet; p. 76: © Nicholas MacInnes; p. 78: © Markel Redondo; p. 81, top: © Markel Redondo; p. 81, bottom: © Markel Redondo; p. 82, top: © Markel Redondo; p. 82, bottom: © Markel Redondo; p. 85, left: © Markel Redondo; p. 85, right: © Nicholas MacInnes; p. 86, left: © Markel Redondo; p. 86, right: © Elisabeth Blanchet; p. 88: © Nicholas MacInnes; p. 89: © Markel Redondo; p. 90, left: © Markel Redondo; p. 90, right: © Markel Redondo; p. 91, left: © Nicholas MacInnes; p. 91, right: © Markel Redondo; p. 92: © Markel Redondo; p. 93, left: © Nicholas MacInnes; p. 93, right: © Markel Redondo; p. 94: © Markel Redondo; p. 95: © Markel Redondo; p. 96: © Markel Redondo; p. 100, top: © Markel Redondo; p. 100, bottom: © Elisabeth Blanchet; p. 101: © Markel Redondo; p. 102: © Markel Redondo; p. 103: © Alden Gewirtz; p. 104: © Markel Redondo; p. 105: © Courtesy Musee Jacquemart-Andre; p. 106: © Markel Redondo; p. 107, top: © Markel Redondo; p. 107, bottom left: © Markel Redondo; p. 107, bottom right: © Markel Redondo; p. 108: © Nicholas MacInnes; p. 109: © Markel Redondo; p. 110, left: © Courtesy Musée Grévin, Photo by Christophe Recoura; p. 110, right: © Markel Redondo; p. 112, top: © Markel Redondo; p. 112, bottom: © Nicholas MacInnes; p. 113, left: © Markel Redondo; p. 113, right: © Markel Redondo; p. 115, left: © Stephanie Lamy; p. 115, right: © Stephanie Lamy; p. 116: © Markel Redondo; p. 119: © Elisabeth Blanchet; p. 120, top left: © Markel Redondo; p. 120, top right: © Markel Redondo; p. 120, bottom: © Elisabeth Blanchet; p. 121: © Elisabeth Blanchet; p. 122: © Markel Redondo; p. 124, top: © Markel Redondo; p. 124, bottom: © Markel Redondo; p. 125: © Markel Redondo; p. 127, top: © Markel Redondo; p. 127, bottom: © Markel Redondo; p. 130: © Markel Redondo; p. 131, left: © Courtesy Hotel Abbaye Saint-Germain; p. 131, right: © Nicholas MacInnes; p. 135: © Elisabeth Blanchet; p. 136: © Andrea Innocenti/CuboImages/Alamy; p. 137, top: © Georgios Makkas; p. 137, bottom: © Markel Redondo; p. 138: © Alden Gewirtz; p. 140: © Nicholas MacInnes; p. 142: © Markel Redondo; p. 144, top left: © Elisabeth Blanchet; p. 144, top right: © Markel Redondo; p. 144, bottom: © Stephanie Lamy; p. 145, left: © Alden Gewirtz; p. 145, right: © Alden Gewirtz; p. 146, top: © Markel Redondo; p. 146, bottom: © Markel Redondo; p. 147: © Markel Redondo; p. 149: © Markel Redondo; p. 152: © Elisabeth Blanchet; p. 154: © Markel Redondo; p. 156, left: © Markel Redondo; p. 156, right: © Markel Redondo; p. 157: © Markel Redondo; p. 158: © Pam Shawcross/Alamy; p. 159: © Markel Redondo; p. 160: © Markel Redondo; p. 162, top: © Elisabeth Blanchet; p. 162, bottom: © Markel Redondo; p. 164: © Markel Redondo; p. 165: © Markel Redondo; p. 166: © Markel Redondo; p. 169: © Markel Redondo; p. 171: © Nicholas